Jurisprudence

Jurisprudence

Fifth Edition

R W M Dias

MA LL B **(Cantab.)**

of the Inner Temple, Barrister
Fellow of Magdalene College
University of Cambridge

Butterworths
London
1985

United Kingdom	Butterworth & Co (Publishers) Ltd, 88 Kingsway, LONDON WC2B 6AB an 61A North Castle Street, EDINBURGH EH2 3LJ
Australia	Butterworths Pty Ltd, SYDNEY, MELBOURNE, BRISBANE, ADELAIDE, PERTH CANBERRA and HOBART
Canada	Butterworth & Co (Canada) Ltd, TORONTO and VANCOUVER
New Zealand	Butterworths of New Zealand Ltd, WELLINGTON and AUCKLAND
Singapore	Butterworth & Co (Asia) Pte Ltd, SINGAPORE
South Africa	Butterworth Publishers (Pty) Ltd, DURBAN and PRETORIA
USA	Butterworth Legal Publishers, ST PAUL, Minnesota, SEATTLE, Washington, BOSTON, Massachusetts, AUSTIN, Texas and D & S Publishers, CLEARWATER, Florida

© Butterworth & Co (Publishers) Ltd 1985

British Library Cataloguing in Publication Data
Dias, R.W.M.
  Jurisprudence.—5th ed.
  1. Jurisprudence
  I. Title
  340'.1   K230

  ISBN Hardcover 0 406 57432 4
  ISBN Soft cover 0 406 57431 6

Made and printed in Great Britain by Butler & Tanner Ltd, Frome and London

DEDICATED TO THE
AUTHORS OF
'THE MEANING OF MEANING' (1923)

Preface

The study of jurisprudence is an opportunity for lawyers to bring theory and life into focus, for it concerns human thought in relation to society. It is always the hope of teachers of law to encourage pupils to learn how to think rather than just what to know, and Jurisprudence is suited to this end because it can set law in wider contexts and proceed by way of stimulation and not simply by instruction. This book does not evolve or demonstrate a particular theory, but seeks instead to provide a way of thinking about law. It tries also to furnish material for the evolution of ideas and the understanding of other theories and in this respect serves as a prelude to these contributions by providing an informed and critical background to them. A guarantee of independence and originality in thought is breadth of view, a sense of perspective and appreciation of what people have said and are saying. No one theory provides the best or exclusive avenue to the 'truth', and those who choose to tread one path rather than another are not for that reason misguided. Jurisprudence is a field traversed by many paths, none being superior to another, since much depends on whither one wishes to go.

To give effect to this aim an attempt has been made to offer guiding threads to the extensive literature on the topics dealt with, which will give readers an idea of those topics and the issues and problems they involve. The reading lists appended to each chapter are no more than pointers. Side by side with this, a parallel attempt has been made to provide fuller references for those wishing to delve more deeply, which are contained in the companion volume, *A Bibliography of Jurisprudence*, the object of which is to enable readers to steep themselves in as many aspects as possible of various topics by consulting a wide range of views and shades of opinion.

The only consistent theme throughout the various editions of this book has been in the Prefaces announcing changes since the previous edition. This stems from the fact that the book was born before being conceived, which is why its gestation has been unusual, to say the least. The 'achievement of justice' as a general concern of law, which was the plan according to which the last edition was revised, is continued. The book is divided back into three Parts, and not two as before, and the material of the whole book has been revised and redistributed. The first three chapters are differently presented and Chapter 3 is new. Other new material has been put in, but there has also been a good deal of shortening and excision so as to prevent the book growing larger; hopefully to make it shorter. The different style and format of this edition make it difficult to gauge how far these hopes have been realised.

The acknowledgment of the debts to others is always the pleasantest task. The help given by those mentioned in previous Prefaces has been of permanent value, and although they have been spared in the preparation of this edition, my gratitude to them can never diminish. However, a special word of thanks should continue to be given to that unfailingly helpful body of critics, the undergraduates, whom I have met over the years in discussions and classes. It is for their successors that this work is designed, and if it proves to be of value to them, that might atone in some measure for the experiments inflicted upon their predecessors.

In conclusion, I would like to record my appreciation of the efficiency and indulgence of the Publishers and Printers, who have made the business of production as smooth as possible.

RWM DIAS
August 1985

Contents

List of cases

Decisions of the European Court of Justice are listed below numerically.
These decisions are also included in the preceding alphabetical list.

Introduction

SUMMARY

CHAPTER 1

Introduction

'Jurisprudence was the first of the social sciences to be born', said Wurzel[1]. Its province has been determined and re-determined because the nature of the subject is such that no delineation of its scope can be regarded as final. On torts or contracts, for example, a student may be recommended to read any of the standard textbooks with the assurance that, whichever book he does read, he will derive much the same idea as to what the subject is about. With jurisprudence this is not so. Books called 'jurisprudence' vary so widely in subject matter and treatment that the answer to the question, what is 'jurisprudence'?, is that it means pretty much whatever anyone wants it to mean—a depressing start indeed. This kind of answer suggests that something is amiss with the question. It would be better to ask: How is this word used?, or more pertinently, What is this book going to do?

Use of the word 'jurisprudence'

The Latin expression, *juris prudentia*, means either 'knowledge of' or 'skill in law'. The Roman jurists, however, never developed any such subject as '*jurisprudentia*'[2]. In the sense of 'knowledge of law', the word sometimes describes expositions of particular branches of the law, eg the name 'Equity Jurisprudence' was once given to a textbook on Equity[3]. This use of the word, current on the Continent, is no longer fashionable in common law countries. In a wide sense 'jurisprudence' is used also to describe the legal connections of any body of knowledge: so 'Dental Jurisprudence', 'Architectural Jurisprudence' or 'Medical Jurisprudence' would be titles for expositions of such aspects of dentistry, architecture or medicine as may be important in law. Some criticisms of this use of the term are somewhat misconceived. There has been a tendency to suppose that the word 'jurisprudence' has, or should have, some 'proper' meaning, which makes it inapplicable to this kind of study[4]. As will appear, no word, least of all 'jurisprudence', has a 'proper' meaning. There is also the argument that such studies as these are not 'scientific'[5], which presupposes some special meaning of the word 'science'. The reason for avoiding a term like 'medical jurisprudence' is that this kind of expression is no longer current in English-speaking countries, although occasional instances may still be found[6]. It may be noted

1 Wurzel 'Methods of Juridical Thinking' in *Science of Legal Method: Select Essays*, p 289.
2 Ulpian's remark in the *Digest*, quoted in the opening of Justinian's *Institutes*, '*Juris prudentia est divinarum atque humanarum rerum notitia, justi atque injusti scientia*' (D 1.1.10.2; *Inst* 1.1.1: jurisprudence is the concept of things divine and human, knowledge of the just and the unjust), was only a piece of rhetoric not pursued by the Romans.
3 Ames *Equity Jurisprudence*. See the comments of Stone *The Province and Function of Law* p 26.
4 Holland *Jurisprudence* p 4, n 4.
5 Gray *The Nature and Sources of the Law* pp 134, 147.
6 The term 'medico-legal jurisprudence' has largely been superseded by 'forensic medicine'.

that in French law *la jurisprudence* is the term applied to the body of law built up by the decisions of particular courts[7].

In England it was not until the time of Bentham and his disciple Austin in the early part of the nineteenth century that the word began to acquire a technical significance among English lawyers[8]. The former distinguished between examination of the law as it is and as it ought to be ('expositorial' and 'censorial' jurisprudence), and he was also much concerned with law reform ('deontology'). The latter, who was the first Professor of Jurisprudence in the University of London, occupied himself with 'expository' jurisprudence, and his work consisted mainly of a formal analysis of the structure of English law. Analytical exposition of the type which Bentham pioneered, and Austin developed, has dominated English legal thought almost to the present. It was therefore inevitable that the word 'jurisprudence' came to mean in this country almost exclusively the analysis of the formal structure of law and its concepts. This was the nearest that the word came to bearing a precise meaning.

Towards the end of the nineteenth century changing human affairs had brought about an ever-increasing preoccupation with conflicting ideologies and troubled social conditions, which resulted in a decisive shift in outlook with the result that jurisprudence came to be envisaged in a broader sense than in Austin's day. Buckland described the change vividly. 'The analysis of legal concepts', he said[9], 'is what jurisprudence meant for the student in the days of my youth. In fact it meant Austin. He was a religion; today he seems to be regarded rather as a disease'. The breadth of the modern attitude is well summed up by Julius Stone who described jurisprudence as:

> 'The lawyer's extraversion. It is the lawyer's examination of the precepts, ideals, and techniques of the law in the light derived from present knowledge in disciplines other than the law'[10].

So vast a coverage may be summed up in the proposition that jurisprudential study nowadays concerns thought about law, its nature, function and functioning, on the broadest possible basis, and about its adaptation, improvement and reform. A convenient way of obtaining an idea of its compass is by explaining this description.

Thought about law

Writings on jurisprudence are not concerned with expositions *of* law, but with disquisitions *about* law[11]. Various branches of substantive law, for example, teach how rights and duties are acquired, whereas jurisprudence would investigate such questions as: What are rights and duties? How are they used? How do they work? It also improves the use of law by drawing together insights from different branches, criminal, constitutional etc, in the solution of problems. Thought about law is also a story of movements in outlook and ever-changing ideas, and developments are taking place in contemporary physical, moral and other social sciences, which make it difficult to decide once and for all how, if at all, these should be taken into account.

---

7 The equivalent of 'jurisprudence' in its Anglo-American sense is *Théorie générale du droit*.
8 For their work, see ch 16 post.
9 Buckland *Some Reflections on Jurisprudence* p 2.
10 Stone *Legal System and Lawyers' Reasonings* p 16.
11 King 'Propositions about Law' (1951) 11 CLJ 31.

'Thought about law' suggests that an important, if not essential, prelude to jurisprudential study should be some thought about thought. The overall aim is not to teach students what they need to know, but how to think profitably and for themselves, as well as to educate and equip them to be efficient lawyers. Thinking is inseparably bound up with the meaning and use of words. This is an aspect of philosophy, known as semantics, which is of especial interest to lawyers since, as Lord Macmillan said, 'The lawyer's business is with words. They are the raw material of his craft'[12]. Laws are articulated in language; logic is controlled by it. Some of the needless difficulties that have arisen in jurisprudence are of linguistic origin. This is because words are not only tools of thought, but also control it; people tend to think in terms of their language structure. Accordingly, learning how to think profitably will be assisted by a sharpened awareness of the possibilities of language, not only to lead thought but also to mislead it[13].

Linguistic precepts

In the first place, the idea that a word must necessarily possess some unique or 'proper' meaning should be abandoned. An explanation of this lies at the basis of a biological theory, known as 'autopoiesis', put forward by Professor Maturana, that no one can 'know' what the world outside him or her 'really' is, for what each person 'knows' is the response of his or her nervous system to external stimuli[14]. This is not a denial of objective reality, but an assertion that no one can ever know what this is outside his or her neuronal response to it. Perception is thus a matter of personal interpretation. Equally, the meaning of a word depends on individual past experience of the contexts in which it is used, its applications as well as its non-applications. Another reason for rejecting 'proper' meanings is that the same 'thing' may be referred to by different words for different purposes, eg the same act may be called trespass to goods or theft or malicious damage in different contexts. The meaning of a word also depends upon how it is used in the context, so its function in the proposition as a whole should be considered[15]. The sense is often lost as soon as one attempts to elucidate the thing referred to, ie the referent. For instance, in the statement 'England expects every man to do his duty', it is useless to elucidate 'England' by reducing it to its referents. The sense here depends, not on the thing or things referred to, but on the function which the word performs in that sentence. The nuances of meaning imparted by context can be illustrated by taking a question and answer by, say, a husband and wife, 'where are you?' and her reply, 'I am here'. If this answer is understood referentially, it is unhelpful, for at the moment of speaking she could only be 'here' on that spot. However, against the background of her husband's knowledge of the geography of the house and the direction from which her voice comes, the answer could mean 'I am in the

---

12 Macmillan *Law and Other Things* p 31.
13 For a different statement of methodological and other errors, see Summers 'Legal Philosophy Today—an Introduction' in *Essays in Legal Philosophy* (ed Summers) pp 7 et seq.
14 See *Autopoiesis, Communication and Society* (a symposium, edited by Benseler, Hejl and Köck) in which there are papers by Maturana and others and references.
15 'The meaning of a word is its use in the language': Wittgenstein *Philosophical Investigations* p 43. For an application of this technique to the elucidation of legal terms, see Hart 'Definition and Theory in Jurisprudence' (1954) 70 LQR 37, especially his elucidation of 'right' at 49. For criticism, see Auerbach 'On Professor Hart's Definition and Theory in Jurisprudence' (1956) 9 Journal of Legal Education 39.

drawing room', or kitchen etc. If she were to announce 'I am here' as soon as she enters the front door after shopping, the function of the statement is not to indicate where she is (her husband knows that), but the completion of the shopping activity and her return. If the baby wakes up crying and she says 'I am here', the function is not to indicate location or completion of an activity, but reassurance (mother is at hand). Similarly, it is futile to elucidate the meaning of 'jurisprudence' by applying reductive analysis; it needs to be understood in the light of how it is used. All this does not deny that words are frequently used to refer to 'things'. Thus, a word may refer to a particular phenomenon as perceived by the user, eg the 'Mona Lisa'; or a class of things, eg 'pencil'; or an inference from a totality of factors, eg 'negligence'.

Secondly, if meaning and experience rest on individual interpretation, it follows that concerted activities can only take place within areas of similar interpretations, 'consensual domains'. It is in such areas that law, morals, ethics etc operate. Likewise, communication takes place within the consensual domain of the 'usual' meaning of words. It is generally accepted that words have an inner 'core' of settled applications surrounded by a 'fringe' of unsettled applications. Problems of interpretation arise in this 'fringe' area. Words may also have more than one usual meaning, in which case the context has to resolve which meaning is being considered, eg 'race', 'capital'. As will be seen later, words such as 'person', 'possession' and even such common legal terms as 'right' and 'duty' are of this type. An American judge has remarked that 'a good deal of warfare has its origin in the confusion that arises when a single term of broad and ill-defined content is made to do duty for two or more ideas'[16]. When a word has undergone shifts in meaning in this way, it is fruitless to speculate about the 'essence' that underlies the shifts; each shift should be elucidated on its own. Equally pointless would it be to condemn one or other application as 'improper'.

Thirdly, however useful it may be in the elucidation of words, especially abstract words, to ask how they are used, this should not imply that reductive analysis is totally valueless. In a good many kinds of discourse it will prove most helpful to identify as closely as possible the 'things' that are being referred to. This may conveniently be done with the aid of such questions as Who? What? When? Where? For instance, people argue at length about 'the class struggle', but discussion of this only becomes meaningful when it is reduced to a less abstract level. There have been many 'class struggles': who? about what? when? where? Corbin evinced a keen appreciation of the point when he said:

> 'It helps us to realize that acts are always individual; that pain and pleasure, emotions and desires, are always individual; that rules of law are made for individuals and that human and social welfare is, in the last analysis, always individual welfare. Labour is not in conflict with capital; but a labourer with no capital may fight a labourer with capital. "Interests of personality" do not conflict with "interests of property", because only *persons* have interests either factual or jural. . . . A state, a corporation, a group, a union, can act and can be affected only through individuals. Societal evolution can take place only by the evolution of individuals. Socialism is always some form of individualism, some combination of individual relations'[17].

---

16 Cardozo *The Growth of the Law* p 30.
17 Corbin 'Jural Relations and their Classification' (1920–21) 30 Yale LJ at p 227 n 2.

Because reductive analysis will not succeed with *all* statements (eg 'England expects every man to do his duty'), it is wrong to imagine that it cannot apply usefully to *some* statements. The method is unquestionably an aid to precision and a valuable corrective to sloppy thinking in terms of slogans. The two methods of elucidation, the functional and reductive, are not mutually exclusive; both are helpful.

Fourthly, some words carry an emotive element which lends illegitimate weight to a statement. Words like 'science', 'law', 'right', are heavily loaded in this way. Indeed, the word 'jurisprudence' is itself an 'imposing quadrisyllable', which, it has been said, 'is constantly introduced into a phrase on grounds of euphony alone'[18].

Fifthly, language has different functions. The most usual is communication, which requires a speaker or writer, a medium of communication and a listener or reader. Each party has a part to play. The speaker or writer should so choose a term that it is likely to be interpreted in the way he wants[19]. 'When I use a word, it means just what I choose it to mean, neither more nor less'[20] is a cavalier and unhelpful attitude unless the author clearly indicates beforehand the special meaning that he attaches to the word. The listener or reader should do his best to understand the word in the intended sense[1], and in this respect the great lesson is that of restraint in criticism. No one should criticise another for something he did not mean. Having understood, it may be proper to point out that his language is misleading, or that what he says is misconceived, or that he does not go far enough; and if indeed he is obscure, suggestions might even be made as to what he might have meant. Subject to this, it is always necessary, as Julius Stone remarked, to 'speak as faithfully as we can *with his voice before we chide him with ours*'[2].

Apart from communication, language is also used performatively, ie to accomplish results[3]. For example, the utterance 'I pronounce you man and wife', is not a communication or a report. It does not state the fact that a couple *are* man and wife, but that they *are to be* man and wife; it constitutes a new state of affairs. This function is closely connected with institutions and procedures. Thus, it is only a clergyman acting officially who can effectively pronounce two persons to be man and wife.

Sixthly, generalisation beyond the field of study should be made with care. As will appear later, some theories of law, though providing valuable insights, are spoiled by over-generalisation.

Seventhly, 'facts' should be distinguished from 'statements of facts'. Some non-verbal thing or event can be the basis of different statements of fact at varying levels of generality. For example, A drove his Rolls Royce car at 30 mph at 2 pm last Wednesday through Piccadilly Circus, knocked down B and broke his right leg. Assuming that this event occurred, the above would be a statement of those facts. It is possible, however, to restate them at a higher level of abstraction thus: a person drove a vehicle negligently on the

18 Holland *The Elements of Jurisprudence* p 4.
19 For a failure to communicate, see *J McGrath Motors (Canberra) Pty v Applebee* (1964) 110 CLR 656.
20 Humpty Dumpty in *Alice Through the Looking Glass* ch 6. For a judicial comment, see Lord Atkin in *Liversidge v Anderson* [1942] AC 206 at 245, [1941] 3 All ER 338 at 361.
 1 Cf Lord Reid's protest in *Mutual Life and Citizens' Assurance Co Ltd v Evatt* [1971] AC 793 at 813, [1971] 1 All ER 150 at 164.
 2 Stone *Legal System and Lawyers' Reasonings* p 2.
 3 JL Austin *How to Do Things with Words*.

highway and inflicted physical injury on another person. At still higher levels of abstractness the following statements might be made: inflicting physical damage negligently on another; or, inflicting damage negligently on another; or, inflicting damage on another. In trial courts 'establishing facts by evidence' is to make statements at the lowest possible, or at least a very low, level of generality; but the concern of lawyers is not confined to this. As will be seen in Chapter 7, the possibility of formulating different statements of fact based on the same event is a clue to understanding the *ratio decidendi*, or principle, of a judicial decision. It also explains how an appellate court, while accepting the findings of the trial court, may nevertheless substitute a different opinion of them[4].

Finally, in so far as statements are capable of being checked at all, they may be checked with a view to establishing either their truth-value (verification) or their admissibility for consideration[5]. It is obvious that the criterion of checking has to lie outside the statement which is being checked, and that this criterion should never be twisted to suit the statement. Some statements may be both checked and verified, eg that a man named A drove his Rolls Royce car at 30 mph at 2 pm last Wednesday through Piccadilly Circus and ran into and injured a man named B. The statement, eg that A drove his car negligently, cannot be verified, since 'negligence' is an inference and a matter of opinion. It may, however, still be checked in order to see whether it is an admissible 'statement of fact' based on that occurrence; which it clearly is. By contrast, the statement that A caused a flood in Piccadilly Circus at 2 pm last Wednesday is inadmissible. It is evident, therefore, that the range of possible statements of fact, though wide, is not unlimited, and that there is a point beyond which they cannot go. With regard to law, propositions of law are incapable of being checked, proved or disproved, eg you ought not to steal. Propositions *about* law, on the other hand, may or may not be checkable. Thus, the statement that judges use the proposition, 'You ought not to steal', in deciding a certain type of case may be checked and verified; but neither the statement that the payment of £50 for pulling the communication cord in a train without cause is a penalty, nor the statement that such payment is only a tax on the indulgence of this pleasure[6] is capable of verification. Both are admissible; which is to be preferred has to be determined with reference to their respective utility for lawyers, and this depends on conformity with the whole background of legal doctrine and way of thinking.

In addition to these linguistic preliminaries, another aspect of thought concerns the methods of reasoning that are used and on which any discipline depends. Gray once said 'The real relation of Jurisprudence to Law depends not upon *what* Law is treated, but *how* Law is treated'[7]. Relationships, however, are seen only by the mind and Gray's use of the word 'real' is a slightly tendentious utilisation of its emotive loading. Had he spoken of the relationship which appealed to him there would be no objection. It would have been

---

4 Eg *Benmax v Austin Motor Co Ltd* [1955] AC 370, [1955] 1 All ER 326; *Wheat v E Lacon & Co Ltd* [1966] AC 552, [1966] 1 All ER 582; *The Wagon Mound (No 2)* [1967] 1 AC 617, [1966] 2 All ER 709.
5 See generally Waismann 'Verifiability' in *Logic and Language I* (ed Flew) ch 7 (reprinted from *Proceedings of the Aristotelian Society* Supplement 1945). Cf Popper's test of 'falsifiability': *Poverty of Historicism*. Is the statement 'Black ravens exist' falsifiable? If not, has it no meaning?
6 Holmes 'The Path of the Law' in *Collected Papers* p 173, and see p 449 post.
7 Gray *The Nature and Sources of the Law* p 147.

better had he said that this relation depends *not so much* upon what law is treated, but how it is treated, for obviously there must be some material for treatment. The main idea, however, is acceptable.

One method of treating the subject might be called the method of logical analysis which is *a priori* and demonstrative, ie breaking down a given hypothesis into its components and implications. Alternatively, there is what may be called the method of synthesis, which is constructive and empirical, ie unifying the data into a coherent whole. There is no question of one being more correct than the other, or indeed of their being kept sharply distinct. They are both useful as well as interdependent. The only point is which of them should predominate; which is a matter of preference.

The method of logical analysis starts with a given concept as embodied in a definition and proceeds to unfold its implications. The pattern into which the material falls is implicit in the definition. The chief points are:

(a) The power and penetration of the demonstration depends on the organising power of the concept.
(b) Definition is always an abstraction, that is, it is selective and does not include everything. It thus represents a model, an approximation, or a hypothetical framework[8].
(c) Emphasis is laid on the logical implications of the premise, that is, on the validity of the inference rather than on its truth-value or desirability. *A priorists* tend, as a rule, to scorn empiricism.
(d) A new concept may well be thought-provoking and offer some new way of looking at the subject.
(e) It may have persuasive force and ultimately mould practice.
(f) Logical thinking is a valuable mental training.

This method is not so much a training in thinking for oneself as thinking along a line determined by another. It may well happen that a particular way of looking at law will lead to one answer only of a problem which might with equal plausibility be resolved in some other way. It is important that each person should be left to decide such a point for himself. As Pollock once put it: 'A definition has no business to prejudge the question how far that is the case'[9]. For example, a much disputed question is whether international law is 'law'. Austin, who thought of 'law' as the sum-total of laws and defined 'a law' as the command of a sovereign supported by sanction, logically refused to apply the word 'law' to international law[10]. No harm is done as long as it is realised that this is only the logical result of *his* use of the word 'law'. What is important is that each should decide for himself and not blindly follow in the footsteps of Austin. There are many ways of defining 'law', some of which would include international law.

Secondly, logical manipulation will only reveal what has been put into a premise. The interesting part is the analysis on which it is based. Definitions, said Julius Stone, are 'essentially mnemonics for clarification. They may be preambulatory mnemonics foreshadowing elucidation to follow, or summation mnemonics recalling what has already been expounded. In either case "definition" cannot fruitfully be more definite nor more definitive than

---

8 Cf Stone *Legal System and Lawyers' Reasonings* pp 53, 55, and generally ch 5.
9 Pollock *A First Book of Jurisprudence* p 29.
10 See ch 22, post.

the exposition which it calls to mind'[11]. What is important is to know why certain ideas and not others were chosen and linked as they are in a definition[12].

Thirdly, obsession with a particular definition is misplaced, for there is no one proper or even supremely useful definition. Different definitions are useful for different purposes and for looking at the subject matter from different points of view[13]. Thus, definitions of law with reference to structure or function or development are all useful; and a definition may reflect the point of view of a legislator, judge, practitioner, jurist, sociologist, moralist or wrongdoer.

Fourthly, every definition is only an approximation to the detail of its subject matter. It is thus useful as a pointer to it and as clarifying the proposed use of a term by the definer. A lawyer will find a definition valuable if its logical implications correspond with the actual ways in which judges and lawyers think and act in deciding disputes. Insofar as the logical analysis of a definition fails to correspond in this way, it is misleading. 'The first call of a theory of law', said Holmes J, 'is that it should fit the facts'[14]. Not all the implications of a definition of 'law' have ever corresponded with the actual language and behaviour of lawyers because, to quote Holmes J again, 'The life of the law has not been logic: it has been experience'[15]. The result is that the method of logical analysis has tended to produce a cleavage between 'jurisprudential thinking' and 'lawyers' thinking', which is unfortunate since efforts should be made towards bridging the gulf that regrettably exists between jurisprudents and practitioners[16].

Fifthly, as to the thought-provoking and persuasive force of definitions, it is submitted that while there is some truth in this, it can be over-estimated. The thought-provoking potentialities have hitherto consisted mostly in evoking critical responses, while the persuasive possibilities would require an unattainable measure of agreement among jurists before there can be any hope of practical achievement[17]. 'In fact', said Sir Ivor Jennings, 'the task which many writers on jurisprudence attempt to fulfil in defining law is a futile one'[18]. Besides, laws develop according to needs, not the logical implications of definitions.

Finally, while nothing should be allowed to impair the value of deductive analysis as a mental discipline, it has to be pointed out that it is not the only one. The alternative constructive or empirical method of synthesis is no less worthy a discipline, about which something must now be said.

This is concerned with the evolution of a concept. Before its logical implications can be worked out, it must have been evolved in some way, which suggests that the constructive process has to precede the demonstrative.

---

11   Stone *Legal System and Lawyers' Reasonings* p 184; and earlier Dias 'The Mechanism of Definition as Applied to International Law' [1954] CLJ at 218–219.
12   As Kantorowicz explains throughout his book *The Definition of Law*.
13   For an amusing example of the definer and definee being at cross purposes, see Buckland *A Manual of Roman Private Law* p xii.
14   Holmes *The Common Law* p 211. See also Stone *Legal System and Lawyers' Reasonings* p 58.
15   *Holmes* p 1.
16   Cf Dicey: 'Jurisprudence is a word which stinks in the nostrils of the practising barrister', quoted in Gray *The Nature and Sources of the Law* p 2.
17   Stone *Legal System and Lawyers' Reasonings* pp 167 et seq, for reasons why no definition is likely to win wide acceptance.
18   'The Institutional Theory' in *Modern Theories of Law* (ed Jennings) p 83; *Jilani v Government of Punjab* Pak LD (1972) SC 139 at 159.

'The definition of a concept must precede, not the investigation of the question, but its presentation, if you wish to avoid discussing alien objects under the cover of an ambiguous word'[19].

The statement expresses the point that every definition is the product of some prior investigation.

The greater part of this book will be concerned with the kind of analysis that could serve as the prelude to the formulation of refined and elaborate definitions rather than with any particular definition. Where, then, should such a study begin? The prior investigation, which precedes the formulation of a definition, requires that the material to be examined should first be identified in some rough, provisional way. The constructive method, therefore, does not claim to dispense with all preconceptions. The point is that these should be both minimal and provisional. The matter was well put as follows:

'While it is true that all observation is in terms of a conceptual scheme, this does not mean that one must have a fully worked out theory in order to do any observation at all'[20].

After the material has been identified, the study may proceed in any direction and progress can be achieved by formulating tentative hypotheses, the logical implications of which may be checked as to accuracy and admissibility, as explained earlier. A 'hypothesis' here means a provisional theory or basis of explanation. No hypothesis can be evolved out of nothing. It presupposes prior knowledge of the problem presented by the material; the deeper the knowledge, the more fruitful the hypothesis. Huntingdon Cairns explained it as follows:

'The general pattern of the inventive process as it has been developed by psychological experiment and analysis is, first, awareness of a need, second, reflection upon the need, third, a sudden illumination, and, finally, painstaking efforts to perfect the insight. All the steps appear essential, but none more so than the demand for previous acquaintance with the subject matter'[1].

Consistently with the foregoing, two kinds of definitions can be distinguished. The first consists of those which merely identify the material for the purpose of examination. The second consists of those which organise the completed study and precede the logical unfolding of the patterns implicit in them, in short, they indicate the sense which the definers impose on their terminology. The latter are more refined than the former, and reflect the purposes and points of view of the definers. Definitions of both types are found in Kantorowicz's book, *The Definition of Law*, in which he begins with a rough definition, as he says, 'provisionally and with intentional vagueness, as an example of what will be in our minds when speaking of law before arriving at a formal definition'; and he then proceeds to refine it into a final definition at the end[2].

A convenient starting point would be to identify legal material by taking

19 Kantorowicz and Patterson 'Legal Science—a Summary of its Methodology' (1928) 28 Columbia Law Review 679 at 681n.
20 Sheldon 'Some Observations on Theory in Social Science' in *Towards a General Theory of Action* (eds Parsons and Shils) 36.
1 Cairns *The Theory of Legal Science* 58, 130; cf M R Cohen 'Law and the Scientific Method' in *Jurisprudence in Action*, p 125.
2 Kantorowicz *The Definition of Law* pp 12, 79.

the applications of the word 'law' by courts. Professor Olivecrona adopts a similar approach. 'The study cannot begin with a definition of law', he says:

'It is impossible to start from a definition since this would mean a *petitio principii*. Before a definition can be reached, the facts must be analysed. The method will be simply to take up such facts as are covered by the expression rules of law. No assumption is made from the beginning concerning their nature. We only use the word "law" so to say as a stick to point to the object of the investigation'[3].

An idea such as this is not precise, but it serves as a provisional means of identifying legal material. Mere identification gives no indication of its nature and prejudges no issues. It only furnishes a starting point with minimal preconceptions and is, above all, provisional and open to refinement. It will certainly bring in the 'core' of agreed applications of the word 'law' without prejudice to 'fringe' meanings, eg international law[4].

The courts have been selected as the focal point because they are observable facts and because much of a lawyer's business centres on them[5]. Whatever the angle of vision, they remain an inescapable landmark. Legislators, jurists and villains are all concerned with them in different ways, whether in trying to control, explain or circumvent their probable reactions. As Professor Cross has observed, this 'is an excellent point of departure for a discussion of the major problems of analytical jurisprudence'[6]. An objection might be advanced that some 'law' must have established courts in the first place, which would prevent 'legal material' being identified as what courts accept. The answer is that this only indicates that in the very beginning a different means of identifying 'legal material' would have been required; it does not prevent it from being so identified *now*.

The courts of every country accept some medium, or media, as capable of imparting the quality of 'law' to propositions. The usual designation for such medium is 'criterion (criteria) of validity' because if a proposition has filtered through it, then it is a valid proposition of law; if it has not done so, it is not a valid proposition of law[7]. In Great Britain the label 'English law' is

---

3 Olivecrona *Law as Fact* (1939) pp 25–26; elaborated in the second edn (1971) pp 1–5, 84–85. Cf Lawson *The Rational Strength of English Law* p 7. It is also to be noted that nowhere in Stone's original treatise, *The Province and Function of Law*, was there a definition of 'law', and after nearly twenty years of reflection he still did not see the need for one: *Legal System and Lawyers' Reasonings*, pp 184–185. So, too, Jennings 'The Institutional Theory' in *Modern Theories of Law* (ed Jennings) p 83.

4 Some argue that a definition of 'a law' should follow on a concept of 'legal system', eg Raz *The Concept of a Legal System* p 2. Perhaps so, but to identify material for study is not to define 'a law'.

5 'Law is basic to orderly society and courts are basic to law': per Salahuddin Ahmed J, in *Jilani v Government of Punjab* Pak LD (1972) SC 139 at 267. For a discussion of 'court' and 'judicial office', see *United Engineering Workers Union v Devanayagam* [1968] AC 356, [1967] 2 All ER 367.

6 Cross *Precedent in English Law* p 151. See also Raz 'The Institutional Nature of Law' (1975) 38 MLR 489.

7 In Roman law, for example, the remuneration, *honorarium*, for services rendered under a contract of mandate was never embodied in any of the law-constitutive media of that system, which is why mandate remained theoretically gratuitous, the *honorarium* being 'extra-legal' and recoverable by procedure *extra ordinem*.

regulated by legislation[8], judicial precedents[9], immemorial customs[10] and after Britain's accession to the European Economic Community its Regulations and Decisions. A caution has to be observed here. The mere fact that a proposition is embodied, or even applied, in a judgment does not *ipso facto* make it 'law'; it has to be enunciated and applied as such. Thus, judges constantly employ rules of arithmetic, but these do not thereby become 'English law' since they are not being applied as such[11].

The expression 'source of law' is sometimes used in this connection. 'Source' has more than one meaning. It may refer to the source of information of a rule (eg a textbook), or the origin of the material content of a rule, or the formal stamp of authority as 'law'. It is the last sense which is relevant in identifying legal material. Failure to bear the distinctions in mind, especially between the second and third meanings, introduces an element of confusion[12].

Discussion of thinking processes would be incomplete without allusion to the special kinds of reasoning involved in the judicial process. In addition to

8 'What the statute itself enacts cannot be unlawful, because what the statute says and provides is itself the law, and the highest form of law that is known to this country. It is the law which prevails over every other form of law, and it is not for the court to say that a parliamentary enactment, the highest law in this country, is illegal': per Ungoed-Thomas J in *Cheney v Conn* [1968] 1 All ER 779 at 782. It might be remarked that some natural lawyers would disagree, for they would want the courts to add the moral quality of the content to the mere fact of enactment as the criterion of validity. This will be discussed later in ch 4 and at pp 500–501. Further, statutes do not become 'law' only when judges apply them; they are applied because they are 'law' on enactment; cf Gray *The Nature and Sources of the Law* pp 125, 170–172, and pp 449, 452–453 post.

9 Cardozo CJ referred to precedent as 'the process by which forms of conduct are stamped in the judicial mint as law, and thereafter circulate freely as part of the coinage of the realm': *The Growth of the Law* p 32. See also MR Cohen: 'It is only when courts, balancing considerations of justice and policy, decide to enforce a moral or political rule that they transform it into a legal rule': 'The Process of Judicial Legislation' (1914) 48 Am LR at 170. As an example may be cited the duty of care towards rescuers, which was a rule of American law summarised by Professor Goodhart as a correct statement of what should also be English law, but which only became a rule of English law when the Court of Appeal adopted Goodhart's statement: *Haynes v Harwood* [1935] 1 KB 146 at 157.

10 By convention the writings of certain ancient jurists, the latest of whom is probably Foster, 1762, can also be quoted as 'English law', but only as 'law' at their respective periods. Lord Denning MR once remarked that in certain types of matters 'the opinion and practice of the profession certainly makes law': *R v Industrial Injuries Comr, ex p Amalgamated Engineering Union* [1966] 2 QB 21 at 28, [1966] 1 All ER 97 at 99. This should not be understood literally, but as referring only to a rule of practice.

11 Eg in *Askinex Ltd v Green* [1969] 1 QB 272 at 285, [1967] 1 All ER 65 at 71, Lord Denning MR added an appendix to his judgment working out the calculations involved in terms of mathematical formulae.

12 Noted by Pound, 'Judge Holmes's Contribution to the Science of Law' (1920–21) 34 Harv LR 449 at 452–453. Salmond in the 7th edn of his *Jurisprudence* (the last by himself) distinguished between 'formal' sources, the will and power of the state, and 'material' sources, relating to the rule itself. The latter were sub-divided into 'legal' sources, chiefly legislation, precedent, custom and 'agreement'; and 'historical' sources, those which become 'law' when filtered through a 'legal' source. The first distinction has been dropped by editors since the 10th edn (see p 530 for reasons). Allen rejected the second distinction between 'legal' and 'historical' sources arguing that the gist of the matter is whether a source will be applied: *Law in the Making* pp 271–272. Salmond's dismissal of 'historical' sources from consideration was too facile, but the difference between these and 'legal' sources is important in a way that Allen overlooks. A judge cannot ignore statute, precedent or custom, but he has a discretion whether or not to resort to historical sources. The latter work differently from 'legal' sources. See chs 2, 10 post, and see also the account in the 3rd edn of the present work, ch 2.

analysis and synthesis, use is frequently made of analogical reasoning and what, for want of a better term, might be called the 'logic of justification'. This is the interpretation and manipulation within permissible limits of the law so as to justify decisions which are thought to be right. All these place judicial reasoning in a class of its own and will be considered in Chapter 7.

Something should also be said about persuasion. When challenging highly abstract propositions, to call for supporting evidence is often asking the wrong question. With statements at a low level of abstraction whose referents are ascertainable, it is important to call for these as evidence. With high-level abstractions, however, which have lost touch with their referential bases, to call for evidence may be an effective way of scoring a debating point, but it is unfair. For instance, the assertion that 'every society has a shared morality' cannot be proved by evidence in the same way as the assertion that 'the Prime Minister inhabits No 10 Downing Street' can be proved. Whereas the acceptability of factual, or near-factual, statements depends on a balance of probability on the evidence, the acceptability of highly abstract statements depends on a 'balance of plausibility', persuasion not proof, to which the following considerations are relevant. First, is there any consideration which might defeat or reduce the plausibility of an argument? Reductive analysis in search of referents will sometimes help. The argument must not be both pro and contra, and it must be relevant, ie not used as a smoke-screen. Also, it will have different weightings according to the sympathies of the audience, which affect its plausibility. Secondly, with intuitive arguments the need is to persuade the other side of the acceptability of one's point of view. Thirdly, persons with no convictions either way on an issue may be persuaded by a balance of plausibility, but those with strong convictions one way have to be prised out of what is often an entrenched position. Here a balance of plausibility alone may not suffice since it has to combat, eg loyalty to a prior commitment, refusal to admit a change of opinion, fear of being thought liberal or illiberal, and similar reactions. In such situations it is often the case that the more persuasive an argument is, the stronger is the resistance to it; which is why debates of this kind seldom seem to 'get anywhere', and this is often the case with jurisprudential disputes.

Nature, function and functioning of law

The nature of legal material, laws and legal system is mainly the concern of this book. Suffice it to say here that law consists largely of 'ought' (normative) propositions prescribing how people ought to behave. The crucial distinction between these and the laws of science lies here. The substrata of scientific laws are the observable uniformities of nature out of which laws are derived. Legal laws express ideas as to hoped-for behaviour; the laws are not derived from the behaviour. Scientific laws, therefore, *describe* observable behaviour patterns of natural phenomena and are a basis for predicting how the phenomena will behave. The phenomena do not 'obey' the laws, and it is nonsensical to say that a scientific law is such and such, but that the phenomena do not conform to it. If they do not conform, the law is wrong and must be changed. There is thus exact correspondence between prediction and behaviour. Legal laws, on the other hand, *prescribe* how people ought to behave.[13] It is not nonsense to say 'X ought not to steal' and also 'But X does steal'. A law is not 'wrong' because people disobey it. Therefore, prescription of behaviour and description of actual behaviour bear only a rough correspondence; the aim is to achieve as much correspondence as possible. The law also consists of material other than prescriptions and these will be dealt with in the next chapter.

The function of law connotes purpose. The 'oughts' of laws are variously dictated by social, moral, economic, political and other purposes. The overall purpose of law may be thought of as the achievement of justice, which will be considered in Chapter 4. The functioning of law concerns its working. On the one hand, there is the application of law in deciding disputes and by way of enforcement. The former involves consideration of the judicial process with all its institutional and conceptual apparatus. On the other hand, there is the extent to which laws are obeyed or disobeyed and the ways in which the behaviour of people diverges over long periods from the norms of the law. All these will be dealt with in various parts of the book.

Broadest possible basis

Law is a social institution. A society may be described as an association of people with a measure of permanence. A 'civic society' is said to comprise (1) territory, (2) perpetuity, (3) a measure of independence, and (4) a culture as manifested in its art, philosophy, law, morality, religion, fashion and opinion[14]. The last five, namely, law, morality, religion, fashion and opinion, are modes of social control in that they prescribe in various ways how people ought to behave. Law is distinguishable from the others with reference to the criteria of validity already mentioned, but the relationship between them is a matter for jurisprudential study.

More important is the inextricable interrelation between law and philosophy, sociology, ethics and politics. The training of lawyers has hitherto failed to take sufficient account of the essential unity of law and these other disciplines. They are not just related to each other, but interwoven; their pattern is not that of circles which touch at their circumferences, but of circles which overlap. Only on such an integrated basis is it possible for lawyers to approach their subject meaningfully and improve its serviceability. Indeed, jurisprudence might well be described as the lifemanship of the law. No one can be a good lawyer who only knows law. As Buckland well said, 'A man will be a better lawyer, as he will be a better architect or physician, if his mind is open to the movements of thought on the profounder issues of

---

13 Thus, Lord Wright said of law: 'Its purpose is to regulate man's conduct in relation to external things and persons, not merely to ascertain and explain what happens in fact': 'Precedents' (1943) 8 CLJ 124. So, too, Goodhart: 'in the physical sciences we have a *description* of conduct, while in the social sciences we have a *prescription* for conduct': *English Law and the Moral Law* p 9. The distinction was expressed by Kelsen in terms of the 'ought' and the 'is', *Sollen* and *Sein*, eg in *General Theory of Law and State* pp xiv, 35–42, and for his theory, see ch 17, post. See also Castberg *Problems of Legal Philosophy* p 53; Hart *The Concept of Law* pp 78–79. For Hall, on the other hand, the legal prescription is also to some extent descriptive of the significance of the rule: 'Concerning the Nature of Positive Law' (1948–49) 58 Yale LJ 560.
14 Johnson *Sociology* p 9.

life, beyond his immediate professional concerns. And, if his mind is so open, he can hardly fail to have some sort of philosophy of his own'[15].

Of the philosophical aspects, which are more or less useful to lawyers, that which is outstandingly relevant is logic and various kinds of reasoning. There are also questions of semantics, method and definition, which have been dealt with. Part III of this book will deal with some philosophies of law, which will reveal the manner in which people in different countries at different times have speculated about some of the problems examined in the preceding Parts. It is not enough to enhance merely the technical efficiency of a lawyer, important though this is; he should also be invited to broaden his outlook by treading along paths from which he will be able to perceive new horizons and be invigorated by scholarship in other spheres. Speculations about law by past and present thinkers are part of intellectual culture. Even where theories are open to criticism they possess value and later theories can be better understood in the light of them. This book can do no more than try to indicate directions along which such inquiries can be pursued and where the wisdom of great thinkers is to be found. It might be convenient to refer to a particular theory alongside the discussion of the problem most nearly connected with it in Parts I and II; but whether one does this, or waits until Part III is a matter of preference. Taken as a whole, therefore, jurisprudential study ranges from minute analytical dissections and sharp distinctions at one end of the intellectual scale to the broad sweep of ideas and philosophies through the ages at the other.

Sociology is a theoretical study of social existence based on descriptions of social facts[16]. From the point of view of the sociologist the administration of law is an observable social fact, while from the point of view of the lawyer it is obvious that laws can only function in a social environment, that they are bound to be influenced by the prevailing climate of opinion and tendencies and that, to a lesser extent, the continued enforcement of laws does in its turn affect people's outlook. More specifically, three aspects of sociology can be singled out as being peculiarly relevant to a lawyer's understanding of law, namely history, anthropology and economics. Historical development frequently accounts for and explains present-day doctrines; anthropology increasingly provides valuable insights into institutions of the modern state; while the influence of the economic order on the structure of both laws and society has been amply demonstrated. With regard to ethics, this, again speaking broadly, is a theoretical study of what is implied by prescriptions of what ought to be or ought not to be[17]. Insofar as the 'oughts' of laws imply aims to be achieved, the element of ethical evaluation inherent in the content of laws becomes clear.

The alleged autonomy of analytical jurisprudence, history, sociology and ethics

It used to be fashionable to draw contrasts between these, but to do so would be to paint a misleading picture. For, in the first place, the suggested

---

15 Buckland *Some Reflections on Jurisprudence* p 47. See also Julius Stone's treatment, *Legal System and Lawyers' Reasonings* pp 18 et seq; Jerome Hall *Foundations of Jurisprudence* (on which see p 485–487, post); Lord Radcliffe *The Law and its Compass* p 93.
16 Emmet *Rules, Roles and Relations* pp 5–6. See generally Sprott *Sociology*; Johnson *Sociology. A Systematic Introduction*, Part I.
17 *Emmet* pp 5–6.

distinction between analytical jurisprudence, on the one hand, and history and sociology, on the other, is non-existent. Ever since Bentham and Austin 'analytical jurisprudence' has been associated with the formal analysis of legal concepts, but the opposition between this and history and sociology is rooted in a confusion between the *subject matter* of a study and the *method* by which it is pursued. 'Analytical' connotes a method of approach which applies not only to formal, but also to historical and sociological study. One may analyse the structure of laws as they are found, or their purpose and operation in society, or their historical evolution. For this reason Salmond's classification, for example, is to be rejected. He divided jurisprudence into Analytical, Historical and Ethical. The former, he explained, is the analysis of the first principles of the law 'without reference either to their historical origin or development or to their ethical significance or validity'[18]. The distinction is not one of kind, but of emphasis. They are both analytical; in the one case attention is fixed on the law as it is today, in the other on development over a period of time. Moreover, insofar as history is only a branch of sociology a similar objection applies to any distinction between analytical and sociological study. Analysis is necessary to any sort of fruitful exposition, and it is misleading even to suggest that sociology is not concerned with analysis. It would be worthless if it were not. Here, too, the contrast is not that one type of study is analytical while the other is not, but that in the one, analysis is applied to the formal structure of law while in the other, analysis reaches beyond this into the way in which it works in society.

In the light of the above objection it might be thought that the word 'analytical' could be shared by these studies, but in such a way as to preserve distinctions between formal analysis, historical analysis and sociological analysis. Even such distinctions, however, are frequently untenable. In the case of many institutions, notably of the common law, formal analysis of them as they are inevitably dovetails in with their historical evolution. Formal, historical and functional analysis cannot always be separated. Legal institutions do not exist *in vacuo*, but are there for some purpose. An important point is that even the formal structure of concepts is constantly being re-shaped according to the functions they are made to perform. Indeed, all analysis is ultimately directed towards an understanding of the subject matter, and formal analysis alone will not provide a complete understanding of legal material because there has also to be an examination of the purpose for which it is there and how it works in the context of actual situations.

Just as analysis cannot be divorced from history and sociology, so, too, sociology is not independent in ethics. Social problems are grounded in ethical evaluation. For instance, as Professor Emmet has observed, the problem of juvenile delinquency is seen to be a *problem*, not because it prevails,

18 Salmond *Jurisprudence* (7th edn). Salmond's view has been discarded in the 12th edn by Fitzgerald. Stone has suggested that the separate identity, traditionally given to historical jurisprudence, sprang from its early emergence on the Continent: *The Province and Function of Law* p 35. Salmond drew another distinction between historical jurisprudence and legal history on the basis that the former was the analytical aspect of history: *Jurisprudence* (7th edn) p 6; and see Keeton *The Elementary Principles of Jurisprudence* p 7. This distinction is wholly unreal. The innuendo is that legal historians do not analyse. Nothing is more untrue, and the point is well made by Allen *Legal Duties* p 13. For a similar distinction between comparative law and comparative jurisprudence, see Wigmore. 'A New Way of Teaching Comparative Law' (1926) JSPTL 6. For a possible distinction between 'sociology of law' and 'sociological jurisprudence', see pp 422–423 post.

but because it is thought to be *bad*. Again, the most suitable method of resolving some social problem often depends upon built-in ethical considerations. As a solution to the over-population problem the periodic slaughter of all new-born babies will not even be contenanced, not because it would not solve the problem, but because it would be unworkable owing to the moral sentiments of people. Finally, many social aims, such as 'stability', 'cohesion', 'education', 'health' and the like are value-laden and are posited as goals of society because they are approved[19].

Ethical evaluation, for its part, cannot be kept apart from sociology. Moral judgment by its very nature implies decision about action in some situation, and all information relevant to that situation needs to be taken into account. Furthermore, the moral judgment passed on conduct is often dependent upon the social relationship, or role, that is involved. For example, the moral judgment on a man who turns his back on a beseeching child will depend not only on the relation of the man to the child (eg parent or stranger), but also on the role which the child is fulfilling (eg collecting for Guy Fawkes, soliciting for immoral purposes and so on).

It is evident, therefore, that the study of jurisprudence should not be insulated from these other disciplines. When it comes to practical techniques their interrelation is no less obvious. Four different techniques are discernible. (a) **Judicial technique.** A point, to be amplified later, is that laws do not of themselves decide disputes, for they have to be applied to the case in hand. This process leaves to the judge an element of choice[20], which is guided by a variety of considerations, philosophical, historical, social and moral[1]. (b) **Legislative technique.** The need to clarify the social problem that requires legislation and to evaluate the objective in view requires no further emphasis. (c) **Administrative technique.** An element of discretion in giving effect to policy decisions is inescapable and the modern tendency is to enlarge this. Such discretion is again guided by social and moral considerations. (d) **Advisory technique.** Lawyers advising clients or arguing in court have to take account, not only of laws, but also of how they are likely to be applied by courts. This combines prediction of how a court is likely to decide and persuasion of the court so that the prediction is fulfilled. They thus have to gauge as best they can the influence on judges of current social, moral and other pressures.

To insist in this way on the unity of legal, sociological and ethical study is not to dismiss purely formal analysis as valueless. All that is urged is that while this is important, it is no more an end in itself than the foundations of a house.

So far stress has been laid on the need to approach jurisprudential study with the aid of every relevant discipline. This, however, is separate from the question whether so broad-based an approach should be directed to speculating about English law in particular, or perhaps just the common law systems, or law generally. Much will depend on the level of abstractness at which the problems are presented. For example, problems of law and order are common to all systems, but problems of binding precedent can only arise in common law systems. A related question is whether the material, which furnishes the basis for speculation, should be drawn from one system, or a

---

19 Emmet *Rules, Roles and Relations* ch 2, especially pp 19 et seq.
20 Pp 151 et seq. post.
 1 Cardozo *The Nature of the Judicial Process* pp 30-31, and passim; ch 10 post.

few, or all systems. Here the limitation is a practical one, and this is what is hinted at by the word 'possible' in the phrase 'broadest possible basis'. These questions, which have not always been distinguished, have given rise to some debate as to whether the study should proceed on a particular, comparative or general basis.

The particular basis derives its material exclusively from one system of law, the comparative basis derives its material from more than one system, while the general basis presupposes certain notions as being common to all, or a large number of systems. Many writers have paid lip-service to general jurisprudence such as Austin, Holland and Allen, but have not adhered to it in their treatment. Austin dealt mainly with English law with occasional allusions to Roman Law. It is possible that underlying his thinking was the belief that the common and civil law between them would cover the civilised world and so constitute 'general' jurisprudence. In any case, his references to Roman law are too few and superficial even for this purpose. Holland, in spite of an uncompromising adherence to general jurisprudence, proceeded mainly with an exposition of English law; Allen's treatment is comparative at most. Besides, the arguments that have been adduced in support of general jurisprudence have not always been convincing, and the following observations of Holland are worthy of comment. He supported his advocacy of general jurisprudence with an analogy drawn from geology.

> 'Principles of Geology elaborated from the observation of England alone hold good all over the globe, in so far as the same substances and forces are everywhere present; and the principles of jurisprudence, if arrived at entirely from English data, would be true if applied to the particular laws of any other community of human beings; assuming them to resemble in essentials the human beings who inhabit England.... The phrase [particular jurisprudence] may however, and probably does, mean: an acquaintance with the laws of a particular people; and the impropriety of describing such merely empirical and practical knowledge by a term which should be used only as the name of a science has been already pointed out'[2].

In the first place, the analogy is false. However true it may be that principles of geology derived from an observation of English data will apply elsewhere as well, this is so only because, as Holland himself says, 'the same substances and forces are everywhere present'. The point, however, is that the 'substances and forces' of law are not the same everywhere. Law is a social institution, and the structures of societies differ, their pressures differ, their traditions and environments differ. Secondly, he glosses over this obvious point by shifting attention from *communities* of human beings to *human beings* themselves, for it seems safe to say that at least human beings elsewhere in the world do 'resemble in essentials the human beings who inhabit England'. Everything then turns on what is signified by 'essentials': 'essential' to human beings as organic entities, or as social units, or what? This vital word is left unexplained. Thirdly, it is not easy to see what is meant by the word 'science' so that it comes to be associated with general, but not with particular, jurisprudence. Fourthly, the passage commits two of the semantic sins mentioned earlier. The word 'jurisprudence' is alleged to possess a 'proper' meaning, which would exclude the term 'particular jurisprudence' as 'improper'. Again, not only is the emotive connotation of 'science' used to evoke a

---

2 Holland *Elements of Jurisprudence* p 11. For criticism, much of which is adopted here, see Buckland *Some Reflections on Jurisprudence* pp 68–69.

favourable response to general jurisprudence, but the derogatory insinuation in the phrase 'merely empirical and practical' is used to evoke a correspondingly disparaging response to particular jurisprudence. It will be seen, therefore, that the passage fails to make out any case for general jurisprudence.

It has been suggested that the answer to the question whether the approach should be general or particular depends on how abstract the problem under review is. It will also depend on whether the study aims at formal or functional analysis, and, if formal, whether it proceeds constructively or demonstratively. If an analysis of form and structure is intended, those who seek to construct formal concepts will find themselves forced of necessity to confine their attention to the particular basis, or at most to the comparative[3]. Only supporters of the demonstrative method will find the general basis manageable. On the other hand, functional analysis may conveniently be conducted on either a particular or general basis. Generalised functional jurisprudence might include such things as general methods of reasoning (eg deduction, analogy etc) and general adaptability to social and moral change.

Adaptation, improvement and reform

Jurisprudence is concerned, not only with the law and its institutions as they are and with their social impact, but also with improving them and changing them in line with social developments. This brings in the pressures behind change and the machinery of change. These matters will be considered in Chapter 15.

Conceptual framework for jurisprudential study

Emphasis has been laid on the need to engage every relevant discipline for the purpose of study. These wide ranging pursuits and the functioning of law in particular make it obvious that law has to be considered in the sense of a legal system, and the conceptual framework needed to unify all this is a temporal one. A legal system, as the word 'system' implies, is a co-ordinated and purposive activity. Now, every activity must occupy some time over its functioning; from which it follows that every functioning phenomenon, together with its component elements, must continue to exist over that period of time. Therefore, the conditions essential to continued existence and factors relating to functioning are implicitly part of the concept of it as a functioning phenomenon. An analogy may help. It is usual to regard, for instance, a human being as a three-dimensional entity possessing length, breadth and depth. This, however, is the concept of an instantaneous person, who has length, breadth and depth for a moment and vanishes. In the real world there is no such thing as an instantaneous person; he or she endures over a period of time, which introduces the dimension of endurance in which length, breadth and depth endure together. The continued existence of a person depends on certain essential conditions, such as a minimum intake of calories, oxygen, parameters of temperature, of states of health and so on. A graph of an enduring human being, if such were possible, would depict a person

3 Cf *Formation of Contracts. A Study of the Common Core of Legal Systems* (ed Schlesinger) for the unwieldly result of trying to encompass a large number of systems even on a single topic.

rather like a four-dimensional worm extending in time[4]. There are thus two frames of thought, the time-frame of the present and that of continuity, ie the continuum. 'Present' does not mean 'instantaneous', but a very limited time-frame covering the immediate concern as distinct from indefinite duration. The idea of a 'four-dimensional worm' may seem abstract and remote from reality until one realises, with some sense of shock, that of the two the familiar, everyday three-dimensional conception is the more abstract and unreal, since it is that of an 'instantaneous person', which does not exist. So, too, with legal system and laws. A law is not designed to be in force for an instant or only for today, but to operate over a period of time. A 'momentary law' is as inconceivable as a 'momentary person'. More important is the point that as soon as one thinks of a legal system or a law as continuing, then everything implied by the idea of continuity becomes an *integral part* of the concept of the continuing phenomenon. Nor can one contemplate continuity without taking account of the factors relating to origin and continued existence and those relating to function (purpose) and functioning (operation).

Which, then, is more 'real': a human being or law which lasts only here and now, or a continuing human being or law? The obvious answer might lead one to reject the present time-frame entirely, but this would be a mistake. Thinking in both frames is useful in different contexts. For the purpose of accommodating persons round a table, for example, the concept of each as a three-dimensional entity suffices; the conditions of continued existence are superfluous. In situations where existence is of moment, such as a prolonged stay in a hotel or in space, the conditions essential to existence become vital. Again, the idea of a living fish implies an environment of water, and so on. Similarly, the validity of a law is all that is needed for immediate purposes, but the idea of a continuing law automatically imports the factors that brought it into being, keep it going, modify, weaken or kill it, as well as those that determine how in fact it works in its social environment.

To regard legal phenomena in a continuum will provide the unifying framework for the study of law in relation to other disciplines, especially sociology and ethics. There is much loose talk about the 'sociological' study of law, which so often ends in platitudinous generalities—the worst kind of mental training. The temporal approach offers a modest but systematic plan by asking: What factors (social, political, moral etc) brought about a rule of law? What factors keep it going? (which need not necessarily be the same as those which brought it about). How does it work? (which calls for an investigation into its structure, its efficiency in fulfilling its task and the factors that affect its working)[5]. Can it be improved? Such questions reach out into sociology, ethics and other fields with limitless ramifications.

The present book will develop this temporal approach in various contexts, and it is submitted that in a time-perspective some traditional puzzles can be resolved, while others assume different proportions. It is also worth pointing out that this approach involves no statement in the form 'Law is ...'.

---

4 This analogy is taken from Eddington *The Nature of the Physical World* pp 53, 87. The expression 'four-dimensional worm' is his. For the temporal approach to law explained above and its relation to Hurst *Justice Holmes on Legal History*, see Dias 'Temporal Approach Towards a New Theory of Natural Law [1970] 28 CLJ 75 at 76 n3. A temporal basis is also implicit in Hall's 'integrative jurisprudence': *Foundations of Jurisprudence* (see pp 485–487 post).

5 Cf Hall's basis of 'law-as-action': *Foundations of Jurisprudence* on which see p 486 post.

What it offers is a way of looking at laws, indeed of any phenomena, and, as such, is entirely non-committal as to the nature of law.

READING LIST

C K Allen *Legal Duties* ch 1.

J Austin *Lectures on Jurisprudence* (5th edn R Campbell) II, pp 1071–1079.

C A Auerbach 'On Professor Hart's Definition and Theory in Jurisprudence' (1956) 9 Journal of Legal Education 39.

J Bryce *Studies in History and Jurisprudence* II, ch 12.

W W Buckland *Some Reflections on Jurisprudence* chs 1 and 6.

H Cairns *The Theory of Legal Science* chs 1, 6 and 10.

M R Cohen *Law and Social Order* pp 184, 219.

W W Cook 'Scientific Method and the Law (1927) 13 American Bar Association Journal 303.

J Dewey *How We Think* chs 8–11.

P Goodrich 'The Role of Linguistics in Legal Analysis' (1984) 47 Modern Law Review 523.

J Hall 'Integrative Jurisprudence' (1976) 27 Hasting's Law Journal 779.

H L A Hart 'Definition and Theory in Jurisprudence' (1954) 70 Law Quarterly Review 37.

W N Hohfeld *Fundamental Legal Conceptions* (ed W W Cook) ch 8.

E W Patterson *Jurisprudence* Part I.

M Rheinstein 'Education for Legal Craftsmanship' (1944–45) 30 Iowa Law Review 408.

R Robinson *Definition*.

J Stone *Legal System and Lawyers' Reasonings* 'Introduction' and ch 5.

R S Summers 'Legal Philosophy Today—an Introduction' in *Essays in Legal Philosophy* (ed R S Summers) p 1.

G L Williams 'Language and the Law' (1945) 61 Law Quarterly Review 71, 179, 293, 384, (1946) 62 Law Quarterly Review 387.

J Wilson *Language and the Pursuit of Truth*.

CHAPTER 2

Legal material

Thought about law presupposes some acquaintance with the law itself; which is why the study of jurisprudence becomes meaningful only towards the middle or, preferably, the end of a first course in law. It has been suggested that legal material can be identified with reference to the use of the word 'law' by courts. The detailed rules so identified are traditionally distributed under various labels such as contract, tort, crime, property and so forth, and new categories keep emerging such as obligations, intellectual property and others. Reflection on the nature of this material, however it may have been presented, shows that it is not of uniform texture. There are, again, different ways of classifying the texture. The one that will be adopted here is according to the functions performed by different kinds of material. There are:

(1) duties prescribing how people ought, or ought not, to behave with regard to others, who are said to have correlative claims or rights;
(2) liberties or freedoms to act and not to act;
(3) powers to alter existing legal situations;
(4) immunities from having existing legal situations altered;
(5) means of achieving legal ends;
(6) definitions;
(7) location of legal relationships;
(8) principles, doctrines and standards.

The first four concern legal relationships between persons and are termed 'jural relations'[1].

JURAL RELATIONS

Claims, liberties, powers and immunities are subsumed under the term 'rights' in ordinary speech, but for the sake of clarity and precision it is essential to appreciate that this word has undergone four shifts in meaning. They connote four different ideas concerning the activity, or potential activity, of one person with reference to another.

(1) Y's duty with regard to X would be expressed by X as 'you ought (must)': (X is then said to have a claim or right, *stricto sensu*).
(2) X's freedom to do something in relation to Y would be expressed by X as 'I may': (X has a liberty or privilege).
(3) X's ability to alter Y's legal position would be expressed by X as 'I can': (X has a power).

---

1 For their importance, see Kohler *Einführung in die Rechtswissenschaft* s 6; Ahrens *Cours de droit naturel* s 23; Savigny *System des heutigen römischen Rechts* ss 4, 52; Pashukanis *Allgemeine Staatslehr und Marxismus*; Kocourek *Jural Relations* chs 1-3.

(4) Y's inability to alter X's legal position would be expressed by X as 'you cannot': (X has an immunity)[2].

The use of the homonym 'right' to denote these separate ideas obscures the distinctions and leads to confusion sooner or later. It would be helpful, therefore, to make the distinctions as obvious as possible by allotting to each a term of its own[3].

These distinctions were arrived at gradually. Hobbes criticised Sir Edward Coke for failing to see the distinction between being bound (claim-duty relation) and being free (liberty)[4]. It is also apparent from a work of Bentham, published only in 1945[5], that he too distinguished, clearly and convincingly, between claim and liberty. His work was lost to his successors until recently, but may have been known to his disciple Austin, who drew the same distinction rather tentatively[6]. In 1862 Windscheid distinguished between claim and power[7]. Thereafter, Thon in 1878[8] and Bierling in 1883[9] distinguished between claim, liberty and power. In 1902 Salmond also distinguished between these three and the corresponding ideas of duty, disability and liability[10]. Finally, in 1913 Hohfeld, an American jurist, rearranged and completed Salmond's scheme by adding a fourth term, immunity, and worked out a table of jural relations with incisive logic[11]. The work so brilliantly pioneered has been developed and expanded in many directions.

Hohfeld set out his table of jural relations as follows:

Jural Correlatives	Right	Privilege	Power	Immunity
	Duty	No-right	Liability	Disability
Jural Opposites	Right	Privilege	Power	Immunity
	No-right	Duty	Disability	Liability

The following presentation of this table is that of Professor G L Williams[12].

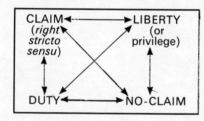
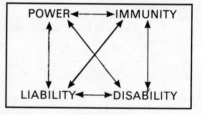

2 The phrases 'you must', 'I may', etc were suggested by Corbin 'Legal Analysis and Terminology' (1919) 29 Yale Law Journal 165.
3 Cardozo *The Growth of the Law* p 30; Stone *Legal System and Lawyers' Reasonings* p 138; Ogden and Richards *The Meaning of Meaning* pp 130–131.
4 Hobbes *Dialogue between a Philosopher and a Student of the Common Laws of England* vi, 30.
5 Bentham *The Limits of Jurisprudence Defined* (ed Everett) ch 2, re-published in 1970 as *Of Laws in General* (ed Hart) ch 10 and Appendix B.
6 Austin *Jurisprudence* I, p 356.
7 Windscheid *Lehrbuch de Pandektenrechts* I, s 37.
8 Thon *Rechsnorm und subjektives Recht* cap 5.
9 Bierling *Zur Kritik der juristischen Grundbegriffe* II, pp 49–73.
10 Salmond *Jurisprudence* (7th edn) ss 74–77.
11 Hohfeld *Fundamental Legal Conceptions* ch 1. His early death prevented him from completing the task he outlined. His scattered writings were collected and published posthumously under the editorship of W W Cook in 1923.
12 In Salmond *Jurisprudence* (11th edn) p 278, and 'The Concept of Legal Liberty' in *Essays in Legal Philosophy* (ed R S Summers) 121. Professor Williams's own terminology is not quite the same as Hohfeld's, for he has suggested certain changes.

An important preliminary point is that a jural relation between two parties should be considered only between them, even though the conduct of one may create another jural relation between him and someone else. In *Chapman v Honig*[13] the defendant's action in terminating the plaintiff's tenancy was lawful (ie he had a liberty) as between them, although it was at the same time unlawful (ie breach of duty) as between defendant and the court (contempt).

When operating the scheme the following formulae will be helpful.

Jural Correlatives (vertical arrows and read both ways): '... in one person, X, implies the *presence* of its correlative, ..., in another person, Y'. Thus, claim in X implies the presence of duty in Y (but in so far as duties may exist without correlative claims[14], the converse proposition is not always true). Again, liberty in X implies the presence of no-claim in Y, and *vice versa*.

Jural Opposites, including what one might here call *jural negations* (diagonal arrows and read both ways): '... in one person, X, implies the *absence* of its opposite, ..., in *himself*'. Thus, claim in X implies the absence of no-claim in himself, and *vice versa*; duty in X implies the absence of liberty in himself, and *vice versa*.

The merit of Professor Williams's presentation is that it is possible to discern at a glance a third set of jural relations not mentioned by Hohfeld. These may be called

Jural Contradictories (horizontal arrows and read both ways): '... in one person, X, implies the *absence* of its contradictory, ..., in *another* person, Y'. Thus, claim in X implies the absence of liberty in Y, and *vice versa*. In the case of duties with correlative claims, a duty in X (absence of liberty) implies the absence of no-claim in Y and *vice versa*. (The question whether there are non-correlative duties will be discussed below).

With these formulae in mind the scheme may now be considered in detail.

CLAIM-DUTY RELATION ('YOU OUGHT')

Hohfeld himself suggested the word 'claim' as a substitute for 'right', but continued to use 'right'. 'Claim', however, will be preferred in this book. He did not deal at length with this relation, believing that the nature of claim and duty was sufficiently clear. This was perhaps rather a facile assumption. He did, however, point out that the clue to claim lies in duty[15], which is a prescriptive pattern of behaviour. A claim is, therefore, simply a sign that some person ought to behave in a certain way. Sometimes the party benefited by the pattern of conduct is able to bring an action to recover compensation for its non-observance, or he may be able to avail himself of more indirect consequences. At other times, he can do nothing[16].

13 [1963] 2 QB 502, [1963] 2 All ER 513.
14 Pp 26-27, post.
15 Hohfeld *Fundamental Legal Conceptions* p 38. Duty is discussed in ch 11, post.
16 Many tests have traditionally been offered for 'rights' in a broad sense. (1) Presence of a duty. This is no test even for 'right' in the narrow sense of claim. Non-correlative duties, discussed in the text, would be one answer; but, apart from that, a contract in which the promisor undertakes to do something for the promisee and a third party confers no claim on the latter. (2) Morality: Grotius *De Jure Belli ac Pacis* 1.1.4; Pufendorff *De Naturae Jure et Gentium* 1.30; Phillips *Jurisprudence* pp 6-8, 27; Rutherford *Institutes of Natural Law* II, s 3;

The correlation of claim and duty is not perfect, nor did Hohfeld assert that it was. Every claim implies the existence of a correlative duty, since it has no content apart from the duty. The statement, 'X has a claim', is vacuous; but the statement, 'X has a claim that Y ought to pay him £10', is meaningful because its content derives from Y's duty. On the other hand, whether every duty implies a correlative claim is doubtful. Austin admitted that some duties have no correlative claims, and he called these 'absolute duties'[17]. His examples involve criminal law. Salmond, on the other hand, thought that every duty must have a correlative claim somewhere[18]. Allen supported Austin[19]. Professor G L Williams treats the dispute as verbal[20]. Duties in criminal law are imposed with reference to, and for the benefit of, members of society, none of whom has claims correlative to these duties. As far as their functioning is concerned, it is immaterial whether the claims are in the Crown, the Crown in Parliament, or whether there are any claims.

Statutory duties furnish other examples. It rests on the interpretation of each statute whether the duties created by it are correlative to any claims in the persons contemplated by the duties. It was held in *Arbon v Anderson*[1] that even if there had been a breach of the Prison Rules 1933, which had been made under the Prison Act 1898, s 2, a prisoner affected by such a breach

---

(possibly) Allen *Legal Duties* p 200. However, a case like *Bradford Corpn v Pickles* [1895] AC 587, shows that a defendant can have a legal 'right' (liberty) to act unmorally and spitefully. (3) Interest: Ihering *Geist des römischen Rechts* III, p 339; Salmond *Jurisprudence* p 217; Heck *The Jurisprudence of Interests: an Outline*, in *20th Century Legal Philosophy Series* (trans Schoch) II, p 33. The House of Lords acted on the interest basis in *Gouriet v Union of Post Office Workers* [1978] AC 435, [1977] 3 All ER 70. See also *Ex p Island Records Ltd* [1978] Ch 122, [1978] 3 All ER 824. However, (a) a 'right' does not always coincide with the interest, eg a trust, where both law and equity acknowledge the legal 'right' in the trustee although the interest is not in him, and common law gives no 'right' to the beneficiary who has the interest. (b) Not all interests give rise to 'rights', eg an employer's interest in not having strikes gives him no 'rights' against his employees; nor does the interest which a husband has in his child being borne by his wife, give him a 'right' against her not to abort her pregnancy: *Paton v Trustees of BPAS* [1979] QB 276, [1978] 2 All ER 987. If anything, 'rights' are only 'protected interests': Salmond *Jurisprudence* p 218. This shows that the protection of some interests, but not others, is not grounded in the mere fact of an interest: *Phipps v Pears* [1965] 1 QB 76 at 84, [1964] 2 All ER 35 at 38. (c) A 'right' is not the interest, but the means by which it is secured: Gray *The Nature and Sources of the Law* p 18; Allen *Legal Duties* pp 218–219; Merkel *Juristische Enzyklopädie* s 159. (4) Attitude of demand: Vinogradoff 'The Foundations of a Theory of Rights' in *Collected Papers* II, p 367. 'Rights', however, inhere in people who have no attitude of demand, eg a baby, or as in *Cooper v Phibbs* (1867) LR 2 HL 149 (a person contracted to take a lease of a fishery, but the contract was held void since the fishery belonged to him all the time, ie the 'right' was in him though he clearly had no attitude of demand). (5) Power of enforcing the correlative duty: Gray *The Nature and Sources of the Law* pp 12, 18; Holland *Elements of Jurisprudence* p 83; to which the objections are, (a) that a person may set enforcement machinery in motion and yet have no 'right' himself, eg criminal law machinery. (b) If enforcement means a successful action, such success depends on the 'right', not *vice versa;* Olivecrona *Law as Fact* (1939) pp 85–86; 'Law as Fact' in *Interpretations of Modern Legal Philosophies* (ed Sayre) ch 25. For enforcement generally, see pp 235–246, post. A possible explanation for these attempts to find some basis for 'rights' may be the mistaken belief that every word must correspond with some 'thing'. Professor Hart, who appreciates this, brought to bear a different technique of elucidation: 'Definition and Theory in Jurisprudence' (1954) 70 LQR at 49.

17 Austin *Jurisprudence* I, pp 401–403
18 Salmond *Jurisprudence* (7th edn) p 240
19 Allen *Legal Duties* pp 183–193
20 In Salmond *Jurisprudence* (11th edn) pp 264–265.
 1 [1943] 1 All ER 154. See also *R V Customs and Excose Comrs, ex p Cooke and Stevenson* [1970] 1 All ER 1068, [1970] 1 WLR 450.

had no action since he had no claim. The decision in *Bowmaker Ltd v Tabor*[2] creates a difficulty. The Courts (Emergency Powers) Act 1939, s 1(2), forbade hire-purchase firms to retake possession of things hired without first obtaining leave of court. The claim to damages was conferred by the statute on any hire purchaser from whom goods were retaken without the necessary leave having been obtained. In this case the defendant purchaser consented to the plaintiffs retaking possession of the article hired, and they did so without obtaining leave of court. The plaintiffs later sued the defendant for arrears of rent, which had accrued up to the time of the retaking, and the defendant counterclaimed for damages under the statute. The Court of Appeal held that he was entitled to damages. This means that there was a duty to pay damages, which was correlative to the claim to receive them. The duty not to retake possession without leave of court was, as the Court pointed out, imposed in the public interest and not for the benefit of an individual. The defendant, therefore, could not absolve the plaintiffs from it. The inference is that the claim was not in him[3]. The further question as to why the defendant's consent to the plaintiffs' course of action did not debar him from exercising his claim to damages was answered by the Court on the ground that consent, or *volenti non fit injuria*, is no defence to a breach of this kind of statutory obligation[4].

Conduct is regulated by the imposition of duties. Claims may assist in achieving this end, but if it can be otherwise achieved, there is no reason why the mere fact that Y is under a duty with regard to X should confer upon X, or anyone else for that matter, a corresponding claim[5]. There is nothing to prevent it being the law that every breach of duty, of whatsoever sort, shall be dealt with by the machinery of the state. Such a state of affairs, though possible, would be inconvenient, for it would stretch state machinery to breaking point. Where duties are of private concern, the remedies are best left to individuals to pursue in the event of their breach. Above all, it is expedient to give aggrieved persons some satisfaction, usually by way of compensation. Every system of law has to decide which breaches of duties shall be taken up by the public authorities on their own motion, and which shall be left to private persons to take up or not as they please. The distinction between 'public' and 'private' law is quite arbitrary. It would seem, therefore, that there is no intrinsic reason why claims should be a necessary concomitant of duties[6]. Indeed, some modern writers, for different reasons, reject the whole idea of claim as redundant[7].

If non-correlative duties are accepted, they do not fit snugly into the Hohfeldian scheme.

2 [1941] 2 KB 1, [1941] 2 All ER 72.
3 This is supported eg by Lord Atkin in *East Suffolk Rivers Catchment Board v Kent* [1941] AC 74 at 88, [1940] 4 All ER 527 at 533, who said that 'a duty imposed by statute is primarily a duty owed to the state'.
4 Cf *Carr v Broderick & Co Ltd* [1942] 2 KB 275, [1942] 2 All ER 441.
5 Kelsen *General Theory of Law and State* p 85.
6 Radin 'A Restatement of Hohfeld' (1938) 51 Harv LR 1149–1150, says that X's claim and Y's duty are the same thing. On the argument above, his statement is unacceptable.
7 Eg Duguit *Law in the Modern State* (trans F and H Laski), and see Laski 'M Duguit's Conception of the State' in *Modern Theories of Law* (ed Jennings) ch 4; Kelsen *General Theory of Law and State*; Olivecrona *Law as Fact* (1939).

LIBERTY-NO-CLAIM RELATION ('I MAY')

Hohfeld distinguished the freedom which a person has to do or not do something from claim, and called it 'privilege'; but the term liberty will be preferred. X's so-called 'right' to wear a bowler hat consists, on Hohfeld's analysis, of a liberty to wear the hat and another liberty not to wear it. The relationship between claim, duty, liberty and no-claim can be explained in the following way.

(1)   Duty and liberty are jurally 'opposite'. If, for example, X were under a duty *to wear* a bowler hat, this would imply the absence in him of any liberty *not to wear* it, ie the Hohfeldian opposite of duty means that there is no liberty to do whatever is opposite to the content of the duty. Similarly, if X were under a duty *not to wear* the hat, this would be the opposite of a liberty *to wear* it, ie there would be no liberty to do so[8]. The jural opposition between duty and liberty does not mean simply that the one cancels out the other, but that they will only have that effect when the content of one is irreconcilable with the content of the other[9]. For example, X normally has the liberty of wearing his hat. If he puts himself under a duty to wear it, his liberty and duty *of wearing* the hat are harmonious and co-exist[10]. It is only when he puts himself under a duty *not to wear* it that his liberty *to wear* it and his duty conflict and are jurally opposite.

The opposition may be illustrated by *Mills v Colchester Corpn*[11]. The owners of an oyster fishery had, since the days of Queen Elizabeth I, granted licences to fish to persons who satisfied certain conditions. The plaintiff, who satisfied them but was refused a licence, brought an action alleging a customary claim correlative to a duty in the defendants to grant him one. The Court held otherwise on the basis that the defendants had always exercised a discretion in the matter. This implied not only a liberty to grant licences, but also a liberty not to grant licences, which implied the absence of a duty to do so. If, then, they were under no duty to grant licences, the plaintiff could have no claim[12].

Sometimes it is held for reasons of policy that the liberty of doing a particular thing cannot be erased by a contrary duty. *Osborne v Amalgamated Society of Railway Servants*[13] lays down that the liberty of a member of Parliament to vote in any way he chooses on a given issue cannot be overridden

---

8   G L Williams suggests 'liberty (not)' instead of privilege to bring out the opposition between duty and privilege: 'The Concept of Legal Liberty' in *Essays in Legal Philosophy* 128-132. For illustrations in Roman law, see *Inst* 1.3.1; *D* 50.17.55.

9   Bentham had earlier demonstrated the logic more incisively than Hohfeld: see pp 338-339 post.

10   G L Williams instances the Larceny Act 1861, s 103, under which a person 'is authorised, and, if in his power, required' to effect an arrest. These words according to him confer both a liberty to arrest ('authorised') and a duty to do so ('required'): 'The Concept of Legal Liberty' p 134.

11   (1867) LR 2 CP 476. A liberty may be limited by circumstances which may create a duty to grant a licence: *David v Abdul Cader* [1963] 3 All ER 579, [1963] 1 WLR 834.

12   See also *Chaffers v Goldsmid* [1894] 1 QB 186, 63 LJQB 59 (a member of Parliament has a liberty to present the petition of a constituent to Parliament and an equal liberty not to present it. Hence he is not under a duty to do so). (This example is in G L Williams, 'The Concept of Legal Liberty' p 142). In *Bradford Corpn v Pickles* [1895] AC 587, a landowner's liberty of abstracting subterranean water implies that he has no duty not to abstract it. See also *Langbrook Properties Ltd v Surrey County Council* [1969] 3 All ER 1424, [1970] 1 WLR 161, and *Chapman v Honig* [1963] 2 QB 502, [1963] 2 All ER 513, and p 25, ante.

13   [1910] AC 87.

by a contractual duty to vote in a certain way. Similarly in *Redbridge London Borough v Jacques*[14], the respondent had for several years stationed his vehicle on a service road in the afternoons of early closing days and had operated a fruit and vegetable stall from the back of it. The local authority was aware of this practice and had raised no objection. It then charged him with obstructing the highway. The justices dismissed the charge on the ground that the local authority had, in effect, given him a licence (liberty). The decision was reversed on the ground that where there is a public duty, created by statute, this prevents the conferment of a liberty to do what the duty forbids.

(2) If Y has a claim, there must be a duty in X. A duty in X implies the absence of a liberty in X. Therefore, a claim in Y implies the absence of a liberty in X, ie claim and liberty are 'jural contradictories'.

(3) Conversely, the presence of a liberty in X implies the absence of a claim in Y. Hohfeld calls this condition 'no-claim'. Therefore, a liberty in X implies the presence of a 'no-claim' in Y, ie liberty and no-claim are 'jural correlatives'. On the opposition between claim and no-claim there is this to be said. The opposition here is different from that between duty and liberty. No question of content arises. No-claim is simply not having a claim, and having a claim is not being in the condition of no-claim, just as having a wife is not being in a state of bachelordom (no-wife). If it is thought necessary to distinguish between the opposition of duty and liberty on the one hand, and no-claim and claim on the other, the latter might be styled 'jural negation' instead.

Distinction between claim and liberty

A claim implies a correlative duty, but a liberty does not. X's liberty to wear a bowler hat is not correlative to a duty in anyone. There is indeed a duty in Y not to interfere, but Y's duty not to interfere is correlative to X's claim against Y that he shall not interfere. X's liberty to wear the bowler hat and his claim not to be prevented from so doing are two different ideas. Thus, X may enter into a valid contract with Y where X gives Y permission to prevent him from wearing the hat, but X says he will nevertheless try to wear it. If X succeeds in evading Y and leaves the scene wearing the hat, he has exercised his liberty to wear it and Y has no cause for complaint. If, on the other hand, Y prevents him from wearing the hat, he cannot complain, for he has by contract extinguished his claim against Y that Y shall not interfere. This shows that the liberty and the claim are separate and separable; the claim can be extinguished without affecting the liberty[15].

It is usual for liberties to be supported by claims, but it is important to realise that they are distinct and separate, and the distinction is reflected in case law. It was held in *Musgrove v Chun Teeong Toy*[16] that at common law an alien has the liberty to enter British territory, but no claim not to be

14 [1971] 1 All ER 260, [1970] 1 WLR 1604.
15 Cf Hohfeld's demonstration *Fundamental Legal Conceptions* p 41.
16 [1891] AC 272. This case was originally quoted by Salmond. Cf Mackenzie King: 'It is not a "fundamental human right" of an alien to enter Canada. It is a privilege. It is a matter of domestic policy', quoted in *Re Hanna* (1957) 21 WWR NS 400. See also *R v Secretary of State for Home Department, ex p Bhurosah* [1968] 1 QB 266, [1967] 3 All ER 831.

prevented; which was re-affirmed in *Schmidt v Secretary of State for Home Affairs*[17]. *Chaffers v Goldsmid*[18] shows that a person has the liberty of presenting a petition to Parliament through his representative member, but no claim against such member that the latter shall comply. *Bradford Corpn v Pickles*[19] shows that a landowner has the liberty of abstracting subterranean water, but no claim against anyone else who, by abstracting the water before it reaches the landowner, prevents him from exercising his liberty. In *Cole v Police Constable 443A*[20], the court considered the position of a non-parishioner in extra-parochial churches, for example Westminster Abbey, which is a Royal peculiar. Although the language of the learned judges is open to criticism, their conclusion, translated into Hohfeldian terminology, was that a non-parishioner has a liberty to be in such a church, but no claim not to be prevented. Therefore, the plaintiff's ejection by the respondent, who acted under instructions from the Dean, gave him no cause for complaint. Again, in *Piddington v Bates*[1] the defendant, a trade unionist, in the course of a trade dispute insisted on going to the rear entrance of certain premises at which two pickets were already standing. To do so would not have been wrongful, for he would merely have exercised a liberty. In fact, however, the complainant, a police officer, who had decided that two pickets were all that were needed in the circumstances, prevented the defendant from going to the rear entrance. The latter then 'pushed gently past' the complainant 'and was gently arrested' by him. The defendant was found guilty of obstructing a constable in the exercise of his duty, since his liberty to stand at the entrance was not supported by a claim not to be prevented.

The failure to distinguish between claim and liberty leads to illogical conclusions. Thus, a member of the public has only a liberty to attend public meetings, which is not supported by a claim not to be prevented[2]. The tribunal in *Thomas v Sawkins*[3] argued at one point that such a liberty to attend was a 'right' and that, therefore, there was a duty not to prevent the person concerned, who happened to be a policeman. The conclusion is a *non sequitur*, since it fails to perceive the distinction between the two uses of 'right' as established by case law. If, as was probably the case, it was sought to create a claim-duty relation for reasons of policy, more convincing reasoning should have been employed. Cases on trade competition, whatever the merits of the decisions, present an array of fallacious propositions, which would have been avoided had the distinction between liberty and claim been perceived[4]. The claim not to be interfered with in trade corresponds to a duty

---

17 [1969] 2 Ch 149, [1969] 1 All ER 904. See also *DPP v Bhagwan* [1972] AC 60, [1970] 3 All ER 97.
18 [1894] 1 QB 186.
19 [1895] AC 587.
20 [1937] 1 KB 316, [1936] 3 All ER 107.
1 [1960] 3 All ER 660, [1961] 1 WLR 162. For other cases involving a similar analysis, see *O'Kelly v Harvey* (1883) 14 LR Ir 105; *Humphries v Connor* (1864) 17 ICLR 1; *Duncan v Jones* [1936] 1 KB 218; *Tynan v Balmer* [1967] 1 QB 91, [1966] 2 All ER 133.
2 *De Morgan v Metropolitan Board of Works* (1880) 5 QBD 155; *Brighton Corpn v Packham* (1908) 72 JP 318; *Bailey v Williamson* (1873) LR 8 QB 118; *R v Cunninghame Graham and Burns* (1888) 16 Cox CC 420; *Ex p Lewis* (1888) 21 QBD 191; *R v Brent Health Authority, ex p Francis* [1985] 1 All ER 74, [1984] 3 WLR 1317. There is a liberty to hold a public meeting, ie it is not unlawful: *Burden v Rigler* [1911] 1 KB 337; *Duncan v Jones* [1936] 1 KB 218.
3 [1935] 2 KB 249.
4 Eg *Mogul SS Co v McGregor, Gow & Co* (1889) 23 QBD 598 at 611 (affd [1892] AC 25); *Allen v Flood* [1898] AC 1 at 29, 84, 112, 132, 138, 151; *Quinn v Leathem* [1901] AC 495 at 534; *A-G (Australia) v Adelaide SS Co* [1913] AC 781 at 793; *Sorrell v Smith* [1925] AC 700 at 727;

not to interfere. There is indeed a duty not to interfere, eg by smashing up the plaintiff's shop; but no duty not to interfere by underselling him. So the question how far a duty not to interfere extends, ie how far the liberty of another person to interfere is allowed, is a delicate decision of policy. This is the real issue, which is thrown into relief when these situations are seen to involve conflicting liberties, but which is masked by the language of duties and claims[5].

The exposure of faulty reasoning also helps in assessing the effect and worth of decided cases. In *Thomas v Sawkins*[6], for example, the very demonstration that the conclusion was illogical when stated in terms of 'rights' and duties shows that the way to reconcile it with the established law is by saying that it has, in effect, created a new rule of law for policemen[7].

Finally, it may be observed that Hohfeld's analysis of claim, duty, liberty and no-claim is useful in many general ways. It may be used for drawing distinctions for purposes of legal argument or decision. It was held, for instance, in *Byrne v Deane*[8] that to call a person an 'informer' was not defamatory. Suppose a case where the allegation is that the plaintiff is a 'conscientious objector'. *Byrne v Deane* is distinguishable. An 'informer' is a person who gives information of crime; there is in law a duty to do so, and *Byrne's* case decides that it is not defamatory to say that a man has performed a legal duty. There is only a liberty to be a 'conscientious objector', and *Byrne's* case is thus no authority for saying that it cannot be defamatory to allege that a person has exercised this liberty[9]. Again, the analysis is useful in considering the relation between common law and equity; in particular, it helps to demonstrate the precise extent to which there was conflict. Thus, the life-tenant had at law the liberty to cut ornamental trees, in equity he was under a duty not to do so. The liberty and duty are jural opposites and the latter cancels out the former. At common law a party had a claim to payment under a document obtained by fraud, in equity he had no-claim. Further, such a person had at law the liberty of resorting to a common law court on such a document, whereas equity imposed on him a duty not to do so (common injunction)[10].

Liberty as 'law'

It has been shown that liberty begins where duty ends. Some have maintained that freedom is outside the law. Thus, Pound declared that liberty is 'without independent jural significance'[11], and Kelsen said, 'Freedom is an

Crofter Harris Tweed Co Ltd v Veitch [1942] AC 435 at 462–466, [1942] 1 All ER 142 at 158–160.
5   G L Williams in 'The Concept of Legal Liberty' in *Essays in Legal Philosophy* p 141, exposes a faulty conclusion reached by Pollock in 'Gifts of Chattels without Delivery' (1890) 6 LQR 446; MacCormick 'A Note on Privacy' (1973) 89 LQR 23, exposes the fallacy in the argument of the majority Report of the Committee on Privacy ((1972) Cmnd 5012).
6   [1935] 2 KB 249.
7   Thus, Goodhart refers to it as 'A Constitutional Innovation' (1936–38) 6 CLJ 22.
8   [1937] 1 KB 818, [1937] 2 All ER 204. See also *Berry v Irish Times Ltd* [1973] IR 368.
9   Hamson, 'A Moot Case in Defamation' (1948) 10 CLJ 46.
10 Hohfeld *Fundamental Legal Conceptions* p 133.
11 'Legal Rights' (1916) 26 International Journal of Ethics 92 at 97.

extra-legal phenomenon'[12]. As to this, it is as well to remember that liberty may result (a) from the fact that legislators and judges have not yet pronounced on a matter, and represents the residue left untouched by encroaching duties, eg invasion of privacy; or (b) it may result from a deliberate decision not to interfere, as in *Bradford Corpn v Pickles*[13], or (c) from the deliberate abolition of a pre-existing duty, eg the statutory abolition of the duty forbidding homosexuality between consenting adults, or an Act of Indemnity absolving a person from a penal duty. There is some plausibility in saying with Pound and Kelsen that liberty in sense (a) lies outside law; but it seems odd to say that the liberty pronounced by a court in (b) and the statutory provisions in (c) are 'without independent jural significance' and 'extra-legal'. Analytically, the resulting position in all three cases is the same, namely, no duty not to do the act.

Kinds of liberties

Some liberties are recognised by the law generally, eg liberty to follow a lawful calling. So, too, are 'Parliamentary privilege' in debate and 'judicial privilege', which are liberties in the Hohfeldian sense in that both connote the absence of a duty not to utter defamatory statements. An infant's position (sometimes called in non-Hohfeldian language an immunity) in contracts for things other than necessaries is more complicated. In some cases it amounts to a power to repudiate the contract; in others it is not clear whether an infant has a liberty not to perform the contract, ie no primary duty to perform[14], or whether there is a sanctionless duty, ie a primary duty which he ought to fulfil, but no sanctioning duty to pay damages and instead an immunity from the power of judgment[15].

Other liberties are recognised by law on special occasions, that is to say, the normal duty not to do something is replaced in the circumstances by the liberty to do it, eg self-help, self-defence, the defences of fair comment and qualified privilege. Lastly, liberty may be created by the parties themselves, eg consent, or *volenti non fit injuria*, one effect of which is that it absolves a defendant from his duty[16].

Limits of liberties

Some liberties are unlimited, even if exercised maliciously, eg, 'Parliamentary' or 'judicial privilege'. *Non omne quod licet honestum est*[17]. In other cases, the exercise of liberties may be limited by the law of 'blackmail', by public

---

12 Kelsen *Das Problem der Souveränität* p 247; cf Kaufmann *Das Wesen der Völkerrechts* p 51; G L Williams 'The Concept of Legal Liberty' pp 122-123. See also p 369, post.
13 [1895] AC 587.
14 *Coutts & Co v Browne-Lecky* [1947] KB 104, [1946] 2 All ER 207.
15 If the infant performs he cannot recover unless consideration has wholly failed: *Valentini v Canali* (1889) 24 QBD 166; *Pearce v Brain* [1929] 2 KB 310; *Steinberg v Scala (Leeds) Ltd* [1923] 2 Ch 452.
16 *Wooldridge v Sumner* [1963] 2 QB 43, [1962] 2 All ER 978; *Stein v Lehnert* (1962) 36 DLR 159. At other times the effect of consent seems to be to leave the duty, but only waive the power of action: *Imperial Chemical Industries Ltd v Shatwell* [1965] AC 656, [1964] 2 All ER 999. For the distinction, see Dias 'Consent of Parties and *Voluntas Legis*' [1966] CLJ 75.
17 *D* 50.17.144; eg *Bradford Corpn v Pickles* [1895] AC 587.

policy[18] or by malice, eg qualified privilege and fair comment in defamation, or by statute[19].

POWER-LIABILITY RELATION ('I CAN')

Power denotes ability in a person to alter the existing legal condition, whether of oneself or of another, for better or for worse[20]. Liability, the correlative of power, denotes the position of a person whose legal condition can be so altered. This use of 'liability' is contrary to accepted usage, but when operating the Hohfeldian table words have to be divorced from their usual connotations. X has a power to make a gift to Y, and correlatively Y has a liability to have his legal position improved in this way[1]. A further point is that a person's legal condition may be changed by events not under anyone's control, eg an accumulation of snow on his roof. A distinction accordingly needs to be drawn between liability, which is correlative to power, ie the jural relation; and what for present purposes may be termed 'subjection', namely, the position of a person which is liable to be altered by non-volitional events. This is not a jural relation.

Distinction between claim and power

On the face of it the distinction is obvious: a claim is always a sign that some other person is required to conform to a pattern of conduct, a power is the ability to produce a certain result. The 'right', for example, to make a will can be dissected into a liberty to make a will (there is another liberty not to make one), claims against other people not to be prevented from making one, powers in the sense of the ability to alter the legal conditions of persons specified in the will, and immunities against being deprived of will-making capacity. The power itself has no duty correlative to it. It would be incorrect to describe this as a 'right' in the testator correlative to the duty in the executor to carry out the testamentary dispositions, for the will takes effect as from death and the executor's duty only arises from that moment. When the testator dies his claims etc cease, so the duty cannot correlate to any 'right' in him.

The distinctions between claim, liberty and power are important for much the same reasons as those considered above. A complex illustration is *Pryce v Belcher*[2]. At an election the plaintiff tendered his vote to the defendant, the returning-officer, who refused to accept it. The plaintiff was in fact disqualified from voting on grounds of non-residence. It was held that he had exercised a power by tendering his vote, which imposed on the defendant the duty to accept it. The latter's refusal to do so was a breach of that duty, which might well have rendered him liable to a criminal prosecution. However, the plaintiff's power to impose such a duty did not carry with it either the liberty of exercising the power or a claim to the fulfilment of the duty.

---

18 Eg covenants in restraint of trade. See also *Thorne v Motor Trade Association* [1937] AC 797, [1937] 3 All ER 157; *Congreve v Home Office* [1976] QB 629, [1976] 1 All ER 697.
19 Eg limits on the liberty to picket: *Broome v DPP* [1974] AC 587, [1974] 1 All ER 314.
20 Cf Roman law, *D* 9.2.37 pr, 28.1.6. pr, 50.17.163.
1 Stone *Legal System and Lawyers' Reasonings* p 147, seems to assume that liability necessarily contemplates a change for the worse. That is not what Hohfeld meant by it.
2 (1847) 4 CB 866.

He, therefore, failed in his action against the defendant for the breach of his duty.

> 'Although a party in the situation of the plaintiff, has the power in this way to compel the returning-officer under the apprehension of a prosecution, to put his name upon the poll, he has not the right to do so [liberty]; that, in doing so, he is acting in direct contravention of the Act of Parliament, the terms of which are express that he shall not be entitled to vote; and that the rejection of his vote cannot amount to a violation of any thing which the law can consider as his right'[3].

In *David v Abdul Cader*[4] the defendant refused to exercise a statutory power to grant the plaintiff a licence to run a cinema. The Supreme Court of Ceylon rejected the latter's action for damages on the ground that an action presupposes violation of a 'right' (claim) in the plaintiff and that until the power had been exercised the plaintiff acquired no 'right'. The fallacy is clear. The 'right' which the plaintiff would have acquired on the exercise of the power is the liberty to run his cinema with appurtenant claims, powers, etc. The acquisition or non-acquisition of these is independent of the question whether the defendant was under a duty to exercise the power and whether there was in the plaintiff a claim correlative to *this* duty. The Judicial Committee of the Privy Council reversed the Supreme Court on this very ground and remitted the case for trial on those issues. Failure to observe the distinction between power and claim results in confusion, though this occurs less often than in the case of liberty and claim. Also, analysis does help to assess the case law. An example is *Ashby v White*[5], where the 'right' to vote was held to import a duty not to prevent the person from voting. The 'right' to vote is a power coupled with a liberty to exercise it, and the whole point was whether there was a claim not to be prevented. The decision in effect created such a claim, although the reasoning was fallacious. The Sale of Goods Act 1893 (now the Act of 1979), s 12 (1), introduces an implied condition that a seller of goods 'has a right to sell the goods'. It is clear from the context, which deals with conditions as to title, that 'right' here means 'power' to pass title. It was held in *Niblett v Confectioners' Materials Co*[6] that the defendant company had no 'right' to sell certain articles because a third party could have restrained the sale for infringement of a trade mark. This is a confusion between power and liberty. For, the fact that the defendants had power to pass title is independent of whether or not they had a duty not to exercise it (ie no liberty to do so).

Distinction between duty and liability

If X deposits or lends a thing to Y, there is no duty in Y to restore it until X makes a demand. Before such demand is made Y is under a liability to be placed under the duty. The demand itself is the exercise of a power. The distinction is important, for instance, in connection with the limitation of

3 Coltman J at 883.
4 [1963] 3 All ER 579, [1963] 1 WLR 834, on which see Bradley 'Liability for Malicious Refusal of Licence' [1864] CLJ 4. For a demonstration of how two disputants might have avoided needless confusion had they employed the Hohfeldian terminology of power, liability, immunity and disability, see Rostow 'The Enforcement of Morals' [1960] CLJ at 195.
5 (1703) 2 Ld Raym 938.
6 [1921] 3 KB 387.

actions. Thus, in *Re Tidd, Tidd v Overell*[7], where money was entrusted to a person for safe-keeping, it was held that the period of limitation only commenced from the time that a demand for restoration had been made. Again, a deposit of money with a bank amounts to a loan, and there is no duty to repay until a demand has been made. *Joachimson v Swiss Bank Corpn*[8] shows that time only runs from demand and not from the time of the original deposit. A sum of money can be attached under a garnishee order if there is a duty to pay, even though the actual time for payment may be postponed. In *Seabrook Estate Co Ltd v Ford*[9], a debenture holder appointed a receiver, who was to realise the assets and then pay off any preferential claims and the principal and interest to the debenture holders, and having done that, to pay the residue to the company. The judgment creditors of the company sought to attach a certain sum of money in the hands of the receiver before he had paid these other debts and which was estimated to be the residue that would be left in his hands. It was held that this could not be done as there was as yet no duty owing to the company. From this kind of situation must be distinguished those where there is a duty owing, but the performance of which is postponed. Such a debt can properly be the subject of attachment[10].

Distinction between duty and 'subjection'

If X promises Y under seal, or for consideration, that he will pay Y £5 on the following day should it rain, there is clearly no duty in X unless and until that event occurs. In the meantime X's position is simply that he is 'subject' to be placed under a duty. The distinction need not be elaborated further and may be dismissed with the comment that this is not liability to a power, but to a non-volitional event and, as such, forms the basis of much of the law of insurance.

An analytical problem arises with such a rule as *Rylands v Fletcher*[11] (under which an occupier has to pay for damage caused by the escape of a substance likely to do mischief) and the rule concerning animals (under which the 'keeper' has to pay for damage done by dangerous animals and trespassing cattle)[12], both of which do not involve fault. There seems to be a distinction between these cases, which are sometimes called 'strict liability' (but might preferably be styled 'strict subjection') and 'strict duties'. A duty prescribes a pattern of conduct, and by 'strict duty' (eg duty to fence dangerous machinery) is meant one to which the actor may not be able to conform no matter how reasonably he behaves in the circumstances. With *Rylands v Fletcher* and animals, the policy of the law is not to prevent people from keeping mischievous substances or animals, ie there is no duty not to keep them[13]. It could be argued, perhaps, that there are duties to prevent *escape*, in which case they would be correlative to claims; but this is not how the rules are

---

7 [1893] 3 Ch 154.
8 [1921] 3 KB 110. See also *Hampstead Corpn v Caunt* [1903] 2 KB 1; *Bradford Old Bank Ltd v Sutcliffe* [1918] 2 KB 833.
9 [1949] 2 All ER 94. See also *Tapp v Jones* (1875) LR 10 QB 591 at 592, especially.
10 See p 242, post.
11 (1868) LR 3 HL 330.
12 Animals Act 1971, ss 2, 4.
13 Cf the duty not to keep a live Colorado beetle and certain wild animals under the Dangerous Wild Animals Act 1976.

framed. What they say, in effect, is that one keeps these things at one's peril, ie liability attaches in the *event* of escape, which makes the position analogous to X having to pay £5 tomorrow if it rains. If so, there is no way of accommodating cases of 'subjection' within the Hohfeldian scheme, except to say that they are not jural relations and therefore are not entitled to a place therein.

Distinction between liberty and power

Buckland disputes the need for any distinction.

> 'All rights [liberties] are rights to act or abstain, not to produce legal effects. To say that he has a right that his act shall produce that effect is to imply that if he liked it would not have that effect, and this is not true. The act will produce the legal effect whether he wishes it or not. If I own a jug of water I have a right to upset it, but it is absurd to say that I have a right that the water shall fall out'[14].

It would appear that Buckland misunderstood the nature of the Hohfeldian power. It is not a 'right' that certain effects shall ensue. Acts that have certain effects are called powers, those that do not are not called powers. That is distinct from the liberty to perform or not to perform such an act. The distinction may be put as follows: the liberty to perform or not applies to all types of conduct, but considered with reference to their effects, it can be seen that some actions result in an alteration of existing legal relations, while others do not.

Rightful and wrongful powers

The significance of the distinction between the nature of the act and the liberty to do it may be demonstrated in this way. Sometimes a power may be coupled with a liberty to exercise it and a liberty not to exercise it, while at other times it may be coupled with a duty to exercise it. In both situations the exercise of the power may be said to be 'rightful'. When a power is coupled with a duty not to exercise it, such exercise would then become 'wrongful'.

Where a power is coupled with a liberty, a party cannot be penalised for having exercised it, or for not having done so. Thus, X may for no considera-tion at all give Y permission to picnic on his land. He may then change his mind with impunity and order Y to depart, ie exercise a power revoking Y's licence and imposing on him a duty to leave. If Y fails to do so within a reasonable time he commits a breach of that duty and becomes a trespasser. In *Clore v Theatrical Properties Ltd and Westby & Co Ltd*[15], Y had a liberty to be on X's land. X assigned his interest to A and Y assigned his interest to B. A exercised his power to revoke B's liberty. It was held that he could do so; since there was no contract between A and B, A was under no duty not to exercise his power, ie he had a liberty to do so. *Wood v Leadbitter*[16] is not

---

14 Buckland *Some Reflections on Jurisprudence* p 96.
15 [1936] 3 All ER 483. See also *Frank Warr & Co Ltd v LCC* [1904] 1 KB 713; *Chapman v Honig* [1963] 2 QB 502, [1963] 2 All ER 513.
16 (1845) 13 M & W 838. Little is left of this case since *Hurst v Picture Theatres Ltd* [1915] 1 KB 1, but the principle is sound.

exactly in point, for the plaintiff's liberty to be on the defendant's premises was created by contract. The defendant ordered the plaintiff to leave and, after a reasonable time, expelled him with reasonable force. The plaintiff did not sue in contract, though there was undoubtedly a contractual duty not to exercise the power, but sued for assault instead. It was held that, since he had become a trespasser, he could be ejected with reasonable force. It was held in *East Suffolk Rivers Catchment Board v Kent*[17] that the Board had a power and a discretion (liberty) as to its exercise. In *R v Board of Referees, ex p Calor Gas (Distributing) Co Ltd*[18], where a statutory power was coupled with a liberty to exercise it and also not to exercise it, the Divisional Court refused an application for an order of mandamus to compel the Board to exercise it[19]. On the other hand, in *David v Abdul Cader*[20], the Judicial Committee of the Privy Council thought that a *malicious* refusal to exercise a discretionary power might amount to a breach of duty; but this is a limit on the liberty.

Where a power is coupled with a duty to exercise it, ie no liberty not to exercise it, there is no question of any 'right' to do the act; the party 'must' do it. A simple example is the power and duty of a judge to give a decision. Generally the presumption is against there being a duty to exercise statutory powers[1]. The word 'may' in an empowering statute is usually taken to confer a liberty to exercise a power and not a duty, so mandamus will not lie[2]. At the same time, it was held in *Trigg v Staines UDC*[3] that a local authority cannot contract not to exercise a power of compulsory acquisition, ie it cannot deprive itself of the liberty to use its power by an opposite contractual duty. Where, however, there is a duty to exercise a power, a remedy will lie for a breach of it. In *Ferguson v Earl of Kinnoull*[4] damages were awarded for the refusal by the Presbytery to take a preacher on trial. In *R v Somerset Justices ex p EJ Cole and Partners Ltd*[5], the Divisional Court held that the statutory power of Quarter Sessions to state a case was coupled with a duty to do so in cases of conviction for crimes, but that in other cases there was only a liberty to do so. Mandamus lies in the former. Under s 17 of the Criminal Appeal Act 1968, the Home Secretary has the liberty to exercise his power to refer a criminal case to the Court of Appeal after the normal time limit for appeal has elapsed. Accordingly, in *ex p Kinally*[6] the Divisional

---

17 [1941] AC 74, [1940] 4 All ER 527.
18 (1954) 47 R & IT 92.
19 See, too, *R v Secretary of State for the Environment, ex p Hackney London Borough Council* [1984] 1 All ER 956, [1984] 1 WLR 592. Discretionary powers may be controlled as follows. (a) Abusive exercise may be held void: *Congreve v Home Office* [1976] QB 629, [1976] 1 All ER 697. (b) If reasons are given, the courts may inquire into their adequacy, eg if reasons are stated in a return to a writ of *habeas corpus* for the release of a person committed for contempt by the House of Commons. See also *Pilling v Abergele UDC* [1950] 1 KB 636, [1950] 1 All ER 76.
20 [1963] 3 All ER 579, [1963] 1 WLR 834.
 1 *Julius v Lord Bishop of Oxford* (1880) 5 App Cas 214 at 225, 241, 245. The presumption may be displaced: *Re Shuter (No 2)* [1960] 1 QB 142, [1959] 3 All ER 481. See also *Cullimore v Lyme Regis Corpn* [1962] 1 QB 718, [1961] 3 All ER 1008.
 2 *Re Fletcher's Application* [1970] 2 All ER 527n.
 3 [1969] 1 Ch 10, [1968] 2 All ER 1.
 4 (1842) 9 Cl & Fin 251, especially at 311; *David v Abdul Cader* [1963] 3 All ER 579, [1963] 1 WLR 834.
 5 [1950] 1 KB 519, [1950] 1 All ER 264.
 6 [1958] Crim LR 474 (decided under s 19 of the Act of 1907). For the creation of a duty by virtue of the degree of control conferred by a power, see *Dutton v Bognor Regis UDC* [1972] 1 QB 373 at 391, 403, [1972] 1 All ER 462 at 470, 480.

Court refused leave to move for an order of mandamus. Subject to certain other limits[7], mandamus generally lies where the duty is a 'public duty'. It is not easy to say what precisely a 'public duty' is[8].

Where a power is coupled with a duty not to exercise it, the party concerned has no liberty to do so. Thus, if a person has a liberty to be on premises by virtue of a contract, *Kerrison v Smith*[9] shows that the exercise of a power revoking the liberty is effective, although it amounts to a breach of the contractual duty. The case of *Pryce v Belcher*[10] has already been considered. Another example is that of a thief who sells a thing in market overt to an innocent purchaser for value. He exercises a power in that he deprives the owner of his title and confers title on the purchaser, but he is under a duty not to exercise this power and commits a fresh conversion by so doing. The simplest example is the commission of a tort: it is a power in that the legal positions both of the victim and of the tortfeasor are altered, but there is a duty, owed to the victim, not to commit the tort. Furthermore, the commission of a tort may operate as a power against a third party. Thus, a servant who commits a tort in the course of his employment alters the legal position of his master by imposing upon him the duty to pay damages vicariously and a liability to be sued therefor, but the servant concurrently owes a duty to his master not to exercise this power of imposing vicarious responsbility upon him for the breach of which the master can recover from the servant by way of indemnity what he has to pay to the victim of the tort[11] In all these situations the act of the party concerned is a power, for it alters the legal position, even though its exercise is a breach of duty. To call such powers 'rights' would be a misnomer, for it would amount to speaking of 'rights' to commit wrongs, ie breaches of duty. Though Hohfeld purported to distinguish between uses of the word 'right', it is clear that not all powers, in the sense in which he used that term, can be called 'rights'. This is hardly a criticism. The power concept is unobjectionable as power; it cannot always be brought under the umbrella of 'rights'; which only reinforces the case for the greater precision and scope of the Hohfeldian terminology.

Kinds of powers

Broadly, they may be divided into 'public' and 'private', but both involve ability to change legal relations. When a public power is coupled with a duty to exercise it, it is termed a 'ministerial' power; when it is coupled with a liberty, it is termed 'discretionary'. Public powers, though numerous especially in administrative law, cannot compete with the profusion of private powers. The appointment of an agent, for instance, is a power, for it confers on the agent further powers to alter the legal position of the principal and

---

7 Broadly, if there is no other more appropriate remedy: *Pasmore v Oswaldtwistle UDC* [1898] AC 387; *R v Dunsheath, ex p Meredith* [1951] 1 KB 127, [1950] 2 All ER 741. For careful discussion, see *Hughes v Henderson* (1963) 42 DLR 743.
8 Eg *Western India Match Co v Lock* [1946] KB 601, [1946] 2 All ER 227.
9 [1897] 2 QB 445; *Thompson v Park* [1944] KB 408, [1944] 2 All ER 477. See also *Wood v Leadbitter* (1845) 13 M & W 838. For a short discussion of the point, see Hutton 'The Remedy of an Ejected Licensee' (1954) 17 MLR 448. Power coupled with an implied duty not to exercise it: *Hounslow London Borough Council v Twickenham Garden Development Ltd* [1971] Ch 233, [1970] 3 All ER 326.
10 (1847) 4 CB 866, for which, see p 33-34 ante.
11 *Lister v Romford Ice and Cold Storage Co Ltd* [1957] AC 555, [1957] 1 All ER 125.

creates in the latter corresponding liabilities. A married woman has power to pledge her husband's credit for necessaries, in contract there is a power to make an offer and a power to accept, and innumerable others in contract, property, procedure and, indeed, in every branch of the law. Private powers may also be coupled with duties to exercise them, eg certain powers of trustees, or they may be coupled with liberties.

IMMUNITY-DISABILITY RELATION ('YOU CANNOT')

Immunity denotes freedom from the power of another, while disability denotes the absence of power. In *Hurst v Picture Theatres Ltd*[12], it was held that where a liberty to be on premises is coupled with an 'interest', this confers an immunity along with the liberty, which cannot therefore be revoked. The relationship between power, liability, immunity and disability may be explained as follows.

(1) If X has a power, Y has a liability. They are therefore 'jural correlatives'. A liability in Y means the absence of an immunity in him. Therefore, immunity and liability are 'jural opposites' (more strictly, 'jural negations', as previously explained).

(2) Conversely, the presence of an immunity in Y implies the absence of a liability in him. The absence of a liability in Y implies the absence of a power in X. Therefore, an immunity in Y implies the absence of a power in X, ie power and immunity are 'jural contradictories'.

(3) The absence of power could have been styled 'no-power', in the same way as no-claim, but Hohfeld preferred to give it the term disability. Power and disability thus become 'jural opposites' ('negations'). It follows from this that immunity in Y implies the presence of a disability in X, ie they are 'jural correlatives'.

Distinction between claim and immunity

An immunity is not necessarily protected by a duty in another person not to attempt an invasion of it. If X is immune from taxation, the revenue authorities have no power to place him under a duty to pay. A demand for payment is ineffectual, but X has no remedy against them for having made the demand. If immunity is the same as claim, there should be a correlative duty not to make a demand. In *Kavanagh v Hiscock*[13] it was held that the relevant section of the Industrial Relations Act 1971 (since repealed) conferred on pickets an immunity from prosecution or civil suit, but no liberty to stop vehicles on the highway and no claim not to be prevented from trying to stop vehicles. Secondly, there may be an immunity in X, which is protected by a duty in Y, but the claim correlative to that duty is not in X. Thus, diplomatic envoys are immune from the power of action or other legal process. Under an old law, since repealed, it used to be a criminal offence for any person 'to sue forth or prosecute any such writ or process' against

---

12 [1915] 1 KB 1 (although the plaintiff could have sued in contract, he sued in tort). See generally Lord Macnaghten in *Vacher & Sons Ltd v London Society of Compositors* [1913] AC 107 at 118.

13 [1974] QB 600, [1974] 2 All ER 177.

them[14]. As pointed out earlier, even if there are claims correlative to duties in criminal law, they are not in the persons for whose benefit the duties exist. Finally, an immunity in X may be protected by a duty in Y and the claim correlative to the duty may also be in X, as in the case of the malicious presentation of a petition in bankruptcy[15]. The failure to distinguish between 'right' in the sense of claim and immunity may be at the root of *Dowty Boulton Paul Ltd v Wolverhampton Corpn*[16]. In 1936 the corporation conveyed to the company a plot of land for 99 years for use as an airfield, and the corporation undertook to maintain it for use by the company. In 1970 the corporation purported to revoke the company's interest in the land. It was held that although the corporation was not entitled to override the company's interest in the land, the latter's only remedy lay in damages and not in an injunction. The effect of the 1936 conveyance would appear to have been to grant, *inter alia*, a liberty to the company; and if the corporation was unable to determine that interest, then that liberty seems to have been coupled with an immunity against revocation. The court refused an injunction on the ground that to issue one would amount to compelling the corporation to fulfil its obligation to maintain the airfield, ie be equivalent to an order for specific performance. It is here that the confusion lies. The 'right' of the company, which the court held could not be overridden, was its liberty plus immunity; but the 'right' correlative to the duty to maintain the airfield was its contractual claim. Breach of this duty is remediable by damages, but the question whether an injunction could be issued to support the immunity ought not to have been related to compelling performance of the contractual duty.

Distinction between liberty and immunity

The position of a diplomatic envoy illustrates this. Such a person is treated as being capable of committing a breach of duty and is under a duty to pay damages, although immune from the power of action or other legal process to compel him to do so. In other words, he has no liberty to do the act, nor a liberty not to pay damages for it, but he has an immunity from process all the same. It was held in *Dickinson v Del Solar*[17] that the fact that an envoy was thus under a sanctionless duty to pay damages was sufficient to involve his insurance company in responsibility. If, on the other hand, he voluntarily pays the damages, he cannot recover them, since there is the duty to pay.

EVALUATION OF HOHFELD'S ANALYSIS

Hohfeld's work has earned as much criticism as praise. One set of criticisms is to the effect that some of Hohfeld's conceptions are without juridical significance, for instance, liberty, liability and disability[18]. The answer, as Hohfeld's editor has pointed out, is that liberty is necessarily related to the other concepts in the first square of the table, and liability and disability are similarly related to the other concepts in the second square[19]. With regard to

---

14 Diplomatic Privileges Act 1708, s 4 (repealed and replaced by Diplomatic Privileges Act 1964).
15 *Chapman v Pickersgill* (1762) 2 Wils 145.
16 [1971] 2 All ER 277, [1972] 1 WLR 204.
17 [1930] 1 KB 376; and see more fully p 243 post.
18 Pound 'Legal Rights' (1916) 26 International Journal of Ethics 92 at 97.
19 Cook 'Introduction' to Hohfeld pp 9-10.

liberty the objection has been considered[20]. With regard to liability and disability, it should be pointed out that once the concept of power is admitted, the others must follow. A power in X to alter the legal condition of Y implies that Y is liable to have his condition altered; if X has no power (disability), then Y is immune.

Kocourek objected to no-claim on logical grounds[1]. That which is not a claim, he observed, could be 'an elephant, a star or an angel'. This is unfair, for it proceeds on the basis of something that Hohfeld never implied. To Hohfeld no-claim simply denoted the position of one who is not in a position to demand the performance of a duty. To allege that it could be 'an elephant' misses the point. Liberty, be it noted, is just as negative as no-claim, the gist of it being no-duty. So, too, immunity and disability might just as well be called no-liability and no-power respectively. Yet, Kocourek was prepared to accept these.

Secondly, various allegations have been made that Hohfeld's analysis was incorrect and incomplete in places. There is truth in this, and many critics have done constructive service in removing the errors. It should be remembered that Hohfeld himself would very likely have corrected these had he lived to revise his work. His premature death was a loss, for the form in which his work is to be found is not that in which he hoped to have left it[2]. It has been pointed out that it requires some straining of language to bring wrongful powers under the label of 'rights', which is not an objection to Hohfeld's analysis of power, but rather to the association of power with 'right'. Non-correlative duties and 'subjections' (as distinct from liability) do not fit into the scheme, but these can be explained on the ground that they are not jural relations, which is what the scheme purports to portray. They reveal its limitations all the same. It has also been objected that the power concept needs greater refinement. On the one hand there is 'capacity' possessed by individuals, eg to make wills, contracts etc; on the other hand there is 'authority' conferred on specially qualified individuals or bodies in special circumstances. While it is true that the exercise of both results in changing jural relations, the categories are so different that they should not be grouped together.

Thirdly, there is the objection that the terminology is unusual and that it is unrealistic to expect the profession to make so radical a change in its vocabulary. The day when the House of Lords will be talking of no-claims is remote, but what is important is not the *words*, but the *ideas* which they represent. One may *think* Hohfeld without *talking* Hohfeld. One can utilise the analysis to keep one's mind clear when grappling with problems, and may then state the result in any other terms. It is not unimportant to note that the American Restatements have adopted Hohfeld's vocabulary as their medium of expression.

Fourthly, there is the objection that the terminology is not unusual enough. Critics, while applauding the effort to dispense with the homonym 'right', have shown that some of the terms which Hohfeld chose are just as ambiguous, that they are, to use a homely phrase of Dr Oliver 'earmarked for other conceptions'. The objection is not fatal. Hohfeld did his best to

---

20 See p 31–32 ante.
 1 Kocourek 'The Hohfeld System of Fundamental Legal Concepts' (1920) 15 Illinois Law Quarterly 23 at 24, 26 et seq.
 2 *Hohfeld* p 64, n 100.

provide synonyms for his terms, and other writers are free to improve the terminology as they think best.

Fifthly, valuable as Hohfeld's work is in distinguishing between claims, liberties, powers and immunities, it is convenient and necessary to retain a general concept of 'right' to denote institutions, such as ownership or possession[3]. Thus, an owner and his bailee have claims etc in relation to the thing bailed, but the interest of the former is distinguished from that of the latter by the 'right of ownership', which carries with it the claims etc[4]. Also, as will appear later, such phrases as 'right to possess' and 'better right' in a thing expresses the general idea of entitlement, which cannot be conveyed adequately if it were reduced to specific claims etc. Such expressions are convenient and do not mislead.

Lastly, the decisive question concerns the utility of the scheme. Cases which accord with Hohfeld's analysis, so the argument might run, were in fact decided without the aid of his scheme. The scheme is therefore superfluous. If, on the other hand, a case is not in accord with the scheme, then the scheme should be altered; for is not case law the criterion by which any theory is tested? Only a superior tribunal can say that a case was wrongly decided. To this kind of argument the answers would be as follows. The first step is to see what justification there is for adopting the Hohfeldian distinctions. It is submitted that they are borne out by such an abundance of case law as to justify their acceptance as a basis for an appraisal of individual decisions. Just as an established line of authority is not discarded as soon as the first aberrant decision turns up, so too the occasional decision not in accord with the Hohfeldian scheme should not of itself be taken as discrediting it. Secondly, it could be of use in assessing the precise effect of an aberrant decision without condemning it as wrongly decided. Thirdly, sometimes, however, it may be permissible to argue that such a decision was indeed wrongly decided as when an appellate court is invited to overrule it. Hohfeld's analysis may furnish reasons why it should be regarded as incorrect. Fourthly, the use of the analysis will enable the law to be developed more in accordance with existing principles and less through exceptions. Fifthly, the analysis is of value in understanding the law. Sixthly, it is an aid to distinguishing. Finally, it is an aid to clear thinking and invaluable as a mental training. Although the hopes that were once entertained of startling achievements with the aid of the scheme have not been realised, yet its value and utility as an aid to clear thinking have been proved.

It is important to apply the Hohfeldian analysis to social and political slogans such as 'Fundamental rights', 'rights of Man', 'Women's rights', 'Prisoners' rights', 'Animal rights', 'Workers' rights' and so forth. As such these are ridiculous bases for serious action. Is a particular campaign launched for claims, liberties of action, powers, or immunities; in whom; in what circumstances; when; where? The point may be illustrated by taking

3 See eg *Re Sykes, Skelton and Dyson v Sykes* [1940] 4 All ER 10, where it was held that a bequest of 'all my ... horses' was not apt to convey the interest which the testator had as a tenant in common of three horses. If ownership is no more than a bundle of claims etc, there is no reason why the testator could not pass his half of the bundle. The language of the judge (at 12) suggests that a mere 'collection of rights' is not equivalent to the idea conveyed by the expression 'the testator's horses'. For a different explanation, see REM in (1941) 57 LQR 23.
4 Honoré 'Rights of Exclusion and Immunities against Divesting' (1959-60) 34 Tulane LR at 456-458.

one of these, 'Workers' rights'. On analysis, it can be seen that one aspect is the claim-right to be given jobs, correlative to a duty in the state to provide them, which deserves sympathy in a climate of unemployment. Next, there is the assertion of an unrestricted liberty-right not to work at the jobs, which are claimed 'as of right', ie the liberty to strike. Side by side with this is the assertion of an unrestricted liberty-right to prevent other workers from working at their jobs by picketing. There is also the assertion of a power to drive workers out of their jobs through the closed-shop doctrine. There is the assertion of immunity from suits in courts of law and immunity from having these various liberties and powers curtailed or abolished. Finally, there is a claim-right to at least some kind of regular payment for workers even while they are not working through various welfare benefits. Any discussion of a legal framework for industrial relationships should surely begin with precise analysis of the different concepts that are involved.

TEMPORAL PERSPECTIVE OF THE HOHFELDIAN SCHEME

The difference between the first square and the second is that the former concerns jural relations at rest, the second with changing jural relations. Of the eight concepts in the scheme, two stand out as the key concepts, one in each square. They are duty and power, the others in their respective squares being only derivatives. Duties regulate behaviour, while powers create, repeal or modify duties and other relations. Professor Hart has unerringly fastened on these two to provide him with the centrepiece for his concept of law, which will be considered later[5].

A point of significance is the relationship between the squares. Each depicts jural relations of correlation, opposition and contradiction as they are to be found presently. The relationship between the squares requires a temporal perspective. Thus, a power and, eg the claim-duty relation created by its exercise, cannot co-exist; the former is anterior to the latter[6]. It has been shown how a power may co-exist with a duty to exercise it, or not to exercise it, but this is the concurrence of two independent jural relations. The situation now being considered concerns the relationship between a duty and a power where the duty has been *created* by the power. If one focuses on the power, the claim-duty relation is in the future; if one focuses on the claim-duty relation, the power which created it is in the past. For instance, there is a power to make an offer and a power to accept it, and once they have been exercised they give rise to a contractual claim-duty relationship. When the contract comes into being, the offer and acceptance are finished and done with. It would be incomplete to take account only of the power and lose sight of the claim-duty relation, or to take account only of the latter and lose sight of the creative power. In order to get both into focus a temporal perspective is necessary. Indeed, 'the law', as commonly understood, is as much concerned with powers as with the jural relations they create. Thus, the 'law of contract' deals with powers to create claim-duty relations as well as the claim-duty relations themselves, which are labelled as different kinds

5 See pp 351–356 post.
6 Hall *Foundations of Jurisprudence* pp 123–125.

of contracts. Accordingly, it is submitted that in order to see the working of the Hohfeldian table a temporal perspective is essential.

OTHER VARIETIES OF LEGAL MATERIAL

Means of achieving legal ends

Certain provisions prescribe how certain ends are to be achieved. Thus, a gratuitous promise must be made under seal, a vote at an election must be exercised by marking a cross at a certain spot on the ballot paper. These resemble duties in that they prescribe what a person ought to do, but they are not duties. They are conditions regulating the effective exercise of powers. The consequence of non-compliance with such directions is that the transaction is null and void. Austin argued that nullity is a sanction and that therefore there is a duty to put the seal etc[7]. The matter was well discussed by Buckland[8]. The question is, Who comes under the duty in these cases? In the example of the gratuitous promise, the duty to put the seal cannot be on the promisee, who need know nothing about it. If there is a duty at all, it must be in the promisor, in which case it is odd that the penalty for non-compliance is that he is not bound by his promise. Secondly, a duty usually has a correlative claim. If there is a duty to put the seal, the claim correlative to it cannot be vested in the promisee, since he only acquires his claim after the seal has been affixed. Nor can it be in the promisor, for it makes no sense to say that he has a claim against himself. (This argument is not, perhaps, strong since, as has been indicated, duties need not always correspond with claims). Thirdly, the major premise of the argument that these are duties because nullity is the sanction, breaks down if sanction is rejected as a test of duty[9]. Fourthly, these rules prescribe how a person can achieve some result for himself rather than what he ought to do for others. The imperative 'must' should not mislead[10]. Thus, 'if you want to talk to X by telephone you ought to (must) ring him up'. This is hardly a duty; it is simply the effective way of bringing about the desired result. It is clear, therefore, that 'ought' here is being used in a different sense from the 'ought' of duty[11]. Finally, the 'ought' behind duty is normative and is not derivable from an 'is' of fact; the 'ought' in the kind of provision under discussion is so derived. For instance, fire burns and throws out heat; therefore, the statement that if one wants to get warm, one ought to/must light a fire is derived from the nature of fire. It is not prescribing a duty to light the fire. Similarly, the provisions being considered only specify the means of achieving certain ends.

The means-to-an-end connection is significant in other ways. For instance,

---

7 Austin *Lectures on Jurisprudence* I, p 505.

8 Buckland *Some Reflections on Jurisprudence* pp 91–92.

9 As to which, see pp 236 et seq. post. Hall substitutes 'privation' for 'sanction': *Foundations of Jurisprudence* pp 104 et seq; p 238 post.

10 Imperative language is not conclusive: *Re Philpot* [1960] 1 All ER 165, explaining *R v Dickson* [1950] 1 KB 394, [1949] 2 All ER 810.

11 *Caldow v Pixell* (1877) 36 LT 469 at 470; *E Ramia Ltd v African Woods Ltd* [1960] 1 All ER 627, [1960] 1 WLR 86; but it is possible for a condition precedent to consist of the performance of some other duty: *Mungoni v A-G of Northern Rhodesia* [1960] AC 336, [1960] 1 All ER 446.

law could be regarded as the application of force conditional on behaviour of a certain kind: 'If a person does X, then punishment Y ought to be visited on him'[12]. This way of looking at it makes the legally approved behaviour the means of achieving the desired end of avoiding punishment. There is, of course, an alternative view, namely, that there are two separate prescriptions here, one prescribing what a person ought, or ought not to do, the other prescribing the punishment for breach of the prescription[13]. Which of these two interpretations is preferable will be discussed later. Further, to take up a point made at the end of the last chapter, when a legal system is considered in a continuum, as it should be, the conditions necessary to its continuity and functioning become part of the concept by virtue of the means-to-an-end connection: such conditions are means of achieving continuity and proper functioning.

Definitions

It is statutorily provided, eg that the word 'person' shall include a corporation, and according to the common law a simple contract is constituted by offer, acceptance and consideration. These and numerous other definitions lay down the legal use of certain terms. It is arguable that a judge, or other official, is under a duty to attach the appropriate label and act accordingly once the requisite conditions are fulfilled, but the specification of the conditions themselves is not a duty but definition.

Location of legal relationships

A different kind of rule determines the incidence of jural relations. For instance, on an intestacy various claims arise in persons entitled to share in the deceased's property and there are duties of administration correlative to them. It is a special kind of rule that lays down that a claim vests in the first instance in X, or failing him in Y, and that the duty of administration shall vest in A. The same applies to the incidence of the duty of supporting an illegitimate child[14]. All such rules help to structure a legal system.

Principles, doctrines and standards

No one disputes that strict and full responsibility are part of the law, nor does anyone doubt that notions such as privity of contract, *mens rea*, presumption of innocence, unjust enrichment, *ex turpi causa non oritur actio* are also part of law. The well-known maxims of equity are the roots from which a crucial body of law has grown up. In the law of tort damages are payable for failure to show reasonable care, or failure in certain circumstances to see that such care was taken by another, or failure to show special skill where this had been professed. What is the status of these and others like them? They do not create jural relations or indicate their location, nor are they

---

12 So Kelsen, as to which see pp 359 et seq. post.
13 So Bentham, p 340 post.
14 A good example from Roman Law is that when a contract was made by a slave or child under paternal power, the civil law vested only the claim against the other contracting party in the father, not the duty. Praetorian law vested a duty, but not necessarily to the full extent of the other's claim.

means to ends or definitions. Professor Dworkin contends that they stand in a category of their own and refers to them as principles, doctrines and standards[15]. He says that they operate differently from rules of law, which, according to him, apply in an all or nothing fashion, whereas these have a dimension of weight and operate persuasively by exerting pressure on the law to develop in their direction. The 'all or nothing' character of rules is perhaps an overstatement, for rules do admit discretion as to how they are applied and, indeed, some expressly allow a judge, eg to make such order as he thinks fit, or to reduce damages in proportion to his assessment of a plaintiff's contributory negligence. The discretion in the application of rules is guided by a host of considerations[16] among which principles, doctrines and standards play an important part. These are distinguishable from other value considerations in that, whereas a good many values are non-legal, these do possess law-quality. This brings up another of their distinguishing features, which is that they do not acquire law-quality through statute, precedent or custom. The presumption of innocence, for instance, was never formally enunciated, nor were the maxims of equity, while the privity of contract doctrine ante-dates English law. They are 'law' because courts accept them as such and they are, therefore, part of legal material.

15 Dworkin 'Is Law a System of Rules?' in *Essays in Legal Philosophy* (ed Summers) p 25; *Taking Rights Seriously* chs 2 and 3. See, however, Tapper 'A Note on Principles' (1971) 34 MLR 628; Coval and Smith 'Some Structural Properties of Legal Decisions' (1973) 32 CLJ 81; 'The Causal Theory of Law' (1977) 36 CLJ 110; Steiner 'Judicial Discretion and the Concept of Law' (1976) 35 CLJ 135; Smith *Legal Obligation* ch 9.
16 See ch 10 post.

READING LIST

W W Buckland *Some Reflections on Jurisprudence* pp 92–110.
W W Cook 'Introduction' to Hohfeld's *Fundamental Legal Conceptions as Applied in Judicial Reasoning* (ed W W Cook).
A L Corbin 'Legal Analysis and Terminology' (1919–20) 29 Yale Law Journal, 163.
R M Dworkin 'Is Law a System of Rules?' in *Essays in Legal Philosophy* (ed R S Summers) p 25.
G. W Goble 'A Re-definition of Basic Legal Terms' (1935) 35 Columbia Law Review 535.
W N Hohfeld *Fundamental Legal Conceptions as Applied in Judicial Reasoning* (ed W W Cook) ch 1.
R Pound 'Fifty Years of Jurisprudence' (1936–37) 50 Harvard Law Review 571–576.
M Radin 'A Restatement of Hohfeld' (1938) 51 Harvard Law Review 1141.
J Stone *Legal System and Lawyers' Reasonings* ch 4.
G L Williams 'The Concept of Legal Liberty' in *Essays in Legal Philosophy* (ed R S Summers) p 121.

CHAPTER 3

Rules, laws and legal system

The varieties of legal material discussed in the last chapter did not include 'rules of law' or 'laws' even though these expressions are among the commonest in legal talk. Their exclusion seems odd at first sight, since one would suppose that they comprise the very stuff of the law. The reason will appear on an examination of 'rule' and 'a law'.

RULES

'Rule' connotes a standard by which to judge conduct, or on which to base one's own conduct. All the kinds of legal material that have been discussed share this rule-quality directly or indirectly. A duty is always a pattern of behaviour that serves as a general standard with reference to which deviance is condemned as being wrong, not just incorrect; means of achieving legal ends are 'standard' procedures for the effective exercise of certain powers; the requirements stipulated in definitions are the bases on which those concerned proceed when using terms; locations of jural relations similarly require such persons to proceed on the basis that claims, duties etc vest in certain parties and not others. The 'rule-ness' of principles, doctrines and standards is self-evident.

Three questions arise: (1) How did the words 'rule' and 'law' come to be associated with 'standard'? (2) What does 'acceptance' of standards mean? (3) How do they come to be accepted?

Association of 'rule' and 'law' with 'standard'

The details of what is a fascinating development lie in the history of Roman Law and have to be sought elsewhere[1]. The story in broad outline is that *lex* (law) meant declared law (derived from *lego*, I declare) as opposed to *jus*, which was customary law crystallised out of decisions. In the course of time *leges* became expressions of popular will through enactment by the assemblies and their function was prescriptive like modern legislation and ceased being declaratory of *jus*. The term *regula* (rule) came in via the Grammarians for whom it connoted 'guide' or 'standard'. One of the most distinguished jurists of the early Principate, Labeo, a Grammarian turned lawyer, pioneered the use of *regula* for certain legal axioms which had prescriptive function. The association of *regula* with *lex* evolved some time during the second century AD via imperial decrees, which had taken over the role of *lex*. During this period Rule Books, *Regulae*, named after the jurists who had been commissioned to prepare them, were issued under imperial authority to subordinate officials as manuals for their guidance. These *regulae* thus had the force of *lex*.

1 Stein *Regulae Juris*.

The *regulae*, which had been worked out privately by certain of the great jurists during the second and third centuries AD, the Classical period of Roman Law, were later officially invested with the force of *lex* by the Law of Citation in AD 426. Finally, Justinian's *Digest*, which codified much of the writings of the Classical jurists, was itself promulgated as a *lex* by the emperor. It is significant that the finale of this monumental work, its concluding Title, Book 50.17, consists entirely of a collection of *regulae*. The association of 'rule', 'law' and 'standard' was thus gradually completed and has formed the basis of legal thinking ever since.

Acceptance of standards

The concept of 'rule' has been examined by Professor Hart whose explanation rests on the distinction between what he calls the 'external' and 'internal' points of view[2]. The former is the point of view of an outside observer, who simply describes behaviour as he sees it: people do in fact behave in such and such a way. The latter is the point of view of a person, who treats the behaviour as a prescriptive pattern of how he and others ought to behave, in other words, he 'internalises' it. Internalised patterns of behaviour are expressed, not just descriptively as the external observer would do, but in terms of 'ought', 'must', 'should'. Conformity is said to be 'right' and non-conformity 'wrong'. The point is not whether people do or do not conform, but that they ought to do so. Internalisation moves from the realm of the 'is' of what happens in fact (*Sein*) into that of the 'ought' (*Sollen*).

The characteristic of a rule, says Professor Hart, lies in internalisation, ie acceptance of a behaviour pattern as a standard. He distinguishes 'rule' from 'habit' in that habits only involve shared behaviour, which is not enough for rules; nor do habits serve as standards. 'Rule' is also said to be at the root of the notion of 'obligation', and here he distinguishes between 'being obliged' and 'having an obligation'. If a gunman claps a pistol at X's head, X may feel obliged to yield his purse, but he has no obligation to do so. Having an obligation results from a rule to that effect; and clearly there is neither rule nor obligation that X should surrender his purse[3]. Professor MacCormick further distinguishes between two forms of internalisation[4]. One is understanding the standard accepted by an actor with a view to explaining what he does and how he does it. Judgment is passed on his skill in acting correctly and deviations are condemned as incorrect. The other form is acceptance of a standard according to which people ought to act and deviations are condemned as wrongdoing. A further distinction might be drawn between internalisation by citizens and by officials. Citizens accept a behaviour pattern as a standard for themselves, but they do not also internalise a duty to pass an official judgment on the conduct of others. Officials do both; they accept it as a guide for their own conduct and also accept a concomitant duty to apply it when judging the conduct of others officially.

There are many rules in society prescribing how people ought to behave, but not all of them are internalised as 'law'. There are, for example, accepted rules in various sports, rules of etiquette, morals and so on. As previously

2 Hart *The Concept of Law, passim.*
3 Hart pp 80 et seq. For 'obligation' see pp 228–229 post.
4 MacCormick *Legal Reasoning and Legal Theory* pp 274 et seq.

indicated, legal rules are distinguished from others with reference to the criterion, or criteria, of validity, which in this country are statutes, precedents and immemorial customs. Rules emanating from the criterion of validity are internalised as rules of law because the criterion itself has been internalised as law-constitutive, a point which will be discussed presently.

If 'having an obligation' results from a rule of law, then 'having an obligation', too, is a matter of law. Underlying this there is a moral substratum of 'having a sense of obligation', which is not congruent with the acceptance of either a legal rule or obligation. Thus, a rule of law may forbid a certain action, which is internalised by a person to the extent that he acknowledges a legal obligation. If he has no sense of obligation with regard to the conduct in question, he may well be inclined to disobey. Every motorist acknowledges that to abide by speed limits is a legal obligation, but vast numbers of them have no sense of obligation with regard to it, which is why the law is disobeyed during every minute of every day. The imposition of a legal duty and the creation of a legal obligation are not the end, for there always remains the underlying moral liberty to obey or disobey; and it is a sense of obligation that inhibits disobedience. A different illustration comes from cases where the law leaves people with liberties to act or not as they please, ie without constraining duties either way. Freedom of action can be exercised abusively or responsibly. Since the law does not restrain, any restraint on liberty cannot come from law. It can only derive from a moral sense of obligation based on the acceptance of moral rules. The distinction between law and morals and between 'having an obligation' and 'having a sense of obligation' is important, but it is even more important that their relationship should not be left out of account. Law without a sense of obligation is unworkable, which means that any discussion of law as a functioning phenomenon has to include this moral dimension.

How do standards come to be accepted?

It is an obvious progression to pass from the acceptance of standards to how and why they come to be accepted. Not only do these questions naturally arise, but they also open up other aspects of 'rule'. Many reasons, moral, social and historical, lie behind the acceptance of standards and these, of course, vary from country to country. They are inextricably interwoven into the 'rule-ness' even of rules of law and it would be arbitrary to cut off the examination of rule at this point. As contended in Chapter 1, the jurisprudential study of legal phenomena cannot be divorced from their social and cultural milieu.

One reason for the acceptance of a rule as a standard lies in its appeal to a sense of moral rightness. This does not apply to every rule, since some are morally neutral, but it is true of others. In bygone days when the pronouncements of a supreme lawgiver were accepted because of his charismatic authority, this derived from trust in his moral sense, often believed to have been divinely inspired, as with Moses and the Ten Commandments, Themistes in Homer, or the Dooms of the Anglo-Saxons. On a more prosaic level, the influence of imitation, the herd instinct to follow what others do, should not be overlooked. The fact of compliance by others exerts psychological pressure on individuals to follow suit, which may stem from reluctance to appear egregious, or from an unthinking assumption that a thing is done because it must be right[5]. Allied to this is the pressure exerted by the traditions and craftsmanship of specialist callings, which have been evolved over long periods of time, and those who enter these vocations accept the rules regulating the practices and ways of going about the jobs[6]. Perhaps the most sophisticated basis of acceptance is reason, which is the judgment of a person who weighs up the pros and cons and concludes that it is in the wider interest to conform, even against his own interest and inclination.

Something more has to be said about acceptance of rules for reasons which are compendiously means of achieving desired ends. In primitive societies a range of activities was regulated by ritual, and rules of ritual were accepted because they were believed to be means towards achieving various ends, such as abundant harvests, rain in times of drought and so on. This came about through belief in word-magic, ie the power of words to influence the material world.

Word-fetishism is a habit that is easily formed[7]. The natural reaction of a baby in its earliest days to discomfort, for instance, is to utter a sound. When sound is uttered, in the majority of cases the offending situation is rectified. The baby's limited appreciation of cause and effect can only register the broad fact that sound succeeded in bringing about an alteration in the world of fact. Food appears, discomforts disappear and persons materialise[8]. As the child grows older it is made to realise that not every time it makes a noise is it going to get its own way. Deep down, however, there remains that unshakeable conviction that sound does have power; obviously, it cannot be any and every sound, but only certain special (magic) sounds. The ground for belief in word-magic is thus prepared very early and during the most receptive period of consciousness. In so far as law gives a person power to control property as well as the actions of other persons, it is not surprising that it should have become associated with word-magic from the earliest times. Nor is it surprising that the earliest exponents of law were priests. To put the machinery of law into operation the proper ceremonial has to be observed and the proper incantations uttered. Adherence to the rules of ritual is to be found in every system and traces remain today. People outgrow it and find ways and means of circumventing it. New uses are found for the original forms and this, together with an element of conservatism, combine to keep formality and ritual alive long after the inner belief in word-magic drops out[9].

Another form of internalisation of rules of behaviour as means to an end lies in the inter-dependence of people in society. As social existence develops and becomes more complex, it evolves a network of interlocking practices so that the activities of individuals, or groups of them, come to depend more and more on the activities of others, so much so that if one group refuses to play its role, other groups are stricken into impotence, or at least

---

5 For imitation, see Tardè *Les Lois de L'Imitation* (trans Parsons).
6 See eg Llewellyn *The Common Law Tradition. Deciding Appeals*, and pp 454-455, 456-459 post.
7 Ogden and Richards *The Meaning of Meaning* ch 2; Ogden *Word-Magic;* Malinowski Supplement I to *The Meaning of Meaning* pp 318-326; Malinowski *Argonauts of the Western Pacific* pp 408 et seq. See also p 462 post.
8 There is a strong connection between the earliest syllabic sound uttered by a baby, *ma,* and the person most prominent in its world, the mother, which may be the reason why *ma* is the common root in a great number of languages of the various words for 'mother'. Malinowski Supplement to *The Meaning of Meaning* p 320.
9 Olivecrona *Law as Fact* (1939) p 116.

inconvenienced. One has only to reflect on the extent to which the daily work and existence of individuals depends on others providing water, heat, food, clothing, housing, transport etc in order to appreciate this[10]. The result is that considerable pressure builds up on people to conform to their roles so as not to unsettle others, which thereby leads to acceptance of conformity to roles in order to achieve smooth co-existence as 'right' and non-conformity as 'wrong'. A good many interlocking practices do crystallise into laws.

A more subtle manifestation of the means-to-an-end connection is the acceptance of a rule as a means of avoiding the unpleasant consequences of non-compliance. A distinction has to be drawn between internalisation of the rule as such and the decision by a particular individual whether or not to obey it in a given situation. The latter aspect does not relate to the matter under discussion, but it needs mention in order to get it out of the way. With regard to disobedience, the influence of fear in inhibiting such acts should not be over-estimated. It does not work uniformly and in all circumstances. Disobedience by officials acting officially can probably be more easily detected and punished than disobedience by ordinary people, so fear of punishment may operate more strongly on the former than on the latter. Even with the latter the influence of fear depends on being caught. It plays no part when the violation of a rule is unintended; but even where it is intended, fear is balanced against the chance of escape, severity of the punishment and so on. All this does not relate to internalisation of rules, but only to obedience of rules already internalised. The way in which fear could lead to internalisation of rules depends on the law being administered firmly and successfully over a long period and the process has been explained by Professor Olivecrona[11]. Fear of unpleasant consequences, he says, does not of itself make a rule; if so, there would be a rule forbidding people to put their hands into the fire. Internalisation of a rule as a result of fear is an indirect and long term consequence. He points out that everyone is aware from his or her infancy of the consequences of breaking laws, domestic in the earliest instance, and the temptation to transgress brings into play this fear of punishment. It is not in the human make-up to accommodate such tension indefinitely, and fear tends to be removed by a psychological adjustment, which accepts conformity as a means of getting rid of it, which then disappears from the surface as a motive. Not only legal rules, but also moral ideas are shaped by the ever-present pressure of legal enforcement[12]. Other people have expressed the same idea. Plato and Aristotle drew attention long ago to the educative function of law; indeed, the latter said, 'Legislators make citizens good by forming their habits[13]. More recently, Lord Simon of Glaisdale observed, 'I would only add that it seems also to have been within Parliamentary contemplation that the law might perform in this field one of its traditional functions, an educative one – namely, to raise moral standards by stigmatising as henceforward socially unacceptable certain hitherto generally condoned conduct[14]. Two jurists said much the same: 'The threat of sanction can deter people from violating the law, perhaps in an important

---

10 Cf, Duguit *Law in The Modern State* (trans Laski) see pp. 436–439 post.
11 *Olivecrona* (1939) pp 147–148; (1971) pp 271–273. See also Lundstedt *Superstition or Rationality in Action for Peace?* Introduction; Tsanoff in 'Round Table Discussion' (1952) 1 Journal of Public Law at 268.
12 *Olivecrona* (1939) p 153.
13 *Ethics* II, 1.5.
14 *Charter v Race Relations Board* [1973] AC 868 at 900, [1973] 1 All ER 512 at 527.

part by inducing a moralistic attitude towards compliance'[15]. Perhaps, the outstanding contemporary example of such an enterprise is that of the Soviet Union, which has been attempting to use laws to educate the masses in the values of communism[16]. This is a gigantic undertaking which will no doubt take time, and may explain why the authorities are so zealous in preventing contacts other than carefully vetted ones between Soviet citizens and the non-communist world.

Valuable as Professor Olivecrona's insight is, it should not be taken too far. Not all moral ideas are shaped by legal enforcement, but, even when they can be, there may be difficulties. One is that the process requires settled conditions and is unworkable in a state of flux. Another is that deep-seated attitudes are peculiarly resistant to re-moulding in this way, especially when the law seeks to go against what large sections of the community like or believe to be right; which is why terror regimes are unlikely to succeed in the long run. In these cases the psychological reaction is to throw up a barrier not only to the influence of laws, but even to propaganda. Thus, the de-segregation laws in America made very little headway in the racially-minded southern States, while even the South African government has occasionally been caught in its own toils. Having used law, amongst other methods, to create the feeling that *apartheid* is morally right, some of its own more liberal laws and policies have thereby been frustrated[17]. The solution to the problem of how such attitudes are to be changed is not yet insight.

Perhaps the most interesting psychological factor behind internalisation is the pressure exerted by the mere fact that the proposition in question possesses the quality of 'law'. To say that such and such is 'law' is to strike an attitude towards it and to evoke one. Professor Olivecrona has examined this too and shows that this feeling derives from the prior internalisation of the institutions and procedures of law making. As soon as one is told that this or that is in an Act of Parliament, judicial precedent or immemorial custom, one accepts it as a rule of law without even knowing of its content. This is coupled with the fact that texts produced by these agencies are published through certain media, eg gazettes, which have associations built round them that what they contain is true[18]. The inquiry thus gets pushed a stage further back into the reasons behind the internalisation of the law-making institution, namely, the criterion of validity. For instance, even if the reigning monarch makes a declaration with the unanimous assent of all the members of both Houses of Parliament assembled at a garden party, that will not have the quality of 'law' nor exert the same pressure as when the established constitutional processes of legislating have been gone through.

> 'Constitutional law-givers gain access to a psychological mechanism, through which they can influence the life of the country ... the significance of legislating is not that the draft acquires a 'binding force' by being promulgated as a law.

---

15 Schwarz and Orleans, 'On Legal Sanctions' (1966–67) 34 U Ch LR at 300.
16 See p 414 post. Cf. the South African *apartheid* legislation which helps to create the feeling of the moral rightness of *apartheid*.
17 Eg the case of Sandra Laing (1967) Times 2 October, where a child was classified as 'white' when born, then re-classified as 'coloured' and re-classified again as 'white'. When, according to a government directive, she was due to be admitted to a white school, most of the parents of the other children threatened to withdraw their children. Again, the very policy of *apartheid* suffered a blow when white miners refused to train Africans for skilled jobs in the mines within designated African homelands.
18 *Olivecrona* (1939) See also 'The Imperative Element in Law' (1964) 18 Rutgers LR at 806.

The relevant point is that the provisions of the draft are made psychologically effective. And this result is attained through the use of a certain form, which has a grip over the mind of the people'[19].

The reason why pressure is associated with agencies and procedures is partly because it is a tradition, and partly because the organised force of the community can be brought to bear in connection with them. Olivecrona illustrates the point with the example of a successful revolution. The explanation of how the new order wins obedience is not just force, but that the revolutionaries control the machinery capable of exerting the necessary psychological pressure. When the revolution is peaceful, they take over the existing machinery and the psychological forces associated with it, and their only problem is to accustom people to the use of this machinery by themselves. This is what happened in the 'Bloodless Revolution' of 1688–1689, and in the Rhodesian Revolution, where after UDI the Rhodesians found no difficulty in continuing to accept the use by the rebels of the existing, local law-making apparatus and its psychological associations, to which they were accustomed, rather than the unfamiliar machinery of Westminster, which the British Government sought to substitute in its place. When the revolution is violent, the revolutionaries may create new machinery and a new psychological association, eg the Russian Revolution. In either case, force and propaganda have to be maintained until the new order becomes established. Propaganda especially is important in creating the new psychological association.

The question remains: why was a particular criterion of validity accepted in the first place? The circumstances in which statute, judicial precedent and immemorial customs came to be accepted reveal underlying historical, social, political and moral factors.

Acts of Parliament, or more fully Acts of the Crown in Parliament, are constituted by the assent of the Crown, the Lords and the Commons. The Crown in Parliament as the supreme law-making institution was accepted in 1689 after a revolutionary break with the past. There was no legal justification for the change; it became 'legal' because the judges internalised it. Previously the position was that, although Parliament did have legislative and judicial functions[20], it was only convened in an advisory capacity. The King used to legislate with the advice of Parliament in important matters and through prerogative legislation in other matters. By Stuart times the national mood had changed. Not only was the Puritan country opposed to the later Catholic Stuarts, but the Kings had been forced into unpopular exercises of prerogative power to raise money. When their legality came to be tested in the courts, notwithstanding the King's alienation of judicial sympathy[1], the judges had to uphold the historic validity of prerogative legislation[2]. The conflict between the King and Parliament erupted into civil war in the seventeenth century ending in a victory for Parliament in 1688–1689 and the acceptance by the judiciary of the Crown in Parliament henceforth as the supreme legislative authority in place of the prerogative. The

19 *Olivecrona* (1939) pp 54, 60; (1971) pp 93 et seq.
20 Fleta II, 2.1.
 1 By setting up the prerogative courts of which the common law courts were intensely jealous, and by interfering with judges by way of arbitrary dismissals, eg of Coke CJ. The judges did seek to impose limits on the prerogative in the *Case of Proclamations* (1611) 12 Co Rep 74.
 2 *Case of Impositions (Bate's Case)* (1610) 2 State Tr 371; *R v Hampden (Case of Ship Money)* (1637) 3 State Tr 826.

judges acted as they did for a variety of reasons. One explanation may lie in the fact that men like Scroggs and Jeffreys had brought the judiciary into such disrepute by the close of the Restoration that the judges dared not risk giving further cause for offence. Another may be weariness after nearly a century of turmoil, which led to the feeling that it was best to let things be rather than provoke needless trouble. A third was the awareness of political realities by the judges themselves. For, if they had refused to recognise the change, an entirely new conflict would have been precipitated between them and the legislature. It was avoided because the judges accepted the change. The fact that the triumph of the doctrine of the supremacy of the Crown in Parliament depended on its acceptance by the judges does not imply that Parliament would not have succeeded had the judges resisted. The battle would in that event have assumed a new dimension and would have resulted in the subordination of the judiciary as well. The point is that Parliament triumphed in the way it did because of the support of the judges.

This leads to a consideration of effectiveness as a reason for accepting a legislative authority. As to this, it should be emphasised that effectiveness is not a condition of its own law-quality or even of its enactments, but only a factor which in time induces courts to accept and continue to accept it[3]. A situation may be supposed in the midst of a revolution where the old order has gone and no new order has effectively replaced it. In such a lacuna the courts can continue to apply as 'laws' the enactments of the old order even though it is no longer effective. The label 'laws' attaches to whatever the courts are prepared to accept as such; their acceptance of the law-creating source is a separate matter. Even if the old order is ineffective and there is a new, effective order, the courts may still treat the old order as 'legal' and the new as 'illegal', or simply '*de facto*'. The Rhodesian revolution provided an example. On 11 November 1965, the Rhodesian government unilaterally declared its independence of Britain, repudiated the Constitution of 1961 and promulgated a new one in its place[4]. The revolutionary régime was undoubtedly effective and remained so despite efforts by Britain to bring it down through the imposition of sanctions. In the test case of *Madzimbamuto v Lardner-Burke*[5] the court of first intance decided in the following September that the régime was illegal, but accepted the decree on which the Minister based the order in question as 'law' on grounds of necessity. The Appellate Division by a majority held in January 1968 that the régime still had not acquired *de jure* validity, although it was effective *de facto*. It also reversed the court of first instance by holding the Minister's order invalid on a technical ground. Later that same year the Judicial Committee of the Privy Council also declared the régime to be illegal.

Not only is the legality of a revolutionary régime independent of effectiveness, but it also has jurisdictional (spatial) and temporal dimensions. Thus, although the Rhodesian régime was eventually accepted as legal by the Rhodesian courts[6], British courts never did so. In *Adams v Adams (A-G*

---

3 *Jilani v Government of Punjab* Pak LD (1972) SC 139 at 159, 232–233, 242.

4 The 1965 Constitution and its successor have since been superseded.

5 Court of first intance: Judgment No GD/CIV/23/66 of 9 September 1966 (published as a Government Blue Book); Appellate Division: 1968 (2) SA 284 of 29 January 1968; Privy Council: [1969] 1 AC 645, [1968] 3 All ER 561. For discussion of some of the points dealt with here, see Dias 'Legal Politics: Norms behind the *Grundnorm*' [1968] CLJ 233.

6 On 13 September 1968 in *R v Ndhlovu* 1968 (4) SA 515, the Appellate Division refused to obey the Privy Council's ruling in *Madzimbamuto*.

intervening a British court refused to recognise a divorce decree pronounced by a Rhodesian judge, who had not taken the oath under the 1961 Constitution. This shows that legality depends on the jurisdiction in which the matter is considered, quite apart from effectiveness[8]. The temporal dimension is brought out by a decision of the Pakistan Supreme Court, *Jilani v Government of Punjab*[9], which rejected effectivness altogether as the criterion of legality. In an earlier case, *The State v Dosso*[10], the Supreme Court had held that a revolutionary régime, which was effectively in power, was legal and had thereby destroyed the previous Constitution no matter how or by whom that change had been brought about. In *Jilani* the Supreme Court rejected this as a wholly unsustainable proposition and overruled *Dosso*. The point, however, is that this decision was given *after* that revolutionary régime had itself been overthrown so that the declaration that it was illegal *ab initio* was retrospective[11].

Madzimbamuto's Case illustrates the further point that the validity of 'laws' and of the law-constitutive medium are separate questions. Effectiveness relates to the acceptance of the latter. Both the Rhodesian courts and one judge on the Judicial Committee held that, although the régime was not lawful, at least some of its enactments could be accepted as 'laws' provided that they conformed to the old 1961 Constitution, the implication of which is that an illegal authority can enact valid 'laws', while the previous and now ineffective authority continues to possess some legal force[12].

In the result it would seem that the effectiveness of the legislative authority is not a condition of the validity either of 'laws' or even of itself. It is a factor which *in time* induces the courts to accept such authority. Nor is it the only such factor. Others are force, propaganda and packing the Bench with judges who will comply, all of which only reinforces the contention that the legality of the law-constitutive medium only comes about when the courts accept, or are made to accept it[13].

There was also a moral factor behind the acceptance of the Crown in Parliament. The sovereignty of the prerogative was rejected because it had been used immorally by the King, and the Crown in Parliament was adopted

---

7 [1971] P 188, [1970] 3 All ER 572, rejecting *Ndhlovu*. Cf *Bilang v Rigg* [1972] NZLR 954; and see Southern Rhodesia (Matrimonial Jurisdiction) Order 1970, SI 1970/1540. In *Re James (an Insolvent) (A-G Intervening)* [1977] Ch 41, [1977] 1 All ER 364, the majority of the Court of Appeal held that the 'High Court of Rhodesia', sitting under the revolutionary Constitution, was not a 'British Court'.

8 The jurisdictional distinction was acknowledged by MacDonald JA in *Madzimbamuto's Case (No. 2)* 1968 (2) SA 457 at 463.

9 Pak LD (1972) SC 139.

10 (1958) SC Pak 533. See also *Uganda v Commissioner of Prisons, ex p Matova* [1966] EALR 514.

11 In view of the heavy reliance on *Dosso* by the Appellate Division in *Madzimbamuto's Case*, it is interesting to speculate what effect, if any, its overruling might have had on the reasoning in *Madzimbamuto*. In post-war West Germany the courts might have declared the formally enacted legislation of the Nazi era to be void retrospectively, but they refrained from actually doing so: see Pappé 'On the Validity of Judicial Decisions in the Nazi Era' (1960) 23 MLR 260.

12 In *Bilang v Rigg* [1972] NZLR 954, a New Zealand court recognised the validity of the appointment of a court officer after UDI on the ground that he had been appointed under a valid statute, that he had acted according to lawful intructions of the Governor and that his action did not contravene UK legislation.

13 Cf. the unanimous opinions in *Jilani v Government of Punjab* Pak LD (1972) SC 139 at 159, 162, 229, 230, 261, 267. In both *Madzimbamuto's Case* and *Dosso's Case* the theory of Hans Kelsen, which is based on effectiveness, was invoked in support; *Jilani* repudiated it *in toto*.

in its place in 1689 in order to guard against such abuse. Similar reasons also underlay the revolt of the American colonies against the abuse of power by the Crown in Parliament and the adoption there of a new institution. In South Africa the form in which the law-making institution came to be accepted stemmed from political compromise. The 'entrenched clauses' of the South Africa Act 1909 sought to safeguard certain minority rights by providing that a statute affecting these had to be passed by at least a two-thirds majority of both Houses of Parliament sitting together. This arrangement was part of the political compact between the four provinces as a condition of their union.

There is thus an arguable case for contending that courts should take account of the moral basis on which a criterion of validity was initially accepted when pronouncing on the validity of subsequent enactments, and this will be considered more fully later[14].

Turning next to the acceptance of judicial precedent as a criterion of validity, a distinction has to be drawn between the doctrine of precedent, which is that like cases should be decided alike and is in no way peculiar to common law systems, and the special doctrine of precedent in the common law, which is that decided cases in certain circumstances possess *law-quality* in themselves and are also *binding* in that they have to be followed or distinguished. A convenient nomenclature for the common law doctrine is *stare decisis*, derived from *stare decisis et quieta non movere*, so as to distinguish it from the broad doctrine of precedent shared by all developed systems.

No system of law can be a 'system' without regularity in the way in which disputes are decided. Therefore, a fundamental reason for the acceptance of a doctrine of precedent is the moral dictate of justice that like cases should be decided alike. If people are required to settle disputes by peaceful process rather than by resorting to self-help, which is a prime consideration in the dawn of society, such process should dispense what they feel is justice in the situation complained of as being unjust. In order to do this, it is essential to foster confidence in the peaceful settlement of disputes. Judgments are pronounced on the facts of individual cases and the chance that the facts of even two cases will be identical in every particular is so remote that, as a practical matter, similarities and dissimilarities can only be viewed on the basis of generalisations and classification of facts into types. So the requirement that like cases should be treated alike reduces itself to minimising arbitrariness and caprice in the perception of similarities and dissimilarities. This is achieved up to a point by using previous cases as paradigms furnishing broad type-situations.

The doctrine of precedent in English law is of considerable antiquity, while that of *stare decisis* is relatively modern. Judges in the twelfth century did listen to citations of earlier cases and were no doubt influenced by them in reaching their decisions. Thus, Richard Fitz-Nigel, writing around 1177 and 1179, said 'There are cases where the courses of events, and the reasons for decisions are obscure; and in these it is enough to cite precedents'[15]. There was not at this time any suggestion that judges were bound by them, nor do the early writers give any such indication. In other words, the mere fact of being forming the basis of a decision did not of itself invest a proposition with the quality of being 'English law'.

14 See pp 91–93 post.
15 Fitz-Nigel *Dialogues de Scaccario* 17.

If one were to inquire why it is that in Britain today precedents have law-quality, it would be difficult to offer a reason. The only reply is that this has come to be one of the accepted bases upon which the system now rests. The genesis of it lies in factors peculiar to this country, principally the absence of a code. The Normans forbore to impose an alien code on a half-conquered realm, but sought instead to win as much widespread confidence as possible in their administration of law. This was achieved through the institution of itinerant justices touring different circuits[16]. There being no central code, these justices had no guidance other than local customs, and their implementation of these gradually won local support for the new system in that it was seen, in the main, to fulfil people's expectations. In the longer term the practice of following like cases was extended over all parts of the realm. In this way lines of similar decisions evolved in time, like cases following upon each other, and eventually it became possible to look back along those lines and to distil general propositions from them, which came to be known as the common custom of the realm or the common law[17]. 'Nor, speaking more generally', said Lord Asquith, 'does English jurisprudence start from a broad principle and decide cases in accordance with its logical implications. It starts with a clean slate, scored over, in course of time, with *ad hoc* decisions. General rules are arrived at inductively, from the collation and comparison of these decisions'[18]. So, too, Lord Denning: 'We do not seek, as Continental jurists do, to lay down principles first by abstract reasoning and then apply them to concrete cases. We decide cases according to their merits and then see what principle emerges from them'[19]. Not only the common law, but equity too developed in this way. So it came about that the principle of justice gave rise to a system of precedent in the broad sense in this country as elsewhere.

The law-quality of precedents is attributable, as already stated, to the absence of a code. Decisions were not illustrations of law to be found elsewhere, but were the only statement that there was of the law. Also, in the early days decisions were believed to be expressions of natural law, and the earlier the decision the more truly was it supposed to reflect ideal law. As the gulf of time widened, judges became increasingly reluctant to challenge old decisions. Bracton and Coke, for example, preferred older authorities. The former, as Plucknett pointed out, attempted in his treatise to persuade his contemporaries that the laws of the day had become distorted and had departed from the earlier 'true' principles. Once this attitude of mind became ingrained in the outlook of lawyers with regard to ancient decisions, its application to all decisions, both old and new, is not hard to appreciate. In the dawn of the nineteenth century the critical spirit of positivism dispelled belief in natural law, and it needed but this to invest decisions themselves with ultimate authority. Even before this, the common law had become the people's champion against governmental oppression, so no one dared to suggest that it should be replaced with a code.

---

16 The assize system was abolished in 1971 by the Courts Act 1971 and replaced by Crown Courts.
17 Cf Gluckman *Judicial Process Among the Barotse*, pp 253–258; Stein *Regulae Juris*, ch II.
18 *Chapman v Chapman* [1954] AC 429 at 470, [1954] 1 All ER 798 at 819.
19 Denning *The Changing Law* p 50; and also *Chic Fashions (West Wales) Ltd v Jones* [1968] 2 QB 299 at 313, [1968] 1 All ER 229 at 236. See also Cardozo *The Nature of the Judicial Process* p 23.

A different factor, which paved the way for *stare decisis*, is the prestige of the judges, who have always been chosen from among the leaders of the Bar and represented the apex of the profession[20]. A historical factor which enhanced that prestige was their successful resistance to the Royal endeavour to override individual rights by virtue of the prerogative.

It may be asked whether the doctrine of *stare decisis* is itself a rule of law. If it were treated as such, it could not be reconciled with the doctrine that the common law has existed from time immemorial; but this, as will presently appear, is a pious fiction. A better way of looking at the matter would be to say that the application of the label 'law' cannot rest on 'legal' considerations. The acceptance of the term 'law' to principles enunciated in precedents evolved historically, but none of them can justify the usage by virtue of which they themselves acquired law-quality. *Stare decisis* is one of the foundations upon which English law rests. The practical question is not what it should be called, but whether it is satisfactory.

The acceptance of immemorial customs as 'law' is bound up with the larger question as to how practices generate the belief that they ought to be followed. It is a philosophical axiom that a normative 'ought' cannot be derived from an 'is', which in the present context means that the fact of a practice does not of itself explain why it ought to be followed[1]. The 'ought' stems from a value-judgment, which is sometimes concealed. Thus, in the statement, 'X is your father; therefore you ought to help him', the 'ought' derives, not from the fact that he is the father, but from the unstated moral attitude attaching to the parent-child relationship[2]. Again, in the statement, 'X is smaller than you; therefore you ought not to hit him', the 'ought' derives from the disapproval of hitting persons smaller than oneself. In the case of the practices of people at large the position becomes more complex, and it is at this point that the pressure exerted by interlocking practices, previously mentioned, comes into play. The greater the number of people involved, the more numerous are the interlocking practices that invariably develop among them, the result of which could make it highly unsettling if individuals refuse to conform. The aversion that is then generally felt towards disruption and inconvenience accounts in good measure for the sense of obligation towards conformity in such cases. For people make plans on the basis of expectations that a practice will be observed, and the more widespread this is, the greater the pressure against frustrating such hopes. Language, too, is an important factor in creating emotional responses towards conduct. Non-conformity, which unsettles the interlocked behaviour-patterns and expectations, is disapproved and comes to be associated with such words as 'wrong', 'irresponsible', 'bad', 'immoral'; while conformity tends to be associated with such words as 'right', 'responsible', 'good', 'moral'. In this way the inherited traditions of words contribute materially to generating feelings of 'ought' and hence of 'duty'. It will be seen, therefore, that it is not

---

20 *Salmond on Jurisprudence* (12th edn) pp 141-12. Cf Goodhart 'Precedent in English and Continental Law' (1934) 50 LQR 60.
1 This thesis is ascribed to Hume *A Treatise on Human Nature* III, 1.1. For discussions, see *The Is/Ought Question* (ed Hudson); Kolakowski *Positivist Philosophy* pp 42 et seq; Samek *The Legal Point of View* pp 181-185; Toulmin *An Examination of the Place of Reason in Ethics* ch 2; Warnock *Contemporary Moral Philosophy*. There is a different sense in which an 'ought' is derived from an 'is' which has been considered earlier. See p 21 ante.
2 See on this Emmet *Rules, Roles and Relations* pp 42 et seq.

the development of a practice as such, but the growth of the conviction that it ought to be followed that constitutes its acceptance as a *rule* of behaviour.

It has already been pointed out that general customs of the realm are the common law. Immemorial customs now under discussion are local variations of the common law. Judges accepted them in the early days because not to have done so would have unsettled local expectations. Besides, respecting them helped to foster confidence in the royal administration of justice, while the judges, for their part, welcomed any guidance they could find in the nascent state of the law.

The foregoing discussions show how far the original inquiry into the internalisation of standards of behaviour can and does reach into realms remote from its prosaic beginnings. Yet, the steps in that progression follow one by one. The factors behind internalisation are imprecise and unpredictable, which may be why they are excluded from formal analyses; but they remain necessary to a full understanding of 'rule'. It shows again that this legal phenomenon cannot be isolated from the moral, social, historical and political context of society except by drawing an arbitrary cut-off point.

LAWS

As with 'rule', the raw material of the law as set out in the previous chapter did not include 'a law'. This is because 'a law' is only a particular way of organising the material and also because its formulation presupposes to some extent a concept of 'legal system'.

The identification, or as Jeremy Bentham put it, 'individuation', of 'a law' is a matter of definition and reflects the definer's way of organising legal material. This can be shown by contrasting Bentham's, John Austin's and Hans Kelsen's ways of 'individuating' a law. Bentham believed that a 'legal system' is only the sum-total of laws and that one only needs to identify 'a law'[3]. This he did in substance by positing an act-situation at the core of each law. Thus, 'You ought not to do X', and 'If you do X, you ought to be punished', are two separate laws dealing respectively with different act-situations. In fastening on acts as the substrate of laws it would appear that he subscribed to the belief that the expression 'a law' had to have a factual counterpart. This is not above criticism, but it is not necessary to enter into the objections here[4]. Kelsen, on the other hand, rolled into one what for Bentham are two separate laws. According to him, a law is in the form: 'If X, then sanction Y ought to follow'[5]. The doing of X is a condition precedent to the ordering of the sanction. Bentham's disciple, Austin, shared his mentor's belief that a 'legal system' is the sum-total of laws, but unlike him went on to define 'a law' as the command of a sovereign backed by a sanction; which is different again[6]. All these ways of 'individuating' a law will be considered later, but the point to be made here is that they all represent different ways of isolating 'a law' out of the same material.

The concept of 'a law' also presupposes 'legal system'. For instance, it would popularly be thought that the statutory prescription of a fine for

3 Bentham *Of Laws in General* (ed Hart), and more generally pp 336, 341 et seq. post.
4 See p 337 post.
5 Kelsen *General Theory of Law and State*; pp 359 et seq. post.
6 Austin *Lectures on Jurisprudence*; p 345 post.

unauthorised parking is 'a law'. Bentham pointed out that such a precept is made up of strands of various other parts of the law just as, to use his own 'coarse allusion', a slice of meat cut by a butcher is a conglomerate cross-section of muscle, bone, tendons, nerves etc. An anatomist's dissection would seek to reveal the whole muscle, tendon etc[7], and, similarly, a jurisprudential analysis of a precept such as the imposition of a fine for unauthorised parking would follow out its various strands, such as the system of courts for trying offenders, the authorisation of parking-meters, appointment of traffic wardens, procedures, ways of obtaining evidence, scales of punishments, and so on. Any particular precept presupposes the whole background and its analysis will unfold the whole system of which it is a part.

Another way of making the same point is by harking back to the concept of liberty, which was discussed earlier[8]. The question was then raised as to whether liberties are part of law. Pound and Kelsen, it will be remembered, denied that they were. This looks plausible in cases where the liberty lies in the area as yet untouched by encroaching duties, but it is less plausible, if not unacceptable, in cases where the liberty is created by the abolition of a duty, eg by statute. The point is that whether liberty is treated as being within or outside law reflects one or other of two ways of regarding 'legal system': as 'open' or 'closed'. An 'open' concept confines 'law' to areas of specific regulation by authority. Areas not yet regulated are then outside 'law', which means that the concept of law remains open in these areas to future regulation. A 'closed' concept treats all areas as falling within 'law', whether regulated positively or negatively in the sense that it is still the law that allows or creates liberty.

Yet another pointer in the same direction is the thesis propounded by Professor Honoré that to understand 'a law' one should begin by understanding 'a group'[9]. Every law is a law of some group, and 'law' in its broad sense is a group structure designed to secure obedience to group prescriptions. For present purposes it is sufficient only to draw attention to Professor Honoré's contention, which will be explained later[10].

The upshot of all this is that neither 'rule' nor 'a law' is part of the basic material. An examination of them is helpful in clarifying the ground. Since in one way and another they reflect 'legal system', it is this that has to be considered.

LEGAL SYSTEM

As stated above, Bentham and Austin believed that 'law' in the sense of 'legal system' is only the sum-total of laws and that elucidation of 'a law' is all that is necessary. This, as will have become evident from the foregoing analysis, was mistaken. In addition there is the further objection that a legal system is more than the sum-total of laws or legal material; it represents the pattern of interrelation of this material and differs from them also in its overall purposes and functioning.

---

7 Bentham *Of Laws in General* p 12.
8 See p 31 ante.
9 Honoré 'Groups, Laws and Obedience' in *Oxford Essays in Jurisprudence* (Second Series) (ed Simpson) ch 1.
10 See pp 443–444 post.

Pattern of interrelation

A railway system, for example, is not just the sum-total of tracks and rolling stock stacked together; the system is the pattern of their linkage and distribution. In areas rich in coal and iron, for instance, and around major ports, the network of railways will tend to be thick and complex, but less so in areas of desert; and the lay-out will vary again in mountainous districts and over plains. With regard to a legal system, as a generalisation it may be stated that the pattern of linkage imparts unity to all its components, which can be discerned through the concept of validity and through the institutional structure.

Validity refers to the law-quality of a proposition: if it has law-quality, it is a valid proposition of law, if not, it is invalid. Validity, therefore, unifies legal material at its foundation; it is what makes it all 'legal' and isolates it from non-legal material. It has been explained that legality depends on the acceptance by courts of some criterion, or criteria, as capable of imparting law-quality to propositions filtering through them. In this country they are Acts of Parliament, judicial precedents, immemorial customs and, by virtue of statute, Regulations and Decisions of the European Economic Community. Because of judicial acceptance of principles, doctrines and standards as 'legal', these, too, come under the umbrella of validity[11].

The institutional structure of a legal system pulls it together in a different way[12]. There are only a certain number of law-making institutions, which between them cover the entire system. The Crown in Parliament stands at the top; bodies with subordinate legislative power are strictly defined and derive their power from Parliament. The courts, which apply the law and also have power to make law through precedents, are strictly defined and limited in number. Immemorial customs occupy an odd position. Theoretically their law-making power is unspecified and amorphous, which reflects the historical past. Since early times, however, the legal system has filled out and become increasingly unified through the expanding activity of statute and precedent with the result that the law-making potentiality of customs has dwindled into virtual nothingness. The point will be dealt with further under custom.

Next, there are law-applying and law-enforcement institutions. Courts come into this category and in addition to those that can make law, there are a number of subordinate courts and tribunals, all of which are defined; and the range of orders and punishments courts can decree is likewise defined. Enforcement through the use of organised force is institutionalised through bodies such as the armed forces, the police and other bodies of officials. As before, the number of such institutions is limited and their powers are defined.

Finally, there are conceptual institutions within the law itself. Its *corpus* is pulled together by institutions which unify fact-situations and legal consequences. Instead of each situation being governed separately by its own

---

11 Theories of validity have variously been based on the will of God (Aquinas); will of the sovereign (Bentham, Austin), the *Grundnorm* (Kelsen); a rule of recognition (Hart). See later in connection with each of these authors.
12 Raz 'The Institutional Nature of Law' (1975) 38 MLR 489; on which see Reid and Schiff (1976) 39 MLR 118.

regulation, there is a single regulation applicable to a class of facts. This is accomplished through unifying concepts, such as possession, ownership etc[13].

Purposes and functioning

The very word 'system' implies that a legal system consists of co-ordinated activities; there cannot be a system without co-ordination and regularity. Co-ordination in turn implies that the activities are not haphazard but purposive in the sense that they are directed towards achieving different objectives. The way in which these tasks are put into effect and the extent of their success or failure involves an inquiry into their actual functioning. The activity of any phenomenon must take time over its functioning and, therefore, the phenomenon must continue in existence over that period.

To list the many tasks which a legal system sets out to achieve would be tedious. Speaking broadly, it can be said that one task is to provide a framework within which people conduct their affairs. Thus, the legal framework shapes many daily activities, eg buying and selling, giving credit etc, are shaped by the way in which promises are enforced. Another more difficult task, previously alluded to, is the educative function of shaping people's ideas. One of the most important, indeed, the overall task is to achieve justice in society[14]. As one of the main purposes of any legal system it is difficult to see how this could be doubted, whatever the problems and difficulties that beset the meaning of 'justice' and the practicalities of its achievement. Justice is integral to the concept of a legal system; the etymology of the word 'law' itself derives from what is fitting and right[15]. Even where injustices are practised, and no one doubts that these do occur, the authorities contrive to hide them behind a veil of justice, however thin, and it is when such practices become intolerable to the masses and the veil becomes threadbare and transparent that revolution tears the system apart in the hope of establishing a new and more just system in its place. The achievement of a minimum of justice is a condition *sine qua non* of the continuity of a legal system, and some of the many aspects of justice will be the concern of the next Part of this book.

13 MacCormick, 'Law as Institutional Fact' (1974) 90 LQR 102.
14 See eg Del Vecchio 'On the Function and Aims of the State' in *Essays in Jurisprudence in Honor of Roscoe Pound* at p 150.
15 Clark *Practical Jurisprudence* p 90 and passim.

READING LIST

J Bentham *Of Laws in General* (ed HLA Hart).
HLA Hart *The Concept of Law*.
A M Honoré 'Groups, Laws and Obedience' in *Oxford Essays in Jurisprudence* (Second Series) (ed A W B Simpson) ch 1.
D N MacCormick 'Law as Institutional Fact' (1974) 90 Law Quarterly Review 102.
K Olivecrona *Law as Fact* (1939 and 1971).
J Raz 'The Institutional Nature of Law' (1975) 38 Modern Law Review 489.
P G Stein *Regulae Juris*.
W L Twining and D Meirs *How to Do Things with Rules*.

Aspects of justice

SUMMARY

CHAPTER 4

Distributive justice

The quest for justice has been as challenging as the quest for the Holy Grail, and as elusive. To some this is because justice is a will-o'-the-wisp, to others because it is too vast to be encompassed by one mind. The master mind of Aristotle (384–322 BC) was superior to most people's and his pioneer analysis still serves as a crucible into which even modern craftsmen continue to pour problems of the 20th century in the hope that an acceptable brew will emerge. At least his discussion provides a starting point. In dealing with 'particular justice', as distinct from 'universal justice', he distinguished between 'distributive' and 'corrective' justice[1]. Distributive justice is based on the principle that there has to be equal distribution among equals[2]. Corrective justice seeks to restore equality when this has been disturbed, eg by wrongdoing, which assumes that the situation that has been upset was distributively just.

The Aristotelian principle suffers from certain weaknesses. The first is: distribution of what? Aristotle spoke of the distribution of 'honours or money or the other things that fall to be divided among those who have a share in the constitution'[3]. Such a formula is imprecise and will be considered presently. More important is the criterion of 'equal' and who decides equality. Equal distribution among equals means that according to a given criterion of discrimination, unequal cases are to be treated differently, which still leaves open the question whether it is just to select that particular criterion[4]. Also, amongst those classed as equals one person may complain of injustice if he is treated worse than the others. What if he is treated better? For instance, if black people are treated as less privileged than white people, but one black man is given the same privileges as whites, this would be unjust as far as other black people are concerned. Would it be just or unjust as far as he himself is concerned; or white people? This harks back to the justice of the criterion for discriminating between the two groups in the first place.

Another difficulty is that equal treatment in law of things unequal in fact, such as power, talents etc, may widen or create inequalities. Thus, for the law to insist on sanctity of contract on the ground that contracting parties stand on an equal footing when in fact there is inequality in their respective bargaining positions, has led to various forms of injustice, eg between employer and employee, or public authorities and individuals. To take account of inequalities in fact there has to be unequal treatment in law, which means that the question when the law should depart from equality has to be determined on some principle other than equality. Lastly, the distinction between

---

1 *Nicomachean Ethics* V (trans Rackham).
2 *Nicomachean Ethics* V, 3.
3 *Nicomachean Ethics* V, 2.
4 Honoré 'Social Justice' in *Essays in Legal Philosophy* (ed Summers) 61 at 68–69.

distributive and corrective equality is by no means clear. The unsatisfactory cases of *DeFunis v Odegaard*[5] and *Regents of the University of California v Bakke*[6] show the difficulty. In both a white student sued a university on the ground of unjust discrimination because the university admitted black and Indian students with lower qualifications than were required of white students. In *De Funis*, since the white student was admitted before the conclusion of the appeal, the American Supreme Court by a bare majority held that there was no issue[7]. In *Bakke* the Supreme Court did decide, again by a bare majority, that the university was in the wrong, but extracting a coherent principle from the judgments defies ingenuity. Both cases, however, raise the question whether this kind of reverse discrimination was designed to create distributive justice by providing equality of educational opportunity, or was a form of corrective justice to redress an inequality through past discrimination.

It should be evident from all this that justice is not synonymous with equality; equality is one aspect of it, no more. Justice is not some 'thing', which can be captured in a formula once and for all[8]; it is a process, a complex and shifting balance between many factors, including equality. As Friedrich observed 'Justice is never given, it is always a task to be achieved'[9]. The tasks of justice submitted in this book are the just allocation of advantages and disadvantages, preventing the abuse of power, preventing the abuse of liberty, the just decision of disputes and adapting to change. Aristotle's distributive justice would be associated mainly with the first three and his corrective justice mainly with the fourth. The five tasks have been listed in this way for the purpose of exposition. They are not disjunctive for, as will appear, the need to curb the abuse of power and liberty underlie the others.

Some modern writers approach justice differently from Aristotle. Professor Honoré suggests that it would at least be 'refreshing to look at justice, not so much from the Aristotelian point of view of the just man, but from that of the citizen to whom just treatment is due'[10]. From a somewhat similar point of view Cahn speaks of the 'sense of injustice'[11]. It is true that persons with grievances are those who raise the question of justice. There is, therefore, much to be said for this angle of approach, but the problem goes deeper. It is not enough to work out a just scheme of distribution, from whatever point of view, but there is the further problem of getting it accepted and keeping it acceptable; which requires constant re-distribution according to changing circumstances. Both initial acceptance and continued acceptance depend on people feeling that the scheme is at least not unjust.

Just allocation of advantages and disadvantages

This is the first of the tasks listed above. The difficulty of securing acceptance of a scheme of allocation and, even more so, of keeping it acceptable arises from the fact that the sense of injustice is a capricious sentiment, which is likely to be influenced, even changed, by the distribution that presently

5 40 L Ed (2d) 164 (1974).
6 438 US 265 (1978).
7 Douglas J alone discussed the merits: see 40 L Ed (2d) 164 (1974) at 171 et seq. See on this case Paulsen '*De Funis*: the Road not Taken' (1974) 60 Virginia LR 917.
8 See eg the theories of Aristotle, Kant, Stammler, Marx and Rawls.
9 Friedrich 'Justice: the Just Political Act' 6 *Nomos, Justice*, at 34.
10 *Honoré* p 62.
11 Cahn *The Sense of Injustice* (1949).

exists. For instance, the welfare state attempts to satisfy 'basic needs'. The word 'basic' implies that over and above certain minima, it is open to some people to enjoy additional amenities, so that there will continue to be 'haves' and 'have-nots'. The tendency sooner or later will be for the latter to start insisting that some of the things which they would like, but do not have, are 'basic' and hence 'needs' and due 'as of right'. As Professor Honoré has observed 'What is at one time a luxury becomes at another time a necessity and need'[12]. Also, no one likes to feel indebted and grateful. Rather than have to feel grateful for benefits received, a not uncommon psychological reaction is to convince oneself that these are due 'as of right' for which there is no call for gratitude, and to start furbishing new demands. All schemes of a just distribution will be brought to nought if the more that is given, the more is demanded 'as of right'[13]. This does not necessarily follow, but, human nature being what it is, the danger does appear to be real[14]. The safeguard lies in a sense of obligation as opposed to a sense only of 'rights'. An unfortunate by-product of the welfare state has been the encouragement of a sense of 'rights' to the virtual exclusion of a sense of obligation. Any scheme of justice is likely to turn sour if nurtured on ideas of 'rights' alone. To adopt the point of view of 'the citizen to whom just treatment is due' should not commit one to consider only his 'rights'; what is due *from him* is just as relevant. To promote and maintain a successful scheme of justice requires the promotion of a sense of obligation, requiring among other things, a curb on the appetite for 'rights', especially when this leads to abuse of liberties.

Another difficulty in the way of winning and preserving acceptance of a scheme of distribution is the need to have confidence in those who decide what are basic needs, how advantages and disadvantages are to be distributed and when they are deemed to be satisfied. The persons who decide these matters have to be invested with powers, and the problem then is one of curbing the abuse of power.

Turning now to the 'things' that fall to be distributed, it is not enough to refer to them simply as 'advantages' and 'disadvantages', or as 'honours or money or the other things that fall to be divided among those who have a share in the constitution'. All such terms need to be categorised more precisely. Different considerations apply to distribution between individuals and over the community, and a sense of injustice works differently with different kinds of advantages and disadvantages. It is here that the Hohfeldian distinctions, considered earlier, prove helpful. Hohfeld was concerned solely with analytical subtleties, not with a theory of justice, although he did remark at the end of his paper that his distinctions make it possible 'to discern common principles of justice and policy underlying the various jural problems involved'[15]. This was not a considered statement, and he has been

---

12 *Honoré* p 78.
13 One recalls Goldsmith's lines:

> 'Ill fares the land, to hastening ills a prey,
> Where wealth accumulates and men decay': (*The Deserted Village*).

14 One example is the abusive demands made on the 'free' health service which has forced retrenchments in various ways. Arguably, welfare benefits enjoyed by families of strikers helps, at least to some extent, to carry out strikes damaging to the very institution that provides the benefits. See on this, 'Financial Strikes', Conservative Political Centre (1974). Cf Lasko, 'The Payment of Supplementary Benefit for Strikers' Dependants—Misconception and Misrepresentation' (1975) 38 MLR 31.
15 Slohfeld *Fundamental Legal Conceptions* (ed Cook) p 64.

criticised for it[16]. However, the application of his distinctions to the problem of distributive justice might posthumously tinge his allusion to justice with some relevance.

Starting with disadvantages, the most abundant of these are duties and liabilities. The imposition of duties is always dictated by policy. Doing justice here involves balancing various considerations, for which no rules can be laid down. With regard to the imposition of liabilities, equality should be a very rough guide so that special variations in their incidence require justification. Thus, various criteria are used to justify the unequal imposition of taxation[17], or liability to expropriation or destruction of property in emergencies, or equal liability to rationing in times of shortage. With regard to disabilities, when these affect large numbers of people the question of justice concerns their removal so as to produce equality of advantage rather than their imposition, eg those attaching to women, Jews, Catholics, agnostics and even today to members of certain races in countries where a racial policy obtains. It is the imposition of disabilities that calls for justification. When they attach to individuals, the reasons why they are imposed cannot stem from equality; the justice behind them derives from other considerations. For instance, a man has a disability to insure against his own intentional wrongdoing. This is based on a moral consideration, not equality[18]. On the other hand, he is allowed to insure against negligence, but here the moral consideration is outweighed by the need to compensate the victim[19]. To talk of a distribution of no-claims has a ring of unreality, which disappears when it is realised that the no-claim of one person corresponds with the liberty of another to perform some action (usually to exercise a power, eg reduce a fee normally payable). The question of injustice here concerns the manner in which the liberty and power are exercised.

Advantages may be divided into claims, liberties, powers and immunities. With regard to claims, Professor Honoré invites his readers to consider 'not primarily the duty to act justly, but the demand for just treatment'; and he continues: 'Following Hohfeld's usage it seems appropriate to use the word "claim" in this context to mark the point that we are here concerned not, as we are in the analysis of liberty, with the question "What are men permitted to do?" but with the question "What are men entitled to demand?"'[20]. For this purpose claims can be divided into those correlative to negative and positive duties. With regard to negative duties, eg the duty not to injure others, no one should be accorded less protection by way of correlative claims than his neighbour unless he forfeits it by choice or his own conduct, eg by consent or aggression. With regard to claims correlative to positive duties, these can be divided into claims against individuals and against the state. The allocation of the former presents no difficulty since they and the fulfilment of the duties rest largely on choice, eg contractual claims and duties. The allocation of the latter type of claim depends on state policy, eg that the

16 J Stone *Legal System and Lawyers' Reasonings* p 161; and see Ch 2 ante.
17 In *Roberts v Hopwood* [1925] AC 578, the House of Lords invalidated a scheme drawn up by a local council on the ground that it distributed the liability to tax unequally among ratepayers. See also *Prescott v Birmingham Corpn* [1955] Ch 210, [1954] 3 All ER 698.
18 *Geismar v Sun Alliance and London Insurance Ltd* [1978] QB 383, [1977] 3 All ER 570.
19 Cf automatic insurance: introduced in New Zealand by the Accident Compensation Act 1972, and Accident Compensation Amendment (No 2) Act 1973; Royal Commission Report *On Civil Liability and Compensation for Personal Injury* (Cmnd 7054-I).
20 *Honoré* pp 62, 63.

state shall provide basic subsistence. Professor Honoré speaks of 'advantages which are generally desired and are in fact conducive to their well-being ... I mean such things as life, health, food, shelter, clothing, places to move in, opportunities for acquiring knowledge and skill, for sharing in the process of making decisions, for recreation, travel etc. Men not only have a claim to these things but to an equal share in them'[1]. The two general points previously made are relevant here, namely, someone has to be vested with power to decide what claims need to be met and when they are satisfied, and there is the possibility that the satisfaction of these and other claims might whet the appetite for increased demands.

With liberties the problem is not one of equal distribution but whether *some* should be allowed at all, eg liberties to kill, maim, steal, and, if they are allowed, how their abuse can be prevented. In the unrestrained exercise of liberties lies the greatest threat to any scheme of distributive justice.

Powers are of various kinds. There should be equal distribution of some, eg power to contract, subject of course to obvious denials, eg to the insane. Other kinds of powers cannot in their nature be equally distributed, eg the power to decide what are basic needs, when they are satisfied and what is a just distribution. The question is, who should have such power? For instance, recent governments in Britain thought that a wages and incomes policy was a just way of staving off economic ruin, but many trade unions did not agree and on occasions thwarted the government. Karl Marx said that in the proletarian dictatorship distribution will follow the formula: 'From each according to his capacity, to each according to his work'; and in a communist utopia distribution will follow the formula: 'From each according to his capacity, to each according to his needs'[2]. Not only is it crucial to know who is to decide these matters, but also how that person is to evaluate capacities, work and needs. For instance, in the Soviet Union a certain dissident mathematician was not allowed to pursue his calling and he had to take a job of shovelling coal in order to avoid being convicted of being a social 'parasite'[3]. Is his capacity gauged as a mathematician or as a coal-heaver? If, as seems to be the case, it is the latter, is his capacity gauged on the basis of his contribution to society? The difficulty still remains of how one evaluates the contribution of a film-star, a coal-heaver, a dustman, or a person whose work has delayed or imperceptible effects, eg a teacher. Further, how does one evaluate the needs of, eg chefs, hospital porters or motor car workers? Finally, does giving people what they deserve according to their needs do away with pay differentials? If two persons have the same needs, should one be given a higher wage because he does a more dangerous or more skilful job than the other? The point is that decisions on such questions as these cannot depend on a formula and the allocation of power to decide them can hardly be determined on a principle of equality. To give it to one person is to court tyranny; to give it to all is not possible. With powers, therefore, the question of justice is not one of equal distribution, but of preventing their abuse.

The problem of the distribution of immunities is different from that of claims. Claims are demandable by all so that denial in a special case needs to be justified, whereas it is not denial but conferment of a special immunity that requires justification. There has been a progressive removal of special

1 *Honoré* pp 63, 82, 94.
2 See p 397 post.
3 See p 414 post.

immunities, eg those of the Crown and of public authorities. What calls for attention is the immunities claimed by trade unions. The original reason for these was the anxiety to preserve their slender resources from being paid out in damages. That reason no longer obtains with anything like the same force; so the question arises as to the justice in persisting with and, perhaps, widening their immunities.

Not only do power and liberty share the danger of abuse, but power, on the one hand, and immunity from power and liberty, on the other, are indissoluably linked as will appear. For these reasons the problem of power and liberty have to be treated as separate aspects of justice, distinct from the distribution of other advantages. Different ages have reacted differently to power and liberty, but have always regarded the issues raised by them as central. These have inspired various versions of natural law theory. In order to gain some idea of their complexity and importance it is necessary to review the changing attitudes towards power, immunity and liberty in a historical perspective.

SPIRALS OF HISTORY

Montesquieu pointed out long ago that power tends to be abused[4], and Lord Acton perceived with equal clarity that 'power tends to corrupt, and absolute power corrupts absolutely'[5]. It is not that wielders of power are inherently evil, but that they get caught up in the toils of power, which gets beyond their control. The contemporary tragedy of Pakistan illustrates this. The chaos into which political factions plunged the country after allegedly rigged elections was halted on 5 July 1977 by a military coup, which promised elections on 16 October and a return to democratic government. Supporters of the deposed President then kept fomenting such unrest that on 1 October it was announced that conditions had deteriorated to such a level that elections would have to be postponed indefinitely. Since then the government, which meant well at first, has found itself having to impose sterner and sterner measures until it has reached an even more unenviable position than its predecessor. In similar ways most holders of power are forced into resisting change, and as pressure for change mounts, are forced to resort to ever-increasing repression. Failure to adapt to change is as much an abuse of power as direct exercises of it. The result is that sooner or later people reach the point when they can stand the abuse of power no more and start agitating for freedom from power.

'Freedom' is a slogan charged with powerful emotive content, which has moved people to nobility, sacrifice and violence. Three meanings of the term should be distinguished. (1) Freedom from power (immunity), eg a freeman is one who is not under anyone's power. (2) Freedom to act and not to act (liberty), eg free speech implies the absence of duty not to speak[6]. (3) Freedom from disability (capacity, the acquisition of powers and liberties), eg coming of age. Aspects of this fall under head (1) or head (2), so it need not be discussed further.

Popular advocates of freedom fail to distinguish between freedom as

4 Montesquieu *L'Esprit des Lois* (1748) 11, 4–6.
5 Acton *Historical Essays and Studies* Appendix.
6 For a similar distinction, see Fuller 'Freedom—a Suggested Analysis' (1954–55) 68 Harv LR 1305; Isiah Berlin *Two Concepts of Liberty* (1958) pamphlet).

immunity and freedom as liberty. The two are linked, but distinct. Liberty to act implies absence of duty not to act; and duty is associated with enforcement and all the paraphernalia of power. Complete liberty cannot exist without complete absence of duty. Although linked in this way, the distinction is vital and much harm results from the loose use of 'freedom' wherein clamour for 'freedom from' power slides into clamour for 'freedom to' act as one pleases. To gratify a desire for freedom from power does not imply freedom to gratify every desire, and because of the failure to see this distinction the deliverance from the evil of abusive power so often ends in the evil of abusive liberty. In the words of Iris Murdoch:

> 'Freedom is, I think, a mixed concept. The true half of it is simply a name of an aspect of virtue concerned especially with the clarification of vision and the domination of selfish impulse. The false and more popular half is a name for the self-assertive movements of a deluded selfish will which because of our ignorance we take to be something autonomous'[7].

It is a sad paradox that the seeds of the abuse of power are sown in the bed of 'freedom'. Those who agitate most strongly for freedom from power are usually foremost in insisting, along with complete freedom of action for themselves, on the use of the utmost power to prevent others from going against them. Naturally they would not wish to see the cause for which they have striven being frustrated. They know, who better?, at what points they succeeded in bringing down the previous power-structure, so they know how best to stifle freedom of action against themselves at precisely those points; which is why the tyranny of those asserting freedom from tyranny is often worse.

Unrestrained freedom of action is the road to chaos. There comes a point in the breakdown of law and order which provokes increasing demand for power to restore stability. At first the call is generally supported by all who have grown weary of chaos. Indeed, it is an age-old tactic of revolutionaries to maintain constant disruption so as to produce just this reaction in order to smooth their own eventual accession to power. Then as memories recede and a new generation grows up, the now established power-structure becomes increasingly irksome and people, weary of power, start to agitate anew for freedom from it.

Striking the right balance between freedom from power and freedom of self-assertion has been a recurrent problem. The spirals of history show that the victory of freedom from abuse of power seems almost fated to end in abuse of freedom of action, which in turn calls for a return to power to keep it in check[8]. Such return is not to the same point as before; the slow march of societies has been a lurching spiral from one side to the other. The whole sorry tale is not a repetition, but goes on developing, like all great stories, as a supreme tragedy. Man just does not seem able to learn. Legal concepts of immunity, liberty and power cannot of themselves guarantee against their misuse, since they are only instruments of policy. Each society has to work out, and keep working out, the balance it wants between power, immunity and liberty. Whether the tide of opinion flows towards power or towards freedom from power and liberty depends on the social need of the age, which

7 Murdoch 'The Sovereignty of Good over other Concepts' *Leslie Stephen Lecture* 1967 (CUP) pp 31-32.
8 For illustration of an aspect of this, see Dietze *Two Concepts of the Rule of Law.*

has been reflected in variations of natural law theory. Such divergent interpretations should not condemn it, for they are necessary for a full grasp of
what it has stood for, namely, as a support for power and stability amidst
instability (or threat of it), or for revolution against power. In either case
the need has had to be justified by appeal to ideals, whether derived from
God or reason, other than the prevailing ones. It might even appear that
natural law theory is always a reaction against force, whether it be the
controlled force of tyranny or the uncontrolled force of anarchy.

Jewish theory

The Jewish doctrine, which is one of the oldest philosophies, possesses the
insight to lay equal stress on immunity from power and restraint in action.

The Israelites learned the value of freedom from power during their en-
slavement under the Egyptians. They desired a society in which Pharaohs
had no place, one which owed allegiance solely to God and was governed by
His laws. Sovereignty resides in His law which, by virtue of its origin and
intrinsic righteousness, cannot be altered by human institutions. So great,
however, was the insistence on freedom that even this law had to be freely
accepted by the people. The foundations of modern democracy and possibly
the earliest version of the social contract, which was destined to play so
prominent a part in later European thought, would seem to lie here. The
result was the theocracy, which is understood to date from the Exodus in the
thirteenth century BC to the establishment of kingship with the anointing of
Saul as King of Israel in 1037 BC. Its main features were the direct rule of
God over the people and insistence on the independence of the individual.
It was because the people were free that even the rulership of God was not
imposed but had to be accepted by them, an occurrence, possibly hypothetical, which is said to have taken place in the covenant with Abraham[9],
renewed with Isaac and Jacob[10], and later in the covenant with the people
at Sinai. The covenant with God was needed because of Man's freedom.
Independence resulted from his acceptance of God in place of dependence
on any other human being or institution, not excluding the state. So sublime
an assertion of human dignity could serve as a powerful means of protecting
the individual against the power of the state. All this embodies the idea of a
social contract transcending anything that was later evolved by European
political philosophers, and holds up a pattern of voluntary restraint on the
part of an omnipotent ruler. There had also to be acceptance of God as a
legislator[11]. It follows that the appointment of Saul as king in 1037 BC
amounted to a rejection by the people of God as their ruler: 'for they have
not rejected thee, but they have rejected me, that I should not reign over
them'[12]. Since Saul was understood to put God's law into effect, he was the
Lord's anointed. Even so, the monarch's position was based on a contract
with the people[13], and this relationship of the ruler to his subjects is of the
utmost significance for democratic limitation of power and constitutional
monarchy.

9 Gen 15.18.
10 Gen 26.3–5; Gen 28.12–16, 35.9–12; Deut 26.16–18.
11 Exod 19.3–8, 24.3, 7 (*quaere* whether 'be obedient' in King James's Bible is correct; cf 'hear').
   See also chs 20–23.
12 1 Samuel 8.7–9.
13 1 Samuel 10.17–25; 2 Samuel 3.21, 5.3.

Yet, amidst these lofty assertions of freedom and independence, the dangers inherent in the abuse of liberty were not overlooked. So another outstanding feature of Jewish philosophy is its insistence on duties alongside its insistence on human freedom from power. Indeed, the liberties are ascertained with reference to the duties, for they are the residue that remain after the delimitation of duties deduced from the co-partnership between God and Man in developing the human race towards holiness. Modern theories, which reach towards the idea of the paramountcy of duties over 'rights', might well be compared with this early expression of the idea.

In these and other ways the concepts of Jewish law offer a striking contribution to jurisprudence. The answers to many problems of Christian Europe had already been worked out in Jewish philosophy. Thus, the relation between Church and state, which occasioned such bitter rivalry in Europe, was no new problem. The immortal words, 'Render unto Caesar the things that are Caesar's, and unto God the things that are God's', crystallised centuries of practical wisdom. Again, the Divine Right of Kings' would appear to be a reflection of the profounder Jewish idea of 'anointed of the Lord'; but Jewish law, insisting as it did on the priority of duties, laid stress on obedience by the king to God's law and thus provided a safeguard against any 'right divine to govern wrong'. Jewish kingship began as constitutional monarchy.

The Greek period

Solon (c 638-558 BC) preached a doctrine of freedom from power, which arose out of the discontent of the poor owing to the tyranny of the rich and the Draconian Code. He was requested by all classes to deal with the social difficulties that had arisen and was invested with the title of *Archon*. His solutions laid the foundations of democracy. Every man should have a say in selecting those to whose rectitude and wisdom he is required to submit, and in this way it was hoped that civic power would be controlled by a sense of moral obligation and measured by public service.

The crucial factor in following later Graecian thought is that it unfolded in a setting of small city states presenting a picture of diversity and unstable equilibrium. Their development induced thinkers to speculate about the nature of the ordering that governed the relations of men. A group of such thinkers of the fifth and fourth centuries BC, the Sophists, distinguished between φυσις, nature, and νομος, law, the former being wise and eternal, the latter arbitrary and born of expediency. With regard to the latter, they developed a scepticism in which they recognised the relativity of human ideas and rejected absolute standards, and which was in its way an anticipation of some modern theories. The basis of law was said to be the self-interest of the law-maker, the only reason for obedience to law being the self-interest of the subject. Law was conceived of as being purely utilitarian and the product of expediency.

As against this, there was the view that law was guided by uniform principles, which gave it stability. Such a theory was more suited to the need of the age, which was stability, than the relativity of the Sophists, since it helped to preserve the *status quo*. This theory also offered a reason for obedience to law other than naked force or the self-interest of the governed, which was incompatible with social order.

The basis of this theory was somewhat as follows. Patterns of behaviour in Nature are not controlled by the objects which conform to them. A flower does not choose its location, nor does a cat make moral decisions. They lead what might be called a 'natural' way of life. Man alone has developed powers of reason and will, by virtue of which he has insight into goodness and badness. He has the choice of developing in either direction, but he ought to devote his powers to developing according to a natural morality, that is to say, a moral, rational and social life. Socrates (c 470–399 BC) set out to urge the existence of immutable moral principles by which all regulation of conduct was to be judged. He refused to admit with the Sophists that human actions were solely governed by inclinations and desires and contended instead that Man possesses the faculty of 'insight' into the nature of conduct, this insight being a knowledge of goodness. Virtue is knowledge, and in this way he propounded a natural morality. He and his pupil Plato (428/7–348/7 BC)[14] with their firm assertion of the discoverability of absolute standards started European thought along a road which it still pursues. Man's insight, the knowledge of goodness, was the criterion by which all regulation and conduct must be examined. Here, already formulated, is the classical dissociation of actual law from ideal 'natural' law. At the same time Socrates went on to propound that one of the dictates of natural law was that authority and positive law should be obeyed. This was a plea for security and stability, which, as already mentioned, was the prime need of the age. This was why he refused to escape from imprisonment and faced death. It was only a short time since the irregular settlement of disputes had been replaced by orderly process; for him to have flouted the court would have been a step towards disorganising society[15]. He did not, however, advocate a blind acceptance of positive law; this, he said, has to be subjected to critical examination in the light of man's insight.

In Plato's ideal state each individual is assigned to the role for which he is best fitted by reason of his capacities. Rulership should be in the hands of philosopher-kings, who could be trusted not to abuse their power. In the absence of such, a state governed by law was the next best thing. Plato was no advocate of immunity from power since, in his view, men are unequal both in status and in their capacity for virtue. Subject classes should not deplore their lot on a supposition that they have lost freedom for servitude; on the contrary, they have exchanged subjection to wisdom for subjection to nature. Side by side with this Plato also preached restraint on freedom of action, which is an essential condition of virtue. Those restraints, which are necessary for the development of excellence, are also those that are essential to political association. People need to be educated in virtue, and it is the lot of the state to do this; to rule is to educate.

The work of Aristotle (384–322 BC)[16] needs special mention. Both the need for authority and restraint on freedom of action were stressed by him. Man is by nature a political animal. The family is instituted by nature for the supply of his daily wants, but for other and wider needs men unite in communities and ultimately in the state. The state is therefore the creature of nature to enable Man to realise the good life. Man is the measure of all things; there is nothing on earth superior to Man. Therefore, the best law for Man is the product of the best men. So men should strive towards perfection. Goodness, to his way of thinking, was the ultimate aim of existence.

14 *Republic.*
15 *Critic* 11, 50.
16 *Politics; Nicomachean Ethics.*

Communities and laws should seek to realise the good life, that is, living according to virtue. He distinguished between particular or positive law and law which is common or natural. The former consists of patterns of conduct regulating behaviour, and these are needed for imposing restraints on freedom of action. The mark of the worst governments, he said, is that they allow people to do as they please, and he condemned societies whose members acknowledge no restraint. Positive laws and fidelity to them are thus essential. At the same time it is not enough just to have laws; they must be just laws. Laws may be criticised, but the aim of this should be improvement, not disobedience. A just law is one which enables individuals to achieve the fullness of their nature in society. To rule is to educate, ie to develop subjects in the virtues with which they have been endowed by nature. It is an important task of the state to be the school of the citizen: 'Legislators make citizens good by forming habits in them'[17]. In this respect Aristotle held the same view as Plato. A just law, then, needs to be moulded in reason, unclouded by passion as well as intelligible. It is hostile to a tyrannous abuse of power and favourable to the proper sort of freedom, and this taming of power is the contribution of his *Ethics* and *Politics*. Freedom and good government go together.

There is also the other sort of law, a perfect law, which is discoverable and unalterable[18]. It is connected with the idea of development, and is inherent in the nature of Man as a potentiality of development; it develops with him as part of his faculties and skill; and it is present in the ultimate goal of his development. This perfect, or natural, law is thus universal in Man and capable of growth. It embraces citizenship and life in society, but slaves may not share in it, for they are only the adjuncts to the citizenship of their superiors in natural virtue. Thus, Aristotle did not advocate complete freedom from power, and he justified slavery on several grounds. In the first place, just as there are physical inequalities between men, so also there are spiritual inequalities. Thus, some people are by nature slaves and slavery is a natural institution. They are less deserving and capable[19]. War is justifiable in that it makes those who are by nature slaves into slaves. Secondly, men need leisure to cultivate virtue, and slaves provide this by relieving them of tedium. Thirdly, slaves for their part derive benefit through being guided by their superiors in virtue. Such a doctrine, it will be observed, avoided the disruptive tendencies implicit in the egalitarian ideas of the Sophists by harnessing natural law to the preaching of an acceptance of the *status quo*; slaves should accept their lot as a dictate of unalterable law. Nevertheless, Aristotle declared, virtue demands that masters should treat them with moderation.

The Roman period

Abstract philosophy played very little part in the practical outlook of the Roman lawyers, who were content for the most part to take over Greek

17 *Ethics* II, 1:5; *Politics* VII, 13-17. The biggest contemporary experiment along this line is that by the Soviet Union to re-educate the masses for communism (see ch 19 post). See also the dictum of Lord Simon in *Charter v Race Relations Board* [1973] AC 868 at 900, [1973] 1 All ER 512 at 527 (quoted p 51 ante); and the abolition of the death penalty in the face of opposition from at least a substantial, if not a majority, body of opinion might also be regarded as an example.

18 *Politics* I, 2.

19 *Politics* I, 5-7.

philosophy. The conditions of empire demanded a power-structure, but the *Corpus Juris Civilis* of Justinian has passages which might support almost any view. Statements of Ulpian, for instance, favour absolute power: the prince is not bound by law[20]; the wish of the prince has the force of law[1] On the other hand, two emperors, Theodosius and Valentinian, declared that their own authority derived from the authority of the law[2].

It was Cicero[3], an orator, not a lawyer, who referred to natural law as superior to positive law. He dwelt on Man's need for government and inquired into the basis of just government and the purpose and function of law. He argued that since divine reason was inherent in the universe, it was more or less identified with the physical ordering of the universe. Man stood highest in creation by virtue of his faculty of reasoning, and his welfare is thus the supreme purpose of creation. In the eyes of this universal law all men are equal, that is, in their possession of reason and ability to discover natural law. Moreover, Man is by nature sociable, and communion with others is made possible by language and reason. Since human welfare is the purpose of creation, men should spare no effort to help others.

Cicero recognised three forms of government, monarchy, aristocracy and democracy. Just as individuals have higher selves that control their ordinary selves, so also should society have a higher and permanent 'self' in the shape of a constitution. Law is the means of achieving just government, for the maximum liberty of action is best guaranteed by legal limitations. He struck off the ringing statement, 'we are slaves of the law in order that we might be free'[4]. He also recognised the need for freedom from the abuse of power, for he added that there are limits to the use of law as an instrument of power. It should be determined by what is sacred and just and be as far as possible a reflection of divine and eternal law as revealed through reason. He realised of course that positive laws had to be detailed and practical, but positive and natural law should not be in conflict. Shortcomings in the former require to be remedied by resort to the rational, social and moral norms of the latter. Natural law is 'right reason in agreement with nature'[5], from which there can be no dispensation either by the senate or the people. To run counter to or try to restrict it by legislation is immoral. This emphasis on Man's nature as the 'true' source of laws bore fruit in later times.

The chief interest of this period lies, not in the contribution of the Roman lawyers, but of the early Christians. Gleanings from the New Testament are unhelpful. There are certainly some clear affirmations of the need for civic authority[6]. On the other hand, when freedom as an absolute value is mentioned, the reference is to freedom of the spirit and freedom from sin[7], and something akin to the Ciceronian paradox appears in repeated statements that to be free is to be the servant of God[8].

The most important of the early Christian philosophers was St Augustine

20 *D* 1.3.31.
1 *D* 1.4.1.
2 *C* 1.14.4.
3 *De Republica*.
4 *Pro Cluentio* 53.146. (Cf Tacitus *Dialogues* 40: only fools identify liberty with licence to do whatever one likes.
5 *De Republica* III, xxii.
6 *Romans* xiii, 1–7; 1 *Peter* ii, 13–14.
7 *John* viii, 32 (cf 34, 36); II *Cor* iii, 17; *Romans* viii, 21.
8 *Romans* vi, 18, 20; I *Cor* vii, 22; ix, 19; *Eph* iv, 3; 1 *Peter* ii, 16.

(AD 345–430). Like many of the Christian fathers he was influenced by the pagan philosophers. They had emphasised the repression of the body and a concentration on things of the mind and soul. St Augustine, who had at one time been a professor of philosophy, preached that mankind had fallen from a state of nature and tended thereafter towards moral death from which the only hope of salvation is Christian grace. The tempting conclusion, which is only round the corner, is that the state of nature is now depraved and corrupt. Indeed, in the centuries which followed nature became synonymous with corruption, in which the body was a *saccus stercoris*, and the task of Man was to overcome by an intense asceticism the nature within him. St Augustine himself cannot be accused of any such inference. He constantly repeated that 'every creature, in so far as it is a part of nature, is good'. There is a distinction between the 'absolute' law of nature, representing the state from which Man fell, now beyond recall, and the 'relative' law of nature, related to the circumstances obtaining after the Fall. The Church, as the exponent of divine law, is entitled to interfere with institutions of positive law; and human law could be ignored if in conflict with divine law, for if it is not just it is not 'law': *lex esse non videbitur quae justa non fuerit*[9]. Had practical possibilities for putting this utterance into effect been worked out, it would have constituted a signal contribution towards preventing the abuse of power through unjust laws. As it stands, it is no more than a grandiloquent declamation. Indeed, it would seem that, on the whole, St Augustine was on the side of power and preservation of the *status quo*. For, apart from the vague privilege of the Church to interfere, institutions, such as law, government, property etc, are the products of reason, which have been devised to meet the situation brought about by original sin[10]. Although positive law is the product of sin, it is also a remedy for the evils of sin (*poena et remedium peccati*); and thus within limits is entitled to obedience. Another interesting feature is St Augustine's acceptance of slavery. Unlike Aristotle, he denied that any man was by nature a slave, since God's grace is distributed uniformly. Nor does he categorically state that slaves must somehow be more sinful than free people. What he does say is that slavery is a form of collective retribution for original sin.

The Medieval period

The social needs of the times were three-fold. The first, as in the early Greek period, was the emergence of some semblance of order from a long period of chaos. Hence there was need, not for freedom, but for power to preserve the newly won stability.

Secondly, there was need to establish the authority of the Church by reason and argument rather than force. Since the Church was intellectually pre-eminent, it fell to churchmen to propound a theory suited to both these needs. The available philosophical material, however, consisted largely of the works of the Greek thinkers. To take over heathen doctrines of natural law would have been inconsistent with the authority of Christianity and of the Church. The obvious solution, which was adopted in the famous *Decretum Gratianum* (c 1140), was to identify the law of nature with the law of God.

9 *De Libero Arbitrio* 1.5.7.
10 *Civitas Dei* ch 5.

The Church thus became the exponent of natural law. It was made possible by faith in the creation. Nature was the product of the will of God, and was regarded as conforming to the prescriptions of the ruler of the universe. Natural law, however, was much more than this: it covered also the rule of the Gospels that one should do as one would be done by. It is supreme and immutable and prevails over custom and enactment.

Thirdly, in these precarious times the produce of the soil was the main, and for most the only, source of subsistence, and men came to depend on landlords for land in return for specified services. In this way the power structure of feudalism, which made land the source and measure of power, stratified Europe into classes. There was an idea of unity, one Church, one faith, one realm, Christendom as opposed to heathendom (especially as the Holy Land was under heathen domination). The most comprehensive attempt to evolve a theory of law, which would harmonise the aims of the Church with contemporary needs, was that of St Thomas Aquinas (1224/5–1274) whose views will be considered later[11]. Suffice it to say here that his cosmic scheme made the Church the ultimate repository of authority in matters concerning 'eternal law' and its 'promulgation' to Man through reason, as well as the interpreter of 'divine law' as revealed in the Scriptures. Side by side with this he preached the significant precept that, although there is a duty to obey human laws in so far as they are reasonable, there is nonetheless a concomitant need to avoid social disruption, which demands compliance with the occasional unjust law. This clearly reflects the social need for stability. The best repository for power is what in modern parlance would be styled a constitutional monarchy, for a monarchy, rather than a republic, represents unity and resembles the rule of God, while its constitutional framework ensures protection from, or at least minimises, the danger of an abuse of power. If a ruler does abuse his power, he may legitimately be overthrown, provided this does not create as bad, or worse, state of affairs. The caveat reflects once more the need for stability.

In this way the Thomist system sought to uphold the authority of the Church, which was in a sense the first sovereign authoritarian 'state' in the western post-Roman world. There were, on the other hand, certain significant secular developments. Teutonic law stressed the fact that law belonged to the community, to the folk, and was thereby the common possession of every individual. Feudalism, in prescribing the duties owed by a vassal to his lord, inspired also the idea of 'right', for no more could be demanded of him than was due. Allied to ideas of Christian equality these left a legacy of freedom from power, which in later years led to parliamentary government and resistance to arbitrary authority, even of the Church itself.

The Reformation and the Renaissance to the Nineteenth Century

The result of the disintegration of the Holy Roman Empire was the replacement of the medieval idea of a united Christendom under the spiritual guidance of the Church by independent national states. The paramount need now was to free the national sovereigns from external authority and to consolidate power in their hands, since more and more strength was required to maintain independence in a world of increasing rivalry. Support for this movement came from various quarters. Individuals wished to free themselves

11 See pp 471–475 post.

from the Church and the shackles of the feudal system which had held Europe for so long in an iron grip, and in particular the rising commercial middle class wanted freedom to pursue its trade. The age of discovery and colonisation was at hand, and these enterprises were left to individuals, who had to be guaranteed liberty to carry on these activities. Individuals, therefore, found that a powerful sovereign was their best guarantee against interference, and the need was to foster the power of the sovereign.

Side by side with these developments natural law theory assumed a more secular aspect, brought about by a combination of factors. It was necessary to adapt theory to meet the above needs. Advances were also being made in knowledge about the physical operations of the material world. The Thomist system contained no scientific treatment of the movement and measurement of bodies and forces, and its exponents found themselves intellectually incapable of assimilating the new knowledge without some adjustment. The effect was not a rejection, but an adaptation of natural law theory. The Protestants denied that the Church had authority to expound the law of God, and in the controversy appeal to the law of nature as based on the reason of the individual came more and more into prominence. The intellectual world came to be actively engaged in the revived study of Roman law, which was now being adapted to meet contemporary local needs. This had two results. The diffusion of Roman law throughout different nationalities in Europe led to an association of it with natural law. It was revered as being supremely reasonable, the spirit of Rome still ruled the world by her reason. In this way the resources of Roman law were always on tap to supply the deficiencies of positive law; it also provided most of the material for constructing a system of international law. Secondly, the adaptation of Roman law had led to local variations. This fostered the belief that there was a 'natural law' which transcended its innumerable applications. The result of this belief was that the study of 'pure' Roman law became mainly an academic discipline[12].

Reflecting these developments and the call of a new age for sovereign power, theory tended to develop in the direction of justifying absolute monarchy. In this connection one thinks immediately of Machiavelli's *Prince* (1513), but his ideas are interesting chiefly on account of what he said in his other work known as *Discourses*. He characterised republics as being 'free' and superior to princedoms in that a high degree of virtue is required of people not to abuse freedom. To the extent that people lack virtue, they are 'corrupt' and have to be governed by a tyrant or prince, and in his *Prince* he elaborated absolute dictatorship. The state and its sovereign have to be supreme and subject to no external control, while moral and ethical principles need to be subordinated to political expediency.

In the hands of Thomas Hobbes (1588–1679), described as a belated medievalist, absolute sovereign power was justified by postulating an imaginary compact between ruler and ruled. In a state of nature everyone is entitled to everything; but this leads to friction. So Hobbes believed that Man's life in a state of nature was one of fear and selfishness. 'The life of man', in his own words, was 'solitary, poor, nasty, brutish and short'[13]. It is a fundamental dictate of the law of nature that people desire peace[14], so to

12 Cf Savigny's attitude: ch 18 post.
13 *Leviathan* ch xiii.
14 *Leviathan* ch xiv.

escape from the state of nature they entered into the social contract, whereby each surrendered his rights to a sovereign ruler, the Leviathan, who, in return for absolute subservience, guaranteed peace and greater security to each than he might otherwise have had. In this way natural law theory had come to support power[15]. It is important to remember that Hobbes lived through the Civil War in England, so his preoccupation was with stable and secure government. His doctrine reflects the idea that the security of the individual can only be found in the exaltation of the power of the sovereign. Liberty is not of men, but of the sovereign[16]. The menace to the individual from the sovereign is not faced. There is a suggestion that the sovereign is bound by natural law, but this is nothing more than a vague morality. The sovereign is expected to allow a harmless liberty, but there is no justification for resisting laws. There is no such thing as an iniquitous law; whatever is law is moral. Since society depends on the sovereign, law in society is what the sovereign commands: form rather than content becomes the determining feature of law. Although Hobbes was not concerned with protecting the individual against oppression by the sovereign, it was of the utmost significance that one precept of his natural law was the individual's entitlement to self-preservation. For herein lay the germ of a new view of natural law as a system of 'rights' in the individual. It is a far cry from the ancient idea of it as laying down duties. In Hobbes's scheme the authority of the Church as the interpreter of God's law is vigorously denied. All power is given to a severely utilitarian secular sovereign. This marked the final break up of the Catholic international order of things.

In this way national sovereigns acquired freedom from external power, but this was taken to imply complete liberty of action in their mutual dealings. Side by side with this they acquired also unfettered power over their own subjects. It was not long before the need arose to curb the abuse of liberties in international relations and the abuse of domestic power over subjects.

It has been pointed out that unlimited freedom to act as one pleases leads ultimately to chaos; and so it proved in the international sphere. Under the guise of the 'sovereignty of states' the unbridled pursuit of selfish policies reduced Europe to a state of barbarity culminating in the Thirty Years War. This abuse of liberty evoked increasingly loud cries for some power-structure whereby such freedom of action might be restrained. Voices, notably that of Hugo Grotius (1583–1645) started to preach the need for restraint[17], and a body of duties, known later as 'international law', began to be worked out in the hope of setting limits to the conduct of states. In his natural law theory Grotius was essentially a child of the time, but a feature of interest and significance in his writings is the shift in emphasis from Divine Providence to the reason of Man. He believed that natural law was rooted in the nature of Man, and would exist even if there were no God. This was not a denial of the Deity, but an assertion that natural law is independent of God and a quality of Man. The binding force of law is its essence. The problem is how men, supposed to be free, could fetter themselves. The answer was: by voluntary submission, by a social contract. Mutual promises have no obligatory

15 *Leviathan* chs xvii–xviii. Cf the Jewish social contract, which was in support of immunity from power.
16 *Leviathan* ch xxi.
17 *De Jure Belli ac Pacis, Prolegomena* 28.

force unless it derives from some rule giving such force to promises; and this rule is a rule of natural law. By virtue of it Grotius sought to explain the adoption of different forms of government by different societies. Reason impels Man to seek society. The state originates in a contract by virtue of which each individual surrenders his sovereignty to a ruler. The group has the liberty to choose the order which it prefers, but once it has chosen it loses all power to restrain its ruler. This was the way in which absolute power emerged. The subjects are bound to an almost blind obedience and only in exceptional circumstances did Grotius concede a liberty to revolt. The only guarantee which they have against an abuse of power by the ruler is that he is bound by natural law, which Grotius explained in these words:

> 'A dictate of right reason, which points out that an act, according as it is or is not in conformity with rational nature, has in it a quality of moral baseness or moral necessity.'

The next, and more important, step was to restrain the absolute sovereign in his relations with other such sovereigns, for it was the absence of restraints that precipitated wars. Grotius accordingly went on to assert that nations were still in a state of nature and so bound by natural law. Man according to its fiat is a sociable being and desires peaceful society. For nations to assert their absolute independence was futile, and the sooner they realised that they, too, should unite to form a society of states the better it would be. It is these doctrines that have earned for Grotius the distinction of being styled the 'father of International Law'. He sought to establish international law on two foundations, the law of nature and consent. From natural law were deduced principles as to how states should conduct themselves, the idea of consent was utilised to infer rules from the observed practice of states. The difficulty about the latter is that one cannot derive an 'ought' from an 'is'; in other words, in view of the variety of reasons why different states at different times behave in a given way it is futile to propound a norm of behaviour. However, Grotius posited natural law as the principal foundation of international law.

In the municipal sphere the individual, who so fondly trusted his sovereign to deliver him from feudal oppression, soon found that he had only ex-changed one tyranny for a worse. This gave rise to domestic struggles for immunity from the abuse of the sovereign's power. The age of the individual was now at hand, an age of commercial adventure and expansion, an age of trading middle classes. In support of this movement natural law doctrine was again called in aid. As early as 1581, when the Netherlands broke away from the overlordship of Philip II of Spain, it was declared in the Act of Abjuration that if a sovereign treats his subjects like slaves he ceases to be their rightful sovereign. In the succeeding age the mythical social contract theory was re-furbished by John Locke (1632–1704)[18]. The reign of the Stuarts in England had revealed what a menace the sovereign could be to the individual. So Locke evolved a theory to protect the individual. The state of nature, which preceded the social contract, was not one of anarchy, as Hobbes had imagined, but was 'a state of liberty, not of license'. It had, however, one defect, namely that 'property' was insecure and by 'property' was meant life, liberty and estate[19]. 'Every man has a *Property* in his own

18 Locke *Second Treatise on Civil Government* (1690).
19 *Locke* para 123.

Person', wrote Locke; and since the source of value lies in a man's labour, whatever a man 'hath mixed his *Labour* with, and joyned to it something that is his own' becomes his[20]. 'Property' in the sense described was insecure because (a) there was no established law, nor (b) an impartial judge, and (c) the natural power to execute natural law was not always commensurate with the claim. Executive powers were regarded as natural powers of a quasi-judicial character. To remedy this flaw Man entered into the social contract by which he yielded to the sovereign, not all his rights, but only the power to preserve order and enforce the law of nature[1]. The individual retained the 'natural rights' to life, liberty and estate, for they were the natural and 'inalienable rights of Man'[2]. This was an innovation of significance inasmuch as the idea of a natural law of society was transmuted into one of individual 'natural rights' which could be used to resist social control. The purpose of government was to protect these; it has no other end than 'to preserve the members of that society in their lives, liberties and possessions'. Its function is in the nature of a trust[3]; as Locke put it, all this 'is *"limited to the publick good* of the society"'[4]. So long as government fulfils this purpose, its laws should be binding. When it ceases to protect or begins to encroach on these 'natural rights', laws lose their validity and the government may be overthrown. In this way Locke championed the revolution of 1688–1689, and his idea that positive law might thus be overborne by natural law sustained the American colonists in their successful defiance of the British Parliament in the fateful years 1775–1781.

It is clear that in Locke's view unlimited sovereignty is contrary to natural law. The basic limitations are (a) that sovereign power cannot justifiably be used in an arbitrary fashion over the lives and fortunes of people. No individual enjoyed such power in the natural state and none could therefore be surrendered to the sovereign. (b) The sovereign may not rule by arbitrary decree, but only through known laws administered by known judges. (c) The people may not be deprived of their possessions without their consent. (d) The sovereign may not transfer the power of making laws to other persons. In order that the sovereign shall not abuse his authority Locke championed a constitutionally limited sovereign and a threefold division of governmental power[5]. Foremost there stands the legislative power for the creation of rules to give effect to and protect the 'inalienable rights'; secondly, there is the executive power by which the law is enforced; and thirdly, there is the 'federative' power, which concerns the making of war and peace and controls the external relations of the state. Locke thought it advisable to confer the legislative and executive powers on different organs, one reason being that the legislature does not, while the executive does, operate continuously, and another being the danger of entrusting law-makers with the power to carry out the laws which they themselves make. He did not advocate a similar separation between the executive and 'federative' powers since both are dependent on force. His views had considerable influence, for the climate of opinion was such as to make them acceptable. Not only was he hailed as the

---

20 *Locke* para 27.
 1 Cf Pratt CJ: 'The great end for which men entered into society was to secure their property': *Entick v Carrington* (1765) 19 State Tr 1029 at 1066. Cf *Locke* para 124.
 2 *Locke* para 135.
 3 The idea of a trust was echoed in *Jilani v Government of Punjab* Pak LD (1972) SC 139 at 182.
 4 *Locke* para 135.
 5 *Locke* ch xii.

intellectual defender of the English constitutional revolution of 1688-1689, but he also influenced the later American Revolution.

The problem of protecting the individual was not to be solved simply by curbing or destroying the sovereign, for power was only transferred from him to a faceless institution known as 'government'. One way of controlling power, whether exercised by sovereign or government, is to postulate the supremacy of law. Long before Locke, Chief Justice Coke (1552-1633) maintained this, and his view of law was essentially naturalistic. Law commands obedience, he said, by virtue of being reasonable; and it is in this context that his doctrine of the avoidance of even Acts of Parliament, which offend against common right and reason, has to be understood[6]. He also introduced an idea of profound significance when, in his famous disputation with James I, he insisted that even the king is under God and the law, and added that the reason of the law is not 'natural reason', but 'artificial perfection of reason, gotten by long study'. The implication of this is that kings and governments are controlled by the very special craftsmanship of the law of which judges, by virtue of their experience and practice, are the exponents. This made the judges the champions of the individual, and stresses the importance of an independent judiciary in controlling power.

Another way of controlling governmental power was put forward by the French philosopher Montesquieu (1689-1755), who purported to base his conclusions on the English constitution. The secret of its success, as he put it, lay in the fact that power was not concentrated in the hands of an individual or group. Unless power is made to check power, it will be abused. An essential prerequisite is that general rules should be laid down in advance of actual situations, but even so there remains the real possibility of abuse if the person laying down the general rules were also allowed to apply them and then carry out his own decisions. So the guarantee against abuse lies in establishing mutual checks between the legislative, executive and judicial functions[7]. All that his doctrine of the 'separation of powers' insists on is the danger of an absolute union of these functions in one person or body. It does not require their respective allocation to three distinct organs with no inter-relation between them. The functions may well be shared as in England, for instance, where the cabinet, which is the executive centre, is an integral part of the legislature and responsible to it; executive departments have legislative functions entrusted to them; justices of the peace perform judicial and executive functions. Montesquieu's doctrine is carried furthest in the United States of America, where the separation is guaranteed by a Constitution, guarded by the courts. The federal legislative power is vested in Congress, the federal executive power in the President and his cabinet; and the federal judicial power in the Supreme Court. A very great deal of inter-relation exists, which enables them to work harmoniously

In France the continuing need to protect the individual against an oppressive monarchy found expression in the theory of Rousseau (1712-1778), in which the idea of the social contract underwent yet another revision. Rousseau set out to evolve a community in which the community as such

---

6 *Bonham's Case* (1610) 8 Co Rep 114a.

7 Montesquieu *L'Esprit des Lois* (1748) 11, 4-6. It is commonly supposed that Montesquieu based his views on the British system. For the view that he was really arguing what ought to obtain in France and that he used Britain as a façade for avoiding domestic censorship, see Merry *Montesquieu's System of Natural Government* (1970).

would protect the individual; but in which at the same time the individual would remain free from oppression. All should participate in policy-making. Accordingly, he argued that in the original contract the individuals did not surrender their rights to any single sovereign, but to society as a whole, and this is their guarantee of freedom and equality. Society, having come into being for this purpose, is expected to restore these rights to its members as civil liberties. Their basis is a moral one. Each individual is not subject to any other individual, but to the 'general will'[8], and to obey this is to obey himself. Government and law are both dependent upon general will, on popular as distinct from parliamentary sovereignty, which may revoke or overthrow them. Enacted law is necessary to avoid arbitrariness, and to get law right to begin with public servants should apply the 'general will' so that law will produce just results[9]. Little wonder that this theory was utilised as the philosophy of the French Revolution in order to get rid of the monarch. Yet again the pattern of history was repeated. Deliverance from the evil of uncontrolled sovereign power only led to the evil of uncontrolled popular liberties as manifested in the excesses of the Revolution; which in turn called for a return to power in Napoleon.

The same sad swing can be detected in Germany[10]. The nineteenth century saw the unification of the Germanic states, which stimulated an upsurge of nationalistic fervour. Although there was some talk of a 'Law State' (*Rechtsstaat*, constitutional government), the trend was towards the glorification of imperial power. The reaction against this after World War I came with the Weimar Republic, which was a 'national-social state'. On the one hand, its socialist character required a planned economy, which meant concentrating power in these matters in government. On the other hand, the extremely permissive attitude adopted by government in its reaction against the authoritarianism of the past allowed disruptive and revolutionary freedom to flourish to the point of eventually reducing the country to economic and social chaos. Little wonder that there was general support for the return to a power-structure under Adolf Hitler to restore stability. There is no need to dwell on the way in which that power was subsequently abused[11]. After World War II West Germany became a 'republican, democratic and social Law State'[12]. Its socialist character requires concentration of power in government in economic planning, but at the same time, as with the Weimar Republic, extreme sensitivity to the excesses of the Hitler régime has induced a permissive attitude towards disruptive movements.

The Soviet Union provides a vivid example of the power-freedom-power swing. The Revolution was a successful bid for freedom from the power of the Czars. In its wake the revolutionary leaders immediately claimed for themselves unlimited freedom to act as they chose, untrammelled by codes or laws[13]. More significantly, they have established an infinitely more ruthless power-structure, rooted in a new ruling class of the Communist Party, which brooks no opposition in any shape or form. This was required, among other things, to stifle all contrary values, which are condemned as 'counter-

8 Rousseau *The Social Contract* (1762, Everyman's Lib) pp 13-15.
9 *Rousseau* pp 26-27.
10 See generally Dietze *Two Concepts of the Rule of Law*.
11 See p 387 post.
12 Bonn Basic Law, art 28.
13 See ch 19 post.

revolutionary', and also to carry out a long-term programme of mass re-education of the populace in the values of communism. The lengths to which the Soviet Union is prepared to carry this power is seen in the way in which she intervened to crush libertarian stirrings in Hungary in 1956 and in Czechoslovakia in 1968.

There have been other power-structures which have filled many people all over the world with misgiving. Traumatic experiences such as these have induced at times an almost hysterical reaction against power and, indeed, any call for law and order. It has the unfortunate result of blinding people to the alternative dangers of the abuse of liberty through overweening per-missiveness. The need to prevent this abuse is at least as great as the need to prevent the abuse of power. Democracy was a device to prevent the latter. Even among a small group of people, as long as the person in authority enjoys their trust, they will be content to leave power in his hands. Once he loses it through wickedness or mismanagement, they will feel driven to de-mand a say in their own government, either personally in the case of very small groups, or through representatives in the case of large groups. Repre-sentation dilutes democracy, unavoidably in the nature of things, and it leaves democratic processes of election and decision open to manipulation by those in quest of power. By means of propaganda and by taking advantage of the apathy of the majority, who do not attend meetings, or by shouting down opposition, they manage to vote themselves on to bodies, which then use the votes of these few as block-votes to represent the whole constituency. Having won power in this way, they seldom risk losing it by allowing any reference back to the constituency on a one man one vote basis. Although such processes as these are claimed to be democratic, they are a perversion of democracy. Apathy may deserve what it gets, but election through the apathy of the majority is not election *by* the majority.

Democracy is workable as long as there is a substantial area of shared values and aspirations among the people and where they have the maturity to rise above differences[14]. Once this willingness to 'rub along together' disappears and differences become irreconcileable, (eg with racial or religious divisions), and fragmentation reaches the point of pluralism without a co-hesive substrate, then government through democratic participation becomes precarious, if not impossible. For it may then not be possible to reach majority decisions, and, even if it were, one section or other may refuse to abide by them[15]. The uncomfortable question arises whether democracy itself is only an intermediate stage in the doom of society, beginning with loss of confidence in a tyrant and ending in anarchy. The answer is that it need not be. The message coming through history is that to break out of the melan-choly spiral of power and liberty a way must be found of curbing both rather than promoting either[16]. This, it would seem, is the paramount need of the present age in its quest for justice.

14 Cf Machiavelli *Discourses*, and p 79 ante.
15 Eg Northern Ireland.
16 Lord MacDermott *Protection from Power under English Law* p 195.

READING LIST

Aristotle *Nicomachean Ethics* (trans H Rackham) V.
Aristotle *Politics* (trans J E C Weldon) 1, chs 1–7.
E Bodenheimer *Jurisprudence* chs 1, 3, 11.
J M Brown 'A Note on Professor Oakeshott's Introduction to the *Leviathan*'
 (1953) 1 Political Studies 53.
E N Cahn *The Sense of Injustice*.
W Friedmann *Legal Theory* (5th edn) chs 2, 7–12.
J W Gough *The Social Contract*.
H Grotius *De Jure Belli ac Pacis* (trans F W Kelsey) I, paras 10–17.
T Hobbes *Leviathan* (ed M Oakeshott) and M Oakeshott's Introduction.
A M Honoré 'Social Justice' in *Essays in Legal Philosophy* (ed R S Summers)
 61.
J W Jones *Historical Introduction to the Theory of Law* ch 4.
H Kelsen 'What is Justice?' in *Essays in Legal and Moral Philosophy* (ed Ota
 Weinberger) 1.
J Locke *Two Treatises of Government* (ed P Laslett) II.
Plato *The Laws* (ed E B England) I and II.
K R Popper *The Open Society and its Enemies* I (5th edn).
R Pound *An Introduction to the Philosophy of Law* chs 1–2.
R Pound *Justice According to Law*.
M S Shellens 'Aristotle on Natural Law' (1959) 4 Natural Law Forum 72.
J Stone *Human Law and Human Justice* chs 1, 2, 8, 10, 11.

CHAPTER 5

The problem of power

Power has two connotations. One is physical force, but this, however great, is inert in itself. It can be dangerous only when exercised, and juridically its exercise is often a matter of liberty to do so or not. The problem of curbing the abusive exercise of physical force is, therefore, the problem of curbing liberty of action, which will be discussed in the next chapter. Power has the other connotation of legal capacity to alter jural relations and this is the sense in which the problem of power is considered here and, even so, only the supreme power of making laws will be dealt with. Abuse of this power by government may be designated 'rule by law' where laws are used as instruments of government policy. 'Rule of law', by contrast, is the use of law, among other things, to curb the misuse of law-making power by government.

The abuse of 'rule by law' manifests itself in the passing of unjust laws. The supreme legislative authority in Britain being the Crown in Parliament, in order to prevent an unjust statute from being treated as 'law', it would be necessary to include a criterion of just quality in the requirements for the validity of a statute in addition to purely formal criteria. The point is that on purely formal criteria an unjust enactment, however heinous, is 'law' provided the requisite procedures have been observed and majorities obtained. The addition of a moral quality of justness is designed to ensure that an enactment is not 'law' merely because it has been passed in due form. Any such suggestion with regard to an Act of Parliament would be dismissed by practically every lawyer as fantasy, quite apart from the immense problems and practical difficulties in the way of its implementation. The purpose of this chapter is to consider the suggestion and the problems and difficulties, even if the conclusion may be to leave the suggestion where it is—as a fantasy.

The idea is not new. The words of St Augustine may be recalled: *lex esse non videbitur quae justa non fuerit*[1]; as well as those of Sajjad Ahmad J: 'A law is not law merely because it bears that label. It becomes law only if it satisfies the basic norms of the legal system of the country [enshrined in the Qur'an] and receives the stamp of validity from the Law Courts'[2]. On the other hand, British courts accepted Acts of Parliament as supreme in 1689 and, as suggested in the last chapter, the change over from the supremacy of the prerogative was to ensure, among other things, that the Crown in Parliament would be a bulwark against the passage of unjust laws like some of those enacted under the prerogative. Notwithstanding the revolutionary nature of the change, the judges' refusal to challenge Parliament by questioning the validity of the new state of affairs enabled them to preserve their independence as well as a measure of power the limits of which have never been defined. The latter manifests itself in relation to the unresolved question as

---

1 *De Libero Arbitrio* 1.5.7.
2 *Jilani v Government of Punjab* Pak LD (1972) SC 139 at 261.

to who decides what constitutes a valid 'statute' and in their power to interpret statutes. As will appear, this power has a part to play when the problem of preventing the abuse of legislative power to be considered.

In the past there have been utterances, both before and after 1689, suggesting that courts could treat as 'void' (but which probably meant no more than side-step or ignore) legislation which contradicts reason or is otherwise repugnant[3]. Such sayings, however, especially after 1689, come from highly suspect reports[4]. At least one modern British judge has expressed a similar view. Lord Cross, alluding to a confiscatory decree of the Nazi Government of Germany, said:

> 'To my mind a law of this sort constitutes so grave an infringement of human rights that the courts of this country ought to refuse to recognise it as a law at all'[5].

The significance of this remark should not be over-estimated, for there is a difference between the application of such a consideration to the discretion, which judges have, with regard to the recognition of a foreign decree and to an Act of Parliament. What is noteworthy is the thinking behind it.

Notwithstanding such dicta, the traditional attitude of judges is to accept Acts of Parliament as unchallengeable, and the following statement of Ungoed-Thomas J is characteristic:

> 'What the statute itself enacts cannot be unlawful, because what the statute says and provides is itself the law, and the highest form of law that is known to this country. It is the law which prevails over every other form of law, and it is not for the court to say that a parliamentary enactment, the highest law in this country, is illegal'[6].

One by-product of this doctrine is that a statute never ceases to be 'law' through disuse. There used to be an idea that an Act need not be applied if it has never been enforced[7], but this is no longer true. There is no doctrine of desuetude[8]. The courts are thus debarred from reacting against the unfairness of applying even an out-of-date statute. In defence of the existing position it might be observed that there are difficulties about desuetude. The period of time varies with the subject matter and complications could well arise in the case of statutes embodying dissimilar material. Moreover, non-application of a statute may be the result of non-violation rather than obsolescence. A statute may indeed expire if there is provision in it to that effect, eg the annual financial legislation and the Armed Forces Acts; and if

---

3 Coke CJ in *Bonham's Case* (1610) 8 Co Rep 114a; Holt CJ in *R v Earl of Banbury* (1693) Skin 517 at 527, and in *City of London v Wood* (1701) 12 Mod Rep 669 at 687.

4 Coke himself emphatically asserted the supremacy of Parliament elsewhere: 2 Inst *Proemium*. Cf Blackstone *Comm* I, pp 90–91, 160–161.

5 *Oppenheimer v Cattermole* [1976] AC 249 at 278, [1975] 1 All ER 538 at 567. So, too, Lord Salmon 'the decree in my judgment should not be recognised by our courts as having any effect in English law for any purpose': at 284, and at 572. See also Lord Hodson at 265, and at 557.

6 *Cheney v Conn* [1968] 1 All ER 779 at 782, [1968] 1 WLR 242 at 247. See also Willes J in *Lee v Bude and Torrington Junction Rly Co* (1871) LR 6 CP 576 at 582; *R v Jordan* [1967] Crim LR 483 where the court refused to entertain the argument that an Act was void as curtailing free speech; *British Railways Board v Pickin* [1974] AC 765, [1974] 1 All ER 609 where the House of Lords held that a court cannot investigate whether an Act had been procured by fraud.

7 *R v Bishop of Lincoln* (1345) YB 19 Edw 3 (Rolls Series) 170, rejected in *Stewart v Lawton* (1823) 1 Bing 374 at 375.

8 Eg *A-G v Prince Ernest Augustus of Hanover* [1957] AC 436, [1957] 1 All ER 49.

the manner in which a statute is to terminate has been specified, it will come to an end only in that way[9]. Another by-product is that Parliament is not bound by a prior Act, which it can always repeal, even by implication, and even though the prior Act had been declared unrepealable[10].

Such being the attitude of British judges, a heavy onus lies on those who contend for a moral check on legislative power to show why this is necessary, and how it can be achieved. With regard to the question why, the following points should be considered. Laws are not just things of the moment, but enduring phenomena. Just quality is a factor of endurance, which means that, in a long view, that quality needs to be taken into account *now*[11]. Also, it is not true to say, as some positivist philosophers do, that nothing is gained by refusing to call an unjust enactment 'law', for there are the emotive associations of that word which work powerfully in influencing public reaction. Thus, one positivist has contended that clarity and honesty might be gained by keeping the juristic and moral issues separate. To accord validity to an unjust enactment, so he argues, does not imply moral approval of it, namely, that 'might is right', but only that it is 'law'. Moral disapproval can be signified by a refusal to obey[12]. The allusion to disobedience betrays a weakness in this argument, for it overlooks the emotive associations of the word 'law', which induce obedience and cast on would-be dissidents the onus of justifying disobedience. Added to this is the fact that the coercive apparatus of the state can be invoked in support of that which is styled 'law'. The whole point of calling a thing 'law' is to evoke a realisation that obedience is called for and that the force of authority lies behind it. This is why fidelity to laws is enhanced by just quality as much as it is weakened by the lack of it. Even formal criteria of validity were often accepted initially because they were thought to guarantee justice, as pointed out earlier. The attack might even be carried into the positivist camp, for positivism itself is grounded in a belief that there shall continue to be an in-built justice in the accepted criterion of validity. When this assumption breaks down, as it did repeatedly in Nazi Germany, then law-quality based on formalism alone becomes suspect. 'The capricious orders of a crazy despot', said Pollock, 'may be laws according to Austin's definition until they are revoked; but if so, it is the worse for the definition'[13]. The positivist attitude enables régimes like that of Nazi Germany to establish themselves through the grossest injustices becoming accepted as 'laws' simply because they satisfy some formal criterion. Finally, even a doctrine such as the 'Rule of Law' becomes a betrayal of the individual if all it means is that formally valid laws shall be administered impartially, for there is neither hope nor comfort in the impartial application of oppressive and degrading rules[14]. It is for such reasons as these that people press for some means of controlling, not just the form of enactment, but its very substance.

---

9 *Willcock v Muckle* [1951] 2 KB 844, [1951] 2 All ER 367.
10 *Vauxhall Estates Ltd v Liverpool Corpn* [1932] 1 KB 733; *Ellen Street Estates Ltd v Minister of Health* [1934] 1 KB 590. Cf *Krause v IRC* [1929] AD 286 (SA).
11 Different considerations will have to apply to temporary but oppressive laws, eg in an emergency. The problem here lies in deciding what constitutes an 'emergency'.
12 Hart *The Concept of Law* p 203, quoted at p 355 post.
13 Pollock *Essays in Jurisprudence and Ethics* p 50.
14 Mr Justice Schreiner argued in his Hamlyn Lectures, *English Law and the Rule of Law in South Africa* Part II, that South Africa today is under a rule of law, on which see the comment of Lazar in his review in (1968) 31 MLR 582.

Apart from the need to do so, the practicalities of achieving a moral check on power present formidable difficulties. Whose moral sense is to count? and, How can any check be made practicable? With regard to the first question, the answer clearly cannot be the moral sense of legislators, for the object of the whole exercise is to protect the community from the immoral values of legislators. Nor could it be that of the community itself, which is too diffuse and whose opinion is likely to be divided and, in any case, cannot be readily ascertained. What remains is some independent and impartial control. This raises the preliminary problem of working out an objective and acceptable moral code. Sets of principles, which may be used as models, are to be found littered throughout history in sundry Bills of Rights, Declarations of Human Rights, Fundamental Freedoms etc. The problem of working out a set of principles cannot be divorced from the question who is to do this, and also the precise manner in which they can be put into effect. As a prelude to such an exercise it is suggested that the following principles might be helpful as a guiding framework. First, power must not be exercised exclusively for the advantage of the power-wielders[15]. Secondly, power must not be exercised so as to exclude, or accord unequal treatment to, another from society by reason of race, religion or opinion without special justification, which, whatever it is, must not infringe any of these principles. Thirdly, in exercising their power, power-wielders must conform to accepted procedures. These may be spelled out in 'due process' clauses, or they may be conventional; but, whichever it be, power-wielders must not go against the way of going about things accepted in the community[16]. Fourthly, no exercise of power should be beyond independent scrutiny and question[17]. Fifthly, power-wielders are not immune from compliance with their own dictates. Sixthly, power-wielders must not become a closed circle, ie the door must be open for participation by other members of the society. Professor Honoré includes as his first proposition of social justice 'opportunity ... for sharing in the process of making decisions'[18]. Eligibility to participate has to be worked out with care. Some of the considerations that would be relevant are: (a) the degree of permanence of the involvement in the particular society, eg whether in a state or in a university, or as a citizen or alien. The more transient the involvement, the more need there is to pay attention to the balance between the desirability of participation and the stability and continuity of the society. (b) The voluntariness or involuntariness of the involvement. If it is voluntary, then

---

15 Eg arguably the action of the late Indian Prime Minister, who, having been convicted of certain offences involving disqualification from Parliament, procured the passing of retrospective legislation validating the acts before the Supreme Court heard the appeal.

16 It has been pointed out, rightly, that 'process values' have hitherto been largely neglected: Summers 'Evaluating and Improving Legal Processes—a Plea for "Process Values"' (1974) 60 Cornell LR 1. His list of ten such values (pp 20–27) relate to evaluating legal process as a good process and is relevant to the whole question of power-wielding processes.

17 Eg *Congreve v Home Office* [1976] QB 629, [1976] 1 All ER 697. See also the Watergate scandal in America where the President attempted to evade scrutiny; dicta in *Mir Hassan v The State* Pak LD (1969), Lah 786 at 808 (quoted at p 92 post). The problem of protecting workers against their unions becomes insoluble if unions have their way in operating outside a legal framework. To say that workers need no protection other than that provided by their union is no answer to the problem of protecting them against the power of the union. The argument that unions exist to protect and not to abuse them might be countered by reference to such cases as *Bonsor v Musicians' Union* [1956] AC 104, [1955] 3 All ER 518; *Rookes v Barnard* [1964] AC 1129, [1964] 1 All ER 367; and several others.

18 Honoré 'Social Justice' in *Essays in Legal Philosophy* (ed Summers) at p 63.

the conditions, if any, attaching to membership of the society are relevant. (c) The nature of the society and the relation between its members. Should participation be forced on members? (d) Ability of participants to contribute, eg depending on the issue, their age, experience, skill etc.

The practical difficulties of introducing a moral control on unjust enactments concerns the methods and agencies through which this might be given effect. Judicial control of the abuse of power will be considered first.

JUDICIAL CONTROL

This has serious limitations of which judges themselves are well aware. 'Judicial review', said Lord Brightman, 'is concerned, not with the decision but with the decision-making process. Unless that restriction on the power of the courts is observed, the court will in my view, under the guise of preventing the abuse of power, be itself guilty of usurping power'[19]. There are, however, certain ways in which judicial control can and does operate. With regard to subordinate legislation, courts may invoke certain principles and doctrines in order to invalidate exercises of power, eg by invoking the principles of natural justice or due process. With regard to Acts of Parliament themselves, something can be accomplished as part of daily business by interpreting statutes so as to obviate or minimise their effects. There is no doubt that wherever possible courts of all countries will prefer this course to the more drastic one of holding statutes void. Since the technique of interpretation applies to all statutes, whether thought to be just or unjust, it will be postponed for consideration in another context[20].

Two other methods are important enough to merit extended discussion. One is to resort to the historical context in order to utilise the moral basis on which a legislative authority came to be accepted as a check on its power. The other is to invalidate an enactment on the ground that it had not been passed in the appropriate manner and form. There· is nothing to prevent even British courts from adopting this course should opportunity arise: courts are not here declaring that a statute acknowledged to be such is void, but that it is not a statute at all.

Historical context

A colourable case can be made out for saying that the moral and other reasons for the acceptance of a new law-constitutive medium become built-in limitations on its competence. What is odd is the manner in which these come to be sloughed off. In Britain the revolution of 1688–1689 was essentially a protest against the abuse of legislative power by the monarch; the revolt of the American colonies was a protest against the abuse of legislative power by the British Parliament. In both cases new power-structures were accepted because they were thought to provide guarantees against certain abuses, and it is therefore arguable that such guarantees become limitations on the power of the new structures. In fact, Sir Matthew Hale used this very

---

19 *Chief Constable of North Wales Police v Evans* [1982] 3 All ER 141 at 154, [1982] 1 WLR 1155 at 1173.
20 See ch 8 post.

argument in answer to Hobbes's view of unlimited sovereign power[1]. In South Africa the union of the four provinces by the South Africa Act 1909 was on the understanding that minority rights would be safeguarded. Honouring that compact could thus be made a condition of the validity of legislation by the Union Parliament[2]. Another example is the Bonn Basic Law of West Germany, article I, which declares that the German people acknowledge fundamental human rights; and the succeeding article provides that the legislature is powerless to contravene the specified rights. The Federal German Constitutional Court has said of these that 'They are referred to in the *Grundgesetz* as inviolable and inalienable human rights; not as guaranteed by the Constitution, but as existing before it and independently of it'[3]. The implication is that these rights do not derive their force from the Constitution, but from the circumstances in which West Germany was established after the collapse of the Hitlerite régime. So, too, in *Maharaj v A-G of Trinidad and Tobago (No 2)*[4] the Judicial Committee of the Privy Council held that chapter 1 of the Constitution of Trinidad and Tobago 1962 protected individuals against infringement of rights by the state, which were declared by section 1 to have been in existence prior to the Constitution. Another interesting example is that of a Pakistani judge, who used the historical context to strike down a piece of legislation by the revolutionary government, and he was fearless enough to do so while that government was still firmly in power. Referring to the avowed basis on which it came into power, the learned judge said:

> 'Martial law was imposed, therefore, with the declared purpose of "restoring sanity", "restoring and saving the country from internal disorder and chaos" and to "ensure that the administration resumes its normal functions to the satisfaction of the people" ... No one, including the Chief Martial Law Administrator, can transcend or deviate from the sole purpose of restoring law and order and democracy and it needs no gainsaying that curbing the jurisdiction of the established judiciary is not a step in that direction'[5].

In a later case the Supreme Court of Pakistan made a broader, and more emphatic averment to the same effect. 'Our own *Grundnorm*', said the Chief Justice,

> 'is enshrined in our own doctrine that the legal sovereignty over the entire universe belongs to Almighty Allah alone, and the authority exercisable by the people within the limits prescribed by Him is a sacred trust. This is an immutable and unalterable norm (as embodied in the Qur'an) which was clearly accepted in the Objectives Resolution passed by the Constituent Assembly of Pakistan on the 7th of March 1949 ... It is under this system that the Government becomes a Government of laws and not of men, for, no one is above the

---

1 'Sir Matthew Hale on Hobbes: an unpublished manuscript', published by Pollock and Holdsworth in (1921) 37 LQR 274, on which see in more detail Yale 'Hobbes and Hale on Law, Legislation and Sovereign' [1972B] CLJ 121. See also Fuller *The Morality of Law* pp 137–139.
2 On this see McWhinney 'The Union Parliament, the Supreme Court and the "Entrenched Clauses" of the South Africa Act' (1952) 30 Can BR 692; *Judicial Review in the English-speaking World* ch 6; Keith *The Dominions as Sovereign States* pp 167–183.
3 Bundesverfassungsgericht 51; see also 3 B Verf G 231; Rommen 'Natural Law in the Decisions of the Federal Supreme Court and of the Constitutional Courts in Germany' (1959) 4 Nat L Forum 1; Pappé 'On the Validity of Judicial Decisions in the Nazi Era' (1960) 23 MLR 260.
4 [1979] AC 385, [1978] 2 All ER 670. See also *De Freitas v Benny* [1976] AC 239.
5 *Mir Hassan v The State* Pak LD (1969) Lah 786 at 808, per Mushtaq Hussain J.

law. It is this that led Von Hammer, a renowned orientalist, to remark that under the Islamic system "the law rules through the utterance of justice, and the power of the Governor carries out the utterances of it" [6].

On this basis the Supreme Court unanimously declared two successive governmental régimes illegal.

A historical control of this kind, however, may suffer from the weakness that it does not go far enough. Thus, the object of the revolution of 1688–1689 was to provide a guarantee against the abuse of power by the prerogative by transferring power to the Crown in Parliament; but this is no safeguard against abuse of power by the latter, which was why the American colonies revolted. The compact between the provinces in South Africa was designed to protect minority rights. Does it forbid *apartheid*? Again, a particular historical context may even enshrine what some may regard as an abuse of power. Thus, the Rhodesian revolution of 1965 occurred because the minority white population wished to deny to the African majority a share in the government. The historical context here would have justified perpetual denial. Other objections are that it might have the ill-effect of impressing a past morality too strongly on the present and so hold back development to suit a different outlook. Also different historical interpretations of events might yield different moral bases; and it may not always be possible to discover a moral basis. The conclusion to be drawn from all this is that the historical context is not a firm enough weapon with which to attack legislation. It is by no means fanciful, however, since it can be and, indeed, has been used.

Manner and form

As an indirect method of controlling legislative power the 'manner and form' check is open to British courts because the question who decides what constitutes a 'statute' has never been decided. Parliament cannot bind itself not to repeal a statute; but the point is whether it is bound to observe a particular procedure in order to pass one. Any requirement as to what constitutes a 'statute' necessarily precedes every statue, for it is this that invests an enactment with that character. It is not of itself a limitation on the substance of an enactment, but prescribes how the power of enactment may be effectively exercised[7]. The one will, however, imply the other whenever there is a provision to the effect that certain things can only be done after a special procedure has been followed[8]. In any case, disregard of appropriate procedures is more likely to occur in passing oppressive or unpopular measures.

The existing requirements for an Act of Parliament are a simple majority in the House of Commons and in the House of Lords and the Royal Assent[9].

---

6 *Jilani v Government of Punjab* Pak LD (1972) SC 139 at 182. See also Yaqub Ali J at 235, Sajjad Ahmad J at 258, Salahuddin Ahmed J at 264, 267.

7 *Bribery Comr v Ranasinghe* [1965] AC 172 at 198–200, [1964] 2 All ER 785 at 792, 793.

8 Ibid. For the presumption that an Act has been properly passed, see *Akar v A-G of Sierra Leone* [1970] AC 853, [1969] 3 All ER 384.

9 *Pylkington's Case* YB 33 Hen fo 6 17 pl 8. See also *Prince's Case* (1605) 8 Co Rep 1a; *College of Phisitians v Cooper* (1675) 3 Keb 587. A Bill before Parliament is not a 'statute': *Willow Wren Canal Carrying Co Ltd v British Transport Commission* [1956] 1 All ER 567, [1956] 1 WLR 213. In making a *discretionary* order a court may take into account a forthcoming change in the law: *Clifford Sabey (Contractors) Ltd v Long* [1959] 2 QB 290, [1959] 2 All ER 462. Cf *Wilson v Dagnall*, [1972] 1 QB 509, [1972] 2 All ER 44. A resolution of the House of Commons is not 'law': *Bowles v Bank of England* [1913] 1 Ch 57. Even in times of political stress Parliament

Parliament can of course alter these requirements and introduce some new manner and form for legislating[10]. Suppose that it passes an Act to the effect that all future legislation shall be passed by at least a two-thirds majority in each House. It is clear that a future Parliament can, by observing this two-thirds majority rule, rescind it and restore the rule of a simple majority.

The question is whether a future Parliament can by a simple majority repeal the two-thirds majority rule. Would such an enactment be a 'statute'? Sir Ivor Jennings said no, and denied that Parliament is competent to do this. It is a rule of law, he argued, accepted by the judges, that statutes are enactments made by the Monarch and passed by simple majorities in the Lords and Commons; and this rule, like any other, is alterable. If, then, a statute, passed in the accepted way, substitutes a different procedure for legislating, the law has been altered and the judges will be bound by the new law. An enactment which does not thereafter conform to the new procedure will not in law be a 'statute'[11]. Sir Ivor added that the only escape from this conclusion is to maintain that the statute, which originally effected the alteration, is void, which would be absurd. Parliament is in this way able to bind a future Parliament to observe a particular manner and form.

Professor H W R Wade has challenged this reasoning. He points out, in the first place, that the question is not whether the original statute is void, but whether it is repealable. No statute, he says, can declare itself to be unrepealable: which is undeniable. The point is whether it can be repealed by an enactment passed otherwise than in the prescribed manner and form[12]. Professor Wade contends that Parliament does not have to comply with that requirement because at rock bottom there lies the principle, which no statute can establish or alter, that the courts will always enforce the latest statute, in other words, the later statute will always, by implication if need be, repeal an earlier[13]. The weakness in this argument is that it begs the question by assuming that the later enactment is a 'statute'. Professor Wade appears to be supported by Sir Owen Dixon of Australia, who has argued that the common law is the source of Parliament's authority, in other words, that the doctrine of parliamentary supremacy is a rule of common law. Constitutional questions of the sort under consideration should accordingly be resolved in the context of the whole of the law of which the common law is an important part[14].

On the other hand, the opinion of the Judicial Committee of the Privy Council in *Bribery Comr v Ranasinghe*[15] would appear to have endorsed Sir Ivor Jennings's view. Section 29 (4) of the Ceylon (Constitution) Order in

has observed the requirements. On occasions the assent of the House of Lords has been obtained by the creation of, or threat to create, peers, eg passing of the Treaty of Utrecht, Reform Bill 1832; Parliament Act 1911.

10 In *Moore v A-G for the Irish Free State* [1935] AC 484, the Privy Council held that the Irish Parliament, while conforming to such requirements as to manner and form as were necessary, could repeal s 2 and amend s 50 of its own constituent Irish Free State Constitution Act 1922. See also *Bribery Comr v Ranasinghe*, [1965] AC 172 at 197–198, [1964] 2 All ER 785 at 792.

11 Jennings *The Law and the Constitution* ch 4.

12 It might be observed that one reason why the XII Tables in Rome acquired their unalterable sanctity was that the very special machinery which produced them was never set up again: Buckland *The Main Institutions of Roman Private Law* p 3.

13 Wade 'The Basis of Legal Sovereignty' (1955) CLJ 172.

14 Dixon 'The Common Law as an Ultimate Constitutional Foundation' (1957–58) 31 ALJ 240.

15 [1965] AC 172, [1964] 2 All ER 785.

Council 1946, requires that any Bill amending or repealing the Constitution should be certified by the Speaker as having been passed by no less than two-thirds of the whole House of Representatives. Section 55 secures the independence of the judiciary by vesting the appointment of judges in the Judicial Service Commission. The Bribery Amendment Act 1958, s 41, provided that members of Bribery Tribunals, established under the Act, were to be appointed by the Governor General on the advice of the Minister of Justice; but there was no certificate of the Speaker in accordance with s 29 (4) of the Constitution. Both the Supreme Court of Ceylon and the Judicial Committee had no difficulty in holding that members of Bribery Tribunals were judicial officers and that the 1958 Act purported to amend the Constitution. Since the established procedure had not been followed, those provisions of the Act which conflicted with the Constitution were invalid. 'Once it is shown that an Act conflicts with a provision in the Constitution, the certificate is an essential part of the legislative process. The court has a duty to see that the Constitution is not infringed and to preserve it inviolate'[16].

In this important case no question arose of a conflict between the legislature and the courts. It does not therefore touch on a deeper issue underlying the debate between Sir Ivor Jennings and Professor Wade, which is this. Granting that the situation envisaged has arisen, the vital question is:

(a) is it for Parliament to decide as a matter of its own internal procedure what constitutes a 'statute', or

(b) is it for the courts to decide this as a matter of law; in brief, is it for Parliament to dictate to the courts what a 'statute' is whenever occasion arises, or is there a testing right in the courts[17]?

These questions determine how 'statute' should be defined, and what the conditions of validity are. The answer would follow on (a) that a 'statute' is simply what the legislature says is a statute, notwithstanding any provisions that may exist as to procedure or voting majorities. Such provisions are not then conditions of validity, no part, in other words, of the rule defining a 'statute'. On the other hand, it would follow on (b) that a 'statute' is something that has to satisfy certain conditions, and on this basis provisions as to procedure or voting majorities would become part of the conditions of validity. Where the requirement for legislating is a simple majority, there is no reason for bringing to the surface the issue between (a) and (b), which is why the point has never been determined in this country[18]. Only when the requirement is anything other than a simple majority is the question likely to arise. When viewed in this way the difference of opinion between Sir Ivor Jennings and Professor H W R Wade becomes explicable. Sir Ivor's argument, now supported by the Judicial Committee, is founded on assumption (b), namely, that the courts decide what a 'statute' is as a matter of law. For

16 [1965] AC 172 at 194, [1964] 2 All ER 785 at 790. For a presumption that it has been properly passed, see *Akar v A-G of Sierra Leone*, [1970] AC 853, [1969] 3 All ER 384. In *A-G of St Christopher, Nevis and Anguilla v Reynolds* [1980] AC 1037, [1979] 3 All ER 129, the Privy Council said that the amendment of an entrenched section of the Constitution without going through the proper procedure was void.

17 It will be noticed that during the first three years of the Rhodesian rebellion the courts firmly maintained that they alone were competent to decide what legislation they would accept as 'laws', and the government accepted this contention inasmuch as it submitted to the jurisdiction of the courts in the matter.

18 As observed in *Bribery Comr v Ranasinghe* [1965] AC 172 at 125, [1964] 2 All ER 785 at 790.

it is then clear that the courts are bound to declare that an enactment, which does not conform to *their* definitive rule, is not a 'statute'. Professor Wade's contention, on the other hand, appears to proceed on assumption (a), namely, that it is for Parliament alone to decide what is a 'statute' as a matter of internal procedure; for only on this basis is it possible for him to maintain that an enactment, which fails to conform to some existing rule as to manner and form, could nevertheless be a 'statute'. The crucial decision, therefore, is between questions (a) and (b).

The argument that legislation will be invalid unless it conforms to the requirement as to manner and form, however this may be expressed[19], is attractive. In other words, it is for the courts to test the validity of legislation. Arguments the other way also merit consideration. One way of maintaining that Parliament may still control what constitutes a 'statute' is to say that once an enactment has been enrolled on the Parliamentary roll it is a 'statute' as far as the courts are concerned, save perhaps where an irregularity is apparent on the face of the record itself. Such a rule would enable Parliament to decide as and how it pleases what a 'statute' is simply by enrolling an enactment as such, notwithstanding any requirement as to manner and form. There are some judicial statements suggesting that the roll is conclusive[20], but none is wholly convincing. The argument only raises the issue between (a) and (b) in another form: is the condition of the validity of a 'statute' simply enrolment, or is the requirement of manner and form itself a condition? It might even be asked, quite apart from manner and form, whether the assent of the Monarch, the Lords and the Commons is a condition of validity or not. For one interpretation of the enrolment rule might be that a statute is such on enrolment notwithstanding the fact that one or other of these parties had not signified its assent. On the other hand, the rule could mean only that, granting that the main conditions of validity are fulfilled, the courts will not inquire into minor rules of procedure and the like which are not themselves conditions of validity, such as the triple reading of Bills, or whether an Act had been procured by fraud[1]. In none of the cases alluded to was there any doubt as to the fulfilment of the constitutive requirements. Would the judges, who appeared to have accepted the enrolment rule, still have upheld it had the assent, for example of the Commons, been wanting? That they would have done so is at least doubtful, and therefore their *dicta* should not be generalised. It is thus equally doubtful that they would have supported the enrolment rule when some special provision as to manner and form had not been observed. Maitland, for one, entertained doubts about the scope of the enrolment rule[2].

Another way of putting the matter is to argue that Parliament exercises

---

19 When this is laid down in a constitution the position is clear; cf *McCawley v R* [1920] AC 691, and *A-G for New South Wales v Trethowan* [1932] AC 526, and see Evershed MR in *Harper v Secretary of State for the Home Department* [1955] Ch 238 at 253, [1955] 1 All ER 331 at 339. See also *R v Military Governor NDU Internment Camp* [1924] IR 32, where the Irish court declared an Act of the Irish Parliament to be invalid because it failed to conform to the required manner and form. The South African case of *Harris v Minister of the Interior* 1952 (2) SA 428 (A) illustrates the same point.
20 Notably *Edinburgh and Dalkeith Rly Co v Wauchope* (1842) 8 Cl & Fin 710 at 724–725. See also *R v Countess of Arundel* (1616) Hob 109; *Lee v Bude and Torrington Junction Rly Co* (1871) LR 6 CP 576 at 582.
1 *British Railways Board v Pickin*, [1974] AC 765, [1974] 1 All ER 609.
2 Maitland *Constitutional History of England* pp 381–382.

exclusive jurisdiction over the regulation of its own internal affairs[3], including the entire legislative process. This, too, is not convincing, since the question would then be how far the privilege of Parliament extends. Is this particular rule, which requires some special procedure or majority, merely a matter of internal procedure or a rule of law? In the one instance in this country where a special procedure may be employed, namely, under the Parliament Acts 1911–1949, there is a specific rule which deprives the courts of any testing right by making the Speaker's certificate conclusive that the appropriate procedure has been followed[4]. It would be unsafe to generalise from this somewhat special type of situation. Indeed, it might even be argued that where there is no definite provision like this the courts do automatically have a testing right; for if not, a rule denying them such a right is meaningless. In the South African case of *R v Ndobe*[5] the Appellate Division rejected the contention that a rule prescribing a particular manner and form for legislating was to be likened to regulations controlling the internal proceedings in Parliament or that the parliamentary roll was conclusive. In *Bribery Comr v Ranasinghe*[6] the Judicial Committee held that the Speaker's certificate was a necessary part of the manner and form of legislation amending the Ceylon Constitution. In its absence enrolment and the presentation of an official copy of an Act is no substitute. 'If Parliament could not make a bill valid by purporting to enact it, it certainly could not do so by reprinting it, however august the blessing that it gives to the reprint'[7].

It will be seen that none of the above considerations is decisive. The solution will have to be sought in the acceptance of one or other of the alternatives posed above, for which purpose considerations outside law will have to be resorted to. The first decision to be made is whether it is desirable that the judiciary should have the power to review the validity of legislation. It might be borne in mind that freedom of the individual means, *inter alia*, freedom from the law-maker, be it monarch or legislature. The judiciary has traditionally safeguarded the individual from oppression by the former; should it not be a bulwark against the latter as well if need be? To this it might be objected that an elected legislature is in power with the approval of the people, and that judges are not elected. Popular approval, however, is a vague idea. It might be conceivable with reference to some specific issue, but hardly as to the details of general administration. Besides, the difficulties arise not so much as to the approval with which a legislature comes into power, but as to how long it might be said to continue to enjoy it. If the power of judicial review is thought to be necessary, then this would weigh in favour of proposition (b), given earlier, rather than (a). It cannot be

---

3 *Bradlaugh v Gossett* (1884) 12 QBD 271; *Bilston Corpn v Wolverhampton Corpn* [1942] Ch 391, [1942] 2 All ER 447; *Harper v Secretary of State for the Home Department* [1955] Ch 238, [1955] 1 All ER 331 (the two latter cases refused an injunction). Cf *Clayton v Heffron* (1960) 34 ALJR 378, where the Australian court similarly refused to issue an injunction and declared that *Trethowan's Case, ubi sup.*, which allowed an injunction, was wrong on this point. None of these cases touch on the question whether the requirement as to manner and form is simply a matter of internal procedure.

4 Parliament Act 1911, s 3. Cf *Akar v A-G of Sierra Leone* [1970] AC 853, [1969] 3 All ER 384.

5 1930 AD 484 (SA), now upheld by *Harris v Minister of the Interior* 1952 (2) SA 428 (A); *contra*, *Ndlwana v Hofmeyr NO* 1937 AD 229 (SA), not followed in *Harris's Case*.

6 [1965] AC 172, [1964] 2 All ER 785.

7 [1965] AC 172 at 195, [1964] 2 All ER 785 at 791. For the power of the courts to interfere with the conduct of members of a colonial legislature when deliberating a measure, see *A-G of Hong Kong v Rediffusion (Hong Kong) Ltd* [1970] AC 1136, [1970] 2 WLR 1264.

emphasised too often that the need to decide between them has not arisen because no conflict has occurred between Parliament and the courts. The apparent docility of the judges in 1689 was deceptive: they sided with Parliament as against the prerogative. By not flaunting their independence of Parliament they preserved to themselves a considerable degree of power the limits of which have never been defined. The fact that the issue has not arisen should not obscure the historical fact that the present position of Parliament and its victory over the prerogative rested on the acceptance by the judges of its authority. Should a conflict now arise between Parliament and the courts, the choice between (a) and (b) will have to be made by the electorate, whose decision will largely be governed by the political *milieu* in which the reference to them is made.

The point has arisen in other jurisdictions. With regard to Scotland the opinion was expressed in *MacCormick v Lord Advocate*[8] that Parliament may be incompetent to alter the Act of Union 1707, since this is in a sense a 'fundamental law'. In relation to the Dominions the Statute of Westminster 1931, s 4, declares that no British statute shall apply to a Dominion 'unless it is expressly declared in that Act that that Dominion has requested and consented to the enactment thereof'. Such request and consent are arguably part of the special manner and form for legislating for the Dominions. If the British Parliament were to repeal s 4 unilaterally, the question whether this would be valid depends on whether it is for Parliament or the courts to decide what constitutes a 'statute'. Viscount Sankey in a dictum said that theoretically such repeal would be valid[9], but Dominion judges have said otherwise[10]. Even accepting that statutes for Dominions require an extra condition of validity, there might be some doubt as to what exactly this is. Must the Dominion concerned in fact have assented, or is it sufficient for the statute merely to recite that it has done so, however untrue this may be? The wording of s 4, read literally, could support the latter view[11]. If, on the other

8 1953 SC 396, per Lord Cooper; cf Lord Russell at 417. It may be noted that in the Universities (Scotland) Act 1853, Parliament did repeal a provision which had been declared to be fundamental in the Act of Union. See also the repeal of the fifth article of the Union between Britain and Ireland, also stated to be fundamental, by the Irish Church Act 1869.

9 *British Coal Corpn v R* [1935] AC 500 at 520. Cf Danckwerts J in *Re Brassey's Settlement, Barclay's Bank Ltd v Brassey* [1955] 1 All ER 577 at 580.

10 Thus, a South African judge, Stratford ACJ, said: 'Freedom once conferred cannot be revoked'. *Ndlwana v Hofmeyr NO* 1937 AD 229 at 237 (SA); and see Lord Denning MR in *Blackburn v A-G* [1971] 2 All ER 1380 at 1382. The Australian case of *Copyright Owners Reproduction Society v EMI (Australia) Pty Ltd* (1958) 32 ALJR 306, came near to the point. In *Re Cunningham, ex p Bennett* (1967) 86 WN (Pt 2) NSW 323 at 328, another Australian judge was clear that a British Act not complying with s 4 would not be law in Australia. See also Dixon 'The Law and the Constitution' (1935) 51 LQR 590, and Hanks 'Re-defining the Sovereign: Current Attitudes to Section 4 of the Statute of Westminster' (1968) 42 ALJ 286. With regard to Northern Ireland the Ireland Act 1949, s 1(2), provides that no part of Northern Ireland shall cease to be part of the United Kingdom without the consent of the Parliament of Northern Ireland. Heuston has argued that without such consent a British Act is invalid: 'Sovereignty' in *Oxford Essays in Jurisprudence* pp 220–221. With regard to Rhodesia it should be noted that Rhodesia remained a colony so that the British Parliament had full legislative power. The convention, which was embodied in s 4 of the Statute of Westminster, was not in statutory form as regards Rhodesia, and the British Parliament is not bound by mere convention. Besides, the act of rebellion arguably released Britain from her obligation to continue to observe it: *Madzimbamuto v Lardner-Burke* [1969] 1 AC 645 at 723, [1968] 3 All ER 561 at 573. The Rhodesian courts refused to accept this interpretation and defied the ruling: *R v Ndlovu* 1968 (4) SA 515 at 525.

11 *Manuel v A-G* [1983] Ch 77, [1982] 3 All ER 786, 822. Cf where a certificate of the Speaker is said to be conclusive and not open to question by a court: Parliament Acts 1911–1949.

hand, the condition is understood to mean actual assent, then it cannot be dispensed with by mere declaration. Whatever the view taken by British courts, the view of Dominion courts is too obvious to need mention.

In South Africa the issue between Parliament and the courts arose squarely in connection with the 'entrenched' clauses of the South Africa Act 1909, which can only be repealed or altered by a two-thirds majority of both Houses of the Union Parliament sitting together[12]. Early in the 1950s the Government sought to place the Cape coloured voters on a separate electoral roll. Such a change could only be made by a two-thirds majority according to the South Africa Act, but the disenfranchising statute was passed by only a simple majority. The Appellate Division held this void as well as a subsequent statute purporting to create a 'High Court of Parliament' for deciding issues of this nature[13]. The nub of the dispute was that Parliament maintained that it alone decides what constitutes a 'statute' and that the courts must accept what it says, while the Appellate Division maintained that the courts decide this. Eventually by the Senate Act 1955 the number of senators was increased so as to provide the necessary two-thirds majority and the South Africa Act Amendment Act 1956, ending the entrenchment of voting rights, was passed in accordance with the South Africa Act[14]. The Government, in effect, bowed to the Appellate Division.

It would seem, therefore, that the manner and form control could be effective, but the occasions for its use are likely to be rare. A powerful government will be in such complete command as to be able to carry out its policies with a scrupulous adherence to procedure, so the manner and form control will be of least avail when most needed.

As against all this, there are several drawbacks to judicial control of power. Whatever form such control may assume, its success depends on judges being independent of those wielding the power. Independence means far more than immunity from interference; it means that they are free to bring their own sense of values to bear in considering legislation and do not simply reflect the values of government. For there can be no protection against abuse of power, even when safeguards are enshrined in a written constitution, if the judges who have to interpret these whenever the government is challenged are only puppets of government. In this respect there lies a distinction be-

---

12 There has been some debate as to whether or not the validity of these clauses depended on the Colonial Laws Validity Act 1865, so that with its repeal in 1931 the clauses ceased to be entrenched. The respect that continued to be paid to them after 1931, even by Nationalist governments, suggests that they remained valid. The Conference on the Operation of Dominion Legislation 1929 (Cmd 3479) para 67: 'In the case of the Union of South Africa the exercise of these powers is conditioned only by the provisions of s 152 of the South Africa Act 1909'; and this was approved by the resolution of both Houses of the South African Parliament. See also the assurances in 1931 by the Nationalist Prime Minister and others (see House of Assembly Debates, April 22 1931, col 2738-2739, 2746); and the statement by the Speaker in 1934 (see House of Assembly Debates, April 25 1934, col 2736). In 1936 Act 12/1936, providing for a separate roll for Africans, was passed as stated in the recital 'in accordance with the requirements of sections thirty-five and one hundred and fifty-five of the South Africa Act 1909'. In *Krause v IRC* 1929 AD 286 (SA), it was held that an Act of the South African Parliament could impliedly alter any part of the South Africa Act, except the 'entrenched' provisions.

13 *Harris v Minister of the Interior* 1952 (2) SA 428 (A); *Minister of the Interior v Harris* 1952 (4) SA 769 (A).

14 *Collins v Minister of the Interior* 1957 (1) SA 552 (A). Schreiner JA dissented on the ground that the artificially enlarged body which passed the 1956 Act was not a 'House of Parliament' within the meaning of the South Africa Act, but merely a piece of political jerrymandering.

tween so-called 'totalitarian' and 'free' countries. In the former the task of the judge is that of reflecting an official set of values; in the latter he has to weigh these against others which may be opposed to them–a more difficult task[15]. A feature of this independence is the way in which the judiciary can switch, overnight if need be, to supporting official values, as in times of crisis[16].

The British judiciary has enjoyed a long tradition of independence. When Chief Justice Coke told King James that the King was under God and the law, he meant the reasoning and values of the common law which requires special expertise and of which the judges are the experts. In the conflict between King and Parliament ending in the revolution of 1689 the judges sided with the latter, so there was no cause for Parliament to suppress them. In this way their independence was preserved and it has now become a cherished tradition. Had they opposed the new order, the position would have been vastly different. The Rhodesian revolution provided a different example. It would appear that the judiciary there played a clever political game; while the government was asserting its independence of Britain, the judges were tacitly asserting their independence of the government so as to prevent the judiciary from being engulfed by the emotional and political tides unleashed by rebellion. They did so by refusing unanimously to recognise the régime as legal and by continuing in this attitude for nearly three years until the Appellate Division, the highest court in the land, had a chance of saying so too. Thus, Lewis J at first instance declared uncompromisingly:

> 'The only course open would then be the drastic one of filling the vacuum by replacing all of the existing judges with revolutionary judges, who, regardless of judicial conscience, would be prepared to accept without question the 1965 Constitution as the *de jure* Constitution of this country, despite the ties of sovereignty and despite the anomalies in the Constitution itself to which I have already referred. ... Once a judge appointed under the 1961 Constitution were to yield to this threat and to swear an oath to uphold the 1965 Constitution, knowing full well it was not the law, he would no longer remain an independent judge; he would become a craven hireling of the executive'[17].

Once the Appellate Division had made clear its own views, the courts then came round in a series of rapid steps to accepting the rebel régime as legal[18].

15 Churchill, HC Debates, March 23 1954, col 1061; Denning 'The Independence of the Judiciary' (1950) Presidential Address to the Holdsworth Club; Lord Denning and Salmon LJ in *Re Grosvenor Hotel, London (No 2)* [1965] Ch 1210 at 1245, 1261, [1964] 3 All ER 354 at 361–362, 372; *Liyanage v R* [1967] AC 259, [1966] 1 All ER 650; *Conway v Rimmer* [1968] AC 910, [1968] 1 All ER 874; *Van der Linde v Calitz* 1967 (2) SA 239. Parliamentary indignation over the *Burmah Oil Co Case* [1965] AC 75, [1964] 2 All ER 348, shows how far removed judicial values were from those of government.
16 In politically immature and emergent countries, which are in the course of evolving their values and of winning acceptance of them, judicial independence dare not be allowed beyond a certain point. For the position in South Africa, see p 99 ante. See also Harvey 'A Value Analysis of Ghanaian Legal Development since Independence' (1964) 1 UGLR 4.
17 *Madzimbamuto v Lardner-Burke* GD/CIV/23/66, Government Blue Book, pp 24, 36. See also Yaqub Ali J in *Jilani v Government of Punjab* Pak LD (1972) SC 139 at 229.
18 For a brief account, see Dias 'Legal Politics: Norms behind the *Grundnorm*', [1968] CLJ at 251–253, to which has to be added *R v Ndhlovu* 1968 (4) SA 525 (A), decided on 13 September 1968 when the Appellate Division finally accepted the régime as legal.

In this way they made it abundantly clear to the government that its legality depended, not on effectiveness, but on the judges saying so[19].

The power of even the most independent judiciary suffers from the weakness that the assertion of values contrary to those of government can only be carried up to a point. All judges will ultimately be helpless in the face of ruthless power. The cynical Hobbes had a keen appreciation of the point when he said: '... in the matter of government, when nothing else is turn'd up, Clubs are Trump'[20]. It is true that this is an extreme situation and before it is reached there is still something that an independent judiciary might accomplish[1]. Another obvious weakness of judicial control is that judges can only act when cases come before them, which means that the principles on which they will operate have to be evolved piecemeal rather in the way in which equity was developed. Such a process is bound to take time, whereas the need to prevent the abuse of power is too urgent for that. This objection might be avoided by having a constitution, perhaps with a Bill of Rights annexed, and guaranteed by the judiciary[2].

Finally, it is questionable whether the judiciary should be used at all for these purposes, which cast judges into a political arena. Moreover, the judicial process of fact-finding and the application of rules is not geared to such matters. Against this it might be pointed out that even the normal process of deciding disputes does import an element of discretion guided by value-judgments as between competing social, individual, governmental and other interests[3]. The difference in the kind of discretion is one of degree, and it becomes a matter of opinion as to whether this is large enough to warrant keeping such questions away from the judiciary.

If, as would appear from the above, judicial control is inadequate and possibly undesirable, it is necessary to consider other ways of preventing the abuse of power. To call in aid the concept of duty not to exercise power in any particular way is not within the sphere of practical politics. It is not possible to impose duties on sovereign legislatures, which have the liberty to enact what they please. As pointed out earlier, the problem becomes one of curbing the abuse of liberty. The nearest approach to the utilisation of the duty concept is to be found in *Teh Cheng Poh (alias Char Meh) v Public Prosecutor, Malaysia*[4], where the Judicial Committee of the Privy Council held that although the proclamation by a ruler, made under statutory power, declaring a specified area to be a security area remained valid until revoked, nevertheless it was an abuse of the ruler's discretion not to have exercised the power of revocation once he considered that the proclamation was no

19 For possible justification of the judicial attitude deriving from an implied provision in the old constitution, or from natural law, or from a moral or social duty to the populace, see Honoré 'Reflections on Revolutions' (1967) 2 Ir Jur (NS) 268.
20 Hobbes *Dialogue between a Philosopher and a Student of the Common Laws of England* sv 'Punishments' p 140.
1 Eg in Rhodesia the revolutionary régime had power to remove judges who refused to swear allegiance to the new constitution. Yet at no time during the three years when the judges refused to accept the régime as legal did it dare to invoke this power. To have done so would have been politically damaging.
2 Powerfully advocated by Lord Justice Scarman in his Hamlyn Lectures *English Law—The New Dimension* pp 76 et seq.
3 See ch 10 post. Perhaps the 'manner and form' check on power is the most mechanical of those that have been considered.
4 [1980] AC 458, [1979] 2 WLR 623.

longer necessary for the purpose for which it was issued. It was held further that, although the ruler was immune from court proceedings, an order of mandamus could be sought against members of his cabinet requiring them to advise the ruler to revoke the proclamation, which implies that they were in breach of their public duty.

The concept of disability provides a more feasible method of controlling legislative power than duty, ie no power to enact unjust laws. By way of analogy it might be noted that there is a disability to create an immoral contract, any such agreement being void. Likewise, it is through disability that the *ultra vires* doctrine operates to limit the power of subordinate legislatures. At these levels there can be disability controls on power, but the step from them to that of sovereign legislatures is very large. Hitherto the most effective way in which this can be, and has been, accomplished is by means of written constitutions.

WRITTEN CONSTITUTION

In countries which possess written constitutions the legislatures are bound by the constitutions and courts can declare statutes invalid on the ground that they are unconstitutional. Montesquieu saw clearly the dangers of power. 'It is the experience of history', he said, 'that power tends to be abused, so power must be used to check power'. The guarantee against its misuse lies in establishing mutual checks between the legislative, judicial and executive functions[5]. What his doctrine of the 'separation of powers' insists on is the danger of an absolute union of these functions in one person or body; it does not require their respective allocation to three distinct organs with no inter-relation between them. The functions may well be shared, as in Britain where the cabinet, which is the executive centre, is an integral part of the legislature and responsible to it; executive departments have legislative and 'quasi-judicial' functions entrusted to them; justices of the peace perform judicial and executive functions. What is crucial is the independence of the judiciary[6]. The paradigm example of Montesquieu's doctrine is the United States of America, where the separation is guaranteed by the Constitution, guarded by the courts. The federal legislative power is vested in Congress, the federal executive power in the President and his cabinet, and the federal judicial power in the Supreme Court; and a great deal of inter-relation exists between them.

An interesting Commonwealth illustration is *Liyanage v R*[7]. The appellants were charged with participation in an abortive *coup d'etat*. By the Criminal Law (Special Provisions) Act No 1 of 1962, the legislature sought retrospectively to legalise their prolonged imprisonment without trial, to create *ex post facto* a new criminal offence so as to cover the situation of the abortive *coup*, to alter the law of evidence so as to render admissible much that would otherwise have been inadmissible, and to prescribe a minimum penalty. All

---

5 Montesquieu *L'Esprit des Lois* 11, 4–6.
6 Where there is a separation of powers guaranteed in a constitution, it is the function of the judiciary alone to interpret the law: *Chokolingo v A-G of Trinidad and Tobago* [1981] 1 All ER 244, [1981] 1 WLR 106.
7 [1967] 1 AC 259, [1966] 1 All ER 650. See also *Hinds v R* [1977] AC 195, [1976] 1 All ER 353.

these remarkable provisions applied only to these appellants and to the circumstances of the *coup*. By another Act a special tribunal, nominated by the Chief Justice, was established to try the case, and this, with reluctance, held itself bound by the legislation. The Judicial Committee of the Privy Council, however, declared the legislation to be invalid because it infringed the doctrine of the separation of powers, which was part of the then Constitution. It was argued that the vesting of the judicial function in the judiciary, as distinct from the legislature and the executive, had occurred before the promulgation of the Constitution, which had continued that state of affairs. Any attempt by the legislature to usurp the judicial function was, therefore, *ultra vires*. Of course, the Constitution might be altered so as to permit this to be done, but that had not occurred. The Judicial Committee was careful to indicate that the legislation was invalid, not because it was *ex post facto* and *ad homines*, but because the nature of the legislation, considered as a whole, constituted a usurpation of the judicial function. The *ex post facto* and *ad hominem* character of the legislation merely showed that the Acts were, in the words of an American judge, 'Legislative judgments, and an exercise of judicial power'[8].

A written constitution provides probably the most effective of all checks on legislative power, but a contrary effect is that, while a constitution may limit legislative power, it may thereby prevent government from dealing with the abuse of liberty, which could be as undesirable as the abuse of power[9]. In any case, the success of a constitution depends on a number of factors. One of the most important is the language in which the limitations are expressed, whether in fairly specific terms or in generalities open to divergent interpretation. Secondly, the safeguards may be effectively cancelled by countervailing provisions elsewhere in the document[10]. Thirdly, if the constitution can be easily amended, a restraint which the government finds irksome will not impose quite such a curb as when the procedure for amendment is complex and elaborate. An interesting case is *Golak Nath v State of Punjab*[11], in which the Supreme Court of India declared that the Indian Parliament was incapable of amending the Constitution so as to abridge or remove fundamental rights. Fourthly, every constitution has to be interpreted, so the effectiveness of its restraints rests ultimately on the interpreters, ie the judges and the measure of their sympathy with and independence of government[12].

A compromise might be a 'non-justiciable Bill of Rights' along the line adopted in a former Rhodesian Constitution[13]. When a measure, usually one

8 Per Chase J in *Calder v Bull* (1789) 3 Dallas USSC 386. Cf *Kariapper v Wijesinha* [1968] AC 717, [1967] 3 All ER 485, where the Act was held to be legislative rather than judicial and did have the effect of amending the Constitution.

9 Eg the First Amendment to the United States Constitution, which inhibits the use of legislative power to curb some of the grossest abuses of liberty, such as anti-social monopolies. See also *New York Times Co v US* 403 US 713 (1971).

10 Hiemstra 'Constitutions of Liberty' (1971) 88 SALJ 45 (comparing the American and German Constitutions).

11 [1967] 2 SCR 762.

12 The American Supreme Court is a good example, eg its obstruction of New Deal Legislation in the 1930s. Cf more recently *Brown v Board of Education* 347 US 483 (1954); *New York Times Co v US* 403 US 713 (1971) ('Pentagon Papers' case).

13 Cf the Protection of Human Rights Bill 1971, introduced into the British Parliament, but which did not get beyond a second reading. It provided for a Commission of Human Rights, which would report to Parliament and whose decisions would be outside the jurisdiction of the courts (cl 14).

before Parliament, is thought likely to infringe a 'fundamental right' contained in the Bill of Rights, the matter might be referred to an independent body of which a judge may well be a member. The adverse report of such a body, even though not binding, could have effect. For it would cast on the legislature the onus of justifying the measure which, if implemented, could impair its prestige and popularity at home and abroad.

SUPRA-NATIONAL CONTROL

There is no external body yet in existence which can prevent the abuse of municipal power over individuals. Two developments, which are steps in that direction, are the European Court on Human Rights and the European Economic Community with its own Court. The former is indeed concerned with the individual, but it is not as significant as the latter which, though confined to economic matters, could be regarded as limiting the legislative competence of member states. If there were to be a Human Rights Treaty with machinery analogous to the relevant aspects of the Treaty of Rome, this would provide a check on power transcending national legislatures[14]. For this reason, and also because of its impact on the doctrine of parliamentary sovereignty, the implications of membership of the European Economic Community need attention.

Community law is *sui generis*, not susceptible to classification either as international or federal law[15]. Both the European Court of Justice and municipal courts have regarded it as a new kind of legal order[16]. Certain aspects of Community law have direct internal effect, ie certain measures have automatic law-quality within the member states. Community law consists of the following:

(1) **Regulations,** which are general legislative measures binding on states as well as individuals if applicable (art 189(2) of the Treaty of Rome)[17].

(2) **Directives,** general or particular, bind only as regards their objectives but leave to member states the manner of their implementation (art 189 (3)). Members are required to take all appropriate steps to ensure fulfilment of the Treaty obligations (art 5)[18].

14 See Lauterpacht *International Law and Human Rights* and his prophecy as to a limitation of parliamentary sovereignty at p 141.

15 *Mirabile quidam monstrum:* Lipstein *The Law of the European Economic Community* p 45.

16 Case 26/62 *Van Gend en Loos v Nederlandse Belastingadministratie* [1963] CMLR 105 at 129; Case 6/64 *Costa v Ente Nazionale per L'Energia Elettrica (ENEL)* [1964] CMLR 425 at 455; Case 28/67 *Molkerei-Zentrale Westfalen-Lippe GmbH v Hauptzollamt Paderborn* [1968] CMLR 187 at 217, [1969] CMLR 300.

17 Case 13/68 *Salgoil SpA v Foreign Trade Ministry of the Italian Republic* [1969] CMLR 181; Case 2-3/69 *Sociaal Fonds voor de Diamantarbeiders, Antwerp v SA Ch Brachfield & Sons and Dougal Diamond Co Antwerp* [1969] CMLR 335; *SAFA v Amministrazione delle Finanze* [1973] CMLR 152; Case 82/72 *Re Frauds on Agricultural Levies* [1974] CMLR 251.

18 See art 169, 170; Case 41/74 *Van Duyn v Home Office (No 2)* [1975] Ch 358, [1975] 3 All ER 190, [1975] 1 CMLR 1; on which see Simmonds '*Van Duyn v Home Office*: the Direct Effect of Directives' (1975) 24 ICLQ 419. Directive 221/64 prohibited the deportation of alien citizens of Member States as a deterrent to other aliens. In *Re Deportation of Aliens* [1977] 2 CMLR 255, the German Bundesverwaltungsgericht held that a ruling on Community law given by the European Court took precedence over a contrary ruling by a national court. Lord Denning MR also spoke of 'giving supremacy to Community': *Shields v E Coomes (Holdings) Ltd* [1979] 1 All ER 456 at 465, [1978] 1 WLR 1408 at 1419.

(3) **Decisions,** which are individual measures, are binding as regards objectives and means (art 189 (4)). In practice the distinction between Directives and the other two is not always clear-cut.

(4) **Recommendations** are advisory and not binding (art 189 (5)).

On Britain's accession to the Community on 1 January 1973, Regulations and Decisions, which under the Treaty have automatic law-quality within member states, were given like effect in Britain by the European Communities Act 1972, s 2 (1)[19]. Directives, which do not *per se* become part of municipal law, have to be embodied in Acts of Parliament, Orders in Council or statutory instruments[20]. Section 2 (2) and (4) of the 1972 Act say that whichever of these organs is used, regard should be paid to the objects of the Community and to its obligations and entitlements. Certain limitations on such enabling legislation are specified in Schedule 2, para 1 (1)[1], but these apply to Orders in Council and statutory instruments, not to statutes.

When considering whether membership to the Community limits the sovereignty of Parliament it is important to distinguish between two aspects of sovereignty: between power to pass a measure which has law-quality, and power to repeal or invalidate some other measure which has law-quality. The conferment of domestic law-quality on Community Regulations and Decisions and the question whether these can invalidate contrary domestic laws are thus distinct. It is a British constitutional axiom that no treaty can have internal effect without an enabling Act; and Community law has become 'English law' by statutory fiat. Because of this there is no difficulty in accepting that Community law existing on the date of incorporation can repeal or amend prior municipal law[2]. Since Britain has no written constitution, no question of conflict between Community law and pre-existing constitutional provisions arises[3].

The 1972 Act has given effect not only to existing, but also to future Community law. Even so, there is nothing to impair the supremacy of Parliament and, indeed, the Command Paper issued in anticipation of entry took the view that future Community instruments, 'like ordinary delegated legislation, would derive their force under the law of the United Kingdom from an original enactment passed by Parliament'[4]. Questions of invalidation

---

19 *Application des Gaz SA v Falks Veritas Ltd* [1974] Ch 381, [1974] 3 All ER 51.
20 It has been held that a provision of the Finance Act 1972, a pre-accession statute in conflict with a prior Community Directive, remained binding on British courts until another statute was passed under s 2(2) of the European Communities Act 1972: EC Commission Decision 73/4 (*Processed Vegetable Growers Association Ltd v Customs and Excise Comrs* [1974] 1 CMLR 113).
1 Legislation imposing taxation, retrospective provisions, new criminal offences punishable with imprisonment for more than two years or fines of more than £400 or £5 per day, or conferment of any power to legislate by means of orders, rules, regulations or other subordinate instruments other than rules of procedure for any court or tribunal.
2 *Re Import of Pork* [1966] CMLR 491 (Germany); *Grundig Werke GmbH and JNJ Sieverding NV v PVBA Common Market Import and Trade Co* [1968] CMLR 97 (Belgium); *Macarthy's Ltd v Smith* [1981] QB 180, [1981] 1 All ER 111; Case 43/75 *Defrenne v SA Belge de Navigation Aérienne* [1976] ECR 455, [1976] 2 CMLR 98, [1981] 1 All ER 122n.
3 For the problems that have beset Germany and Italy, see *Lipstein* pp 22–27, and *Internationale Handelsgesellschaft mbH v Einfuhr-und Vorratsstelle für Getreide und Futtermittel* [1974] 2 CMLR 540; *Administration des Douanes v Sociète Cafés Jacques Vabre and J Weigel et Cie Sarl* [1975] 2 CMLR 336.
4 *Legislative and Constitutional Implications of United Kingdom Membership of the European Economic Communities* 1967 (Cmnd 3301) paras 22–23; *Internationale Handelsgesellschaft mbH v Einfuhr-und Vorratsstelle für Getreide und Futtermittel* [1974] 2 CMLR 540.

could arise in two ways: (a) a future Community instrument may conflict with pre-existing statute law, or (b) a future statute may run counter to Community law. With regard to (a), the avoidance of existing statute law by a future Community instrument need raise no problem if the latter's authority has been delegated from Parliament[5]. With regard to (b), however, there is difficulty. The Command Paper evaded it by suggesting simply that Parliament will have to take care to avoid conflict, or, if this did occur, will have to pass the necessary amendment or repeal. A problem could confront a court before Parliament has had time to act. What is likely to happen is that an unsuspected inconsistency will come to light for the first time before a court. Perhaps, a distinction should be drawn between implied and express contravention of Community law. Even with regard to the former, Lord Denning MR has said that such a contravention would be valid in English law[6]. Parliament could of course disable itself in advance from contravening Community law impliedly by inserting into every statute a clause 'and in accordance with European Community law'.

As to express contravention, it is by no means inconceivable that an anti-Community government may deliberately go against Community laws. The possibility of conflict is then real. The alternatives are: on the one hand, British courts may take the view that an Act of Parliament expressly contravening Community law remains valid in British municipal law and leaves Britain answerable to the Community. On the other hand, Community law may be regarded as akin to supra-national law so as to disable Parliament from going against it.

The answer is not easy. The evolution of Community law suggests that the issue wears a dual aspect. From the point of view of the Community, the European Court and some municipal courts have accepted the 'priority' of Community law and have even talked in terms of a partial surrender of sovereignty by member states[7]. Moreover, the European Court has pointed out that the Treaty demands the supremacy of Community law over domestic law and that art 189 (2) would be pointless otherwise. Such a view, especially when garnished in the language of surrender of sovereignty, could mean that subsequent contrary municipal legislation is void[8]. In Case 106/77 *Amministrazione delle Finanze dello Stato v Simmenthal SpA (No 2)*[9] the European Court ruled that directly applicable Community law automatically invalidates prior conflicting national law; prevents validity of future conflicting national law; and that every national court must set aside conflicting national measures. This places municipal courts in an unenviable position. From the point of view of municipal law the simple solution would be that Community law has domestic validity by virtue of a municipal statute, and that, therefore, on the principle *lex posterior derogat legi priori* a later statute

---

5 The Dutch Tariefcommissie held that EEC regulations override national law: *Re Import Duties on Processed Beef* [1966] CMLR 346.
6 *Felixstowe Dock and Rly Co and European Ferries Ltd v British Transport Docks Board* [1976] 2 CMLR 655 at 664.
7 Case 26/62 *Van Gend en Loos v Nederlandse Belastingadministratie* [1963] CMLR 105 at 129; Case 6/64 *Costa v Ente Nazionale per L'Energia Elettrica (ENEL)* [1964] CMLR 425 at 455; *Alma SpA v The High Authority* [1965] CMLR 290 (Italian); *FA Max Neumann v Hauptzollamt Hof/Saale* [1969] CMLR 284; *Molkerei-Zentrale Westfalen-Lippe GmbH v Hauptzollamt Paderborn* [1969] CMLR 300 (Germany).
8 Cf Case 57/65 *Firma Alfons Lütticke GmbH v Hauptzollamt Sarrelouis* [1971] CMLR 674; *Re Fees for Examination of Imported Oranges* [1975] 2 CMLR 415.
9 [1978] ECR 629, [1978] 3 CMLR 263.

overrides prior Community law[10]. On the other hand, a municipal court must also pay heed to the opinion of the European Court, which means that this simple solution is only to be adopted, if at all, in the last resort[11].

As far as Britain is concerned s 2 (4) of the 1972 Act does not, indeed cannot, declare that future Acts inconsistent with the Treaty shall be void. What it says is that 'any enactment passed or to be passed ... shall be construed and have effect subject to the foregoing provisions of this section' (ie the objects of the Community and its obligations and entitlements and Schedule 2 of the Act itself). This puts the burden on the courts, which will no doubt construe an Act so as to avoid conflict as far as possible. If this is not possible, the unavoidable question is whether they can declare it void, or even hold it ·to be inapplicable to the extent of conflict. If the inconsistency was not intended by Parliament, it is submitted that the latter course is more likely, for courts will hardly assume so revolutionary a power as to declare statutes void. If, however, Parliament were to go deliberately against a Community law while continuing to remain in the Community (ie without repealing the 1972 Act), it is tempting to say that the courts in accordance with age-old tradition will follow Parliament. Yet, as long as membership lasts, the courts are also under certain obligations deriving from that fact, and it remains to be seen whether they will adopt the bold course of holding such a statute inapplicable. If so, it would appear that here at least there is a possibility of a limitation on parliamentary sovereign power.

This leads to the related problem whether Parliament can withdraw from the Community by repealing the 1972 Act. The Treaty itself is indefinite in duration (art 240), which means presumably that on the ordinary principles of international law it will end by unanimous consent or fundamentally changed conditions (*rebus sic stantibus*). As to the validity of unilateral resignation by Britain[12], the crucial question for a British court will be: does the

---

10 *Syndicat Général de Fabricants de Semoules de France* [1970] CMLR 395; *Felixstowe Dock and Rly Co and European Ferries Ltd v British Transport Docks Board* [1976] 2 CMLR 655 at 664; *contra: Administration des Contributions Indirectes et Comité Interprofessional des Vins Doux Naturels v Ramel* [1971] CMLR 315 (France); *Fromagerie case* [1970] CMLR 219 (Belgium); 2695/70: *Amministrazione delle Finanze dello Stato v SACE SpA* [1975] 2 CMLR 267 (Italy); Netherlands Constitution, art 66.

11 Thus, the Italian Constitutional Court in Case 6/64 *Costa v ENEL* [1964] CMLR 425, at 456, upheld subsequent municipal legislation contrary to Community law. Cf the opinion in [1968] CMLR 267. In *Macarthys Ltd v Smith* [1979] 3 All ER 325, [1979] 1 WLR 1189, it was said that the Treaty of Rome could not contradict the clear wording of the Act of Parliament, especially as the Treaty provision was ambiguous. The Court of Appeal stayed proceedings until a reference to the European Court had been made under art 177, as to which see further Case 129/79 [1981] QB 180, [1981] 1 All ER 111.

12 The position under s 4 of the Statute of Westminster 1931 is not analogous. (1) As has been pointed out, it is arguable, even from the British point of view, that the Statute imposes a special manner and form of legislation by Parliament for Dominions so that a statute not conforming to this procedure would be void. Membership of the Community imposes no special manner and form for passing British Acts so that the procedural bar, which might hinder the repeal of the Statute of Westminster, does not stand in the way of the repeal of the 1972 Act. (2) Whereas the Statute of Westminster freed Dominion subjects from Parliament's unilateral power to legislate for them, the 1972 Act in no way frees British subjects from Parliament's power, but only grants a limited, concurrent legislative power to the Community authorities. (3) Even if Parliament were to repeal the Statute of Westminster unilaterally, she is powerless to coerce Dominion subjects into accepting the change, but she can coerce British subjects into accepting a unilateral repeal of the 1972 Act; and even if British courts were to accept as valid the unilateral repeal of the Statute of Westminster, despite the unenforceability of such a measure, it would be quite another thing for them to say that the enforceable repeal of the 1972 Act is invalid.

Community's power derive solely from the 1972 Act, or does it have independent validity once it has been let in by the Act? There are arguments and persuasive authority both ways, and a court will have to pronounce when the point arises[13]. Only if it were to be accepted that Parliament cannot repeal the 1972 Act, or legislate contrary to Community law, would the doctrine of parliamentary sovereignty as hitherto understood have to be revised. Otherwise it remains unimpaired except, possibly, in the minor respect suggested above. Indicative of a future possibility is the attitude of the left wing of the Labour Party and trade union movement, which have been increasingly defying the authority of Parliament by disobeying statutes, but which at the same time call for Britain's withdrawal from the Community. Withdrawal means that there will not be even the possibility of a supranational restriction on the omnicompetence of Parliament, so that if and when they assume to governmental power, nothing can stand in their way in establishing a 'rule by law' if they so wish[14].

In the result it would seem that there are possibilities of restraining power, though less in Britain than in countries with written constitutions. Even with reference to Britain the idea is perhaps not as starry-eyed as it might seem at first sight. All countries have still a long way to go, so this challenge of the age has not yet been met.

13 In *Blackburn v A-G* [1971] 2 All ER 1380 at 1383, [1971] 1 WLR 1037 at 1040, the Court of Appeal declined to anticipate the answer. Lords Diplock and Scarman have since said that British courts should follow Parliament.
14 On this see Dias, '*Götterdämmerung*: Gods of the Law in Decline', (1981), Legal Studies 1 at p 21.

READING LIST

H E Cohen *Recent Theories of Sovereignty*.
D V Cowen *Parliamentary Sovereignty and the Entrenched Sections of the South Africa Act*.
D V Cowen 'Legislature and the Judiciary' (1952) 15 Modern Law Review 282; (1953) 16 Modern Law Review 273.
A T Denning *Restraining the Misuse of Power* (Holdsworth Club, 1978).
R F V Heuston 'Sovereignty' in *Oxford Essays in Jurisprudence* (ed A G Guest) ch 7.
O Hood Phillips 'Self-limitation by the United Kingdom Parliament' (1975) 2 Hastings Constitutional Law Quarterly 443.
R T E Latham 'The Law and the Commonwealth' in W K Hancock *Survey of British Commonwealth Affairs* pp 522–595 (also published separately).
H Lauterpacht *International Law and Human Rights*.
K Lipstein *The Law of the European Economic Community* ch 2.
Lord MacDermott *Protection from Power under English Law* (Hamlyn Lectures Series).
G Marshall *Parliamentary Sovereignty and the Commonwealth* chs 2–11.
E McWhinney *Judicial Review in the English-Speaking World* (2nd edn) chs 2, 6 and 10.
K W B Middleton 'New Thoughts on the Union between England and Scotland' (1954) 66 Juridical Review 37.
Sir Leslie Scarman *English Law—The New Dimension* (Hamlyn Lectures Series).
J van der Vyver 'Parliamentary Sovereignty, Fundamental Freedoms and a Bill of Rights' (1982) 99 South African Law Journal 557.
H ver Loren van Themaat 'The Equality of Status of the Dominions and the Sovereignty of the British Parliament' (1933) 15 Journal of Comparative Legislation (3rd ser) 47.
H W R Wade 'The Basis of Legal Sovereignty' (1965) Cambridge Law Journal 172.

CHAPTER 6

Control of liberty

Abuse of liberty is not the path to freedom or justice. In the case of liberty, as with power, the achievement of justice lies, not in equal distribution, but in disallowing certain liberties altogether and in restraining the exercise of those that are allowed[1]. The crucial point is the criterion by which it has to be decided that a particular liberty should or should not be allowed, or that its exercise is in need of restraint. 'Control of liberty' is an apparent contradiction in terms, since to abolish a liberty by replacing it with a jurally opposite duty is to restrict the overall area of freedom. Control by such curtailment will be referred to as 'limitation of liberty'. Where, on the other hand, liberty is allowed to remain, the problem of control concerns how its exercise might be restrained; and this aspect will be distinguished from the former by the expression 'restraint of liberty'.

With regard to limitation, it is clear that liberty ends where duty begins, and *vice versa*. Although the phrases 'liberty to do something' and 'absence of duty not to do it' denote the same result, their connotations are different. A régime, which forbids everything save only those things that are expressly allowed, would be regarded as a bullying power-structure, while a régime, which permits everything save only those things that are expressly forbidden, would be counted liberal by contrast. Yet, in content they may be identical.

LIMITATION OF LIBERTY

Duty not to exercise power

As pointed out earlier, duties cannot be imposed on sovereign legislatures not to exercise their power to make laws. The most that can be hoped for in this direction is to restrict the power itself by attaching disabilities, the possibilities of which were explored in the last chapter. Sovereign legislatures can of course impose duties on their subjects not to exercise certain liberties, whether by way of exercising powers or in any other way.

With regard to the limitation of liberty, it is superficially attractive to contend that there should be equal liberty all round, or that it should be curtailed equally. The matter is not so simple, however; whether minorities or individuals are allowed certain liberties at all depends, not on equality, but on the priority of values. Suppose that a government has been established by rebels. They will find it difficult to accord liberties to anyone else to express opposition[2]. For, if they believe in their own cause and the values

---

1 The Conservative Party Political Centre document *Public Order* (1970) speaks of 'a synthesis of freedom and order. It is a notoriously difficult task, but it is necessary to try to achieve it as the basis for a satisfactory system of law in a democratic society'.
2 This is so whether it is a right-winged rebellion against a left-wing régime, eg Franco's rebellion against the previous communist government, or *vice versa*.

which they espouse, they clearly cannot allow others to act on values against which they rebelled and which could imperil their hard-won position by inspiring the same sort of agitation by which they themselves weakened and eventually overthrew the previous régime. From their point of view, such agitation will be an abuse of liberty, which cannot be allowed. The result is usually two-fold: the imposition of a severe discipline consisting of sundry prohibitions and the intensive use of propaganda vilifying other points of view as 'counter-revolutionary', 'fascist', 'communist' etc, so as to justify repression. In this way a worse power-structure than that which it replaces comes into being; but the point is that the limiting of liberties, which all this entails, reflects the priority accorded to the values of those in power. Should governments have liberty to destroy liberty by the exercise of such power? If it is thought not, then the possibilities will have to be explored of imposing disabilities on them, as considered earlier. If these prove to be of no avail, it is difficult to see how any curbs can be imposed on governmental liberties to use power other than the moral self-restraint of the individuals composing government.

Apart from government there are other kinds of liberties to exercise powers. Courts may sometimes protect individuals against the abuse of power by the executive[3]; but certain other liberties to abuse power can only be dealt with by government. A Conservative Prime Minister once spoke of the 'unacceptable faces of capitalism', such as profiteering and monopolies. Employers used to be at liberty to drive unconscionable bargains with workers, and trade unions evolved to redress the unequal bargaining position. That is now a thing of the past. Here and there some abuses have been dealt with, eg by monopoly legislation, anti-trust laws etc, but others remain, as where building speculators and landlords have contributed to the land and house price problem; and so forth. Workers, who are asked to hold back on wage demands, have indeed cause for complaint when such people as these are left free to pick their way around and betwixt the law and to misuse the liberties allowed to them. These are not cases of allowing everyone equal opportunity to exercise them; the question is whether such liberties should be allowed at all. The competing values here are those of individual liberty of action and the social interest, and it is submitted that in these kinds of situations the latter should prevail. There are also 'faces of socialism' which many would regard as equally unacceptable, eg the 'closed shop' principle, which reflects a conflict between the value of individual liberty to join or not join a trade union and the collective interest of workers in a trade[4]. Again, there is the liberty to strike to the detriment of the national economy or sections of the public, which is a conflict between other values writ large.

Liberty and anarchy

At the opposite end to dictatorship is the permissive society, which allows liberties to the point where society becomes fragmented. Slogans such as 'liberality', 'tolerance', 'reasonableness', are so emotively charged that many

---

3 *Congreve v Home Office* [1976] QB 629, [1976] 1 All ER 697; *Secretary of State for Education and Science v Tameside Metropolitan Borough Council* [1977] AC 1014, [1976] 3 All ER 665; *Laker Airways Ltd v Department of Trade* [1977] QB 643, [1977] 2 All ER 182.
4 See the decision of the European Court of Human Rights against the British Government: *Young, James and Webster v United Kingdom* [1981] IRLR 408.

people become obsessed with being thought 'illiberal', 'intolerant', or 'unreasonable', which colours their approach. Also, people react justifiably against abuses of power, of which there are numerous examples, but in stepping backwards from that danger they fail to pay heed to the abyss of anarchy at their heels. To condemn an abuse of power is obviously not a denial of all exercises of power. Some exercise of it there must be to avoid chaos. If everyone insisted on complete liberty of action in using the highway, traffic would seize up; so certain limitations on liberty are imposed in the interests of all. Likewise, limitations have to be imposed on various other kinds of liberties in order to hold society together. Obviously there should be no liberty to murder, maim, steal etc, but these are extreme examples. The question is always one of the degree of latitude that should be given to the free expression of divergent views and actions.

Law and morality

Toleration of a minority implies a majority that does the tolerating; but there could come a point when so many minorities are in being that there is no majority left. Democracy itself can only work so long as the differences between groups do not impair a broad substrate of shared values. Once this disintegrates the groups will tend to become increasingly alienated from each other, and democratic government could not possibly work any more. If society does fragment in this way, distributive justice in that society ends with it, and the problem becomes one of co-existence between groups and justice between them will pose new problems to be worked out afresh. Permissive societies are always in danger of becoming weak societies unless a stand is taken at some point to uphold a broad basis of cohesive values. One of the most important cohesive factors is the shared morality of a society, and the extent to which efforts should be made to uphold a minimum morality has become the subject of dispute.

One question is whether certain moral liberties should be allowed at all, ie how far prohibitory laws should be used to uphold moral positions. First, what is the significance of the word 'should'? No one denies that many laws do reflect moral considerations[5], while many are morally neutral. The question is not whether they do or do not, but whether they should uphold morals, ie the moral justification for using laws in this way[6]. Justification is said to be needed because (i) the imposition and enforcement of legal duties limit liberty of action; any interference with liberty is said to need justification since 'liberty is ancient; it is despotism that is new'. (ii) Much of the legal reinforcement of morals involves interference with sexual freedom; and the psychological problems that can arise through the inhibition of such deep-seated drives demand that sufficient reasons be given. (iii) The freezing of moral attitudes by laws may hinder the processes of moral change; so hindrance needs justification.

Morality has hitherto been largely bound up with religion, and it is said that once a state leaves religion to private judgment it should do likewise with morality. There is, however, a distinction. Moral ideas of right and wrong dictate behaviour, but religion is a matter of belief and only influences behaviour through the moral attitudes which it fosters. Many ideas about

5 Pollock *Essays in the Law* pp 53-79.
6 Hart *Law, Liberty and Morality* pp 4, 28.

everyday morals are not peculiar to any particular religion, or any religion at all. Since the state is very much concerned with the behaviour of its citizens, it may rightly continue to concern itself with moral attitudes while renouncing interest in beliefs, except when these are thought to be conducive to undesirable behaviour, eg Scientology.

Another reason is that social existence depends upon co-ordination, which in turn requires restraint in individual action. As has been pointed out, such restraint may spring from laws imposing duties to limit liberties, or it may spring spontaneously from moral sense. Liberty and duty are jurally opposite, each beginning where the other ends. Accordingly, legal restrictions may only be relaxed safely when there is a sufficient degree of self-control bred from moral discipline[7]. This has hitherto been linked to religion, but today religion is fast losing its former appeal and with this the influence of its moral teaching. To relax legal restraints at a time when there is less and less assurance of self-discipline is the path to social destruction; which is why some reinforcement of moral discipline by law must continue.

The problem confronting law-makers is a difficult one, made worse by the modern tendency of people who, though largely apathetic, bestir themselves to protest, not against indiscipline, but against any insistence on discipline. This may be a reaction against the terrible experiences under Nazi and Fascist and similar contemporary dictatorships, which induces people to associate any sort of discipline with tyranny. A different reason may be the desire of the individual to assert his identity which, it is felt, is in danger of being lost amidst the standardised and machine-like structure of modern society.

Finally, the message which comes through history is that, although emphasis may be laid now on power and now on freedom from it, depending upon the paramount need at any particular time, thinkers of all ages have acknowledged that some restraint through laws on liberty of action is necessary if anarchy is to be avoided[8].

Next comes the interpretation of 'moral position', which is central to the problem of how far laws should uphold morality. Two persons may debate whether the law should allow or forbid the doing of something which both acknowledge to be immoral. What of the man who asks, On what basis is it judged immoral? Answers based on religion cannot appeal to non-believers and so fall outside the scope of this chapter. A secular answer given by Professor Hart is that '*some* shared morality is essential to the existence of any society'[9]. 'Essential' has two aspects. On the one hand, it means that some shared morality is an ingredient of any and every community, ie a part of every community is its morality. On the other hand, it may also connote certain additional moral ideas which have become part of the fabric of a particular society[10]. This distinction provides the respective bases for what

7 Thus, freedom of contract led to exploitation of workers by employers, so legal restrictions had to be imposed. Supporters of *apartheid* in Southern Africa sometimes resort to the argument that to give liberties and powers to Africans, who lack self-discipline not to abuse them, will lead to chaos. This needs to be set against the point that to base legal restrictions on a racial distinction and to give those who benefit from the discrimination the power to decide what amounts to a sufficient degree of self-discipline and how fast Africans should be allowed to acquire it create grave long-term problems.

8 See pp 70–85 ante.

9 *Hart* p 51. He appears to regard this as self-evident. See also Milne 'Bentham's Principle of Utility and Legal Philosophy' in *Bentham and Legal Theory* (ed James) at p 31.

10 See Mitchell *Law, Morality and Religion in a Secular Society* for elaboration.

might be termed the 'institutional' and the 'utilitarian' interpretions of 'moral position'.

The 'institutional' basis

In a lecture to the British Academy a distinguished judge, Lord Devlin, criticised the Report of the Wolfenden Committee, which had advocated lifting the ban of the criminal law from homosexuality between consenting adults[11]. He maintained that the law should continue to support a minimum morality. In the light of the widespread controversy which the lecture aroused, his position may be outlined as follows. An important point, which has subsequently been clarified, is that his case rests on the fact that each society has evolved certain moral institutions which form part of its own particular fabric. Marriage, for intance, is an institution of societies generally; but monogamy is not essential to every kind of society though it is to Christian societies, and is thus a part of their particular fabric. Just as most institutions of a society are interrelated and interdependent, so also is its particular morality; one cannot pluck one strand without puckering the whole. It has been suggested, rightly it is submitted, that Lord Devlin's case is best understood on the basis of moral intitutions which are necessary to the existence of particular societies[12].

In so far, then, as some moral ideas are part of the fabric of a given society, that society is entitled to preserve them, and thus itself, against anything capable of destroying them; which is why Lord Devlin compares contravention of this morality to treason. The law cannot undertake not to interfere[13]. For such moral institutions are like the legs of a chair; if one is pulled out, the chair may not necessarily topple over, but it will be more prone to do so. He does *not* seek to preserve moral ideas against change, as some critics have alleged; what he urges is that responsible persons should be slow to change laws protecting them.

In order to preserve itself society is entitled to use its laws when the limit of tolerance is reached. This is gauged with reference to the reasonable man, a juryman. What should count are opinions reached after informed and educated discussion of all relevant points of view (not excluding religious or any other). When opinion is divided, the majority view should prevail, as it does in the ordinary legislative process on even the weightiest matters. The following are the limits within which legislators should act. (a) There should be the maximum of freedom consistent with the integrity of society. (b) The limit of tolerance is reached when the ordinary man would feel indignation and disgust. (c) Law-makers should be slow to change. (d) Privacy should be respected as far as possible. (e) Laws should be concerned with minimum, not maximum, standards.

Lord Devlin has been attacked and defended. One objection is that his thesis involves practical difficulties which are difficult to overcome. The

---

11 Devlin 'The Enforcement of Morals' *Maccabaean Lecture in Jurisprudence* 1959, reprinted in *The Enforcement of Morals* ch 1. In the Introduction Lord Devlin considers some criticisms of his thesis. See also the later chapters.

12 *Mitchell* p 25.

13 Rostow 'The Enforcement of Morals' [1960] CLJ at 191, cites two cases, *Reynolds v US* 98 US 145 (1878) and *Musser v Utah* 333 US 95 (1948), where the Supreme Court upheld laws against polygamy notwithstanding the provision in the Constitution that 'Congress shall make no law respecting an establishment of religion or prohibiting the free exercise thereof'.

reasonable man test is too vague to apply in a given case; and so is the criterion of indignation and disgust. The workings of a juryman's mind are not entirely reassuring, while the influences that work on it in a court of law are different from those that operate outside, eg on moral issues. Also, an inevitable tendency of his thesis is that it lends itself to upholding intitutions as such without regard to those very considerations and points of view which he said should be taken into account.

The 'utilitarian' basis

Lord Devlin's principal opponent, Profesor Hart, proceeds from John Stuart Mill's utilitarianism[14]. He admits that '*some* shared morality is essential to the existence of any society[15], but the significance of this is that it connotes morality which is the *sine qua non* of the existence of any and every kind of society, not just of a particular society. Mill's thesis, adopted by the Wolfenden Committee and Professor Hart, was as follows. Strong monarchs were needed in the past to repel aggressors and to maintain order. Because power tends to be abused, they developed into tyrants; so democracy was resorted to. However, the idea that democratic government cannot be tyrannical is false, since tyranny can be exercised in ways other than by law, namely by the morality of a ruling class. 'Wherever there is an ascendant class, a large portion of the morality of the country emanates from its class interests, and its feelings of class superiority[16]. Accordingly, his plea for liberation was that laws should not uphold morality of such, but should only seek to prevent harm to others as this is disruptive of any kind of society.

As to this, it is obvious in the first place that Mill's position conceals a moral premise, namely that it is morally wrong to uphold morality as such[17]. Next, there is difficulty over the idea of 'harm to others' which includes many things. No one doubts that it covers physical hurt, but the legal prohibition of 'harm' on a broader scale is in fact acceptable even to utilitarians. Professor Hart justifies this wider interference on grounds of 'paternalism', ie the concern of the law to prevent people from harming themselves. This enables him to support the continued prohibition of certain kinds of harm even when the victim has consented[18]. An extension of the idea is seen in the question: Should a man be free to make himself unfree? Mill was quite clear that the answer is: No. 'The principle of freedom', he said, 'cannot require that he should be free not to be free. It is not freedom to be allowed to alienate his freedom'[19]. Again, Professor Hart supports the continued prohibition of homosexuality with youths by using the argument of paternalistic concern to protect them from corruption. He is here hoist with his own petard, for the very word 'corruption' implies a moral position. His concern is for the moral welfare of youth, so he is using the law to uphold morality as such after all[20]. He also resorts to paternalism in order to justify

---

14 *On Liberty*, in Mill *Utilitarianism, Liberty and Representative Government* (ed Lindsay) p 65.
15 *Hart* p 51.
16 *Mill* p 70.
17 Cf *Hart* p 17.
18 Eg the rule that consent is no defence to a criminal charge of inflicting grievous bodily harm (*R v Donovan* [1934] 2 KB 498), or to breach of statutory duty (apart from the limited exception recognised by *ICI Ltd v Shatwell* [1965] AC 656, [1964] 2 All ER 999).
19 *Mill* p 158.
20 For this and the following objections, see *Mitchell* ch 4.

the prohibition of acts which are 'offensive' to the public. Thus, it is not immoral for a husband and wife to have intercourse with each other, but it would be offensive for them to do so in public, which is why such public behaviour is rightly forbidden. Accordingly, he subscribes to the distinction drawn by the Wolfenden Committee between 'public' and 'private' behaviour, between public and private spheres of morality. The latter is not the concern of law.

There are objections to this. In the first place, public offensiveness and the immorality of conduct cannot always be separated. Thus, accosting in public is not offensive if done by a girl collecting for, say, a university rag; but it would be if done for purposes of prostitution. What makes the latter offensive is the knowledge of her immoral purpose. Nor is it possible to demarcate public from private behaviour, for what a person does in private can have repercussions outside because society is made up of a net-work of moral institutions. Because of the difficulty of marking out the boundaries of the influence of so-called 'private' actions, it is not possible to exclude these *a priori* as having no bearing on the problem. Nor can one meaningfully draw lines of demarcation between 'private' and 'public' spheres of morality, because the same action can have private or public significance depending, eg on the individual involved. Thus, a factory hand, who has an illegitimate baby, does not impinge upon the populace as does a public figure whose similar behaviour is more likely to be invoked as an example. This interrelation cuts across the public-private division, which is, therefore, unhelpful in deciding whether or not law should uphold a moral institution. Another difficulty arises out of Professor Hart's explanation of the prohibition of bigamy as analogous to public nuisance in that it is not only an affront to a public ceremony, but also throws the legal obligations of parties into confusion. Here he seems to be underlining Lord Devlin's point that both the affront and confusion stem from the fact that monogamy is the accepted institution and part of the fabric of *this* society[1].

As Lord Devlin himself has pointed out[2], if the law is entitled to show a paternalistic interest in the matters which Professor Hart specifies, why should it not show paternalistic zeal in maintaining the morals of a community? It seems curiously contradictory if people insist, as they do, that the state nowadays should assume responsibility by means of laws for education, health, trade etc, and at the same time deny it responsibility for morals. The survival of a country in a crisis depends on the resilience of its people, and moral discipline is as necessary to such strength as physical discipline is to an athlete. Self-indulgence weakens the character of individuals and ultimately of the state; which is contrary to the interests of the state. In this connection it may be noted that Professor Lloyd, supporting Professor Hart, says that 'the other side of the coin is *moral pluralism*. Would this lead to antagonism, to a society in the state of nature depicted by Hobbes, or rather to mutual tolerance, to co-existence of divergent moralities? What evidence there is comes down firmly in favour of co-existence'[3]. He gives no indication of what this evidence is, nor how there could be evidence while a situation is in flux. People on the edge of a landslide may truly say that at that precise moment collapse has not occurred. What needs to be stressed against this kind of view

1 *Mitchell* p 28.
2 *Devlin* ch 7.
3 Lloyd *Introduction to Jurisprudence* p 52.

is that there is a point at which fragmentation of values destroys cohesion, and co-existence becomes unworkable. As long as that point has not been reached people can talk about co-existence, but once divergent groups agree to differ in important respects, the very importance of these and the insistence on maintaining the respective points of view will create gulfs, which will become increasingly unbridgeable as time goes on and will lead eventually to the groups having less and less in common. The Russians perceive this very clearly. Their apparatus of secret police, exclusive propaganda and the like are designed to prevent any fragmentation of the socialist morality. They portray an extreme,which no advocate of moral pluralism could recommend. What these advocates do not appear to face is that at the other extreme moral pluralism itself will eventually cease to be, for 'pluralism', 'co-existence' and 'tolerance' presuppose that underneath the divergences there still remains some unity without which 'co-existence' and 'toleration' have no meaning. The question is whether it is possible to preserve that underlying unity simply by drawing the line of legal interference at 'harm to others'. For the reasons given, this seems inadequate.

Finally, the moral standards of a community influence the handing on of a way of life, which means that a state's concern with education cannot stop short of this point. Ideals are part of laws when these are viewed in the context of social life, and they enter into the broadest concept of 'harm to others'.

Both sides agree that laws should uphold some moral positions, though they advance different reasons. The dispute touches on the limits which should be set on their use. According to utilitarians, they should only uphold that aspect of morality which is a *sine qua non* of any type of society, whereas according to Lord Devlin they should be concerned with all the morality that constitutes the *sine qua non* of the particular society[4]. Apart from this, the utilitarians only mask, and fail to expel morality from consideration, while Lord Devlin fails to provide a workable test as to where legal reinforcement should stop.

Much of the argumentation in this debate illustrates what was said at the beginning of the book about persuasion[5]. Appeal to 'evidence' is misplaced. For intance, Professor Hart's assertion that '*some* shared morality is essential to the existence of any society' cannot be 'proved' or 'disproved' by 'evidence'. Further, morality is an area in which people hold strong views so that arguments, however persuasive, are not enough in themselves to prise them out of fixed positions; which is why this particular debate is destined to remain inconclusive. It certainly cannot be resolved by applying a single formula, like 'harm to others', or any other. In addition to what has already been discussed, it seems necessary to take account also of the type of legal machinery that might be used.

Machinery of the law

Granting that laws should uphold morality, at least to some extent, something has now to be said about the word 'uphold'. The two concepts that may be invoked are disability and duty.

---

4 *Mitchell* ch 2, especially at p 25. For a different analysis, see Samek 'The Enforcement of Morals: A Basic Re-examiniation in its Historical Setting' (1971) 49 Can BR 188; also Lord MacDermott *Protection from Power under English Law* pp 8, 195.
5 See p 14 ante.

DISABILITY. Abolishing the duty not to indulge, eg in homosexuality, does not affect its immoral quality, just as adultery remains immoral though it is no longer an offence in this country. The moral attitude might still be 'upheld' by rules attaching disabilities with regard to immoral conduct. Thus, contracts to commit homosexuality could continue to be void, and ground no collateral claims for unfair dismissal[6]; and there may still be disability to sue *ex turpi causa*. The law may go further and 'uphold' the moral attitude in other collateral ways, eg by punishing advertisement of homosexuality as a conspiracy to corrupt[7], and by treating an allegation of homosexuality as an imputation against character[8].

DUTY. Direct prohibition of immoral conduct by means of duty is more troublesome. Its functioning should be taken into account along with other considerations. The following factors would seem to be relevant. (i) The danger of the activity to others; (ii) the danger to the actor himself; (iii) economy of forces needed for detection and pursuit; (iv) equality of treatment; (v) the nature of the sanction; (vi) possible hardship caused by the sanction; and (vii) possible side-effects. It is submitted that the question whether or not laws should be used to uphold morality through direct prohibition is better dealt with on the basis of a calculus such as this rather than on some simple formula like 'harm to others'.

The machinery of the civil law is inappropriate for two reasons. Its remedy is usually compensation, but this is owing only to unwilling victims and is thus inapplicable to cases of consent or of immorality with animals. Besides, compensation may easily develop into a trade in vice. The machinery of the criminal law has the advantage that it is already geared to giving effect to the interests of the state, but it also has disadvantages. One is that punishment is not the cure. When meted out as revenge, it presupposes a victim, and there is no victim when he has consented. Its deterrent effect depends on the likelihood of being caught. If this is small, as is usually the case with sexual misconduct, the deterrent influence is small too. Again, punishment can have deleterious effects, for sexual immorality stems from deep-seated drives which need channelling, not punishment. One strives to cure disease, not to punish sufferers. Finally, the words 'crime' and 'criminal' are emotively charged. People who object to the epithet 'criminal' might not object to 'treatment', or some equivalent. Ideally what is required is some machinery that will give effect to the interests of the state in upholding moral institutions without the stigma of 'criminal' attaching to it and which will provide curative treatment. Something along the lines of juvenile courts, where reference to 'criminality' is avoided, seems to be indicated.

RESTRAINT OF LIBERTY

Restraint of liberty is a more deep-seated problem than power. In the first place, liberty stands behind the very exercise of power. Whatever kind of

6 *Coral Leisure Group v Barnett* [1981] ICR 503.
7 *Knuller (Publishing, Printing and Promotions) Ltd v DPP* [1973] AC 435, [1972] 2 All ER 898. Approaches for homosexual purposes between adults are approaches for 'immoral purposes' within s 32 of the Sexual Offences Act 1956: *R v Ford* [1978] 1 All ER 1129, [1977] 1 WLR 1083.
8 *R v Bishop* [1975] QB 274, [1974] 2 All ER 1206.

power one has, there is usually a liberty to exercise it or not[9]. The danger of abuse has to be met by abolishing the power and replacing it with a disability, which was considered in the last chapter; or by abolishing the liberty and replacing it with an externally imposed duty not to exercise that power; or through voluntary restraint in its exercise. Secondly, at the other end of the scale and removed from oppression is permissiveness, which gives free rein to liberties of action. The giving of equal liberties could reach the point of anarchy and the question then is how liberties, which are destructive if exercised abusively, are to be restrained. Finally, even where the law limits liberty by replacing it with a duty not to do some act so that the individual no longer has any liberty *at law*, he still has an inner *moral liberty* to obey the law or to disobey. Law here reaches its limit. For restraint on liberty beyond this point can only derive from self-restraint and self-discipline, and all that law can ever hope to do so is to help in indirect ways to promote the necessary moral sense of obligation. It is for these reasons that the problem of liberty cuts far deeper than that of power.

Forces of moderation appear to be in retreat at the present time and a sense of obligation is at low ebb. Strikers, for intance, seek to cast on government, or other body against which they act, the responsibility for their own calculated exercise of liberty to hit the public, arguing that they have been driven to such action. The justice of their cause is not the point; it is the justice of the means adopted[10]. Is liberty to hit the innocent a just way of furthering a cause? When the point of moral liberty is reached, any restraining influence on it must spring from inner motivations, whether through fear of punishment or through a sense of obligation, which in turn is bound up with the extent to which people are prepared to accept standards and have a sense of purpose and faith in a way of life. The law is directly involved in the imposition and enforcement of punishment, but with regard to promoting the acceptance of standards and faith in a way of life it can only play an indirect part at most.

Within limits the courts can sometimes restrain governmental exercises of liberty. If reasons are given for a certain action, they can inquire into their adequacy; if none are given, they are powerless. More important is their use of 'unreasonableness' as a check on the exercise of executive discretion the details of which must be sought in books on administrative law[11].

With regard to individual liberties of action, the inhibition of the liberty to disobey through fear of punishment has been touched on[12]. Leaving that aside, the abandonment of standards might also be discouraged to some extent, as pointed out above, by attaching disabilities to certain activities. Neither of these methods promotes a sense of obligation; they do no more

---

9 For power coupled with a duty to exercise it or not to exercise it, see pp 36–38 ante.
10 Most kidnappers and hi-jackers, who kill, or threaten to kill, innocent victims, are also convinced of the justice of their cause and they, too, seek to cast responsibility for what they do away from themselves.
11 See, eg *Roberts v Hopwood* [1925] AC 578, *Laker Airways Ltd v Department of Trade* [1977] QB 643. Cf *Secretary of State for Education v Tameside Metropolitan Borough Council* [1977] AC 1014, [1976] 3 All ER 665. In *Asher v Secretary of State for the Environment* [1974] Ch 208, [1974] 1 All ER 156, a Minister exercised his discretion to uphold the law and the court supported him. Cf *Gouriet v Union of Post Office Workers* [1978] AC 435, [1977] 3 All ER 70, where the court upheld the Attorney General's discretion to refuse to uphold the law, which seems wrong, since it was upholding the latter's use of law as an instrument of government policy, ie 'rule by law'.
12 See p 51 ante. See also pp 313 et seq. post.

than indicate the probable consequences when such sense is lacking[13]. Nor is fear the only, or even decisive, factor in securing obedience[14].

A more powerful inducement towards obedience comes from an acceptance of the standards underlying the law[15]. Indeed, resort to legal prohibition of undesirable behaviour may safely be kept to a minimum as long as there is acceptance of moral standards which discourage it, for the self-restraint which these inspire will check any abuse of the liberty allowed at law. The law can only help indirectly in the acceptance of standards by discouraging their abandonment. For instance, where there are laws, especially those embodying the standards of that shared morality, which, according to Professor Hart, is essential to any society, the upholding of such laws not only points to the existence of the standards, but also helps to preserve them by acting as a brake on their abandonment. It is precisely at a time when standards are being questioned that it becomes socially suicidal to relax laws simply because they are being questioned or are difficult to apply. This is not to argue that there should be no change; questioning is only the first wind of this. It is quite another thing to abolish legal restraints at a time when moral restraints are already on the wane since this could end in destroying society, not changing it.

Upholding laws, therefore, helps by preserving a 'moral atmosphere', which is essential to preserving that shared morality, which in turn is essential to encouraging obedience and social existence. It gives heart to those who support standards and wish to conform. *Their* point of view should not be overlooked, for they too deserve to be heard and have been ignored for too long. Laws also set criteria by which non-conformity is acknowledged to be disobedience and illegal even by dissidents. Conformity must remain the norm; it is for non-conformists to justify themselves[16]. This is most important, for to remove a sense of disobedience and illegality by removing the law is to remove a support of the social fabric[17]. Besides, the standards embodied

---

13 Cf: 'Students who are accorded the coveted privilege of attending an educational institution, founded and maintained from public funds, and who grossly abuse that privilege by resorting to public violence, will be dealt with severely when they come before the courts. The privilege conferred upon them imposes a duty to act in a responsible and mature way and the privilege of attendance does not confer on them the right to interfere in any way in the day-to-day administration of the institution during their brief sojourn there': Macdonald JP in *State v Katsande* 1974 (1) SA 355 at 362. The duty referred to is clearly not the duty not to cause criminal damage, since it would be a *non sequitur* to say that the liberty to attend a university imposes that duty. What is referred to is the moral duty to exercise liberty responsibly.

14 This was pointed out by Bryce *Studies in History and Jurisprudence* II pp 6 et seq. See pp 48 et seq. ante and p 248 post.

15 This is the essential point in Goodhart *English Law and the Moral Law*. Llewellyn *Jurisprudence: Realism in Theory and Practice* ch 18, points out that obedience is a matter of habit and practice; Fried 'Moral Causation' (1963–64) 77 Harv LR 1258, distinguishes moral causation of obedience from psychological causation and moral persuasion.

16 Puner 'Civil Disobedience: an Analysis and Rationale' (1968) 43 NYULR 651 (and see also the other contributions to this issue); Wasserstrom 'The Obligation to Obey' in *Essays in Legal Philosophy* (ed Summers) 274.

17 In the 'Clay Cross' Affair (1974) certain local councillors exercised their private judgment that an Act of Parliament passed by a Conservative government was unjust, and they disobeyed it. The succeeding Labour government not only repealed the Act, but also sought to remove the illegality of their disobedience retrospectively. Such a vindication of the liberty to disobey strikes a damaging blow to the upholding of law. Even more disastrous for law and the authority of Parliament was the refusal by the Attorney General to take action to prevent an organised defiance of an Act of Parliament: *Gouriet v Union of Post Office Workers*

in the law are the criteria by which the outside world judges a country, and no country can now live in isolation or afford to ignore world opinion altogether. The presence of laws is also helpful in persuasion and reform of dissidents and in providing points of reference when weighing up the pros and cons of proposed action[18]. Indeed, upholding laws may even in time shape the *mores* of the community. It has been said with some degree of truth that forcing people not to behave in certain ways does not make them moral; it merely sets up taboos. This is true up to a point, but there is also the countervailing influence that the regular enforcement of law does produce a psychological adjustment towards acceptance of its standards[19]. The law can have an educative function to perform, which could be impaired by failures to uphold laws. Besides, every failure estops the authorities from trying to uphold a law on a subsequent occasion.

A commonly advanced reason for abolishing laws, especially those concerning moral standards, is that these may have become difficult to enforce ie detect and visit with sanctions, which is said to lead to discrimination in punishment in that only some people are punished and not others. This is a fallacious argument, for it confuses discrimination in punishment with catching offenders. Even if many violations of a law go undetected, it is important to deal firmly with cases that are detected. A large number of murders may go undetected, but is that an argument for abolishing the law against murder? Unenforceability is a matter of degree, and difficulty of enforcement, however great, should never be a ground *per se* for abolishing any law[20]. The argument rests on the premise that only enforceable laws should be preserved. But enforceability is less significant in ensuring obedience than the psychological pressure towards conformity exerted by the fact of other people's conformity. Successful disobedience by one person relaxes the pressure to obey by setting an example to someone else to disobey in circumstances in which the first person would still have obeyed, and he is estopped from protesting that the second person has gone further than he would have desired. The more numerous the cases of disobedience, the weaker becomes the pressure. Even so, some residue of pressure always remains by virtue of the fact that *some* persons continue to obey and by virtue of the mere existence of something possessing the quality of 'law', which casts on deviants the onus of justifying themselves. The danger of abolishing a law because it it unenforceable and is being disobeyed is that it weakens at one stroke the pressure to conform even to other enforceable laws; which is how laws once enforceable *become* unenforceable in time. In short, to talk of maintaining only enforceable laws is to take the first step towards undermining *their* enforceability.

Enforceability of a law depends on the observance by the officials concerned of other laws giving effect to the penalty. Once they are discouraged

---

[1978] AC 435, [1977] 3 All ER 70, on which see Dias *Götterdämmerung: Gods of the Law in Decline'* (1981) 1 Legal Studies 1.
18 Palley 'Constitutional Devices in Multi-racial and Multi-religious Societies' (1968) 19 NILQ 381 et seq.
19 Olivecrona *Law as Fact* (1939) pp 147-148; Lord Simon in *Charter v Race Relations Board* [1973] AC 868 at 900, [1973] 1 All ER 512 at 527. Plato and Aristotle taught that to rule is to educate; while the Soviet Union is engaged in a gigantic effort to educate the masses for communism. See pp 51-52, and ch 19 post.
20 On the need to enforce laws particularly in this kind of situation, see Dietze *Two Concepts of the Rule of Law* especially ch II.

because of lack of interest in upholding laws, the practical foundation of law-enforcement as a whole is eroded[21].

Another argument is that the support of dissidents may be won back by removing laws against which there is widespread protest; otherwise the disobedience that is likely to ensue might bring all law into disrepute. This, too, is a dangerous argument, particularly when discontent threatens to be general. For in such a climate there has invariably been a prior loss of support for the standards involved independently of the laws reflecting them; criticism of the latter is only the consequence. Support for those same standards used to be forthcoming, often for generations, and in some cases along with more stringent laws than exist presently. If, then, support for the standards has been lost independently of laws, abolition of the latter will not win back or preserve one jot of support even for what is left. Instead, the abolition will simply be accepted as of course and become a basis for demanding the relaxation of yet other standards and laws. It is important to remember that those loyal to standards and laws should not be betrayed. Removal of laws as a concession to dissidents is more likely to bring about the loss of *their* confidence and faith. The easing of laws and penalties on anti-social conduct may conceivably result in less freedom and safety for the law-abiding. As Dietze puts it: 'Just as the despotic variant of democracy all too often has jeopardised human rights, its permissive variant threatens these rights by exposing citizens to the crimes of their fellow-men'[22]. Mere condemnation of such behaviour and words of sympathy with victims are never enough without firm action giving practical effect to such sentiments. The more law-abiding people lose confidence in the law and those in authority to protect them, the more will they be driven to the alternative of taking matters into their own hands, the perils of which are unthinkable and are nearer than some liberally-minded philanthropists seem inclined to allow[1].

Something more positive than just the preservation of a moral atmosphere is needed to foster the acceptance of common standards and moral restraint in liberties of action. A unifying force is required, which can only derive from a sense of common purpose and faith in a way of life. Such a sense of unity becomes manifest in times of national crisis, such as a war; but these are of short duration. To achieve lasting unity a lead has to come from a common moral inspiration and a sense of obligation. It must be a *lead* if it is to inspire people with a sense of social responsibility and induce them to 'pull together'. If morality is regarded simply as a reflex of socieiety, it will only tend towards greater and greater diversification in permissive societies[2]. The irresistible conclusion is that such a lead must come from religion, whatever its form or name. Simply to have faith in a way of life is not enough. This may pull people together and provide inspiration for a time, as national-socialism did in Hitlerite Germany. It has to be a just way of life,

---

21 Constant criticism by the Labour left of police action to uphold the law during the miners' strike of 1984 induced at least one leading police officer to say that the police might have to reconsider their position when the next Labour government comes into power. His view was repudiated, but the point was made.

22 *Dietze* p 54.

1 Northern Ireland is an example. Cf Green 'Law and Morality in a Changing Society' (1970) UTLJ 422 at 433.

2 A democratic system where elected representatives are only 'mandated mouthpieces' of their particular constituencies can work as long as there is a measure of shared values throughout the entire electorate. Once this ceases to exist, the mandate system becomes unworkable.

particularly one in which neither power not liberty is abused, if it is to last. In the past it was religion that inculcated moral restraints on action, and as long as religious dictates held sway the law could hold back. Today when so many religions are losing their hold, the need is to re-establish their appeal. The little that law can conceivably do towards this end is to lend its techniques and discipline to a re-examination of established religious ideas, which could make them more acceptable[3]. An exploration of these possibilities will overstep the bounds of this book, but this is not to imply that they have nothing to do with jurisprudential study. The problems of liberty and obedience are very much its concern. The 'legal' and 'non-legal' motivations behind them are mutually influential and to draw a boundary between them is like trying to draw a line between night and day.

The last aspect of this problem is the promotion of liberty with a sense of obligation[4]. At present too much emphasis is placed on 'rights' and too little on duties. Law *serves* society; it should, therefore, help to promote a sense of obligation and to ascribe primacy to duties rather than to 'rights'[5]. The welfare state has done much to foster insistence on rights. It is not that welfare services are bad, but that they can have undesirable side-effects unless there is a corresponding emphasis on what people owe to society in return for the benefits they receive[6]. How a sense of obligation is to be instilled through law involves delicate questions of policy. Perhaps, something might be done by withholding welfare benefits from the families of those who strike at society, which has to bear the responsibility for them; but what constitutes 'striking at society' and who decides this need to be worked out with the utmost care. Industrial action by workers and unions is a sphere of activity that springs immediately to mind and is a peculiarly sensitive one. Nowadays the inter-dependence of people in society is such that whole sections of the nation, sometimes the nation itself, can be stricken into impotence

3 With regard to Christianity, for instance, a comparison of the 'facts' on which it is based with the legal conception of 'facts' and methods of establishing these might induce a revised and perhaps more acceptable attitude towards 'belief'. For the unpreparedness of lawyers to cope with religious 'belief', see *US v Ballard* 322 US 78 (1944); 329 US 187 (1946), on appeal twice to the Supreme Court from 138 F (2d) 540, and 152 F (2d) 941, concerning Ballard's belief that he had talked and shaken hands with Jesus Christ in San Francisco. Also, the legal techniques of interpreting precedents and statutes might be deployed in interpreting religious texts. For a suggestion, see Dias 'Law at the End of its Tether' [1972B] CLJ at 312-314.

4 See on this problem Cole 'Private Morality and Public Law' (1968) 54 Am BAJ 158; Morris 'American Society and the Rebirth of Civil Obedience' (1968) 54 Am BAJ 653.

5 For this reason Honoré's treatment of justice from the angle of claims alone seems unduly one-sided: 'Social Justice' in *Essays in Legal Philosophy* (ed Summers) p 61. Some of the greatest philosophies, notably that of the ancient Jews, stress the primacy of obligation (see pp 72-73 ante). It is also central to the theory of Duguit, eg *Law in the Modern State* (trans F and H J Laski) (see pp 436-439 post). In a recent analysis of justice, Rawls brings in, subject to qualification, the obligation towards society to uphold just institutions as long as one accepts its benefits: *A Theory of Justice* (see pp 000, 000 post). Some of those who currently produce pornography assert a liberty to indoctrinate children with their views. They may be sincere in what is to them a crusade. But (a) it is curious that they are also foremost in opposing indoctrination of children with religion on the ground that they cannot think for themselves. Besides, (b) indoctrination is not a bad thing as such; it depends on what is instilled. Religious indoctrination at least teaches service and duty to others; pornographic indoctrination teaches self-indulgence. From a social point of view, the former is tolerable, the latter is not.

6 See p 67 ante.

by one group or other taking strike action[7]. As long as the liberty to do this sort of thing is neither limited nor controlled[8], the law would appear to condone a form of blackmail, especially when such action is calculated to coincide with occasions when maximum hardship and inconvenience can be inflicted on countless numbers of persons, who are in no way responsible for or involved in the disputes. In a different sphere, that of crime, criminals could be made to do social work as reparation in proportion to their offences; but this is hedged by difficulties with trade unions[9].

The development of no-fault insurance to replace the traditional basis of liability in tort law in many areas[10] poses a problem of conflict. On the one hand, it meets the need to compensate victims, especially those who sustain catastrophic loss through some trivial fault, by protecting them against impecunious defendants. On the other hand, in so far as it may reduce or abandon emphasis on wrongdoing it could have a long term effect on standards. Severing the link between compensation for plaintiffs and the fault of defendants is beneficial provided the inadmissible inference is not drawn that because compensation for victims is not dependent on fault, therefore fault is irrelevant. Other means, administrative perhaps, should be devised to register disapproval of fault, eg loss of bonuses, increased premiums, contributions to insurance funds etc, the extent of which might well be related to the degree of fault[11]. Popular psychology has spread the idea that deviant behaviour is the result, not of the delinquent's moral shortcoming, but of the failure of others (parents, environment etc). The incessant barrage along this line through the mass media does not help with the problem of instilling a sense of obligation, if it does not actually hinder. The broad proposition has some truth, but it has come to be regarded as if it represents the whole truth; which it does not. For, logically, if the failure of the present generation is attributable to the past, the failure of the next generation must be attributable to the present. In short, to foist responsibility away from oneself and onto others in the past, *is* to accept responsibility now for others in the future.

It is the latter aspect of this proposition that needs to be put across, since as soon as a person can be made to appreciate the responsibility of others and of circumstances for what he is, that is precisely the moment at which he has become capable of appreciating his own responsibilities. The present-day tendency, however, is such that there is no lack of persons to raise an outcry against any insistence on self-discipline or show of firmness in dealing with trouble-makers, or potential trouble-makers, at any rate on those occasions that achieve publicity[12]. The consequences of this are

7 Cf Duguit's doctrine of 'social solidarity', pp 436-439 post. For the problem, see *Lord Mac-Dermott* ch 7.
8 In *Collymore v A-G* [1970] AC 538, [1969] 2 All ER 1207, the Privy Council held that the liberty of association was not impaired by limiting the liberty to strike.
9 McClean 'Reparation by the Offender' (1971) 34 MLR 436; Wootton 'Community Service' [1973] Crim LR 16; Powers of Criminal Courts Act 1973, ss 14-17.
10 New Zealand: Accident Compensation Act No 43 of 1972 (amended by the Accident Compensation Amendment (No 2) Act 1973). For Great Britain, see the Report of the Royal Commission *On Civil Liability and Compensation for Personal Injury* (Cmnd 7054-1).
11 Thus meeting Viscount Simond's point in *The Wagon Mound* [1961] AC 388 at 426-427, [1961] 1 All ER 404 at 413.
12 Eg the Archbishop of Canterbury's call to the nation for a spiritual regeneration was condemned by the Bishop of Southwark, who chose to treat it as a defence of capitalism (see *The Times* 16 October and 1 November 1975); the Editorial in the *Law Guardian* July/August 1970 (No 61) protested against the sentences passed on the 'Garden House' rioters; Drewry 'Freedom and Order' (1970) 120 NLJ 1142 criticised *Public Order* (Conservative Party Pol-

incalculable: it discourages the law-abiding, it undermines law-enforcement and, worst of all, minimises the chance of inculcating any sense of obligation.

Psychologists and psychiatrists will probably admit that their subjects are still in their infancy, for they have not yet evolved the wherewithal by which they can know when their theories are wrong[13]. There is seldom any difficulty in weaving plausible theories in these subjects; the difficulty lies in testing them. A sense of social obligation is certainly not promoted by plunging into penal reform on such hypotheses or by ameliorating punishments without at least substituting some sort of compulsory service by wrongdoers either to society or to their victims. Be kind by all means, but not at the expense of standards. To be merciful to a wrongdoer is one thing; to carry that to the point of refusing to see any wrongness in the doing is quite another. It is as foolish to have a sense of compassion without a sense of social obligation as it is to have no sense of compassion at all.

There is now greater distrust and lack of confidence in authority than used to be the case. So obsessed are certain people with the perils of the abuse of power that they are blind to the perils of the abuse of liberty. To advocate liberty as such is to adopt a negative attitude, for the gist of liberty is the *absence* of duty. However much its champions may believe that they are taking up a positive stand, they are not mindful of what people actually do with their liberties, but are far more concerned to see that there shall be fewer and fewer limitations and controls, or even none at all. Added to this is the point that the doom of liberty itself lies at the end of the road of unlimited liberty. A more positive and constructive approach would be to concentrate on duty, on obligations towards society, and to work outwards from these towards liberties. *Some* exercise of power there must be to prohibit certain forms of liberty; and a sense of values and standards will help to keep in perspective the dangers of the misuse of both power and liberty[14]. The absence of such a sense is all the sadder in those critics of authority, who are usually so well meaning.

The prevention of the abuse of power and liberty must end on a speculative and inconclusive note. They remain problems because the solutions to them, which are two of the main tasks of justice, are as yet far away.

---

itical Centre pamphlet) on the ground that there should have been prior 'agreement about basic definitions'; Hepple 'Aliens and Administrative Justice: the Dutschke Case' (1971) 34 MLR 501, criticised the deportation of an acknowledged agitator. How do any of these help in dealing with future situations in the present climate? Neither casuistry nor legalistic arguments derived from the analysis of bygone incidents take account of the fact that in the days when the British 'rule of law' gave sanctuary to Marx, Engels, Kropotkin and others, it was operating in a vastly different social, political and world arena from that of today.

13 For an apt statement about sociology, see Sprott *Sociology* p 39, quoted at p 421 n 2 post.

14 For Lord MacDermott the preservation of public order effectually 'is a first task': *Lord MacDermott* p 7; and for the moral quality in law, see pp 8, 195. Goodhart 'Freedom under the Law' (1960) 1 Tasm LR 375, shows how legal control came to be thought of as necessary to freedom. See also Carritt 'Liberty and Equality' (1940) 56 LQR 61; Hale *Freedom Through Law*. On the need to uphold authority for the sake of human freedoms, see Humphrey 'Human Rights and Authority' (1970) 20 UTLJ 412.

READING LIST

N Anderson *Liberty, Law and Justice* (Hamlyn Lecture Series).

E F Carritt 'Liberty and Equality' (1940) 56 Law Quarterly Review 6.

P Devlin *The Enforcement of Morals* chs 1, 6.

M Ginsberg *On Justice in Society* ch 12.

A L Goodhart *English Law and the Moral Law* (Hamlyn Lectures Series).

A L Goodhart 'Freedom under the Law' (1960) 1 Tasmanian Law Review 375.

L C Greene 'Law and Morality in a Changing Society' (1970) 20 University of Toronto Law Journal 422.

R L Hale *Freedom Through Law*.

H L A Hart *Law, Liberty and Morality*.

J Humphrey 'Human Rights and Authority' (1970) 20 University of Toronto Law Journal 412.

J S Mill *Utilitarianism, Liberty and Representative Government* (ed A D Lindsay) 65.

B G Mitchell *Morality and Religion in a Secular Society*.

E F Morris 'American Society and the Rebirth of Civil Obedience' (1968) 54 American Bar Association Journal 653.

N W Puner 'Civil Disobedience: an Analysis and Rationale' (1968) 43 New York University Law Review 63.

N St John Stevas *Law and Morals*.

K W Wasserstrom 'The Obligation to Obey' in *Essays in Legal Philosophy* (ed R S Summers) 274.

C H and W M Whiteley *The Permissive Morality*.

CHAPTER 7

Justice in deciding disputes: precedent

The fourth major task of justice, and one which lies especially within the province of lawyers, is giving just decisions in disputes. In Aristotelian terms this would fall under 'corrective justice'.

Deciding disputes involves three kinds of knowledge: knowing the facts, knowing the law applicable to those facts, and knowing the just way of applying the law to them. Knowing the law involves knowing how to find it in judicial precedents, statutes and immemorial customs and will be dealt with in that order in this and the following two chapters; knowing the just way of applying the law will be dealt with in Chapter 10.

As mentioned before, the doctrine of precedent in Britain has assumed a special form, known as *stare decisis*, the effect of which is that judicial decisions have binding force and enjoy law-quality *per se*. Bindingness depends on the hierarchy of courts; higher courts bind lower courts, never *vice versa*. Law-quality relates to the principle behind a decision, its *ratio decidendi*, as stated by Jessel MR: 'The only thing in a Judge's decision binding as an authority upon a subsequent Judge is the principle upon which the case was decided'[1]. The two aspects are independent. A decision of the High Court, for example, is 'law' although it is not binding on any court superior to itself. Two conditions had to be satisfied before *stare decisis* could become established. (1) There had to be a settled judicial hierarchy before there could be any clear-cut doctrine of *binding* authority, for until then it could not be known whose decisions bound whom. (2) There had also to be reliable reports of cases; if cases are to be authoritative as 'law', there should be precise records of what they lay down. Only about the middle of the last century were these conditions fulfilled, and it is from about then that the modern doctrine emerges.

Stare decisis should also be distinguished from another doctrine known as *res judicata*, which means that the final judgment of a competent court may not be disputed by the parties or their successors or any third parties in any subsequent legal proceeding. The main differences between the two doctrines are:

(1) *Res judicata* applies to the decision in the dispute, while *stare decisis* operates as to the ruling of law involved.
(2) *Res judicata* normally binds only the parties and their successors. *Stare decisis*, relating as it does to the ruling of law, binds everyone, including those who come before the courts in other cases.
(3) *Res judicata* applies to all courts. *Stare decisis* is brought into operation only by decisions of the High Court and higher courts.

1 *Osborne v Rowlett* (1880) 13 ChD 774 at 785.

(4) *Res judicata* takes effect after the time for appealing against a decision is past. *Stare decisis* operates at once[2].

HIERARCHY OF COURTS

As long as the hierarchy of courts remained unsettled, the modern doctrine of bindingness could not come into existence. It assumed substantially its present shape in the Judicature Acts 1873–1875, and is now modified by the Courts Act 1971. Rivalry used to exist, not only between the common law courts and Chancery, but between the common law courts themselves. After these had passed away, and even before the Judicature Acts, the modern doctrine began to make its appearance[3]. The Judicature Acts finally reorganised the courts into an unified structure surmounted by the House of Lords as the ultimate appellate court. Such a clear pyramid of authority was essential to the operation of any doctrine of bindingness, the full rigour of which was achieved when the House of Lords decided in 1898 that it was bound by its own decisions[4]. Since then the difficulties of too rigid an application of the doctrine led to the admission of exceptions, and in 1966 the House of Lords announced that it will no longer be bound by its decisions[5].

Only decisions of the High Court and above are quotable as 'law'[6]. With regard to the binding force of decisions, the rule is that higher courts bind lower courts; courts of co-ordinate authority do not bind each other. The High Court does not bind itself. Where two High Court decisions are in conflict, the judge in a third case should follow the later decision, unless he is convinced that the judge in the later decision was wrong in not following the earlier case[7]. The Court of Appeal and possibly Divisional Courts still consider themselves bound by their own decisions. The detailed rules govern-

2 Art 59 of the Statute of the International Court of Justice expressly applies the doctrine of *res judicata* to its decisions, and expressly rejects *stare decisis*. It does not specifically allude to the wide doctrine of precedent which has in fact been acted on. See eg *The Lotus* (1927) PCIJ Ser A No 10; *The Corfu Channel Case* (1948) ICJ Reps 15.

3 See eg the classic statement of Parke J in *Mirehouse v Rennell* (1833) 1 Cl & Fin 527 at 546.

4 *London Tramways Co v LCC* [1898] AC 375. On the persistent miscitation of this case as 'London Street Tramways Co', see Leach 'Revisionism in the House of Lords: the Bastion of Rigid *Stare Decisis* Falls' (1967) 80 Harv LR 800 n 11.

5 *Note (Judicial Precedent)* [1966] 3 All ER 77, [1966] 1 WLR 1234. The Court of Appeal has also declared itself bound by its own decisions, subject to certain qualifications: *Young v Bristol Aeroplane Co Ltd* [1944] KB 718, [1944] 2 All ER 293; and see *Miliangos v George Frank (Textiles) Ltd* [1975] QB 487, [1975] 1 All ER 1076. Since the Note (Judicial Precedent) in the House of Lords, the Court of Appeal has reaffirmed the fact that it continues to be bound by a decision of the Lords, however questionable it may be: *Conway v Rimmer* [1967] 2 All ER 1260, [1967] 1 WLR 1031, subsequently reversed by the House of Lords [1968] AC 910, [1968] 1 All ER 874, which was the first case since the Note (Judicial Precedent) which their Lordships refused to follow their own previous decision.

6 Crown Courts, established by the Courts Act 1971, are 'superior courts' according to s 4 (1). This is so when they hear cases on indictment, but they are also said to bear some of the 'stigmata of inferior courts': *Sirros v Moore* [1975] QB 118, [1974] 3 All ER 776.

7 *Colchester Estates (Cardiff) v Carlton Industries plc* [1984] 2 All ER 601, [1984] 3 WLR 693. *Young v Bristol Aeroplane Co Ltd* [1944] KB 718, [1944] 2 All ER 293, CA; *Huddersfield Police Authority v Watson* [1947] KB 842, [1947] 2 All ER 193, DC; *R v Greater Manchester Coroner, ex p Tal* [1985] QB 67, [1984] 3 All ER 240. The Criminal Division of the Court of Appeal is bound in the same way as the Civil Division except where the liberty of the subject is involved, in which case the court will not follow a previous decision in the interests of justice: *R v Spencer* [1985] 1 All ER 673, [1985] 2 WLR 197.

ing the hierarchy of authority will not be discussed here for want of space, but they are readily accessible elsewhere[8]. Certain special aspects, however, do require mention. The first concerns the rule that the Court of Appeal is bound by its own decisions. This is known as the rule in *Young v Bristol Aeroplane Co Ltd*[9], and it is subject to significant qualifications:

(1) If two decisions are in conflict, the Court of Appeal must choose between them.

(2) If a decision, although not overruled, is inconsistent with a decision of the House of Lords or of the Judicial Committee of the Privy Council[10], the Court of Appeal is not bound by it.

(3) If a decision was given *per incuriam*, ie in ignorance of a statute or other binding authority, the Court of Appeal is not bound by it; nor may it be bound where the previous court had followed an incomplete report of a still earlier case[11]. The *incuria* rule does not apply where the previous court, which is alleged to have overlooked an earlier case, had in fact alluded to it[12]; nor does it apply where the earlier of the conflicting cases exerted only persuasive authority[13].

These exceptions create difficulties. The first allows the Court of Appeal to choose between two of its own conflicting decisions[14], which seems eminently necessary. Its application, however, is far from straightforward. In *Fisher v Ruislip-Northwood UDC and Middlesex County Council*[15] the Court of Appeal refused to be bound by earlier decisions of its own which distinguished a still earlier case. It held instead that they were in conflict and proceeded to follow the decision which had been held in the later cases to be distinguishable. This seems inconsistent with the decision in *Hogan v Bentinck West Hartley Collieries*[16] where the Court of Appeal held that it was not competent to consider two earlier decisions as being in conflict when it had previously treated them as not inconsistent. More serious is the implication of saying that two decisions are in conflict. Logically the exception contradicts the rule. For, if the Court of Appeal propounds a rule in one case and a different rule in another, the later of the two must either have been decided

---

8 Eg Cross *Precedent in English Law*, chs 3–4; for literature, see Dias *Bibliography* pp 26–32.

9 [1944] KB 718, [1944] 2 All ER 293.

10 *Re Polemis & Furness Withy & Co Ltd* [1921] 3 KB 560, disapproved in *The Wagon Mound* [1961] AC 388, [1961] 1 All ER 404, not followed in *Doughty v Turner Manufacturing Co Ltd* [1964] 1 QB 518, [1964] 1 All ER 98. See also *Worcester Works Finance Ltd v Cooden Engineering Co Ltd* [1972] 1 QB 210 at 217, 219, [1971] 3 All ER 708 at 711, 712–713.

11 *Industrial Properties (Barton Hill) Ltd v Associated Electrical Industries Ltd* [1977] QB 580, [1977] 2 All ER 293.

12 For an inadmissible application of the *incuria* rule, see *Broome v Cassell & Co Ltd* [1971] 2 QB 354, [1971] 2 All ER 187, disapproved on appeal by the House of Lords [1972] AC 1027, [1972] 1 All ER 801. For a limit on the *incuria* rule, see *Miliangos v George Frank (Textiles) Ltd* [1976] AC 443, [1975] 3 All ER 801.

13 *Johnson v Agnew* [1978] Ch 176 at 189, 198, [1978] 3 All ER 314, 320, 328 (varied [1980] AC 367, [1979] 1 All ER 883).

14 *The Nowy Sacz* [1979] QB 236 at 249–250, [1978] 2 All ER 297 at 305; *W A Sherratt Ltd v John Bromley (Church Stretton) Ltd* [1985] 1 All ER 216, [1985] 2 WLR 742.

15 [1945] KB 584, [1945] 2 All ER 458, preferring *Morrison v Sheffield Corpn* [1917] 2 KB 866 to *Lyus v Stepney Borough Council* [1941] 1 KB 134, [1940] 4 All ER 463; *Wodehouse v Levy* [1940] 2 KB 561, [1940] 4 All ER 14, and *Fox v Newcastle-upon-Tyne Corpn* [1941] 2 KB 120, [1941] 2 All ER 563.

16 [1948] 1 All ER 129.

in ignorance of the earlier, in which event it falls under the third exception and is accordingly invalid; or it must have violated the rule that the court is bound, in which event also it is invalid. To assert that the court may choose between them and perhaps prefer the later case is in effect to escape from the rule itself by according validity to the very case which has violated it. If, on the one hand, it is thought that the exception applies only to decisions prior to *Young's Case*, not only is there nothing in support of such a view, but it would also be difficult to reconcile it with the declaratory theory of precedent. If, on the other hand, the logical view is followed that it must be the earlier case that is the binding authority, a curious possibility is opened up. In *Wynne-Finch v Chaytor*[17] the Court of Appeal refused to be bound by its own previous decision; therefore, the later pronouncement in *Young's Case* that it is bound must be invalid. Even if so radical an assault on *Young's Case* is considered too venturesome, the Court of Appeal might still be able to argue that these two cases are in conflict and that, being free to choose under the rule in *Young's Case*, it chooses to abide by *Wynne-Finch v Chaytor*. Whatever view is taken of these odd possibilities, it is clear that by virtue of this exception the court has liberty to escape from the rigour of its own doctrine.

The position of the High Court when confronted with conflicting decisions of the Court of Appeal is also not clear. Oliver J suggested that the High Court, like the Court of Appeal, should be free to choose or, if not, he felt he should follow the later case[18]. Donaldson J, on the other hand, felt bound to follow the earlier of the conflicting decisions since the latter had violated the doctrine of *stare decisis* and following it would be inconsistent with that doctrine[19].

The second exception to the rule in *Young's Case* is where the earlier decision of the Court of Appeal is regarded as inconsistent with a subsequent decision of the House of Lords. Is it open to the court to differ from a previous decision on the ground that that decision was inconsistent with a decision of the House of Lords which preceded it? This would seem to be what was done in *Fitzsimons v Ford Motor Co Ltd (Aero Engines)*[20], and in *Wilson v Chatterton*[1], where the Court of Appeal refused to follow previous decisions of its own on the ground that they were inconsistent with still earlier decisions of the House of Lords. They amount to asserting that a decision of the Court of Appeal which came after a decision of the House of Lords and which distinguished it, could be disregarded as wrongly decided, but under the principle of *Young v Bristol Aeroplane Co Ltd*, this is exactly what is not permissible. However, in *Williams v Glasbrook Bros Ltd*[2], the Court of Appeal returned to the statement of principle in *Young's Case* and held that if in a previous decision of the court a decision of the House of Lords had been considered, the court could not now say that that previous decision was inconsistent with the decision of the House of Lords. *Fitzsimons' Case* was not brought to the notice of the court in *Williams v Glasbrook Bros Ltd*, and no member of the court in the former case was sitting in the later appeal. The

17 [1903] 2 Ch 475.
18 *Midland Bank Trust Co Ltd v Hett, Stubb & Kemp (a firm)* [1979] Ch 384 at 404-405, 432, [1978] 3 All ER 571 at 584-585.
19 *Uganda Co (Holdings) v Government of Uganda* [1979] 1 Lloyds Rep 481.
20 [1946] 1 All ER 429.
 1 [1946] KB 360, [1946] 1 All ER 431.
 2 [1947] 2 All ER 884.

scope of this second exception may yet prove to be very far-reaching and it is to be noted that the Divisional Court of King's Bench has since held itself at liberty to ignore an earlier decision of the Court of Appeal on the ground that the Court of Appeal had not examined a decision of the House of Lords[3].

The third exception raised by the Court of Appeal in *Young's Case* to the doctrine that the court is bound by its own decisions is where the previous decision was given *per incuriam*, that is to say, in ignorance of a statutory provision or binding authority[4]. If the Court of Appeal had misapprehended the principle or material point in a previous decision, it would appear that the case, in which the error had been made, is not binding. Mere inadequacy of argument does not bring a case within the *incuria* rule, but if relevant authorities have not been cited to the court the rule will apply. If the reasoning behind a decision is shown to have been faulty by a higher court, or even by a court of co-ordinate authority, that decision may again be disregarded. This third exception opens a wide gap in the doctrine of *stare decisis*, for, as Sir Carleton Allen has demonstrated[5], in these days of the multiplication of reports and decisions it is increasingly easy for a court to come to a decision without having considered all the relevant authorities. In the result, the exceptions to the rule in *Young's Case* are more significant than the rule itself, for they point towards a relaxation in the strict doctrine of *stare decisis*[6].

Turning next to the House of Lords, it might be noted that the House, which for long used to be bound by its own decisions subject to some exceptions, has altered this practice since 1966 and now considers itself free to depart from its previous decisions[7]. The Judicial Committee of the Privy Council, as the highest appellate court from different parts of the Commonwealth (more so in the past than now), used to hear appeals from jurisdictions where different systems of law prevail, eg Roman–Dutch law. Clearly, a decision given in one system could not be binding in a case coming from a different system. With regard to any one particular system, the Privy Council has stated that as long as there is a higher court of appeal, such as itself, a lower appellate court is right to consider itself bound by its own

---

3 *R v Northumberland Compensation Appeal Tribunal, ex p Shaw* [1951] 1 KB 711, [1951] 1 All ER 268 (affd [1952] 1 KB 338, [1952] 1 All ER 122).

4 Explained in *Morelle Ltd v Wakeling* [1955] 2 QB 379 at 406, [1955] 1 All ER 708 at 718; on which see Note in (1955) 18 MLR 602. As to decisions given in ignorance of authoritative cases, see Lord Goddard CJ's views in *Moore v Hewitt*, [1947] KB 831 at 835, [1947] 2 All ER 270 at 272; and *Nicholas v Penny* [1950] 2 KB 466 at 473, [1950] 2 All ER 89 at 92. Quaere as to a decision in ignorance of a rule of statutory interpretation: *Royal Crown Derby Porcelain Co Ltd v Russell* [1949] 2 KB 417, [1949] 1 All ER 749.

5 Allen *Law in the Making*, Excursus C.

6 Possible new exceptions: (i) decisions overruled by statute, eg *Thomson v Moyse* [1961] AC 967 at 989, 1006, [1960] 3 All ER 684 at 699; (ii) decisions with more than one *ratio decidendi*, as to which see p 143 post; (iii) narrower conception of the *ratio*, on which see Cross 'Stare Decisis in Contemporary England' (1966) 82 LQR 203; (iv) an interlocutory order made by only two Lords Justices if it is thought to be wrong: *Boys v Chaplin* [1968] 2 QB 1, [1968] 1 All ER 283 (affd [1971] AC 356, [1969] 2 All ER 1085).

7 *Note (Judicial Precedent)* [1966] 3 All ER 77, [1966] 1 WLR 1234. The first case in which the House refused to follow a previous decision of itself was *Conway v Rimmer* [1968] AC 910, [1968] 1 All ER 874. For an examination of the position in the Court of Appeal and the House of Lords, see Cross *Precedent in English Law* chs 3–4; Blom-Cooper and Drewry *Final Appeal* ch 4; Dias *Bibliography* pp 28–31.

decisions[8]. However, it has also said that whether such lower appellate court should or should not follow a decision of itself, which is thought to be wrong, is a matter of policy of which the local court is a better judge than the Privy Council[9].

Finally, since Britain's accession to the European Economic Community the status of Community case law in British courts needs to be considered. Art 177 of the Rome Treaty lays down that when questions concerning the interpretation of the Community Treaties or the validity of measures taken by Community institutions (Commission, Council of Ministers, European Court) come before national courts, a subordinate court *may*, and final court *must*, request the European Court to give a preliminary ruling[10]. The European Court will only provide an abstract interpretation of the law; it will not consider the merits of the dispute, or its facts, or relevance of the facts to the point at issue, or the validity of any rule of national law; nor does the European Court's pronouncement invalidate such rule. The municipal court should then try to avoid conflict if possible[11]. Only within these limits is a decision of the European Court 'binding', if that is the appropriate word, on the municipal court which requests a ruling. What effect has such a decision on the courts of other member states? The European Court has ruled that its judgments are not binding precedents for national courts generally, but that the courts of any country may give them that effect if they wish[12]. Decisions of other municipal courts enjoy no more than persuasive force in British courts as they have always done, perhaps with the difference that such persuasive force may be greater in Community matters than in others because of the shared aim of member states to harmonise their economic development. Decisions of British courts will of course continue to bind other British courts in the ordinary way[13].

Are the rules regulating the binding force of precedents rules of law or of practice? The point has been discussed principally in connection with the

---

8 *A-G of St Christopher, Nevis and Anguilla v Reynolds* [1980] AC 637 at 659-660, [1979] 3 All ER 129 at 139-140.

9 *Geelong Harbor Trust Comrs v Gibbs Bright & Co (a firm)* [1974] AC 810 at 818-819, [1974] 2 WLR 507 at 512.

10 For an important discussion, see *H P Bulmer Ltd v J Bollinger SA* [1975] Ch 401, [1974] 2 All ER 1226; and also *Van Duyn v Home Office* [1974] 3 All ER 178, [1974] CMLR 347. The European Communities Act 1972, s 3, says that questions of Community law are to be treated as questions of law, not of fact.

11 See pp 106-108 ante.

12 Municipal courts may put the question again in order to invite the European Court to review its practice: Case 28-30/62 *Da Costa en Schake NV v Nederlandse Administratie van Belastingen* [1963] CMLR 224 at 237, 238; Case 28/67 *Molkerei Zentrale Westfalen-Lippe v Hauptzollamt Paderborn* [1968] CMLR 187 at 217. A French court has held that the decision of the European Court on a preliminary ruling was binding on all courts involved in the particular case: *Caisse Regionale de Sécurité Social du Nord-Est v Goffart* [1969] CMLR 24 (following the ruling of the European Court in [1967] CMLR 343). The German Federal Supreme Court has held such a decision to be binding even in other cases: *Re A Brewery Solus Agreement* [1975] 1 CMLR 611. Cf *SAFA v Amministrazione delle Finanze* [1973] CMLR 152 at 156.

13 This follows from the position with regard to any other rule of international law. 'A rule of international law, once incorporated into our law by decisions of a competent court, is not an inference of fact but a rule of law. It therefore becomes part of our municipal law and the doctrine of *stare decisis* applies as much to that as a rule of law with a strictly municipal provenance': Scarman LJ in *Thai-Europe Tapioca Service Ltd v Government of Pakistan, Ministry of Food and Agriculture, Directorate of Agriculture Supplies (Import and Shipping Wing)* [1975] 3 All ER 961 at 969-970, [1975] 1 WLR 1485 at 1495. See also Lawton LJ [1975] 3 All ER at 967, [1975] 1 WLR at 1493.

former rule that the House of Lords was bound by its own decisions. By abolishing this in a *Note (Judicial Precedent)*[14] the House has treated it merely as one of practice[15], which means simply that a new rule of practice has been substituted for the old and is descriptive of what the House is now doing without prejudice to what it may decide to do in future. If, on the other hand, it were treated as a rule of law, there might be a doubt as to whether a rule of law can be unsettled by a practice statement forming no part of the decision of any dispute. Such speculation is devoid of practical significance, for it is clear that the House will continue for the foreseeable future to abide by the *Note (Judicial Precedent)*, which makes it futile to suggest that the old rule has not been changed. Even if the House had overthrown it in a decided case, then all this would have meant is that the prior pronouncement was an erroneous statement of law; but the new statement could in turn be dismissed as an error tomorrow, and so on. The point is that a pronouncement as to practice is indicative of what the House is now doing, so any question as to whether it should be labelled 'law' or 'practice' is quite unfruitful. Precisely the same argument applies to the Court of Appeal, which continues to be bound by its own decisions, but with the further point that even the House of Lords cannot decide as a matter of law whether or not the Court of Appeal is bound by itself. Any such pronouncement is bound to be *obiter*, since the matter will be resolved by the Lords on its merits and not on the point whether the Court of Appeal bound itself; which is what happened in *Young v Bristol Aeroplane Co Ltd*, itself[16].

LAW-QUALITY OF PRECEDENTS

Before any kind of doctrine of precedent can operate, there have to be reliable records of the decisions in previous cases and this is especially necessary for the doctrine of *stare decisis*.

Law reports

It has been pointed out by many writers that the history of *stare decisis* is the history of law reporting. Although the strict doctrine could not come into existence until reporting had attained an efficient standard, it is equally true

---

14 'Constitutional convention having the force of law': per Lord Simon in *Miliangos v George Frank (Textiles) Ltd* [1976] AC 443 at 472, [1975] 3 All ER 801 at 816. See generally Evans 'The Status of Rules of Precedent' (1982) 41 CLJ 162; Goldstein 'Some Problems about Precedent', and Evans 'The Status of Rules of Precedent - a Brief Reply' (1984) 43 CLJ 88, 108.

15 [1966] 3 All ER 77, [1966] 1 WLR 1234.

16 [1946] AC 163 at 169, [1946] 1 All ER 98 at 100, where Viscount Simon approved of the practice of the Court of Appeal, but the observation was *obiter*. Cf Salmon LJ: 'The point about the authority of this court has never been decided by the House of Lords. In the nature of things it is not a point that could ever come before the House for decision': *Gallie v Lee* [1969] 2 Ch 17 at 49, [1969] 1 All ER 1062 at 1082 (affd sub nom *Saunders (Executrix of Will of Gallie) v Anglia Building Society* [1971] AC 1004, [1970] 3 All ER 961. For a suggested distinction between 'prescriptive' and 'descriptive' practice, see J Stone (1969) 69 Col LR 1162 at 1168. Thus, the *London Tramways* rule had no binding effect in 1898, but by virtue of judicial practice since that date became 'a rule both *descriptive* of past procedure, and also *prescriptive* of a rule of law binding in the future'. The same would apply to the *Note (Judicial Precedent)* of 1966. The difficulty is to see how the prescriptive 'ought' derives from the descriptive 'is'.

that it was the habit of relying on precedents that gradually improved law reporting. The absence of reports, though inconvenient, did not preclude recourse to previous decisions. Memory was often relied on; and in the early days of equity, for instance, the absence of reports only led judges to refer to the Registrar's Books in which the facts, the steps in suit and the principles were set out[17].

Among the earliest writers no reliance on cases is to be found. Glanvil, writing at the end of the twelfth century, cited only one judgment in his treatise; Fleta and Hengham at the end of the thirteenth century quoted hardly any. The same is true of Fortescue in the late fifteenth century. The notable exception was Bracton, who compiled a *Notebook* of some two thousand cases as material for his treatise and employed some five hundred of them[18]. There was nothing resembling the modern use of precedent; he stated his view of what a rule should be and added an illustrative case.

It is possible that Bracton's use of cases may have had something to do with the appearance of the Year Books. These constituted the earliest law reports, but bore no resemblance to modern reports. Many were anecdotal in character, the authors being concerned to record asides and points of pleading rather than principle, and the decisions often passed unmentioned. Nevertheless, the Year Books were used by students and it is clear from occasional statements that judicial decisions were being treated as authoritative pronouncements of the law. Thus, Prisot CJ said in 1454:

> 'And moreover if this plea were now adjudged bad, as you maintain, it would assuredly be a bad example to the young apprentices who study the Year Books, for they would never have confidence in their books if now we were to adjudge the contrary of what has so often been adjudged in the Books'[19].

An utterance like this should not, however, be overestimated, and there was as yet no doctrine of *stare decisis*.

The Year Books, though useful, were not reliable reports and citation remained largely a matter of memory. The original record was the only official source of information[20], but resort to this was impractical in the daily work of the courts and, indeed, access to records was normally accorded only to lawyers acting for the Crown. The appearance of private compilations of cases was therefore the next landmark. Among the first, and of deservedly high repute, were the reports of Dyer and of Plowden, followed by the famous reports of Coke, which ceased in 1616. None of them was in modern dress for they consisted of lengthy accounts of pleadings and disquisitions upon the branches of the law involved. Shortly after this, but still in the seventeenth century, there emerged the idea that decisions of the Court of Exchequer Chamber were of binding authority[1]. This was perhaps because such decisions were given by groups of judges. The same idea did not apply to decisions of the King's Bench, Common Pleas or even of the House of

17 Winder 'Precedent in Equity' (1941) 57 LQR 245, 249.

18 Cf the *Practicks* of early Scots law in which important decisions were noted by judges and counsel for their own use: Smith *The Doctrine of Judicial Precedent in Scots Law* p 2.

19 YB 33 Hen VI Mich 17, fo 41. See also YB 32 & 33 Edw I (Rolls Series) 32, for a statement by counsel that 'the judgments to be given by you will be hereafter an authority in every *quare non admisit* in England'; and YB 3 & 4 Edw II (Seldon Series iv), 161, for a statement by Bereford CJ that 'by a decision on this avowry we shall make a law throughout all the land'.

20 For the distinction between 'record' and 'report', see Pollock 'Judicial Records' in *Essays in the Law* ch 9, especially at p 233; *A First Book of Jurisprudence* p 293.

1 Herbert CJ in *Godden v Hales* (1686) 11 State Tr 1166 at 1254–55.

Lords. Indeed, decisions of the last mentioned body, which enjoy such authority today, enjoyed virtually none in those days. One reason was that lay
peers took part in the deliberations, often to the confusion and embarrassment of lawyers, and it was not until 1844 that they ceased to participate in
purely judicial matters[2]. Another reason was that this assembly did not
distinguish between its legislative and judicial functions, both of which were
covered by parliamentary privilege. The publication even of judicial proceedings would have constituted a breach of it. Only in 1813 did Dow begin
a series of House of Lords reports.

After Coke a period of indifferent reporting set in until the publication of
Burrow's Reports, which cover the period from 1757 to 1771. These admirable compilations marked the beginning of the modern practice, for they
distinguished between headnote, facts, argument and decision with a proper
report of the judgment. The doctrine of *stare decisis* was beginning to cast its
shadow. Thus, Blackstone spoke of 'an established rule' to follow previous
cases 'unless flatly absurd or unjust'[3]. It would appear also that from about
1785 judges began to favour particular reporters chosen for each court and
to prefer citation from them and no other[4]. Eighty years later, in 1865, the
series of reports known as the 'Law Reports' was inaugurated by the Incorporated Council of Law Reporting. These enjoy the advantage of being
revised by the judges before publication, but beyond that they are in no
sense official. Law reporting remains, as always, a matter of private enterprise.

The question what cases should be reported bristles with problems. The
decision rests ultimately with the individual reporter. 'Utility to the profession is the only test', said Pollock[5]. Another aspect of the matter is that there
is, on the one hand, a need for as expeditious a service as possible, and on
the other, that it is no easy matter to decide how useful a particular case is
likely to prove. In 1936 the All England Law Reports began providing a
rapid weekly service of cases both useful and otherwise. In 1953 the Council
of Law Reporting introduced an alternative weekly service with an indication as to which of the reported cases would subsequently be more fully
reported in the 'Law Reports'. These are by no means all; there are other
current series.

Assessment of reports

A 'law report' means any account of a case vouched for by a barrister who
was present at the hearing[6]. Today it is usual for a report to begin with
catch-words indicating the main points involved, followed by a headnote
summarising the facts and decision, then the arguments of counsel, but these
are included only in some series, and finally the judgment or relevant portion
of it.

2 *O'Connell v R* (1844) 11 Cl & Fin 155 at 421–426.
3 Bl *Com* I, 70.
4 Daniel *The History and Origin of 'The Law Reports'* p 265. For a list of 'authorised reporters'
   just prior to 1865, see Moran *The Heralds of the Law* p 20.
5 Pollock *Essays in the Law* p 249.
6 Pollock *Essays in the Law* p 243. It must be by a barrister: *Birtwistle v Tweedale* [1953] 2 All
   ER 1598, [1954] 1 WLR 190, on which see Megarry 'Reporting the Unreported' (1954) 70
   LQR 246. Cf Moran *The Heralds of the Law* p 13, where there is no mention of barrister; but
   see also p 102. For a solicitor's note of proceedings, see *Thompson v Andrews* [1968] 2 All ER
   419, [1968] 1 WLR 777.

The following points may be borne in mind in estimating the value of a report. In the first place, any of the old reports may be consulted, but their authority varies. Some, for example those of Coke or Burrow, are viewed with approval, while others, for example those of Barnardiston or Epinasse, are not[7]. In all old reports it is important to observe how fully the facts are stated and whether the judgment is reported *verbatim* or not. Secondly, if a case is reported in more than one report, all the versions should be compared, for significant discrepancies may appear[8]. Thirdly, as a general rule the Law Reports version, by virtue of having been revised by the judges, should be consulted in preference to others[9]. The question may be asked: Which is more authoritative—the original as taken down in court, or the subsequent revision? The Court of Appeal has ruled that it is the latter, since the former is only provisional and awaits approval by the judge. The judge should not, of course, alter the whole character of his judgment[10]. Fourthly, the best type of report is one which indicates the arguments of counsel and sets out the judgment, or relevant portion of it, *verbatim*. A report which only summarises the judgment should only be used in the absence of a fuller report, but may not even then carry much weight[11]. Finally, in the absence of all else the oral

---

7 Eg Denman CJ in *Small v Nairne* (1849) 13 QB 840 at 844; Evershed LJ in *Hamps v Darby* [1948] 2 KB 311 at 317-318, [1948] 2 All ER 474 at 475-476; Denning LJ in *Warren v Keen* [1954] 1 QB 15 at 20-21, [1953] 2 All ER 1118 at 1121.

8 See Pollock *A First Book of Jurisprudence* p 317, who also points out the importance sometimes of comparing the report with the record: *Essays in the Law* p 231. On *Williams v Carwardine* as reported in (1833) 4 B & Ad 621, and in 5 C & P 574, see Goodhart *Essays in Jurisprudence and the Common Law* p 11. Other examples of significant divergences: *Edwards v Jones* [1947] KB 659 at 664, [1947] 1 All ER 830 at 833 where not quite the same reason is given for refusing to follow a prior decision; *Barker v Levinson* [1951] 1 KB 342, [1950] 2 All ER 825 where a statement as to the criminal liability of masters for the acts of servants does not appear in the latter report; *Perry v Stopher* [1959] 1 WLR 415 at 420, where Hodson LJ alludes to a difference in the report of a previous case in [1953] 2 All ER 1599 and in [1953] 1 WLR 1486, and his observation is in fact omitted in [1959] 1 All ER 713; the report of *Woods v Martin's Bank Ltd* [1959] 1 QB 55 at 72, is preferable to those in [1958] 3 All ER 166 and [1958] 1 WLR 1018; *Re Philpot* [1960] 1 All ER 165 at 168, where attention is drawn to the reports of *R v Dickson* in [1950] 1 KB 394 at 398, and in [1949] 2 All ER 810 at 812, in which the phrases 'must be' and 'should be' appear respectively with reference to a point of procedure; in *R v Agricultural Land Tribunal for the South Eastern Area, ex p Bracey* [1960] 2 All ER 518, the applicant relied on a statement reported in [1953] 2 All ER 4 at 6, but which is omitted in [1953] 2 QB 147. The weekly issue (Part 14) of the All England Law Reports version of *Schlesinger v Schlesinger* [1960] P 191, contains a fuller report than that which subsequently came out in the bound volume of the same parts.

9 *Leather Cloth Co v Lorsont* (1869) LR 9 Eq 345 at 351; *Brentnall and Cleland v LCC* [1944] 2 All ER 552 at 555; *Duke of Buccleuch v IRC* [1967] 1 AC 506 at 527-528, [1967] 1 All ER 129 at 133; *National Bank of Greece SA v Westminster Bank Executor and Trustee Co (Channel Islands) Ltd* [1970] 3 All ER 656 n, [1970] 1 WLR 1400. Cf *CHT Ltd v Ward* [1963] 3 All ER 835 at 842, where the LR version of a case was rejected as unsatisfactory.

10 *Bromley v Bromley* [1965] P 111, [1964] 3 All ER 226. See also *Young v North Riding Justices* [1965] 1 QB 502 at 508, [1965] 1 All ER 141 at 143-144, where the omission from the revised version of a point included in the Justices of the Peace Report was considered; and *R v Cockburn* [1968] 1 All ER 466 at 468, [1968] 1 WLR 281 at 283-284, where the court repudiated a remark in another case, which is reported in the All England Law Reports and Weekly Law Reports, but is eliminated from the Law Reports and Criminal Appeal Reports.

11 Hallett J in *Rivoli Hats Ltd v Gooch* [1953] 2 All ER 823 at 824, [1953] 1 WLR 1190 at 1192, commenting on the summarised report of *Clayton Newbury Ltd v Findlay* in (1951) Current Law Consolidation 65 (a fuller report was immediately included in [1953] 1 WLR 1194, and, less fully, in [1953] 2 All ER 826). See also *Haley v London Electricity Board* [1965] AC 778, [1964] 3 All ER 185, commenting on *Pritchard v Post Office* as reported in [1950] WN 310 and (1950) 114 JP 370.

account of a case by a barrister is admissible, though again this may be of limited value[12].

Application of precedents

A precedent influences future decisions. Every decision is pronounced on a specific set of past facts and from the decision on those facts a rule has to be extracted and projected into the future. No one can foresee the precise situations that will arise, so the rule has to be capable of applying to a range of broadly similar situations against a background of changing conditions. It has therefore to be in general terms and 'malleable'. As pointed out at the beginning of the book, no word has one proper meaning, nor can anyone seek to fix the meaning of words for others, so the interpretation of the rule remains flexible and open-ended[13].

Applying a precedent to the instant case is a process of matching the fact-pattern of the precedent and the ruling thereon with the fact-pattern of the instant case; if they match, the rule is applied, if not, it is distinguished. This involves the first two kinds of knowledge mentioned at the start of this chapter, namely, knowing the facts and knowing the law applicable to those facts.

Knowing the facts

Knowing the facts of the instant case involves an exercise of discretion. This lies initially in believing or disbelieving the testimony of witnesses and weighing it on a balance of probability. Judges are human, so the quirks of individual personalities may also play some part occasionally[14]. The discretionary element is most significant in knowing how to *state* the facts, for, as pointed out in Chapter 1[15], it is not knowledge of facts, but knowledge of how to state facts that is relevant; and this applies to the statement of facts of both the instant and the precedent cases. As Lord Simon has said, 'What is relevant is not only the statement of material facts by the deciding judge, but also their re-statement by other judges in later cases'[16].

First, the art of knowing how to state facts involves the distinction between statements of primary and secondary (or inferential) facts: between saying, eg that A did so and so at such a time in such a place and saying that A acted negligently. 'Negligence' is commonly treated as a question of fact, but since it is a matter of inference from a set of primary facts two courts may state the inferential fact differently while agreeing on the primary facts[17].

Secondly, there is knowledge of how to state facts at different levels of generality, which makes it possible for the deciding judge and a judge in a later case to make different statements of facts. Thus, A may have driven a Rolls Royce car at 30 mph through Piccadilly Circus at 2 pm on a certain

12 See the observations of Lord Morton in *Chapman v Chapman* [1954] AC 429 at 464–465, [1954] 1 All ER 798 at 815–816.
13 See Stone *Legal System and Lawyers' Reasonings* pp 35–36.
14 See pp 220–225 post.
15 See pp 7–8 ante.
16 *F A & A B Ltd v Lupton (Inspector of Taxes)* [1972] AC 634 at 658, 659, [1971] 3 All ER 948 at 964, 965.
17 *Benmax v Austin Motor Co Ltd* [1955] AC 370, [1955] 1 All ER 326.

Wednesday, run into B and broken his right leg. The individual A may be generalised into 'person'; the Rolls Royce car may be generalised into 'vehicle'; Piccadilly Circus into 'public highway'; 30 mph through Piccadilly Circus at 2 pm on Wednesday into 'negligence'; and B's broken right leg into 'physical injury to the person'. A restatement of these facts at a more general level would be: 'a person inflicted physical injury on another person by the negligent driving of a vehicle on the public highway'. An even more general form of it would be: 'the negligent infliction of physical damage'; and more generally still: 'the negligent infliction of damage'. The higher the level of generality, the wider the scope of the proposition. It is clear at a glance that 'negligent infliction of damage' is wider than just 'the breaking of a given person's right leg by the careless driving of a Rolls Royce car'. A later judge is at liberty to accept as the fact-statement of *A v B* a proposition at any level along the scale. Thus, one who is confronted with a situation in which a careless false statement has caused damage to person or property, and who wishes to utilise the decision in *A v B* in order to hold the defendant liable, would no doubt regard that case as authority for 'the negligent infliction of physical damage', since only at this level of generality would the ruling become wide enough to cover the instant case[18]. On the other hand, another judge, wishing to impose liability for pecuniary loss would no doubt prefer the widest interpretation of *A v B*, namely, 'the negligent infliction of damage'[19].

Thirdly, it is necessary to know how to select the material facts. The fewer material facts included in a statement, the wider is its scope. In *Rylands v Fletcher*[20] the facts were as follows: (i) A had a reservoir built; (ii) A employed B to build it; (iii) A was not himself negligent; (iv) B was negligent; (v) water escaped owing to B's negligent construction of the reservoir and damaged C's property. Only facts (i) and (v) were treated as material by the court. By ignoring the absence and presence of negligence in A and B respectively, and by generalising fact (i) into 'anything likely to do mischief', the decision creates the sweeping rule that whoever brings a 'mischievous substance' on to his land is liable for damage[1] caused by its escape, irrespective of negligence.

Connected with this, **fourthly,** is the ability of a later judge to review the material facts of the precedent and add to or subtract from the sum-total of facts selected by the deciding judge; or he may re-state the facts at a different level of generality. Such re-statements extend or restrict the ambit of the precedent. In *Wilsons and Clyde Coal Co Ltd v English*[2] the employers were held liable for the death of one of their employees owing to the default of another employee. At that date a servant could not hold his employer vicariously

18 Eg Asquith LJ in *Candler v Crane, Christmas & Co* [1951] 2 KB 164 at 189, [1951] 1 All ER 426 at 439; *Clayton v Woodman & Son (Builders) Ltd* [1962] 2 QB 533, [1961] 3 All ER 249 (revsd on the facts without affecting the principle [1962] 2 QB at 546, [1962] 2 All ER 891).
19 Eg *Ross v Caunters* [1980] Ch 297, [1979] 3 All ER 580; *Junior Books Ltd v Veitchi Co Ltd* [1983] 1 AC 520, [1982] 3 All ER 201.
20 (1868) LR 3 HL 330, and see Goodhart 'The *Ratio Decidendi* of a Case' in *Essays in Jurisprudence and the Common Law* pp 17–18.
 1 Subsequent interpretation of 'damage' leaves open whether it includes personal injury: *Miles v Forest Rock Granite Co (Leicestershire) Ltd* (1918) 34 TLR 500; *Shiffman v Order of St John* [1936] 1 All ER 557; *Hale v Jennings* [1938] 1 All ER 579; *Perry v Kendricks Transport Ltd* [1956] 1 All ER 154, [1956] 1 WLR 85. Cf *Read v J Lyons & Co Ltd* [1947] AC 156, [1946] 2 All ER 471.
 2 [1938] AC 57, [1937] 3 All ER 628.

liable for an injury inflicted by a fellow-servant because of the prevailing doctrine of common-employment, which has since been abolished. Therefore, to hold the employers liable, it was essential to the *ratio decidendi* to ignore the fact that the party at fault was a servant and to say that the employers were being held liable, not vicariously, but for the breach of a personal non-delegable duty to ensure that reasonable care would be taken. So stated, the rule would attach liability to the employer of even an independent contractor. In *Davie v New Merton Board Mills Ltd*[3], however, Viscount Simonds and Lord Reid appeared to place an interpretation upon *Wilsons' Case* which would dismantle this rule. They stressed the materiality of the fact that it was not a contractor but a servant who had been at fault, which would involve a fundamental reinterpretation of the case[4]. The Employer's Liability (Defective Equipment) Act 1969, has now overruled *Davie* and restored the original interpretation of *Wilsons* in statutory form. The point is even more vividly brought out in the two *Wagon Mound* cases. A quantity of furnace oil was carelessly allowed to spill overboard from the SS Wagon Mound into the waters of a harbour. In *Wagon Mound*[5] the Judicial Committee of the Privy Council proceeded on the finding of the lower court that, according to scientific opinion at that date, the ignition of the oil in such circumstances was not reasonably foreseeable, and accordingly held that there was no answerability in negligence for damage by fire. In *Wagon Mound (No 2)*[6], however, brought by different plaintiffs but based on the same occurrence, the lower court stated that a bare possibility of fire might have been foreseeable, but that the chance was so remote that it should be ignored. Accordingly, the defendants were held not liable on the basis that fire was not reasonably foreseeable. The Judicial Committee fastened on this advertence to even a bare possibility of fire as constituting a material difference between the first and the second case, and, reversing the lower court, held the defendant liable in negligence for fire damage after all. It will thus be seen how stressing one factor as material not only enabled two different courts to reach opposite results in the same case, but also enabled the same court to reach opposite results in two cases based on the same happening.

Fifthly, there is the art of knowing how to make different statements by taking different combinations of facts. The facts in *Donoghue v Stevenson*[7] may be listed as follows. (i) A was a manufacturer of ginger beer; (ii) A was assumed to have been negligent in that a snail was alleged to have been found in one of the bottles; (iii) acting under contract with a retailer, B, A delivered the tainted bottle to B without knowing that it contained a snail and thereby committed a breach of his contract with B; (iv) B, acting under contract with C, innocently passed the bottle to C, thereby committing a breach of his contract with C; (v) C innocently passed the bottle to D; (vi) there had been no opportunity for an intermediate examination of the bottle

---

3 [1959] AC 604, [1959] 1 All ER 346 (overruled by the Employer's Liability (Defective Equipment) Act 1969).
4 [1959] AC at 621–622, 631, [1959] 1 All ER at 351–353, 358. See now *Clerk & Lindsell on Torts*, § 10-102. See also the attenuation of *Bailey v Geddes* [1938] 1 KB 156, [1937] 3 All ER 671, in *Knight v Sampson* [1938] 3 All ER 309; *Chisholm v London Passenger Transport Board* [1939] 1 KB 426, [1938] 4 All ER 850; *Wilkinson v Chetham-Strode* [1940] 2 KB 310, [1940] 2 All ER 643; *London Passenger Transport Board v Upson* [1949] AC 155, [1949] 1 All ER 60.
5 [1961] AC 388, [1961] 1 All ER 404.
6 [1967] 1 AC 617, [1966] 2 All ER 709.
7 [1932] AC 562.

at any stage since it left A; (vii) D was allegedly poisoned by drinking the remains of the snail; (viii) this being a Scottish case, D sued A in the Scottish courts, and the case was referred to the House of Lords on a preliminary point. It was held that, assuming A had been negligent in leaving a snail in the bottle, A would be liable to D. The case was remitted to the Scottish court for a decision on fact (ii), namely, whether there had in truth been a snail in the bottle. Different *rationes decidendi* can be extracted by taking different combinations of the above facts. In the first place, on fact (viii) alone it might have been argued that an appeal from Scotland is not binding on English courts, since Scots law is a different system[8]. Secondly, on facts (i), (ii), (vi) and (vii) it could be said that a negligent manufacturer is liable for damage to the ultimate consumer where there is no likelihood of an intermediate examination—the 'manufacturer' proposition. Thirdly, on facts (ii), (iii) and (vii) it could be said that any one who negligently misperforms a contract and physically damages a third party, whom he ought reasonably to have contemplated as likely to be affected, is liable to such third party in tort, though he would not be liable in contract. Fourthly, on facts (ii) and (vii) it could be said that anyone who negligently damages another, whom he ought reasonably to have contemplated as likely to be affected, is liable— the 'neighbour' proposition. Only in the light of later cases is it possible to determine the *ratio decidendi* of this important case. In recent years courts have come to regard the fourth proposition as being its ratio[9], while previously they generally adopted the second[10]. It is clear, therefore, that until recently tribunals had the choice of adopting one or the other[11]. In this way a case may even be given an interpretation quite other than that of the deciding judge[12].

Finally, as an aside, it may be remarked that *Donoghue's* case strikingly illustrates the point that what is important in law is the statement of facts rather than even their truth. The House of Lords remitted the case to the Scottish court for trial on the ruling laid down by the House, but this did not take place because of the death of one of the parties. So the truth as to whether or not there was a snail in the bottle was never established and is irrelevant to the ruling.

Wide though the possibilities are of making different statements of facts, they are limited by the consensual domain of the usual meanings of words. The facts of *Donoghue's* case would support any of the statements given above, but not, eg the statement that the defendant caused a public nuisance.

Knowing the law

What is 'law' in a precedent is its ruling or *ratio decidendi*, which concerns future litigants as well as those involved in the instant dispute. Knowing

---

8 Not after *Heyman v Darwins* [1942] AC 356 at 401, [1942] 1 All ER 337 at 361.

9 *Home Office v Dorset Yacht Co Ltd* [1970] AC 1004, [1970] 2 All ER 294; *Anns v Merton London Borough Council* [1978] AC 728, [1977] 2 All ER 492; *Ross v Caunters* [1980] Ch 297, [1979] 3 All ER 580; *Junior Books Ltd v Veitchi Co Ltd* [1983] 1 AC 520, [1982] 3 All ER 201.

10 Eg *Howard v Walker and Lake (Trustees) and Crisp* [1947] KB 860 at 863.

11 'Wherever the court wishes to find for the plaintiff, that doctrine (the fourth proposition) will be invoked, just as it will be disregarded when the defendant is the favoured party': Landon in *Pollock on Torts* p 329.

12 Danckwerts LJ said that the decision in a previous case 'may be supportable, but not for the reasons given in the case by the learned judge with which I find myself unable to agree': *East Ham Borough Council v Bernard Sunley & Sons Ltd* [1965] 1 All ER 210 at 217, [1965] 1 WLR 30 at 40 (revsd [1966] AC 406, [1965] 3 All ER 619).

the law in this context means knowing how to extract the *rationes decidendi* from cases. Statements not part of the *ratio decidendi* are distinguished as *obiter dicta* and are not authoritative. Three shades of meaning can be attached to the expression '*ratio decidendi*'. The first, which is the translation of it, is 'the reason for (or of) deciding'[13]. Even a finding of fact may in this sense be the *ratio decidendi*. Thus, a judge may state a rule and then decide that the facts do not fall within it. Secondly, it may mean 'the rule of law proffered by the judge as the basis of his decision'; or, thirdly, it may mean 'the rule of law which others regard as being of binding authority'.

There is a temptation to suppose that a case has one fixed ruling which is 'there' and discoverable here and now and once and for all. This is not so, for the *ratio* is not only the ruling given by the deciding judge for his decision, but any one of a series of rulings as elucidated by subsequent interpretations[14]. The pronouncement of the judge who decided the case is a necessary step towards ascertaining the *ratio*, but the process by no means ends there; subsequent interpretation is at least as significant, sometimes more so. 'It is not sufficient', said Jessel MR,

> 'that the case should have been decided on a principle if that principle is not itself a right principle, or one not applicable to the case; and it is for a subsequent Judge to say whether or not it is a right principle, and, if not, he may himself lay down the true principle'[15].

Cases of overruling and reversal by superior authority are obvious instances of subsequent correction, but they are not within the scope of the immediate discussion. For, apart from these, the judge in a later case may restrict or enlarge the ruling as stated by the deciding judge, or he may reinterpret that ruling in such a way as to relegate it to the status of an *obiter dictum*. Accordingly, *ratio* is best regarded as a pointer towards the direction which subsequent decisions should take within a broad spectrum of variations. It is not something identifiable once and for all, but a continuing process, and as such it has to be viewed in a continuum of time.

(1)   Difficult though the task of finding the *ratio* is, there would be a measure of agreement in propounding that no rule should be treated as *ratio* which would not support the ultimate order[16]. Where a stated-

---

13   Lord Denning MR in *Paal Wilson & Co A/S v Partenreederei Hannah Blumenthal* [1983] 1 AC 854 at 873, [1982] 3 All ER 394 at 400, (varied [1983] 1 AC 854, [1983] 1 All ER 34, HL).

14   Goodhart *Essays in Jurisprudence and the Common Law* pp 2, 25, says that 'the reason which the judge gives for his decision is never the binding part of the precedent', but 'never' is too strong a word, as pointed out by Schreiner JA in *Pretoria City Council v Levinson* 1949 (3) SA 305 at 316–317.

15   *Osborne v Rowlett* (1880) 13 ChD 774 at 785. Lord Reid, in attempting to find the *ratio decidendi* of an earlier case, said: 'If I had to try, the result might depend on whether or not I was striving to obtain a narrow *ratio*': *Scruttons Ltd v Midland Silicones Ltd* [1962] AC 446 at 477, [1962] 1 All ER 1 at 12. Cf Devlin J in *Behrens v Bertram Mills Circus Ltd* [1957] 2 QB 1 at 24, [1957] 1 All ER 583 at 594.

16   The reason *sine qua non*: Cardozo 'Jurisprudence' in *Selected Writings* (ed Hall) p 33. See also Lord Denning in *Penn-Texas Corpn v Murat Anstalt (No 2)* [1964] 2 QB 647 at 660–661, [1964] 2 All ER 594 at 597; *Harper v National Coal Board (Intended Action)* [1974] QB 614 at 621, [1974] 2 All ER 441 at 446. In *Pinchin v Santam Insurance Co Ltd* 1963 (2) SA 254 (WLD) the ruling on a point which did not affect the ultimate decision was nevertheless made part of the *ratio* by being made the basis of the order on costs. See also *The Wagon Mound (No 2)* [1967] 1 AC 617, [1966] 2 All ER 709, for the relationship between rulings and the ultimate order.

rule obviously bears no relation to the facts, it is no more than a *dictum*.

(2) Even when the deciding judge has given no reason for his decision, it may be possible for a subsequent tribunal to extract one from it[17]. However, no judge is required to accomplish the impossible. 'If it is not clear', said Viscount Dunedin, 'then I do not think it is part of the tribunal's duty to spell out with great difficulty a *ratio decidendi* in order to be bound by it'[18].

(3) It follows from what has previously been said that different *rationes* may be extracted from a case depending on different ways of stating the facts.

(4) More rarely, a judge may demote a proposition in a previous case from its status of *ratio* to that of *dictum*. Thus, the 'neighbour' proposition in *Donoghue v Stevenson* used to change its category according to whether the plaintiff or the defendant was thought entitled to succeed[19].

(5) Certain types of cases do not deserve to be authorities. One type, already alluded to, is that in which there is no discoverable *ratio decidendi*. Others are cases turning purely on facts[20], those involving the exercise of discretion[1], and those which judges themselves do not think worthy of being precedents[2]. Decisions on the interpretation of documents are sometimes used as precedents, which is regrettable since a court may find itself construing, not the document before it, but judicial interpretations of similar wording in other, slightly different documents[3]. 'I do not think it right', said Lord Denning MR, 'to look at previous cases in this way. The only legitimate purpose is to use them as a guide towards the meaning of words, so as to help in the search for the testator's intention. They should never be used so as to defeat his intention'[4].

The difficulties so far considered by no means exhaust the problems that may arise, some of which are incapable of solution. A case may involve two points, A and B, and a decision on either in favour of the defendant, be it

17 Eg *Giles v Walker* (1890) 24 QBD 656, discussed in *Davey v Harrow Corpn* [1958] 1 QB 60 at 71–72, [1957] 2 All ER 305 at 309–310.

18 *Great Western Rly Co v Mostyn (Owners), The Mostyn* [1928] AC 57 at 73. A remark by Lord Reid in *Nash (Inspector of Taxes) v Tamplin & Sons Brewery, Brighton, Ltd* [1952] AC 231 at 250, [1951] 2 All ER 869 at 880, to the effect that every case must have a *ratio decidendi* and that this should either be applied or distinguished appears to have been contradicted by Lord Reid himself in *Scruttons Ltd v Midland Silicones Ltd* [1962] AC 446 at 479, [1962] 1 All ER 1 at 14, where he despaired of finding the *ratio decidendi* of a previous case.

19 See *Fairman v Perpetual Investment Building Society* [1923] AC 74, as interpreted by Scott LJ in *Haseldine v C A Daw & Son Ltd* [1941] 2 KB 343, [1941] 3 All ER 156, and in *Boylan v Dublin Corpn* [1949] IR 60, and in *Pearson v Lambeth Borough Council* [1950] 2 KB 353, [1950] 1 All ER 682. See also *Jacobs v LCC* [1950] AC 361, [1950] 1 All ER 737. See further *Adam v Ward* [1917] AC 309, as interpreted in *Egger v Viscount Chelmsford* [1965] 1 QB 248, [1964] 3 All ER 406.

20 *Simpson v Peat* [1952] 2 QB 24 at 28, [1952] 1 All ER 447 at 449; *R v Young* [1953] 1 All ER 21.

1 *Bragg v Crosville Motor Services Ltd* [1959] 1 All ER 613 at 615, [1959] 1 WLR 324 at 326.

2 *R v Stokesley (Yorkshire) Justices, ex p Bartram* [1956] 1 All ER 563 at 565, [1956] 1 WLR 254 at 258.

3 See the observations of Jessel MR in *Aspden v Seddon* (1875) 10 Ch App 394 at 397, 398. As to whether such cases should be reported, see Moran *The Heralds of the Law* ch 7, summarising the views of Lord Lindley, Mews and Burrows.

4 *Re Jebb, Ward-Smith v Jebb* [1966] Ch 666 at 672, [1965] 3 All ER 358 at 361.

supposed, is conclusive of the matter, while the plaintiff has to win on both A and B in order to win. Suppose that the judge decides in the defendant's favour on both issues. Which is the *ratio*, since either is sufficient to support the decision?[5] On the other hand, if he decides in favour of the plaintifff on point A, but in favour of the defendant on point B, who accordingly wins, and if it is accepted that no ruling can be *ratio* unless it supports the order made, then the decision on point A is *obiter*. Even as a *dictum* it may never-theless carry such authority that a subsequent tribunal may feel obliged to follow it. If so, the nomenclature *ratio decidendi* or *obiter dictum* for the decision on point A ceases to matter. In *Hedley Byrne & Co Ltd v Heller & Partners Ltd*[6] the House of Lords overthrew a rule by virtue of which the defendant had succeeded in the Court of Appeal and propounded a different rule, but with a qualification attached so that the defendant was still able to win. This rule and qualification together constitute the *ratio*; but even if it were said to be a *dictum*, the distinction is immaterial at this level of authority.

A judge may embark upon a line of reasoning involving a rule which justifies a certain conclusion. He may then proceed along another line of reasoning involving a different rule, wider or narrower, which also justifies that conclusion[7]. Lord Simonds once declared that if two reasons are put forward by a court for its decision, both should be accepted as part of the *ratio decidendi*[8]. One may later be rejected, as in *Fisher v Taylor's Furnishing Stores Ltd*[9] where the Court of Appeal rejected as incorrect one of the two grounds which it had given in an earlier case, and the rejection was later confirmed by both the Court of Appeal and the House of Lords[10]. Again, if the House of Lords has given two reasons for a decision, and declares sub-sequently that one of them is correct and the other wrong, the authoritative ruling is the correct one[11]. This shows how subsequent interpretation deter-mines the *ratio decidendi* as between two stated rulings. Another illustration of the difficulty is *Donoghue v Stevenson*[12] in which there are three rulings justi-fying the result, the wide 'neighbour' rule, the narrower 'manufacturer' rule and the 'fallacy of contractual privity' rule. It has been pointed out that judges used to regard the first as being *ratio* or *dictum* according to the way in which they wished to decide. On the other hand, even the considered

---

5 In *Said v Butt* [1920] 3 KB 497, the judge made it clear that his decision on point B was additional, which makes it a *dictum*.
6 [1964] AC 465, [1963] 2 All ER 575. In the South African case of *Pinchin v Santam Insurance Co Ltd* 1963 (2) SA 254 (WLD) the judge made his decision for the plaintiff on point A part of the *ratio decidendi* by basing his order as to costs on it. See also *The Wagon Mound (No 2)* [1967] 1 AC 617, [1966] 2 All ER 709.
7 Eg Denning LJ in *Broom v Morgan* [1953] 1 QB 597 at 609–610, [1953] 1 All ER 849 at 854–855.
8 *Jacobs v LCC* [1950] AC 361 at 369–371, [1950] 1 All ER 737 at 741–742. To the same effect, Lord Bramwell in *Membery v Great Western Rly Co* (1889) 14 App Cas 179 at 187; Lord MacNaghten in *New South Wales Taxation Comrs v Palmer* [1907] AC 179 at 184; Greer LJ in *London Jewellers Ltd v Attenborough* [1934] 2 KB 206 at 222; Pearce LJ in *Cane (Valuation Officer) v Royal College of Music* [1961] 2 QB 89 at 114, [1961] 2 All ER 12 at 24; Stamp J in *Rogers v Longsdon* [1967] Ch 93 at 109, [1966] 2 All ER 49 at 57.
9 [1956] 2 QB 78, [1956] 2 All ER 78.
10 *Craddock v Hampshire County Council* [1958] 1 All ER 449, [1958] 1 WLR 202; *Betty's Cafés Ltd v Phillips Furnishing Stores Ltd* [1959] AC 20, [1958] 1 All ER 607.
11 Per Lord Denning MR in *Re Holmden's Settlement Trusts, Holmden v IRC* [1966] Ch 511 at 530, [1966] 2 All ER 661 at 666, 667 (affd [1968] AC 685, [1968] 1 All ER 148).
12 [1932] AC 562.

opinion of a judge on a point not raised or argued will probably be treated as a *dictum*[13]. The same applies to a proposition which is 'merely a proposition of law assumed by the [Board] to be correct for the purpose of that particular case'[14].

These complications multiply in appellate tribunals where there is a plurality of judgments. It may happen that all the judges agree in the result for different reasons. Suppose that each of five judges gives a different reason for arriving at the same result and without disagreeing with the reasons given by the other four. Such a case may be said to have five competing *rationes* and a subsequent tribunal may adopt any of them for the purpose of deciding the case before itself. Suppose instead that each of the five not only gives a different reason for the same conclusion, but also rejects the reasons given by the other four[15]. Here the difficulty in the way of adopting any one opinion is that it has been condemned in four others. Such a case, it is submitted, has no discoverable *ratio* and is, in any event, worthless as an authority. It has so far been assumed that the judges agree in the result. Where they disagree, further difficulties arise. As long as three at least out of five, or two out of three, concur in the result for the same reason, their view may be said to constitute the *ratio*[16]. Where the majority differ in their reasons while the minority agree on the reason for their dissent, it is difficult to say what the *ratio* is. The judge in a subsequent case will once more be able to exercise his discretion[17]. Finally, if a case has more than one issue and the tribunal is not only divided as to the result but also divided on each issue, the difficulties that arise cannot be resolved by any test. The judge in a subsequent case will be free to reject the case as having no *ratio*, or to place whatever interpretation he chooses upon it[18]. All this does not imply that the solution would be to have only one judgment, even if the court is agreed. Differences in presentation and wording will avoid the danger of any one judge's utterance being treated like an Act of Parliament[19].

Obiter dicta

Pronouncements of law, which are not part of the *ratio decidendi*, are classed as *obiter dicta* and are not authoritative. *Rationes* and *dicta* tend to shade into

13 Eg the views of Lord Denning in *Rahimtoola v HEH Nizam of Hyderabad* [1958] AC 379 at 423, [1957] 3 All ER 441 at 464.
14 *Baker v R* [1975] AC 774 at 789, [1975] 3 All ER 55 at 64, per Lord Diplock; *Barrs v Bethel* [1982] Ch 294 at 308, [1982] 1 All ER 106 at 116, per Warner J.
15 Lord Simonds is reported to have given this very example in the course of argument: REM in (1950) 66 LQR 298, quoting (1949) 23 Austr LJ 355, and contrasting the Scottish practice.
16 Eg *Amalgamated Society of Railway Servants v Osborne* [1910] AC 87; *Jones v Secretary of State for Social Services* [1972] AC 944 at 1004, [1972] 1 All ER 145 at 180, per Lord Diplock.
17 *George Wimpey & Co Ltd v British Overseas Airways Corpn* [1955] AC 169, [1954] 3 All ER 661, analysed by Lord MacDermott CJ in *Walsh v Curry* [1955] NI 112. In *Harper v National Coal Board (Intended Action)* [1974] QB 614, [1974] 2 All ER 441, the Court of Appeal held itself free to adopt any of the reasons which supported the majority decision. It is to be noted that the rule adopted in South Africa is that in a five-judge court no proposition is to be regarded as being the *ratio decidendi* unless at least three judges give the same reason: *Fellner v Minister of the Interior* 1954 (4) SA 523 (A).
18 See the example discussed by Coutts in (1955) 71 LQR 24.
19 On this see Lord Reid 'The Judge as a Law-Maker' (1972) 12 JSPTL (NS), especially at pp 28–29; and in *Cassell & Co Ltd v Broome* [1972] AC 1027 at 1084–1085, [1972] 1 All ER 801 at 836.

each other. The former have law-quality and are binding on lower courts; *dicta*, too, have law-quality, but are not binding at all. *Vis-a-vis* a higher court even the *ratio decidendi* of a lower court decision has only persuasive force like that of a *dictum*. It has been pointed out that some *dicta* are so authoritative that the distinction between *ratio* and *dictum* is reduced to vanishing point. *Dicta*, which have no force, are propositions stated by way of illustration or on hypothetical facts[20]. Greater difficulties attend rulings of law which are subsequently relegated to the status of *dicta* by interpretation. The distinction in such cases between *ratio* and *dictum* is but a device employed by subsequent courts for the adoption or rejection of doctrine expressed in previous cases according to the inclination of the judges. An example would be the treatment of Lord Atkin's 'neighbour' proposition in subsequent cases.

The weight accorded to *dicta* varies with the type of *dictum*. Mere casual expressions carry no weight at all. 'Not every passing expression of a judge, however eminent, can be treated as an *ex cathedra* statement'[1]. On the other hand, *dicta* which have been acted upon over the years may acquire increasing respect[2]. A *dictum* may also be adopted as the *ratio decidendi* of a subsequent decision and will then acquire the authority of that tribunal. In *Zeidman v Owen*[3] Lord Goddard CJ said 'If we thought that the dicta, though *obiter*, expressed the true construction of the Act, we should feel we ought to follow them'. Finally, a suggestion has been offered that a distinction be drawn between *obiter dicta*, those irrelevant to the case, and *judicial dicta*, those relevant to some collateral matter but no part of the *ratio*[4]. The latter will generally be more persuasive than the former.

Subsequent history of a case

It should be abundantly clear from all this that the *ratio decidendi* of a case depends on the interpretation put upon it no less than on what the deciding judge himself propounded. Later history is thus an indispensable and continuing part of *ratio*. It also shows the limits of bindingness.

Reversal

A case may be reversed on appeal. The effect of reversal is normally that the first judgment ceases to have any effect at all. The situation is different if the case is affirmed or reversed by an appellate court on a different point from that on which the decision in the lower court was based. In one case, a Master of the Rolls said that in such a situation the previous decision will be 'of no effect at all'[5]. This probably goes too far, and in another case it was

---

20 A ruling on *assumed* facts, eg on a preliminary point, may well be treated as *ratio decidendi*, eg *Donoghue v Stevenson* [1932] AC 562; *Weller & Co v Foot and Mouth Disease Research Institute* [1966] 1 QB 569, [1965] 3 All ER 560.
1 Lord Porter in *London Graving Dock Co Ltd v Horton* [1951] AC 737 at 748, [1951] 2 All ER 1 at 6.
2 Hodson LJ in *Triefus & Co Ltd v Post Office* [1957] 2 QB 352 at 360, [1957] 2 All ER 387 at 389. For the rejection of such a *dictum*, see *Public Trustee v IRC* [1960] AC 398, [1960] 1 All ER 1.
3 [1950] 1 KB 593 at 596, [1950] 1 All ER 290 at 291.
4 Megarry in a Note in (1944) 60 LQR 222.
5 *Hack v London Provident Society* (1883) 23 Ch D 103 at 112.

said that the first judgment remains binding[6]. The truth seems to be that in such a situation a later court has freedom to deal as it pleases with the earlier decision.

Refusal to follow

Before the doctrine of *stare decisis* came into being, judges freely refused to follow cases which they considered to be contrary to principle. A judge may even now refuse to follow a decision of co-ordinate authority, in which event the conflict awaits resolution by a superior tribunal. Repeated refusals to follow will weaken the authority of a case; as also the refusal by a higher court to adopt the rule enunciated by a lower court, but only if such refusal implies disapproval of it[7].

The growing volume of reported cases often leads to an unavoidable overlooking of relevant authorities. Sometimes, however, a precedent may be deliberately put on one side, though this is done rarely and perhaps as a last resort. Thus, Sellers LJ once said 'the best way to deal with that case is to say that it goes into the limbo of lost causes'[8].

Distinguishing

Repeated distinguishing of a case is evidence that the decision is not approved, and the effect may also be to confine it more and more closely to its own special facts.

It should be evident already that the bindingness in *stare decisis* is not rigid since judges have some latitude in evading unwelcome authorities[9]. All that the doctrine means is that a judge must follow a precedent except where he can *reasonably* distinguish it; but the possibilities of the latter are such that they reduce buidingness to the semblance of a cloud, solid looking and clear-cut when viewed from afar, but less so when one actually gets into it. A judge may, in the first place, restate the factual part of the precedent by lowering the level of generality in order to effect the necessary distinction. 'A case is only an authority for what it actually decides. I entirely deny that it can be quoted for a proposition that may seem to follow logically from it':

6 *Curtis Moffat v Wheeler* [1929] 2 Ch 224. See also *The Parlement Belge* (1879) 4 PD 149, revsd on a different point (1880) 5 PD 197, but the ruling at first instance remains an authority; *Barratt v Gough-Thomas* [1945] 2 All ER 414, revsd on a different point [1945] 2 All ER 650, but the ruling at first instance was upheld in [1951] Ch 242, [1950] 2 All ER 1048. The rule in *Young v Bristol Aeroplane Co Ltd* [1944] KB 718, [1944] 2 All ER 293 remains an authority despite the fact that the decision was affd on a different point [1946] AC 163, [1946] 1 All ER 98.
7 *Dutton v Bognor Regis UDC* [1972] 1 QB 372 at 394, 401–402, [1972] 1 All ER 462 at 473, 478–479.
8 *Matthews v Kuwait Bechtel Corpn* [1959] 2 QB 57 at 69, [1959] 2 All ER 345 at 351. In *Herschtal v Stewart and Ardern Ltd* [1940] 1 KB 155, [1939] 4 All ER 123, Tucker J refused to follow *Dransfield v British Insulated Cables Ltd* [1937] 4 All ER 382, and ignored *Otto v Bolton and Norris* [1936] 2 KB 46, [1936] 1 All ER 960. In *Elias v Pasmore* [1934] 2 KB 164, Horridge J made no mention of the classic case of *Entick v Carrington* (1765) 19 State Tr 1029, though it had been cited to him.
9 Llewellyn listed sixteen distinguishing techniques and sixteen for providing a 'fresh start': *The Common Law Tradition, Deciding Appeals* pp 85–91.

so said Lord Halsbury[10], and his words are classic authority for this particular distinguishing technique. The two decisions then, as Lord Simon put it, are like 'binary stars each part of which lives within the field of the other and is essentially influenced by it'[11]. In this way it is theoretically possible to confine the authority of *Donoghue v Stevenson*[12] to the manufacture of ginger beer and to distinguish it from a case concerning the manufacture of fruit-salad; but it is obvious that the lengths to which this technique can be carried have to be regulated by common sense. A distinction has to be *reasonable*, else it will not satisfy the desire that justice should be done. Alternatively, a judge may restate the factual part of the precedent by treating as material such additional facts as will move it away from the case in hand[13]. Again, it is possible to evade a precedent by treating the less appropriate of alternative principles as its *ratio*. Or, the ruling hitherto regarded as being the *ratio* may be rejected as *dictum*. Asquith LJ once quoted the following remark: ' "the rule is quite simple: if you agree with the other bloke you say it's part of the *ratio*; if you don't, you say it's *obiter dictum*, with the implication that he is a congenital idiot". And this may well, as a matter of pure psychological fact, have more underlying truth than we know, or care to avow'[14].

On occasions it may be difficult to decide whether a case has been overruled in a subsequent decision, or merely distinguished. Where the House of Lords, for example, has commented adversely on earlier decisions of inferior courts, there is often a great deal of discretion for future courts in deciding whether the House of Lords has by its comments destroyed the authority of those cases, or merely distinguished them and left their authority unimpaired[15].

Changed conditions

Although a case has neither been reversed nor overruled, it may cease to be 'law' owing to changed conditions and changed law: *cessante ratione cessat ipsa lex*. It is not easy to detect when such situations occur, for as long as the traditional theory prevails that judges never make law, but only declare it, two situations need to be carefully distinguished. One is where a case is rejected as being no longer law on the ground that it is now thought never to have represented the law[16]; the other is where a case, which is acknowledged to have been law at the time, has ceased to have that character owing

---

10 *Quinn v Leathem* [1901] AC 495 at 506. See also Lord Denning in *Close v Steel Co of Wales Ltd* [1962] AC 367 at 388, [1961] 2 All ER 953 at 960; Lord Upjohn in *Ogden Industries Pty Ltd v Lucas* [1969] 1 All ER 121 at 126. See, however, Lord Diplock in *D v NSPCC* [1978] AC 171 at 220, [1977] 1 All ER 589 at 596-597.

11 *FA & AB Ltd v Lupton (Inspector of Taxes)* [1972] AC 634 at 659, [1971] 3 All ER 948 at 965. In *Jones v Secretary of State for Social Services* [1972] AC 944, [1972] 1 All ER 145, the House of Lords refused to distinguish a previous case which the Court of Appeal and Divisional Court had held to be distinguishable.

12 [1932] AC 562.

13 Eg *Haley v London Electricity Board* [1965] AC 778, [1964] 3 All ER 185 where the House of Lords distinguished a previous decision by stressing the materiality of a certain fact; and *The Wagon Mound (No 2)* [1967] 1 AC 617, [1966] 2 All ER 709, where the Judicial Committee stressed one small fact so as to distinguish its own previous decision on the same occurrence.

14 Asquith 'Aspects of the Court of Appeal' (1950) 1 JSPTL(NS) 359.

15 *Consett Industrial and Provident Society Ltd v Consett Iron Co Ltd* [1922] 2 Ch 135.

16 Eg *R v Jackson* [1891] 1 QB 671, where, on the question of a husband's power to confine and chastise his wife, the case of *Re Cochrane* (1840) 8 Dowl 630, giving him such a power, was overruled as never having represented English law.

to altered circumstances. It is the latter that is under consideration. If the law-making function of courts is admitted, then it would be easy to reject out-of-date precedents openly on the ground of changed conditions and not have to resort to the threadbare fiction that cases only reflect what always has been law.

Willes CJ once said 'When the nature of things changes, the rules of law must change too'[17]. This is a truism in that the legislature and, within limits, the courts should change rules to keep the law abreast of change. The question under review is whether changed conditions may deprive a case of its law-quality. For instance, the decision of the Court of Appeal in *Re Polemis and Furness, Withy & Co Ltd*[18] was disapproved by the Privy Council in *The Wagon Mound*[19], but although it has never been overruled, it has been declared to be no longer law in the light of the change in the law of remoteness of damage that had taken place. There is also a strong suggestion in *The Heron II*[20] that *The Parana*[1], which had laid down a rule for assessing damages in the bygone days of sailing ships, had ceased to be law in the conditions of modern transport. When sterling changed from being a stable to a floating currency and after Britain's entry into the EEC, the Court of Appeal departed from the rule laid down by the House of Lords in an earlier case[2]. Later, in following their decision, Lord Denning MR remarked 'When the nature of sterling changes, the rule of law may change too'[3]. On appeal, the House of Lords affirmed the Court of Appeal and refused to follow their previous decision, but indicated that it was for the House, and not the Court of Appeal, to do so. The 'changed conditions' rule applies only to decisions which are not binding. In an important statement of the position Lord Simon said:

> 'To sum up on this part of the case: (1) the maxim in the form "cessante ratione cessat ipsa lex" reflects one of the considerations which your Lordships will weigh in deciding whether to overrule, by virtue of the 1966 declaration, a previous decision of your Lordships' House; (2) in relation to courts bound by the rule of precedent the maxim "cessante ratione cessat ipsa lex", in its literal and widest sense, is misleading and erroneous; (3) specifically, courts which are bound by the rule of precedent are not free to disregard an otherwise binding precedent on the ground that the reason which led to the formulation of the rule embodied in such precedent seems to the court to have lost cogency; (4) the maxim in reality reflects the process of legal reasoning whereby a previous authority is judicially distinguished or an exception is made to a principal legal rule; (5) an otherwise binding precedent or rule may, on proper analysis, be held to have been impliedly overruled by a subsequent decision of a higher court or impliedly abrogated by an Act of Parliament; but this

---

17 *Davies v Powell* (1737) Willes 46 at 51.
18 [1921] 3 KB 560.
19 [1961] AC 388, [1961] 1 All ER 404. If one accepts the view that courts only declare, but do not make, law, it is arguable that *Polemis* never did reflect the 'true' law.
20 [1966] 2 QB 695, [1966] 2 All ER 593; affd [1969] 1 AC 350, [1967] 3 All ER 686.
 1 (1877) 2 PD 118. In *British Railways Board v Herrington* [1972] AC 877, [1972] 1 All ER 749 the House of Lords took account of the changed attitude with regard to the relative sanctity of person and property and, in effect, treated a previous decision of itself on the nature of an occupier's duty as no longer law.
 2 *Schorsch Meier GmbH v Hennin* [1975] QB 416, [1975] 1 All ER 152, not following *Re United Railways of the Havana and Regla Warehouses Ltd* [1961] AC 1007, [1960] 2 All ER 332.
 3 *Miliangos v George Frank (Textiles) Ltd* [1975] QB 487 at 504, [1975] 1 All ER 1076 at 1085.

doctrine is not accurately reflected by citation of the maxim "cessante ratione cessat ipsa lex" '[4].

Overruling

This refers to the action of a superior court in upsetting the *ratio* laid down by a lower court in some other case. Reversal, which is the overthrow of a decision on appeal in the same case, may involve disapproval of the *ratio* as stated by the lower court; but it need not, as where the decision is reversed on some other point. Overruling necessarily involves disapproval of the *ratio*, but never affects the previous *decision* so that the parties in the overruled case continue to be bound by the decision under the doctrine of *res judicata*; and accounts that have been settled also are not affected[5]. A theoretical question arises when a superior court declares that a *ratio* enunciated previously by a lower court is wrong, but at the same time decides the present case with similar facts in the same way but for a different reason. If it is accepted that, whatever is held to constitute the *ratio decidendi* of a case, at least nothing can be *ratio* which does not support the order that is made, then the new ruling is *ratio*; but even if it is not, it may well prove to be so authoritative as to reduce the distinction between *ratio* and *dictum* to vanishing point[6]. If a case is overruled by statute, there is some ground for saying that its *ratio* is no longer authoritative[7]. A case may first be overruled and then reversed, as when the *ratio* is overthrown by superior authority in another case while there is still time within which to appeal in the first case, and an appeal is then lodged against the decision, which is duly reversed[8]. It is also possible for a case to be first reversed and then overruled, as when the decision is reversed on appeal on some other point without affecting the *ratio*, and the *ratio* is then overthrown in another case. If a case is overruled and the overruling case is itself reversed[9], or overruled[10], the first will revive. Statutory repeal operates prospectively, unless the statute itself provides otherwise. Suppose that case A is overruled by case B, which is itself subsequently overruled by statute. Does case A revive? By analogy with the case law position it is submitted that it does[11].

---

4 *Miliangos v George Frank (Textiles) Ltd*[1976] AC 443 at 476, [1975] 3 All ER 801 at 820. In the light of this one wonders if *Re Polemis* [1921] 3 KB 560 is still binding on the Court of Appeal.

5 *Thomson v St Catharine's College, Cambridge* [1919] AC 468; *Re Waring, Westminster Bank v Burton-Butler* [1948] Ch 221, [1948] 1 All ER 257. Cf *Re Koenigsberg, Public Trustee v Koenigsberg* [1949] Ch 348, [1949] 1 All ER 804. Accounts settled: *Henderson v Folkestone Waterworks Co* (1885) 1 TLR 329.

6 This might have occurred in *Hedley Byrne & Co Ltd v Heller & Partners Ltd* [1964] AC 465, [1963] 2 All ER 575, but here the order was in fact based on the new principle as formulated.

7 *Thomson v Moyse* [1961] AC 967 at 989, 1006, [1960] 3 All ER 684 at 688, 699.

8 *Ainley v Ainley* [1945] P 27, [1945] 1 All ER 265, overruled by *Beard v Beard* [1946] P 8, [1945] 2 All ER 306; revsd [1946] 1 All ER 311n.

9 *Watson Bros v Hornby* [1942] 2 All ER 506, overruled by the Court of Appeal in *Sharkey v Wernher* [1954] Ch 713, [1954] 2 All ER 753, revived by the House of Lords, which revsd the Court Appeal, [1956] AC 58, [1955] 3 All ER 493.

10 It was on this principle that Denning LJ revived *Cann v Willson* (1888) 39 ChD 39, in his dissenting judgment in *Candler v Crane, Christmas & Co* [1951] 2 KB 164, [1951] 1 All ER 426. The House of Lords agreed with him in *Hedley Byrne & Co Ltd v Heller & Partners Ltd* [1964] AC 465, [1963] 2 All ER 575.

11 Cf the restrictive interpretation of *Wilsons & Clyde Coal Co Ltd v English* [1938] AC 57, [1937] 3 All ER 628, in *Davie v New Merton Board Mills Ltd* [1959] AC 604, [1959] 1 All ER 346, and the overruling of *Davie* by the Employer's Liability (Defective Equipment) Act 1969. The gist of the *Wilsons* ratio was re-stated in the statute, so the point did not arise. It is submitted that that *ratio* would have revived even apart from the Act.

It is not possible to lay down a rule as to when it is or is not permissible to overrule[12]. There will sometimes be a bold rejection even of settled doctrine[13]; at others there will be a timid refusal to eradicate obsolete and obstructive rules[14]. In *Jones v Secretary of State for Social Services*[15] the House of Lords considered whether or not to overrule a previous decision of its own. Various considerations were mentioned. In the first place, it was said to be important on grounds of public policy not to weaken certainty or finality. (a) Finality is necessary in developing the law; (b) a tenable view taken in case 1 should not be cast aside by an equally tenable opposite view in case 2, or this in turn may be cast aside in case 3; and (c) it is important not to encourage the re-opening of questions. Secondly, overruling is legitimate when broad issues of legal principle are involved, or if a decision has been disapproved, or distinguished on inadequate grounds. Thirdly, it is easier to overrule a recent decision before it has been acted on. Fourthly, overruling should rarely occur in matters of statutory construction according to two of their Lordships, but two others thought otherwise[16]. In the result, even though a majority of their Lordships thought the earlier case to have been wrongly decided, only a minority were prepared to overrule it[17].

Circumstances which might tend to strengthen the authority of a case and which would work against it being overruled are the unanimity of the court, the eminence of the judges who composed it, the approval of the decision in later cases and by the profession at large, the evidence in the report that the issue was fully and carefully argued by counsel and that the court took time to deliberate, and the length of time for which the decision has stood. This last is especially important since the longer a case has stood, the more people will have governed their transactions on the basis of what is thought to be law[18]. Similarly, factors which might make a court more ready to overrule

---

12 See the remarks of Lord Loreburn in *West Ham Union v Edmonton Union* [1908] AC 1 at 4.

13 Eg *Morgan v Fear* [1907] AC 425; *Bowman v Secular Society* [1917] AC 406; *Fibrosa Spolka Akcyjna v Fairbairn Lawson Combe Barbour Ltd* [1943] AC 32, [1942] 2 All ER 122; *Holmes v DPP* [1946] AC 588, [1946] 2 All ER 124; *Public Trustee v IRC* [1960] AC 398, [1960] 1 All ER 1; *Button v DPP* [1966] AC 591, [1965] 3 All ER 587; *R v Bow Road Domestic Proceedings Court, ex p Adedigba* [1968] 2 QB 572, [1968] 2 All ER 89.

14 Eg *Foakes v Beer* (1884) 9 App Cas 605; *Admiralty Comrs v SS Amerika* [1917] AC 38; *Searle v Wallbank* [1947] AC 341, [1947] 1 All ER 12; *Westminster Bank v IRC* [1958] AC 210, [1957] 2 All ER 745.

15 [1972] AC 944, [1972] 1 All ER 145.

16 See, however, *Farrell v Alexander* [1977] AC 59, [1976] 2 All ER 721; *Vestey v IRC* [1980] AC 1148, [1979] 3 All ER 976.

17 In *British Railways Board v Herrington* [1972] AC 877, [1972] 1 All ER 749, the House of Lords had no doubt that the principle in *Addie & Sons (Collieries) Ltd v Dumbreck* [1929] AC 358 was outdated, and three judges thought it wrong. Yet there was some hesitation about overruling it formally, but a preference instead to interpret it in a way which deprives it of effect. This may be because the Privy Council only a few years previously had emphatically upheld it in *Railways Comr v Quinlan* [1964] AC 1054, [1964] 1 All ER 897. Nevertheless, *Herrington* has given the clearest hint that the *Addie-Quinlan* principle is no more. See also *The Johanna Oldendorff* [1974] AC 479, [1973] 3 All ER 148. J Stone thought that (1) the House of Lords should first determine what the law ought to be; (2) the precedent challenged should be measured against what it ought to be; and (3) if it falls short, the degree of shortfall should be weighed against the effect of departing from it, or, alternatively, the possibility of narrowing its *ratio* should be weighed against the evil of an over-refined distinction: 'On the Liberation of Appellate Judges—How not to do it!' (1972) 35 MLR 449.

18 Eg *The Annefield* [1971] P 168, [1971] 1 All ER 394 (construction on a commercial document, which had been acted on for fifty-six years, should not be upset). In *Knuller Ltd v DPP* [1973] AC 435, [1972] 2 All ER 898, the House of Lords declined to overrule *Shaw v DPP*

an earlier case are a lack of unanimity in the judgments, the failure to take notice of relevant authorities, the lack of eminence of the judges who decided it, the fact that the report is of poor quality, the fact that the issue was not fought out fully but was compromised, the fact that the judgment was extempore and the matter had not been properly argued, the fact that the case has been doubted or criticised in subsequent decisions or by the profession or in commentaries of jurists, and, by no means least, if the decision is thought to be plainly wrong.

Overruling may be express or implied. It is implied when the *ratio* of the later decision of a superior court is inconsistent with that of the inferior court. In view of the difficulty of ascertaining the *ratio* of a case, it follows that it is equally difficult to decide whether a case has been impliedly overruled or not[19], but it does give courts a loophole for escaping from *stare decisis*.

The effect of overruling is retroactive except that it does not unsettle matters which are *res judicata* as between the parties to the overruled decision, and accounts which have been settled[20]. Retroactivity is logically reconcilable with the theory that judges do not make law but only declare what always has been law on the hypothesis that the overruled decision was an erroneous declaration of the law and hence void *ab initio*. This reason may be an *ex post facto* rationalisation. A more fundamental reason seems equally plausible, namely that just quality is inherent in every law. Therefore, an unjust (hence erroneous) precedent can never have been 'law'. However, the retroactive rule creates a difficulty. The House of Lords insists that only the House can declare its own decisions wrong and that lower courts must follow them. This implies that such previous decisions are 'law', albeit 'bad law', since no court can be bound to follow that which is not 'law'. If so, the overruling by the House of Lords of one of its own decisions must operate prospectively. On the other hand, all transactions entered into prior to the overruling are governed by the new decision. This differs from statute where repeal operates prospectively, unless there is express provision to the contrary. Everything that occurred prior to repeal remains governed by the repealed statute.

Even if it be conceded that judges do make law, the question of hardship would remain in that those who had acted in reliance on the law prevailing at the time would be judged on the basis of a different law made *ex post facto*. This consideration weighs powerfully against overruling except for compelling reasons. A suggestion that merits serious attention is that overruling, like repeal, should take effect for the future only, and that the decision in the instant case should abide by the previous law for the last time[1]. The

---

[1962] AC 220, [1961] 2 All ER 446, because the decision had been acted on in a great many cases since. Lord Reid, who had dissented in *Shaw* and still thought it to have been wrongly decided, refused to overrule it on grounds of certainty.

19 Eg *Leathley v John Fowler & Co Ltd* [1946] KB 579, [1946] 2 All ER 326. See also the effect on *Norris v Edmonton Corpn* [1957] 2 QB 564, [1957] 2 All ER 801 of *Francis v Yiewsley and West Drayton UDC* [1958] 1 QB 478, [1957] 3 All ER 529, as discussed in *Eastbourne Corpn v Fortes Ice Cream Parlour (1955) Ltd* [1958] 2 QB 41, [1958] 2 All ER 276 (revsd [1959] 2 QB 92, [1959] 2 All ER 102).

20 Blackstone *Commentaries* I, p 87; *Re Waring, Westminster Bank v Burton-Butler* [1948] Ch 221, [1948] 1 All ER 257; *Henderson v Folkestone Waterworks Co* (1885) 1 TLR 329.

1 Wigmore, Preface to *Science of Legal Method* p xxxviii. The doctrine has been applied in the United States: *Great Northern Rly v Sunburst Oil and Refining Co* 287 US 358 (1932); *Johnson v New Jersey* 384 US 719 at 733-735 (1966). The Indian Supreme Court in a bold and imaginative judgment showed readiness to hold a statute void prospectively: *Golak Nath v State of Punjab* [1967] 2 SCR 762. In *Jones v Secretary of State for Social Services* [1972] AC 944 at 1015, 1026-27, [1972] 1 All ER 145 at 189, 198-199, Lords Diplock and Simon thought

objections do not appear to be conclusive. It might be said that if the new rule, which is to supplant the old, does not support the actual decision it can only be a *dictum*. This might be countered by the argument that the tribunal is only freeing itself for the *future* from any constraining effect of its own decision, thus enabling itself to adopt the *dictum* later. It might also be objected that a litigant would not be encouraged to appeal against a bad precedent if the overruling of it would not avail him. There is probably some substance in this in a limited number of cases, but against it there is a possible advantage in that the new practice should remove the inhibiting factor which often stands in the way of much-needed reform. Besides, the objection would be met by coupling prospective overruling with a discretion to overrule for the future and for the instant case, or for the future only, or for the future, the instant case and retrospectively. Prospective overruling will be helpful where the object is to create a new criminal offence, or extend an existing one, by overruling a case which had held that there is no liability in that situation; for this would avoid having to punish the accused in the instant case for conduct which was not a crime when he did it[2].

Following and applying

The *ratio decidendi* of a previous case may be followed or applied in a subsequent case. If a case has been repeatedly followed, this is a factor which enhances its authority. A case may be said to be 'followed' when the use made of it does not affect its *ratio*, for example, when the judge only trims the facts of the case before him to fit it into the precedent. A case may be said to be 'applied' when the use made of it does affect its *ratio*, which could occur when the judge raises the level of its generality by reducing the material facts, or selects the more appropriate of alternative *rationes*. He may also adopt a *dictum* in it as the *ratio* of the case before him[3].

Explaining

A judge may place a certain interpretation on a precedent and he may then follow it, or he may refuse to follow it, or he may distinguish it. Explaining is an indication that the *ratio decidendi* is being reshaped.

JUDICIAL DISCRETION

Since there is no fixed *ratio* of a case, there is an element of choice in determining it. The orthodox Blackstonian view, however, is that judges do not make law, but only declare what has always been law[4]. This doctrine is

---

that prospective overruling should be considered; and see Lord Simon's 'Afterword' in *Miliangos v George Frank (Textiles) Ltd* [1976] AC 443 at 490, [1975] 3 All ER 801 at 832. Contra Lord Devlin 'Judges and Lawmakers' (1976) 39 MLR at 11. See also Traynor '*Quo Vadis*, Prospective Overruling: a Question of Judicial Responsibility' (Birmingham University 1975).

2 See on this Friedmann 'Limits of Judicial Lawmaking and Prospective Overruling' (1966) 29 MLR 593.

3 Llewellyn listed thirty-two techniques of following and applying: *The Common Law Tradition, Deciding Appeals* pp 77–84.

4 *Blackstone* I pp 88–89. See also Hale *History of the Common Law* p 90; Lord Esher in *Willis v Baddely* [1892] 2 QB 324 at 326; Viscount Dilhorne in *Home Office v Dorset Yacht Co Ltd* [1970] AC 1004 at 1045, 1051, [1970] 2 All ER 294 at 313, 318; and in *Cassell & Co Ltd v Broome* [1972] AC 1027 at 1107, [1972] 1 All ER 801 at 854.

the product of many factors. It would appear to result from thinking exclusively in the present time-frame, which gives rise to the belief that there must
be some rule which is always 'there' at any given moment and waiting to be
applied. In Blackstone's day another important foundation for the doctrine
was the belief in natural law, which was supposed to be part of English law.
Despite the derision which this theory encountered[5], and in the face of
evidence to the contrary, its vitality is remarkable. Again, during the
seventeenth-century struggle against the prerogative the judges maintained
that the king was subject to the law and could not legislate, the corollary of
which was that they, too, were subject to the law and unable to make law
and bound only to apply it. The doctrine of the separation of powers also
insisted upon the theoretical dissociation of judicial and legislative functions.
The climate of opinion in the nineteenth century was favourable to the
theory in so far as the prevailing positivism concerned itself only with the
law as found, whether thought to have been produced by custom or laid
down by sovereign authority. Also, public confidence is more easily retained
by fostering the illusion that judges do but administer the law impersonally
and that none of them can make the rules, especially since judicial law-
making is necessarily retroactive. The theory is also borne out in the simplest
disputes, particularly those in lower tribunals, which constitute the bulk of
litigation. Judges, for their part, seek refuge in the theory when giving a
harsh decision. Indeed, it has even been suggested that the theory satisfies
the psychological preference of human beings to be led rather than have to
find their own way, the need, in short, for a 'father-symbol'. Another factor
is that judicial decisions in their nature have to pronounce on the legality of
conduct after it has taken place[6]. Anything savouring of attainder is unpopular and the orthodox theory conceals this suggestion under the pretence
that the law has always been there. It should also be noted that, whether or
not a creative element enters into a particular decision, it becomes for future
purposes evidence of what the law is, and this evidential function overlays
the creative factors that operated to bring it into being.

Finally, and by no means least, the orthodox theory finds support in the
syllogistic form of reasoning by which the conclusion is ultimately reached.
For a syllogism requires that the premises, from which the conclusion is
deduced, should already be in existence. Thus: 'All men are mortal' (major
premise); 'X is a man' (minor premise); 'Therefore X is mortal' (conclusion).
In a judgment the syllogism assumes the following form: 'Facts of Type A
are governed by Rule B, (major premise); 'Facts of the instant case are of
Type A' (minor premise); 'therefore the facts of the instant case are governed
by Rule B', (conclusion)[7]. A syllogism can only make explicit that which is
implicit in the premises; it neither creates nor reveals anything new. With
reference to a judicial decision this gives rise to the idea that the result is
deducible from a rule, which is already 'there'[8].

The syllogistic form appears only in the way the conclusion is stated at

5 Austin *Jurisprudence* II p 634, who called it 'the childish fiction employed by our judges, that
  judiciary or common law is not made by them, but is a miraculous something made by
  nobody, existing, I suppose, from eternity, and merely *declared* from time to time by the
  judges'.
6 Cf Bentham *Works* V, p 235, who called it 'dog law'.
7 Summarised by Lord Simon in *FA and AB Ltd v Lupton* (*Inspector of Taxes*) [1972] AC 634 at
  658–659, [1971] 3 All ER 948 at 964.
8 See MacCormick *Legal Reasoning and Legal Theory*; Aarnio *On Legal Reasoning*.

the end of a judgment. Before a judge can deduce his conclusion, however, he has to find, and sometimes make, suitable premises and there is flexibility at every stage of the decisional process. First, he has to establish the major premise that 'Facts of Type A are governed by Rule B' by finding it in a precedent, statute or custom; or, if not, he creates one by analogy with other rules or by a process akin to induction or, in the absence of any other guide, he creates one out of his own sense of justice. When there is a rule of precedent, he has to consider whether or not to follow it either because it is binding and is not reasonably distinguishable, or, if not binding, because it is consonant with his sense of justice.

Next, he has to establish the minor premise that 'Facts of the instant case are of Type A'. Every case begins with the facts, but the finding of facts depends on opinion as to the credibility of witnesses and interpretation of the evidence generally. The facts have then to be stated at an appropriate level of generality and the statement is governed by linguistic conventions. It may also be coloured by a convenient rule which is to hand. The rule-statement, too, for its part is often trimmed according to the view taken of the facts so that it can be made to yield the conclusion which the judge wants to reach. The formulation of fact-statements and rule-statements are parallel processes.

In establishing that the facts of the instant case are of Type A, a distinction to be borne in mind is that between 'similarity' and 'identity'. It is unlikely that the factual part of a rule will be identical with the facts of the instant case because the chance of identity between facts in different situations occurring at different times is inconceivably remote and because rules are stated in general terms so as to accommodate variations and often utilise vague concepts, such as 'negligence', and 'possession'. As will be seen later, these have no fixed content and can be given different meanings in different contexts. What is crucial, therefore, is the perception of similarity, not identity, between the fact-situation of the case and the fact part of the rule; which is subjective, since perception of similarities and dissimilarities is a matter of choice and a desire to reach a just decision[9].

Finally, there is the conclusion that 'The facts of the instant case are governed by Rule B. Once the major and minor premises have been manipulated so as to show that the fact-statement in the instant case is similar to that of the rule, the conclusion will appear to follow syllogistically. The judicial process thus stands in a class of its own; it involves different kinds of reasoning.

A INDUCTION. This applies to finding a major premise. The term 'induction' is not a happy one but will serve for want of a better. The process bears only a broad parallel to scientific induction in so far as it proceeds from instances of particular cases to a generalised rule. 'Facts of case A were decided Y'; 'Facts of case B were decided Y'; 'Therefore, strictly, facts A and B should be decided Y'. It may, however, be reasonable to extract a broader proposition capable of yielding decision Y in situation C (and perhaps D and E)

9 See eg the extension of 'cattle' in the old cattle-trespass rule. Dogs were not similar to cattle for the purpose of this rule, but they were similar for the purpose of the rule (since abolished) of non-liability for straying on the highway: *Ellis v Johnston* [1963] 2 QB 8, [1963] 1 All ER 286. Cf *Upton-on-Severn RDC v Powell* [1942] 1 All ER 220. See also MR Cohen 'Law and Scientific Method' in *Jurisprudence in Action* pp 125-126.

as well[10]. Any such broader proposition has to be reasonably warranted by
the material out of which it was extracted, or it is liable to be cut down as
being too wide by a later court[11].

There are differences between this type of reasoning and scientific induction:

(a) A scientist can repeat his experiment and verify his principle; a judge
cannot.

(b) Scientific principles result from observations of data; judicial principles
result from statements of fact and value-judgments.

(c) A judge can reason by analogy and choose between competing analogies; a scientist does not.

(d) A scientific principle has to be modified so as to accommodate new
data; judicial principles are modified in response to moral and policy
considerations.

(e) A judge induces a principle in order to decide the case before him; for
a scientist the case before him is part of the data out of which the
principle is drawn, or by which it is tested[12].

(f) A scientist must accommodate all the data and has no choice; a judge
can select his material by discarding unwelcome cases.

B ANALOGY. This applies to finding the minor premise. The reasoning proceeds
case-by-case and by means of contrasting examples, first one way and
then another to see which way one's judgment is swayed. In this way the
scope of the 'facts' contained in the major premise is widened so that it can
accommodate a new set of facts[13]. Professor Wisdom expressed it best when
he said:

> 'It is a presenting and re-presenting of those features of the case which *severally
> co-operate* in favour of the conclusion, in favour of saying what the reasoner
> wishes said, in favour of calling the situation by the name by which he wishes
> to call it. The reasons are like the legs of a chair, not the links of a chain'[14].

Analogical reasoning accommodates change with certainty painlessly and
is, therefore, popular in the common law. The pressure exerted by the need
for certainty in law is a powerful incentive to develop the law analogically
when possible. It also helps to preserve confidence by abiding within existing

10 See Lord Asquith in *Chapman v Chapman* [1954] AC 429 at 470, [1954] 1 All ER 798 at 819;
Lord Denning MR in *Chic Fashions (West Wales) Ltd v Jones* [1968] 2 QB 299 at 313, [1968]
1 All ER 229 at 236; and in *The Changing Law* p 50. See also Cardozo *The Nature of the
Judicial Process* p 23.

11 Cf the treatment of Lord Atkin's speech in *Donoghue v Stevenson* [1932] AC 562, by Asquith
and Denning LJJ in *Candler v Crane, Christmas & Co* [1951] 2 KB 164, [1951] 1 All ER 426.
See also Jenkins LJ in *Re Ulverstone and District New Hospital Building Fund, Birkett v Barrow
and Furness Hospital Management Committee* [1956] 2 Ch 622 at 641, [1956] 3 All ER 164 at
174-175; *Haley v London Electricity Board* [1965] AC 778, [1964] 3 All ER 185 (rejecting
Pritchard v Post Office (1950) 114 JP 370 as being too widely stated).

12 Dickinson 'Legal Rules and their Function in the Process of Decision' (1931) 79 U Pa LR
833.

13 Lord Simon in *FA and AB Ltd v Lupton (Inspector of Taxes)* [1972] AC 634 at 659, [1971] 3
All ER 948 at 965.

14 'Gods' in *Philosophy and Psycho-Analysis* pp 157-158, 248-254. See also Cohen 'Law and
Scientific-Method' in *Jurisprudence in Action* pp 125-126; Bracton *De Legibus* f 1(b); Parke B in
Mirehouse v Rennell (1833) 1 Cl & Fin 527 at 546; Roxburgh J in *Re House Property and
Investment Co Ltd* [1954] Ch 576 at 601, [1953] 2 All ER 1525 at 1536.

authority. The case-by-case method is thus a way of making one's own sense of justice plausible.

c JUSTIFICATION The judge reaches a provisional conclusion and then tries to find authority to support it. The provisional conclusion may be the result of his trained instinct, or his opinion as to the merits of the dispute, or his sense of public need and social expediency; and he interprets and manipulates his authorities so as to justify that conclusion in a publicly satisfying way[15]. The 'public' for this purpose includes not only those charged with applying and administering the decision, but also all those interested in and affected by its application, which varies with the kind of rule[16]. Distinguishing depends on *plausibly* stating the facts of the instant case differently from the factual part of the rule that is being distinguished, or *plausibly* restating the rule so as to move it away from the instant case. Such techniques call for considerable skill and experience in handling authority. As Lord Wright once said 'A good judge is one who is the master, not the slave, of the cases'[17]. MacKinnon LJ also gave a pointed hint when he said

> 'So far as I am concerned, I freely avow that, inasmuch as in common-sense and decency Mr Heap ought to be able to recover against somebody, and in the circumstances of this case and having regard to the correspondence which has taken place, in common-sense and decency he ought to recover against these defendants if the law allows, my only concern is to see whether upon the cases the law does allow him so to recover. I think that it does'[18].

Viscount Radcliffe began a speech by speculating on the merits of a particular conclusion before considering what support it had in law.

> 'My Lords, it sometimes helps to assess the merits of a decision, if one starts by noticing its results and only after doing that allots to it the legal principles upon which it is said to depend.' (Having done that, he proceeded) 'I start, then, with the assumption that something must have gone wrong in the application of legal principles that produce such a result'[19].

A well-known ploy in this type of reasoning is for a judge to set out one line of argument leading to a certain conclusion, and then to set out a different line of argument also leading to the same conclusion[20]. They are alternative justifications.

Although all these methods play important parts in judicial reasoning, the first two types are frequently pressed into the service of the last[1]. Thus, induction can be much influenced by the conclusion which the judge may

---

15 Dewey 'Logical Method and Law' (1924) 10 Cornell LQ 17. 'The decision is a matter of outlook and impression rather than one for logical argument': per Porter J in *Philadelphia National Bank v Price* [1937] 3 All ER 391 at 397.

16 They may be sections of the community, eg motorists or trade or pressure groups, such as the National Council for Civil Liberties. The need for the judicial process to retain confidence was stressed by the Privy Council in *Geelong Harbor Trust Comrs v Gibbs Bright & Co* [1974] AC 810, [1974] 2 WLR 507.

17 Wright *Legal Essays and Addresses* p 79.

18 *Heap v Ind Coope and Allsop Ltd* [1940] 2 KB 476 at 483, [1940] 3 All ER 634 at 636-637.

19 *ICI Ltd v Shatwell* [1965] AC 656 at 675-676, [1964] 2 All ER 999 at 1005-1006. See also Lord Radcliffe *The Law and its Compass*.

20 Eg Denning LJ's judgment in *Broom v Morgan* [1953] 1 QB 597 at 609-610, [1953] 1 All ER 849 at 854-855.

1 For an examination of reasoning, see Lord Diplock in *Home Office v Dorset Yacht Co Ltd* [1970] AC 1004 at 1058 et seq, [1970] 2 All ER 294 at 324 et seq.

want to reach. In scientific induction *all* the facts have to be accommodated in the rule, whereas in law the judge can and does get rid of inconvenient precedents by distinguishing them. In this way he *selects* the material out of which to induce a rule and can thereby bend legal development in a certain direction.

The case-by-case method likewise lends itself to finding justification for a provisional conclusion. The perception of similarities is a matter of choice. Cases are not labelled 'similar' or 'dissimilar'; they can be made to appear similar or dissimilar according to the way in which they are presented[2]. The words of Professor Wisdom, quoted earlier, are worth repeating. The process, he said, is a presenting and re-presenting of those features of a case which co-operate 'in favour of saying what *the reasoner wishes said*, in favour of calling the situation by the name by which *he wishes to call it*'[3].

It is clear, therefore, that analogy can be pressed into the service of justification, but a caution needs to be uttered in case an exaggerated impression is created. Judges, like all human beings, prefer to avoid having to make personal decisions[4] and they are very much aware of the need for consistency, which is an important dictate of justice. The position may be put as follows. If a judge has no strong feelings in the matter, and the resemblances thrown up by the case-by-case method are obvious, these are likely to exercise a compelling influence. Even where the resemblances are not obvious, different ways of presenting the material may still help to sway the beam of judgment by weighting the similarities one way rather than another[5]. It should not be forgotten, however, that similarities are creations of the mind, not something given, and that some element of choice, perhaps imperceptible, underlies the application of every rule.

If a judge has strong feelings, then, however obvious the resemblances may be the other way, he will contrive, as far as he can reasonably do so, to manipulate the authorities to suit the decision he wants to give. 'If I thought that injustice had been done to him', said Lindley LJ 'I should have found some method, I have no doubt, of getting rid of the technical objection'[6]. Lord Denning, too, made a similar remark: 'I confess that I should do my best to distinguish it in some way if I was quite satisfied that it was wrong'[7]. A candid avowal of judicial technique came from Lord Diplock:

> 'Yet all nine judges who have been concerned with the instant case in its various stages are convinced that the plaintiff's claim ought to succeed; and if I may be permitted to be candid, are determined that it shall. The problem of judicial technique is how best to surmount or to circumvent the obstacle presented by the speeches of the Lord Chancellor and Viscount Dunedin in *Addie's* case, and the way in which those speeches were dealt with in the Privy Council in the comparatively recent Australian appeal of *Railways Comr v Quinlan*'[8].

---

2 See p 153 ante.

3 See p 154 ante (italics added). See also p 183 note 9 ante.

4 Wright 'Precedents' (1943) 8 CLJ 144; Goodhart *Essays in Jurisprudence and the Common Law* ch 13.

5 Decisions as to whether a servant acted in the course of employment are an outstanding example.

6 *Re Scowby, Scowby v Scowby* [1897] 1 Ch 741 at 751.

7 *Scruttons Ltd v Midland Silicones Ltd* [1962] AC 446 at 487, [1962] 1 All ER 1 at 19.

8 *British Railways Board v Herrington* [1972] AC 877 at 931, [1972] 1 All ER 749 at 787. The case is an example of different judicial techniques to arrive at the same result. The Court of Appeal, which was bound by a House of Lords decision that a trespasser can only recover

These statements should not be misunderstood to imply that bindingness is illusory and that judges decide as they please. To say that the doctrine is not rigid does not mean that it is non-existent. There are many pressures on judges to keep within the law, so their ability to manipulate rules is limited, and whenever they do so, their interpretations have to be reasonable and plausible. Far from being always free to decide as they please, they frequently confess that they are compelled by authority to decide in a certain way, even against their own inclinations.

When there is no rule of law

When there is no rule of precedent, statute or custom, knowing the law requires knowing how to create a rule. This may be done by the process akin to induction, which has been explained, or, failing all else, a judge may simply create a rule out of broad principle or doctrine, eg the fault principle or the maxims of equity, or out of his own sense of justice. In *Sommersett's Case*[9] the question arose for the first time whether English law should countenance slavery. There was no authority and counsel on both sides resorted to current philosophy in their arguments. Lord Mansfield made short work of the matter and declared that the slave should go free. In *Wilson v Glossop*[10] a husband turned his wife out of doors and she pledged his credit for the 'necessaries of life. When he sought to evade liability, the Court of Appeal held him liable on grounds of justice. If there had been no rule to that effect until then, there was one from then on. In *Corbett v Corbett (otherwise Ashley)*[11] an English court had to address itself for the first time to the question, What is a 'woman'? when a person, who had undergone a sex-change operation converting himself into an apparent female, went through a ceremony of marriage. Part of the judgment consists of a biological exposition of male and female organisms, the rest deals with the purpose and function of marriage. In the result the judge held the marriage to be void, since the person in question was still a biological male.

A study of the judicial process, its reasonings and techniques, helps to assess the significance of a case. Where there is an existing rule, a judge may do any one of several things.

(a) He may find complete similarity between the facts of the case before him and those contemplated by the rule. Not only is such a situation rare, but as a precedent the decision in such a case is, in any event, valueless.

(b) The statement of facts in the rule may be sufficiently general to cover the more specific facts of the instant case. A rule which contemplates, for example, the fact of 'negligence' will cover a multitudinous variety of situations. The decision in the instant case is then only illustrative.

(c) If the facts of the case before him differ from those stated in the rule, he may ignore the differences so as to be able to make a statement of

---

in respect of intentional or reckless injury, deplored the narrowness of the rule but interpreted the facts as amounting to recklessness so as to give the trespasser a remedy. The House of Lords interpreted the facts as amounting to negligence only, but upheld the Court of Appeal by utilising its power not to follow its own previous decision.

9 (1772) 20 State Tr 1.
10 (1888) 20 QBD 354.
11 [1971] P 83, [1970] 2 All ER 33. It is interesting that the judge had been a qualified doctor.

fact which will fit into the rule. Since this does not affect the rule, the decision is again only illustrative.

(d) He may also, in the last situation, reinterpret the statement of facts of the rule so as to extract a sufficient measure of resemblance to the case in hand. Such reinterpretation will vary the scope of the rule and the decision is important because it thereby alters the rule.

(e) Notwithstanding a difference between the statement of facts in the rule and in the case, he may apply the rule. The decision is again important because it has extended the rule to cover new facts.

(f) If he dislikes the rule he may distinguish it on account of some difference in the statement of facts in the case before him. Such a distinction does not affect the rule; it means only that the rule has not been extended. The importance, if any, of such a decision will rest on other factors.

(g) He may create a distinction by lowering the level of generality at which the facts in the rule are stated. Such a decision is again important because it has narrowed the rule.

(h) He may deny the rule the dignity of 'law' by interpreting it as an *obiter dictum*. Such an interpretation is important for it has, in effect, unmade law.

(i) In appropriate circumstances he may destroy the rule directly by reversing or overruling it.

(j) He may select one of alternative or conflicting rules[12]. Such a case is important in that it settles a point previously uncertain.

(k) Where there is no existing rule, he has to find one, and a creative decision of this kind is of the highest importance.

FACTORS THAT KEEP *STARE DECISIS* IN BEING

The reasons why *stare decisis* continues to be a criterion of validity are not the same as those which brought about its acceptance, though some do continue to play their part. The factors may be listed as the ethos of the profession, more doubtfully the continued absence of a code, and continued service of the requirements of justice. These, it will be noticed, are moral, sociological and practical requirements, and essential to the continuance of *stare decisis*. This is not to imply that an unjust or inconvenient precedent is not 'law' *here and now*; the point is that injustice or inconvenience will *in time* kill it and, if this were to occur on a large enough scale, may even bring about the demise of *stare decisis* itself.

Professional ethos

Every specialist vocation evolves its own expertise and habits of thought, ie a way of going about the job[13]. It has been pointed out how, because of the absence of a code from the earliest days, lawyers were compelled to seek guidance in precedents and to distil principles from lines of decisions. This became so much the lawyers' way of thinking that it should now be regarded

12 Eg *Thorne v Motor Trade Association* [1937] AC 797, [1937] 3 All ER 157; *Armstrong v Strain* [1951] 1 TLR 856; (affd [1952] 1 KB 232, [1952] 1 All ER 139).
13 See Llewellyn *The Common Law Tradition, Deciding Appeals* pp 19, 21–23.

as one of the most influential factors in keeping *stare decisis* alive. The thinking habits of centuries as well as the individual perfecting of this craft over a lifetime make it difficult, if not impossible, for most lawyers to think in any other way[14].

Absence of a code

The lack of a code was an important factor in bringing *stare decisis* about, but what part this still plays is doubtful. Even if the common law were to be codified now, this would not dispel the ingrained habits of thinking of the profession and, moreover, there is no reason why *stare decisis* could not flourish under a code. The two are not incompatible, but complementary. The kind of code one has in mind would enunciate only the broad principles and what it would gain by way of economy of wording it would lose in detail[15]. In the result, numberless decisions will mushroom forth to fill in the outlines, which will lead to a system of case-law hardly distinguishable from *stare decisis*—as Continental experience has shown[16]. Therefore, where, as in Great Britain, *stare decisis* is the accepted practice, the introduction of a code is unlikely to produce a significant change in outlook[17].

Continued service of justice

The need to continue treating like cases alike and so achieving equality, consistency and impartiality remains constant. It may be argued that the broad doctrine of precedent achieves all this no less than *stare decisis*. So a better way to put it is this: while failure to satisfy the needs of equality, consistency and impartiality will be fatal to *stare decisis*, fulfilment does not of itself account for its continuance. The other factors that have just been considered are responsible for this. In view of this, it will be useful to compare briefly the working of *stare decisis* and its Continental counterpart.

Equality of treatment, consistency and impartiality are bound up with the need for certainty and predictability. Complete certainty and predictability are elusive goals, for if law is to develop at all, uncertainties are bound to arise and, moreover, it may not be the rule that is uncertain, but which of competing rules should apply. So far as certainty can be achieved at all, there is no reason why precedent in the broad sense may not succeed as well as *stare decisis*. On the contrary, *stare decisis* is in some danger of making certainty in law become certainty of injustice. For a binding authority, however erroneous, has to be followed unless it can be distinguished, and a tenuous distinction to avoid an unwelcome precedent is not the happiest alternative. Again, it is important that there should be uniformity of treatment for all; but this, too, can be achieved without *stare decisis*. There should also be some limit to litigation, and if by this is meant that repeated agitation of a point that has once been determined should be discouraged, then, as the Continental experience has shown, it can be achieved as successfully

---

14 This may be why lawyers are thought to develop personality traits that favour the *status quo*, on which see Weyrauch *The Personality of Lawyers passim*. Cf Shklar *Legalism passim*, for a call to lawyers to abandon their specialist outlook.

15 Silving *Sources of Law* pp 84–86.

16 Eg in France.

17 Cf the *Note (Judicial Precedent)* [1966] 3 All ER 77, [1966] 1 WLR 1234, which suggests that the practical effect of the House of Lords' refusal to bind itself is likely to be small.

without *stare decisis* as with it. No judge departs from previous decisions except for compelling reasons, and legal advisers do not encourage vain hopes in their clients. If a decision is clearly erroneous, an attempt will probably be made to get it overruled; which happens here as elsewhere. Finally, it is desirable not to discount the experience of the past, but this is of limited value. It cannot avail in cases *primae impressionis* and it may also be that such wisdom is out-dated. In so far as past wisdom should be preserved, both precedent and *stare decisis* seem equally apt for this purpose. Summing up one might say that *stare decisis* does not seem to fulfil the requirements of justice any better than the doctrine of precedent. There is, however, another way of regarding the matter. It is because the things that *stare decisis* and precedent can accomplish are desirable that the two doctrines have now moved so near to each other as to be barely distinguishable.

One of the most important aspects of continued justice is that *stare decisis* should be adaptable to changing needs. This requires the avoidance of inconvenience and technicality and, above all, functioning flexibility.

Avoidance of inconvenience and technicality

A practical drawback is the growing number of reported decisions, which may reach such proportions as to make *stare decisis* physically unworkable. The chances of relevant authorities being overlooked increases and this strikes at the roots of the doctrine, for a decision can hardly be treated as authoritative if it was given *per incuriam*. Digests of cases and comparable services are just about able to make the system work, but these may become inadequate in time. It might be possible to make less use of the decisions of judges sitting alone, or to have one opinion only in all appellate courts; and in order to avoid encumbering the court house the use of looseleaf reports has been advocated. The possibilities of computerised storage of decisions opens up new vistas altogether, but these are beset with other difficulties and will be discussed later[18]. A different objection to *stare decisis* is that in this overwhelming mass of cases there is the danger of losing sight of principle. This may well be, but it can be minimised to some extent by the work of legal authors whose business it is to expound and illuminate principle. It is also maintained that case law based on *stare decisis* is inconveniently slow in adapting itself to a rapidly changing society. However, rapidity of change depends, not on the system, but on the judges who work it. The charge had more substance as long as the House of Lords was bound, in effect, even by its own mistakes, but now that that rule has gone, the position has been eased and might become easier still if the Court of Appeal, too, refuses to be bound by itself.

Allied to the above is the inconvenience caused by the growing technicality of an ever increasing multitude of rules and sub-rules and exceptions, which was castigated by Tennyson as 'that wilderness of single instances'. The common law possesses, however, the remarkable faculty of self-simplification, which from time to time saves *stare decisis* from collapsing under its own weight. This ability to slough off the top-heavy overgrowth and to start budding afresh has given it much of its resilience. Sometimes a single broad principle is drawn out of a number of precedents, thereby relegating them to the category of mere illustrations, an outstanding instance of which was Lord

18 See pp 307–308 post.

Atkin's review of a large number of authorities in *Donoghue v Stevenson*[19], and his formulation from them of a rule of liability for negligence of epoch-making significance. Again, in *Hedley Byrne & Co Ltd v Heller & Partners Ltd*[20] the House of Lords fused a number of diverse exceptions to the rule of non-liability for careless mis-statements[1] into a rule of liability for such statements[2].

Negligence, which is the branch of law in which decisions proliferate more rapidly perhaps than in any other, provides other examples of self-simplification. For instance, if the hosts of decisions as to whether a defendant's conduct was or was not careless were treated as laying down rules of law as to what does and does not constitute carelessness, the resulting state of affairs would be unthinkable. There has been an increasing tendency of recent years for courts not to treat such cases as 'law', but simply as illustrations of the rule that if a person causes damage carelessly he is liable, if he has not been careless he is not liable. 'The basic rule' said Pearson J 'is that negligence consists in doing something which a reasonable man would not have done in that situation, or omitting to do something which a reasonable man would have done in that situation, and I approach with scepticism any suggestion that there is any other rule of law properly so called in any of these cases'[3].

Notwithstanding these tendencies, negligence is still over-complex. 'There is no room today for mystique in the law of negligence' said Diplock LJ[4], but the rules relating eg to 'foreseeability of harm' are of such artificiality and technicality as to belie that remark[5]. Obviously, courts do not indulge in artificialities for their own sake; what they strive to do is to give fair decisions in particular cases, and it is *stare decisis* that produces the complications. Just as considerations such as the degree of likelihood of injury, cost and practicability of measures to avoid it, the end to be achieved, and so forth, are regarded only as helpful guidelines in determining whether a defendant has acted carelessly or not, might not the foreseeability rules of today similarly become guidelines for applying tomorrow's principle that in cases of negligence liability shall be attributed according as the court deems just[6]? Such a development would be in keeping with the genius of the common law.

19 [1932] AC 562.
20 [1964] AC 465, [1963] 2 All ER 575.
1 Originating in *Derry v Peek* (1889) 14 App Cas 337.
2 Where such a principle has been constructed, it is unnecessary to cite illustrative cases, per Lord Diplock in *Lexmead (Basingstoke) Ltd v Lewis* [1982] AC 225 at 274-275, [1981] 1 All ER 1185 at 1189-1190.
3 *Hazell v British Transport Commission* [1958] 1 All ER 116 at 118, [1958] 1 WLR 169 at 171. In three cases the House of Lords expressly declared that decisions on what constitutes carelessness should not be treated as laying down rules of law: *Qualcast (Wolverhampton) Ltd v Haynes* [1959] AC 743 at 755, [1959] 2 All ER 38 at 42 per Lord Keith, and at 757, 758, and at 43, 44 per Lord Somervell; *Cavanagh v Ulster Weaving Co Ltd* [1960] AC 145 at 163-164, [1959] 2 All ER 745 at 751, per Lord Keith; *Brown v Rolls-Royce Ltd* [1960] 1 All ER 577 at 581, [1960] 1 WLR 210 at 214 per Lord Keith, and at 582 and at 214 per Lord Denning.
4 *Doughty v Turner Manufacturing Co Ltd* [1964] 1 QB 518 at 531, [1964] 1 All ER 98 at 103.
5 Cf eg *The Wagon Mound* [1961] AC 388, [1961] 1 All ER 404, with *The Wagon Mound (No 2)* [1967] 1 AC 617, [1966] 2 All ER 709. For the difficulties of the foreseeability test generally, see *Clerk & Lindsell on Torts* ch 11.
6 Cf *Dutton v Bognor Regis UDC* [1972] 1 QB 373 at 397, [1972] 1 All ER 462 at 475; *Spartan Steel and Alloys Ltd v Martin & Co (Contractors) Ltd* [1973] QB 27 at 37, [1973] 3 All ER 557 at 562-563.

Similar to the complexity in negligence is the 'course of employment' doctrine in vicarious liability. The only rule of law here should be the broad and simple one that if a servant commits a tort while acting within the course of his employment, his master is answerable, but that if he was acting outside it, his master is not answerable. The question whether a servant was within or outside the course of employment, like the question whether a person was careless or not, is one of fact; to reduce it to rules of law governing types of situations is to reduce it to chaos. The sensible attitude has prevailed with regard to the question of carelessness; why not here? The opinion is ventured that it is perhaps writers of textbooks, rather than judges, who have been responsible for undue technicality by trying to evolve rules of law. The judges themselves do not appear to be obsessed in this way, for, as Finnemore J once said: 'The answer to a lot of the arguments on both sides in this case is, I think, as it so often is in the law of this country, that there is no one test which is conclusive or exhaustive or exclusive by which this particular problem can be solved'[7]. It is not easy to gauge how far this remark represents the judicial attitude as a whole, but even if it does not, it may well be a pointer in the direction of future simplification.

CONCLUSIONS

1. Judges do make law. A scrutiny of the judicial process shows that the Blackstonian doctrine is unacceptable. It fails to explain how the common law and certainly equity have grown[8]. No judge may refuse to give a decision. If no rule is at hand, he invents one. 'It may be' said Lord Denning MR 'that there is no authority to be found in the books, but, if this be so, all I can say is that the sooner we make one the better'[9]. In such a situation declaring what the law is and what it ought to be amount to the same[10]. More usually a judge narrows, extends, or otherwise modifies some existing rule, but all rules, whether created or adapted, are subject to modification in their turn. The *ratio* of a case may be likened to a pellet of clay, which a potter can stretch and shape within limits. If he wants to stretch it, he can; or he can press it back into a pellet. A *ratio* cannot be stretched indefinitely any more than clay, for there is a limit beyond which the generalisation of the statement of specific facts cannot go. When an unmanageable number of

7 *Staton v National Coal Board* [1957] 2 All ER 667 at 669 [1957] 1 WLR 893 at 895. Cf Asquith LJ 'I am not unaware that a prohibition has been held in some cases not to curtail the scope of employment, as in *Limpus v London General Omnibus Co* (1862) 1 H & C 526, but I think it does so in this case': *Conway v George Wimpey & Co Ltd* [1951] 2 KB 266 at 276, [1951] 1 All ER 363 at 367.

8 Mellish LJ in *Allen v Jackson* (1875) 1 Ch D 399 at 409; Jessel MR in *Re Hallett's Estate, Knatchbull v Hallett* (1880) 13 Ch D 696 at 710. A new doctrine, the 'deserted wife's equity', was created in 1952 (*Bendall v McWhirter* [1952] 2 QB 466, [1952] 1 All ER 1307); but this was overthrown by the House of Lords thirteen years later (*National Provincial Bank Ltd v Ainsworth* [1965] AC 1175, [1965] 2 All ER 472).

9 *A-G v Butterworth* [1963] 1 QB 696 at 719, [1962] 3 All ER 326 at 329. For examination of judicial creativity, see Lord Diplock in *Home Office v Dorset Yacht Co Ltd* [1970] AC 1004 at 1058 et seq, [1970] 2 All ER 294 at 324 et seq; Lord Hailsham in *Cassell & Co Ltd v Broome* [1972] AC 1027 at 1075, [1972] 1 All ER 801 at 827. See also the examples given on p 157 ante.

10 So Sir Garfield Barwick CJ in *Mutual Life and Citizens Assurance Co v Evatt* (1968) 42 ALJR 316 at 318 (quoted on p 333 post).

pellets accumulate, they may be gathered together and rolled into a single big pellet; and the moulding process begins anew. The analogy also holds in one further respect. The longer a decision has stood, the more brittle and less malleable does it become; it then has to be accepted as it stands or destroyed.

The line between creation and adaptation is a thin one, and the fact that judges do make law has been avowed by judges as well as writers. There is, however, a difference between judicial and legislative creativity. Allen put the matter thus:

> 'the creative power of the courts is limited by existing legal material at their command. They find the material and shape it. The legislature may manufacture entirely new material'[11].

This is approximately true, the difficulty being the sense in which a judge may be thought to use 'existing legal material' when he decides a case purely out of a sense of justice. If Allen's expression refers to any source of inspiration for a decision, natural law for example, the proposition is true, but then Blackstone's orthodoxy would be equally true. If, on the other hand, it connotes only existing material labelled 'English law', it is untrue, for the judge is not, in the situation envisaged, using such material. Such cases may be rare, but that does not alter the fact that the judge does here legislate.

It is true also that the legislature may make entirely new material. It often happens, of course, that a statute only shapes existing material, as when it codifies; and besides, even new material has a better chance of success if it keeps within the spirit of existing material[12]. A semantic point is involved in the word 'make'. One can 'make' logs out of a tree trunk, but the material of wood is already 'there'; and this seems to be the idea behind Allen's statement. The weakness of his position is that there are times when judges do make new material. Perhaps, the distinction between statute and judge-made law may be put as follows. Every decision is concerned primarily with a specific set of facts, and the rule for which it is then quoted as a precedent is derived *from* the decision on the facts as stated. Statutes only seek to control the future (except for retrospective legislation) and accordingly deal with classes of facts. So statutes aim at laying down rules applicable *to* specific sets of facts as and when they arise. At the normative level, ie for future purposes, rules, whether created by precedents or statutes, operate alike. So, the distinction between statute and judge-made law does not lie in the bare fact that the former manufactures new material while the latter only shapes it, but in the manner in which and the degree to which they respectively resort to existing material or create wholly new material.

2. The bindingness of *stare decisis* operates up to a point. It means that a judge is bound to follow a precedent unless he can reasonably distinguish it.

---

11 *Law in the Making* p 310. See also Pound *Interpretations of Legal History* p 127; Cardozo *The Nature of the Judicial Process* p 166. Holmes J: 'I recognise without hesitation that judges must and do legislate, but they do so only interstitially; they are confined from molar to molecular motions': *South Pacific Co v Jensen* 244 US 205 (1917); Lord Reid: 'If we are to extend the law it must be by the development and application of fundamental principles. We cannot introduce arbitrary conditions or limitations: that must be left to legislation': *Myers v DPP* [1965] AC 1001 at 1021, [1964] 2 All ER 881 at 885 (this case has since been overruled by the Criminal Evidence Act 1965). He made a similar observation in *Pettitt v Pettitt* [1970] AC 777 at 794-795, [1969] 2 All ER 385 at 390.

12 Cf Savigny *On the Vocation of our Age for Legislation and Jurisprudence* (see ch 18 post).

Since distinguishing techniques are numerous, the element of bindingness is correspondingly limited.

3. Such discretion as judges have in handling precedents is guided by values, which concerns knowing the just way of applying the law to the facts. This will be dealt with in Chapter 10.

4. Legal thinking is *sui generis*. Its logic is instrumental and functional, and though precise, it is not mechanical. It is creative and purposive, but not haphazard.

5. The mechanics of the judicial process shows the genius of the common law in combining the need for certainty and the need to keep the law abreast of changing ideas and social conditions[13]. Certainty is preserved within the limits of rules and concepts; flexibility and adaptability are achieved through their interpretation and through the varieties of fact-statements.

6. Every decision pronounces on the legality or otherwise of conduct after it has been performed. This may seem hard on the litigant where a new rule or variation of a rule is enunciated, but it is the sort of imperfection that is unavoidable in a human institution such as this. The answer to any protest must be that the position cannot be otherwise, for it is beyond the wit of man to provide in advance for all contingencies. Besides, it would be true to say that in an immense number of situations the conduct of the persons concerned would not have been influenced even if the rule had been clear beforehand, while the value of having a rule for the future might be thought to outweigh any hardship that could occur by applying it retrospectively to the case in hand.

7. An unjust precedent is 'law' here and now, but this is sometimes too high a price for certainty in law. 'Certainty in law' said Maitland 'must not become certainty of injustice'[14]. Injustice is a factor that will in time either minimise its effect through distinguishing or bring about its demise through overruling. Neither is a satisfactory way of dealing with unjust precedents, since distinctions introduce needless complexity through exceptions, while overruling by higher authority or statute is slow and chancy. Should unjust precedents become numerous, then the future of *stare decisis* itself would be in jeopardy.

---

13 Lord Evershed: 'If it be said that your lordships are making new law, that is only because, whatever may have been the facts and circumstances reasonably to be contemplated a hundred years or more ago, at the present time it must be accepted ... that the ancient rules of the English common law have—and have as one of their notable virtues—the characteristic that in general they can never be said to be finally limited by definition but have rather the capacity of adaptation in accordance with the changing circumstances of succeeding ages': *Haley v London Electricity Board* [1965] AC 778 at 800–801, [1964] 3 All ER 185 at 194. Lord Reid: 'The common law must be developed to meet changing economic conditions and habits of thought, and I would not be deterred by expressions of opinion in this House in old cases': *Myers v DPP* (see p 163, n 11 ante).

14 Maitland *Collected Papers* III, pp 486–487.

READING LIST

A Aarnio *On Legal Reasoning*.

C K Allen *Law in the Making* (7th edn) chs 3–4.

B N Cardozo *The Nature of the Judicial Process*.

A R N Cross *Precedent in English Law* (3rd edn).

J Dewey *How We Think* ch 8.

J H Farrar *Introduction to Legal Method*.

R N Gooderson 'Ratio Decidendi and Rules of Law' (1952) 30 Canadian Bar Review 892.

A L Goodhart 'Precedent in English and Continental Law' (1934) 50 Law Quarterly Review 40.

A G Guest 'Logic in the Law' in *Oxford Essays in Jurisprudence* (ed A G Guest) ch 7.

K Lipstein 'The Doctrine of Precedent in Continental Law with Special Reference to French and German Law' (1946) 28 Journal of Comparative Legislation (Part III) 34.

D Lloyd 'Reason and Logic in the Common Law' (1948) 64 Law Quarterly Review 468.

D N MacCormick *Legal Reasoning and Legal Theory*.

R E Megarry *Judges and Judging* (The Child & Co Lecture 1977).

J L Montrose *Precedent in English Law and Other Essays* (ed H G Hanbury) ch 1.

C Morris *How Lawyers Think* chs 3–5 and 8.

C Mullins *In Quest of Justice* chs 3–6.

G W Paton and G Sawer 'Ratio and Obiter Dictum in Appellate Courts' (1947) 63 Law Quarterly Review 461.

R Pound *An Introduction to the Philosophy of Law* pp 100–129.

R Pound *Jurisprudence* III, ch 19.

J Stone 'The Ratio of the Ratio Decidendi' (1959) 22 Modern Law Review 597.

J Stone 'Reason and Reasoning in Judicial and Juristic Argument' in *Legal Essays, A Tribute to Frede Castberg* p 170.

A Tunc 'The Not So Common Law of England and the United States, or, Precedent in England and in the United States, a Field Study by an Outsider' (1984) 47 Modern Law Review 150.

A T von Mehren *The Civil Law System: Cases and Materials* ch 16, ss 3–4.

R A Wasserstrom *The Judicial Decision*.

CHAPTER 8

Statutory interpretation

The law applicable to the facts of a dispute may be contained in an Act of Parliament, and knowing the law then involves interpreting a legislative text. Unlike case law, where judges construct their own texts out of precedents (*rationes decidendi*), with statute law the texts are presented to them.

Legislation may be described as law made deliberately in a set form by an authority, which the courts have accepted as competent to exercise that function[1]. From sparse and scanty beginnings, its use steadily increased until now the output of statutes has assumed formidable proportions. Although the volume and the nature of certain kinds of legislation may be subjected to criticism, there is universal agreement that deliberate law making of this kind is indispensable to the regulation of the modern state. The part played by the judges in the struggle between the prerogative and Parliament enabled them to preserve in their hands a considerable measure of power, one aspect of which is that what becomes 'law' is their interpretation of statute through the operation of *stare decisis*. As Lord Devlin has put it:

> 'The law is what the judges say it is. If the House of Lords were to give an Act of Parliament a meaning which no one else thought it could reasonably bear, it is their construction of the words used in preference to the words themselves that would become the law'[2].

In this way the judicial doctrine of *stare decisis* has come to be superimposed upon the doctrine of the supremacy of the Crown in Parliament.

When confronted with the task of interpreting a statute judges say that their task is to ascertain the 'intention of Parliament' as can be gathered from the meaning of the words used. This quest is no less elusive than the search for the *ratio decidendi* of a case. For instance, where Parliament enacts a provision on a mistaken view of the law, the courts will give effect to it according to what the law really was in their view[3]. This may be a by-product of the rule that express words, or necessary implication, are required to change the law. Such being the case, the point is: if Parliament did take a mistaken view of the law, in what sense are courts giving effect to the intention behind the enactment? Reference to intention seems to be superfluous.

Secondly, whose intention is it that is relevant? It cannot be the intention of the body which may have recommended the measure, such as the Law

1 On this description of legislation see *Jilani v Government of Punjab* Pak LD (1972) SC 139 at 159.
2 Devlin *Samples of Law Making* p 2. See also Lord Reid in *London Transport Executive v Betts* [1959] AC 213 at 232, [1958] 2 All ER 636 at 645. If, of course, the court is not bound by the previous decision it will consider the statute *de novo*: cf *R v Board of Control, ex p Rutty* [1956] 2 QB 109, [1956] 1 All ER 769, with *Richardson v LCC* [1957] 2 All ER 330.
3 *Birmingham City Corpn v West Midland Baptist (Trust) Association (Incorporated)* [1969] 3 All ER 172 at 179-180, 188, 190.

Reform Committee, nor of the draftsman[4], nor even of the members of Parliament who voted it through, for a good many of them may not have attended on that day, or may have voted only in obedience to party dictates[5]. An Act is the product of compromise and the interplay of many factors, the result of which is expressed in a set form of words[6]. Ascertaining the 'intention of the legislature', therefore, boils down to finding the meaning of the words used—the 'intent of the statute' rather than of Parliament[7].

Further difficulties arise from the fact that 'meaning' and 'intention' are ambiguous words. Does the present case fall within what the legislature 'meant' to refer to by the wording it has used (reference), or does it fall within the purpose which it 'meant' to accomplish (purpose)[8]? The two methods of treating a statute represented by these questions might be designated respectively as 'interpretation' and 'construction', but the activities of the judiciary cannot be separated in this way, for the distinction between interpretation and construction is not clear-cut. Where language is equivocal, the decision whether the wording was 'meant' to refer to the situation before the court, which no one may have contemplated at the time of the passing of the statute, inevitably imports a measure of 'construction'[9]. In such cases it is difficult to see where 'interpretation' leaves off and 'construction' begins. As to the ascertainment of legislative purpose, this would appear on the face of it to permit a court to venture outside the enactment for available evidence as to the policy behind it so that the wording may be construed in the light of this. The practical question is how far a court is expected to go in search of such evidence, for without some limit the inquiry might be pursued to unreasonable lengths. English tribunals have evinced reluctance to venture outside the enactment itself, which means that its wording is to be construed in the light of policy only in so far as this can be gleaned within the four corners of the statute. This limitation narrows still further the distinction between 'construction' and 'interpretation'.

Another difficulty derives from the fact that statutes seek to control the future by using broad terms of classes and categories. These are man-made, and there are inevitably *casus omissi*, so that a measure of discretion is imported into every decision as to whether a provision applies to the case in hand or not.

Nor do words have proper meanings. A word may bear the meaning put upon it by the user, that understood by the recipient[10], or the usual meaning.

---

4 Lord Simon thought that in ordinary cases the intention of the draftsman would be sufficient: *Ealing London Borough Council v Race Relations Board* [1972] AC 342 at 360-361, [1972] 1 All ER 105 at 113-114; and in *Maunsell v Olins* [1975] AC 373 at 391, [1975] 1 All ER 16 at 26.

5 For the difficulties, see Lord Wilberforce in *British Railways Board v Pickin* [1974] AC 765 at 796, [1974] 1 All ER 609 at 625-626.

6 For changes during the passage of a controversial Bill producing inconsistency in the use of words, see Lord Diplock in *Jones v Secretary of State for Social Services* [1972] AC 944 at 1008, [1972] 1 All ER 145 at 183-184.

7 Holmes 'The Theory of Legal Interpretation' (1898-99) 12 Harv LR 417; Fuller *The Morality of Law* p 87. Is the quest for intent a relic of the theory that laws are commands of a sovereign? As to this see ch 16 post.

8 Lord Watson in *Salomon v Salomon & Co Ltd* [1897] AC 22 at 38.

9 Eg *Re Regulation and Control of Radio Communications in Canada* [1932] AC 304 (whether 'telegraphs' in the British North America Act 1867, includes broadcasting).

10 See Lord Reid's protest against the way in which his words had been interpreted: *Mutual Life and Citizens' Assurance Co Ltd v Evatt* [1971] AC 793 at 813, [1971] 1 All ER 150 at 164.

The last is a compromise between the first two[11], and is complicated by the fact that although most words do have an area of agreed application they are also surrounded by a hinterland of uncertainty, which is where disputes arise. Ideally one ought to proceed on the meaning intended by the user, but this is impossible with emanations from a body like the legislature. There is no one legislator or group, whose assistance can be invoked, and it is obviously impractical, whenever a statute comes up for consideration, to ask members of Parliament to elucidate what they individually or collectively 'had in mind'[12]. Moreover, in the case of antique enactments, whose framers have long since disappeared, the present members of Parliament are in no better position than judges to explain what their predecessors may have intended. It is the judges on whom the task devolves to ascertain the meaning as best they can.

It would seem on outward appearances that judicial interpretation of statutory provisions does follow a syllogistic style of reasoning, and that the major premise being 'given' in the form of some statutory rule, the judge is at least relieved of the task, which he has to perform so often with case law, of finding an appropriate major premise. Such a view is misleading. For words are often ambiguous, so it still remains necessary for a judge to elucidate the major premise. Also, in cases of doubt, which are the ones that present difficulty, it is not possible to separate the settlement of the major and minor premises. Fact-finding and premise-finding are interrelated: a court hears the evidence and determines the facts, and any doubt as to the scope and applicability of a given statutory provision may well be resolved by the view taken of the facts. So discretion even in the application of statute, is unavoidable.

The discretionary element is given another slant through the relationship between the courts and Parliament over the centuries. The tendency has been on the whole towards a restrictive rather than a liberal exercise of discretion, which prompted Pollock to comment caustically that the attitude of judges

> 'cannot well be accounted for except on the theory that Parliament generally changes the law for the worse, and that the business of the judges is to keep the mischief of its interference within the narrowest possible bounds'[13].

It would be unfair to attribute this restrictive attitude to judicial wickedness, because historical factors combined to produce it.

In the Middle Ages it was felt that the task of interpreting the law should be discharged by those who ordained it, for the very word 'interpretation' connoted evasion. Parliament, meeting at random, was hardly the body best suited to do this, and judges were the persons on whom the responsibility was placed because the need for interpretation more often than not arose before them and, more especially, because at that time they took part in the legislative processes. 'Do not gloss the statute', Hengham CJ admonished

---

11 *McInerny v Lloyds Bank Ltd* [1974] 1 Lloyd's Rep 246.
12 Lord MacDermott: 'There is no means of ascertaining parliamentary intention by scrutinising the minds of those who voted for the enactment in question': 'Some Requirements of Justice' [1964] JR 109; Lord Morris: 'It is well accepted that the beliefs and assumptions of those who frame Acts of Parliament cannot make the law': *Davies, Jenkins & Co Ltd v Davies* [1968] AC 1097 at 1121, [1967] 1 All ER 913 at 922.
13 Pollock *Essays in Jurisprudence and Ethics* p 85, and see also p 242: 'catastrophic interference'. So, too, Stephen J speaking as a draftsman said 'it is necessary to attain if possible to a degree of precision, which a person reading in bad faith cannot misunderstand': *Re Castioni* [1891] 1 QB 49 at 167.

counsel 'for we know better than you; we made it'[14]. In course of time judges ceased to partake in legislation and so lost their knowledge of the background and context of statutes. With the rise of the Court of Chancery the common law courts may have felt inclined to relinquish to it the exercise of discretion, in interpretation as well as in other matters. The attitude of judges shifted in this way to something more like what it is today. A statute was viewed as a text and judges could only infer the policies of Parliament from what was said in it. Another historical development started with the fact that much early legislation was concerned with special privileges and particular derogations from the common law. This should be set alongside the belief, which then prevailed, that the common law was self-sufficient and ought not to be interfered with lightly. Both factors prompted judges not to accord wider effect than was necessary to what were, in fact, exceptions created by statute, and it is to this tendency that Pollock refers. Again, doctrines concerning the inalienable rights of Man began to make headway in the eighteenth century, and were no doubt influential in restricting statutory encroachments on the rights of individuals. The penalties of the criminal law, too, used to be among the most savage of their day and the growing humanitarianism of the age made judges interpret penal legislation more narrowly than they might otherwise have done.

The restrictive attitude towards statute induced by these factors had an unfortunate effect. Statutes of the nineteenth century came to be drafted in meticulous detail so as to provide for every conceivable contingency, since judges could not be relied on to help out with omissions. This abundance of detail only inspired a still more restrictive attitude, for Parliament was taken to have specified everything that needed to be covered and a *casus omissi* was assumed to have been intentionally left out. This is probably the reason behind judicial reluctance even now to fill in the gaps in a statute. The point shows incidentally how unhelpful the phrase 'intention of Parliament' is. A different influence in more recent times has been the ever increasing regulation by statute of more and more spheres of activity, which has sometimes inspired in courts a desire to preserve the common law from being engulfed. The following utterance of Lord Tucker is an example:

> 'It appears to me desirable in these days, when there are in existence so many statutes and statutory regulations imposing absolute obligations upon employers, that the courts should be vigilant to see that the common law duty owed by a master to his servants should not be gradually enlarged until it is barely distinguishable from his absolute statutory obligations'[15].

There are other factors of a more general nature. For instance, much may depend on the merits of the dispute, and in this connection it is important to stress that the finding of the facts does sometimes influence the view taken of the statutory premise. A decisive part is also played by the degree of sympathy which the court entertains towards the objective in view. Judges do weigh up considerations of social and individualist policy and the balance

14 YB 33 & 35 Edw 1 (Rolls Series) 82. The same judge accepted Royal explanations of doubtful enactments, YB 30 & 31 Edw 1 (Rolls Series) 441. At times the judges themselves inquired of the King's Council what a statute meant: Thorpe CJ in YB 48 Edw 3, fo 34b.

15 *Latimer v AEC Ltd* [1953] AC 643 at 658, [1953] 2 All ER 449 at 455. See also *Harding v Price* [1948] 1 KB 695 at 700-701, [1948] 1 All ER 283 at 284; *Davie v New Merton Board Mills Ltd* [1959] AC 604 at 627, [1959] 1 All ER 346 at 355. See on this Friedmann *Law and Social Change* pp 93 et seq.

does not always work out in favour of the administration. The details of this will be postponed until Chapter 10.

It has also long been the fashion to treat statutes and other documents alike. The sanctity that used to attach to the seal and to the wording of written instruments is proverbial, and the reluctance of courts to redraft a document for the parties has been carried over to statutes. The unhelpful attitude towards Parliament may also be a carry-over of the *contra proferentem* rule applicable to documents to the effect that 'where doubt arises the words must be construed most strongly against him who uses them'[16]. Such treatment of statutes and documents as if they are alike is mistaken, for there are important differences. Documents are often only records of past events, and are mostly confined to specific transactions; they also affect specified parties and not the public at large. Statutes differ in each of these respects. Finally, the aversion to giving an appearance of acting outside the judicial function by legislating, attributable perhaps to the doctrine of the separation of powers, may also be responsible.

The present state of statutory interpretation suggests that something is amiss with the judicial approach to the whole exercise. Statutes are designed to operate over indefinite periods of time, so they should be viewed in a continuum. Unfortunately, the reverse has been the case. The distinction may be expressed by differentiating between the referential approach as to what a statute 'means', ie what its words refer to here and now, and the purposive approach as to how it is to be 'applied'. 'Application' is a continuing process and the application of a provision to a particular case is only one step in a journey[17]. There are, of course, limits to the continuous adaptation of statutes, which are not easily specified. It should stop short of altering the character of a statute, eg changing a procedural provision into a substantive one, or the introduction of wholly new doctrine[18]. A comparison might be made with laying a line of bricks. If a bricklayer simply lays each brick, moment by moment, in line with the previous brick as straight as he thinks it should be positioned, the line will soon start to meander this way and that. No competent bricklayer does this; he has a line stretching out in front so that he can lay each brick with a guide to the whole linear extension. The policy of a statute may be likened to its plumb-line extending into the future and the constructions placed on its wording should be in accordance with that policy. This method of approach is becoming more fashionable, but it has not been so in the past because there has been too little appreciation of the fact that statutory regulation continues and has temporal extension. Instead, the tendency has been for cases to be decided on a moment to moment basis, with the result that the ins and outs of the lines of cases on scores of statutes have made this one of the sorriest corners of British jurisprudence[19].

There is no single set of rules of statutory interpretation. It would be truer to speak of conflicting approaches and guidelines, largely supported by *dicta*. Lord du Parcq, while not regretting that the so-called rules of construction had 'fallen into some disfavour' went on to add:

16 *Langham v City of London Corpn* [1949] 1 KB 208 at 212, [1948] 2 All ER 1018 at 1020 (applying the rule to a private Act of Parliament).
17 *Keys v Boulter* [1971] 1 QB 300 at 305, [1971] 1 All ER 289 at 292.
18 For an extreme example of the difference in approach, contrast the views of Lord Denning MR and the House of Lords in *Pettitt v Pettitt* [1970] AC 777, [1969] 2 All ER 385.
19 For one example, see Jennings 'Judicial Process at its Worst' (1937-39) 1 MLR 111.

'It must be remembered, however, that the courts have laid down, indeed, not rigid rules, but principles which have been found to afford some guidance when it is sought to ascertain the intention of Parliament'[20].

The Employment Appeals Tribunal has said that the guidelines laid down by courts or industrial tribunals in applying statutes to particular facts are not binding legal rules. The statute alone is law and judges cannot add to or subtract from the law as expressed in it[1]. A shrewd writer summed up the position admirably:

'A court invokes whichever of the rules produces a result that satisfies its sense of justice in the case before it'[2].

REFERENTIAL APPROACH

'Literal' or 'Plain Meaning Rule'

Judges frequently use the phrase 'the true meaning' of words in the pursuit of their task. The most widely used canon of interpretation, the so-called '*Literal*' or '*Plain Meaning Rule*', is best summed up in the words of Jervis CJ:

'If the precise words used are plain and unambiguous, in our judgment, we are bound to construe them in their ordinary sense, even though it do lead, in our view of the case, to an absurdity or manifest injustice'[3].

There is a tendency to imagine that the courts are thereby giving effect to the intention of Parliament on the hypothesis that 'the words themselves do, in such a case, best declare the intention of the lawgiver'[4]. On the contrary, it would seem that whenever the '*Literal Rule*' is being applied any reference to the intention of Parliament is better avoided, since there is something comic in ascribing to Parliament an *intention* to enact absurdities or injustices. Moreover, since Parliamentary intention is to be gathered from the words used, it is no more than what the judges interpret Parliament as having intended.

'What we must look for' Lord Reid once said 'is the intention of Parliament, and I also find it difficult to believe that Parliament ever really intended the

---

20 *Cutler v Wandsworth Stadium Ltd* [1949] AC 398 at 410, [1949] 1 All ER 544 at 550. See also *Croxford v Universal Insurance Co Ltd* [1936] 2 KB 253 at 281, [1936] 1 All ER 151 at 166; *Hamilton v National Coal Board* [1960] AC 633 at 641-642, [1960] 1 All ER 76 at 79; *Cheng v Governor of Pentonville Prison* [1973] AC 931 at 949, [1973] 2 All ER 204 at 212; the Law Commission *The Interpretation of Statutes* p 14.

1 *Wells v Derwent Plastics* [1978] ICR 424.

2 Willis 'Statute Interpretation in a Nutshell' (1938) 16 Canadian BR p 16. Llewellyn in *The Common Law Tradition, Deciding Appeals* Appendix C, lists twenty-eight opposing canons of 'Thrust and Parry' and nineteen of 'Thrust and Counterthrust'.

3 *Abley v Dale* (1851) 11 CB 378 at 391. See also Lord Bramwell in *Hill v East and West India Dock Co* (1884) 9 App Cas 448 at 464-465; Lord Esher in *R v City of London Court Judge* [1892] 1 QB 273 at 290; Lord Atkinson in *Vacher & Sons Ltd v London Society of Compositors* [1913] AC 107 at 121-122.

4 Tindall CJ in *Sussex Peerage Case* (1844) 11 Cl & Fin 85 at 143; Lord Reid in *IRC v Hinchy* [1960] AC 748 at 767, [1960] 1 All ER 505 at 512 (quoted in n 5 infra, and see also the other references).

consequences which flow from the appellants' contention. But we can only take the intention of Parliament from the words which they have used in the Act'[5].

The rigid exclusion until very recently of extrinsic evidence relating to the contextual background of a statute reinforces the point that the concern of courts with Parliamentary intention does not often go deeper than words. There is thus no point in referring to such an intention as if this is something apart from judicial interpretation and to which they are giving effect. Indeed, there are judicial utterances of the highest authority to that effect[6].

The *'Plain Meaning Rule'* suffers from the inherent weakness that it is not always easy to say whether a word is 'plain' or not.

> 'The cases in which there is real difficulty' said Lord Blackburn 'are those in which there is a controversy as to what the grammatical and ordinary sense of the words, used with the reference to the subject matter, is'[7].

In *Liversidge v Anderson*[8] the majority of the House of Lords thought that the words, 'If the Secretary of State has reasonable cause to believe', were ambiguous, since they might mean either that the Secretary of State *has* reasonable cause to believe, or that he *thinks that he has* reasonable cause to believe. Lord Atkin, on the other hand, was of opinion that there was no ambiguity, and he concluded his powerful dissent speech in these words:

> 'After all this long discussion the question is whether the words "If a man has" can mean "If a man thinks he has". I am of opinion that they cannot, and that the case should be decided accordingly'[9].

A vivid illustration of the point is *IRC v Hinchy*[10]. The Income Tax Act 1952 provided that a person who fails to deliver a correct tax return shall 'forfeit the sum of £20 and treble the tax which he ought to be charged under this Act'. The defendant made a return under a particular heading which was £32 19s 9dless than it should have been. The tax assessable on this amount, which he should have declared, was £14 5s. The rest of his tax assessment came to £125 6s 6d, which would have made up a total assessment of £139 11s 6d. The Court of Appeal held that the Act meant that he should pay £62 15s, being £20 plus treble the sum of £14 5s. The House of Lords, however, held that it meant that he should pay £438 14s 6d, being £20 plus

---

5   *IRC v Hinchy* [1960] AC 748 at 767, [1960] 1 All ER 505 at 512. See also Lord Macmillan in *IRC v Ayrshire Mutual ·Insurance Co Ltd* [1946] 1 All ER 637 at 641 (literal interpretation adopted even though parliamentary design was admittedly otherwise. 'The legislature has plainly missed fire'); Lord Guest in *Davies, Jenkins & Co Ltd v Davies* [1968] AC 1097 at 1123, [1967] 1 All ER 913 at 923.

6   *Leader v Duffey* (1888) 13 App Cas 294 at 301; *Wicks v DPP* [1947] AC 362 at 367, [1947] 1 All ER 205 at 207; *Magor and St Mellons RDC v Newport Corpn* [1952] AC 189 at 191, [1951] 2 All ER 839 at 841; *IRC v Dowdell O'Mahoney & Co Ltd* [1952] AC 401 at 426, [1952] 1 All ER 531 at 544.

7   *Caledonian Rly Co v North British Rly Co* (1881) 6 App Cas 114 at 131-132. 'There were those who thought that the meaning of this word [premises] was clear (Lord Diplock and Lord Simon of Glaisdale) and there were those who thought it ambiguous (Lord Reid, Viscount Dilhorne and myself): per Lord Wilberforce in *Farrell v Alexander* [1977] AC 59 at 72, [1976] 2 All ER 721 at 725; *Croxford v Universal Insurance Co Ltd* [1936] 2 KB 253 at 280, [1936] 1 All ER 151 at 166; *Goldman v Hargrave* [1967] 1 AC 645 at 664-665, [1966] 2 All ER 989 at 997.

8   [1942] AC 206, [1941] 3 All ER 338.

9   [1942] AC 206 at 245, [1941] 3 All ER 338 at 361.

10 [1960] AC 748, [1960] 1 All ER 505.

treble the sum of £139 11s 6d[11]. Both tribunals were applying the 'plain meaning'.

The 'plain meaning' canon of interpretation is ill-suited to modern social legislation, which inaugurates whole schemes and policies, nor does it give guidance in marginal cases. A further drawback is that it requires that words are given their ordinary meaning at the time of enactment[12]. If this were rigidly adhered to it would stand in the way of interpreting statutes so as to adapt them to the changing needs of a developing society.

The '*Plain Meaning Rule*' has evolved many explanatory riders, sub-rules and a host of 'presumptions of legislative intent', into which it is not proposed to enter here[13]. None of these presumptions is binding for a variety of reasons: (a) there is no order of precedence between conflicting presumptions; (b) presumptions themselves are often doubtful, being the subject of contradictory judicial pronouncements; (c) in case of conflict with a presumption a court may adopt an interpretation without referring to the presumption; and (d) there are no means of resolving a conflict between a presumption and the purpose of a statute.

'Golden Rule'

An appreciation of some of the difficulties inherent in the '*Literal Rule*' led to a cautious departure, styled the '*Golden Rule*': the literal sense of words should be adhered to unless this would lead to absurdity, in which case the literal meaning may be modified[14]. It contradicts the '*Literal Rule*' according to which, as explained, the plain meaning has to be adhered to even to the point of absurdity. The difficulty of deciding when words are plain and when they are not has already been mentioned. Presumably, for the purpose of the '*rule*' now being considered, the words though plain should not be too plain,

11 See now Finance Act 1960, s 44, on assessment of penalties. See generally *R v Davis* (1870) LR 1 CCR 272; *Richards v McBride* (1881) 8 QBD 119; *Edwards v Porter* [1925] AC 1; *R v Board of Control, ex p Winterflood* [1938] 2 KB 366, [1938] 2 All ER 463; *London Brick Co Ltd v Robinson* [1943] AC 341, [1943] 1 All ER 23; *Fisher v Bell* [1961] 1 QB 394, [1960] 3 All ER 731.

12 Eg *Nokes v Doncaster Amalgamated Collieries Ltd* [1940] AC 1014 at 1022, [1940] 3 All ER 549 at 553; *Ewart v Ewart* [1959] P 23 at 31, [1958] 3 All ER 561 at 564; *Pettitt v Pettitt* [1970] AC 777, [1969] 2 All ER 385.

13 See pp 114-132 of the second edition of this book, and any work on statutory interpretation. See also Dias *Bibliography* pp 86-90 for literature.

14 *Becke v Smith* (1836) 2 M & W 191 at 195. See also *Grey v Pearson* (1857) 6 HL Cas 61 at 106; *River Wear Comrs v Adamson* (1876) 1 QBD 546 at 549; *Vacher & Sons Ltd v London Society of Compositors* [1913] AC 107 at 117; *Re Sigsworth, Bedford v Bedford* [1935] Ch 89 at 92; *Francis Jackson Developments Ltd v Hall* [1951] 2 KB 488 at 494-495, [1951] 2 All ER 74 at 78-79; *HRH Prince Ernest Augustus of Hanover v A-G* [1955] Ch 440, [1955] 1 All ER 746 (first instance); *Sumner v Robert L Priestly Ltd* [1955] 3 All ER 445 at 447; *Thompson v Thompson* [1956] 1 All ER 603 at 607; *Re Lockwood, Atherton v Brooke* [1958] Ch 231, [1957] 3 All ER 520; *London Transport Executive v Betts* [1959] AC 213 at 247, [1958] 2 All ER 636 at 655; *R v Oakes* [1959] 2 QB 350 at 355-356, [1959] 2 All ER 92 at 94-95; *Corocraft Ltd v Pan American Airways Inc* [1969] 1 QB 616 at 655, 658, [1969] 1 All ER 82 at 88, 90; *Re Parkanski* (1966) 56 DLR (2d) 475 (Can); *Bromilow and Edwards Ltd v IRC* [1970] 1 All ER 174, [1970] 1 WLR 128. The '*Golden Rule*' was considered by Lord Simon in *Cheng v Governor of Pentonville Prison* [1973] AC 931 at 949-950, [1973] 2 All ER 204 at 212-214; he also considered absurdity: see at 957-958, and at 219-200. In *Applin v Race Relations Board* [1975] AC 259 at 283, [1974] 2 All ER 73 at 90-91, he seems to give the name '*Golden Rule*' to the '*Plain Meaning Rule*'. The '*Golden Rule*' was again considered by him in *Maunsell v Olins* [1975] AC 373 at 390, [1975] 1 All ER 16 at 25.

but the apparent plain meaning would lead to a result too unfair to be countenanced. Lord Reid put the matter as follows:

> 'To apply the words literally is to defeat the obvious intention of the legislature and to produce a wholly unreasonable result. To achieve the obvious intention and to produce a reasonable result we must do some violence to the words ... The general principle is well settled. It is only when the words are absolutely incapable of a construction which will accord with the apparent intention of the provision and will avoid a wholly unreasonable result that the words of the enactment must prevail'[15].

If absurdity is considered at all, it is apparently judged as at the time when the statute was passed[16]. Moreover, the rule is hardly suited to giving effect to social policies. The paucity of authority reflects the uncertainties of its application.

The absence of a coherent set of rules of interpretation is best seen when judges adopt opposing canons in the same case. Thus, in *A-G v HRH Prince Ernest Augustus of Hanover*[17], a statute of 1705, 4 Anne c 4 (or 4 and 5 Anne c 16), declared

> 'that the said Princess Sophia, Electress and Duchess Dowager of Hanover, and the issue of her body, and all persons lineally descending from her, born or hereafter to be born, be and shall be, to all intents and purposes whatsoever, deemed, taken, and esteemed natural born subjects of this kingdom'.

The appellant, who was born in 1914, and was admittedly a lineal descendant of the Princess, claimed that he was a British subject by virtue of the Act. By s 12 of the British Nationality Act 1948 all persons who, on a specified date, were British subjects were to become citizens of the United Kingdom and Colonies. The House of Lords, upholding the Court of Appeal, held that on the plain meaning of the words a lineal descendant of Princess Sophia, born over 200 years after the passing of the Act of 1705 and before the Act of 1948, enjoyed United Kingdom citizenship, notwithstanding the somewhat startling implications of such a conclusion. For, according to this decision, The German Kaiser must have been a British subject, while Prince Ernest himself had fought against this country in the Second World War. In the court of first instance Vaisey J, while acknowledging that statutes do not lapse, alluded to the absurdity of interpreting the wording literally and held that this particular statute was limited in its operation to the lifetime of Queen Anne; but the Court of Appeal and the House of Lords rejected this interpretation, adhering to the literal meaning[18].

15 *Luke v IRC* [1963] AC 557 at 577, [1963] 1 All ER 655 at 664; *Adler v George* [1964] 2 QB 7, [1964] 1 All ER 628.
16 *Prince Ernest Augustus of Hanover v A-G* [1956] Ch 188 at 218, CA (affd [1957] AC 436 at 461–462, 466, 472, [1957] 1 All ER 49 at 54, 56–57, 60, HL). The Court of Appeal revsd the decision at first instance: [1955] Ch 440, [1955] 1 All ER 746.
17 See n 16 supra.
18 In the House their Lordships in the course of argument questioned whether the Act of 1705 had survived the Act of Union with Scotland 1707, which introduced an entirely new conception of British, as distinct from English, nationality. Counsel on both sides declined to argue the point, and a majority of their Lordships expressly reserved their opinions as to what their conclusion might have been had the point been considered. Nor was the point taken as to whether the Prince's claim was affected by the Royal Marriages Act 1772. On the nationality issue, therefore, the decision is worthless, since it was reached without taking material statutes into account: see pp. 128, 130 ante.

PURPOSIVE APPROACH

'Mischief Rule'

Statutes are generally of indefinite duration, and consideration of them in this way takes account of their changing functions and functioning. It has also been pointed out that words possess an inner core of agreed applications surrounded by a fringe of unsettled applications. The former indicates the general direction of development, while manipulation occurs in the fringe area.

The canon of interpretation that is best suited to give effect to this approach is known as the *'Mischief Rule'*, which was propounded as long ago as 1584. In *Heydon's Case*[19] it was stated that

> 'four things are to be discussed and considered: 1st, What was the Common Law before the making of the Act; 2nd, What was the mischief and defect for which the Common Law did not provide; 3rd, What remedy hath Parliament resolved and appointed to cure the disease of the commonwealth; and 4th, The true reason of the remedy; and then the office of all the judges is always to make such construction as shall suppress the mischief and advance the remedy, and to suppress subtle inventions and evasions for continuance of the mischief, and *pro privato commodo*, and to add force and life to the cure and remedy according to the true intent of the makers of the Act *pro bono publico*'.

The approach here laid down clearly contemplates inquiry into the policy and purpose behind the statute. There are echoes of it in several other judgments[20].

It is obvious that 'meaning' with reference to this *'rule'* connotes purpose, ie what the statute 'means' to accomplish. As Lord Denning MR has said 'We no longer construe Acts of Parliament according to their literal meaning. We construe them according to their object and intent'[1]. This canon also harmonises with the modern tendency to see how words are used[2].

On the other hand, the propositions in *Heydon's Case* were probably adequate to deal with the limited kind of legislation that then existed. Today, however, statutes put into effect new social experiments and operate on a scale much larger than before. *Heydon's Case* itself is thus somewhat

---

19 3 Co Rep 7a at 7b.
20 Plowden, note on *Eyston v Studd* (1574) 2 Plowd 463 at 465; *Eastman Photographic Materials Co Ltd v The Comptroller-General of Patents* [1898] AC 571 at 573; *London and County Property Investments Ltd v A-G* [1953] 1 All ER 436 at 441; *Barnes v Jarvis* [1953] 1 All ER 1061 at 1063; *Wycombe Marsh Garages Ltd v Fowler* [1972] 3 All ER 248, [1972] 1 WLR 1156. The *'Mischief Rule'* has been considered by Lord Simon in *McMillan v Crouch* [1972] 3 All ER 61 at 68–70, [1972] 1 WLR 1102 at 1109–1111; *Cheng v Governor of Pentonville Prison* [1973] AC 931 at 952–954, [1973] 2 All ER 204 at 214–216; *Applin v Race Relations Board* [1975] AC 259 at 286–287, [1974] 2 All ER 73 at 89–90; *Maunsell v Olins* [1975] AC 373 at 393–395, [1975] 1 All ER 16 at 27–29.
1 *Engineering Industry Training Board v Samuel Talbot (Engineers) Ltd* [1969] 2 QB 270 at 274, [1969] 1 All ER 480 at 482. See Lord Denning's statement in *Nothman v London Borough of Barnet* [1978] 1 All ER 1243 at 1246, [1978] 1 WLR 220 at 228, repudiated by Lord Russell on appeal [1979] 1 All ER 142 at 151, [1979] 1 WLR 67 at 77. Cf Roskill LJ in *R v Duncalf* [1979] 2 All ER 1116 at 1121, [1979] 1 WLR 918 at 923. See further *Marshall v BBC* [1979] 3 All ER 80, [1979] 1 WLR 1071.
2 'Seeing that the words of the document are ambiguous, it is permissible to look at what was done under it': per Lord Denning MR in *IRC v Educational Grants Association Ltd* [1967] Ch 993 at 1008, [1967] 2 All ER 893 at 896. The case did not concern a statute but a document and Harman LJ thought that the remark should be confined to ancient documents: at 1012 and at 898.

inadequate; it needs to be broadened and adapted to meet the conditions of today. Lord Simon has suggested that five considerations might be taken into account: (1) the social background to identify the social or juristic defect; (2) a conspectus of the entire relevant body of law; (3) long title and preamble stating legislative objectives; (4) the actual words used; and (5) other statutes in *pari materia*. The exclusion of extrinsic material limits very largely the operation of this approach, and it is these exclusionary rules which have operated to displace the '*rule*', though they themselves are of later development. The most that a tribunal can do is to take judicial notice of the existing law[3]. Finally, it would require a greater degree of judicial legislation than under any other approach. Lord Denning used to be prepared to 'supplement the written word so as to give "force and life" to the intention of the legislature'[4]. The House of Lords pronounced emphatically against this 'naked usurpation of the legislative function'[5], and Lord Denning has since accepted this restriction[6]. A judge may not add words that are not in the statute, save only by way of necessary implication; nor may he interpret a statute according to his own views as to policy, but if he can discover this from the statute or other material, which it is permissible for a court to consult, he may interpret it accordingly[7].

The courts have adopted the '*Mischief Rule*', or an approach akin to it, in the following types of situations.

(1) The question whether or not a person is entitled to compensation for harm sustained as the result of a breach of a statutory duty depends upon whether the mischief, which the statute was designed to eradicate, contemplated damage to him or to the class of which he was a member[8].

(2) The decision whether *mens rea* is an ingredient of a statutory offence seems to rest upon whether the object and policy of the statute would thereby be defeated[9].

(3) Where statutory penalties are imposed on certain kinds of behaviour, the courts take account of the policy behind the statute in question to decide whether or not contracts contemplating such behaviour are void. The contract is void if the penalty is imposed in the interests of the public[10], but not if imposed in the interests of revenue[11].

---

3 *Escoign Properties Ltd v IRC* [1958] AC 549 at 566, [1958] 1 All ER 406 at 414. In *Dullewe v Dullewe* [1969] 2 AC 313, [1969] 2 WLR 811, the Judicial Committee consulted the report of a commission in order to elucidate the mischief that was being remedied.

4 *Seaford Court Estates Ltd v Asher* [1949] 2 KB 481 at 498 499, [1949] 2 All ER 155 at 164 (on appeal [1950] AC 508, [1950] 1 All ER 1018); *Magor and St Mellons RDC v Newport Corpn* [1950] 2 All ER 1226 at 1236.

5 *Magor and St Mellons RDC v Newport Corpn* [1952] AC 189 at 191, [1951] 2 All ER 839 at 841.

6 *London Transport Executive v Betts* [1959] AC 213 at 247, [1958] 2 All ER 636 at 655; but see the reference on p 181 n 19. See also Lord Reid in *Goodrich v Paisner* [1957] AC 65 at 88, [1956] 2 All ER 176 at 185.

7 *Shah v Barnet London Borough Council* [1983] 2 AC 309, [1983] 1 All ER 226.

8 *Gorris v Scott* (1874) LR 9 Exch 125; *Knapp v Railway Executive* [1949] 2 All ER 508; *Hartley v Mayoh & Co* [1954] 1 QB 383, [1954] 1 All ER 375.

9 *R v St Margaret's Trusts Ltd* [1958] 2 All ER 289; *Wiltshire v Barrett* [1966] 1 QB 312, [1965] 2 All ER 271; *Rogers v Dodd* [1968] 2 All ER 22, [1968] 1 WLR 548; *Fletcher v Budgen* [1974] 2 All ER 1243 at 1247, [1974] 1 WLR 1056 at 1061–1062.

10 *Anderson Ltd v Daniel* [1924] 1 KB 138 at 147.

11 *Smith v Mawhood* (1845) 14 M & W 452 at 463. The mischief may also help to determine the penalty itself: *Kennedy v Spratt* [1972] AC 83, [1971] 1 All ER 805. 'Or' interpreted as 'either or both': *Federal Steam Navigation Co Ltd v Department of Trade and Industry* [1974] 2 All ER 97, [1974] 1 WLR 505.

(4) The approach to statutes of a predominantly 'social' nature has been anything but consistent. There have, however, been cases in which the judges have taken a broad view of the background and policy of the statutes in question[12].

(5) The *'Mischief Rule'* is sometimes invoked in support of a literal interpretation[13].

(6) It has also been used in interpreting statutes giving effect to international treaties[14].

COMPROMISE APPROACH

Something can be said in justification of both the referential and purposive approaches. A combination of the two has been suggested by Lord Devlin so as to give effect to purpose so far as this can be ascertained from the meaning of the words used. 'I remain unconvinced' he said,

> 'that there is anything basically wrong with the rule of construction that words in a statute should be given their natural and ordinary meeting. The rule does not insist on a literal interpretation or require the construction of a statute without regard to its manifest purpose'[15].

Unfortunately, this does not resolve the difficulties. The 'natural and ordinary meaning' is what presents difficulty, as has been pointed out. Secondly, when is purpose 'manifest'? If the natural and ordinary meaning would lead to absurdity, such a result is manifestly not Parliament's purpose; so to this extent Lord Devlin's statement is akin to the *'Golden Rule'*. The question is how far beyond the statutory words a court may go in order to ascertain purpose.

Use of extrinsic material

It has been remarked that judges are reluctant to venture outside the statute for information as to its contents. The extent to which they do so is worth reviewing.

(1) The preparatory materials of an Act, the *travaux prèparatoires*, were formerly taken into account more than they are now. The attitude of Hengham CJ who admonished counsel that he knew best what an enactment meant since he had helped to make it[16], should be contrasted with that of Lord Halsbury, who declined to deliver judgment

---

12 *Howard de Walden v IRC* [1942] 1 KB 389 at 397, [1942] 1 All ER 287 at 289; *Latilla v IRC* [1943] AC 377 at 381, [1943] 1 All ER 265 at 266 (social need for taxation); *Summers v Salford Corpn* [1943] AC 283 at 293, [1943] 1 All ER 68 at 72 (policy of the Housing Act 1936); *Okereke v Brent London Borough Council* [1967] 1 QB 42, [1966] 1 All ER 150 (Housing Act 1961); *Brown v Brash and Ambrose* [1948] 2 KB 247 at 254, [1948] 1 All ER 922 (policy of the Rent Restriction Acts); Lords Diplock and Simon in *Jones v Secretary of State for Social Services* [1972] AC 944 at 1005, 1017-1018, [1972] 1 All ER 145 at 181, 190-191.
13 *R v Males* [1962] 2 QB 500, [1961] 3 All ER 705; *Letang v Cooper* [1965] 1 QB 232 at 240, [1964] 2 All ER 929 at 933.
14 *Fothergill v Monarch Airlines Ltd* [1981] AC 251, [1980] 2 All ER 696.
15 Devlin 'Judges and Lawmakers' (1976) 39 MLR 1 at 13.
16 YB 33 & 35 Edw 1 (Rolls Series) 82; and see p 169 ante.

because he had participated in drafting the enactment concerned[17]. Even recourse to Hansard is not permitted[18]. The modern attitude dates from the second half of the eighteenth century[19], and there are various explanations for it. One might be the principle that courts will not inquire into the legislative process. Another might be that the reporting of debates was for long prohibited. Perhaps also the association of statutes with other types of documents led to the extension of the rule which excludes extrinsic evidence as to the contents of documents. The vast and indeterminate nature of the inquiry, which the admissibility of such matter would open up, has shed a discouraging influence. 'These words may be ambiguous', said Viscount Simonds, 'but even if they are, the power and duty of the court to travel outside them on a voyage of discovery are strictly limited'[20].

(2) Extrinsic considerations may be allowed, not to interpret the Act, but to explain the state of the law at the time it was passed[1]. Thus, Viscount Simon referred to the Report of the Law Revision Committee on contributory negligence, not in order to interpret the Law Reform (Contributory Negligence) Act 1945, but to ascertain causation in relation to the 'last opportunity' rule[2].

(3) Schemes framed under a statute may not be consulted. They may, however, be used to confirm the interpretation of the words of the statute themselves[3].

17 *Hilder v Dexter* [1902] AC 474 at 477. In *Lucy v W T Henleys Telegraph Works Co Ltd* [1970] 1 QB 393 at 407, [1969] 3 All ER 456 at 465, Edmund Davies LJ, who was chairman of a committee, whose report led to the Limitation Act 1963, declined to look at his own report, saying: 'Unfortunately ... that is an irrelevant consideration, as the law is to be found not in reports but in statutes'. See also *Vacher & Sons Ltd v London Society of Compositors* [1913] AC 107 at 113, 126.
18 *Hadmore Productions Ltd v Hamilton* [1983] 1 AC 191, [1982] 1 All ER 1042.
19 *Millar v Taylor* (1769) 4 Burr 2303 at 2332; *Salkeld v Johnson* (1848) 2 Exch 256 at 273.
20 *Magor and St Mellons RDC v Newport Corpn* [1952] AC 189 at 191, [1951] 2 All ER 839 at 841. Lord Simon has supported the use of preparatory material in *McMillan v Crouch* [1972] 3 All ER 61 at 76, [1972] 1 WLR 1102 at 1119; and *Charter v Race Relations Board* [1973] AC 868 at 900, [1973] 1 All ER 512 at 527; but he has also pointed out certain difficulties in *Ealing London Borough Council v Race Relations Board* [1972] AC 342 at 361, [1972] 1 All ER 105 at 114. In *Davis v Johnson* [1979] AC 264, [1978] 1 All ER 841, Lord Denning MR advocated the need to look at reports or other *travaux prèparatoires* and confessed that he had done so in order to elucidate the meaning of the provision under consideration; but his view was repudiated by the House of Lords ([1979] AC 264, [1978] 1 All ER 1132). In *Firman v Ellis* [1978] QB 886, [1978] 2 All ER 851, he said that in construing a wholly new type of provision he was entitled to consider the report of the Law Reform Committee; but his view was repudiated by his brethren. If a statute incorporates without change a draft Bill attached to a committee report to Parliament, a majority in the House of Lords expressed the view that the report might be looked at, at least for information as to the mischief and the existing state of the law: *Black-Clawson International Ltd v Papierwerke Waldhof-Aschaffenburg AG* [1975] AC 591, [1975] 1 All ER 810.
1 *Vacher & Sons Ltd v London Society of Compositors* [1913] AC 107 at 113; *Assam Railway and Trading Co Ltd v IRC* [1935] AC 445 at 457-459.
2 *Boy Andrew (Owners) v St Rognvald (Owners)* [1948] AC 140 at 149, [1947] 2 All ER 350 at 353; Lord Denning MR in *Letang v Cooper* [1965] 1 QB 232 at 240, [1964] 2 All ER 929 at 933; *Black-Clawson International Ltd v Papierwerke Waldhof-Aschaffenburg AG* [1975] AC 591, [1975] 1 All ER 810.
3 *Billings v Reed* [1945] KB 11 at 17, [1944] 2 All ER 415 at 419; *Howgate v Bagnall* [1951] 1 KB 265 at 274 [1950] 2 All ER 1104 at 1109. Regulations made under powers conferred by the words have been held to be inadmissible: *Stephens v Cuckfield RDC* [1960] 2 QB 373, [1960] 2 All ER 716; *Jackson v Hall* [1980] AC 854, [1980] 1 All ER 177; but cf *Britt v Buckinghamshire County Council* [1963] 2 All ER 175. A Government White Paper has also been held inadmissible: *Katikiro of Buganda v A-G* [1960] 3 All ER 849.

(4) International treaties, which have been given municipal effect by statutes, may not be consulted if the wording of the statute is clear and unambiguous[4], but if the statute itself refers to the treaty as the authoritative text and its own wording would lead to absurdity or is ambiguous, it is permissible to do so[5]. The use of *travaux prèparatoires* in the interpretation of statutes giving effect to treaties was considered by the House of Lords in *Fothergill v Monarch Airlines Ltd*[6]. Lord Wilberforce was prepared to consult such material only if it was public and accessible and clearly pointed to a definite legislative intention. Lord Diplock thought that courts should have regard to any material, which the delegates to an international conference considered would be available to clarify possible ambiguities; 'a court', he said, 'may even be under a constitutional obligation to do so'. Lord Scarman said that since in the great majority of states preparatory material is available as an aid to the construction of the particular treaty that was being considered, and since such material is used in the practice of international law generally, it should also be available to English courts, but only if there is doubt or ambiguity in the statute, or if the literal meaning appears to conflict with the purpose of the treaty.

A treaty will not cut down the scope of the plain and ordinary meaning of words in a statute, which have a wider application than the treaty[7].

The European Economic Community Treaty stands in a class by itself[8]. Lord Denning MR has said that British courts 'must follow the European pattern. No longer must they examine the words in meticulous detail. No longer must they argue about the precise grammatical sense. They must look to the purpose or intent. To quote the words of the European Court in the *Da Costa* case; they must limit themselves to deducing from "the wording and the spirit of the treaty the meaning of the Community rules" ... They must not confine themselves to the English text. They must consider, if need be, all the authentic texts, of which there are now eight .. They must divine the spirit of the treaty and gain inspiration from it. If they find a gap, they must fill it as best they can. They must do what the framers of the instrument would have done if they had thought about it. So we must do the same'[9].

An indication as to how far this attitude may permeate through to the interpretation of statutes giving effect to other treaties came when

---

4 *Ellerman Lines Ltd v Murray* [1931] AC 126; *IRC v Collco Dealings Ltd* [1962] AC 1, [1961] 1 All ER 762; *Warwick Film Productions Ltd v Eisinger* [1969] 1 Ch 508, [1967] 3 All ER 367. When the statute is ambiguous, see *The Banco* [1971] P 137, [1971] 1 All ER 524; *Medway, Drydock and Engineering Co v The Andrea Ursula* [1973] 1 QB 265, [1971] 1 All ER 821. When the treaty is ambiguous, see *Macarthys Ltd v Smith* [1979] 3 All ER 325, [1979] 1 WLR 1289.
5 *Pyrene Co Ltd v Scindia Steam Navigation Co Ltd* [1954] 2 QB 402 at 421, [1954] 2 All ER 158 at 165; *Riverstone Meat Co Pty Ltd v Lancashire Shipping Co Ltd* [1961] AC 807, [1961] 1 All ER 495; *Salomon v Customs and Excise Comrs* [1967] 2 QB 116, [1966] 3 All ER 871; *Post Office v Estuary Radio Ltd* [1967] 3 All ER 663, 679, [1967] 1 WLR 847, 1396; *Corocraft Ltd v Pan American Airways Inc* [1969] 1 QB 616, [1969] 1 All ER 82.
6 [1981] AC 251, [1980] 2 All ER 696.
7 *The Norwhale, Owners of the Vessel Norwhale v Ministry of Defence* [1975] QB 589, [1975] 2 All ER 501.
8 See pp 104 et seq. ante.
9 *H P Bulmer Ltd v J Bollinger SA* [1974] Ch 401, [1974] 2 All ER 1226 at 1237-1238.

the Court of Appeal said that in construing an Act like the Carriage of Goods by Road Act 1965 the Court should apply the rules used by the courts of the countries which are parties to the treaty, not the traditional canons of English construction, such as the *ejusdem generis* rule[10].

(5) Prior and subsequent legislation may be resorted to where both are laws on the same subject, or *in pari materia*, as it is put, and the portion of the statute under consideration is 'fairly and equally open to diverse meanings', and the Act which is called in aid must itself be unambiguous[11]. Sometimes a statute may provide that a provision or provisions in it shall be construed as part of some other statute. In such a case the two parts must be construed as if they are contained in a single Act, but even so the later Act may not be used to interpret the clear terms of the earlier Act[12].

(6) The Judicial Committee of the Privy Council has referred to extraneous matter more frequently than English tribunals. So in *British Coal Corpn v R*[13] it examined the resolutions of the Commonwealth Conference in order to interpret the Statute of Westminster 1931, and in *Edwards v A-G for Canada*[14] it consulted a report in Hansard of a Parliamentary debate. In *Patel v Comptroller of Customs*[15] it took account of the interpretation of similar legislation in other parts of the Commonwealth, and in *Dullewe v Dullewe*[16] it consulted the report of a commission on the mischief to be remedied.

It will thus be apparent that English courts have been on the whole reluctant to look outside the statute. This attitude is castigated by some writers as a needless fetter. There are, no doubt, occasions when a rigid attitude does lead to odd results. Nevertheless, the criticism can be overestimated. It may be contended that once extraneous considerations are allowed, there is no limit to the inquiry, but this is also an argument which can be carried too far. There is some evidence that the contrary practice elsewhere is not wholly satisfactory, and experience has shown that all such extrinsic material is less helpful than had been supposed. In America the suspected insertion by astute politicians of colouring matter into Congress debates and the proceedings of committees with a view to persuading the

10 *J Buchanan & Co Ltd v Babco Forwarding & Shipping (UK) Ltd* [1977] QB 208, [1977] 1 All ER 518; affd on other grounds [1978] AC 141, [1977] 3 All ER 1048. For the difficulty when there are conflicting foreign interpretations, see *Ulster-Swift Ltd and Pig Marketing Board (Northern Ireland) v Taunton Meat Haulage Ltd, Fransen Transport NV (Third Party)* [1977] 3 All ER 641, [1977] 1 WLR 625.
11 *Re Macmanaway* [1951] AC 161 at 177. For use of prior statutes, see *R v Titterton* [1895] 2 QB 61 at 67. For use of subsequent statutes, see *Rolle v Whyte* (1868) LR 3 QB 286 at 300; *Fendoch Investment Trust Co Ltd v IRC* [1945] 2 All ER 140 at 144, *Kirkness (Inspector of Taxes) v John Hudson & Co Ltd* [1955] AC 696, [1955] 2 All ER 345; *Crowe (Valuation Officer) v Lloyds British Testing Co Ltd* [1960] 1 QB 592 [1960] 1 All ER 411; *Ealing London Borough Council v Race Relations Board* [1972] AC 342 at 362, [1972] 1 All ER 105 at 115.
12 *Sanderson v IRC* [1956] AC 491, [1956] 1 All ER 14; *Kirkness (Inspector of Taxes) v John Hudson & Co Ltd* [1955] AC 696, [1955] 2 All ER 345; *John Walsh Ltd v Sheffield City Council and Tranter* [1957] 3 All ER 353. Interpretation of consolidating statutes: *R v Heron* [1982] 1 All ER 993, [1982] 1 WLR 451; statutory code: *Pioneer Aggregates (UK) Ltd v Secretary of State for the Environment* [1984] AC 132, [1984] 2 All ER 358.
13 [1935] AC 500.
14 [1930] AC 124 at 143.
15 [1966] AC 356, [1965] 3 All ER 593.
16 [1969] 2 AC 313, [1969] 2 WLR 811.

courts to take a certain view of a statute when it has been passed is proving to be something of an embarrassment, and, apart from that, matter can be extracted from preliminary discussions of legislation which could support almost any interpretation. It should also be borne in mind that the amorphous composition of a legislative body compels a tribunal to address itself to what the *enactment* means, not what particular persons may have meant Notwithstanding these factors, there is a residue of force in the criticisms. It is suspected that these are all ultimately directed at the attitude of the courts.

JUDICIAL ATTITUDE

It will have become evident that the vagaries of statutory interpretation reflect differences in the spirit of approach rather than in rules[17]. Much depends on whether judges read statutes in a restrictive or liberal spirit. The difference is vividly illustrated by contrasting the following utterances in the same case:

> 'We sit here' said Denning LJ (as he was then) 'to find out the intention of Parliament and of Ministers and carry it out, and we do this better by filling in the gaps and making sense of the enactment than by opening it up to destructive analysis'[18].

When the case went up to the House of Lords, Viscount Simonds sharply disapproved of what Denning LJ had said.

> 'This proposition which re-states in a new form the view expressed by the lord justice in the earlier case of *Seaford Court Estates Ltd v Asher* (to which the lord justice himself refers), cannot be supported. It appears to me to be a naked usurpation of the legislative function under the thin disguise of interpretation, and it is the less justifiable when it is guesswork with what material the legislature would, if it had discovered the gap, have filled it in. If a gap is disclosed, the remedy lies in an amending Act'[19].

Yet, in another case Viscount Simonds himself asserted in ringing tones the power, and indeed duty, of judges to fill in gaps in the common law without waiting for Parliament.

> 'When Lord Mansfield, speaking long after the Star Chamber had been abolished, said that the Court of King's Bench was the *custos morum* of the people and had the superintendence of offences *contra bonos mores*, he was asserting, as I now assert, that there is in that court a residual power, where no statute has yet intervened to supersede the common law, to superintend those offences which are prejudicial to the public welfare ... But gaps remain and will always remain since no one can foresee every way in which the wickedness of man may disrupt the order of society ... must we wait until Parliament finds time to deal with such conduct? I say, my Lords, that if the common law is powerless in such an event, then we should no longer do her reverance. But I say that

---

17 See eg *Jones v Secretary of State for Social Services* [1972] AC 944 at 966, 996, 1024, [1972] 1 All ER 145 at 149, 174, 196, per Lords Reid, Pearson and Simon.

18 *Magor and St Mellons RDC v Newport Corpn* [1950] 2 All ER 1226 at 1236. See also *Escoign Pties Ltd v IRC* [1958] AC 549 at 565, [1958] 1 All ER 406 at 414; *Ministry of Housing and Local Government v Sharp* [1970] 2 QB 223 at 264, [1970] 1 All ER 1009 at 1015.

19 [1952] AC 189 at 191, [1951] 2 All ER 839 at 841. For a suggestion that Denning LJ was referring to 'linguistic' gaps, not 'substantive' gaps, see Montrose 'The Treatment of Statutes by Lord Denning' in *Precedent in English Law* (ed Hanbury) ch 9.

her hand is still powerful and that it is for Her Majesty's judges to play the part which Lord Mansfield pointed out to them'[20].

The reason for this difference in attitude seems obvious. Judicial sympathy is more likely to be forthcoming with enactments touching on 'common lawyers' law' than with those concerning welfare and other social schemes. Whereas judges have a complete understanding of the problems and background of the former, they are in the main unfamiliar with the latter, due partly to the legal training of lawyers, both at universities and professionally. In view of the present day increase in legislative activity, judges are more and more concerned with statute interpretation, which has overshadowed the slower process of judicial reform of the common law. Even common law reform has come mainly via statute, so it is not surprising that statutes reforming common law receive more imaginative treatment at the hands of the courts than social reform statutes. A good example is the contrast between the judicial interpretation of housing legislation and the property legislation of 1925, which is but an aspect of the broader fact that judges are on the whole less ready to handle social doctrines and policies in the same spirit as traditional common law material. The common law is, after all, the creature of the judges, which is why, as Lord Devlin admitted, 'Judges, I have accepted, have a responsibility for the common law, but in my opinion they have none for statute law; their duty is simply to interpret and apply it and not to obstruct'[1].

A restrictive attitude to statute does not always coincide with literal interpretation as opposed to broad construction, nor *vice versa*. A restrictive desire may, for example, induce a tribunal to place a construction upon the provision in question quite other than what the plain meaning of the words would suggest. In *Roberts v Hopwood*[2] statutory power had been conferred upon a local authority to pay such wages 'as they may think fit'. The plain meaning of these words, one would suppose, is that the widest discretion shall be conferred. Yet the House of Lords, in the interests of a more equitable distribution of the financial burden among the inhabitants of the locality, felt disposed to cut down the apparently unlimited scope of the discretion by interpreting 'as they may think fit' to mean 'as they may *reasonably* think fit', and so enabling itself to decide what was 'reasonable'. The wage itself and the equality of wages for men and women were held to be unreasonable and the scheme was pronounced void. In *Liversidge v Anderson*[3] the question turned on whether a regulation to the effect that the Home Secretary had to have 'reasonable cause to believe' meant 'reasonable' in his opinion or in the opinion of the court. The House of Lords here, unlike the previous case, decided that it was for the Home Secretary, and not the tribunal, to decide the reasonableness of the grounds. The change in the judicial attitude was no doubt prompted by the war emergency and a desire not to hinder executive action at such a time. After the war the Judicial Committee of the Privy Council in *Nakkuda Ali v Jayaratne*[4] returned to an interpretation similar to that in *Roberts v Hopwood*, while in *Prescott v Birmingham Corpn*[5], the Court

20 *Shaw v DPP* [1962] AC 220 at 268, [1961] 2 All ER 446 at 452–453.
1 Devlin 'Judges and Lawmakers' (1976) 39 MLR 1 at p 13.
2 [1925] AC 578.
3 [1942] AC 206, [1941] 3 All ER 338.
4 [1951] AC 66.
5 [1955] Ch 210, [1954] 3 All ER 698.

of Appeal declared unreasonable the provision of free travel facilities for elderly persons by the Corporation, which was acting under statutory power to charge such fares 'as they thought fit'. In *Ross-Clunis v Papadopoullos*[6] a regulation required that a local commissioner should 'satisfy himself' that the inhabitants of a local area had appreciated the nature of the inquiry that had to be held before the imposition of a collective fine. The Judicial Committee, while agreeing that it was sufficient for the commissioner to be satisfied in his own mind, nevertheless expressed the opinion that a court might, if there were no grounds, review the honesty or reasonableness of the view formed by the commissioner. Turning to another context, judicial dislike led to construction as well as interpretation of s 4 of the Statute of Frauds 1677. The attitude of the judges was generally approved and no regret was expressed when in 1954 the Law Reform (Enforcement of Contracts) Act dispatched the substantial portion of the section to history with no scruple or apology. These examples show that the method employed, whether of interpretation or construction, depends very much on the attitude of the court towards the legislative provision in question. The factors that influence, and have in the past influenced, its attitude have been discussed.

CONCLUSIONS

First, judges are reluctant to intrude into Parliament's job. With case law they create their own texts as they proceed (*rationes decidendi*) and play variations on their interpretation. With statutes they only play more limited variations on texts created by Parliament.

Secondly, an inescapable corollary of the demand that judges should be more helpful to Parliament in their treatment of statutes is that a measure of creativeness has to be conceded to them. As Lord Diplock said:

> 'By intervening to change the common law Parliament has relegated the courts within this field to the lesser role of interpreting the written law that Parliament has enacted; but the power to state authoritatively what the words that Parliament has used mean for the purpose of applying them to particular circumstances necessarily involves a power in the courts to make law even though this be, in the phrase of Justice O W Holmes, but interstitially'[7].

Thirdly, statutes should be thought of in a continuum, which would make functional considerations an integral part of the whole problem of their application.

Fourthly, such application requires that information should be provided about the context of the provision. Statutes are no longer the minor departures from common law that they used to be; they now inaugurate new policies and social experiments. It is not possible to give these sympathetic consideration without some appreciation of their background. Some statutes may have no single or readily discoverable policy; yet, the rigid exclusion of all extrinsic material does seem to be undesirable, however hard it might be to set limits to the kind of material that should be admitted. On the other hand, one should not overlook the problem confronting judges, nor the sobering experience of countries which have admitted such material. A rule

---

6 [1958] 2 All ER 23 especially at 32-33.
7 *Geelong Harbor Trust Comrs v Gibbs Bright & Co* [1974] AC 810 at 819, [1974] 2 WLR 507 at 513.

of inclusion might well be as hampering as a rule of exclusion, and the matter may be better left, after all, to judicial discretion. On the occasions when judges have exercised it their efforts have, on the whole, met with success. Objection is levelled at cases in which they might as easily have exercised a similar discretion, but did not.

The information that could be provided is two-fold, in the words of the Law Commission, descriptive and motivating. *Descriptive* information explains the problem. In this connection legislators might perhaps give some thought to attaching explanatory memoranda to statutes. An important example of this is the Commentary accompanying the highly successful Uniform Commercial Code in America, which cannot be understood fully without the Commentary. The experiment of the 'Brandeis Brief' in America is another device which should be considered. This consists of evidence as to the problem, derived from statistics, reports, practice, psychiatric and sociological analyses and the like. It was first employed by Mr Brandeis, later a judge of the Supreme Court, when he appeared as counsel[8], and has since become accepted practice in constitutional cases. There is the danger, however, of increasing costs and the question of whether an undue advantage might lie with the party who can afford to engage the best experts. *Motivating* information gives reasons for the measure, and in this connection the admission of the Parliamentary history of a measure had been a much discussed issue[9]. It has its dangers[10]. As pointed out, unscrupulous politicians might be tempted to introduce colouring matter into debates with a view to influencing the courts. Apart from that, a statute is the product of the *interplay* of several factors. The mere records of debates and such like do not indicate the effect of this interplay on the minds of the legislators. Also, parliamentary history presents its own problem. The older a statute is, the more outdated its context. Should courts interpret it according to its historical context, even if this no longer obtains, or according to modern needs? If it is the latter, then the Parliamentary history is useless[11].

Fifthly, it is submitted that the doctrine of *stare decisis* should not be applied to statute interpretation, and indeed judges themselves have occasionally deprecated it[12]. *Stare decisis* works with case law because the 'statement of facts-reasons-decision' combination lends itself to variation so that the *ratio decidendi* of a case can be adapted; the process is one of making different statements of fact out of some unique, non-verbal event. With statute this is not the case. No facts and reasons are given, and the question is what different interpretations can be placed upon a given statement. The *ratio* of

---

8 *Miller v Oregon* 208 US 412 (1907). See also Frankfurter's brief in *Bunting v Oregon* 243 US 426 (1916); *Adkins v Children's Hospital* 261 US 525 (1923) (overruled in *West Coast Hotel Co v Parrish* 300 US 379 (1937)); *Brown v Board of Education* 347 US 483 (1954).

9 *Sagnata Investments Ltd v Norwich Corpn* [1971] 2 QB 614 at 623, [1971] 2 All ER 1441 at 1444.

10 *Ealing London Borough Council v Race Relations Board* [1972] AC 342 at 361, [1972] 1 All ER 105 at 114; *Dockers Labour Club and Institute Ltd v Race Relations Board* [1974] 3 All ER 592 at 601.

11 In *R v Bow Road Justices, ex p Adedigba* [1968] 2 QB 572, [1968] 2 All ER 89, the court preferred the modern context. On Parliamentary history, see the Law Commission *The Interpretation of Statutes* pp 31-37.

12 Eg in *Wright v Walford* [1955] 1 QB 363 at 374-375, [1955] 1 All ER 207 at 210; *Paisner v Goodrich* [1955] 2 QB 353 at 358, [1955] 2 All ER 330 at 332 (revsd [1957] AC 65, [1956] 2 All ER 176); *Bewlay (Tobacconists) Ltd v British Bata Shoe Co Ltd* [1958] 3 All ER 652 at 655; *Ogden Industries Pty Ltd v Lucas* [1969] 1 All ER 121 at 126.

a decision concerning statute interpretation is thus totally different from that of a non-statute law decision[13].

Sixthly, drafting techniques are better than they used to be. Nothing can ease the despairing complexities caused by poor draftsmanship. It is, of course, unfair to hold legislators always at fault, but, on the other hand, judicial impatience with some choice pieces of legislative obscurity can well be understood. Criticism by judges could be of valuable assistance to Parliament, since they know best the practical shortcomings of the statutes which they have to apply[14]. Drafting technique has not only improved, but has changed. Statutes are not now drafted in as much detail as they used to be in the last century, a factor which gave an additional filip to the literal approach. The more generously worded provisions of modern statutes invite a more liberal approach.

A further point is that statutes are designed to control behaviour and, like every communication, involve an author, a medium and an audience[15]. They are not addressed solely, or even primarily, to judges. The task of the judge is to see whether or not X's actual behaviour came within the statutory prescription. Interpretation has thus to be performed, not only by judges, but also by those whose behaviour is being regulated. This requires that the language used should be graded to suit the type of audience that is likely to be primarily involved, eg the language of traffic laws should be graded to suit the driver in the street; but not the language of company laws, for here the ordinary person will normally seek professional advice, and it is sufficient if such laws contemplate an expert audience[16].

Seventhly, legislators might perhaps give more thought than they do to the remedy in relation to the mischief. In particular, it would be helpful if they provide examples of the sort of thing that is designed to be covered[17]. Arguing by analogy from such examples should have a powerful appeal to judges, who are well versed in this technique of reasoning.

Finally, a suggestion has been made that different methods of interpretation should be applied to different types of statutes[18]. This does not appear

13 In *R v Bow Road Justices, ex p Adedigba* (see n 11 supra) *stare decisis* was not applied and a decision 118 years old was rejected. Where there is conflicting interpretation of a statute, the preponderant interpretation should be followed in the interests of consistency: *Re Electrical Installations at Exeter Hospital Agreement* [1971] 1 All ER 347, [1970] 1 WLR 1391.

14 Eg *Trevillian v Exeter Corpn* (1854) 5 De GM & G 828; *Fell v Burchett* (1857) 7 E & B 537 at 539; *Wankie Colliery Co v IRC* [1922] 2 AC 51 at 71; *LCC v Lees* [1939] 1 All ER 191 at 194; *Langford Property Co Ltd v Batten* [1951] AC 223 at 231, [1950] 2 All ER 1079 at 1080; *Customs and Excise Comrs v Top Ten Promotions Ltd* [1969] 3 All ER 39 at 93, 95, [1969] 1 WLR 1163 at 1175, 1178; *Merkur Island Shipping Corpn v Laughton* [1983] 2 AC 570 at 612, [1983] 2 All ER 189 at 198-199. See also the First Report of the Statute Law Commissioners 1835. Denning LJ has put the case for both sides very fairly: *Seaford Court Estates Ltd v Asher* [1949] 2 KB 481 at 499, [1949] 2 All ER 155 at 164 (on appeal [1950] AC 508, [1950] 1 All ER 1018); and in his Presidential Address to the Holdsworth Club 1950 p 10.

15 Dickerson *The Fundamentals of Legal Drafting* p 19.

16 'Modern statutes are drafted by professional legal draftsmen and intended to be read and understood by professional lawyers': per Lord Diplock in *Prestcold (Central) Ltd v Minister of Labour* [1969] 1 All ER 69 at 75, [1969] 1 WLR 89 at 96; and Lord Simon in *Maunsell v Olins* [1975] AC 373 at 391, [1975] 1 All ER 16 at 26. See also the remark by the Law Commission *The Interpretation of Statutes* p 3.

17 Lord Denning in *Escoign Properties Ltd v IRC* [1958] AC 549 at 565-566, [1958] 1 All ER 406 at 414. See also *London Transport Executive v Betts* [1959] AC 213 at 240, [1958] 2 All ER 636 at 651. Examples are incorporated into sections of the Consumer Credit Act 1974, and the Torts (Interference with Goods) Act 1977.

18 Friedmann *Law in a Changing Society* pp 34 et seq; 'Judge, Politics and the Law' (1951) 29 Can BR pp 825-834; *Legal Theory* pp 451-462.

to be workable, for difficulties are bound to arise as to how a particular statute is to be classified and how one should treat a statute of a hybrid character. Classification will help very little, for the heart of the matter rests in the attitude of the judges.

READING LIST

C K Allen *Law in the Making* (7th edn) ch 6.

F Bennion *Statutory Interpretation*.

J A Corry 'Administrative Law and the Interpretation of Statutes' (1935–36) 1 Toronto Law Journal 286.

A R N Cross *Statutory Interpretation*.

C P Curtis 'A Better Theory of Legal Interpretation' in *Jurisprudence in Action* 135.

D J LL Davies 'The Interpretation of Statutes in the Light of their Policy by the English Courts' (1935) 35 Columbia Law Review 519.

F R Dickerson *The Interpretation and Application of Statutes*.

E R Hopkins 'The Literal Canon and the Golden Rule' (1937) 14 Canadian Bar Review 689.

D G Kilgour 'The Rule Against the Use of Legislative History: "Canon of Construction or Counsel of Caution"?' (1952) 30 Canadian Bar Review 769.

Law Commission and the Scottish Law Commission. *The Interpretation of Statutes* (HMSO).

E H Levi *An Introduction to Legal Reasoning* pp 19–40.

D J Payne 'The Intention of the Legislature in the Interpretation of Statutes' (1956) 9 Current Legal Problems 96.

R Pound 'Common Law and Legislation' (1907–8) 21 Harvard Law Review 393.

M Radin 'Statutory Interpretation' (1929–30) 43 Harvard Law Review 863.

A Ross *On Law and Justice* ch 4.

J W Salmond on *Jurisprudence* (12th edn P J Fitzgerald) 131–140.

J Willis 'Statutory Interpretation in a Nutshell' (1938) 16 Canadian Bar Review 1.

Science of Legal Method: Select Essays by Various Authors (trans E Bruncken and L B Register), J H Wigmore 'Preface' pp xxvi–xxxvi; A Kocourek 'Preface' pp lvii–lxvii.

CHAPTER 9

Custom

The term 'custom' is used in a variety of senses: local custom, usage (some-times known as conventional custom), general custom and the custom of the courts. The first three will be considered here; the fourth relates to precedent and *stare decisis*, which have been dealt with. There are also allusions, espe-cially in the early records, to the custom of the realm or general custom, which, on examination, appear to refer to the custom of the courts. For instance, it was said in one case that a man, who negligently failed to control his fire so that it spread to his neighbour's house, was answerable according to 'the law and custom of the realm'[1]. It is not easy to see which custom was being referred to. If it was the award of damages, then that would be more appropriately regarded as resting on the custom of the courts.

Customs are of slow growth. When a person has been doing a thing regularly over a substantial period of time, it is usual to say that he has grown accustomed to doing it. His habit may not concern anyone but him-self, or at most only those within his immediate circle. When a large section of the populace are in the habit of doing a thing over a very much longer period, it may become necessary for courts to take notice of it. The reaction of people themselves may manifest itself in mere unthinking adherence to a practice which they follow simply because it is done. Indeed, M Tarde found in sheer imitation the drive behind the evolution of all practices, from passing fashions to abiding customs[2]. People's reaction may go further and develop into a conviction that a practice should continue to be observed, because they approve of it as a model of behaviour. It is the latter that is of interest, since it raises the question of how factual occurrences develop into prescrip-tive models of behaviour, which was dealt with earlier[3]. Many such models spring up in society, but not all of them are 'laws', eg that of wearing black at funerals. The question is when and in what circumstances the label 'law' comes to be attached to an 'ought' resting on practices. Historical and an-thropological inquiries into the influence of custom on social and legal de-velopment will be considered later[4]. In considering the law-constitutive character of practices, it is necessary to distinguish between local customs, usages and general custom.

LOCAL CUSTOMS

Customs of particular localities are capable of being recognised as laws in derogation of the common law[5]. Their acceptance by the courts is hedged

1 *Beaulieu v Finglam* (1401) YB 2 Hen 4, f 18, pl 6.
2 Tarde *Les Lois de l'Imitation* (trans E C Parsons).
3 See pp 58–59 ante.
4 See ch 18 post.
5 This seems to be the sense in which Coke referred to custom: *Co Litt* 110b.

by a number of conditions which have been evolved by the judiciary. The geographical limits, too, within which they are allowed to operate need precise definition. To make sense of these conditions it is essential that they should be considered in the perspective of time. The traditional presentation of them on a flat canvas as if they were co-eval produces a contra dictory and confusing picture, which has raised unnecessary problems. Classic accounts will be found in Blackstone's *Commentaries*[6], and in more modern investigations by Sir Carleton Allen and Mr Salt[7].

When custom is considered as an evolutionary phenomenon, the first question is why it came to be accepted by courts as a law-constitutive medium in the first place. There are two answers. Before the common law had filled out, the itinerant justices had to find the law somehow. In the absence of a code, local customs usually were the only available guides and the justices were glad to avail themselves of these. By doing this they also helped to win local confidence in the Royal system of justice. For local people had built up expectations based on local practices and to have ignored these would have caused injustice. The only question with which the judges of old were concerned was whether a practice exerted sufficient local pressure to be acceptable to them. At that date the necessary conditions, which had to be fulfilled, were obvious.

(1) The custom had to possess a sufficient measure of antiquity. 'Sufficient' means today that it must have existed since before 1189[8], but this was by no means the original interpretation. For instance, Professor Plucknett quotes Azo (d 1230) who said

> 'A custom can be called *long* if it was introduced within ten or twenty years, *very long* if it dates from thirty years, and *ancient* if it dates from forty years'[9].

The way this requirement works now is that the onus of proving antiquity is upon the person who sets up the custom, but his task is helped by a presumption of existence since before 1189 on proof of the existence of the custom for a substantial period. The burden of rebutting it then lies on the other party[10].

(2) The custom must have been enjoyed continuously. This refers, not to the active exercise of the custom, but rather to its assertion[11].

(3) The custom must have been enjoyed 'as of right', *nec vi nec clam nec precario*[12]. For without this there is no evidence that it exerts obligatory pressure to conform.

(4) The custom must be certain and precise[13].

6 BI Com I pp 74–79.
7 Allen *Law in the Making* chs 1–2; Salt 'Local Ambit of a Custom' in *Cambridge Legal Essays* p 279.
8 The first year of the reign of Richard I and the start of the Plea Rolls. The date was established to accord with the period of limitation set by the Statute of Westminster 1275, for the bringing of writs of right.
9 Plucknett *A Concise History of the Common Law* p 308.
10 *Simpson v Wells* (1872) LR 7 QB 214; *Bryant v Foot* (1868) LR 3 QB 497; *Iveagh v Martin* [1961] 1 QB 232, [1960] 2 All ER 668; *Egerton v Harding* [1975] QB 62, [1974] 3 All ER 689.
11 *Mercer v Denne* [1904] 2 Ch 534; *Wyld v Silver* [1963] Ch 243, [1962] 3 All ER 309; *Estler v Murrells* (1959) 173 Estates Gazette 393; *New Windsor Corpn v Mellor* [1975] Ch 380, [1975] 3 All ER 44.
12 *Mills v Colchester Corpn* (1867) LR 2 CP 476; *Alfred F Beckett Ltd v Lyons* [1967] Ch 449, [1967] 1 All ER 833, 839.
13 *Broadbent v Wilks* (1742) Willes 360; *Wilson v Willes* (1806) 7 East 121.

(5) The custom had to be consistent with other customs in the same area. The fact that it conflicted with local customs elsewhere did not matter. For if a custom was a departure from the common law itself, it could equally well diverge from some other local departure.

It is not enough to stop with the original acceptance of local customs; it is necessary also to investigate under what conditions they continued to be accepted. As time went on the original reasons disappeared and the altered state of affairs introduced even more restrictive conditions.

1. The common law filled out and more and more statutes appeared on the statute book. There was then no longer the same need as before to seek guidance in local customs, and so arose the limiting condition that custom should not infringe 'fundamental rules of the common law'[14], or conflict with statute. Who decides what is a 'fundamental rule'? The answer is: the court. It is in the very nature of local custom to derogate from the common law, but the condition is that it should not contravene a 'fundamental rule'. The distinction between what is an ordinary and what is a fundamental rule is clearly of such vagueness that it gives courts considerable discretion over the admission of local customs. Even in the earliest times, although they used to find much of the law locally, they were also concerned to give effect to the Royal policy of centralising its development and administration. Therefore, side by side with their readiness to accept local customs, they also kept an eye on securing a measure of overall consistency. The latter aim only began to inhibit the acceptance of local customs when the overall picture filled out, and it is at this stage that the vague condition under consideration came to be articulated.

2. With the development of travel and communication local areas ceased to be isolated, which led to a progressive shrinking of what was understood to be 'local'. According to Mr Salt, this means that 'it has for its scope a class of persons limited by inhabitancy and a right whose subject matter lies in the same defined district'[15]. If the ambit of the rule is widened in respect of either the class of persons or the subject matter of the claim, it cannot exist as a local custom but must be a rule of common law, or not law at all.

3. Finally, as pointed out before, an essential condition of the continued acceptance of any criterion of validity is that it should be adaptable to changing ideas. The introduction of reasonableness as a condition of the acceptability of local customs has virtually sapped them of vitality, for it is the courts who pronounce on what is reasonable.[16] Theoretically, they should decide the question according to the standards of 1189, and this is indeed the test sometimes adopted. More often, however, it would appear that they judge reasonableness by the contemporary standards of the time when the case comes to be heard[17]. The point is that, if the courts adopt a contemporary standard for reasonableness, they are largely undermining the assertion that the custom is binding on them and that they are bound to enforce

---

14 *Tanistry Case* (1608) Dav IR 28; *Johnson v Clark* [1908] 1 Ch 303.
15 *Salt* p 279, after an examination of the cases; *New Windsor Corpn v Mellor* [1975] Ch 380, [1975] 3 All ER 44.
16 Cross does not think that the discretion is unlimited: *Precedent in English Law* pp 158–159.
17 *Bryant v Foot* (1868) LR 3 QB 497; *Alfred F Beckett Ltd v Lyons* [1967] Ch 449, [1967] 1 All ER 833, 839 (unreasonable in 1189). Cf *Lawrence v Hitch* (1868) LR 3 QB 521. See also *Tanistry Case* (1608) Dav IR 28.

it, and are in effect subordinating it to judicial discretion. If reasonableness is judged by the standards of 1189, then it can be argued with some force that the test of reasonableness is only evidential of the existence of the custom from time immemorial, for if it was not reasonable in 1189, it probably did not exist then. According to this view, the courts do not exercise any vital discretion over the admission of a custom on grounds of reasonableness, but only use that test to help in deciding whether was in existence in 1189. *Dicta* can be found to support both sides.

LOCAL CUSTOM AS 'LAW'

Customs are undeniably a 'source' of law in the sense that they have provided material for other law-constitutive agencies, such as legislation and precedent. Whether they are of themselves law-constitutive has been debated; in other words, is a practice 'law' only when statute or precedent stamps it as such, or is it able to stamp itself when the necessary conditions are satisfied? It is submitted that the failure to separate the two time-frames of thought has led to a fruitless controversy in this regard. For the changing attitudes of the judges over centuries present an irreconcilable picture if they are all viewed as something given at any particular moment of time, and pose a problem which is incapable of a tidy solution. On the one hand, judges say that they are bound by custom, and this derives support from the fact that local customs are essentially derogations from the common law, from which they will not deviate unless compelled to do so. On the other hand, their liberty to throw out customs, which they regard as unreasonable or as contravening some fundamental principle of the common law, appears to belie their words. It is impossible to say beforehand whether a judge will follow a given custom or not, yet once he has decided to follow it he says that he does so because he is bound by it. This point was perceived by Jethro Brown, who observed that

> 'What judges do, and what they profess to do, are not always the same, and the latter is only evidence of the former—often very misleading evidence'[18].

Austin approached the matter *a priori* on the basis of his definition of a law as the command of a sovereign backed by sanction. Custom accordingly cannot be law of itself, but only by virtue of sovereign command, which might be express, as in the form of a statute, or 'tacit', which can be seen when a judicial decision recognising a custom is carried out[19]. If this were so, later courts should not be concerned with the custom at all but only with the precedent. Yet they do continue to interest themselves in the custom itself. Allen took the opposite view. Custom is law of itself because a court will recognise and accept it as such[20]. Moreover, a local custom is a variation of the common law, and a judge does not depart from the common law unless constrained by law to do so. Against this, there is the substantial discretion which judges exercise in accepting or rejecting custom, which makes it difficult to maintain that they are bound to accept as law something over which they exercise such extensive control. Buckland proffered the solution that the position is analogous to the law of contract. Here, what is law is not a particular contract, but the statement of the characteristics

18 Brown *The Austinian Theories of Law* p 310.
19 Austin *Lectures on Jurisprudence* I, pp 101–103.
20 Allen *Law in the Making* pp 152 et seq.

which a contract should possess before it will be accepted. So, too, in the case of custom 'what is law is not the custom but the statement of the characteristics which it must have'[1]. The analogy, it is submitted is false. For, even if it is usual to *say* that the terms of a particular contract are not 'law', it is certainly usual to say that a particular custom is 'law' for those who come within its ambit. The phrase 'law of contract' undoubtedly refers to the statement of the characteristics which contracts should possess and not to particular contracts as law-constitutive in themselves, whereas with custom the question is precisely whether a given custom is itself law-constitutive. In short, it is not the 'law of custom' that is under review, but customs as 'laws'[2].

When customs are considered as the products of development over time the problem disappears. There is no doubt that in the early days customs were accepted as law-constitutive because, in the absence of other guidance, judges were glad to avail themselves of them. With the expansion of the common law and legislation, there was less and less need to turn to them, and judicial control over their admission became tighter, thereby reducing their law-constitutive potentiality to vanishing point. Indeed, one might say squarely that as the original reasons for accepting them no longer obtain, they should now cease to be regarded as law-constitutive. Courts, however, still pay lip-service to their force even while exercising such extensive control. The question, therefore, is why they do this. Judges say that they are bound because they *feel* bound, and this feeling is preserved through the language of bygone times when they used to say they were bound because they had little or no choice in the matter. So gradual was the process by which they came to acquire their control that at no point of time in all that development were they themselves conscious of the change. So they continued to talk, and still talk, the language of the past, and it is this that perpetuates the feeling of being bound. In the result, it might be said that local custom was a law-constitutive agency in the past and remains potentially so today, but that the likelihood of its operation is now very small. When looked at in this way, the controversy whether or not custom is 'law' *ex proprio vigore* does not arise[3].

USAGES

Society is never still. As it develops it moves away from the letter of the law by evolving practices that may influence or simply by-pass existing rules. Such practices only acquire the label 'laws' when incorporated into statute or precedent, but they have immeasurably greater significance and operation apart from this.

One sphere is in contract. If transactions in a particular trade, or of a particular kind in a particular locality, have long been carried on subject to a certain understanding between the parties, it is but natural that in the course of time everyone in the trade, or in the locality, who carries on such transactions, will assume that they will be done in the light of this understanding, if nothing is said to the contrary. Since one of the purposes of law

1 Buckland *Some Reflections on Jurisprudence* p 55.
2 For other objections, see Cross *Precedent in English Law* pp 159–160.
3 It may be useful at this point to turn to the theory of Savigny, who based all law on custom as the expression of the spirit of the people: see ch 18 post.

is to uphold the settled expectations of men, courts sometimes incorporate these settled conventions as terms of the contract[4].

The following conditions have to be satisfied before they will do so:

(1) The usage must be so well established as to be notorious. No particular period of longevity, however, is necessary to satisfy this requirement of notoriety[5].

(2) The usage cannot alter the general law of the land, whether statutory or common law. Usage derives its force from its incorporation into an agreement and, therefore, can have no more power to alter the law than express agreement.

(3) The usage will have to be a reasonable one[6].

(4) It need have no particular scope. Usages may be, and usually are, limited to a trade or locality, but they may be common to the whole country, or even be international.

(5) The usage will not be enforced in a particular case if it purports to nullify or vary the express terms of the contract. Its sole function is to imply a term when the contract is silent. The parties cannot be understood to have contracted in the light of a usage which they have expressly contradicted[7].

The operation of such conventional usages is also an illustration of the potency of practice in influencing other law-constitutive processes. At first courts insist on specific proof of some usage, then when it becomes notorious they may take judicial notice of it, and finally it may be embodied in statute. Usages are thus not 'laws' *ex proprio vigore*. Buckland's suggestion, which was considered in the previous context, seems more appropriate here: what is 'law' is not usage, but the statement of the characteristics which it should possess.

Besides commercial usages, there are other kinds of practices that produce divergences from the norms prescribed by laws. For instance, developing skills and techniques, or the introduction of some new kind of machinery, may induce workmen to ignore some pre-existing safety regulation, which in time becomes a dead letter. Behavioural study of what Ehrlich called the 'living law', ie norms of conduct that actually govern behaviour, is of the profoundest importance in keeping 'formal law' abreast of the times and in understanding how it operates, or fails to operate, in society[8].

GENERAL CUSTOM

It has long been commonplace in English judicial pronouncements that a custom prevailing throughout the land and existing since before 1189, is part of the common law[9]. This identity between general custom and the common

---

4 *Hutton v Warren* (1836) 1 M & W 466.
5 *Eastern Counties Building Society v Russell* [1947] 2 All ER 734. See also the speech of Lord O'Hagan in *Tucker v Linger* (1883) 8 App Cas 508.
6 *Tucker v Linger* (1883) 8 App Cas 508.
7 *Les Affréteurs Réunis Société Anonyme v Walford* [1919] AC 801.
8 Ehrlich's views might be considered at this point, for which see pp. 425–427 post.
9 Eg Tindal CJ in *Veley v Burder* (1841) 12 Ad & El 265 at 302, 'Such a custom existing beyond the time of legal memory and extending over the whole realm, is no other than the common law of England'; Best J in *Blundell v Catterall* (1821) 5 B & Ald 268 at 279; Blackstone *Commentaries* I, 63.

law was a matter of historical development, for the common law from its earliest days was no more than the creation of the judges. The reliance by Royal justices on decisions given in one part of the realm, based on local customs, as precedents for decisions in other parts gradually produced principles of general application, which came to be known as the 'common custom of the realm' or the 'common law'. It was part of the process of acquiring a monopoly for the Royal administration of justice. It was also usual for judges to buttress the ideas which they drew from civil and canon law and good sense with the impressive assertion that these were the 'general custom of the realm'. Since only the judges were in a position to declare what was the general custom of the realm, such custom and judge-made law signified one and the same thing[10].

The question that remains open is whether a custom of the realm, which has come into existence after 1189 and contrary to doctrines established by case law, can be law *ex proprio vigore*. The instance where this has occurred is that of negotiable instruments, as to which there was a conflict of judicial opinion[11], but no proposition should be founded on a single instance. The answer should be that general custom now has no law-constitutive effect of its own.

10 A W B Simpson, in his treatment of common law as general custom, puts the matter as follows: 'Just as the statement of a particular custom is not to be identified with the practice itself, so too common law rule-statements are not identical with 'the common law'; which consists of the acceptance as more or less correct by a specialist profession of statements in rule form of received ideas and practices. This, in his view, explains why there is no one authentic text of a common law rule, and why decisions were long treated as illustrative of 'the common law': 'The Common Law and Legal Theory' in *Oxford Essays in Jurisprudence* (2nd Series, ed Simpson) ch 4.
11 *Goodwin v Robarts* (1875) LR 10 Exch 337. Cf *Crouch v Credit Foncier of England* (1873) LR 8 QB 374. See also Salmond on *Jurisprudence* pp 205-212.

READING LIST

C K Allen *Law in the Making* (7th edn) chs 1-2.
J Austin *Lectures on Jurisprudence* (5th edn R Campbell) I, pp 101-103; II pp 536-543.
W Blackstone *Commentaries on the Laws of England* I, pp 67-79.
E K Braybrooke 'Custom as Sources of English Law' (1951) 50 Michigan Law Review 71.
W W Buckland *Some Reflections on Jurisprudence* pp 52-56.
A R N Cross *Precedent in English Law* (2nd edn) pp 155-163.
T F T Plucknett *A Concise History of the Common Law* (5th edn) Book I, Part III, ch 3.
J W Salmond on *Jurisprudence* (12th edn, P J Fitzgerald) ch 6.
H E Salt 'Local Ambit of a Custom' in *Cambridge Legal Essays* (eds P H Winfield and A D McNair) 279.
A W B Simpson 'The Common Law and Legal Theory' in *Oxford Essays in Jurisprudence* (ed A W B Simpson) ch 4.
P Vinogradoff 'Customary Law' in *The Legacy of the Middle Ages* (ed C G Crump and E F Jacob) 287.

CHAPTER 10

Values

The foregoing Chapters will have shown the element of discretion that is necessarily involved in the interpretation and application of precedents, statutes and customs. This is why it can be said that valid rules do not decide disputes. As Holmes J put it 'General propositions do not decide concrete cases'[1]. The judicial oath does not enjoin a judge simply to do justice, nor simply to apply law; it requires him to do justice according to law. Allen said 'one of the most important interpretative factors is a trained sense of *discretionary* justice'[2]. It is here that the third kind of knowledge involved in the decisional process comes in, namely, knowing the just way of applying the law to the facts. The drive behind doing 'justice according to law' is provided by values, which constitute what Holmes J described as 'the inarticulate major premise of judicial reasoning'[3]; 'inarticulate' because there is seldom an openavowal of their influence. Yet, although courts have frequently disclaimed to dispense justice pure and simple[4], there are occasions when they do and say so.

> 'If I thought that injustice has been done to him' said Lindley LJ 'I should have found some method, I have no doubt, of getting rid of the technical objection'[5].

Justice may also help to decide between alternative rules or interpretations. As Lord Reid said 'If a decision in one sense will on the whole lead to much more just and reasonable results, that appears to me to be a strong argument in its favour'[6]. Where there is no authority, the decision may well rest on justice.

---

1 *Lochner v New New York* 198 US 45 at 76 (1905). So, too, Lord Reid: 'Legal principles cannot solve the problem': *British Railways Board v Herrington* [1972] AC 877 at 897, [1972] 1 All ER 749 at 756; Lord Macmillan: 'In almost every case, except the very plainest, it would be possible to decide the issue either way with reasonable legal justification': *Law and Other Things* p 48; Lord Wright: 'Notwithstanding all the apparatus of authority, the judge has nearly always some degree of choice': *Legal Essays and Addresses* p xxv. See also Holmes *The Common Law* pp 35–36; Cardozo *The Nature of the Judicial Process* pp 10–11; Ungoed-Thomas J in *Duchess of Argyll* [1967] Ch 302 at 317, [1865] 1 All ER 611 at 616; Lord Morris in *Australian Consolidated Press Ltd v Uren* [1969] 1 AC 590 at 644, [1967] 3 All ER 523 at 538.
2 Allen *Law in the Making* p 415.
3 *Lochner v US* 118 US 45 at 74 (1905).
4 *Baylis v Bishop of London* [1913] 1 Ch 127 at 140, CA.
5 *Re Scowby, Scowby v Scowby* [1897] 1 Ch 741 at 751, CA. See also *Millar v Taylor* (1769), 4 Burr 2303 at 2312, 2398; *Gardiner v Heading* [1928] 2 KB 284 at 290; *Heap v Ind Coope and Allsopp Ltd* [1940] 2 KB 476 at 483, [1940] 3 All ER 634 at 636–637, CA; *Falmouth Boat Construction Ltd v Howell* [1950] 2 KB 16 at 23, [1950] 1 All ER 538 at 541, CA (affd sub nom *Howell v Falmouth Boat Construction Ltd* [1951] AC 837, [1951] 2 All ER 278, HL); *Kitchen v RAF Association* [1958] 2 All ER 241, [1958] 1 WLR 563 at 568, CA; *Scruttons Ltd v Midland Silicones Ltd* [1962] AC 446 at 487, [1962] 1 All ER 1 at 19, HL.
6 *Starkowski v A-G* [1954] AC 155 at 170, [1953] 2 All ER 1272 at 1274, HL.

'In the end and in the absence of authority binding on this House' said Viscount Simonds 'the question is simply: What does justice demand in such a case as this? ... If I have to base my opinion on any principle, I would venture to say it was the principle of rational justice'[7].

The meaning of legal concepts may vary in different contexts according to the demands of justice. In *Dodworth v Dale*[8], A married B in 1927 and was allowed a deduction in income tax. The marriage was later declared null and void. When the Inland Revenue authorities claimed to re-assess the tax payable by him, it was held that he had been 'married' during that period and their claim therefore failed. On the other hand, in *Re Dewhirst, Flower v Dewhirst*[9], A left money to his widow for as long as she did not re-marry. She did re-marry, but the marriage was declared void. It was held that this was not 'marriage' and she accordingly kept the money. Entire new doctrines owe their origin to broad sentiments of justice, eg equity, quasi-contract and various other special rules[10]. Denning LJ once remarked 'If the rules of equity have become so rigid that they cannot remedy such an injustice, it is time we had a new equity to make good the omissions of the old'[11]. Sometimes discretion is conferred on courts to refuse to apply foreign law if it is unjust[12]; and statute used to empower them to refuse the extradition of fugitive offenders to other parts of the Commonwealth if it would be unjust or oppressive to do so[13].

The reason why, apart from the above, courts prefer not to stress the influence of justice is that popular confidence stems from the belief that 'law is law' and that judges have only to apply it[14]. The very nature of the judicial process shows that this is intrinsically impossible. On the other hand, respect for law would be impaired if it were felt that cases were decided on personal whims, which again is not the case. There is indeed a personal element, but it is far from capricious; judges do have to administer laws as they find them, but there is more discretion in the process than is popularly supposed. This discretion, however, is controlled by a sense of values, which constitute a consensual domain that keeps prejudice in check. Distinctions should here be made between the existence of a particular value, an individual's knowledge of its existence, and his approval or disapproval of it. His knowledge of its existence is akin to his knowledge of 'objective reality'[15]; his approval or disapproval is an additional response. Consensual domains 'exist' apart from an individual's knowledge of it and his approval or disapproval. It is in this way that they operate as checks on personal quirks and go towards preserving public confidence in the judicial settlement of disputes. The inspiration for

---

7 *National Bank of Greece and Athens SA v Metliss* [1958] AC 509 at 525, [1957] 3 All ER 608 at 612-613, HL.
8 [1936] 2 KB 503, [1936] 2 All ER 440.
9 [1948] Ch 198, [1948] 1 All ER 147.
10 Eg *Moses v Macferlan* (1760) 2 Burr 1005 at 1012; *Wilson v Glossop* (1888) 20 QBD 354, CA.
11 *Solle v Butcher* [1950] 1 KB 671 at 695, [1949] 2 All ER 1107 at 1121, CA; cf *Campbell Discount Co Ltd v Bridge* [1961] 1 QB 445 at 459, [1961] 2 All ER 97 at 103, CA (revsd *Bridge v Campbell Discount Co Ltd* [1962] AC 600, [1962] 1 All ER 385 sub nom). See also *Sinclair v Brougham* [1914] AC 398 at 458, HL.
12 *Kaufman v Gerson* [1904] 1 KB 591, CA; *Short v A-G of Sierra Leone* [1964] 1 All ER 125, [1963] 1 WLR 1427; *Oppenheimer v Cattermole* [1976] AC 249, [1975] 1 All ER 538, HL.
13 Fugitive Offenders Act 1881, s 10 (repealed). See now the Fugitive Offenders Act 1967, s 4.
14 Scrutton LJ in *Hill v Aldershot Corpn* [1933] 1 KB 259 at 263-264; Lord Radcliffe *Law and its Compass* p 39.
15 See pp 5-6 ante.

'doing justice according to law' derives from the consensual domain of shared values. Judicial reflection of these in turn sets a kind of official seal on standards, which then act as a brake on social fragmentation.

Every decision reflects a value-judgment on conflicting interests. If interests did not conflict there would be no disputes. 'Values' for present purposes consist of those considerations, which are viewed as objectives of the legal order and which shape, provisionally at least, the decisions of courts and guide their handling of the law by providing yardsticks for measuring the conflicting interests that are involved. By 'value-judgment' is signified the choice of a particular yardstick of valuation as well as the result of measuring interests with reference to the chosen value. A case is important when it introduces something new. The very word 'new' implies that there is nothing in the existing law to cover the precise situation, so the inspiration for such new element has to come from outside. There are, of course, degrees of importance. Case law develops imperceptibly over a period and the new element introduced by a particular decision may be small. In the majority of cases disposed of by lower courts the new element may be non-existent because they allow little scope for discretion. Such cases give the appearance of being straightforward applications of rules to fact[16]. Yet, even in these the possibility of exercising some discretion is there, however minimal.   At the other end of the scale, decisions which create or extinguish some rule, or play some tangential variation thereon, are very important, although they are numerically fewer[17].

The extent to which value-judgments may be given effect depends upon the texture of the law. (a) It is always possible to make different statements of facts in the case before the court; or (b) different statements of law, as where the *ratio decidendi* is open to diverse formulations, or a statutory rule is capable of more than one construction. (c) Some rules are stated in terms of ill-defined content, eg 'negligence', 'possession', the meanings of which in different contexts are governed by values. (d) There may be alternative or conflicting rules, eg where there are conflicting authorities[18]; or (e) there may be no rule at all; and here judicial latitude is at its widest. (f) An authoritative case might be reversed on appeal, overruled, or simply put to one side[19]. (g) Some rules deliberately confer a discretion on the court[20].

'Doing justice according to law' is thus a continuous operation and the process reveals the whole system of norms that hold society together. Values concern the functioning of laws in society. Therefore, they need to be studied with reference to those cases which introduce some new rule, or else play some variation on an existing rule. Speculation about law in society is useful only in proportion to one's appreciation of how it actually operates. For this reason the foundation for any such speculation should be laid, among other things, in actual cases. It follows from this that cases should be thought of in

---

16 MacCormick *Legal Reasoning and Legal Theory*.

17 Diplock 'The Courts as Legislators' in *Presidential Address to the Holdsworth Club* 1965 p 1. See also his remarks on policy behind principle in *Cassell & Co Ltd v Broome* [1972] AC 1027 at 1124, 1129, [1972] 1 All ER 801 at 869, 873; and on changing society and law [1972] AC at 1128, [1972] 1 All ER at 872.

18 Eg *Thorne v Motor Trade Association* [1937] AC 797, [1937] 3 All ER 157; *Fisher v Taylors Furnishing Stores Ltd* [1956] 2 QB 78,]1956] 2 All ER 78. Cf *R v Immigration Appeal Tribunal, ex p Martin* (1972) 116 Sol Jo 697.

19 *Matthews v Kuwait Bechtel Corpn* [1959] 2 QB 57, [1959] 2 All ER 345.

20 Eg Fugitive Offenders Act 1881, s 10. (repealed) See now the Fugutive Offenders Act 1967, s4.

series, since it is from a series that it becomes possible to discern the consensual domain of the values being invoked. There will no doubt be individual variations in interpretation, so the most that can be said is in terms of tendencies.

The principal yardsticks by which conflicting interests are evaluated may tentatively be listed as national and social safety; sanctity of the person; sanctity of property; social welfare; equality; consistency and fidelity to rules, principle, doctrine and tradition; morality; administrative convenience; and international comity. A case may involve any one but not others, or a judge may not take a possible consideration into account. The above list represents some at least of the criteria to which appeal is usually made. Moreover, no judge should be pictured, even remotely, as measuring the activities in the dispute before him against each standard in turn.

Finally, when yardsticks compete the judge has to choose between them, and it is only by collating such cases that it becomes possible to see whether there is a hierarchy of values. It is submitted that national and social safety override all other considerations and sanctity of the person is superior to sanctity of property, but beyond this the pattern is kaleidoscopic, not hierarchical. Every social twist alters the balance and settles the values in a new pattern; the position today is different from what it was five years ago, and vastly different from what it was thirty years ago[1].

SANCTITY OF THE PERSON

The choice between personal liberty and property sometimes presents difficulty, but there is a discernible tilt in favour of the former. In the pioneer decision in *Sommersett's Case*[2] the assertion of ownership by a slave-owner over his slave was rejected. There was no authority, so there was no question of deciding according to a rule of law. Lord Mansfield made short work of the point, saying that slavery was so repugnant to English ideas that Sommersett should go free. In *Horwood v Millar's Timber and Trading Co Ltd*[3] the court rejected as unreasonable a contract which would have reduced a person to a condition of virtual slavery; and in *Eastham v Newcastle United Football Club Ltd*[4] Wilberforce J avoided a form of contract whereby it was sought to operate the retention and transfer system of engaging professional footballers. In both cases the courts might have upheld the contracts by invoking the doctrine of the sanctity of contract, but they found it as easy to invalidate them on grounds of unreasonable restraint of trade. The point is that either doctrine could have been applied, and the question which was to be preferred did not rest on law. Again, there was an ancient rule that a husband could sue another for depriving him of his wife's consortium. In *Best v Samuel Fox & Co Ltd*[5] the House of Lords reluctantly refused to allow a wife a corresponding action in respect of the loss of her husband's consortium. It would seem that equality and justice demanded the same power of action for a wife as for a husband; but since the action was historically based on the idea of

1 The author has relied on his paper 'The Value of a Value-study of Law' (1965) 28 MLR 397, and is indebted to the Editor for permission to make use of it.
2 (1772) 20 State Tr 1. See also *Chamberline v Harvey* (1696) 5 Mod 186; *Forbes v Cochrane* (1824), 2 B & C 448. For a re-appraisal of *Sommersett's Case*, see Shyllon *Black Slaves in Britain*.
3 [1917] 1 KB 305.
4 [1964] Ch 413, [1963] 3 All ER 139.
5 [1952] AC 716, [1952] 2 All ER 394.

a husband owning his wife as a quasi-chattel, the court preferred to perpetuate a very minor inequality between spouses rather than extend so antiquated and repugnant a rule. As Lord Porter put it,

> 'a husband's right of action for loss of his wife's consortium is an anomaly and [I] see no good reason for extending it. If a change is to be made I should prefer to abolish the husband's right rather than to grant the like remedy to the wife'[6].

Not only are courts averse to treating an individual as property, but they are also averse to allowing an individual's labour to be treated as property[7]. The superior weight attaching to personal safety rather than to sanctity of property induced the House of Lords in *British Railways Board v Herrington*[8] to get rid of a previous decision of its own disallowing trespassers to sue in negligence. Also, in judging the reasonableness of a decision taken in a dilemma the House of Lords held it to be reasonable to run the risk of damaging property rather than injuring people[9].

These examples reveal two things. In *Sommersett* there was no rule, in *Horwood* and *Eastham* the question was which of two competing doctrines should be invoked, in *Best* the question was whether an existing rule should be extended, and in *Herrington* the question was whether an existing rule should be abolished. None of these could have been decided simply by applying a rule; the decisions had to rest on value considerations. They also reveal that a basic liberty of the person ranks superior to property and contract.

Two different kinds of cases illustrate the sanctity of life generally. In *Re B (a minor) (wardship: medical treatment)*[10] the parents of a mongol child refused to give their consent to an operation, which might give it a probable lifespan of 20 to 30 years, on the ground that it was kinder to let the child die rather than live handicapped. The Court of Appeal ordered that the operation be performed. In *McKay v Essex Area Health Authority*[11] the Court of Appeal held that a child born deformed as a result of its mother having contracted rubella during pregnancy had no claim against a doctor for not having aborted it. To allow such an action would be contrary to public policy and a violation of the sanctity of life.

SANCTITY OF PROPERTY

This is important in itself. *Entick v Carrington*[12] emphasised that a general warrant is no justification for the seizure of private papers. Pratt CJ basing his view on the contemporary social contract theory said:

---

6 [1952] AC 716 at 728, [1952] 2 All ER 394 at 396. The rule was abolished by the Administration of Justice Act 1972, s 2(a).

7 *Nokes v Doncaster Amalgamated Collieries Ltd* [1940] AC 1014, [1940] 3 All ER 549.

8 [1972] AC 877, [1972] 1 All ER 749. The Court of Appeal, though bound by the earlier House of Lords decision, condemned it nevertheless, and Salmon LJ ascribed the rule of non-liability to trespassers to a time 'when rights of property, particularly in land, were regarded as perhaps more sacrosanct than any other human right': [1971] 2 QB 107 at 120, [1971] 1 All ER 897 at 901.

9 *Ketch Frances v Highland Loch* [1912] AC 312.

10 [1981] 1 WLR 1421, CA.

11 [1982] QB 1166, [1982] 2 All ER 771, CA.

12 (1765) 19 State Tr 1029. It is noteworthy that the trial was engineered so as to come before Pratt CJ, a liberal, rather than before Lord Mansfield, who was a supporter of the government.

'The great end for which men entered into society was to secure their property. That right is preserved sacred and incommunicable in all instances where it has not been abridged by some public law for the good of the whole'[13].

The plea of state necessity was brushed aside with the remark that 'the common law does not understand that kind of reasoning'. In the group of 'General Warrant' cases, to which this case belongs, sanctity of the person and sanctity of property went hand in hand and there was no question of priority. In *Ghani v Jones*[14] the court refused to allow the police to retain passports and letters when no one has been arrested or charged unless certain conditions were fulfilled.

Respect for property has given rise to the rule that there should be no deprivation without compensation. *Attorney General v De Keyser's Royal Hotel Ltd*[15] shows that a prerogative power in the Crown to expropriate private property without compensation has to give way to a statutory power of expropriation subject to compensation. The House of Lords could have decided either way, but they made their creative choice in pursuance of the ideal under consideration. *Burmah Oil Co (Burma Trading) Ltd v Lord Advocate*[16] concerned only the prerogative power to destroy property without compensation in time of war. By restricting it to a situation where hostilities are actually in progress, as distinct from their imminence, the House of Lords insisted on compensation being paid.

NATIONAL AND SOCIAL SAFETY

Both sanctity of the person and of property yield to the safety of the nation or society. Thus, in *Liversidge v Anderson*[17] the validity of the Home Secretary's order for Liversidge's incarceration was in question. The authority under which he acted, namely, the words of the regulation, 'if the Secretary of State has reasonable cause to believe' that a person's continued freedom was prejudicial to the safety of the realm, was ambiguous. It could, on the one hand, have been given the objective interpretation that 'reasonable cause' meant 'reasonable' in the opinion of the court, and, on the other, the subjective interpretation that as long as the Home Secretary was satisfied in his own mind no more was required. The majority of the House of Lords adopted the subjective interpretation[18]. The point is that the choice between

13 (1765) 19 State Tr 1029 at 1060.
14 [1970] 1 QB 693, [1969] 3 All ER 1700. Cf *Garfinkel v Metropolitan Police Comr* [1972] Crim LR 44, where the conditions were fulfilled. Contra, *MacFarlane v Sharp* [1972] NZLR 64: no seizure of documents without an arrest; and *Jeffrey v Black* [1978] QB 490, [1978] 1 All ER 555: no search of premises without a warrant for evidence unconnected with the offence for which a person has been lawfully arrested.
15 [1920] AC 508. See also *Re Petition of Right* [1915] 3 KB 649; *Universities of Oxford and Cambridge v Eyre & Spottiswood* [1964] Ch 736, [1963] 3 All ER 289; *Minister of Housing and Local Government v Hartnell* [1965] AC 1134, [1965] 1 All ER 490. In *IRC v Rossminster Ltd* [1980] AC 952, [1980] 1 All ER 80, the House of Lords allowed seizure according to the wording of a statute.
16 [1965] AC 75, [1964] 2 All ER 348 (the decision was nullified by the War Damage Act 1965).
17 [1942] AC 206, [1941] 3 All ER 338. See the parallel case of the First World War *R v Halliday*, [1917] AC 260.
18 It is interesting to contrast *Liversidge*'s case with *Roberts v Hopwood* [1925] AC 578, where also the ultimate question was whether a reasonable wage was to be determined objectively, ie what the court thought to be reasonable, or subjectively, ie what the local authority that fixed it thought to be reasonable. Here the court, for wholly different considerations, adopted

the two interpretations was not determined by logic or law. In his dissenting speech Lord Atkin was concerned to uphold individual liberty and he was not prepared to allow the courts to surrender their supervisory power in this regard[19]. By contrast, the attitude of the majority is to be explained on the ground that at the time when the situation arose, a most critical phase of the 1939–45 war, the courts were not going to hamper the executive, and every consideration, including that of freedom from arbitrary arrest, was made to yield to the national interest[20].

Even in time of peace the sanctity of the individual may have to yield before national security. In *R v Secretary of State for the Home Department, ex p Hosenball*[1] the principles of natural justice were modified in the national interest and the Court of Appeal held that in the interests of security the Secretary of State did not have to disclose the source of highly confidential information on which he made a deportation order. In *Council of Civil Service Unions v Minister for the Civil Service*[2] the House of Lords held that courts will not inquire into the exercise of the prerogative if this was in the interest of national security. In *Francis v Chief of Police*[3] the Privy Council held that the use of a loudspeaker without obtaining police permission as required by a statute was illegal despite the Constitution, which guaranteed a fundamental freedom of communication. Public order required that the public should be protected from excessive noise and that the statute was not contrary to the Constitution, since everything depended on how the power to withhold permission was exercised. The European Court of Justice has ruled that restrictions on the freedom of movement of individuals within the European Economic Community, allowed by art 48(3) of the Treaty of Rome and Directive No 64/221, art 3, for reasons of public policy may be justified by a genuine and serious threat to a fundamental interest of the state[4].

When no such emergency prevails the courts will not relinquish so readily their power to review executive action, and may well be astute in interpreting regulations in such a way as to preserve at least some measure of control. So, the Judicial Committee of the Privy Council in *Ross-Clunis v Papadopoullos*[5] observed *obiter* that the form of words, 'the commissioner shall satisfy himself', which may well have been devised with the *Liversidge* ambiguity in mind, did not import a wholly subjective test and that a court could still inquire into whether there were any grounds at all on which a reasonable commissioner might have satisfied himself. In *A-G of St Christopher, Nevis and Anguilla v Reynolds*[6] the Emergency Powers Regulations 1967, reg 3(1), ran: 'If the Governor is satisfied that any person has recently been concerned in acts

---

the objective interpretation. A purely formal comparison of the two cases is pointless; they are intelligible only on the basis of value-judgments.

19 [1942] AC 206 at 244, [1941] 3 All ER 338 at 361. Cf the dissenting speech of Lord Shaw in *R v Halliday* [1917] AC 260.

20 A vivid American illustration in point is *Korematsu v US* 323 US 214 (1944) where the forcible removal of some 112,000 persons from their homes along the western seaboard merely because of Japanese ancestry was upheld. For criticism on Kelsenian grounds, see Paulson 'Material and Formal Authorisation in Kelsen's Pure Theory' (1980) 39 CLJ 172, 180 et seq.

1 [1977] 3 All ER 452, [1977] 1 WLR 766, CA.

2 [1984] 3 All ER 935, [1984] 3 WLR 1174, HL.

3 [1973] AC 761, [1973] 2 All ER 251, PC.

4 Case 30/77 *R v Bouchereau* [1978] QB 732, [1981] 2 All ER 924n.

5 [1958] 2 All ER 23, [1958] 1 WLR 546. See also *Reade v Smith* [1959] NZLR 996.

6 [1980] AC 637, [1979] 3 All ER 129, PC.

prejudicial to the public safety ...'. The Privy Council held that since the statement made to the plaintiff in the case gave no details of any reasonable grounds for his detention and since, on the facts, there was no other evidence of reasonable grounds, his detention was invalid.

Likewise with regard to the seizure of property, the national interest in times of peril might be held to justify it[7]. An interesting contrast is to be found between *Entick v Carrington* (1765)[8] and *Elias v Pasmore* (1934)[9]. The former decided that the seizure of private papers, not specified in a warrant, was illegal and the argument of state necessity was rejected. This case was decided at a time when the courts were anxious to protect the individual against arbitrary action by the executive. In the other case the seizure by the police of documents, not specified in a warrant and which they retained for the purpose of a prosecution, was held to be justified on grounds of state necessity[10]. *Entick's* case, though cited, appears to have been ignored. This case, too, should be interpreted in the light of the times. In 1934 the country was confronting a social danger in the form of subversive political organisa- tions of a quasi-military character. A deeper question than that of protecting the individual against executive action was involved, namely, that of pro- tecting society against a formidable peril. Little wonder that the common law was by then ready to admit a plea of state necessity. It is also of interest to note that in 1936 Parliament enacted the Public Order Act, one of the most drastic enactments in force, conferring extensive powers to deal with quasi-military organisations and their property. What happened in 1934 was that the judiciary reacted ahead of the legislature to the needs of society. Reminiscent of the wording of the regulation in *Liversidge's* case is a statutory provision, which reads 'If the appropriate judicial authority is satisfied on oath given by an officer of the board that—(a) there is reasonable ground for suspecting that an offence ... has been committed'. In *IRC v Rossminster Ltd*[11] The House of Lords held that these words justified entry and search of premises and seizure of documents. In *Southwark London Borough Council v Williams*[12] the need to circumscribe the defence of necessity in the interests of law and order was explained in these words by Lord Denning MR:

> 'Necessity would open a door which no man could shut ... So the Courts must, for the sake of law and order, take a firm stand. They must refuse to admit the plea of necessity to the hungry and the homeless; and trust that their distress will be relieved by the charitable and the good'.

The growing crime rate is another factor which induces the courts to countenance interference with property more than they used to. In *Chic Fashions (West Wales) Ltd v Jones*[13], Lord Denning MR said:

---

7 *King's Prerogative in Saltpetre* (1606) 12 Co Rep 12; *R v Hampden, Ship Money Case* (1637) 3 State Tr 826. See also Dyer 36b. If it is possible to accommodate both the national and individual interests, the courts will adopt that course, eg *A-G v De Keyser's Royal Hotel Ltd* [1920] AC 508.

8 (1765) 19 State Tr 1029.

9 [1934] 2 KB 164; but see *Reynolds v Metropolitan Police Comr* [1984] 3 All ER 649, [1985] 2 WLR 93, CA.

10 So, too, in *McPherson v HM Advocate* 1972 SLT (Notes) 71. Cf *Ghani v Jones* [1970] 1 QB 693, [1969] 3 All ER 1700; *Garfinkel v Metropolitan Police Comr* [1972] Crim LR 44; contra, *McFarlane v Sharp* [1972] NZLR 64. Seizure under a search warrant of a forged power of attorney in the hands of a solicitor: *R v Peterborough Justices, ex p Hicks* [1978] 1 All ER 225, [1977] 1 WLR 1371.

11 [1980] AC 952, [1980] 1 All ER 80, HL.

12 [1971] Ch 734 at 744, [1971] 2 All ER 175 at 179.

13 [1968] 2 QB 299, [1968] 1 All ER 229.

'The society in which we live is not static, nor is the common law, since it comprises those rules which govern men's conduct in contemporary society on matters not expressly regulated by legislation ... The balance between the inviolability of personal liberty and the pursuit of public weal in this case [felony] came down upon the side of him who acted reasonably in intended performance of what right-minded men would deem a duty to their fellow men; the prevention and detection of crime'[14].

Public safety influences the law in many other ways. Thus, if a mental defective is harmless the courts are vigilant to see that the conditions, which have to be complied with before he or she can be restrained, are fulfilled to the letter, but where a person is dangerous they will not allow technicalities to stand in the way of protecting the public[15]. Again, in shaping the defence of automatism considerations of public safety have played a big part. At first the traditional line was adopted that if there was no conscious action on the part of the accused he was not guilty, since one of the ingredients of criminal responsibility was lacking[16]. It then came to be appreciated that if the absence of mental control was due to causes likely to recur, eg brain tumours, it is incumbent on the courts to ensure the safety of others from future attack. This consideration led, on the one hand, to the development in criminal law that all such cases should be regarded as cases of insanity so that sufferers can be isolated for appropriate treatment; and, on the other, to the emphasis laid in civil law on the need for such persons, if they know of their disabilities, to take due precautions in advance[17]. In these ways value-considerations are constantly giving the law new dimensions, as the defence of insanity bears witness. Lord Denning went so far as to say: 'The old notion that only the defence can raise a defence of insanity is now gone. The prosecution are entitled to raise it and it is their duty to do so rather than allow a dangerous person to be at large'[18]. The state of the law did not warrant so sweeping a proposition as this, but statute has since taken a step in this very direction[19], which means that the courts should be given credit once more for having reacted ahead of Parliament to a social need.

Where public interest other than safety, eg the health of the race, is in

---

14 [1968] 2 QB 299 at 315-316, [1968] 1 All ER 229 at 237-238. See also Salmon LJ at 319, and at 240. See also *Butler v Board of Trade* [1971] Ch 680, [1970] 3 All ER 593; *P S Jennings v W P Quinn & F Dooris* [1968] IR 305; *R v Lewes Justices, ex p Home Secretary* [1972] 1 QB 232, [1971] 2 All ER 1126; *McPherson v HM Advocate* 1972 SLT (Notes) 71. For the need for reasonable grounds of suspicion and for not detaining property longer than is necessary, see *Ghani v Jones* [1970] 1 QB 693, [1969] 3 All ER 1700; *Garfinkel v Metropolitan Police Comr* [1972] Crim LR 44; *Jeffrey v Black* [1978] QB 490, [1978] 1 All ER 555. *Ghani* was not followed in *McFarlane v Sharp* [1972] NZLR 64; nor does it apply where it would hamper the administration of justice: *Malone v Metropolitan Police Comr* [1980] QB 49, [1979] 1 All ER 256. See also *Frank Truman Export Ltd v Metropolitan Police Comr* [1977] QB 952, [1977] 3 All ER 431.

15 Cf *R v Board of Control, ex p Rutty* [1956] 2 QB 109, [1956] 1 All ER 769, and *R v Board of Control, ex p Winterflood* [1938] 2 KB 366, [1938] 2 All ER 463, CA, with *Richardson v London County Council* [1957] 2 All ER 330, [1957] 1 WLR 751, CA, and *Re Shuter (No 2)* [1960] 1 QB 142, [1959] 3 All ER 481.

16 *R v Harrison-Owen* [1951] 2 All ER 726; *R v Charlson* [1955] 1 All ER 859; *Hill v Baxter* [1958] 1 QB 277, [1958] 1 All ER 193; and see pp 310-312 post.

17 *Green v Hills* (1969) 113 Sol Jo 385; *Boomer v Penn* (1965) 52 DLR (2d) 673.

18 *Bratty v A-G for Northern Ireland* [1963] AC 386 at 411, [1961] 3 All ER 523 at 534. See also *R v Kemp* [1957] 1 QB 399, [1956] 3 All ER 249; *R v Russell* [1964] 2 QB 596, [1963] 3 All ER 603.

19 Criminal Procedure (Insanity) Act 1964, s 6; Criminal Justice (Northern Ireland) Act 1966, s 2.

opposition to the interests of the individual, the balance comes down on the side of the latter. Such an issue arose in *Re D (a minor)*[20], where an application was made to court to sterilise a mentally retarded girl, aged eleven, who was a ward of court. Heilbron J refused it on the ground that to do so would deprive her of a basic human right. Similarly the courts have to balance opposing considerations when deciding whether documents are privileged against discovery. Such protection is given to government departments, statutory bodies and even other independent bodies whenever public interest is involved[1].

The law of torts furnishes many illustrations of the influence of social and individual values. In the earliest times the principle was one of strict responsibility, that is, a *prima facie* case did not require actual proof of fault. This arose out of the need to suppress private vengeance and self-help, which were incompatible with any kind of social order. The nascent authority was not strong enough to stamp them out and the most it could do was to regulate their exercise. In this way state-regulation of self-help came to be the beginning of litigation. Vengeance was regulated in due proportion to the injury: an eye for an eye (only one eye, not two)[2]. In order to appease victims of wrongdoing and to encourage them not to resort to blood-feuds and the like, early law adopted their point of view. The emphasis was on the *deed*, not the character of the *doing*: if the defendant was shown to have caused the harm, fault was presumed and rebutting defences were allowed only sparingly. It is therefore arguable that this strict principle in favour of plaintiffs was the product of the need to preserve social stability. In the course of time state power became established, and changing ideas insisted more on moral fault as the basis of responsibility. The emphasis then shifted away from the plaintiff's to the defendant's point of view, from presumption of fault to actual proof of fault, and the principle took root that there was not to be even a *prima facie* case without this. In more recent times, however, the pendulum has swung back towards the re-introduction of the strict principle in the social interest[3]. The need today is to accommodate both the plaintiff's and the defendant's points of view, which is leading towards automatic insurance[4].

As the law stands, the existence of a duty-situation, whether of fault or strict responsibility, is determined by the balance between the many complex and conflicting interests that make up modern society. Until the 1970s the question whether the law, on grounds of policy, saw fit to give a remedy depended on the kind of harm complained of, the manner of its infliction and with reference to the categories of person to which the plaintiff and defendant respectively belonged[5]. Thus, any decision to extend or not to extend

20 [1976] Fam 185, [1976] 1 All ER 326.
1 *Duncan v Cammell Laird & Co Ltd* [1942] AC 624, [1942] 1 All ER 587, HL, not followed in *Conway v Rimmer* [1968] AC 910, [1968] 1 All ER 874, HL; independent body: *D v NSPCC* [1978] AC 171, [1977] 1 All ER 589, HL.
2 For general examples, see XII Tables, 8.2, 8.3, 8.4; *Exodus* 21.24–25; *Leviticus* 24.20; *Deuteronomy* 19.21; *Leges Henrici Primi* 90.7 (on which see Holdsworth *History of English Law* ii, 47; contra, Pollock and Maitland *History of English Law* i, 46).
3 Eg *Rylands v Fletcher* (1868) LR 3 HL 330; and there has been an enormous increase in strict statutory duties.
4 See Accident Compensation Act 1972, and the Amendment (No 2) Act 1973 (NZ); Royal Commission *On Civil Liability and Compensation for Personal Injury* (Cmnd 7054-I).
5 See eg *Clerk & Lindsell on Torts* §§10–06 et seq.

the ambit of duty-situations was not based on law, but on a value-judgment[6]. The position now is that whenever harm is foreseeable to another, there will prima facie be liability unless policy considerations dictate otherwise[7].

The law of negligence, in particular, is a standing illustration of the fluctuating balance of value-considerations. Whether conduct is careless or not depends on the degree of likelihood that harm will occur, the cost and practicability of measures to avoid the risk, the gravity of the consequences, the importance and social utility of the end to be achieved and the demands of emergencies, dilemmas or sport[8]. Moreover, it is also in the social interest to prevent harm rather than to award damages thereafter, and with that in view the courts do try to improve the prevailing standards of careful behaviour by making the criteria of what constitutes negligence stricter[9].

On the other hand, factors other than those of safety may lead to a relaxation of the legal attitude. For instance, although the highest standards of care are to be expected of the medical profession, there are factors which make it undesirable for the courts to take too strict a view of negligence. For one thing, to do so may inhibit initiative, which would not enure to social advantage; and, for another, the profession itself is so vigilant in maintaining the highest standards that there is no danger of these being lowered.[10] Again, where personal danger was not involved, it was said of a local authority that its varied activities and limited financial resources should 'lead to the application of a somewhat less exacting standard than ordinarily prevails'[11].

SOCIAL WELFARE

There is a detectable priority at least as between national and social safety, sanctity of the person and property in that order. Beyond this no hierarchy is discernible. It is difficult, for instance, to foretell in any given case, whether property rights or social welfare will be preferred, and the most that can be said is that there has been increasing awareness of the interests of society, especially within the past fifty years. The words of Bean J indicate the present tendency:

6 See MacDonald J in *Nova Mink Ltd v Trans-Canada Airlines* [1951] 2 DLR 241 at 254; Lord Pearce in *Hedley Byrne & Co Ltd v Heller & Partners Ltd* [1964] AC 465 at 536, [1963] 2 All ER 575 at 615. A classic instance of the widening of a manufacturer's responsibility, in the social interest, towards the ultimate consumer is *Donoghue v Stevenson* [1932] AC 562. See also *Dorset Yacht Co Ltd v Home Office* [1969] 2 QB 412 at 426, [1969] 2 All ER 564 at 567, affd [1970] AC 1004, and see especially at 1034, 1059; [1970] 2 All ER 294 at 304, 324-325. See also *Dutton v Bognor Regis UDC* [1972] 1 QB 373 at 397-398, 400, 406-408, [1972] 1 All ER 462 at 475-476, 478, 482-485. Note also Lord Reid: 'Legal principles cannot solve the problem. How far occupiers are to be required by law to take steps to safeguard such children must be a matter of public policy': *British Railways Board v Herrington* [1972] AC 877 at 897, [1972] 1 All ER 749 at 756-757.
7 *Anns v Merton London Borough Council* [1978] AC 728, [1977] 2 All ER 492, HL; *Ross v Caunters* [1980] Ch 297, [1979] 3 All ER 480; *Junior Books Ltd v Veitchi Co Ltd* [1983] 1 AC 520, [1982] 3 All ER 201, HL; but see *Leigh and Sillivan Ltd v Aliakmon Shipping Co Ltd* [1985] 2 All ER 44, [1985] 2 WLR 289, CA.
8 *Clerk & Lindsell on Torts* §§10-32 et seq.
9 *Clerk & Lindsell on Torts*, §§10-41 et seq.
10 These opposing considerations may account for the contrast in spirit between *Cassidy v MOH*, [1951] 2 KB 343, [1951] 1 All ER 574, and *Roe v MOH*, [1954] 2 QB 66, [1954] 2 All ER 131; on which see the comment of Denning LJ who was a judge in both cases, 'Law in a Developing Community' (1955) 33 Pub Ad, pp 1, 4-6.
11 Per Lord Thankerton in *East Suffolk Rivers Catchment Board v Kent* [1941] AC 74 at 95-96, [1940] 4 All ER 527 at 539.

'It is another example of the inroad often made into individual rights in the interests of the wider community. In a modern civilised society, there must always be a delicate balance between the right of the individual and the need of the community at large. Authorities who act on behalf of the community are often given powers which, so long as they exercise them reasonably, do entitle the authority to encroach, usually with compensation to be paid, on the rights of the individual'[12].

This vast field can only be touched on with the aid of a few random examples. Thus, in deciding whether statutory authority to exercise a power justifies interference with private rights the old criterion was whether interference was the inevitable consequence of the act which Parliament had authorised. If so, no action lay. Where power had been given to run a railway, it was held that this inevitably implied some interference with the comfort of individuals by way of noise, vibration and smoke[13]; but the power to erect a smallpox hospital was held not to imply authority to erect it in such a place as to interfere with the amenities of individuals[14]. In more recent years there has been a tendency to take account of the social utility of an operation. For instance, it has been held that the utility of a public shelter outweighed the degree of interference with private rights that it caused[15], and the Judicial Committee of the Privy Council has held that a statute, which empowered a local authority to supply 'pure water', should be given a liberal construction so that the addition of fluoride was permissible as this was conducive to improved dental health[16]. Again, efficient farming is now a matter of public importance and since a farmer cannot farm efficiently without a telephone on the premises, a landowner, who refused to consent to the installation of a telephone over and across her land, was held to have acted contrary to the public interest[17]. On the other hand, even the social utility of an authorised activity will not justify causing widespread inconvenience[18].

In connection with the exercise of planning powers, the considerations involved were described by Holmes J as follows:

'The general rule at least is, that while property may be regulated to a certain extent, if regulation goes too far it will be recognised as a taking'[19].

Particular interest has attached to the relaxation of judicial control over executive action in this matter by a narrowing of the concept of

12 *Pattinson v Finningley Internal Drainage Board* [1970] 2 QB 33 at 39-40, [1970] 1 All ER 790 at 793-794.
13 *Vaughan v Taff Vale Rly Co* (1860) 5 H & N 679.
14 *Metropolitan Asylum District Managers v Hill* (1881) 6 App Cas 193; *BC Pea Growers v City of Portage La Prairie* (1965) 49 DLR (2d) 91.
15 *Edgington, Bishop and Withy v Swindon Borough Council* [1939] 1 KB 86, [1938] 4 All ER 57. See also *Oakes v Minister of War Transport* (1944), 60 TLR 319; *Ching Garage Ltd v Chingford Corpn* [1961] 1 All ER 671, [1961] 1 WLR 470.
16 *A-G of New Zealand v Lower Hutt Corpn* [1964] AC 1469, [1964] 3 All ER 179.
17 *Cartwright v PO*, [1969] 2 QB 62, [1969] 1 All ER 421.
18 *Birmingham and Midland Motor Omnibus Co Ltd v Worcestershire County Council* [1967] 1 All ER 544, [1967] 1 WLR 409.
19 *Pennsylvania Coal Co v Mahon* 260 US 393 at 415 (1922), quoted by Viscount Simonds in *Belfast Corpn v OD Cars Ltd* [1960] AC 490 at 519, [1960] 1 All ER 65 at 70. See important dicta by Denning J in *Green & Sons v Minister of Health* [1948] 1 KB 34 at 38, [1947] 2 All ER 469 at 470-471; Lord Evershed MR in *A-G v Crayford UDC* [1962] Ch 575 at 589, [1962] 2 All ER 147 at 153. See also *Ransom ,and Luck v Surbiton Borough Council* [1949] Ch 180, [1949] 1 All ER 185; *Government of Malaysia v Selangor Pilot Association* [1977] AC 337, PC.

'quasi-judicial'[20]. With regard to taxation, too, it is interesting to contrast the old attitude that taxation is an interference with the wealth of individuals and that evasions should be benevolently regarded with the modern attitude that takes account of the social need for taxation. Viscount Sumner represented the old attitude when he said:

> 'It is trite law that His Majesty's subjects are free, if they can, to make their own arrangements, so that their cases may fall outside the scope of the taxing Acts. They incur no legal penalties and, strictly speaking, no moral censure if, having considered the lines drawn by the legislature for the imposition of taxes, they make it their business to walk outside them'[1].

With this should be contrasted the changed attitude expressed by Lord Greene:

> 'For years a battle of manoeuvre has been waged between the legislature and those who are minded to throw the burden of taxation off their own shoulders on to those of their fellow subjects. In that battle the legislature has often been worsted by the skill, determination and resourcefulness of its opponents of whom the present appellant has not been the least successful. It would not shock us in the least to find that the legislature has determined to put an end to the struggle by imposing the severest penalties. It scarcely lies in the mouth of the taxpayer who plays with fire to complain of burnt fingers'[2].

The above are instances of what might be described as forms of official action; but social considerations also come in when taking account of the interests of individuals. A case in which the court had to balance publicity and the freedom of the press against the interest of the individual was *Re X (a minor)*[3], where freedom to publish discreditable details about a deceased person was held to outweigh the possibility of harm to his child through the latter getting to know of them. On the other hand, *Medway v Doublelock Ltd*[4] was a case where two public interests came into conflict, namely, the disclosure of a person's means in a matrimonial suit, which being done under compulsion needed to be kept confidential, and the disclosure of the same information for the purpose of litigation in another suit. The court held that the purpose for which the information was required in the latter was giving security for costs and that this was of lesser importance than the former; so the confidentiality attaching to the former should also attach to the latter. In *Waugh v British Railways Board*[5] there was conflict between the principle that all relevant evidence should be placed before a court and the principle that communications between lawyer and client should be confidential. This was resolved by appeal to public interest, which was best served by confining the professional privilege within narrow limits. In *Trapp v Mackie*[6] Lord

---

20 *R v Electricity Comrs.* [1924] 1 KB 171. Cf *Franklin v Minister of Town and Country Planning* [1948] AC 87, [1947] 2 All ER 289.
1 *Levene v IRC* [1928] AC 217 at 227. See also *Partington v A-G* (1869) LR 4 HL 100 at 122.
2 *Howard de Walden v IRC* [1942] 1 KB 389 at 397, [1942] 1 All ER 287 at 289. Cf Lord Denning MR in *Ionian Bank Ltd v Couvreur* [1969] 2 All ER 651 at 655-656, [1969] 1 WLR 781 at 787.
3 [1975] Fam 47, [1975] 1 All ER 697. See also *Re R (MJ) (an infant) (proceedings transcripts: publication)* [1975] Fam 89, [1975] 2 All ER 749, where public interest in the administration of justice was held to outweigh the interest of the infant.
4 [1978] 1 All ER 1261, [1978] 1 WLR 710.
5 [1980] AC 521, [1979] 2 All ER 1169, HL. Public interest also prevailed in *London and County Securities Ltd v Nicholson* [1980] 3 All ER 861, [1980] 1 WLR 948. See also *Williams v Home Office* [1981] 1 All ER 1151.
6 [1979] 1 All ER 489 at 494-495, [1979] 1 WLR 377 at 383, HL.

Diplock pointed out that the privilege of a witness with regard to evidence given before a court or tribunal rests on a balance between the interest of the individual, whose good name has been traduced, and the interest in ensuring that witnesses should feel free to give evidence without fear of legal proceedings.

The law of nuisance is governed by the consideration that there has to be a measure of give and take between persons. As long as interference is reasonable it is protected, but when it becomes unreasonable the protection is withdrawn. The concept of 'reasonableness' depends on value-judgments. Thus, in *Lyons Son & Co v Gulliver*[7] it was held that theatre queues, which hampered access to and from the plaintiff's premises, constituted a nuisance; but in *Dwyer v Mansfield*[8] it was held not to be a nuisance to allow queues to obstruct access to the plaintiff's shop. The defendant in this case was a greengrocer dealing in commodities that were in short supply during the 1939–45 war. His activity was vital to the community. In *Miller v Jackson*[9] a cricket club had played on their cricket field for over 70 years and when some private houses were recently built adjoining it, householders were disturbed by cricket balls being hit occasionally into their premises. The public interest in having a sporting facility had to yield to the individual interest in non-interference and the disturbance was held to be a nuisance. Much might also be said of the part played by the concept of 'public policy' in the law of contract into which it is not possible to enter. As is well known, the courts may interfere with contracts on this ground[10].

Social considerations have also influenced the interpretation of statutory obligations attaching to contracts. Thus, of a landlord's duty to keep his house 'in all respects reasonably fit for human habitation' Lord Wright said:

> 'The sub-section must, I think, be construed with due regard to its apparent object and to the character of the legislation to which it belongs. The provision was to reduce the evils of bad housing accommodation and to protect working people by a compulsory provision out of which they cannot contract against accepting improper conditions. Its scheme is analogous to that of the Factory Acts. It is a measure aimed at social amelioration, no doubt in a small and limited way. It must be construed so as to give proper effect to that object'[11].

Appeal to the social interest might also have been used by the courts in restraining anti-social monopolies[12], but unfortunately in the sphere of trade

7 [1914] 1 Ch 631.
8 [1946] KB 437, [1946] 2 All ER 247.
9 [1977] QB 966, [1977] 3 All ER 338, CA. Two of the three judges refused to grant an injunction, but the third judge was prepared to grant one and suspend its operation for a year. In *Kennaway v Thompson* [1981] QB 88, [1980] 3 All ER 329, the public interest in a recreational activity did not override interference with private rights and here an injunction was granted.
10 Lord Truro in *Egerton v Earl Brownlow* (1853) 4 HL Cas 1 at 196; *Beresford v Royal Insurance Co Ltd* [1938] AC 586, [1938] 2 All ER 602; *Kores Manufacturing Co Ltd v Kolok Manufacturing Co Ltd* [1959] Ch 108, [1958] 2 All ER 65. For an extreme instance, see *Wyatt v Kreglinger and Fernau* [1933] 1 KB 793.
11 *Summers v Salford Corpn* [1943] AC 283 at 293, [1943] 1 All ER 68 at 72. Cf the earlier attitude: *Jones v Green* [1925] 1 KB 659 at 668, where Salter J said 'the standard of repair required by those Acts is naturally ... a humble standard'; and *Morgan v Liverpool Corpn* [1927] 2 KB 131.
12 Eg *R v Waddington* (1801) 1 East 143 at 155, where cornering a market was described as 'a most heinous offence'. See also *J H Pigott & Son v Docks and Inland Waterways Executive* [1953] 1 QB 338, [1953] 1 All ER 22.

and industry they proceeded instead on the narrower criteria of conspiracy and blackmail[13]. In the result, Parliament had to step in[14]. However, they have not shown themselves to be altogether impotent, for the Court of Appeal has declared that the refusal by the Jockey Club to grant a trainer's licence to a woman was an unreasonable exercise of discretion by a monopolistic concern[15].

EQUALITY

The popular notion of 'justice' is based, however vaguely, on a sense of equality, either distributive or corrective[16]. Of more specific manifestations of justice in the sense of distributive and corrective equality the following may be mentioned.

1. Redress for wrongdoing, whether in the form of punishment or payment of compensation, has to be proportionate to the injury. This has been the concern of law from primitive regulation of self-help[17] down to contemporary versions of making the punishment fit the crime.

2. In the exercise of judicial or quasi-judicial powers the rules of natural justice should be observed. 'Justice' said Lord Hewart CJ 'should not only be done, but should manifestly and undoubtedly be seen to be done'[18]; and speaking of natural justice in rather wide terms, the Judicial Committee of the Privy Council spoke of this as incorporated into the common law.[19] In a narrower sense, the first rule of 'natural justice' is that no one shall be judge in his own cause[20]. Secondly, no one may be condemned unheard, the corollary of which is that he or she should be given reasonable notice of the nature of the case to be met[1]. The remaining rules are not directly concerned with the principle of equality, but may be mentioned all the same. The tribunal must act in good faith[2]. The Report of the Committee on Ministers' Powers added two more doubtful rules. One is that a party is entitled to know the reasons for a decision, but this is not necessarily accepted even in

---

13 Eg *Thorne v Motor Trade Association* [1937] AC 797, [1937] 3 All ER 157.

14 Restrictive Practices Act 1956.

15 *Nagle v Feilden* [1966] 2 QB 633, [1966] 1 All ER 689, especially Lord Denning MR at 644–645 and at 693; and Danckwerts LJ at 651 and at 697.

16 Aristotle *Nicomachean Ethics V*: see p 65 ante.

17 As to which, see p 203 ante.

18 *R v Sussex Justices, ex p McCarthy* [1924] 1 KB 256 at 259. The test is applied objectively: *Lake District Special Planning Board v Secretary of State for Environment* (1975) 119 Sol Jo 187.

19 *Ong Ah Chuan v Public Prosecutor* [1981] AC 648 at 670, [1980] 3 WLR 855 at 965, PC.

20 *Dimes v Grand Junction Canal (Proprietary)* (1852) 3 HL Cas 759; *R v Sussex Justices. ex p McCarthy cf1 supra; R v Hendon RDC, ex p Chorley* [1933] 2 KB 696.

1 *Errington v Minister of Health* [1935] 1 KB 249. For limits on its application, see *Local Government Board v Arlidge* [1915] AC 120; *Franklin v Minister of Town and Country Planning* [1948] AC 87, [1947] 2 All ER 289; *Pillai v City Council of Singapore* [1968] 1 WLR 1278; *John v Rees* [1970] Ch 345, [1969] 2 All ER 274; *R v Aston University Senate, ex p Roffey* [1969] 2 QB 538, [1969] 2 All ER 964. Not applicable to binding over: *R v Woking Justices, ex p Gossage* [1973] QB 448, [1973] 2 All ER 621; *R v North London Metropolitan Magistrate, ex p Haywood* [1973] 3 All ER 50, [1973] 1 WLR 965; *Herring v Templeman* [1973] 3 All ER 569. Prohibition of legal representation: *Enderby Town Football Club, Ltd v Football Association, Ltd* [1971] Ch 591, [1971] 1 All ER 215; *Fraser v Mudge* [1975] 3 All ER 78, [1975] 1 WLR 1132.

2 *Byrne v Kinematograph Renters Society Ltd* [1958] 2 All ER 579 at 599, [1958] 1 WLR 762 at 784.

judicial decisions[3]. The other is that in a public inquiry held by an inspector to guide a Minister in reaching a decision, the inspector's report should be available to the parties, but this is not accepted either[4]. The House of Lords has stated that the rules of natural justice apply equally to final and preliminary hearings[5].

3. Distributive justice requires equal distribution of benefits among equals[6], and it was in accordance with this principle that the Court of Appeal insisted in *Nagle v Feilden*[7] that the refusal by the Jockey Club to grant a trainer's licence to a woman was contrary to public policy. On the other hand, a superior principle may prevail over that of equality, as in *Best v Fox*[8], where the House of Lords reluctantly decided to perpetuate an inequality between the sexes in the entitlement to sue for loss of consortium, because to have done otherwise would have extended an anachronism based on an ancient quasi-proprietary right of husbands over wives.

4. Distributive justice also requires equality of burdens as of benefits. Thus, in *Roberts v Hopwood*[9] the House of Lords invalidated a welfare scheme introduced by a local authority on the ground that expensive social experiments should not be introduced by local authorities at the expense of one section only of the local community without Parliamentary authority.

5. The need to ensure equality of treatment for all persons is a justification for the doctrine of precedent, though not necessarily of *stare decisis*. It is, incidentally, interesting to note that while justice in one sense demands certainty in the law through reliance on precedents[10], justice in another sense demands the rejection of erroneous or outdated precedents. 'Certainty in law must not become certainty of injustice', said Maitland[11]. The conflict here is between distributive equality of treatment and corrective equality requiring redress in the individual case. To meet this difficulty some limited departures from *stare decisis* have been evolved, principally the change in practice by the House of Lords that they will no longer be bound by their own decisions, as well as the established techniques of overruling, not following and distinguishing[12]. It is not easy to predict how a court is likely to resolve conflict on any given occasion.

6. The removal of special advantages and disadvantages of certain individuals and bodies is another example of the leaning towards distributive

---

3 *Giles v Walker* (1890) 24 QBD 656; *William Denby & Sons Ltd v Minister of Health* [1936] KB 337; *Automatic Wood Turning Co Ltd v Stringer* [1957] AC 544 at 550, [1957] 1 All ER 90 at 93; *R v Gaming Board of Great Britain, ex p Benaim and Khaida* [1970] 2 QB 417, [1970] 2 All ER 528. Giving clear reasons was, however, required in *French Kier Developments Ltd v Secretary of State for the Environment* [1977] 1 All ER 296.

4 *Local Government Board v Arlidge* [1915] AC 120.

5 *Wiseman v Borneman*[1971] AC 197, [1969] 3 All ER 275, disapproving *Parry-Jones v Law Society* [1968] Ch 1, [1968] 1 All ER 177.

6 See ch 4 ante.

7 [1966] 2 QB 633, [1966] 1 All ER 689. See the Sex Discrimination Act 1975, and the EEC Treaty, art 119.

8 [1952] AC 716, [1952] 2 All ER 394; doctrine now abolished by the Administration of Justice Act 1982, s 2(a).

9 [1925] AC 578. See also *Prescott v Birmingham Corpn* [1955] Ch 210, [1954] 3 All ER 698; *Taylor v Munrow* [1960] 1 All ER 455, [1960] 1 WLR 151. Cf *Re Walker's Decision* [1944] KB 644, [1944] 1 All ER 614.

10 *Mirehouse v Rennell* (1833) 1 Cl & Fin 527 at 546.

11 *Collected Papers* III, pp 486–487. See also Cardozo *The Nature of the Judicial Process* p 51.

12 See pp 127 et seq. ante. See also the unanimous utterances in the Supreme Court of Pakistan in *Jilani v Government of Punjab*, Pak. LD (1972) SC 139 at 168–169, 249, 259, 269.

equality, eg the Crown, husband and wife, certain religious and non-religious groups[13].

7.   In order to achieve as well as preserve equality the courts tend to lean on the side of the underdog, and it is their shifting attitude that makes it impossible to discern a hierarchy of values beyond the first three that were mentioned. For instance, as between government and the individual, there was a time when the monarch, by virtue of his prerogative, sought to oppress the subject, and the judiciary came to the latter's rescue. Today, after the evolution of representative government, there is no longer quite the same menace to the individual, though when occasion arises the courts will still intervene on his behalf[14]. The attitude has now changed to an appreciation of the fact that government is not out to oppress and has an enormously difficult task. The courts, therefore, no longer consider themselves the watchdogs on government, but are ready to assist. The more complex and diverse society becomes, the more its cohesion has to be considered, which means that courts are readier than before to apply 'social' yardsticks of evaluation in preference to 'individual' yardsticks. As Lord Parker CJ put it:

> 'The traditional function of the judiciary has always been to supervise and overlook duties exercised under the law by administrative tribunals and authorities. Accordingly, there is a natural tendency to identify judicial action with the control of abuses of governmental power, and to identify "government under law" with judicial intervention against executive action. But, to regard the sole concern of the courts in their supervisory capacity as the restraining of abuses is, I think, to misconceive their proper role. In addition to this negative task, there is a positive responsibility to be the handmaiden of administration rather than its governor. This positive task involves, first, the recognition that national policy requires a measure of administrative freedom; second, the affirmation by the courts of their responsibility in facilitating the objectives of administrative action as approved and authorised by Parliament; and third, the appreciation by the judiciary that the methods of judicial control and action are not always appropriate to the solution of disputes between the individual and the State'[15].

The law of contract, too, provides some interesting examples. The axiom upon which its rules traditionally developed is that there should be equality in the bargaining positions of the parties[16], and when that is lost the courts attempt to restore it. Thus, the public are at a disadvantage as against commercial concerns when contracts for services are in 'standard form'. There is no freedom to bargain; one has either to accept the terms set out or do without the service. Such a situation lends itself to abuse and, although the courts can do little once the customer has appended his signature to the document, they have striven to give such relief as they can[17].

13 Crown Proceedings Act 1947; Law Reform (Husband and Wife) Act 1962: *Bowman v Secular Society Ltd* [1917] AC 406; *Bourne v Keen* [1919] AC 815. In connection with public corporations, see *Tamlin v Hannaford* [1950] 1 KB 18, [1949] 2 All ER 327. What is contrary to this tendency is the increase in special immunities and liberties of trade unions, which were curtailed somewhat by the 1980's legislation.
14 *Congreve v Home Office* [1976] QB 629, [1976] 1 All ER 697.
15 Parker (1959) *Lionel Cohen Lectures* V, 25. For an example of judicial control of executive action, see *Bradbury v Enfield London Borough Council* [1967] 3 All ER 434, [1967] 1 WLR 1311.
16 *Printing and Numerical Registering Co v Sampson* (1875) LR 19 Eq 462 at 465.
17 By means of the doctrine of notice, reasonableness and the *contra proferentem* rule, though older in origin. On the use of the doctrine of fundamental term in this connection, see Lord Denning MR in *Levison v Patent Steam Carpet Cleaning Co Ltd* [1978] QB 69 at 80–81, [1977] 3 All ER 498 at 504, but the doctrine was rejected by the House of Lords in *Photo Production Ltd v Securicor Transport Ltd* [1980] AC 827, [1980] 1 All ER 556, HL.

The best examples are to be found in the sphere of employment. There used to be no equality in the bargaining position between employer and employee and accordingly the courts leaned on the side of the latter. Lord Denning MR has commented on inequality of bargaining power and has said that the strong should not be allowed to push the weak[18]. Thus , courts have always been less ready to countenance covenants in restraint of trade between employer and employee than between vendors and purchasers, who are on a more equal footing. As Scrutton LJ said:

> 'It is now well established that the Courts will view restraints of trade which are imposed between equal contracting parties for the purpose of avoiding undue competition and carrying on trade without excessive fluctuations and uncertainties with more favour than they will regard contracts between master and servant in unequal positions of bargaining'[19].

In the law of torts, the defence of consent was all but eliminated[20]; the unpopular defence of 'common employment' was whittled away to vanishing point before its abolition by statute[1]; conformity with standard practice in providing safety measures will not always absolve an employer from negligence[2]; and employers are required to take precautions suited to the known frailties of individual workmen[3]. Statutory provisions for safety are likewise construed strictly against employers. As Lord Wright said:

> 'It has been established by a series of decisions of this House that the employer's obligation to comply with statutory provisions for the safety of his employees is generally absolute ... If the duty is not fulfilled, the employer is liable for the consequences to his workmen, however blameless he may be, at least in the absence of some qualifying words in the Act or regulation. Even then the onus is on the employer to prove that he is entitled to rely on the qualification'[4].

The trade union movement developed to redress the unequal bargaining position between employer and employee, and the fact that a union is entitled to intervene on behalf of one of its members is recognised[5]. The result now of the established power of trade unions, coupled with the increase in statutory protection and welfare schemes for workmen, is that they are not as much in need of judicial protection as they used to be. On the contrary, it is employers who are at a disadvantage. Hence, since about 1950 the courts have leaned slightly in their favour. For instance, with regard to statutory and common law duties, Lord Tucker said:

18　*Clifford Davis Management Ltd v WEA Records Ltd* [1975] 1 All ER 237 at 240–241, [1975] 1 WLR 61 at 64–65.
19　*English Hop Growers Ltd v Dering* [1928] 2 KB 174 at 180; and see *Ronbar Enterprises Ltd v Green* [1954] 2 All ER 266 at 270. An important decision, where inequality was not involved and the employee's obligation to act fairly by his employer was taken into account, is *Hivac, Ltd v Park Royal Scientific Instruments Ltd* [1946] Ch 169, [1946] 1 All ER 350.
20　*Smith v Baker & Sons* [1891] AC 325; but see *ICI, Ltd v Shatwell* [1965] AC 656, [1964] 2 All ER 999.
1　*Priestley v Fowler* (1837) 3 M & W 1, abolished by the Law Reform (Personal Injuries) Act 1948, s 1 (1).
2　*Cavanagh v Ulster Weaving Co Ltd* [1960] AC 145, [1959] 2 All ER 745.
3　*Paris v Stepney Borough Council* [1951] AC 367, [1951] 1 All ER 42.
4　*Riddell v Reid* [1943] AC 1 at 24, [1942] 2 All ER 161 at 172.
5　*R v Industrial Disputes Tribunal, ex p Queen Mary's College, University of London* [1957] 2 QB 483, [1957] 2 All ER 776; *Beetham v Trinidad Cement Ltd* [1960] AC 132, [1960] 1 All ER 274. Where two unions are entitled to represent a workman, the employer may withdraw recognition from one: *Gallagher v Post Office* [1970] 3 All ER 712.

'It appears to me desirable in these days, when there are in existence so many statutes and statutory regulations imposing absolute obligations upon employers, that the courts should be vigilant to see that the common law duty owed by a master to his servants should not be gradually enlarged until it is barely distinguishable from his absolute statutory obligations'[6].

The modern law has gone so far in redressing the balance of power between master and servant that the mere relationship will not give rise to a presumption of undue influence[7]. Again, the courts have come to imply a term in contracts of service whereby the employee has to indemnify his employer if the latter is held vicariously answerable for his negligence[8], and they have also revived the defence of consent within limits[9]. Finally, there was also a tendency to call in question an employer's non-delegable duty to provide for the safety of his employees. The idea of non-delegable duty had been used as a means of restricting the defence of 'common employment'[10], but with the abolition of that defence there was an attempt to re-interpret the duty in a less extensive form, especially as the sociological reasons for pushing personal responsibility to its logical conclusion no longer obtain[11]. The non-delegable duty appears, however, to have been restored[12].

As has been mentioned, trade unions developed to protect workmen against employers, but the trade union movement has raised problems of its own. The idea that trade unions are there to protect workmen against over-mighty employers is fast becoming anachronistic at the present day, and the strike weapon is more and more damaging to the national economy. Some occasions when it has been resorted to, especially when used to interfere with an individual's liberty to work and also in inter-union disputes, show how anti-social and anti-individual it can be. Any legal restriction of the freedom to strike must come from legislation, but judicial interpretation of this will inevitably be governed by a value-sense[13]. Moreover, the individual workman is still not free to bargain as he likes, but is subordinated to the contract as negotiated between his union and the employer[14]. A more serious menace is that the union can deprive him of work by bringing pressure to bear on the employer not to employ him. The problem of the over-mighty unions has to be faced by government, but the courts in their limited way have striven on occasions to redress the inequality by giving the workman relief. An example is *Rookes v Barnard*[15] in which the plaintiff, the workman,

6 *Latimer v AEC Ltd* [1953] AC 643 at 658, [1953] 2 All ER 449 at 455.
7 *Matthew v Bobbins* (1980) 256 Estates Gazette 603.
8 *Lister v Romford Ice and Cold Storage Co Ltd* [1957] AC 555, [1957] 1 All ER 125. Under a 'gentlemen's agreement' employers will not now claim indemnities.
9 *ICI Ltd v Shatwell* [1965] AC 656, [1964] 2 All ER 999. The limitations are that the employer's answerability has to be purely vicarious, not personal, and it would not be contrary to public policy to allow the defence. See also *O'Reilly v National Rly and Tramway Appliances Ltd* [1966] 1 All ER 499 at 504.
10 *Wilsons & Clyde Coal Co Ltd v English* [1938] AC 57, [1937] 3 All ER 628.
11 Viscount Simonds and Lord Reid in *Davie v New Merton Board Mills Ltd* [1959] AC 604, [1959] 1 All ER 346. As to the effect on the *ratio* of *Wilsons case* (note 10 supra), see pp 137-138 ante. See also *Sullivan v Gallagher & Craig* 1960 SLT 70.
12 The Employer's Liability (Defective Equipment) Act 1969, has overruled *Davie's* case (note 11 supra) and has imposed a statutory non-delegable duty with regard to equipment.
13 In *Collymore v A-G of Trinidad and Tobago* [1970] AC 538, [1969] 2 All ER 1207, the Privy Council decided that freedom of association is not impaired by restricting the freedom to strike. In *Associated Newspapers Group v Flynn* (1970) 10 KIR 17, a token strike in protest against proposed legislation was held not to be a trade dispute.
14 *National Coal Board v Galley* [1958] 1 All ER 91, [1958] 1 WLR 16.
15 [1964] AC 1129, [1964] 1 All ER 367; overruled by the Trade Disputes Act 1965.

was lawfully dismissed by his employers, who succumbed to the threat of the union, to which the plaintiff belonged, that the union would induce their other workmen to strike in breach of their contracts with the employers and so cause them loss. The House of Lords decided in favour of the plaintiff. A reading of the speeches will reveal how their lordships found a loophole in the Trade Disputes Act 1906. It is also to be noted that the judges of the Court of Appeal and of the House of Lords came to opposite conclusions as a result of their respective interpretations of the law. It is difficult to assert with confidence that any particular value, or set of values, underlies such a decision as this where there is a difference of opinion among the judges and where, in any case, the values, whatever they may be, are not explicit. As against allegations of class-bias, anti-trade unionism and the like it is suggested that a sense of distributive equality is at least as likely an explanation. For this reason, if for no other, the decision deserved to be applauded.

CONSISTENCY AND FIDELITY TO RULES, PRINCIPLES, DOCTRINES AND TRADITION

Some believe that judicial reasoning proceeds exclusively by means of the case-by-case method and that the influence of values is infinitesimal, if not non-existent. They overlook two points. One is that the perception of similarities and dissimilarities, which is the essence of this mode of reasoning, is subjective[16]. The other is the need for consistency and what is here called fidelity to rules, principles, doctrines and tradition, which are important values in themselves.

'In legal matters, some degree of certainty is at least as valuable a part of justice as perfection', said Lord Hailsham[17]. It has many manifestations. An obvious one is the doctrine of precedent and *stare decisis*, which was carried to an extreme when both the House of Lords and the Court of Appeal declared themselves bound by their own decisions. The House, as has been mentioned, has now relaxed its practice as a concession to flexibility, but the need for certainty ensures that the power to depart from its prior decisions will only be exercised very sparingly[18]. The Court of Appeal, however, continues to be bound by its decisions, which means that 'flexibility has to this extent to be sacrificed to certainty'[19].

16 See pp 153, 156 ante.
17 *Cassell & Co Ltd v Broome* [1972] AC 1027 at 1054, [1972] 1 All ER 801 at 809. He repeated this in *R v Cunningham* [1982] AC 566 at 581, [1981] 2 All ER 863 at 870. See also Megaw LJ in *Ulster-Swift Ltd v Taunton Meat Haulage Ltd Fransen Transport NV (Third Party)* [1977] 3 All ER 641 at 646–647, [1977] 1 WLR 625 at 632.
18 *Note (Judicial Precedent,* [1966] 3 All ER 77, [1966] 1 WLR 1234. In *Conway v Rimmer* [1968] AC 910, [1968] 1 All ER 874 the House preferred to distinguish a previous decision rather than overrule it. So, too, the House stressed the importance of not weakening certainty when it declined, after careful consideration, to overrule a previous decision although the majority thought it to have been wrongly decided: *Jones v Secretary of State for Social Services* [1972] AC 944, [1972] 1 All ER 145; and the same consideration applied in *Knuller (Publishing, Printing and Promotions) Ltd v DPP* [1973] AC 435, [1972] 2 All ER 898. In the latter case it is particularly noteworthy that Lord Reid, who had dissented emphatically in the previous case, followed it nevertheless expressly on the ground of certainty. On the other hand, in *British Railways Board v Herrington* [1972] AC 877, [1972] 1 All ER 749, the House in effect overruled a previous decision. See also *The Johanna Oldendorff* [1974] AC 479, [1973] 3 All ER 148.
19 Per Geoffrey Lane LJ in *Miliangos v George Frank (Textiles) Ltd* [1975] QB 487 at 507, [1975] 1 All ER 1076 at 1088; so, too, Scarman LJ in *Farrell v Alexander* [1976] QB 345 at 371, [1976] 1 All ER 129 at 147, CA (revsd [1977] AC 59, [1976] 2 All ER 721, HL, but Scarman LJ's point was specifically approved: see at 92, and at 741–742).

Even within the framework of *stare decisis*, consistency works powerfully in inducing judges to prefer to play variations on fact-statements than on law-statements[20]. For instance, to take an extreme example, the situation where a dead snail is found in a bottle of ginger beer is different from that where a snail is found in a tin of fruit salad; but there is irresistible pressure not to stress such a difference. Similar pressure applies in varying degrees to less obvious situations. One reason lies in the inertia of human nature, which prefers guidance to the agony of decision. 'The instinct of inertia' said Lord Wright 'is as potent in judges as in other people'[1]. Another is that people often regulate their conduct with reference to existing rules, which makes it important for judges to abide by them. This is especially so in commercial dealings[2]. Innovations can be unsettling and lead to a loss of confidence[3]. The Privy Council expressed the policy aspect of this clearly:

> 'If the legal process is to retain the confidence of the nation, the extent to which the High Court exercises its undoubted power not to adhere to a previous decision of its own must be consonant with the consensus of opinion of the public, of the elected legislature and of the judiciary as to the proper balance between the respective roles of the legislature and of the judiciary as lawmakers ... Such consensus is influenced most of all by the underlying political philosophy of the particular nation as to the appropriate limits of the law making function of a non-elected judiciary'[4].

This need to abide by existing rules is all the stronger at a time when the judiciary happens to be under attack, or viewed with suspicion. A discretionary element is unavoidable in the judicial process, but it is important that this should be played down by conforming with rules as far as possible. In other words at such a time the value of consistency acquires very high priority, so much so that fidelity to rules may even override the sense of justice for the individual and public interest[5].

It follows that judicial discretion should only be exercised within limits, since otherwise confidence in the administration of the law would be shaken. The problem is to determine what those limits are. The point may be illustrated by taking liability for negligence in tort, the requirements of which are the existence of a duty of care owed to the plaintiff, a breach of that duty causing damage, which is not too remote. 'Duty', 'breach', 'causation' and 'remoteness' are terms with a variety of meanings, all of which are controlled by value considerations[6]. It was, therefore, no more than a candid avowal of the actual state of affairs when Lord Denning MR stated:

> 'The more I think about these cases, the more difficult I find it to put each into its proper pigeon-hole. Sometimes I say: "There was no duty". In others

---

20 Llewellyn *The Common Law Tradition, Deciding Appeals*, speaks of 'situation-sense': see especially pp 121 et seq. His fourteen 'steadying factors' in this connection are examples of the value of consistency. For the use of fiction in combining certainty with adaptability, see Maine *Ancient Law* ch 2; Fuller *Legal Fictions*; Stein and Shand *Legal Values in Western Society* pp 32-40.
1 Wright 'Precedents' (1943) 8 CLJ 144.
2 *A/s Awileo v Fulvia SpA di Navigazione, The Chikuma* [1981] 1 All ER 652 at 659, [1981] 1 WLR 314 at 322, HL, per Lord Bridge.
3 Cf *Llewellyn* p 3 et seq. He was concerned at the alleged loss of confidence in the Supreme Court.
4 *Geelong Harbor Trust Comrs v Gibbs Bright & Co* [1974] AC 810 at 820-821, [1974] 2 WLR 507 at 514, per Lord Diplock.
5 *Duport Steels Ltd v Sirs* [1980] 1 All ER 529, [1980] 1 WLR 142, HL.
6 *Clerk & Lindsell on Torts* pp 588-591.

I say: "The damage was too remote". So much so that I think the time has come to discard these tests which have proved so elusive. It seems to me better to consider the particular relationship in hand, and see whether or not, as a matter of policy, economic loss should be recoverable, or not'[7].

His Lordship is here drawing attention to the importance of values; he should not be misunderstood as advocating the abandonment of the rules concerning duty, breach etc. The important thing is to fit value-judgements into them. Policy paraded in its nakedness is more disturbing than when it is fitted into traditional garments. If the ambiguous requirements are to be removed, then negligence liability in its entirety should be abolished and replaced by a different scheme; but as long as such liability is retained, its rules must be seen to be applied. The task of the judge is not only to see that justice is done, but that it is seen to be done according to law.

Apart from rules, there are principles and doctrines, eg *mens rea*, fault, *ex turpi causa non oritur actio*, privity of contract, presumption of innocence etc. The part which these play has been explained in an earlier chapter[8]. Fidelity to them is no less important than fidelity to rules.

It is obvious that the balance between certainty and flexibility can never be fixed. Both can be combined in the case of concepts of indeterminate content, eg negligence, possession, since the rules, which embody them, can remain fixed and at the same time allow flexibility in their application. Also, perhaps with less frequency, new rules can be created within some established concept, principle or doctrine[9]. Greater restraint has to be observed in creating or overturning an established rule or doctrine.

A different kind of pressure is exercised by traditions as distinct from rules, principles and doctrines. Public confidence is also retained by adhering to tradition. One aspect of this derives from the pressure of office. It is commonplace that even the most radical innovators are tamed in the saddle of power. The traditions of the judicial office impose a sense of responsibility and conformity with its standards and values. Above all, there is an ingrained way of thinking, which is the product of training and the expertise of the craft. The lawyer's way of 'going about the job', as Llewellyn put it, inculcates an attitude of mind of keeping to what is known and this becomes standard practice[10].

MORALITY

There can be little doubt that moral considerations *do* influence rules of law, but this aspect has to be distinguished from the question how far laws *should* give effect to moral attitudes, which was discussed earlier[11].

Allen said that 'our judges have always kept their fingers delicately but

---

7 *Spartan Steel and Alloys Ltd v Martin & Co (Contractors) Ltd* [1973] QB 27 at 37, [1972] 3 All ER 557 at 562, CA.
8 See pp 45-46 ante.
9 Eg *Hedley Byrne & Co Ltd v Heller & Partners Ltd* [1964] AC 465, [1963] 2 All ER 575, HL.
10 *Llewellyn* pp 19 et seq. Simpson has argued that the 'common law' is not the sum-total of stated rules, but the acceptance as more or less correct by a specialist profession of formulations of a mass of ideas and practices, which are used in deciding disputes rationally. In this sense common law is the general custom of the realm; and this is also how professional ethics generates pressure to conform: 'The Common Law and Legal Theory' in *Oxford Essays in Jurisprudence* (2nd series, ed Simpson) ch 4. See also Weyrauch *The Personality of Lawyers*; Shklar *Legalism*.
11 See pp 111 et seq. ante.

firmly upon the pulse of the accepted morality of the day'[12]. How far in fact they do so it is not easy to say. Lord Mansfield went so far as to assert that 'the law of England prohibits everything which is *contra bonos mores*'[13]; but other judges have been more cautious[14]. Viscount Simonds, however, forcibly re-asserted the judicial task of preserving moral standards in words which have been quoted earlier[15].

So it is that the courts will contrive to suppress dishonesty. The purchase of honours has long been held illegal[16] and further instances of the manipulation of legal concepts to this end will be found in Chapters 12 and 13. The attitude towards sexual immorality has changed, generally speaking, from one of prohibition to a refusal to assist the parties in the enforcement of claims based on immorality. Adultery used to be an offence, but is not now; an immoral consideration still avoids a contract[17]. In *R v Prince*[18], it was a sense of the immorality of Prince's conduct in abducting a girl that influenced the court to reject his defence of a *bona fide* mistake that she was of statutory age; while in *R v Tolson*[19], Mrs Tolson intended to do nothing immoral by re-marrying when she reasonably believed that her first husband had died; so the court allowed her *bona fide* belief to be a defence. In *Parry v Parry and Adams and MacKay*[20], a co-respondent in a divorce case, who disputed having to pay costs to the husband on the ground that he did not know the wife was married, was nevertheless cast in costs since he should not have had intercourse with a woman other than his wife. So, too, 'unlawful sexual intercourse' in the Sexual Offences Act 1956, s 19 (1) has been held to mean 'illicit', ie outside marriage[1].

With regard to the marriage tie, the attitude towards it can become complicated by differing religious views. For instance, has a marriage been consummated if the parties use contraceptives? The House of Lords said, yes[2]. The sanctity of the marriage bond has produced the rule that there can be no conspiracy between spouses, nor publication of defamatory matter. Any condition attached to a bequest, which might encourage separation or strife, is void[3]; and so is a condition that a wife (as distinct from a widow) shall assume the testator's name and arms[4]. Under the old Rent Acts a tenant husband, who deserted his wife, was deemed to remain in possession of the premises so that the wife could be protected from eviction by the landlord[5]; but the same did not apply to a mistress[6]. In *R v Wheat; R v Stocks*[7], it was

12 Allen *Legal Duties* p 201.
13 *Jones v Randall* (1774) 1 Cowp 17 at 39; *R v Delaval* (1763) 3 Burr 1434 at 1438-1439.
14 Eg Scrutton LJ in *Re Wigzell, ex p Hart* [1921] 2 KB 835 at 859.
15 *Shaw v DPP* [1962] AC 220 at 268, [1961] 2 All ER 446 at 452-453, quoted at p 181 ante.
16 *Egerton v Brownlow* (1853) 4 HL Cas 1; *Parkinson v College of Ambulance Ltd and Harrison* [1925] 2 KB 1.
17 *Ayerst v Jenkins* (1873) LR 16 Eq 275; *Alexander v Rayson* [1936] 1 KB 169.
18 (1875) LR 2 CCR 154. Cf *R v Hibbert* (1869) LR 1 CCR 184.
19 (1889) 23 QBD 168.
20 (1962) 106 Sol Jo 288.
 1 *R v Chapman* [1959] 1 QB 100, [1958] 3 All ER 143.
 2 *Baxter v Baxter* [1948] AC 274, [1947] 2 All ER 886.
 3 *Re Johnson's Will Trusts* [1967] Ch 387, [1967] 1 All ER 553.
 4 *Re Howard's Will Trusts* [1961] Ch 507, [1961] 2 All ER 413.
 5 *Old Gate Estates Ltd v Alexander* [1950] 1 KB 311, [1949] 2 All ER 822.
 6 *Thompson v Ward* [1953] QB 153 [1953] 1 All ER 1169; *Colin Smith Music Ltd v Ridge* [1975] 1 All ER 290, [1975] 1 WLR 463. See also *Diwell v Farnes* [1959] 2 All ER 379, [1959] 1 WLR 624.
 7 [1921] KB 119; disapproved in *R v Gould* [1968] 2 QB 65, [1968] 1 All ER 849. See also *Wiggins v Wiggins and Ingram* [1958] 2 All ER 555, [1958] 1 WLR 1013.

held that after a decree nisi had been granted on a divorce petition, but before it had been made absolute, the marriage still existed technically so that a party committed bigamy by re-marrying within that time, notwithstanding an honest belief that a decree nisi meant that the marriage had ended. In *Fender v Mildmay*[8], on the other hand, a contract to marry another person before the decree nisi was made absolute was upheld by a majority of the House of Lords. Here the conflict of values was between the sanctity of contract and the mere outward shell of a marriage which had come to an end for all practical purposes.

ADMINISTRATIVE CONVENIENCE

No orders will be made unless their working can be effectively supervised[9]. In *Paton v British Pregnancy Advisory Service Trustees*[10] the point arose for the first time whether a husband was entitled to an injunction to stop his wife from having an abortion as allowed by the Abortion Act 1967, but against his wish. Sir George Baker P refused an injunction, saying, 'it would be quite impossible for the courts in any event to supervise the operation of the Abortion Act 1967. The great social responsibility is firmly placed by the law upon the shoulders of the medical profession'. Apart from this, convenience may determine the interpretation that is to be placed upon a rule[11], and in the absence of authority convenience may help to decide an issue[12].

INTERNATIONAL COMITY

The desire to conform to the practice of other nations and to maintain friendly relations with them has shaped a number of rules. In default of any statutory or common law rule, a court may adopt a rule of customary international law. There is a view put forward by international lawyers that international law 'is *per se* part of the law of the land'[13], which was originally based mainly on dicta in certain ancient cases the decisions in which, however, were based on statute. More recently the Court of Appeal accepted it in *Trendtex Trading Corpn Ltd v Central Bank of Nigeria*[14], and the rule that was adopted from international law has since been made statutory. It is not

8 [1938] AC 1, [1937] 3 All ER 402.
9 Eg *Chapman v Honig* [1963] 2 QB 502, [1963] 2 All ER 513.
10 [1979] QB 276 at 281, [1978] 2 All ER 987 at 991.
11 *Fry v IRC* [1959] Ch 86, [1958] 3 All ER 90; *Gatehouse v Vise (Inspector of Taxes)* [1956] 3 All ER 772 at 776-777 (affd [1957] Ch 367, [1957] 2 All ER 183).
12 *Adams v National Bank of Greece SA* [1961] AC 255 at 276, [1960] 2 All ER 421 at 426. Inconvenience: *Cattle v Stockton Waterworks Co* (1875) LR 10 QB 453 at 457. Where the inconvenience is not too great: *Rodriguez v Speyer Bros*, [1919] AC 59 at 132. It has been held to prevail over sanctity of contract: *Taunton-Collins v Cromie* [1964] 2 All ER 332 at 333, 334, [1964] 1 WLR 633 at 635, 637.
13 Lauterpacht (1939) 25 Grotius Society 51; *Private Law Sources and Analogies* 75n; *Oppenheim's International Law* (8th edn) pp 37-47; McNair (1945) 30 Grotius Society 11; Dickinson (1932) 26 American Journal of International Law 239; Scott (1907) 1 American Journal of International Law 831; Westlake (1906) 22 LQR 14 (reprinted in *Collected Papers* 498); Morgenstern (1950) 27 BYIL 42; Seidl-Hohenveldern (1963) 12 International and Comparative Law Quarterly 88.
14 [1977] QB 529, [1977] 1 All ER 881, CA. See also *The Playa Larga* [1983] 1 AC 244, [1981] 2 All ER 1064; and now the State Immunity Act 1978, s 3. *Trendtex* was not followed in *Uganda Co (Holdings) Ltd v Government of Uganda* [1979] 1 Lloyd's Rep 481, but this case has been disapproved.

possible to express an opinion on this view until the meaning of '*per se*' has been clarified. No one disputes that international treaty law does not become part of English law until the treaty provisions are incorporated in an Act of Parliament. With regard to customary international law, no one disputes that a rule of customary international law cannot go against statute or precedent and that, where these exist, British courts have a duty to follow their own binding authority. Nor, further, does any one dispute that, in the absence of statute or precedent, a court has the power to adopt a rule of international law. The nub of the matter is whether this power is coupled with a duty to adopt the international law rule, or only a liberty to do so. If it is a duty, then customary international law would have to be included in the criteria of validity in English law alongside statute, precedent, immemorial custom and EEC Directives, the consequence of which for constitutional and municipal lawyers would be profound. They have rejected such a doctrine[15]. The precise implication of '*per se* part of the law of the land' has never been faced, which makes even *Trendtex* inconclusive. Moreover, it has to be remembered that what judges say is not always indicative of what they do; and the position here seems similar to that with regard to immemorial custom where also judges say that they are bound by such customs though in fact they exercise discretion whether to adopt them or not[16]. There is the further difficulty of identifying rules of international law, especially customary rules, because the criteria of validity vary with different kinds of tribunals[17]. On the other hand, if '*per se* part of the law of the land' means only that courts have the power and liberty to adopt rules of customary international law without these having to be incorporated in Acts of Parliament, no one will disagree, though '*per se*' is tendentious and misleading. Such, it is submitted, is the position, which is why international law is here included among the persuasive factors that guide judicial discretion.

Further points are (a) Statutes will be construed so as to avoid conflict with international law[18]. (b) Acts giving offence to friendly powers will receive no assistance from the courts[19]. (c) The law of extradition shows an elaborate pattern of rules that are the outcome of accommodating the need

15 Jennings, *The Law and the Constitution* pp 173–176; Holdsworth *HEL* XIV (eds Goodhart and Hanbury) pp 23–74. See also the author's 'Mechanism of Definition as Applied to International Law' (1954) CLJ 226–231. Their view is supported by *Commercial and Estates Co of Egypt v Board of Trade* [1925] 1 KB 271 at 295; *Compania Naviera Vascongada v The Cristina* [1938] AC 485 at 497–498, 502, [1938] 1 All ER 719 at 725, 728; *Chung Chi Cheung v R* [1939] AC 160 at 167 168, [1938] 4 All ER 786 at 790; *The Tolten* [1946] P 135 at 142, [1946] 2 All ER 372 at 375; *R v Bottrill, ex p Kuechenmeister* [1947] KB 41 at 54, [1946] 2 All ER 434 at 436; *Riverstone Meat Co Pty Ltd v Lancashire Shipping Co Ltd* [1961] AC 807, [1961] 1 All ER 495; *R v Secretary of State for the Home Department, ex p Thakrar* [1974] QB 684, [1974] 2 All ER 261.
16 See pp 190–191 ante.
17 See p 496–497 post.
18 Lauterpacht (1939) 25 Grotius Society at 76; *Oppenheim* at p 41. The statement of Lord Mansfield in *Heathfield v Chilton* (1767) 4 Burr 2015 at 2016, is not viewed seriously even by supporters of the doctrine of incorporation. The correct view is to be found in *Mortensen v Peters* 1906 14 SLT 227; *Naim Molvan v A-G for Palestine* [1948] AC 351; *Theophile v SG* [1950] AC 186 at 195, [1950] 1 All ER 405 at 407–408; *IRC v Collco Dealings* [1959] 3 All ER 351 at 355 (affd [1962] AC 1, [1961] 1 All ER 762); *Salomon v Customs and Excise Comrs* [1967] 2 QB 116, [1966] 3 All ER 871; *Cheney v Conn* [1968] 1 All ER 779, [1968] 1 WLR 242; *Corocraft Ltd v Pan American Airways Inc* [1969] 1 QB 616, [1969] 1 All ER 82; *R v Secretary of State for Home Affairs, ex p Bhajan Singh* [1975] 2 All ER 1081 at 1083. With regard to the European Convention on Human Rights, later British statutes will be interpreted so as not to conflict with the Convention: *R v Deery* [1977] Crim LR 550.
19 *De Wutz v Hendricks* (1824) 2 Bing 314; *Foster v Driscoll* [1929] 1 KB 470.

to co-operate with other countries in suppressing crime and to uphold the liberty of the individual[20]. (d) Where courts have discretion, the manner of its exercise will be influenced by considerations of comity[1]. (e) Delicate considerations are also involved in defining the attitude of the courts to foreign confiscatory decrees. The validity of such decrees in the country in which they were passed will not be questioned by British courts, for indeed no point would be served by so doing[2]; but they will not be given effect in Great Britain[3]. (f) When a diplomat has committed a tort or breach of contract, international comity demands, on the one hand, that he be accorded immunity from suit, but corrective justice demands, on the other hand, that the victim be given a remedy. Use has accordingly been made of the 'sanctionless duty' idea, ie that the diplomat is under a duty to pay, but is immune from process. The significance of this is that third parties, such as insurers and sureties, can be held responsible while the diplomat himself goes free[4]. Conflicting considerations of this kind have shaped the concept of duty. (g) Since Britain's entry into the European Economic Community the Court of Appeal has held that courtesy towards other member states requires the revision of certain traditional rules[5].

CONCLUSIONS

In the first place, the part played by values shows the essential relation between law and its social setting in the widest sense. Just as one's knowledge of a fish, for example, is incomplete until one sees it living in its habitat, so, too, knowledge of laws is incomplete without seeing how they live and behave in their social habitat. Furthermore, inquiry into the formation of values can provide insights into the phenomenon of social control through power structures[6].

Secondly, values are the life-blood of the law, the motive-power of a machine which would otherwise be inert. As Holmes J put it:

'The very considerations which judges most rarely mention, and always with an apology, are the secret root from which the law draws all the juices of life.

---

20 Eg *Schtraks v Government of Israel* [1964] AC 556, [1962] 3 All ER 529; *R v Godfrey* [1923] 1 KB 24; *Factor v Laubenheimer and Haggard* 290 US 276 (1933); *US v Rauscher* 119 US 407 (1886); *R v Governor of Brixton Prison, ex p Kolczynski* [1955] 1 QB 540, [1955] 1 All ER 31; *Royal Government of Greece v Brixton Prison Governor* [1971] AC 251 [1969] 3 All ER 1337. See also the Fugitive Offenders Act 1967.

1 *Seyfang v GD Searle & Co* [1973] 1 QB 148, [1973] 1 All ER 290 (on appeal 117 Sol Jo 16); *Buttes Gas & Oil Co v Hammer (No 3)* [1982] AC 888, [1981] 3 All ER 616; *TimberLane Lumber Co v Bank of America* (1984) 66 ILR 270.

2 *Aksionairnoye Obschestvo A M Luther v James Sagor & Co* [1921] 3 KB 532; *Princess Olga Paley v Weisz* [1929] 1 KB 718.

3 *Banco de Vizcaya v Don Alfonso de Bourbon y Austria* [1935] 1 KB 140; *Oppenheimer v Cattermole*, [1975] 1 All ER 538. Cf *Lorentzen v Lydden & Co Ltd* [1942] 2 KB 202 (in time of emergency); *A-G of New Zealand v Ortiz* [1982] 3 All ER 432, [1982] 3 WLR 570 (on appeal [1984] AC 1, [1983] 2 All ER 93). Cf *The Rose Mary* [1953] 1 WLR 246.

4 *Dickinson v Del Solar* [1930] 1 KB 376 at 380; *Zoernsch v Waldock* [1964] 2 All ER 256 at 265–266, [1964] 1 WLR 675 at 691–692; *Magdalena Steam Navigation Co v Martin* (1859) 2 E & E 94 at 115. On the sanctionless duty idea, see pp 236 et seq. post.

5 Eg judgments need no longer be expressed in pounds sterling: *Schorsch Meier GmbH v Hennin* [1975] QB 416, [1975] 1 All ER 152; *Miliangos v George Frank (Textiles) Ltd* [1975] QB 487, [1975] 1 All ER 1076.

6 See chs 19 and 20 post.

I mean, of course, considerations of what is expedient for the community concerned. Every important principle which is developed by litigation is in fact and at bottom the result of more or less definitely understood views of public policy; most generally, to be sure, under our practice and traditions, the unconscious result of instinctive preferences and inarticulate convictions, but nonetheless traceable to views of public policy in the last analysis'[7].

Thirdly, nothing could be further from the truth than the belief that judges simply apply laws. The very nature of the process imports choice and discretion which are guided by values. The idea that judges represent the blindfold figure of justice, brooding over a machine, is an illusion that pleases, but the truth is that the machine can be made to work in different ways, and to do this in a socially acceptable manner they have to keep their eyes open and their fingers on every thread of the social pulse[8].

Fourthly, the judicial task is a highly responsible one since the leeways of discretion could be utilised in a socially cohesive or divisive way. Of the cult of doing justice lawyers have been hailed as the priests[9]; the quality of justice depends even more on the quality of the judges than on the quality of legislators.

Fifthly, a study of values also reveals a difference between what are loosely described as 'totalitarian' and 'free' societies. In the former the task of the judge is to reflect an official set of values. In the latter he has to consider these alongside others, which may be opposed to them—a more difficult task. Judicial independence therefore means independence in the choice of values, and it is in this way that the individual can be protected[10].

Finally, a study of values raises the question of judicial impersonality. In a large number of cases the personal element is minimal, but even here, as pointed out, some choice is inescapable. It becomes more pronounced when the question is one of evaluating interests and choosing appropriate standards of evaluation. It was Cardozo CJ who spoke of

> 'other forces, the likes and the dislikes, the predilections and the prejudices, the complex of instincts and emotions and habits and convictions, which make the man, whether he be litigant or judge'[11].

This raises a point of importance. As long as it is believed that judges are merely mechanical appliers of laws it is proper that they should be immune from criticism. Indeed, one reason why the judiciary has been able to preserve its aloofness for so long is this belief. Another reason has been the judges' refusal to enter into areas which clearly and obviously involve policy considerations. They are being forced to do so increasingly in modern conditions, and when, in addition to that, it is realised that policy and discretion, in whatever degree, are inseparable from the judicial process, then their conduct is at once open to comment and criticism[12]. Are judges socially and

---

7   Holmes *The Common Law* p 35; Lord Wright: 'In one sense every rule of law, either common law or equity, which has been laid down by the Courts, in that course of judicial legislation which has evolved the law of this country, has been based on considerations of public interest or policy' (*Fender v St John-Mildmay* [1938] AC 1 at 38, [1937] 3 All ER 402 at 424).
8   Cf Robson *Justice and Administrative Law* ch 5.
9   Cf Ulpian *Digest* 1.1.1. *pr-1*.
10   See pp 99–101 ante.
11   Cardozo *The Nature of the Judicial Process* p 167.
12   Stevens 'Justiciability: The Restrictive Practices Court Re-examined' [1964] PL 221, considered the wisdom of Parliament in entrusting the Restrictive Practices Court, which is there to make policy decisions, to the judiciary, thereby laying it open to criticism.

politically prejudiced? This accusation is being levelled increasingly at the judiciary and merits close attention. The whole question illustrates better than any other the point made at the start of this book that jurisprudential study has to include, *inter alia*, the politics of the law[13].

JUDICIAL IMPERSONALITY

Some exercise of discretion, be it large or small, is unavoidable in the very nature of the judicial process. The point that needs to be stressed now is that there is a difference between allowing this discretion to be guided by one's personal likes and dislikes and by one's sense of current values assessed as objectively as possible. Mr Justice Frankfurter said:

> 'It is not the duty of judges to express their personal attitudes on such issues, deep as their individual convictions may be. The opposite is the truth: it is their duty not to act on merely personal views'[14].

Subjectivity, however, cannot be excluded altogether, since the pattern of values is what the individual thinks it is. Hence the need to stress 'as objectively as possible'. Both these points were appreciated by Slesser LJ:

> 'Yet, even here, it is suggested, the Judge should apply, not his own private opinions, but an objective test. The customary prevailing moral habits and assumptions of the good citizen should be his criterion, not his own personal preference, to quote Dr Wurzel of Vienna in his famous *Judicial Thinking*. If all interpretation were nothing but a sort of artistic function, then nobody could ever foresee how any law would be understood or what effect it would have. Nevertheless, in matters such, for example, as protection of liberty, the views of the Judge on the respective rights of the citizen and state can hardly be excluded, more particularly where society, as a whole, entertains divided opinions. In this case, where the Judge cannot obtain a consensus, what standard has he except his own opinion?'[15].

The thrust of the attack on judicial values is not so much that judges are consciously prejudiced, but that they are subconsciously influenced by the fact that they come from a narrow social stratum and reflect the values of a minority class[16]. There can be no question but that subconscious influences of this kind do exist, but the submission made here is that the charge is prone to exaggeration[17].

In the first place, if subconscious influences are taken into account, as indeed they should be, then account should be taken of all such influences, including those that tend to counteract and minimise prejudice. One of these is fidelity to rules, principles and doctrines. Even if a judge were to have some prejudice and wants to give effect to it, he has to do so as plausibly as possible within the framework of rules; the leeways of doing so are not unlimited and this does operate as a brake on personal prejudice[18]. It has to

---

13 See p 15 ante.
14 Frankfurter 'Marshall and the Judicial Decision' (1955) 69 Harv LR 228.
15 Slesser *The Art of Judgment* pp 32–33.
16 Eg Griffith *The Politics of the Judiciary*, and *Administrative Law and the Judiciary* (Pritt Memorial Lecture 1978).
17 For further analysis, see the author's '*Götterdämmerung*: Gods of the Law in Decline' (1981) 1 Legal Studies pp 14–20; and see Lord Wilberforce 'Educating the Judges' (1969) 10 JSPTL (NS) 254, 258.
18 See p 213–215 ante, and the remark of Lord Diplock in *Duport Steels Ltd v Sirs* [1980] 1 All ER 529 at 542, [1980] 1 WLR 142 at 157.

be remembered that cases are argued, often with great ingenuity, by counsel, and if one side puts forward an interpretation of a statutory provision or a precedent, which cannot be countered plausibly, the judge has to decide accordingly, however much his own wishes are to the contrary. Then there is 'role pressure', ie the pressure exerted by the judicial office with its tradition of impartiality. The conditioning influence of roles has been examined by sociologists and will be discussed later[19]. The more ancient the office and its traditions, the stronger the pressure. Most important of all, perhaps, is the training at the Bar, which is unique in de-personalised thinking. Judges are recruited from the leaders of the profession, and these are people who have learned over many years how to throw the whole of their expertise, intelligence and personalities into the causes of their clients, regardless of their own sympathies and preferences, arguing with equal force whether they sympathise with their clients or not. The effect of such a training over the greater part of a working life is indelible. It is because of such factors as these that inquiries into the psychology, upbringing, health, wealth etc of individual judges are unlikely to be helpful. The movement known as American Realism was originally keen to emphasise the significance of the personal element, but this aspect of the movement has virtually disappeared with the appreciation of other factors that neutralise or minimise it[20].

Subconscious influences are also countered by conscious appreciation of the danger of such influences, and such appreciation lies at the root of responsible action in general. British judges have long been aware of the possible influences of class and background, so the following remark of Scrutton LJ is less weighty in favour of critics of the judiciary than they suppose, for it could cut both ways:

> 'Labour says: "Where are your impartial Judges? They all move in the same circle as the employers, and they are all educated and nursed in the same ideas as the employers. How can a labour man or a trade union get impartial justice?" It is very difficult sometimes to be sure that you have put yourself into a thoroughly impartial position between two disputants, one of your own class and one not of your class.'[1].

The learned Lord Justice is here saying that the task is difficult, not that it is impossible; and consciousness of the danger is itself a safeguard. Judges sometimes bend over backwards to avoid it. Thus, in *Ex p Church of Scientology*[2] the Church succeeded in getting their appeal heard by a panel of the Court of Appeal not presided over by Lord Denning MR, who had heard eight cases concerning the Church in the previous ten years and who, it was alleged, had 'an unconscious adverse influence'. Shaw LJ said that the grounds of the application were not merely slight, but non-existent; yet in order to avoid even the possibility or appearance of influence he acceded to the request.

The debate on judicial impersonality is typical of persuasive argumentation, which was mentioned at the beginning of this book[3]. People tend to approach this issue with convictions already formed one way or the other,

19 See p 440 post; and see also p 50 ante.
20 See Chapter 21 on American Realism, and especially the views of Llewellyn, who in his last major work drew attention to what he called 'steadying factors'.
1 Scrutton 'The work of the Commercial Court' (1921) 1 CLJ 8.
2 (1978) Times, 21 February.
3 See p 14 ante.

which makes arguments favourable to one's prejudice more persuasive than contrary arguments. As pointed out earlier, appeals for evidence in this kind of situation are either misplaced, or else such evidence as there is carries greater or less weight according to whether or not it supports the conclusion one likes. Evidence of judicial prejudice comes mainly, though not exclusively, from the area of industrial law and here the allegation is often made that judges are prejudiced against trade unions. A preliminary point that needs to be made is that reported cases do not reveal the whole picture because not all decided cases are reported. Court records show that many pro-union decisions are seldom reported, and, even when they are, evoke no public protest. Only anti-union decisions tend to receive publicity and spark off criticism of judicial prejudice. Since praise of pro-unions decisions is either lacking, or so muted as to pass unheard, this makes the allegation of prejudice no more than a political attack[4].

After the demise of the Industrial Court, its former President provided statistical data of the cases decided by it during its life, and in the overwhelming number of these there was union and judicial accord[5]. Cases of industrial disputes decided by courts other than the Industrial Court were examined by two left-wing scholars, who concluded: 'Clearly there was less statistical evidence of the influence of judicial bias than might *a priori* have been expected'[6]. Even the oft-quoted dictum of Lord Atkinson in *Roberts v Hopwood*[7] needs to be understood in its context. In this case the House of Lords invalidated a scheme of wages, including equal wages for men and women, drawn up by a socialist local authority. In the course of his speech his Lordship remarked that the local councillors should not allow themselves to be guided 'by some eccentric principles of socialist philanthropy, or by a feminist ambition to secure the equality of the sexes in the matter of wages in the world of labour'. These words certainly indicate his Lordship's own prejudices, but the actual decision of the House reflected a variant of the Aristotelian principle of justice that there has to be equal distribution of burdens as of benefits; the financial burden of an expensive scheme as proposed by the council should not be imposed only on one section of the community without parliamentary authority. Even the chauvinist sentiment deploring equal wages for men and women would probably not have been resented so much at that date as it would be now. The case occurred more or less on the eve of the General Strike and the onset of the Depression, and it is pertinent to ask if trade unions would, or would not, have objected to women taking away yet more jobs from men, let alone equal pay for them.

Objection is sometimes taken that judges are not elected. As to this, it has to be remembered that in the daily administration of the country many

---

4 In *Gouriet v Union of Post Office Workers* [1977] QB 729, [1977] 1 All ER 696, CA (revsd [1978] AC 435, [1977] 3 All ER 70, HL) the Court of Appeal ruled against the unions involved and the Attorney General and provoked an immediate attack in Parliament on judicial prejudice against unions. The House of Lords reversed the Court of Appeal and no comment was made. Was it only the Court of Appeal that was prejudiced? Critics cannot have it both ways: in the House of Lords either there was no prejudice, or, if there was, then as long as it favoured unions, it merited no criticism.
5 Donaldson 'Lessons from the Industrial Court' (1975) 91 LQR 181.
6 O'Higgins and Partington 'Industrial Conflict: Judicial Attitudes' (1969) 32 MLR 53. Their *a priori* expectation of bias perhaps betrays their own prejudice.
7 [1925] AC 578 at 594, HL. See also *Prescott v Birmingham Corpn* [1955] Ch 210, [1954] 3 All ER 698, CA; *Bromley London Borough Council v Greater London Council* [1983] 1 AC 768, [1982] 1 All ER 129, HL.

decisions are entrusted to civil servants, who are not elected; if so, why not judges? Also, why are elected representatives more trustworthy? Even they have to be trusted to do many things on which the electorate is not and cannot be consulted. Election of judges tends to make judicial values equivalent to political values, and judges elected in one political climate may lose confidence when the climate changes. If judges changed with political change, that would spell the end of certainty and continuity. A political judiciary could operate successfully in a one-party state, in which it will constitute one organ of 'rule by law'. Under such a system election would seem pointless, or at most a useless formality.

It has also been said that judges should bring to bear a 'collectivist' outlook on their job rather than an 'individualist' one. If this means that they should think in terms of people's obligations towards society, of duties rather than 'rights', there is much to be said in favour of such a contention; but this has nothing to do with class prejudice. The attitude of judges in the past may have been unduly narrow, but it has changed since the end of the 1939-45 war. If, on the other hand, the contention is that judges should always give more weight to union interests than to individual interests, this is tantamount to a demand that judges should reflect a new class interest, namely, that of trade unions. It is not easy to see why judges should not think 'collectively' and at the same time also pay heed to individual interests; otherwise, the individual will be subordinated to collective interests, which would result in a totalitarian society. Much of the criticism on this point may stem from a failure to appreciate the historic role of the judiciary of siding with the under-dog so as to preserve distributive equality[8].

The foregoing considerations may not wholly dispel the charge of prejudice, but they do go some way towards blunting its edge. A foremost critic of the judiciary concluded his survey by observing that in capitalist and communist societies judges are, after all, only doing their respective jobs. 'That this is so', he says,

> 'is not a matter for recrimination. It is idle to criticise institutions for performing the task they were created to perform and have performed for centuries ... To expect a judge to advocate radical change, albeit legally, is as absurd as it would be to expect an anarchist to speak up in favour of an authoritarian society'[9].

It would seem that underlying this statement is a regretful acknowledgement of the fact that judges have to espouse values other than those which the author would like them to espouse; but it is veiled as a complaint against the pretence by unspecified persons 'that judges are somehow neutral in the conflicts between those who challenge existing institutions and those who control those institutions'. As has been pointed out, few, if any, doubt that a sense of values is subjective, but the point that seems to be overlooked is the significance and power of consensual domains of shared values. The same author also remarks: 'I am not sure what would be the attitude of judges in the ideal society. Perhaps they would not be needed because conflict between Government and the governed would have been removed'[10]. There is an echo in this of the now defunct Marxist doctrine of the 'withering away of law', which has long been dropped from even communist legal philosophy[11].

8 See pp 91 et seq. ante, and note 7.
9 *Griffith* p 215.
10 *Griffith* pp 214-215.
11 See pp 402-405 post.

It is also naive to believe that there can be even an 'ideal society' without tensions between governors and the governed. There will always be reaction against authority by groups, and to eliminate this all minorities will have to be suppressed; which will not appeal to peoples with traditions of freedom and, in particular, accords ill with this critic's own fervent championing of minority interests.

In a 'free' as opposed to a 'totalitarian' society an independent judiciary is essential, with a sense of values, which is not merely a reflection of governmental values. Whatever the kind of society, confidence has to be reposed in judges if they are to keep the day to day administration of the law on an even keel during its passage through the years.

READING LIST

C K Allen, *Law and Orders* (2nd edn).

B R Bamford 'Aspects of Judicial Independence' (1956) 73 South African Law Journal 380.

E Bodenheimer *Jurisprudence* chs 11–13 and 17.

B N Cardozo *The Nature of the Judicial Process.*

B N Cardozo *The Growth of the Law.*

F C Cohen 'Modern Ethics and the Law' (1934) 4 Brooklyn Law Review 33.

F S Cohen 'Field Theory and Judicial Logic' (1950) 59 Yale Law Journal 238.

A T Denning *The Changing Law.*

P Devlin 'Judges, Government and Politics' (1978) 41 Modern Law Review 501.

J Dickinson 'The Law Behind Law' (1929) 29 Columbia Law Review 285.

R M Dworkin *Taking Rights Seriously* chs 2–3.

W Friedmann *Law in a Changing Society* chs 1–8 and 10.

A L Goodhart *English Law and the Moral Law.*

J A G Griffith *The Politics of the Judiciary.*

D Lloyd *Public Policy.*

H L Parker 'Recent Developments in the Supervisory Powers of the Courts over Inferior Tribunals' (1959) *Lionel Cohen Lectures* V.

H Potter *The Quest of Justice.*

R Pound *Justice According to Law.*

P Vinogradoff *Collected Papers* II, ch 18.

R A Wasserstrom *The Judicial Decision.*

P H Winfield 'Ethics in English Case Law' (1931–32) 45 Harvard Law Review 112. *Science of Legal Method. Select Essays by Various Authors* (trans E Bruncken and L B Register).

CHAPTER 11

Obligation and duty

This and the next three chapters are devoted to certain concepts. Conceptual analysis has declined in popularity, so something needs to be said about its inclusion here.[1] The lawyer is a craftsman and the analysis of concepts may be likened to a dissection of the tools of his trade in order that knowledge of their structure and functioning will enhance his skill in their use. 'To be a good craftsman of the law' said Professor Rheinstein 'students must not only learn the law, but also become proficient in the use of its tools. These tools are concepts, logic, and language'[2]. This kind of examination cannot be conducted in courses on substantive law. For example, various branches of substantive law show how one acquires rights, duties, ownership, possession and so on. They are not concerned with the question, What is a 'right', or 'duty'?, which involves a different type of inquiry. Conceptions like possession vary from branch to branch and a unifying study of them has to fall within the province of a separate course, whether this is called 'jurisprudence' or not.

Many rules are expressed in terms of concepts, and concepts, are means of unifying clusters of fact-situations and rules and so provide the machinery for assigning benefits and burdens. They are institutions in themselves, distinct from rules, and as such should not be overlooked[3]. In other words, they are tools of judicial reasoning and the art of doing justice according to law depends in part on the apparatus of the law being so structured as to preserve certainty and also allow room for the play of value-judgments. The efficiency with which the job is done depends on the efficiency of the tools; and the requirements of the job shape and re-shape the tools. The structure of concepts has been moulded by the functions they perform, which, as set out earlier, may broadly be called the tasks of justice. If the functioning of rules is considered at all, then it cannot be divorced from the instruments with the aid of which they function. It has been emphasised repeatedly that law is a social institution and that its study should not be divorced from its social *milieu*. Many useful insights into the moral and social problems of law can be obtained by seeing how concepts are used in different contexts to give effect to such value considerations.

Conceptual analysis is sometimes denigrated as not being 'jurisprudential'.

---

1 For a different treatment of conceptual study, see Summers 'Legal Philosophy Today—an Introduction' in *Essays in Legal Philosophy* (ed Summers) p 1.

2 'Education for Legal Craftsmanship' (1944-45) 30 Iowa Law Review 408.

3 Simpson 'The Analysis of Legal Concepts' (1964) 80 LQR 535, says that to understand what is peculiar about legal concepts it is necessary to investigate the way in which legal terms diverge from and also are related to their extra-legal meanings with explanation as to how, when, why and with what consequences this occurs. For the importance of concepts as institutions, see MacCormick 'Law as Institutional Fact' (1974) 90 LQR 102, who says that a concept requires (a) a set of constitutive rules specifying the type of facts; (b) consequential rules specifying the legal consequences; and (c) terminative rules specifying how it ends.

The immediate response to such a charge should be that it is based on the assumption that 'jurisprudence' has some 'proper' meaning which excludes such analysis. Further, if the way this word is used is considered, it will be found frequently to have included the study of concepts[4]. The charge is reminiscent of the occasional rejection from university courses of certain topics on the ground that they are 'vocational' in a pejorative sense and not 'educational'. Whether a subject is 'vocational', 'educational' or 'jurisprudential' depends on *how* it is treated. The moral, ethical and social dimensions of law are now regarded as falling within the sphere of jurisprudence. Concepts are inlets through which these influences are brought to bear, and if conceptual analysis is conducted in relation to these, as indeed it should be, then there is nothing amiss in treating this, too, as 'jurisprudential'. Part of the objection stems from a belief that 'jurisprudence' should be concerned with generalisations, which remain fairly constant. Such a belief results from thinking exclusively in the time-frame of the here and now in which, it is true, as will appear, that the meanings of concepts vary from branch to branch. From what has been said above it should be evident that concepts need to be studied with reference to the task of doing justice, which requires thinking in a continuing time-frame. This can and does provide a unifying framework within which local variations can be brought together. Finally, analysis of the stuff of the law will provide a background to the study of at least some theories about the nature of law. It should sharpen one's critical awareness of what such theories are about by deepening one's insight. The wider and deeper the analysis of concepts, the greater the chance of appreciating the purport of those theories.

THE IDEA OF 'OUGHT'

The principal function of laws is to prescribe how people ought or ought not to behave. 'Ought' has many significations, not all of which are relevant to lawyers.

(a) It may connote shortcomings, eg 'you ought to know better'.

(b) It may connote probability, eg 'you ought to win your match'.

(c) It may connote recommended conduct, eg 'you ought to see that film'.

(d) It may connote conduct which is due (obligation or duty, eg 'you ought to pay your debt'[5].

(e) It may connote propriety (correct or accepted usage), eg 'you ought to say 'food', not 'grub' '.

(f) It may connote the effective means to an end, eg 'if you want to talk to X by telephone, you ought to ring him up'.

The last three have legal significance: (d) concerns obligation and duty, (e) concerns definitions and the special use of certain terms, and (f) concerns the effective exercise of powers. As (e) and (f) have been dealt with earlier[6], only obligation and duty will be considered here.

---

4 Eg, *Oxford Essays in Jurisprudence* (ed Guest) especially chs 1, 2, 4, 5 and 6; Goodhart *Essays in Jurisprudence and The Common Law* chs 1, 3-7.

5 This is borne out by the etymology: *deü* (past participle of *devoir*), *dueté* (Anglo-French). Cf *debitum* and 'debt'. See *Oxford English Dictionary*; *Thesaurus Linguae Latinae* s vv; Co Litt 291a.

6 See pp 44-45 ante.

OBLIGATION

The analysis by Professor Hart provides the basis for approaching this concept[7]. His treatment of it is bound up with the analysis of 'rule' since, according to him, an obligation exists by virtue of a rule. 'Rule' has been examined earlier, and what was said in connection with it needs to be borne in mind[8]. Every obligation is a normative judgment, and normative judgments imply social rules. These require that the patterns of behaviour enjoined by them are generally 'repeated when occasion arises by most of the group', and 'some at least must look upon the behaviour in question as a general standard to be followed by the group as a whole', ie some at least must internalise the behaviour patterns[9]. Internalisation derives from the fact that these 'are thought important because they are believed to be necessary to the maintenance of social life or some highly prized section of it'; also, the required behaviour 'may, while benefiting others, conflict with what the person who owes the duty may wish to do'[10].

Internalisation is manifested in criticism, felt to be justified or legitimate, of deviance and in demands for compliance; and 'great social pressure' is brought to bear[11]. It is also manifested in the expressions 'right', 'must', 'should', 'wrong', 'ought', and 'obligation'. An obligation is thus a statement from the internal point of view and exists 'when the general demand for conformity is insistent and the social pressure brought to bear on those who deviate or threaten to deviate is great'[12]. The adverse reaction against deviance may or may not ensue; so it is neither a condition for the existence of an obligation, nor does obligation imply a prediction that it is likely.

Obligations can be moral as well as legal[13]. Both kinds are supported by pressure for conformity, which is exerted irrespective of individual consent. Both concern behaviour in everyday situations, and deviance from either kind of obligation justifies criticism. Conformity, on the other hand, is not a matter for praise, since the desired patterns of behaviour are thought to be necessary for society and conformity is a condition *sine qua non* of its existence. The differences between moral and legal obligations are listed as follows:

(a) every moral rule is treated as being important, but this is not so with every legal rule;
(b) moral rules are not changed by deliberate, single acts, while legal rules can be so changed;
(c) breach of moral rules requires voluntary and blameworthy conduct, but many legal rules can be broken without fault;
(d) moral pressure is applied mainly through appeal to the morality of the conduct, not by coercion as with legal rules.

One criticism of Professor Hart's thesis is probably based on a misunderstanding. This is that the existence of social rules being a fact, the 'ought' of obligation cannot logically be derived from an 'is' of fact. Professor Hart

7 Hart *The Concept of Law* pp 79–88.
8 See pp 47 et seq. ante.
9 *Hart* pp 54–55.
10 *Hart* p 85.
11 *Hart* p 84.
12 *Hart* pp 84 et seq.
13 *Hart* pp 168–176.

does not say this: he only says that obligation implies social rules, not that it is logically derived. Leaving this aside, it does appear that there is some unclearness as to what is signified by 'social group'. Most members of a large criminal organisation, eg the Mafia, may regard certain patterns of behaviour as standards among themselves and exert pressure against deviance. In what sense is this a 'social group' and are its behaviour patterns 'social rules'? They are certainly not legal rules; which leads to the next point. Obligation cannot be wholly divorced from moral soundness, despite Professor Hart's firmly positivist stance. It is true that people may acknowledge a legal obligation to do something which they think is morally bad. This conflict stems from the obligatoriness attaching to whatever possesses law-quality, which derives from the original acceptance of the criteria of validity. As pointed out, moral considerations are among the reasons for such acceptance[14].

DUTY

Duty is a species of obligation, and it will be helpful to examine first its function, then its structure and lastly its functioning in society.

FUNCTION OF DUTY

The factors that call duties into being may be summed up very generally: they are prescriptions of conduct towards the achievement of some end, moral, social or other[15]. The ends may also determine the form of the prescription.

A more important question is why a duty continues to exist, by which is meant: continues to be 'law'. The first and obvious requirement is the continuance of the purpose for which it was introduced. It has also to be consonant with, or at least not diverge too much from, prevailing moral ideas. The connection between legal and moral ideas is close[16], but not congruent. On the one hand, moral ideas bring about the creation, modification or abolition of laws[17], and influence their application. On the other hand, there is also truth in the view that certain moral ideas have been moulded through the immemorial administration of the law[18]. It may also happen that after a duty has been created, its moral source changes or even disappears, in which case the duty separates itself from the prevailing morality and the pressure behind it is then solely respect for 'law'. The morality of yesterday may thus find itself perpetuated as an anachronism in legal form[19]. Or it may be that considerations other than morality gave rise to a duty, in which case again the duty is independent of morality. To a greater or lesser extent such tensions between duties and moral ideas can be tolerated, but there comes a point at which the conflict becomes acute and the duty has to be either altered or extinguished. This is why, as Allen remarked, duties should

14 See pp 49–59 ante.
15 See infra, and ch 10 ante.
16 Eg Lord Coleridge CJ in *R v Instan* [1893] 1 QB 450 at 453, and in *R v Dudley and Stephens* (1884) 14 QBD 273 at 287. As to how far they ought to do so, see pp 111, 116 ante.
17 Eg capital punishment, adult homosexuality, matrimonial guilt as the basis of divorce.
18 See further pp 51, 52 ante.
19 Eg some forms of strict liability.

not reach too far beyond accepted moral ideas if they are to command respect[20]. Laws should have a future, which will not be the case unless people have faith in them.

Another factor in the continuance of a duty is its ability to fulfil its function. Two of its tasks, which will now be examined, are: to prescribe a pattern of behaviour and to serve as a norm with reference to which judges decide the legality of actual behaviour. The general conditions for regulating behaviour were stated by Professor Fuller[1]. A duty has to be (i) general (though limited exceptions are allowable); (ii) promulgated; (iii) prospective (though limited exceptions are allowable); (iv) intelligible; (v) consistent in itself; (vi) capable of fulfilment (though exceptions are to be found); (vii) constant through time; and (viii) congruent with official action. These eight points constitute what he called the 'inner morality' of law, and are distinguishable from its 'external morality', which concerns ideals. It should be obvious that these are relevant only in the continuing time-frame and in that context are part of the concept of duty since the task of regulating behaviour could not be performed otherwise. Thus, apart from occasional exceptions, a duty should be general and not designed for an individual, else there would be no cohesion, but only myriads of separate duties severally addressed to each member of the community. Again, no one can be expected to regulate his conduct according to the prescription unless this is made known to him, ie published and intelligible; it must also refer to the future, be unself-contradictory and within the bounds of human possibility. Without a measure of constancy through time there would be no continuity and hence no stable legal order.

The last condition, congruence with official action, carries an implication not developed by Professor Fuller. It has been stated that, apart from regulating behaviour, a duty has also to serve as a norm of judicial decision, and it is here that the requirement of congruence comes in. What it means is that there has to be a satisfactory degree of conformity between the prescription and the action of the judge (or other official); 'satisfactory', that is, from the point of view of both litigants and officials. The extent to which this is achieved depends as much on the *structure* of the duty as on the ability, integrity etc of the judge. Since prescription is usually directed to the future, the control has to be in expansive terms; and since justice in its widest sense has to be done in the resolution of disputes, the structure of duty must allow for the interplay of value considerations. This, as will now be shown, is not fixed.

STRUCTURE OF DUTY

The picture revealed by analysis is not clear-cut because the part played by values in the judicial process makes it necessary that instruments of reasoning should allow a measure of flexibility. Courts use different conceptions of duty so as to do justice in different situations.

Behaviour is regulated chiefly through duties; to conceive of them except in relation to conduct is impossible.

1.   Since duties do not describe, but only prescribe behaviour, it follows

---

20 Allen *Legal Duties* pp 196–200. See also Gray *The Nature and Sources of the Law* pp 11–15; Kelsen *General Theory of Law and State* p 58.
1 Fuller *The Morality of Law* ch 2.

that they express notional patterns of conduct to which people ought to conform. Thus they 'exist' only as ideas, and they remain expressions of 'oughts' even though they may be expressed imperatively as 'must' or 'shall'. This imperative phraseology has given rise to the view that duties have been commanded[2]. Many writers have been at pains to refute the command theory, but only one objection need be mentioned here. Professor Olivecrona maintains that the connection between the imperative form and command is purely psychological[3]. Everyone has a store of experience of actual commands dating from infancy, which have always been expressed in the imperative form. Experience thus accustoms one to associate the command *form* with actual commands. The result is that when faced with this form, as in the case of duties, there is an erroneous tendency to infer that they must have been commanded. Professor Olivecrona concludes that duties are not commanded, but only *expressed* in command form, and for that reason refers to them as 'independent imperatives'[4]. Not only are they independent of a personal relation between commander and commanded, but they also operate independently through the power of suggestion and not by the direct communication of wishes.

The idea of command, therefore, should be discarded. The most that need be said is that duties are notional patterns of conduct that are *phrased* in an imperative form.

2. An 'ought' is legal if it is embodied in one or other of the criteria of validity. Not all legal rules create duties, but even when they do not, they always address an additional duty to officials to treat them as 'law'. Rules conferring powers may confer mandatory or discretionary powers. In the case of the former there is the further duty in officials to exercise them.

3. A duty prescribes a person's behaviour primarily for some purpose other than his own interest, ie it is other-regarding. The duty to perform a contract relates to the other party to the bargain, the duty not to steal X's hat exists not only for X's benefit, but also in the interests of social stability, while the duty not to be cruel to one's own animals is likewise imposed in the interests of the community. Austin, it is true, recognised a category of duties, which he called 'self-regarding duties', and which are imposed, according to him, in the interest of the person obliged by them[5]. Allen, however, showed that all these concern the criminal law and that the behaviour involved has a bearing on the community, or on some section of it[6]. Perhaps, the most that can be argued is that some duties exist not only for the benefit of other persons, but also in one way or another for the benefit of the person obliged, for example, the duty on the driver of a vehicle to observe road signs.

4. The conduct envisaged in duties need not necessarily refer to the future, although this is in fact the case with the majority of them. A duty can be created with reference to past conduct, in which case it represents a notional pattern of conduct as to how people ought to have behaved. If the behaviour of any person is found to have been contrary to what it ought to have been, he is regarded as having committed a breach of that duty. Such

2 Austin *Jurisprudence* I, pp 89-91. See ch 16 post.
3 Olivecrona *Law as Fact* (1939) pp 42-49, and in 'Law as Fact', in *Interpretations of Modern Legal Philosophies*, pp 545-546. See too Von Mises *Positivism* chs 25-26.
4 Cf Kelsen: 'de-psychologized command' *General Theory of Law and State* p 35.
5 *Austin* I, p 401.
6 *Allen* pp 183-193.

ex post facto creation of duties, of which Acts of Attainder are examples, is unusual and is on the whole disfavoured[7].

5. Conduct can be conceived as an omission, an action by itself, an action in relation to circumstances, or an action in relation to both circumstances and results. Thus, there may be:

DUTIES WHICH CONTEMPLATE BEHAVIOUR ALONE. The behaviour may be conceived of simply as acts or omissions. Such duties may be imposed by contract for instance.

DUTIES WHICH CONTEMPLATE BEHAVIOUR IN SPECIFIED CIRCUMSTANCES. An example would be an engagement to sing at a concert. Likewise, there is no duty which restrains a person from getting drunk, but there is a duty not to be drunk when driving or attempting to drive a motor vehicle on a road or other public place[8]. So, too, there is a duty not to carry 'offensive weapons' in public places[9].

DUTIES WHICH CONTEMPLATE BEHAVIOUR BOTH IN RELATION TO SPECIFIED CIRCUMSTANCES AND CONSEQUENCES. In this category are found the largest number of variations. Criminal law and tort furnish the best illustrations. Sometimes the result only is emphasised, at other times it is the result brought about in a certain manner or in certain circumstances. Also, when considering the result it is necessary at times to distinguish between the types of persons who have been affected. Duties compounded in these various ways cannot be classified neatly under the headings of kind of conduct, kind of result, or kind of person affected; yet for purposes of exposition it will be convenient to emphasise each of these aspects individually.

Considering, first, the kinds of behaviour contemplated by different kinds of duties:

(a) A distinction has to be drawn between acts and omissions. In crime and tort this is vital. The duties in these branches contemplate specific results, and are generally negative, ie not to produce certain results. The disapproval here is of acts which produce them. Exceptionally there is disapproval of results produced by failure, in which case the duties are positive, ie to do something[10].

(b) Within the category of acts, some duties contemplate certain types of conduct, but not others. Thus, there is no duty in tort not to cause loss by trade competition[11], or by abstracting subterranean water flowing in undefined channels, even though it is done maliciously[12].

(c) A large number of duties enjoin people not to conduct themselves in

---

7 It has been argued that the Nuremburg War Crimes Trials were not *ex post facto* creation of offences, but that duties not to commit the acts in question had always existed at international law though lacking the machinery of punishment, and that what the Nuremburg Charter did was to provide the latter: Paulson 'Classical Legal Positivism at Nuremburg' (1975) 4 Phil & Pub Affairs 132.

8 Road Traffic Act 1972, s 5.

9 See the Public Order Act 1936, s 4, Prevention of Crime Act 1953, s 1.

10 See Clerk & Lindsell on *Torts* §§ 1–68, 69; 10–19; G L Williams *Criminal Law, General Part*, pp 3–8. For the duty of a police officer to preserve the peace and protect persons, see *R v Dytham* [1979] QB 722, [1979] 3 All ER 641, CA.

11 *Mogul SS Co v McGregor Gow & Co* (1889) 23 QBD 598.

12 *Bradford Corpn v Pickles* [1895] AC 587.

a blameworthy manner. Different duties contemplate different degrees of blameworthiness. Scaled according to their degree of strictness, at one end are those duties which require no blameworthiness at all, ie strict duties. In all such cases the duties simply forbid the production of certain results. Blame is irrelevant. Next in strictness are the duties which require people not to act carelessly, but these are also conditioned by the kind of result that ensues. In the law of tort where the question is less relevant now than it used to be, it is still the law that there is a duty not to interfere intentionally in a contract between two persons, but not carelessly[13]; malicious prosecution, as its name implies, cannot be committed carelessly. Of course, wherever there is a duty not to inflict a particular type of injury negligently, there is *a fortiori* a duty prohibiting the reckless, intentional, or malicious infliction of it[14], even though in the latter cases such duty may, for historical reasons, be classed under a different label. Thus, the intentional infliction of physical injury on the person is classified as battery or trespass, while the careless infliction of such an injury falls under negligence[15]. Again, causing pecuniary loss by wilful or reckless misstatements is actionable as deceit[16], and only in 1963 was it made actionable under negligence[17]. Some duties prohibit only the reckless or wilful infliction of certain types of damage. In such cases, there is no duty not to be negligent. Other duties enjoin people not to act maliciously, for example, in injurious falsehood, malicious prosecution and malicious issue of civil process[18].

Turning to duties in relation to the result of conduct, there is, once more, a great deal of variation in particular duties. In tort the result contemplated by the various duties is, broadly speaking, damage. It used to be possible to distinguish more sharply than now between physical damage (personal and proprietary) and non-physical damage. Duties imposed in respect of the latter used to be narrower in scope than the former. Since the 1970s duties not to inflict non-physical damage have developed apace, but it is still true that some kinds of non-physical damage are not recognised at all[19], while in other cases the duty is not to produce the non-physical damage wilfully or recklessly, but no duty in negligence[20].

Finally, duties may contemplate some classes of persons and not others. No duties in tort or crime are owed to the Queen's enemies, and (in the past) outlaws; the victim of an act of perjury[1], or a contempt of court is not

---

13 *Cattle v Stockton Waterworks Co* (1875) LR 10 QB 453; Prosser 'Palsgraf Re-visited' (1953–54) 52 Michigan Law Review 10: 'a contract interest is not entitled to protection against mere negligence'.

14 Plowman J in *Langbrook Properties Ltd v Surrey County Council* [1969] 3 All ER 1424 at 1440. Exception: *W B Anderson & Sons Ltd v Rhodes (Liverpool) Ltd* [1967] 2 All ER 850.

15 *Letang v Cooper* [1965] 1 QB 232 at 239–240, [1964] 2 All ER 929 at 932, per Lord Denning MR.

16 *Derry v Peek* (1889) 14 App Cas 337.

17 *Hedley Byrne & Co Ltd v Heller & Partners Ltd* [1964] AC 465, [1963] 2 All ER 575. For the development, see Clerk & Lindsell on *Torts* §§ 10–12, 13.

18 Clerk & Lindsell on *Torts* §§ 1–76 and further references.

19 Eg invasion of privacy.

20 Eg interference with contract. In *Corbett v Burge, Warren and Ridgley Ltd* (1932) 48 TLR 626, it was stated that conduct had to be malicious in relation to the type of harm involved, negligence being insufficient.

1 *Hargreaves v Bretherton* [1959] 1 QB 45, [1958] 3 All ER 122.

recognised in the law of tort as entitled to damages[2]. The Fatal Accidents Acts 1846-1976, mark the progressive widening of the class of dependants entitled to sue for the tortious killing of the breadwinner. A statutory duty may contemplate only a particular class of persons and not others[3]. As with the recognition of plaintiffs, so too with defendants. Some, eg the Queen or very young infants, are not recognised as bearing duties in tort or crime, while trade unions refuse to accept contractual duties.

In its most abstract form the idea of duty may be stated simply as a prescriptive pattern of conduct recognised as legal by courts. 'Recognition' is technical, for this may be of conduct alone, or conduct qualified in any of the ways considered. The existence of a duty implies that the courts accept as a model a certain form of behaviour with reference, it may be, to certain types of persons and results; and this is the criterion by which the actual behaviour of an individual is judged. In any given case, therefore, the existence of a duty depends on whether the particular kind of result, the manner of its production and the kind of persons involved are recognised by law. To the vital question: how is one to know whether these are recognised? the answer is: *by knowing the law*. Only in this way can one know whether a duty exists in a given case or not and what its scope is, and it is for this reason that the question of duty is always one of law for the judge[4]. The decision to recognise or not to recognise any of the above factors, in short, to create or refuse to create a duty, cannot be anything other than a policy decision. 'There is always' said MacDonald J 'a large element of judicial policy and social expediency involved in the determination of the duty-problem, however it may be obscured by the use of traditional formulae'[5]. The duty represents the official idea as to how people ought to behave, and adaptations of this idea to suit the needs of changing society reflect the prevailing scheme of distributive justice in society and its curbs on liberty.

Approval and disapproval

The phrasing of a duty signifies the kind of approval or disapproval that is given. Where a duty is embodied in a judicial precedent, the approval or disapproval is traceable to the policy decision of the judge or judges who laid it down; where it is embodied in a statute, the policy that ultimately finds expression in the statute-book is the result of an inextricable interplay of considerations, as explained in Chapter 8. Where it is embodied in custom, the approval of the community is generated out of established practice and, as explained in Chapter 9, there is at least the absence of disapproval on the part of some judge. So, by approval and disapproval in the present context is signified the official acceptance of the 'ought' and 'ought not' patterns of conduct as 'laws'. Even though the 'ought' or 'ought not' of a particular duty may have originated in the opinion of some individual, once it becomes 'legal' through finding expression in one or other of the law-making media, the opinion of the individual fades into the background and may vanish

2 *Chapman v Honig* [1963] 2 QB 502, [1963] 2 All ER 513.
3 *Knapp v Railway Executive* [1949] 2 All ER 508; *Hartley v Mayoh & Co* [1954] 1 QB 383, [1954] 1 All ER 375.
4 Lord Kinnear in *Butler or Black v Fife Coal Co* [1912] AC 149 at 159; du Parcq LJ in *Deyong v Shenburn* [1946] KB 227 at 233, [1946] 1 All ER 226 at 229.
5 *Nova Mink Ltd v Trans-Canada Airlines* [1951] 2 DLR 241 at 254-256. For further references, see Clerk & Lindsell on *Torts* §10-28.

altogether, for the 'ought' has then attracted to itself a value of its own, that of fidelity to law. The approval and disapproval become depersonalised and are adhered to in spite of one's personal sympathy to the contrary. To say that a pattern of conduct is required or prohibited by a duty implies respectively that it is approved or disapproved in the above sense. However, conduct may be approved or disapproved in ways other than through duty. Appreciation of altruistic behaviour, for instance, may be shown in several ways without obliging it as a duty, just as disapproval of wagering may be signified without prohibiting it in the form of a duty.

Sometimes the attitude of the law expressed in duties is one of approval and at others of disapproval. The performance of a contract is approved and there is a duty to perform; on the other hand, stealing is disapproved and there is a duty not to steal. Conduct which amounts to a *breach* of a duty is always disapproved, but the way in which duties are phrased may vary. A duty is positively framed when approval is given to the conduct required by it, eg to perform a contract; it is negatively framed to register disapproval of the conduct contemplated in it, eg not to steal.

The attitude of the law, whether of approval or disapproval, is based on the purpose to be achieved, which in turn may be governed by social values, morality, justice, or may be a relic of a bygone age. Thus, the strict duty not to trespass on land derives from the early days when the law contemplated only the result of conduct and, for reasons which have long since disappeared, remained largely indifferent to the blameworthiness of a defendant's conduct. On the other hand, various strict duties have been introduced in modern times, chiefly by statute, for wholly different reasons. Duties are strict when they may be broken without fault on the part of the person who breaks them. It is therefore untrue to say *lex non cogit ad impossibilia*, that the law does not expect people to accomplish the impossible, for in cases of strict duties people are held responsible even when they could not have done otherwise. Strict duties apart, there are other variations in the attitude of the law, for example, those that depend upon the manner in which the act is done, eg intentionally, carelessly and so on.

Enforceability

As a tool of reasoning 'duty' has alternative meanings, both of which are judicially employed: (a) prescriptive pattern of conduct which is enforceable; (b) prescriptive pattern of conduct even if unenforceable. This ambiguity is utilised in giving effect to the varied play of value-considerations. If (b) can be substantiated, enforceability cannot be essential to the concept of duty.

'Enforceability' itself may mean one of two things: compelling observance of the pattern of conduct enjoined by the duty, or the indirect method of inflicting a penalty, or 'sanction', in the event of a failure to observe it. Considering, first, compelling actual observance of duties, it is necessary to distinguish further between what are known as 'primary' and 'secondary' duties. The latter only come into existence on the breach of the former and have, as it were, an independent existence[6].

The carrying out of primary duties is termed 'specific enforcement'. Where

---

6 Thus, the statutory rule, which extinguishes a primary duty on the death of the defendant, does not affect the secondary duty to pay damages for the breach of it ordered by a court: *Rysak v Rysak and Bugajaski* [1967] P 179, [1966] 2 All ER 1036.

the primary duty is negative, ie not to do something, there is no convenient method of ensuring its continued observance. 'Duty' said Allen 'cannot be enforced by anything but individual conscience'[7]. X is under a duty not to assault Y. There is no way, short of locking X or Y up permanently, by which it can be ensured that X will not assault Y. It is impossible to lock up every member of the community so as to prevent assaults being committed and, indeed, if this were done society would cease to exist. All one can do is hedge the prohibition with deterrent sanctions in the hope that fear of them may succeed in securing obedience if all else fails.

Even where the primary duty is positive, ie to do something, it is generally not possible to ensure that it is carried out. Thus, if the primary duty under a contract is to sing at a concert, it is not possible to make the person sing. Only in exceptional situations are primary positive duties specifically enforced. Thus, if the primary duty is to pay a debt, the party obliged can be sold up in execution and made to pay it; in very special cases of contract specific performance may be ordered; a person may be compelled to repay money received by mistake; he may also be compelled to restore land and chattels wrongfully detained, and *habeas corpus* is available to obtain the release of persons wrongfully detained.

Secondary duties, on the other hand, can be, and are carried out, for no system will be so futile as to impose them unless they can be carried out. Most secondary duties, which are one form of sanctions, consist of the payment of money. It is therefore the case that, apart from the exceptional primary duties mentioned, only secondary duties are enforced in the sense of their observance being ensured. Since this is so, either those primary duties, which are 'unenforceable' in this sense, should not be called duties[8], or else the conclusion must be that this sort of enforcement is no test of duty; and this has in fact been judicially asserted[9].

The alternative meaning of 'enforcement', namely, the attachment of some sanction, whether in the form of a secondary duty or otherwise, leads to the question how far the presence of a sanction should be taken as a test of duty.

Sanction

A number of authorities contend that a duty can be distinguished as 'legal' whenever a sanction attaches to its breach. The corollary of this view is that the presence of a sanction is the test of legal duty. It is true that sanctions attend most duties, but the ideas of duty and of sanction should be kept separate and, as will be shown, sanction is no test of a legal duty. There are several objections to the view that it is a test. In the first place, sanctions only contemplate breach of duty, and the need to pay attention to conformity

---

7 *Allen* p 197.
8 So Holmes, who rejected the whole idea of primary duties, except in certain cases which he regarded as unimportant: 'The Path of the Law' in *Collected Papers* 167 at 173-174. There are many objections to this view. (1) Courts do take primary duties into account when applying the well-known rule that the performance of, or promise to perform, an existing primary duty is not sufficient consideration in contract: *Pinnel's Case* (1602) 5 Co Rep 117a; *Stilk v Myrick* (1809) 2 Camp 317; *Collins v Godefroy* (1831) 1 B & Ad 950. (2) The primary duty is as much a pattern of conduct that ought to be followed as the secondary pattern of conduct. Why reject the one and accept the other? (3) The implications of the exceptions admitted by Holmes, some of which have now been altered by statute, are more far-reaching than he seems to have imagined.
9 *Kaye v Sutherland* (1887) 20 QBD 147 at 151; *Tassell v Hallen* [1892] 1 QB 321.

to duties is just as important as non-conformity. Laws are required at least as much, if not more, for the law-abiding, who wish to know how they ought to regulate their behaviour. For them the importance of a duty lies, not in the sanction, but in the behaviour-pattern that is prescribed. Even in Utopia there will still be a need for guiding behaviour-patterns, though sanctions will never be required. Therefore, to argue, as Kelsen did, that 'law arrives at its essential function' only when a wrong is committed[10], is not the whole way of looking at the matter. Thus, the sanction test gives at best an incomplete and misleading picture.

The word 'sanction' has three different meanings. According to Pollock, it is 'the appointed consequences of disobedience'[11]; but what does 'consequence' mean? The statement 'sanction is a test of legal duty', may mean

1. That a duty exists whenever something called sanction actually happens, or will probably happen, or can be made to happen, in consequence of some action[12]. As to this, (a) the sanction may fail to operate, as where the culprit escapes detection, dies or becomes bankrupt, but the duty remains none the less. (b) The mere fact that something is actually made to happen as the result of doing a certain thing does not imply the presence of a duty forbidding the doing of that thing. Contrast the following examples. If X appropriates Y's property, he is made to pay Y its value. It might be argued that a sanction has operated and that, therefore, this points to a duty in X not to appropriate (convert) Y's property. Suppose now that X, a local authority, has statutory power to expropriate Y's property subject to the payment of compensation. Here, too, if X takes the property, X has to pay Y its value; but there is no duty in X not to do so, for the act of expropriation lacks the element of wrongfulness which it had in the first example[13]. The point is that the wrongfulness of the original taking, in other words, a duty forbidding it, cannot be deduced from the mere fact that X is made to pay Y a sum of money. Indeed, in the latter example, it is because the taking was not a breach of duty that the consequential payment is not called a 'sanction'; or, putting the matter in another way, it is the presence of a duty that makes the term 'sanction' appropriate for the given consequence. Sanction is therefore not a test of duty; on the contrary, it is the other way about. (c) To speak of sanction as what happens, or will probably happen, or can be made to happen, is inadequate. Austin defined sanction as 'the eventual or conditional evil'[14]; and to him, sanction and duty were correlative terms, the sanction being that which ought to be done to a person who breaks a duty. The operation of a sanction depends on the observance of duties by those charged with its execution. Thus, the sanction of imprisonment for theft depends upon a police officer performing his duty of arresting the offender, upon various other persons performing their duties in bringing him to trial, upon the judge performing his duty of passing sentence if the case is proved, and upon the prison authorities performing their duties in imprisoning him. Each of these duties depends in turn upon others and so on in regression[15]. Since, therefore, the operation of the sanction depends on the

10 Kelsen 'The Pure Theory of Law' (1934) 50 LQR 474 at 487.
11 Pollock *A First Book of Jurisprudence* p 23.
12 This meaning seems to underlie the argument of Kadish and Kadish *Discretion to Disobey* as to which see pp 315–317 post.
13 *Crown Lands Comrs v Page* [1960] 2 QB 274 at 286, [1960] 2 All ER 726 at 732.
14 *Austin* I p 444; see also p 89.
15 Timasheff *An Introduction to the Sociology of Law* p 264; Haesaert *Théorie Générale du Droit* p 97.

observance of duties, it is unsatisfactory to make the operation, or likely operation, of duties the test of duty.

2.   To surmount the last-mentioned difficulty it is said that sanction as a test of legal duty is simply the prescriptive formula: 'If A, then sanction B ought to follow', regardless of its actual operation. Kelsen emphasised the distinction between propositions of law and their efficacy[16], and said that a sanction applies only in the event of a certain pattern of conduct not being observed. The sanction is therefore what the law prescribes: 'If A, then B ought to follow'. He treated the prescription of sanctions as 'primary norms', and the patterns of conduct that have to be observed to avoid sanctions as 'secondary' (inverting the terminology in this chapter). Since the proposition, 'if you steal, you ought to be punished', implies the proposition, 'you ought not to steal', it is only the first that is necessary. He did admit all the same that it is sometimes useful to refer separately to the second, but not essential[17]. The difficulties of using sanction in this sense as a test of duty are as follows. (a) As the example of statutory expropriation given above shows, the mere prescription in the form that if X takes Y's property ('If A'), then X ought to pay Y its value ('then B ought to follow'), does not of itself imply a duty in X not to take the property. It leads to a *reductio ad absurdum*: if one reaches the age of 65 ('If A'), then one ought to receive an old age pension ('then B ought to follow'). Is entitlement to pension a 'sanction', and is there a duty not to reach 65? Whether the 'then B' part is to be called a sanction or not depends, as already stated, on whether the 'if X' part imports a duty or not. (b) The thesis of this chapter is that duty is an 'ought' prescribing behaviour and that sanction, though usually associated with duty, is independent. In Utopia primary duties prescribing behaviour are all that would be required, as Austin himself admitted[18]. Theoretically, therefore, duties could exist other than in the 'If A, then B ought to follow' form. (c) As will be demonstrated in detail below, there are numerous occasions when sanctionless duties are recognised by the courts[19].

3.   Another possible meaning of sanction as a test of legal duty is that a duty exists when there is an automatic worsening of one's legal condition or liability to something being done, regardless of whether it is in fact done or not; and on much the same line the term 'privation', rather than sanction, has been offered[20]. To both these suggestions the statutory expropriation example provides an objection. Also, some of the sanctionless duty situations to be mentioned will show that duties can exist without there being any worsening of one's legal condition.

Leaving aside the imprecision of the term 'sanction', another objection to the use of sanction as a test of legal duty is that tribunals do not deduce the presence of a duty from a sanction. On the contrary, they apply the sanction because they first recognise that a duty has been broken. The sanction is applied, not just because a person has done something, but because he has done it when he *ought not* to have done so. The point becomes obvious when one considers a case in which a duty has been recognised for the first time. For instance, the Court of Appeal did not recognise a duty of care towards rescuers because they awarded damages; they awarded damages because

16   Kelsen *General Theory of Law and State* pp 29-30.
17   *Kelsen* pp 58-62.
18   Austin p 763; Holland *The Elements of Jurisprudence* p 148.
19   See pp 239-246 post.
20   J Hall *Foundations of Jurisprudence* pp 104 et seq.

they decided to recognise the duty[1]. It is only by way of retrospective ration-alisation that one is able to say: because a sanction has been imposed, the presence of a duty must now be inferred. A dynamic and prospective view is just as admissible, in which case one has to decide whether or not to recognise a duty before the question of sanction can arise.

To make sanction the test of legal duty is to confuse two different ideas, that of prescribing behaviour and that of ensuring obedience. How people ought to behave is one thing; what ought to be done if they fail to behave is another. The fact that sanctions are often required to induce people to conform to duties should not obscure the separateness of the two ideas. Besides this, there are many reasons why people obey duties of which fear of sanctions is only one[2]. Even if it were true that fear of sanction provides the chief reason why the individual regulates his conduct in accordance with a duty, sanction cannot explain why the behaviour pattern required to avoid it is accepted by the legislature and the courts as a standard for the com-munity. It is their acceptance of the 'ought' that accounts for this.

Professor Hart formulates a different objection by distinguishing between 'having an obligation' (duty) to do something and 'being obliged' to do it. If a gunman claps a pistol at X's head and demands his purse, X may 'be obliged' to comply, but he 'has no obligation' to do so[3]. Here the threatened evil, or even its execution, does not give rise to, or indicate the presence of, any duty. To use sanction as a test of duty, he says, is only the gunman situation writ large.

Finally, judges and lawyers do think in terms of duty even when there is no sanction[4]. It cannot be emphasised too often that judges do not follow a path of undeviating logic; they act according to policy, and the conceptions which they employ have to be flexible for use in this way. Duty, one of the commonest of legal conceptions, is no exception. Judges frequently think and talk in terms of duty even though there is no sanction, but when it suits their purpose they are equally ready to annex sanction as necessary to it. Any concept should allow for such variations; to freeze it in terms of sanction is to distort what actually goes on in the courts.

The case law on 'sanctionless duties' is overwhelming and can only be

1 *Haynes v Harwood* [1935] 1 KB 146. So too the structure of the formula of a Roman action at civil law, which directed the judge, 'if it appears that the defendant ought (*oportere*) to do so and so, then condemn him', shows that the idea of duty preceded that of sanction. *Actiones in factum* do not contradict this. The formulae of these ran: 'if such and such facts are proved, then condemn'. They were not civil law actions but praetorian, not *in jus conceptae* but *in factum conceptae*. Although *oportere*, which is the technical term for a duty at civil law, does not figure in them, the idea of 'ought' was nevertheless implied. For it was only when the praetor decided to recognise a new duty-situation that he published in his edict the formula that he would give.

2 See pp 51–52 ante.

3 Hart *The Concept of Law* pp 19, 80 et seq, and see p 48 ante. Speaking of a usurper who became President of Pakistan, Yaqub Ali J said 'He obligated the people to obey his behests, but in law they incurred no obligation to obey him': *Jilani v Government of Punjab* Pak LD (1972) SC 139 at 229.

4 In an Australian case, *Tooth & Co Ltd v Tillyer* [1956] ALR 891, the idea of a sanctionless duty was rejected as 'a metaphysical unreality'. So too Boreham J in *Mutasa v A-G* [1980] QB 114, [1979] 3 All ER 257. J Hall says that laws conferring powers are sanctionless laws, but goes on to argue that in so far as powers are so closely tied to duties that they cannot be understood apart, the theory of sanctionless laws is said to be discredited: *Foundations of Jurisprudence* p 122. This does not follow, since he assumes that duties are always sanctioned. For his substitution of 'privation' for sanction as the coercive element behind laws, see Hall pp 104 et seq; and p 238 ante.

referred to in outline[5]. Some of the examples to be mentioned have since been altered, but they are relevant as illustrations of judicial thinking.

1. Section 4 of the Statute of Frauds 1677 (the greater part of which has now been repealed by the Law Reform (Enforcement of Contracts) Act 1954), and s 40(1) of the Law of Property Act 1925 (replacing s 17 of the Statute of Frauds), say respectively that in the absence of a note or memorandum in writing signed by the party to be charged 'no action shall be brought' and 'no action may be brought'. Judicial policy towards the Statute of Frauds, as is well known, sought to minimise its operation with the result that its provisions were interpreted to mean that the lack of a memorandum did not affect the existence of a duty, but only its actionability.

> 'I think it is now finally settled' said Lord Blackburn 'that the true construction of the Statute of Frauds, both the 4th and 17th sections, is not to render the contracts within them void, still less illegal, but is to render the kind of evidence required indispensable when it is sought to enforce the contract'[6].

The fact that the duty remains notwithstanding the absence of an action is evidenced in many ways. The Rules of the Supreme Court require the want of writing to be pleaded, otherwise the party is answerable[7]. In other words, the duty is there and it is for the defendant to avail himself of the procedural advantage. Again, if an action is brought in Great Britain on a contract entered into abroad, it has been held that it is not the validity of the transaction but its actionability in the English courts that is affected by the requirement of writing[8]. The absence of writing does not of itself render a transaction void, since it could become void for other reasons, eg want of consideration. The writing may come into existence at any time between the agreement and the action. Finally, if one party alone has signed the memorandum, the action may be brought against him, but not by him[9]. By contrast whenever a transaction is void, a statute will say so.

2. Where acts of part performance are relied on in place of a note or memorandum in writing to make the transaction actionable, the courts do not treat these as creating the duty, but only as supplying the necessary evidence[10].

3. The fact that property rights pass under non-actionable transactions shows that they do create legal relationships. Devlin J once said,

> 'If the Act said that it was void, then of course the character of Murphy's possession could not be altered by it. But the Act says merely that it is to be

---

5 In an article, entitled 'The Unenforceable Duty' (1959) 33 Tulane Law Review 473, the author endeavoured to convey some idea of the volume of authority on the subject in Roman and English law.

6 *Maddison v Alderson* (1883) 8 App Cas 467 at 488. This is all the more significant because this case disposed of the old view that there was no duty: *Carrington v Roots* (1837) 2 M & W 248. For an equally important statement, see *United Dominions Corpn (Jamaica) Ltd v Shoucair* [1969] 1 AC 340 at 347, [1968] 2 All ER 904 at 906-907 (quoted at pp 242-243 post). For acceptance that the contract remains valid in all other respects: *Wauchope v Maida* (1971) 22 DLR (3d) 142.

7 RSC Ord 18 r 8 on which see (1985) *Annual Practice* p 267; *Craxfords (Ramsgate) Ltd v Williams and Steer Manufacturing Co Ltd* [1954] 3 All ER 17 at 18.

8 *Leroux v Brown* (1852) 12 CB 801 at 824. Conversely, a contract unenforceable abroad may be sued on in Britain: *Harris v Quine* (1869) LR 4 QB 653. See also *Compania Colombiana de Seguros v Pacific Steam Navigation Co* [1965] 1 QB 101, [1964] 1 All ER 216.

9 *Laythoarp v Bryant* (1836) 2 Bing NC 735; *Britain v Rossiter* (1879) 11 QBD 123 at 132.

10 *Rawlinson v Ames* [1925] Ch 96; *Broughton v Snook* [1938] Ch 505, [1938] 1 All ER 411.

unenforceable. This must mean that it is effective to alter the rights of the parties but that the altered rights cannot be enforced'[11].

4. Statutes of Limitation only bar the action and do not extinguish the duty, which continues to be sanctionless.

'I think' said Cotton LJ 'that "due" included everything that was owing, whether barred by the statute or not. Statute-barred debts are due, though payment of them cannot be enforced by action'[12].

Nield J discussing the effect of the Statute of Limitations said:

'The Act of 1939 does not provide that after such period the plaintiff's remedy shall be extinguished or even wholly cease to be enforceable, and indeed the remedy is not extinguished, not does it wholly cease to be enforceable; for if a defendant elects not to plead the Statute of Limitations, the remedy may be pursued after the period of limitation. Further than that, the benefit which a defendant derives from the Statute of Limitations is not I think properly described as a substantive benefit but really is merely as a right to plead a defence if he chooses to, so that the plaintiff is barred from prosecuting his claim'[13].

Diplock J has said that 'a cause of action does not cease to exist because a limitation period has expired'[14]; and so also Donaldson LJ 'it is trite law that the English Limitation Acts bar the remedy and not the right; and, furthermore, that they do not even have this effect unless and until pleaded'[15].

5. Acknowledgment or part payment of a statute-barred debt makes it actionable again. If it is argued that the statute, by removing the sanction, thereby extinguished the duty, then acknowledgment or part payment can only result in the creation of a wholly new duty. This is not so. The fact that no new consideration is required is consistent with the idea that acknowledgment operates only as a waiver of the procedural bar rather than with the creation of a new duty; and judges have said that it only revives the old duty. So Lord Sumner:

'Surely the real view is, that the promise, which is inferred from the acknowledgment and 'continues' or 'renews' or 'establishes' the original promise laid in the declaration, is one which corresponds with and is not a variance from or in contradiction of that promise ... If so, there is no question of any fresh cause of action'[16].

If, then, it is the original duty which is rendered actionable again, lapse of time can only have made it unenforceable. It is worth noting, however, that judicial policy has introduced some inconsistency in practice. Judges have not viewed the Statutes of Limitation with favour, especially when they are

---

11 *Eastern Distributors Ltd v Goldring (Murphy, third party)* [1957] 2 QB 600 at 614, [1957] 2 All ER 525 at 534 (overruled without affecting this point by *Worcester Works Finance Co Ltd v Cooden Engineering Co Ltd* [1972] 1 QB 210, [1971] 3 All ER 708).

12 *Curwen v Milburn* (1889) 42 Ch D 424 at 434.

13 *Rodriguez v Parker* [1967] 1 QB 116 at 136, [1966] 2 All ER 349 at 363. For equally important statements, see Lord Esher in *Coburn v Colledge* [1897] 1 QB 702 at 705 (quoted in *O'Connor v Issacs* [1956] 2 QB 288 at 341, [1956] 2 All ER 417 at 428); and Lord Denning MR in *Mitchell v Harris Engineering Co Ltd* [1967] 2 QB 703 at 718, [1967] 2 All ER 682 at 686.

14 *Airey v Airey* [1958] 2 All ER 59 at 62 (affd on other grounds [1958] 2 QB 300, [1958] 2 All ER 571; nullified by the Proceedings Against Estates Act 1970, s 1).

15 *Ronex Properties Ltd v John Laing Construction Ltd* [1983] QB 398 at 404, [1982] 3 All ER 961 at 965, CA.

16 *Spencer v Hemmerde* [1922] 2 AC 507 at 524; *Busch v Stevens* [1963] 1 QB 1, [1962] 1 All ER 412.

used to evade obligations[17]. As between the original promisor and promisee they are ready to hold the promisor strictly to his original bargain and for this purpose regard acknowledgement merely as the waiver of a procedural bar so as to make the original promise actionable once more. With the promisee's executor, on the other hand, there may not be the same reason for insisting on the original promise being carried out to the letter, and there has been a tendency in these cases to say that acknowledgment creates a new promise so that its terms may be qualified[18]. So it would appear that where it would be consonant with policy to say that the duty is the old one or a new one, the idea of the sanctionless duty will be pressed into service or not as the case may be.

6.   It is because a sanctionless duty is still conceived of as a duty that payment under it cannot be recovered, whereas payment under a void transaction can be. The reason is that even though the duty is sanctionless the party who pays fulfils the requirement that he ought still to pay. The fact that he cannot be made to do so does not alter the continuing legal 'ought'. Where the transaction is void, there is no 'ought' at all[19].

7.   A duty, the performance of which is postponed, is in the meantime a sanctionless duty. Speaking of an agreement to give time to a debtor Denning LJ once said,

> 'the effect of it was that the debt remained due, but not enforceable. Between November 17 and 30, it was *debitum in praesenti, solvendum in futuro*'[20].

Judgment creates a duty to satisfy it, even though it is not enforceable by action until a future date; but the period of limitation starts to run from judgment[1].

8.   There has to be an existing duty before a payment or part payment can be appropriated to it. A sanctionless duty is for this purpose recognised as a duty. Thus, in *Seymour v Pickett*[2], one part of the creditor's claim was actionable, the other was not. The debtor, who was aware of this, paid only sufficient money to cover the actionable part without specifically saying so. The creditor thereupon appropriated the payment to the non-actionable part and sued in respect of the actionable part. He was held entitled to do so.

9.   Security can only be given in support of an existing duty, and a sanctionless duty will suffice for this purpose[3].

10.   An unenforceable contract, ie one in which the duty is sanctionless, is valid in the sense that it may be used to discharge a prior contract, provided there is an intention to rescind it even though the new contract is itself unenforceable. If the intention is only to vary the prior contract, then the unenforceable character of the new one leaves the old unamended.

> 'At the root of the problem' said Lord Devlin 'there lies the concept of unenforceability, first introduced into English law by the Statute of Frauds and

---

17   *Re Baker, Nichols v Baker* (1890) 44 Ch D 262 at 270; *Stamford Spalding and Boston Banking Co v Smith* [1892] 1 QB 765 at 770.
18   See Williston *Contracts* ch 7, and authorities collected in Dias 'The Urien forceable Duty' (1959) 33 Tulane Law Review at 485–86 n 49.
19   *Bize v Dickason* (1786) 1 Term Rep 285. Cf *Chillingworth v Esche* [1924] 1 Ch 97 at 112.
20   *Midland Counties Motor Finance Co Ltd v Slade* [1951] 1 KB 346 at 353, [1950] 2 All ER 821 at 824.
1   *Berliner Industriebank Aktiengesellschaft v Jost* [1971] 2 QB 463, [1971] 2 All ER 1513.
2   [1905] 1 KB 715. See also 5th Interim Report of the Law Revision Committee, 32.
3   *Spears v Hartly* (1800) 3 Esp 81; *Low v Fry* (1935) 152 LT 585.

since made use of in a number of other settings, including the Moneylenders Act 1927. If the statute made the amending contract void and of no effect, there would be no problem at all. An attempt at changing the original contract would have failed altogether and so left it quite untouched. But unenforceability creates only a procedural bar. The substance of the contract is good; yet, although the contract is alive and real, the court will not give effect to it unless its existence can be proved in the way prescribed by the statute ... On this view the old contract cannot be enforced because it has been rescinded and the new contract cannot be enforced because it is not properly evidenced'[4].

Similarly, an unenforceable contract may be used by way of defence. Where, for instance, a compromise is unenforceable by one party for lack of writing, that party may nevertheless raise the agreement as a defence to an action brought against him[5].

11. Where work has been done under an unenforceable contract, the question has arisen whether reimbursement can be claimed on the basis of an implied contract. It has been held that the unenforceable contract is an existing contract, and that where an express contract already exists no other contract can be implied[6].

12. The position of diplomats is a good example of how the idea of the sanctionless duty is used to give effect to the conflicting demands of policy. International courtesy requires, on the one hand, that diplomats should be protected, but the claims of private persons, on the other hand, also deserve satisfaction. The solution is to recognise sanctionless duties in diplomats so that, although no action can be brought against them without waiver of the immunity, others, such as insurance companies and sureties, can be made responsible collaterally[7].

'Diplomatic agents' said Lord Hewart CJ 'are not in virtue of their privilege as such, immune from legal liability for any wrongful acts. The accurate statement is that they are not liable to be sued in the English courts unless they submit to the jurisdiction. Diplomatic privilege does not import immunity from legal liability, but only exemption from local jurisdiction'[8].

Furthermore, *Musurus Bey v Gadban*[9] and *Empson v Smith*[10] are authorities for saying that the diplomat will himself be answerable on the expiry of a reasonable time after the termination of his mission if he remains within the jurisdiction. This is not a new duty which suddenly emerges; it is his original duty which becomes actionable.

13. The position in tort of husband and wife before 1962 was another

4 *United Dominions Corpn (Jamaica) Ltd v Shoucair* [1969] 1 AC 340 at 347, [1968] 2 All ER 904 at 906-907. See also *Morris v Baron* [1918] AC 1.
5 *Auckland Bus Co v New Lynn Borough* [1965] NZLR 542.
6 *Britain v Rossiter* (1879) 11 QBD 123 at 127; approved in *James v T H Kent & Co Ltd* [1951] 1 KB 551, [1950] 2 All ER 1099.
7 Insurance: *Dickinson v Del Solar* [1930] 1 KB 376; surety: *Magdalena Steam Navigation Co v Martin* (1859) 2 E & E 94 at 115; excise: *A-G v Thornton* (1824) 13 Price 805; *Schneider v Dawson* [1960] 2 QB 106, [1959] 3 All ER 583. On immunity generally, see Diplomatic Privileges Act 1964.
8 *Dickinson v Del Solar* [1930] 1 KB 376 at 380. See also Diplock LJ in *Zoernsch v Waldock* [1964] 2 All ER 256 at 265-266, [1964] 1 WLR 675 at 691-692.
9 [1894] 2 QB 352. See the Swiss case: *V v D* (1927) 54 JDJ 1175; Briggs *The Law of Nations* pp 786, 801.
10 [1966] 1 QB 426, [1965] 2 All ER 881. A petition under the Matrimonial Causes Act 1973 against a husband, who enjoyed immunity at the time, was valid even though the suit could not be heard; but by the time the matter came to court the husband lost his immunity, so there was no longer a procedural bar: *Shaw v Shaw* [1979] Fam 62, [1979] 3 All ER 1.

instance of sanctionless duty being utilised to serve policy. A trifling exception
aside, one spouse used not to be able to sue the other, but the other's
employer was vicariously responsible[11]. The House of Lords has declared
that vicarious means vicarious, and that no one can be answerable vicariously unless his servant has himself committed a tort[12]. If, then, an employer was answerable vicariously for one of the spouses, there must have
been an unenforceable tort committed between them[13]. The judgment of
Denning LJ in *Broom v Morgan*[14] is of especial interest in this connection. He
first grounded the employer's answerability on a special view that this is not
a vicarious, but a primary responsibility; but he went on to proffer the
sanctionless tort between spouses as an alternative ground for the decision
should it be said that the employer's answerability has to be vicarious.

'If I am wrong on this point, however, and the liability of the master is,
properly speaking, a vicarious liability only (so that he is only liable if his
servant is also liable), then I still think that the employer here is liable ... That
section disables the wife from suing her husband for a tort in much the same
way as the Statute of Frauds prevents a party from suing on a contract which
is not in writing, but it does not alter the fact that the husband has been guilty
of tort. His immunity is a mere rule of procedure and not a rule of substantive
law. It is an immunity from suit and not an immunity from duty or liability.
He is liable to his wife, though his liability is not enforceable by action: and,
as he is liable, so also is his employer, but with the difference that the employer's liability is enforceable by action'.

This shows how, in order to reach a particular decision, the sanctionless
duty, or some other line of argument, will be utilised if suitable.

14. A joint obligation consists of one duty which rests on more than one
person. Anything which ends the duty of one, such as a release, ends the
duty of all. A mere agrement not to sue one party does not free the others,
because such an agreement does not extinguish the duty, but only makes it
unenforceable against him[15].

15. Even in criminal law, where sanctions abound if anywhere, before
the Suicide Act 1961 effected a change, there was a sanctionless duty not to
commit suicide. It is absurd to say that, because in the nature of things there
could be no sanction, therefore there was a liberty to commit suicide. For,
the policy of the law was to forbid, not to permit, suicide. Suicide used to
be a felony of violence and it is a contradiction in terms to speak of a liberty
in law to commit a felony. Attempt at suicide was a punishable misdemean-
our; to admit that there was a sanction and hence a duty not to attempt
suicide, but no duty not to complete the attempt is to overstep the limits of
sense. Finally, the survivor of a suicide pact used to be guilty of murder as

---

11 *Smith v Moss* [1940] 1 KB 424, [1940] 1 All ER 469; *Broom v Morgan* [1953] 1 QB 597,
[1953] 1 All ER 849.
12 *Staveley Iron and Chemical Co Ltd v Jones* [1956] AC 627, [1956] 1 All ER 403; *Imperial Chemical
Industries Ltd v Shatwell* [1965] AC 656, [1964] 2 All ER 999.
13 'Unless the servant is liable the master is not liable for his acts; subject only to this, that the
master cannot take advantage of an immunity from suit conferred on the servant': per Lord
Pearce in *ICI Ltd v Shatwell* [1965] AC 656 at 686, [1964] 2 All ER 999 at 1012.
14 [1953] 1 QB 597 at 609-610, [1953] 1 All ER 849 at 854-855.
15 *Duck v Mayeu* [1892] 1 QB 511 at 513; *Apley Estates Co Ltd v De Bernales* [1947] Ch 217,
[1947] 1 All ER 213; *Cutler v McPhail* [1962] 2 QB 292, [1962] 2 All ER 474; *Gardiner v
Moore (No 2)* [1969] 1 QB 55, [1966] 1 All ER 365.

a principal in the second degree, which can only imply that suicide constituted the principal offence[16].

All this should establish that a legal duty is the expression of an 'ought',
reinforced no doubt by sanctions in the majority of cases, and that a duty is
conceived as such even though the sanction is withdrawn or may not exist.
In the face of this evidence it is to be wondered why sanction is so persistently
thought of as essential to the concept of duty. An obvious reason is that most
duties do have sanctions. It is possible also that attention tends to be focused
on general duties which each person owes to everyone else, such as those in
criminal law and tort, which are duties not to do certain things. With these
it is the sanction arising out of their breach that attracts attention. Where
the duty is positive, one of active performance, one thinks primarily of what
ought to be done and secondarily of sanction. Usually such duties have to be
specifically created and they are owed to particular persons, which is why
they do not spring so readily to the mind as general duties. Another reason
may be that the fear of sanction is a factor in securing obedience; but it is
wrong to assume that this is exclusive, or even of paramount importance[17].
Again, it is necessary to distinguish legal from moral duties and a good deal
of comfort appears to be derived by fastening on sanction as the distinctive
feature. As pointed out, the distinction lies in the use of the label 'law'. Every
country has accepted certain criteria which govern this; in Britain these are
precedent, statute and custom. If an 'ought' is embodied in any of these, it
is 'legal'; if not, it is not 'legal', whatever else it may be. This test is simpler
to apply than the ambiguous sanction test. Besides, as mentioned earlier in
this chapter, sanction itself consists of duties.

The fallacy underlying the sanction test of duty is the result of an illegitimate transposition of a conclusion drawn when thinking in a continuum of
time into the time-frame of the present. The functioning of duties in a
continuum inevitably brings in the machinery of enforcement as an observable feature of their working. Duty, however, is also a tool of legal reasoning
applied *ad hoc* in this and that case, and the nature of it in the context of
here and now is not to be elucidated with reference to its operation as part
of the entire system[18]. In brief, sanctions are among the observable facts of
a 'legal system' and constitute part of the 'is' of society as a going concern.
It is a mistake to deduce from this that they are, therefore, part of the
concept of 'duty' as an 'ought'. A 'legal system' is not merely the sum-total
of laws[19]. It is thus logically consistent to say that the phenomenon of sanction is a feature of 'legal system', but not necessarily of every 'law'. It is true
that a complete picture will be obtained not only by considering duties as
prescriptions of conduct and tools of judicial reasoning, but also the actual
working of these prescriptions in society. The point, however, is that in order
to obtain as true a picture as possible of each aspect it is best to deal with
them separately. To present a unified picture of two dissimilar contexts,

---

16 The need for at least a principal offence, though not necessarily a principal offender, who
   may have a defence, is seen in *R v Bourne* (1952) 36 Cr App Rep 125. See generally *Beresford
   v Royal Insurance Co Ltd* [1938] AC 586, [1938] 2 All ER 602; *Pigney v Pointers Transport
   Services Ltd* [1957] 2 All ER 807; [1957] 1 WLR 1121; *R v Doody* (1854) 6 Cox CC 463; *R
   v Croft* [1944] 1 KB 295, [1944] 2 All ER 483.
17 See pp 51–52 ante.
18 Cf Fuller, who rejects the sanction criterion for another reason: *The Morality of Law* pp 108–
   110.
19 See p 60 ante.

based on a feature appropriate to one only, inevitably results in a distortion of case law. For duty is a weapon of judicial thought and should be elucidated with reference to the way in which it is used to give effect to policy and other such considerations in individual cases. To tie it rigidly to sanction is to fail to allow for that complex interplay of values so necessary to the application of laws, and also to fall into the 'jurisprudence of conceptions' habit justly derided by Ihering. The sanction-oriented concept of duty is appropriate to a sociologist who, like a natural scientist, is seeking to derive *descriptive* laws of social existence. It is not appropriate to a lawyer, even one concerned with the social working of laws, for to him laws are also prescriptive and he has to take account of all the processes, which include law-making, law-applying, reasoning and the operation of laws[20].

Conflicting duties

Before discussing the conflict of duties, some explanation is required as to what is meant by 'conflict'. Two situations are distinguishable: the first is where the two duties are in opposition to each other, one saying in effect, 'You ought to do X', and the other, 'You ought not to do X'; the second is where the duties are not of opposite content, but the fulfilment of one involves a breach of the other.

Duties of opposite content may be found in different jurisdictions or systems of law, eg in the conflict between municipal and international law, as the war criminals found to their cost, or between the civilian and military duties of a soldier. The nearest approach to a conflict within the same system is the *Case of the Sheriff of Middlesex*[1], where the sheriff, who fulfilled his duty by levying execution on the property of Hansard in pursuance of a judgment of the court, found himself committed for contempt by the House of Commons for having done so. Cases are naturally hard to discover, for no system of law will tolerate such situations for long. A more fruitful line of inquiry is whether a person by contract may subject himself to conflicting duties. If A enters into a contract with B, knowing of a prior inconsistent duty in B, the second contract will probably be void; but where it has been entered into without such knowledge in A, the answer is not clear[2]. In so far as people are left to make their own bargains, there is no reason why a person, who has been so foolish as to place himself under conflicting duties, should not be held bound by both.

Although the duties themselves may not be in conflict, their performance may not be reconcilable. An example is the now, as it would seem, discredited case of *R v Larsonneur*[3], in which the defendant was deported under police escort and placed in custody at Holyhead, and was then held guilty of being found in the United Kingdom without having a permit to land. Had she refused to be brought there so as not to commit a breach of the

---

20 See pp 422-423 post.
1 (1840) 11 Ad & El 273. The conflict was resolved shortly afterwards by the Parliamentary Papers Act 1840. In *Johnson v Phillips* [1975] 3 All ER 682, one duty was held to override a contrary duty.
2 See *Beachey v Brown* (1860) EB & E 796; *British Homophone Co Ltd v Kunz* (1935) 152 LT 589; Salmond & Winfield on *Contracts* pp 145-146; Salmond & Williams on *Contracts* pp 366-367; Pollock on *Contracts* p 355; Lauterpacht 'Contracts to Break a Contract' (1936) 52 LQR 494; Rattigan *The Science of Jurisprudence* pp 33-37.
3 (1933) 97 JP 206. Cf *Lim Chin Aik v R* [1963] AC 160, [1963] 1 All ER 223.

duty for which she was found guilty, she would have committed a breach of her other duty not to resist the police in the discharge of their duties. Whichever duty she complied with, she was bound to commit a breach of the other. Another situation is illustrated by *Daly v Liverpool Corpn*[4], where it was acknowledged that the fulfilment of the duty by an omnibus driver to drive with due care and attention was not reconcilable with the discharge of his duty to adhere to a reasonable time-schedule. A person may place himself by contract under two duties which cannot both be fulfilled. A possible illustration is *Eyre v Johnson*[5], in which the defendant by virtue of a pre-war tenancy contract was under a duty to keep the premises in repair and to restore them eventually in a state of repair. At the end of the tenancy he applied for a licence under the Defence (General) Regulations 1939, reg 56A, to effect the necessary repairs, but was refused permission. To have carried out the repairs none the less would have amounted to a breach of the regulations, and not to have done so would have been a breach of the contract. The court held him answerable in contract, but it should be noted that the breach of the contractual duty here was not inevitable, since, as the court found, had he maintained the premises in repair over the years, as he should have done, no licence would have been needed.

Where there is conflict in the sense under consideration between a legal and moral duty, the former prevails[6].

BREACH OF DUTY

Duty is a prescriptive pattern of conduct, which 'exists' in the sense that ideas exist. The breach of duty, however, can only occur as a result of conduct in a given situation, which is why it is always a *question of fact*.

What amounts to a breach of any given duty must follow from the formulation of that duty. If the duty is simply to behave or not to behave in a certain way, then the breach of it is not behaving or behaving in that way. If the duty is to produce or not to produce a given result, the breach of it is the failure to produce or the production of that result. So, too, if the duty is not to produce a given result in a particular manner, the breach of it is constituted by the production of that result in the manner specified[7].

Also, depending on the formulation of the duty, ascription of responsibility for conduct may turn on whether this is an act or an omission, a distinction which has additional significance as to the moment of time when a breach of duty occurs. Thus, in relation to limitation of actions time starts to run from breach. If the conduct in question is an act, then breach of duty occurs at that moment; if it is an omission, breach begins with the failure to act and continues thereafter[8].

In some cases breach of duty requires that the conduct has to be blameworthy (malicious, intentional, reckless or negligent), in others it occurs even

4 [1939] 2 All ER 142.
5 [1946] KB 481, [1946] 1 All ER 719. See also *Sturcke v Edwards* (1971) 23 P & CR 185.
6 *Pancommerce SA v Veecheema BV* [1983] 2 Lloyd's Rep 304, CA.
7 For an application of the above analysis to the confusion attending the 'duty of care' concept in negligence, reference might be made to Dias 'The Duty Problem in Negligence' (1955) CLJ 198, and 'The Breach Problem and the Duty of Care' (1956) 30 Tulane Law Review 377.
8 *Midland Bank Trust Co Ltd v Hett, Stubbs & Kemp (a firm)* [1979] Ch 384, [1978] 3 All ER 571.

without blameworthiness (strict responsibility). Further questions concern the result of conduct, namely, causation and remoteness of consequence. Each of these possesses a range of application giving courts latitude to arrive at just decisions[9].

FUNCTIONING OF DUTY

Professor Fuller is undoubtedly right in saying that one cannot even *hope* to regulate behaviour unless his eight desiderata are satisfied. There is more to it, however, than hope. Duties *do* by and large succeed in regulating the conduct of people. This leads to the question why duties are in fact obeyed, which is sometimes associated with the 'binding force' of duties. What this seems to mean is that the jurisdiction of certain institutions, such as the legislature and courts, extends to all spheres of behaviour and such jurisdiction is supreme. Their decisions cannot be ignored by officials or citizens, even when they are thought to be wrong. Officials are said to have duties in respect of the law, that is, to apply it honestly whether they like it or not; citizens have duties under the law many of which they are powerless to change. This is what gives rise to the idea of the 'bindingness'. So put, it conjures up a mystical entity, but which is only the product of language form. Instead of asking, Why are duties binding? it is more profitable to ask, What machinery is there for dealing with disobedience? and, Why do people in fact obey?

Machinery for dealing with disobedience

This provides the sanctions that support the majority of duties. It has been pointed out that sanction is a feature of the working of duties when these are considered in a continuum. Sanctions are of many kinds; they may operate on the individual himself (eg imprisonment) or on his property (eg damages); they may provide compensation, retribution, deterrence or reformation.

Why do people obey?

There are many reasons why people comply with duties. Bryce long ago tabulated them in the following order: indolence, deference, sympathy, fear and reason[10]. This list does not take sufficient account of psychological, social and moral pressures. All this is another way of approaching the manner in which rules are internalised and continue to be internalised, and for this reference should be made to an earlier part of this book[11].

9 See eg G L Williams *Criminal Law: The General Part* (2nd edn) ch 1, especially §§8-13, and chs 2-3; Clerk & Lindsell on Torts §§1-111 et seq, 11-35 et seq.
10 Bryce *Studies in History and Jurisprudence* II, pp 6 et seq.
11 See p 48 et seq. ante. Some mention might be made of Olivecrona's application of his psychological basis of internalisation to the notion of duty: *Law as Fact* (1971) pp 126 et seq. He distinguishes between the '*imperantum*', which is the part that creates 'the impression that the behaviour in question shall be observed', and the '*ideatum*', which is the part that refers to the conduct. The *imperantum* is the whole background creating the attitude of submission, namely, the organisation, procedures etc. He also followed JL Austin's insight that certain statements are 'performative' in that they produce effects in the world, eg 'I pronounce you man and wife' (see p 7 ante). Such statements are not to be understood as being true or false. Similarly, says Professor Olivecrona, legal statements 'are not statements about realities within the system; they form part of the regularised use of language which makes the system work' (pp 261-262).

READING LIST

C K Allen *Legal Duties* pp 156–220.
J Austin *Lectures on Jurisprudence* (5th edn, R Campbell) Lecture 1.
J Bryce *Studies in History and Jurisprudence* II ch 9.
L L Fuller *The Morality of Law* chs 1 and 2.
A. L Goodhart *English Law and The Moral Law* (Hamlyn Lecture Series).
H L A Hart *The Concept of Law* pp 33–41, 55–56, 79–88.
H Kelsen *General Theory of Law and State* (trans A Wedberg, 20th Century Legal Philosophy Series I).
J U Lewis 'John Austin's Concept of "Having a Legal Obligation": a Defence and Reassessment in the face of some Recent Analytical Jurisprudence' (1975) 14 Western Ontario Law Review 51.
K Olivecrona 'Law as Fact' in *Interpretations of Modern Legal Philosophies* (ed P Sayre) ch 25.
J C Smith *Legal Obligation.*

CHAPTER 12

Persons

The legal use of the word 'person' has attracted an assortment of theories which is probably second to none in volume. Before turning to them, it is necessary to have an idea of the way in which various problems that have arisen in this connection are dealt with, and what part the term 'person' plays in relation to them. This word has undergone many shifts in meaning, so two questions have to be asked: how has it been used? and, how does it function?[1].

With regard to its uses, it might be noted that originally it meant a mask[2], then the character indicated by a mask, the character in a play, someone who represents a character, a representative in general, representative of the Church, a parson[3]. In Roman law another shift in meaning seems to have occurred from a character in a play to any human being. Law takes account of human beings so far as their jural relations are involved and this in Roman law, with its emphasis on remedies, meant the power to sue as well as the recognition of interests in property. The development of such capacities in bodies, such as the *municipium* and the *collegium*, may have helped to abstract the idea. Despite this it would be wrong to suppose that the word *persona* was used in any technical sense in Roman law: there was only a tendency in that direction in late law.[4] Some such idea seems to have been present in the mind of Tertullian, who brought his legal ideas to bear on the interpretation of the 'person' of Christ, which gave the word another shift in meaning as connoting the 'properties' of divinity and humanity[5]. English law has taken over the popular reference of the word to human beings with all its emotive overtones, but the legal significance centres on the jural relations that are focused on an individual. This represents a technical shift in the meaning of 'person'. The law has gone still further and applied it to corporations, which is yet another technical shift and does not rest on any similarity, pretended or real, between human beings and groups. One may acknowledge that a group is a unit without feeling impelled to call it a person; which indeed is the case with unincorporated associations. Had the law stopped at human beings in its use of the word 'person' a good deal of needless perplexity would have been avoided. As a unit of jural relations, however, the term has lent itself to applications other than to human beings and hence serves different functions. This chapter will consider the ways in which it serves various purposes of justice as set out earlier.

1 See Hart 'Definition and Theory in Jurisprudence' (1954) 70 LQR 37.
2 πρόσωπον = face or visage.
3 Greenough and Kittredge *Words and their Ways in English Speech* p 268, quoted by Ogden and Richards *The Meaning of Meaning* p 129.
4 Duff *Personality in Roman Private Law* ch 1.
5 Bethune-Baker *An Introduction to the Early History of Christian Doctrine* ch 10.

ALLOCATION OF BENEFITS AND BURDENS

The concept 'person' focuses large numbers of jural relations, but it allocates them differently in different cases.

Human beings

Individuals are the social units and pre-existed both laws and society. Since laws are made by them and for them, and since jural relations are relations between individuals, it is no wonder that the jural relations of each individual came to be one of the first and most important unities for legal purposes[6]. The legal concept of a human being as a person is simply a multitude of claims, duties, liberties etc treated as a unit; as such there is no distinction in law between 'natural' and 'legal' persons[7].

Corporations sole

From an early time it was found necessary to continue the official capacity of an individual beyond his lifetime, or tenure of office. The common lawyers accordingly created a second 'person' who, though passing under the same name as the flesh and blood individual, enjoys legal existence in perpetuity. This is the corporation sole, which is a personification of official capacity. Unity of jural relations is thus assured a continuity which it would not otherwise have. 'The living official comes and goes', said Salmond in a passage which has become classic, 'but this offspring of the law remains the same for ever'[8]. The idea originated, according to Maitland, with a piece of land, known as the parson's glebe, which was vested in a parson in his official capacity. Difficulties arose over the conveyance of the seisin to a parson for the benefit of the Church. The corporation sole was invented so that the seisin could be vested in it[9]. Maitland went on to show that lawyers nevertheless did not avail themselves of the services of this child of their imagination for certain old rules stood in the way[10].

The main purpose of the corporation sole is to ensure continuity of an office. Moreover, the occupant can acquire property for the benefit of his successors, he may contract to bind or benefit them, and he can sue for injuries to the property while it was in the hands of his predecessor. Today there are many corporations sole, eg a parson, a bishop, Public Trustee, and a great many others[11]. The most spectacular is the Crown about which something more needs to be said.

---

6 Slavery in England died out before Norman times. The attribution of rights or responsibility to animals has likewise long been obsolete. The responsibility of animals is common in primitive systems: Exodus xxi 28; XII Tables 8.8: *D* 9.1.1 *pr*. In English law the responsibility of wrongdoing things, *deodands*, was abolished by statute in 1846, though the institution had long been obsolete. The Privy Council had occasion to deal with the position of an idol in Hindu law, *Pramatha Nath Mullick v Pradyumna Kumar Mullick* (1925) LR 52 Ind App 245.

7 Cf Kelsen *General Theory of Law and State* pp 93 et seq; *Pure Theory of Law* (trans M Knight) p 173.

8 Salmond *Jurisprudence* p 311.

9 Maitland 'The Corporation Sole' in *Collected Papers* III, p 200.

10 Maitland pp 230-243.

11 A Buddhist temple in Ceylon (now Sri Lanka) has been held not to be a corporation sole: *M B Thero v Wijewardene* [1960] AC 842. See also *Land Comr v Pillai* [1960] AC 854; *Salih v Atchi* [1961] AC 778.

THE CROWN AS A CORPORATION SOLE[12]. Personification of the Crown has obviated the need to personify the state in English law as in other systems. The
Crown Proceedings Act 1947, s 40 (1), sharply underlines the distinction
between the sovereign as an individual and the corporation sole. Maitland
said that the notion of the parson's glebe was applied to the Crown, adding
a Gilbertian touch that in this way the Crown was duly 'parsonified'[13]. The
chief manifestation of this is seen in the maxim 'the King never dies', while
the proclamation on the death of the reigning monarch, 'the King is dead,
long live the King' refers both to the individual who has died and to the
corporation which survives[14]. There have been rules, however, which were
inconsistent with this idea of the continuity of the Crown. In early days the
King's peace used to die with the King[15]. Pending actions in the Royal
courts used to lapse on the King's death and had to be restarted in the next
reign until statute altered the rule[16]. Petitions of right also lapsed, but could
never be renewed[17]; and this rule lasted until the Crown Proceedings Act
1947 abolished petitions of right[18]. Further, Crown appointments were automatically terminated[19] and Parliament was automatically dissolved[20].

An archaic attribute of the Crown is that it is *parens patriae*, which confers
upon it prerogative jurisdiction over infants, idiots and lunatics. This is now
exercised by means of Ward of Court procedure[1]. It is also well known that
'the monarch can do no wrong'. The origin of this is that a feudal lord was
not suable in his own court, and the monarch, as the highest feudal lord in
the land, was not suable in any court. The question is whether the monarch
is capable of legal wrongdoing but enjoys a procedural immunity, or whether
there is no initial breach of duty. The opinion is ventured with reserve that,
in early times at any rate, the monarch could do wrong, but was not suable[2].

12　*A-G v Köhler* (1861) 9 HL Cas 654 at 671. Cf *Madras Electric Supply Corpn Ltd v Boarland* [1955]
　　AC 667, [1955] 1 All ER 753.
13　Maitland 'The Crown as a Corporation Sole' in *Collected Papers* III, p 245.
14　*Calvin's Case* (1608), 7 Co Rep 1a; Blackstone *Commentaries* I, p 249. For an anthropological
　　explanation, see Hocart *Kings and Councillors* pp 132 et seq.
15　Stubbs *Select Charters* p 98.
16　1 Edw 6 c 7, *Discontinuance of Process & by the Death of the Queen* 7 Co Rep 29b. (Mr D E C
　　Yale courteously furnished this reference.)
17　*Canterbury (Viscount) v A-G* (1842) 1 Ph 306; *A-G v Köhler* (1861) 9 HL Cas 654.
18　G L Williams *Crown Proceedings* p 8, thinks the abolition of the Petitions of Rights Act 1860
　　(Crown Proceedings Act 1947, s 39 (1) and Sch 2) still leaves the possibility of bringing
　　petitions of right against the sovereign personally under the provisions of s 40 (1) and the
　　pre-1860 rules. See Hood Phillips *Constitutional Law* p 689. For case law, see *Franklin v AG*
　　[1974] QB 185, [1974] 1 All ER 879; *Franklin v R (No 2)* [1974] QB 205, [1974] 3 All ER
　　861.
19　Altered by statute: Tenure of Judges Act 1761; Demise of the Crown Act 1901.
20　Altered by statute: Succession to the Crown Act 1707; Meeting of Parliament Act 1797;
　　Representation of the People Act 1867.
　1　*Re M (an infant)* [1961] Ch 328, [1961] 1 All ER 788; *Re G (infants)* [1963] 3 All ER 370,
　　[1963] 1 WLR 1169.
　2　Pollock & Maitland *HEL* I, pp 515–517; Kenny's *Outlines of Criminal Law* (18th edn) p 69.
　　Cf Stephen *A History of the Criminal Law of England* II p 3. Although the Crown is now liable
　　to process, the personal immunity of the monarch has been retained: Crown Proceedings
　　Act 1947, s 40(1). So a theoretical point could still arise as to whether a private individual
　　might be held answerable for aiding and abetting a mischief perpetrated by the monarch.
　　Following the suggestion given above, the answer would be in the affirmative. (1) The feudal
　　origin suggests only a procedural immunity. (2) There seems to be no reason why the king
　　cannot infringe his own peace. If so, his act is wrongful whatever immunity there might be
　　from process. (3) A subordinate cannot plead Royal orders as a defence. This is because, on
　　the Parliamentarian interpretation, the maxim 'the king can do no wrong', meant that it

Another peculiarity of the Crown is that in relation to the Commonwealth it is regarded for some purposes, not as one person, but as a number of different personalities, each representing one part of the Commonwealth[3]. So, in the 1939–45 war the Crown in each Dominion declared war on Germany at different times, while the Crown in Eire (at that time still a Dominion) remained neutral throughout; also, the abdication of King Edward VIII and the accession of King George VI was confirmed at different times by the Dominions.

Corporations aggregate

The development of trade has enlarged the grouping of jural relations in such a way as to embrace collections of individuals organised into what are known as corporations aggregate. There is no doubt that these are 'persons' in English law. The expression 'person' shall, 'unless the contrary intention appears', include 'a body of persons corporate or unincorporate': so runs the Interpretation Act 1978, s 5 and Sch 1[4]. They can be created (a) by royal charter, (b) by special statute, eg the old railway companies, and (c) by registration under the Companies Act 1985, s 1, which is now the most usual method of creation[5].

In dealing with this topic it might be helpful to note, first, that there is an instinctive tendency to unify groups. This is a surface reaction, for a corporation, like a crowd, is ultimately reducible to a large number of individuals; but both are thought of apart from collections of individuals and a mental effort is always required to perform the analytical dissection. For reasons to be considered, the law, too, sometimes reacts in this way. Secondly, it is important to keep distinct the unity of a group and how the word 'person' is used. There is no necessary connection between them and the belief that there is has engendered needless confusion. In order to explain the

---

was *ultra vires* for the monarch to authorise wrongdoing. (4) The original basis of diplomatic immunity was that foreign sovereigns and their envoys enjoyed the same position at English law as that of the English sovereign. Since such envoys are responsible and only immune from process, it can be inferred that such also is the position of the English sovereign. (Mr H C Whalley-Tooker and Mr E Garth Moore very kindly offered helpful suggestions on this question.)

3 So Griffith CJ in *Municipal Council of Sydney v The Commonwealth* (1904) 1 C LR 208 at 231, and after the Statute of Westminster 1931, the Dominions are regarded as sovereign states.

4 See ibid, Sch 2, Part I, para 4(b), for the application of penal enactments to corporations. See also *Re Pilkington Bros Ltd, Workmen's Pension Fund* [1953] 2 All ER 816. *National and Grindlays Bank Ltd v Kentiles Ltd and the Official Receiver* [1966] 1 WLR 348; *A-G v Antigua Times Ltd* [1976] AC 16, [1975] 3 All ER 81. The position prior to the Act is not clear. Harman LJ in *Penn-Texas Corpn v Murat Anstalt* [1964] 1 QB 40 at 70, [1963] 1 All ER 258 at 270–271, thought that 'person' in the Foreign Tribunals Evidence Act 1856, s 1, did not cover corporations; and Walton J in *Re Dodwell & Co Ltd's Trust Deed* [1979] Ch 301, [1978] 3 All ER 738, held that a corporation was not a person within the meaning of the Accumulations Act 1800, even though such an interpretation went against the mischief contemplated by the the Act.

5 Salmond gives another method of creation, viz immemorial custom, but he gives no example: *Jurisprudence* p 320. Perhaps, the University of Cambridge may be cited, for it is described in the Preface to the University Statutes as a 'common law corporation'. These corporations may depend upon a 'lost grant', *Re Free Fisherman of Faversham (Co or Fraternity of)* (1887) 36 ChD 329. It is possible also that the common law regarded corporations as unlawful, which would favour the 'lost grant' justification; and see the Companies Act 1985, s 716, prohibiting partnerships above twenty.

application of the word 'person' to groups attempts have been made to invest them with the attributes of human beings, whereas the use of the word is purposive, not descriptive. There is also an unfortunate tendency to react to the emotional connotation of 'person' regardless of whether it is used with reference to human beings or corporations. Thirdly, appreciation of unity is dependent on the viewpoint and context. Thus, a team of footballers would be regarded as a unit by subscribers to the pools, whereas in the eyes of the caterer, who has to provide the celebration after a match, they would be a collection of individuals. So too in law, but here the viewpoint and context are governed by purpose.

The term 'person' in connection with corporations performs different functions from those in connection with human beings. One objective is to facilitate the conferrment of powers on collective undertakings. When large numbers of individuals are involved, it is difficult, if not impossible, to deal with them individually. So the power is conferred on the group as a unit. Corresponding to this is the ascription of collective liability to action at law for what has been done, for which purpose, too, emphasis shifts to the unit. This is only one aspect of the general convenience of unifying the common interests of a large number of people and of working out as one unit a host of similar individual jural relations. Another important advantage is undoubtedly the ability to carry on business with limited liability, that is to say, no member need shoulder the debts of the company to an extent greater than the amount outstanding, if any, on the value of his shares. By contrast, in partnerships for example each partner is fully liable for the debts of the firm[6]. Incorporation is particularly advantageous to the one-man trader, who by forming a company is able to control and profit from the undertaking, and at the same time keep the debts of the company distinct from his own. To achieve this end, courts treat a corporation as having an existence apart from its members. The classic illustration is the celebrated case of *Salomon v Salomon & Co*[7]. Salomon formed a company, consisting of himself, his wife and five children, to which he sold his business at an exorbitant price. Payment took the form of 20,000 fully-paid £1 shares and £10,000 in debentures, ie Salomon purported to lend to the company £10,000, which was the balance owing to him on the purchase price, and he secured this loan by means of debentures. When the company went bankrupt shortly afterwards it owed debts amounting to £17,000, of which £10,000 were owed to Salomon on the purchase price and £7,000 to other unsecured creditors. Its assets only totalled £6,000. The trial judge and the Court of Appeal held that the creditors had the prior claim to the assets since the company was a mere sham. Salomon *was* the company. The House of Lords unanimously reversed this, holding that the company was in law a person distinct from Salomon and that, therefore, Salomon was preferentially entitled to the assets as the secured creditor[8]. An American case illustrating the same point is *People's Pleasure Park Co v Rohleder*[9], where the question arose

---

6 Subject to a slight exception created by the Limited Partnerships Act 1907, ss 4(2) and 6(1).
7 [1897] AC 22. See also *Lee v Lee's Air Farming Ltd* [1961] AC 12, [1960] 3 All ER 420; *Davies v Elsby Bros Ltd* [1960] 3 All ER 672, [1961] 1 WLR 170; *Tunstall v Steigmann* [1962] 2 QB 593, [1962] 2 All ER 417; *R v Arthur* (1967) 111 Sol Jo 435.
8 Cf *Houldsworth v City of Glasgow Bank* (1880) 5 App. Cas. 317. Parliament immediately stepped in to prevent such abuses in future.
9 61 South Eastern Rep 794 (1909). See *Underwood (AL) Ltd v Bank of Liverpool* [1924] 1 KB 775; *Ebbw Vale UDC v South Wales Traffic Area Licensing Authority* [1951] 2 KB 366, [1951] 1 All ER 806; *Pegler v Craven* [1952] 2 QB 69, [1952] 1 All ER 685.

whether a restrictive covenant that title to land should never pass to a coloured person operated to prevent a transfer to a corporation of which all the members were negroes. It was held that the corporation was distinct from its members and that the transfer was valid.

A question that is also asked is whether a corporation can survive the last of its members. Professor Gower mentions a case in which all the members of a company were killed by a bomb while at a general meeting, but the company was deemed to survive[10].

There is also perpetuity of succession, the ability to sue and be sued in the corporate name by outsiders and by members, the ability to acquire and dispose of property as a unit, and the advantage that members may derive the profits while being relieved of the tedium of management. This is the case with large-scale undertakings, especially those in which the public are invited to invest money. The great technicality of modern commercial enterprise requires management by experts, a task which the majority of shareholders are incapable of discharging. This has brought about a cleavage, on the one hand, between membership and management, and, on the other, between ownership, which is in the company, and power, which is exercised by managers. This development is sometimes referred to as the 'managerial revolution'. There is often no effective control over management, for the corporation, being a figure of straw, is incapable of exercising it, nor can the members, who usually lack technical knowledge and, in any case, are too large and diffuse a body to be co-ordinated effectively. It is thus true, as has been said, that shareholders have tended to become little more than recipients of dividends[11].

It follows from the distinction between the corporation and its members that the property of the corporation is not the joint property of the members. What they own are their shares[12]. As Evershed LJ (as he then was) put it,

'Shareholders are not, in the eye of the law, part owners of the undertaking. The undertaking is something different from the totality of the shareholders'[13].

CONTROL OF POWER

The separation of power from ownership of the corporate property and ownership of 'notional property', namely shares, has been taken a step further with parent and subsidiary companies. Company A may own the controlling shares in Company B. The result is that, although Company B remains owner in law of its property, the power of control has passed to Company A, which holds the majority of shares. Power also attaches in different degrees to the ownership of even the shares themselves, for a share in A clearly carries more power than one in B. Control of power in all these kinds of situations has to be applied to its actual source and not to the façade

---

10 *Modern Company Law* p 76 n 45. See also Savigny *System des heutigen römischen Rechts* II, 89; Windscheid *Lehrbuch des Pandektenrechts* I, 61.

11 Berle and Means *The Modern Corporation and Private Property* pp 3, 7–8; Jones 'Forms of Ownership' (1947–48) 22 Tulane Law Review 82–93.

12 As to what is a 'share', see Farwell J in *Borland's Trustees v Steel Bros & Co Ltd* [1901] 1 Ch 279 at 288; *Colonial Bank v Whinney* (1885) 30 ChD 261 at 286, (1886) 11 App Cas 426 at 439; *IRC v Crossman* [1937] AC 26 at 66, [1936] 1 All ER 762 at 777.

13 *Short v Treasury Comrs* [1948] KB 116 at 122, [1947] 2 All ER 298 at 301 (affd [1948] 2 All ER 509). See also Lord Buckmaster in *Macaura v Northern Assurance Co* [1925] AC 619 at 626.

of the legal person. Accordingly, statute stepped in and required, *inter alia*, consolidation of the balance sheet and profit and loss account so as to bring to light assets otherwise hidden[14]. Similarly, Sch 13 of the Transport Act 1947 attached statutory responsibilities to controller companies; and the Health and Safety at Work etc Act 1974, s 37, makes managers and directors personally responsible rather than the company.

The best known method of controlling power is nationalisation of large concerns in the hope that state ownership would prevent anti-social abuses of power. Yet, even this step has not provided the hoped-for safeguard. The reason lies partly in the 'managerial revolution', alluded to earlier[15]. Owing to the technicalities of modern industrial and commercial enterprises the actual power lies in the experts, who manage the business, and not in the company, which is only the formal owner in law. Unless parallel measures are taken to ensure control over managers, nationalisation is simply locking the stable door after the horse has bolted. The dual or multi-party system of government in Western democracies makes it imperative that the managerial boards of nationalised concerns should remain independent of the government of the day if they are to enjoy continuity and function efficiently; and such independence limits control[16]. Another drawback to nationalisation is that it adds political power to economic power, which could leave the individual more oppressed than ever; and a centrally planned economy, which nationalisation is designed to secure, not only brings in its wake a vast bureaucracy and a mass of regulations, but it is also debateable whether it may not in fact hamper rational planning[17].

CONTROL OF LIBERTY

Liberty is freedom of action, and actions can only be performed by human beings, not by abstractions like companies. When it becomes necessary to control freedom of action, the courts 'pierce' or 'lift the veil' of corporate personality in order to take account of the conduct of individuals, whose actions are in question. Courts, therefore, do not always adhere to the separateness of corporate existence, which excludes any consistent theory and emphasises the need to look at what courts do in particular situations.

'Lifting the mask' is an imprecise phrase covering different kinds of inquiries. It is not used in connection with individuals. Yet even with a human being it has to be remembered that 'person' is a purely legal conception and that one is looking at his conduct all the time and imputing it to his legal *persona*. What is special about 'lifting the mask' of corporate personality is that only the conduct of certain individuals is looked at with a view to imputing it to the corporation. A further point is that treating the act of a company as being in reality the act of some individuals is different again when treating the act of Company X as being in reality the act of Company Y, for here the act of some individual has first to be imputed to Company X (to make it the act of X), and then imputed to Y. All three situations are fundamentally alike, but it is pointless to consider what should be the correct

---

14 See *Littlewoods Mail Order Stores Ltd v IRC* [1969] 3 All ER 855, [1969] 1 WLR 1241, CA, where Lord Denning MR was prepared to ignore the separate *persona* of the subsidiary.
15 See p 255 ante.
16 See eg HC Debates of 3rd March 1948 (448 HC Deb 391–455 (5th series) 1948).
17 Cf the editorial comment in *The Soviet Legal System* (eds Hazard, Shapiro and Maggs) p 180.

use of the phrase 'lifting the veil' and then to argue that one of its applications is 'proper' and others 'improper'. It is better simply to describe some of the ways in which courts deal with certain situations.

In the first place, whenever courts find it necessary to take account of behaviour, they have to look at the flesh and blood actors behind the corporate façade. In *Gilford Motor Co v Horne*[18] H entered into a covenant not to compete with the plaintiffs. Later, having left the plaintiffs, he formed a company of his own family and this company then sought the custom of the plaintiffs' customers. H argued that his company could not be bound by the covenant, since it had not entered into one; nor could he be personally answerable, since it was not he but the company which committed the breach. The contention was rejected and the plaintiffs were granted an injunction. In certain other cases the acts of members are imputed to the company, even when they act outside its constitution, provided they still keep within the objects of the company. In *Parker and Cooper Ltd v Reading*[19], an informal ratification by the members was held to bind the company. When considering the misperformance or non-performance of duties only the conduct of individuals can be considered. Thus, a rule designed to promote the performance of duties, eg keeping holy the Sabbath day, is inapplicable to a corporation. 'A limited company is incapable of public worship or repairing to a church, or of exercising itself in the duties of piety and true religion, either publicly or privately, on any day of the week'[20].

Questions of imputation are important in tort and crime. In tort it is usual to distinguish between *intra vires* and *ultra vires* torts. Strictly speaking, the commission of torts is never within the powers of a corporation; what is referred to by *intra vires* torts is torts committed in the course of doing something which is within the powers of the corporation. As to these there is no difficulty: a corporation is answerable on the ordinary principles of vicarious responsibility, which has nothing to do with 'lifting the mask'. However, the law has gone further: the actions of members of the 'supreme directorate' may sometimes be regarded as the 'personal' acts of the corporation. This doctrine is invoked wherever responsibility attaches to a personal or wilful breach of duty, as may be the case, for example, when the duty is statutorily imposed[1]. The utterance of Viscount Haldane LC in *Lennards Carrying Co Ltd v Asiatic Petroleum Co Ltd*[2], has become the *locus classicus*:

> 'In such a case as the present one the fault or privity is the fault or privity of somebody who is not merely a servant or agent for whom the company is liable upon the footing *respondeat superior*, but somebody for whom the company is liable because his action is the very action of the company itself'.

The doctrine is not limited to cases of fault, for it has also been applied in

18 [1933] Ch 935.
19 [1926] Ch 975, distinguishing *Re George Newman Ltd* [1895] 1 Ch 674, on the ground that in that case the acts were *ultra vires* the company itself. See *EBM Co Ltd v Dominion Bank* [1937] 3 All ER 555.
20 Per Mocatta J in *Rolloswin Investments Ltd v Chromolit Portugal Cutelarias e Produtos Metálicos SARL* [1970] 2 All ER 673 at 675, [1970] 1 WLR 912 at 915.
1 Eg the Pipe-lines Act 1962, s 54, imposes responsibility on a corporation where the act is done with the consent or connivance of a senior executive.
2 [1915] AC 705 at 713–714. See on this case *Mackenzie-Kennedy v Air Council* [1927] 2 KB 517 at 533. For breach by wilful act, see *Wheeler v New Merton Board Mills Ltd* [1933] 2 KB 669. See also *HMS Truculent, The Admiralty v The Divina (Owners)* [1952] P 1, [1951] 2 All ER 968.

ascertaining the intention of a landlord company in landlord and tenant law[3].

As to *ultra vires* torts there is a theoretical difficulty. For one thing, chartered corporations do not come within the *ultra vires* rule[4]. With statutory corporations the rule may be that no authority will be implied from the corporation to perform the acts in the course of which such torts were committed[5], or it may be that responsibility is to be determined on the ordinary rule concerning the course of a servant's employment. If there is express authority, Winfield argued that the corporation should be answerable as a joint tortfeasor[6]. A contrary view was put forward by Professor Goodhart[7]. Even where there is no express authority, many writers submit that the corporation should be answerable for the acts of its governing body. The only decided case, not a very satisfactory one, is *Campbell v Paddington Corpn*[8], which is in support of responsibility.

In criminal law the old procedural difficulties were removed by statute[9]. The theoretical difficulties have been overcome, partly by statute and partly by bold decisions, so that now a corporation can be made answerable even for crimes involving *mens rea* on the basis that the acts of the 'supreme directorate' are the personal acts of the corporation[10].

In the interests of national safety courts have also sought to ascertain whether a company is to be treated as an 'enemy company' in time of war. During the 1914–18 war in *Daimler Co Ltd v Continental Tyre and Rubber Co (Gt Britain) Ltd*[11], a company, which was incorporated in England, was nevertheless held by the majority of the House of Lords to possess enemy character because all its directors and shareholders except one were Germans. This is not a departure from the rule that a company is distinct from its members, but only shows that its friendly or enemy character is to be ascertained by looking behind the mask. It was held in another case that a company, which

3 *H L Bolton (Engineering) Co Ltd v T J Graham & Sons Ltd* [1957] 1 QB 159 at 173, [1956] 3 All ER 624 at 630. Shipping law: *The Lady Gwendolen* [1965] P 294, [1965] 2 All ER 283. For the residence of a company see *Unit Construction Co Ltd v Bullock* [1960] AC 351, [1959] 3 All ER 831. Where a company is the victim, the knowledge of its directors is not notionally transmitted to it: *Belmont Finance Corpn Ltd v Williams Furniture Ltd* [1979] Ch 250, [1979] 1 All ER 118, CA.
4 *Sutton's Hospital Case* (1612) 10 Co. Rep. 23a.
5 Arguing from *Poulton v London and South Western Rly Co* (1867) LR 2 QB 534.
6 Winfield on *Tort* (7th edn) pp 82–83; see now 12th edn, pp 692–693.
7 Goodhart 'Corporate Liability in Tort and the Doctrine of Ultra Vires' in *Essays in Jurisprudence and the Common Law* ch 5.
8 [1911] 1 KB 869.
9 Criminal Justice Act 1925, s 33(3); Magistrates' Courts Act 1980, Sch 3; Companies Act 1985, ss 210, 732.
10 *DPP v Kent and Sussex Contractors Ltd* [1944] KB 146, [1944] 1 All ER 119; *R v ICR Haulage Ltd* [1944] KB 551, [1944] 1 All ER 691; *Moore v Bresler (I) Ltd* [1944] 2 All ER 515. Where defendant is the sole responsible person in a company, there can be no conspiracy between him and the company: *R v McDonnell* [1966] 1 QB 233, [1966] 1 All ER 193. There is no imputation of acts of persons who are not in responsible positions: *J Henshall (Quarries) Ltd v Harvey* [1965] 2 QB 233, [1965] 1 All ER 725; *Magna Plant v Mitchell* (1966) 110 Sol Jo 349. In *Essendon Engineering Co Ltd v Maile* [1982] RTR 260, it was said that for a company to be guilty of a crime involving *mens rea*, the company must have given the individual full discretion to act independently of instructions from the company and have the necessary knowledge.
11 [1916] 2 AC 307. So, too, a company in a neutral country which becomes effectively controlled by the enemy owing to occupation: *V/O Sovfracht v Gebr van Udens Scheepvaart en Agentuur Maatschappij* [1943] AC 203, [1943] 1 All ER 76.

acquires enemy character in this way, still remains an English company, at all events if it had been registered in England[12].

Public policy may make it necessary to look at the realities behind the corporate façade. Covenants in restraint of trade are viewed more strictly when imposed on employees than on others[13]. In the leading case of *Nordenfelt v Maxim Nordenfelt Guns and Ammunition Co*[14], it was held that for this purpose covenants by the managing director of a company were to be treated as covenants by a seller and not an employee. In another type of case, *Dimes v Grand Junction Canal Co*[15], the Lord Chancellor himself had an interest as a shareholder in the litigant company. The judges advised the House of Lords that the Lord Chancellor's interest disqualified him from sitting as a judge in the case.

Courts are always vigilant to prevent fraud or evasion[16]. Thus, they will not permit the evasion of statutory obligations. In *Re FG (Films) Ltd*[17], a film was made nominally by a British company, which had been formed for this purpose with £100 capital of which £90 were held by the director of an American company. The film was financed and produced by the American company, and it was held that the British company was not the maker of it within the meaning of the Cinematographic Films Act 1948, ss 25(1)(a) and 44(1), but that it was purely the nominee of the American company[18]. This case and others like it are examples of the mask of corporate unity being lifted and account being taken of what lies behind in order to prevent fraud. The converse situation is also true: if a person finds it to his advantage to disregard corporate unity, he may discover to his discomfiture that the courts refuse to do so[19].

Devlin J once said 'the legislature can forge a sledge-hammer capable of cracking open the corporate shell[20], and the legislature has done so in a variety of statutes, principally to prevent the evasion of tax and other forms of revenue[1]. The Companies Act 1985, s 24, casts responsibility personally on members of a company which carries on business for longer than six months after the membership has fallen below a stated minimum, provided that they know it has fallen. Sections 348–350 similarly cast responsibility on the individuals concerned for a failure to publish the name of the company

---

12 *Kuenigl v Donnersmarck* [1955] 1 QB 515, [1955] 1 All ER 46.
13 *Ronbar Enterprises Ltd v Green* [1954] 2 All ER 266, at 270; p 211 ante.
14 [1894] AC 535. See also *Connors Bros Ltd v Connors* [1940] 4 All ER 179.
15 (1852) 3 HLC 759. For a different sort of situation, see *Littlewoods Mail Order Stores Ltd v IRC* [1969] 3 All ER 855, [1969] 1 WLR 1241.
16 See *Pioneer Laundry and Dry Cleaners Ltd v Minister of National Revenue* [1940] AC 127 at 137, [1939] 4 All ER 254 at 259.
17 [1953] 1 All ER 615.
18 See also *S Berendsen Ltd v IRC* [1958] Ch 1, [1957] 2 All ER 612; *Unit Construction Co Ltd v Bullock (Inspector of Taxes)* [1960] AC 351, [1959] 3 All ER 831; *Barclays Bank Ltd v IRC* [1961] AC 509, [1960] 2 All ER 817; *IRC v Harton Coal Co Ltd* [1960] Ch 563, [1960] 3 All ER 48; *Jones v Lipman* [1962] 1 All ER 442, [1962] 1 WLR 832; *Wallersteiner v Moir* [1974] 3 All ER 217 at 237–238, [1974] 1 WLR 991 at 1013; *US v Lehigh Valley RR Co* 220 US 257 (1911) (American); *McDuff Co Ltd v Johannesburg Consolidated Investment Co Ltd* 1924 AD 573 (SA).
19 *Macaura v Northern Assurance Co* [1925] AC 619; *Pioneer Laundry and Dry Cleaners Ltd v Minister of National Revenue* [1940] AC 127 at 137, [1939] 4 All ER 254 at 259.
20 *Bank Voor Handel en Scheepvaart v Slatford* [1953] 1 QB 248 at 278, [1951] 2 All ER 779 at 799.
1 Various Finance Acts eg: 1936, s 18; 1937, s 14(5); 1940, ss 44, 46, 55; 1950, ss 26, 46; *Gramophone and Typewriter Ltd v Stanley* [1908] 2 KB 89 at 95–96.

in the appropriate manner. In s 458 it is laid down that if on winding up it appears that the business of a company has been conducted for fraudulent purposes, all persons who were knowingly parties to such transactions are to be personally responsible.

Even apart from express legislative provision, courts will take account of the realities of a situation in order to give effect to legislative purpose[2].

MISCELLANEOUS PURPOSES

There are various other cases in which the courts have proceeded on what can only be described compendiously as justice and convenience. Even with the *persona* of a human being there is flexibility in the attitude of the law. Thus, courts are free to decide when the jural relations vest. Normally, this occurs at birth, although pre-natal existence is recognised for many purposes. Thus, a child can succeed in tort after it is born on account of damage caused by a pre-natal injury to its mother[3]. Damages may also be recovered under the Fatal Accidents Act 1976, for the benefit of a posthumous child[4]. Ownership may be vested in a child *en ventre sa mère*, and such a child constitutes a 'life' for the purpose of the rule against perpetuities[5]. So, too, such a child can be a 'child of the family' within s 16(1) of the Matrimonial Proceedings (Magistrates' Court) Act 1960[6]. In criminal law the infliction of a pre-natal injury on a child, which is 'capable of being born alive', and which prevents it from being so born could amount to the offence of child destruction[7], while a similar injury which brings about the death of the child after it has been born alive could amount to homicide[8]. It has also been held that to incite someone to murder a child when it is born, but which at the time of inciting is unborn, amounts to soliciting to murder a 'person'[9]. The present relaxation of the law against abortion has not affected the legal concept of person, although it has, of course, raised grave moral and social issues[10]. These vital debates may conceivably bring about a change in the moment at which a person is deemed to 'exist' in law; but this is another matter. Another instance of the recognition of life not yet in being was contained in the old rule that a pregnant murderess was not to be executed until after her child had been born, and the Sentence of Death (Expectant Mothers) Act 1931, substituted life imprisonment for the death penalty in such a case.

The precise moment when a child is deemed to be 'born' cannot be embodied in a neat formula. The point is important in criminal law, where the present state of the law is the result of individual decisions. Thus, the child must have emerged completely and alive from the mother's body, but it is not necessary for the umbilical cord to have been severed, nor is

---

2 *Merchandise Transport Ltd v British Transport Commission* [1962] 2 QB 173, [1961] 3 All ER 495.
3 Congenital Disabilities (Civil Liability) Act 1976.
4 Even prior to the Act: see *The George and Richard* (1871) LR 3 A & E 466.
5 *Elliot v Lord Joicey* [1935] AC 209; *Re Stern, Bartlett v Stern* [1962] Ch 732, [1961] 3 All ER 1129. See also Variation of Trusts Act 1958, s 1(1).
6 *Caller v Caller* [1968] P 39, [1966] 2 All ER 754.
7 Infant Life (Preservation) Act 1929, s 1.
8 *R v Senior* (1832) 1 Mood CC 346.
9 *R v Shephard* [1919] 2 KB 125.
10 G L Williams *The Sanctity of Life and the Criminal Law* ch 5.

breathing the sole test of being 'alive'[11]. Once a child has been born it is a 'person' and becomes the focus of a host of jural relations.

Since their attribution and continued attribution are a contrivance of law, it is possible to withdraw them during life. Thus, at one time a human being who had been declared an 'outlaw' ceased to be a 'person' in the eyes of the law, and killing him was not homicide. A few other points are also worthy of mention. There is a misleading expression that 'husband and wife are one in law'. Taken literally this would imply that there could never be murder of one spouse by the other, but only a form of suicide. It is a clumsy way of expressing the operation of certain special rules that apply to husbands and wives, and by no means the assertion of single personality[12]. For certain other purposes, however, several individuals may be treated as one person. Thus, the Income Tax Act 1952, s 256(3), says that in order to determine the control of a company, 'persons who are relatives of one another, persons who are nominees of any other person together with that other person, persons in partnership and persons interested in any shares or obligations of the company which are subject to any trust or are part of the estate of a deceased person shall respectively be treated as a single person'[13].

Again, it is possible to categorise and sub-divide an individual's jural relations. When such groupings are related to certain types of individuals (distinguished, eg by role, social, or racial characteristics), they constitute 'status', which may be limited or extensive, eg status of parent, husband etc. When groupings are related to certain types of jural relations, they constitute 'capacity'. Different groupings of these latter may be vested in the same individual, in which case he is said to possess different capacities. He may, for instance, convey property to himself or contract with himself acting in different capacities[14], but none of this connotes dual personality[15].

A human being ceases to be a person, in law as in fact, at death. The moment of death used to present few, if any, problems, but modern survival techniques and the transplanting of living organs has opened up possibilities with profound moral, social and legal implications. Techniques are still in an experimental stage and medical experts have much to perfect and discover. This being the case, lawyers must inevitably await clarification of the data before they can re-shape the concept of death and others associated with it.

Although legal interest in a human being as a person ceases at his death, it continues in some other respects. The most important of these is the law of testamentary succession, by which the wishes of the deceased as to the disposal of his property are given effect. The criminal law ensures a decent burial for his body[16], and the law of criminal libel protects his reputation, but only when an attack upon it affects living persons[17]. Certain actions at

11 *R v Poulton* (1832) 5 C & P 329; *R v Reeves* (1839) 9 C & P 25; *R v Enoch* (1833) 5 C & P 539. For discussion, see *Williams* ch 1.
12 Maule J in *Wenman v Ash* (1853) 13 CB 836 at 844; and see now Law Reform (Husband and Wife) Act 1962.
13 *Morrison Holdings Ltd v IRC* [1966] 1 All ER 789, [1966] 1 WLR 553. See now the Income and Corporation Taxes Act 1970, s. 533 (2), (4).
14 *Rowley, Holmes & Co v Barber* [1977] 1 All ER 801, [1977] 1 WLR 371 (contract).
15 Cf Re *Neil McLeod & Sons, Petitioners* 1967 SLT 46, Ct of Sess: articles of association required a quorum of three members to be personally present. Two shareholders attended. Held that the requirement was satisfied, since one attended both as an individual and as a trustee. It is submitted that this is incorrect, because trusteeship does not constitute a different *persona*.
16 *R v Stewart* (1840) 12 Ad & El 773 at 777–778.
17 *R v Ensor* (1887) 3 TLR 366.

law which he would have had during his life, or which would have lain against him, are continued for or against his estate[18].

The *persona* of a company may likewise be disregarded in the interests of justice and convenience. Thus at times a company may be treated merely as the agent of its members, particularly when the members themselves are companies. In *The Roberta*[19] company X acted admittedly as the agent of company Y, which was in turn wholly owned by company Z, and Z was held liable. A different situation arose in *The Abbey, Malvern Wells Ltd v Ministry of Local Government and Planning*[20], where a trust on which the shares in a company were held affected the company. In *Jones v Lipman*[1] the transfer of property by the defendant to a company, which he controlled, in order to avoid specific performance was held to be a sham, and specific performance was ordered. In *DHN Food Distributors Ltd v Tower Hamlets London Borough Council*[2] the corporate *personae* of three separate concerns were pierced so as to take account of the essential unity of all their claims and of the enterprise as a whole. Finally, in *Lonrho Ltd v Shell Petroleum Co Ltd*[3] it was held that documents in the possession of the directors of subsidiary companies do not indicate that the parent companies have power over them for the purpose of discovery of documents. Whether parent companies have such power or not depends on the facts of each case.

In carving these exceptions out of the doctrine of the separateness of the corporate entity the legislature and the courts seem to have proceeded on value considerations. That they have not been acting on a consistent principle is only too obvious. The point gains force from the fact that the law has found ways of dealing with group activities without resorting to the concept of 'corporate person'.

UNINCORPORATED ASSOCIATIONS

It is not necessary to deal with these in any detail. A few remarks might be made about trade unions, friendly societies and partnerships[4].

Registered trade unions have the power to bring actions[5], while other unincorporated associations cannot do so but their members must proceed

18 Law Reform (Miscellaneous Provisions) Act 1934, as amended by the Proceedings Against Estates Act 1970, and Law Reform (Miscellaneous Provisions) Act 1971, s 2.
19 (1937) 58 Ll L Rep 159 at 159, 169; *Rainham Chemical Works Ltd v Belvedere Fish Guano Co Ltd* [1921] 2 AC 465.
20 [1951] Ch 728, [1951] 2 All ER 154. See also *Re Bugle Press Ltd, Re Houses and Estates Ltd* [1961] Ch 270, [1960] 3 All ER 791.
 1 [1962] 1 All ER 442, [1962] 1 WLR 832.
 2 [1976] 3 All ER 462, [1976] 1 WLR 852.
 3 [1980] 1 WLR 627. See also *Orri v Moundreas* [1981] Com LR 168; *Canada Enterprises Corpn Ltd v Macnab Distilleries Ltd* [1981] Com LR 167, CA.
 4 These are not exhaustive, eg Universities Central Council on Admissions, on which see *Willis v Association of Universities of the British Commonwealth* [1965] 1 QB 140 at 148, 152, [1964] 2 All ER 39 at 42, 44, where Lord Denning MR spoke of the Council as 'a separate entity', while Salmon LJ spoke of it as 'a separate entity' although not 'a separate legal entity'. The Victorian Supreme Court held that the Victorian Soccer Federation was an unincorporated association, which could be sued in its collective name: *Bailey v Victorian Soccer Federation* [1976] VR 13. The Central Office of the Conservative Party is not an unincorporated association: *Conservative and Unionist Central Office v Burrell* [1982] 2 All ER 1, [1982] 1 WLR 522.
 5 *National Union of General and Municipal Workers v Gillian* [1946] KB 81, [1945] 2 All ER 593; *Willis v Brooks* [1947] 1 All ER 191; *British Motor Trade Association v Salvadori* [1949] Ch 556, [1949] 1 All ER 208.

by what are known as representative actions[6]. Further, it was held in *Taff Vale Rly Co v Amalgamated Society of Railway Servants*[7] that a trade union could be sued in tort. The effect of this decision has been modified by successive statutes reflecting the political persuasion of the government in power[8]. It is not clear whether a trade union can commit a tort, but no action can be brought[9], or whether no tort at all is committed. In *Longdon-Griffiths v Smith*[10] it was held that a friendly society can be sued in tort in its registered name. In *Bonsor v Musicians' Union*[11] the House of Lords held that a member can sue a trade union as a legal entity for breach of contract. Thirdly, the Trade Union Act 1871, s 8, laid down that the property of trade unions was to be held by trustees, and it was to protect this property, collected with such trouble, that the Trade Disputes Act 1906, was passed. Making trade unions suable, as in *Bonsor*'s case, created a difficulty as to how judgments against them were to be enforced, since the property was in the hands of trustees[12]. Another difficulty was illustrated by the case of *Free Church of Scotland (General Assembly) v Lord Overtoun*[13], in which the House of Lords refused to sanction the use of the funds for purposes other than those to which they were devoted according to the terms of the trust, despite the fact that the religious views of the majority had changed in the meantime. 'The dead hand of the law fell with a resounding slap on the living body' said Maitland, and in the end the legislature had to step in and allow the desired change. Trade unions and other unincorporated associations also have powers in regard to the treatment of their members and the trend with regard to unions has been to reduce the supervision by courts[14]. As to the criminal, or quasi-criminal responsibility of unincorporated associations, it is to be noted that the Road Traffic Act 1960, s 118(3)(a) spoke of 'any association of persons (whether incorporated or not)'. Earlier in *Wurzel v Houghton Main Home Delivery Service Ltd, Wurzel v Atkinson*[15], where two societies, one of which was incorporated and the other unincorporated, had delivered coal to their members, it was held that the former, being an entity apart from its members, had infringed the terms of its vehicle licence, but not the latter. On the other hand, in *Trebanog Working Men's Club and Institute Ltd v Macdonald*[16], the mask was

6 RSC Ord 15, r 12: eg *Woodford v Smith* [1970] 1 All ER 1091, [1970] 1 WLR 806; unregistered trade union: *Hodgson v National and Local Government Officers Association* [1972] 1 All ER 15, [1972] 1 WLR 130.
7 [1901] AC 426; see the remarks of Lord Brampton at 442 to the effect that a trade union is a legal person. Cf *Rookes v Barnard* [1964] AC 1129, [1964] 1 All ER 367.
8 Trade Disputes Act 1906, s 4. Subsequent and current legislation should be sought in books on industrial law.
9 The words of Farwell LJ in *Conway v Wade* [1908] 2 KB 844 at 856 'the legislature cannot make evil good, but it can make it not actionable', suggest that there is a tort but that it is unenforceable. Cf *Electrical, Electronic, Telecommunication and Plumbing Union v Times Newspaper Ltd* [1980] QB 585, [1980] 1 All ER 1097, where it was held that the Trade Union and Labour Relations Act 1974, deprived trade unions of their quasi-corporate status so that a union cannot be defamed.
10 [1951] 1 KB 295, [1950] 2 All ER 662.
11 [1956] AC 104, [1955] 3 All ER 518.
12 Lord Somervell in *Bonsor*'s case [1956] AC 104 at 157, [1955] 3 All ER 518 at 543, suggested that the trustees should be made parties to the action. See *Keys v Boulter* [1971] 1 QB 300, [1971] 1 All ER 289.
13 [1904] AC 515.
14 The degree of control has varied under different governments.
15 [1937] 1 KB 380. See also the Insurance Companies Act 1982, s. 92 (1).
16 [1940] 1 KB 576, [1940] 1 All ER 454. It is to be noted that the same judge decided both cases. See *Heatons Transport (St Helens) Ltd v Transport and General Workers Union* [1973] AC 15, [1972] 3 All ER 101.

lifted from an incorporated society and the sale of liquor to its members was held not to be a sale between two distinct persons.

Partnerships are invariably contrasted with corporations and are not called 'persons'. Nevertheless, a firm can sue and be sued in its own name[17], and partnership property is distinct from the property of its members. Thus, it is the firm that is placed under the duty to indemnify its members in respect of payments made or responsibilities incurred in the course of partnership business[18]. However, a partnership is not a legal entity in the sense that a partner may make a contract of employment with the firm[19].

ADAPTATION TO CHANGE

The greatest social change has been the introduction of nationalisation, which was effected through the concept of the public corporation.

Public corporations

These have been in existence for some time, but they came into prominence with nationalisation[20]. The principal features are, firstly, that they have no shareholders, ie no human sub-stratum. The Minister appoints the managing boards. Secondly, they have no subscribed share capital. In some cases where an existing company was nationalised, its share capital was nationalised too[1]. Generally where industries have been nationalised, the assets have also been transferred to the public corporations. Thirdly, the extent of the claims, liberties, powers and immunities enjoyed by them is regulated by the statutes which create them[2].

When these corporations were created it was sought to make them independent of the government of the day and political influence generally in order to assure them of continuity, and at the same time to provide 'democratic' methods of control, namely, through the courts and through ministerial responsibility in Parliament. This is a matter of the closest concern to constitutional lawyers[3].

Is the legal concept of 'person' efficient?

'Efficiency' is always relative to the task to be accomplished and the end in view. So one answer is that the flexibilities inherent in treating 'person' as a unity of jural relations does enable courts to do 'justice' in its broadest sense. On the other hand, the way in which the idea has been extended to corporations is no longer suited to modern commerce. Here it is not flexible enough, for the influence of the *Salomon* doctrine[4] has a stultifying effect. So experienced a judge as Lord Wilberforce drew attention to this[5]. For instance, as

17 RSC Ord 81 CCR Ord 5, r 9.
18 Partnership Act 1890, s 24(2).
19 *Re Thorne and New Brunswick Workmen's Compensation Board* (1962) 33 DLR (2d) 167 (Canadian).
20 Friedmann 'The New Public Corporations and the Law' (1947) 10 MLR 236-237.
1 Eg Bank of England Act 1946; Cable and Wireless Act 1946.
2 A judicial description of the public corporation comes from Denning LJ in *Tamlin v Hannaford* [1950] 1 KB 18 at 23, [1949] 2 All ER 327 at 328.
3 For Parliamentary control, see House of Commons Debates, March 3 1948; Report of the *Select Committee on Nationalised Industries* (HC 235 of 1952/1953/1955).
4 [1897] AC 22; p 254 ante.
5 'Law and Economics' Presidential Address to the Holdsworth Club 1966, especially at pp 6-13.

he pointed out, the separate *persona* of a corporation fails to cope with the problems of parent and subsidiary companies. Again, there are other urgent questions which the *Salomon* doctrine does not even begin to answer, eg what is 'capital' and 'income' when deciding whether a gain is taxable? How should directors balance the interests of society, shareholders and workers? Should a company go in for long term or short term profits? How far, if at all, should profits be apportioned between welfare purposes and shareholders? What of a company carrying on diverse activities some of which prosper while others fail? Even the great boon of limited liability could be achieved by means of a rule limiting the responsibility of members to shares without tying this to a doctrine of separate *persona*. A more useful basis of approaching some at least of these problems is to take the corporate *enterprise* as the unit, rather than the corporation[6].

On the other hand, the value of personifying group activities is further reduced by the fact that courts have evolved ways of dealing with such activities without resorting to the device of *persona*. The power and liability of unincorporated associations to sue and be sued, sometimes in their own names and sometimes by representative actions, has been mentioned. The relationship between their members can be regulated by holding that the payment of subscription constitutes a contract between them. The property of such organisations can be dealt with by utilising trust ownership, or a form of co-ownership. The latter would be rather special, since the owners are a changing body and enjoyment of the property is limited by membership[7].

From all this the uneven treatment of corporations and groups may be appreciated. The courts have refused to commit themselves to any single theory about the nature of legal persons[8], so the views of some writers on the subject will now be considered.

THEORIES OF THE NATURE OF 'LEGAL PERSONS'

Professor Wolff has observed that on the Continent legal writers may be grouped into two categories: those who have written on the nature of legal persons and those who have not yet done so[9]. In dealing with some of these theories it is as well to bear in mind that the attitude of the law has not been consistent and also that there is a distinction between appreciating the unity of a group and the way the word 'person' is used.

'PURPOSE' THEORY

This theory, that of Brinz primarily, and developed in England by Barker[10], is based on the assumption that 'person' is applicable only to human beings; they alone can be the subjects of jural relations. The so-called 'juristic'

6 *DHN Food Distributors Ltd v Tower Hamlets London Borough Council* [1976] 3 All ER 462, [1976] 1 WLR 852; and see p 266 post.
7 As to when a club ceases to exist, see *Re GKN Bolts and Nuts Ltd Sports and Social Club, Leek v Donkersley* [1982] 2 All ER 855, [1982] 1 WLR 774.
8 For the use of 'quasi-corporation', see *IRC v Bew Estates Ltd* [1956] 2 All ER 210 at 213; *Knight and Searle v Dove* [1964] 2 QB 631, [1964] 2 All ER 307.
9 Wolff 'On the Nature of Legal Persons' (1938) 54 LQR 494.
10 Brinz *Lehrbuch der Pandekten* 1, pp 196–238; III, pp 453–586; Barker in his translation of Gierke *Natural Law and the Theory of Society* lxxiii–lxxxvii.

persons are not persons at all. Since they are treated as distinct from their human sub-stratum, if any, and since jural relations can only vest in human beings, they should be regarded simply as 'subjectless properties' designed for certain purposes. It should be noted that this theory assumes that other people may owe duties towards these 'subjectless properties' without there being correlative claims, which is not impossible, although critics have attacked the theory on this ground. As applied to ownership, the idea of ownerless ownership is unusual, but that is not necessarily an objection. The theory was designed mainly to explain the foundation, the *Stiftung* of German law, and it would also explain the vacant inheritance, the *hereditas jacens*, of Roman law. It is not applicable to English law. Judges have repeatedly asserted that corporations, for instance, are 'persons', and it is this use of the word that needs explaining. If they say that these are 'persons', then to challenge this usage would amount simply to using the word differently from judges.

To Duguit 'purpose' assumed a different meaning. To him the endeavour of law in its widest sense is the achievement of social solidarity. The question is always whether a given group is pursuing a purpose which conforms with social solidarity. If it does, then all activities falling within that purpose deserve protection. He rejected the idea of collective will as unproven; but there can be, he said, a collective purpose[11].

THEORY OF THE 'ENTERPRISE ENTITY'

Related, though somewhat removed from the above, is the theory of the 'enterprise entity'. The corporate entity, it is said, is based on the reality of the underlying enterprise[12]. Approval by law of the corporate form establishes a *prima facie* case that the assets, activities and responsibilities of the corporation are part of the enterprise. Where there is no formal approval by law, the existence, extent of responsibility and so forth of the unit are determined by the underlying enterprise.

This way of looking at it does explain the attitude of the law towards unincorporated associations and also leaves room for the miscellaneous situations in which corporate unity is ignored. The theory is an utilitarian one.

'SYMBOLIST' OR 'BRACKET' THEORY

According to Ihering[13] the members of a corporation and the beneficiaries of a foundation are the only 'persons'. 'Juristic person' is but a symbol to help in effectuating the purpose of the group, it amounts to putting a bracket round the members in order to treat them as a unit. This theory, too, assumes that the use of the word 'person' is confined to human beings. It does not explain foundations for the benefit of mankind generally or for animals[14]. Also—and this is not so much an objection as a comment—this theory does not purport to do more than to say what the facts are that underlie

11 See Duguit *The Progress of Continental Law in the 19th Century* pp 87-100.
12 Berle 'The Theory of Enterprise Entity' (1947) 47 Columbia Law Review 343; Lord Wilberforce in *British Railways Board v Herrington* [1972] AC 877 at 911, 922, [1972] 1 All ER 749 at 769, 779; *DHN Food Distributors Ltd v Tower Hamlets London Borough Council* [1976] 3 All ER 462, [1976] 1 WLR 852.
13 Iherling *Geist des römischen Rechts* III, 356.
14 *Wolff* p 497.

propositions such as, 'X & Co owe Y £5'. It takes no account of the policy of the courts in the varying ways in which they use the phrase, 'X and Co'; whether they will, for instance, lift the mask, ie remove the bracket, or not.

Closely related to this theory is that of Hohfeld, which may be considered next.

HOHFELD'S THEORY

Hohfeld[15] drew a distinction between human beings and 'juristic persons'. The latter, he said, are the creation of arbitrary rules of procedure. Only human beings have claims, duties, powers and liabilities; transactions are conducted by them and it is they who ultimately become entitled and responsible. There are, however, arbitrary rules which limit the extent of their responsibility in various ways, eg to the amount of the shares. The 'corporate person' is merely a procedural form, which is used to work out in a convenient way for immediate purposes a mass of jural relations of a large number of individuals, and to postpone the detailed working out of these relations among the individuals *inter se* for a later and more appropriate occasion.

This theory is purely analytical and, like the preceding one, analyses a corporation out of existence. Although it is reminiscent of a person who fails to see a wood and sees only a collection of trees, it would be unfair to suggest that Hohfeld was advocating that corporations should be viewed in this way. He was only seeking to reduce the corporate concept to ultimate realities. What he said was that the use of group terminology is the means of taking account of mass individual relationships. It is to be noted, however, that he left unexplained the inconsistencies of the law; his theory was not concerned with that aspect of it. Finally, to say that corporate personality is a procedural form may seem to be rather a misleading use of the word 'procedural'. What seems to be meant is that the unity of a corporation is a convenient way of deciding cases in court.

KELSEN'S THEORY

Kelsen[16] began by rejecting, for purposes of law, any contrast between human beings as 'natural persons' and 'juristic persons'. The law is concerned with human beings only in so far as their conduct is the subject of rules, duties and claims. The concept of 'person' is always a matter of law; the biological character of human beings is outside its province. Kelsen also rejected the definition of person as an 'entity' which 'has' claims and duties. The totality of claims and duties *is* the person in law; there is no entity distinct from them. Turning to corporations, he pointed out that it is the conduct of human beings that is the subject matter of claims and duties. A corporation is distinct from one of its members when his conduct is governed not only by claims and duties, but also by a special set of rules which regulates his actions in relation to the other members of the corporation. It is this set of rules that constitutes the corporation. For example, whether the contract of an individual affects only him or the company of which he is a member will depend on whether or not the contract falls within the special set of rules regulating his actions in relation to his fellow members.

15 Hohfeld *Fundamental Legal Conceptions* chs 6 and 7.
16 Kelsen *General Theory of Law and State* pp 93–109; *Pure Theory of Law* pp 168–192.

This theory is also purely analytical and accurate as far as it goes. It omits the policy factors that bring about variations in the attitude of the courts, and it does not explain why the special set of rules, of which Kelsen spoke, is invoked in the case of corporations, but not, eg partnerships. In fairness to Kelsen it must be pointed out that he expressly disclaimed any desire to bring in the policy aspects of the law. All he was concerned to do was to present a formal picture of the structure of the law, and to that extent he did what he set out to do.

'FICTION' THEORY

Its principal supporters are Savigny and Salmond[17]. Juristic persons are only treated *as if* they are persons, ie human beings. It is thought that Sinibald Fieschi, who became Pope Innocent IV in 1243, was the first to employ the idea of *persona ficta; 'cum collegium in causa universitatis fingatur una persona'*[18]. It is clear that the theory presupposes that only human beings are 'properly' called 'persons'. 'Every single man and only the single man is capable of rights', declared Savigny[19]; and again, 'The original concept of personality must coincide with the idea of man'[20]. The theory appears to have originated during the Holy Roman Empire and at the height of Papal authority. Pope Innocent's statement may have been offered as the reason why ecclesiastical bodies could not be excommunicated or be capitally punished. All that the fiction theory asserts is that some groups and institutions are regarded as if they are persons and does not find it necessary to answer why. This gives it flexibility to enable it to accommodate the cases in English law where the mask is lifted and those where it is not, cases where groups are treated as persons for some purposes but not for others, and those where some groups are treated as persons but not others. The popularity of this theory among English writers is explained partly by this very flexibility, partly by its avoidance of metaphysical notions of 'mind' and 'will', and partly by its non-political character.

'CONCESSION' THEORY

This is allied to the fiction theory and, in fact, supporters of the one tend also to support the other. Its main feature is that it regards the dignity of being a 'juristic person' as having to be conceded by the state, ie the law. The identification of 'law' with 'state' is necessary for this theory, but not for the fiction theory. It is a product of the era of the power of the national state, which superseded the Holy Roman Empire and in which the supremacy of the state was emphasised. It follows, therefore, that the concession theory has been used for political purposes to strengthen the state and to suppress autonomous bodies within it. No such body has any claim to recognition as a 'person'. It is a matter of discretion for the state. This is consistent with the deprivation of legal personality from outlaws; but on the other hand it is possible to argue that the common law corporations of English law discredit it somewhat though, even with these, there is a possibility of arguing that they are persons by virtue of a lost royal grant.

17 Salmond *Jurisprudence* 7th edn, s 114.
18 Gierke *Das deutsche Genossenschaftsrecht* III, 279 n 102.
19 Savigny *System des heutigen römischen Rechts* II, 2–3.
20 *Savigny* II, 60.

'REALIST' AND 'ORGANISM' THEORY

The 'realist' theory, of which Gierke is the principal exponent and Maitland a sympathiser[1], asserts that 'juristic persons' enjoy a real existence as a group. A group tends to become a unit and to function as such. The theory is of German origin. Until the time of Bismarck Germany consisted of a large number of separate states. Unification was their ideal, and the movement towards it assumed almost the character of a crusade. The very idea of unity and of collective working has never ceased to be something of a marvel, which may be one reason for the aura of mysticism and emotion which is seldom far from this theory.

The theory opposes the concession theory. Human beings are persons without any concession from the state and, so the argument runs, so far as groups are 'real', they too are automatically persons.

The 'organism' theory, with which the 'realist' theory is closely associated, asserts that groups are persons because they are 'organisms' and correspond biologically to human beings. This is based on a special use of the term 'organism', and the implications of such biological comparison can lead to absurdity[2]. It is said that they have a 'real life'. Professor Wolff points out that if this were true, a contract between two companies whereby one is to go into voluntary liquidation would be void as an agreement to commit suicide[3]. It is also said that they have a 'group will' which is independent of the wills of its component members. Professor Wolff has pointed out that the 'group will' is only the result of mutually influenced wills[4], which indeed every fictionist would admit. To say, on the other hand, that it is a single will is as much a fiction as ever the fictionists asserted. As Gray, quoting Windscheid, said 'To get rid of the fiction of an attributed will, by saying that a corporation has a real general will, is to drive out one fiction by another.'[5]

It has also been stated that group entities are 'real' in a different sense from human beings. The 'reality' is psychical, namely the unity of spirit, purpose, interests and organisation. Even so, it fails to explain the inconsistencies of the law with regard to corporations.

Connected with the realist theory is the 'Institutional' theory which marks a shift in emphasis from an individualist to a collectivist outlook. The individual is integrated into the institution and becomes part of it. The 'pluralist' form of this theory allowed the independent existence of many institutions within the supreme institution of the state. The 'fascist' form of it, however, gave it a twist so as to make the state the only institution, which integrated all others and allowed none to survive in an autonomous condition.

CONCLUSIONS

In the first place, no one explanation takes account of all aspects of the problem, and criticism becomes easy. Two questions should be kept clear:

1 Maitland Introduction to Gierke's *Political Theories of the Middle Ages*.
2 Discussed by Wolff pp 498-499. See, however, Denning LJ in *H L Bolton (Engineering) Co Ltd v T J Graham & Sons Ltd* [1957] 1 QB 159 at 172, [1956] 3 All ER 624 at 630. A 'realist' interpretation can be given to certain aspects of English law, eg when a corporation is said to act, 'personally' through its supreme directorate. See also *Riverstone Meat Co Pty Ltd v Lancashire Shipping Co Ltd* [1961] AC 807 at 861, [1961] 1 All ER 495 at 516.
3 *Wolff* p 501.
4 *Wolff* p 501.
5 *Gray* pp 54-55.

What does any theory set out to explain? and, What does one want a theory to explain? Those that have been considered are philosophical, political or analytical: they are not so much concerned with finding solutions to practical problems as with trying to explain the meaning of the word 'person'. Courts, on the other hand, faced with the solving of practical problems, have proceeded according to policy, not logic. The objectives of the law are not uniform. One of its main purposes in the case of human beings is to regulate behaviour; so there is, on the one hand, constant concern with the performance or non-performance of duties by individuals. With corporations the main purpose is to organise concerted activities and to ascribe collective responsibility therefor; so there is, on the other hand, emphasis on collective powers and liabilities.

Secondly, as has been pointed out by more than one writer, English lawyers have not committed themselves to any theory. There is undoubtedly a good deal of theoretical speculation, but it is not easy to say how much of it affects actual decisions. Authority can sometimes be found in the same case to support different theories[6].

Thirdly, two linguistic fallacies appear to lie at the root of much of the theorising. One is that similarity of language form has masked shifts in meaning and dissimilarities in function. People *speak* of corporations in the same language that they use for human beings, but the word 'person' does not 'mean' the same in the two cases, either in point of what is referred to or function. The other fallacy is the persistent belief that words stand for things. Because the differences in function are obscured by the uniform language, this has led to some curious feats of argumentation to try and find some referent for the word 'person' when used in relation to corporations which is similar to the referent when the word is used in relation to human beings[7]. A glance at the development of the word *persona*, set out at the beginning of this chapter, shows progressive shifts in the ideas represented by it.

There is no 'essence' underlying the various uses of 'person'. The need to take account of the unity of a group and also to preserve flexibility are essential, but neither is tied to the word. The application of it to human beings is something which the law shares with ordinary linguistic usage, although its connotation is slightly different, namely a unit of jural relations. Its application to things other than human beings is purely a matter of legal convenience. Neither the linguistic nor legal usages of 'person' are logical. If corporations aggregate are 'persons', then partnerships and trade unions should be too. The error lies in supposing that there should always be logic. Unless this has been understood, the varied uses of the word will only make it a confusing and emotional irritant.

6 So Pollock *A First Book of Jurisprudence* pp 110-111; 'Has the Common Law Received the Fiction Theory of Corporations?' in *Essays in the Law* p 151; Duff *Personality in Roman Private Law* p 215.
7 *Hart* pp 49-59. Cf Auerbach 'On Professor Hart's Definition and Theory in Jurisprudence' (1956) 9 Journal of Legal Education 39.

READING LIST

A A Berle 'The Theory of Enterprise Entity' (1947) 47 Columbia Law Review 343.

A A Berle and G C Means *The Modern Corporation and Private Property*.

J Burnham *The Managerial Revolution*.

P W Duff *Personality in Roman Private Law* chs 1 and 9.

O Gierke *Political Theories of the Middle Ages* (trans F W Maitland) chs 3, 4 and 8; and F W Maitland's 'Introduction' pp xviii–xliii.

O Gierke *Natural Law and the Theory of Society 1500–1800* (trans E Barker); and E Barker's 'Introduction' pp lvii–lxxxvii.

A L Goodhart *Essays in Jurisprudence and the Common Law* ch 5.

F Hallis *Corporate Personality*.

W N Hohfeld *Fundamental Legal Conceptions as Applied in Judicial Reasoning* (ed W W Cook) chs 6–7.

H Kelsen *General Theory of Law and State* (trans A Wedberg) pp 93–109.

D Lloyd *The Law Relating to Unincorporated Associations* especially the 'Introduction' and 'Conclusion'.

F W Maitland *Collected Papers* (ed H A L Fisher) pp 210, 244, 271, 321.

G W Paton *A Text-Book of Jurisprudence* (4th edn G W Paton and D P Derham) ch 16.

F Pollock and F W Maitland *The History of English Law before the Time of Edward I* pp 511–526.

W A Robson 'The Public Corporation in Britain Today' in *Problems of Nationalised Industry* (ed W A Robson) ch 1.

J W Salmond on *Jurisprudence* (12th edn P J Fitzgerald) ch 10; (see also the 7th edn).

F F Stone 'Ultra Vires and Original Sin' (1939–40) 14 Tulane Law Review 190.

G L Williams *The Sanctity of Life and the Criminal Law* chs 1, 5–6, 8.

P H Winfield 'The Unborn Child' (1942) 8 Cambridge Law Journal 76.

M Wolff 'On the Nature of Legal Persons' (1938) 54 Law Quarterly Review 494.

I M Wormser *The Disregard of the Corporate Fiction and Allied Corporate Problems* chs 1–2.

CHAPTER 13

Possession

Physical control of a thing by a person is a fact external to and independent of laws. When laws came into existence, this fact, known as 'possession'[1], was taken into account in the sense that certain advantages attached to the possessor. In Roman law the chief of these were (a) that possession was *prima facie* evidence of ownership. (b) Possession was the basis of certain remedies, especially the possessory interdicts. Even a wrongful possessor was protected, not only against the world at large, but also against the true owner who dispossessed him without due process of law. (c) Possession was an important condition in the acquisition of ownership in various ways. (d) In the law of pledge possession of the thing pledged constituted the creditor's security without any presumption of ownership. These apply substantially in English law as well where there is also the advantage that the possessor may exceptionally confer a good title on another though he has none himself. In both systems there are other advantages besides these.

If the idea of possession had remained wedded to physical control, the position would have been relatively simple. Difficulties arose when it became necessary, because of the widening of legal activity, to attribute to persons who were not actually in control some or all of the advantages that were enjoyed by persons actually in control. Tradition and technicality combined to complicate the matter. Traditionally possession was the basis in law of these advantages. They attached to a man because he had physical control, which was synonymous with 'possession', but when it became necessary to give the same benefits to a man who was not in control, 'possession' came to be ascribed to him without the need for control. Reasoning then took the form that whenever a man has these advantages, this must be because he has possession[2].

The consequence was to bring about a contrast between actual holding and possession as well as a shift in the meaning of the term 'possession'[3]. Physical control came to be distinguished from possession under the nomenclature of 'custody' or 'detention'. In Roman law it was designated sometimes by the phrase '*in possessione esse*' (as distinct from '*possidere*')[4] or by coupling the word '*possessio*' with such words as '*corporaliter*', '*naturalis*' and '*naturaliter*'. It is suggested that the terms 'custody' for English law and '*detentio*' for Roman law would be the least confusing terminology to adopt.

Three situations had thus become possible. A man could have physical

---

1 For the basis of *possessio* as the Romans saw it, see *D* 41.2.1 *pr*, 41.2.3.5, 43.26.19 *pr*.

2 Neatly summarised by Maitland: Pollock & Maitland *HEL* II, p 31. The same sort of reasoning is found in Roman law: *D* 8.1.20.

3 *Parmee v Mitchell* [1950] 2 KB 199 at 203, [1950] 1 All ER 872 at 874; *Newcastle City Council v Royal Newcastle Hospital* [1959] AC 248 at 255, [1959] 1 All ER 734 at 736; *Towers & Co Ltd v Gray* [1961] 2 QB 351 at 364, [1961] 2 All ER 68 at 73; *R v Purdy* [1975] QB 288 at 298, [1974] 3 All ER 465 at 473; *Sullivan v Earl of Caithness* [1976] QB 966, [1976] 1 All ER 844.

4 In *D* 41.2.10.1 Ulpian explains the distinction.

control without possession and its advantages; he could have possession and its advantages without physical control; or he could have both. Possession, therefore, became a technicality of law. The separation of possession from physical control gave it a flexibility, which the administrators of the law have not been slow to utilise in fulfilling the demands of policy and convenience.

An understanding of the way in which lawyers employ the term 'possession' has been obscured by too much theorising and, worse still, by the distortion of actual decisions so as to fit them into preconceived ideas[5]. Much of this speculation originated in attempts to elucidate possession in Roman law and has been carried over into English law. In order to clarify the approach to the latter, it is worthwhile considering what exactly the Roman jurists did say.

POSSESSION IN ROMAN LAW

A cardinal tenet of the Roman law of property was the protection of *dominium*, or ownership at civil law. The purpose of prescription, *usucapio*, was to avoid leaving ownership in doubt for too long: G 2.44, *Inst* 2.6 *pr*. To complete prescription continuous possession was essential. The object of the institution of pledge, on the other hand, was to secure the creditor by protecting his possession by means of the possessory interdicts. The policies of the law in these two branches could come into conflict as when an usucaptor pledged the thing. The jurists saw no difficulty. Javolenus said that for the purpose of completing prescription, the usucaping debtor possessed the thing, while for (most) other purposes the creditor possessed it: *D* 41.3.16, 41.2.1.15. Similarly, when the usucaptor died, his heir was deemed to continue possession of the thing so as to complete prescription without interruption. For other purposes, however, the heir's possession of it was a new possession beginning at the moment when he actually took it: *D* 4.6.30 *pr*, 41.2.23 *pr*, 41.2.30.5. Again, the basis of the interdicts was possession. In order to make them available to owners, it was necessary sometimes to extend possession artificially. Certain things, such as summer and winter pastures and some wild creatures, which have the *animus revertendi*, were deemed to remain in possession even when they were beyond reach: *D* 41.2.3.15–16, 41.2.3.11, 43.16.1.25.

Possession for the purpose of prescription and the interdicts was not the same as possession for other purposes. Thus, possession of a thing was one of the bases for acquiring through it. Where a thing was given in pledge by an usucaptor, both the pledgor and the pledgee, as just indicated, were deemed to be in possession of it for different purposes; but neither of them was in possession for the purpose of acquiring through it: *D* 41.1.37 *pr*, 41.2.1.15, 41.3.16. Possession of a thing in deposit remained with the depositor and the depositee got only *detentio*. The depositor could thus continue prescribing it. *Sequestratio* was but a form of deposit with someone pending the settlement of a dispute, and the *sequester*-depositee also got only *detentio*. Where, however, the object of the particular *sequestratio* was to halt the prescription of one of

5 The view of possession set out in this chapter was originally suggested by Professor G L Williams and by Dr J W C Turner.

the depositing parties to the dispute, the *sequester* was given possession so as to prevent that party from acquiring title and forestalling the decision: D 16.3.17.1, 41.2.39. This shows that within the contract of deposit itself the incidence of possession varied according to the purpose in hand.

Another way in which the flexibility of possession was utilised was as follows. The person with an immediate 'right' to obtain physical control had an interest worthy of protection by the interdicts; but a person must actually have possession in order to bring them. There was no difficulty; for the purpose of bringing an interdict the person with a 'right' to possess was deemed to be in possession: D 41.2.17 *pr.* A curious extension of possession was to interests, such as servitudes and usufruct. The rule was that holders did not possess the things over which they enjoyed their interests: G 2.93; but their exercise needed protection, especially of the interdicts. The magistrates would appear to have given such protection without regard to theoretical difficulties: *Vatican Fragments* 90, D 46.13.3.13, 17. Later the jurists in attempts at rationalisation argued that the interdicts were given because these persons must in some way have possession. They did not possess the things themselves, so the uncouth solution was to say that they 'possessed the right', not the thing, '*possessio juris*', D 8.4.2; or that they were treated 'as if they possessed', or had a 'sort of possession' of the thing itself, '*quasi possessio*', G 4.139.

Policy was not the only factor that induced the inconsistencies of possession. Convenience played a part. *Traditio brevi manu*, where X held Y's thing and Y purported to transfer it to X, and *constitutum possessorium*, where X transferred a thing to Y but continued to hold it with Y's permission, were both cases where possession was shifted artificially so as to avoid the thing having to be handed back and forth. *Traditio longa manu*, where large and cumbersome objects were transferred by pointing them out to the transferee, was also a means whereby possession shifted in law without the inconvenience of actual delivery.

The dictates of convenience are best illustrated by the acquisition, continuance and loss of possession. Possession was acquired and lost when certain facts existed or ceased to exist, but what these were varied. As a broad generalisation, the facts needed to acquire possession were physical control, '*corpus possessionis*', and an awareness of the situation, '*animus*': *Pauli Sententiae* 5.2.1, D 41.2.3.1. The mental element had to be supplied personally by the acquirer, but the physical element could be supplied either by him or by an instrument, whether inanimate or another person acting in an instrumental capacity: *Pauli Sententiae* 5.2.1. In certain cases the *animus* element was dispensed with, eg the acquisition of possession by a *paterfamilias* through the allowance made to slaves and children, D 41.2.44.1; and by a principal through an agent acting with prior authority, *Pauli Sententiae* 5.2.2, C 7.32.1. Both these relaxations of the normal rule were expressly based on convenience. Fewer facts were needed to continue a possession once acquired than were necessary to acquire it, but they varied from case to case. In some, possession continued despite loss of *animus*, whether temporarily or permanently, and the rule was expressly grounded in convenience: D 41.3.44.6. There are other cases, however, in which loss of *animus* alone did not involve loss of possession: D 41.2.3.6. In some cases a person did not lose possession by losing *corpus* alone, and this rule is also expressly based on convenience: D 41.2.1.14, 41.2.40.1; but there are others in which it was so lost: D 41.2.3.13. A runaway slave continued to be possessed, certainly for the purpose of acquiring ownership of him through continued possession, and this rule, too, was based on convenience: *D* 41.2.1.14; *D* 47.2.17.3. Again, it is said on occasions that both *animus* and *corpus* have to be lost before possession can be lost: *D* 41.2.8, 50.17.153; but at other times that possession was retained even though both were lost: *D* 41.2.27. It is thus obvious that these cases cannot reflect any single principle. Most of them were decisions given in actual situations and were designed to meet the practical requirements of the particular cases.

The way should now be clear towards a general conception of the Roman view of possession. Possession was not one idea, but many. The element common to all these applications seems to be that it was a device of convenience, utilised chiefly to effectuate the policy of the law in different branches. It is in the light of the foregoing that the classic theories on the subject need to be reviewed.

SAVIGNY'S THEORY

The theory which has had enduring influence is that of Savigny, whose pioneer work, *Das Recht des Besitzes*, appeared in 1803[6]. Its appeal lay not only in the fact that it was the first in the field on this topic, but also in that it marked a new departure in scholarship, returning as it did to the Roman originals the silt of gloss and commentary. It also foreshadowed the historical approach with which Savigny's name is for ever associated. The work is the more impressive when it is realised that it was the product of a man as yet in his early twenties. Yet for all that, its substance bears little relation to Roman law and is no more than a brilliant *tour de force*.

Basing his theory mainly on the texts of Paul, Savigny said that possession consisted of two ingredients, *corpus possessionis*, effective control, and *animus domini*, the intention to hold as owner. Since possession involved both these elements the permanent loss of one or the other brought possession to an end. He could not escape, however, from the cases in which possession continued although one was lost, and he sought to explain them by conceding that the temporary loss of one did not matter, provided it was reproducible at will[7]. The proviso was essential to his thesis that possession 'was' both *corpus* and *animus*.

As an explanation of Roman law this theory is demonstrably wrong. In the first place, Savigny overlooked the shift in meaning of the word 'possession', to which attention has been drawn, and he seems to have fallen into the fallacy that words must correspond with some factual counterpart. Hence his desire to find such a content for possession. He also based his statement of this content on the utterances of one jurist, Paul. Academic speculation was never the strong point of the Romans, and Paul was no exception. In any case, it was erroneous to assume that *corpus* and *animus*, which were only *conditions* sometimes required for the acquisition and loss of possession, constituted possession itself. Even Paul's texts, on which Savigny relied so much (*D* 41.2.3.1, *Pauli Sententiae* 5.2.1.), only say, '*apiscimur possessionem corpore et animo*', and again, '*possessionem adquirimus et animo et corpore*': we *acquire* possession by means of *corpus* and *animus*, not that possession

---

6 Savigny *Possession* (Translated by Perry (1848)).
7 *Savigny* pp 253, 266.

is both these things. Savigny's idea of *animus domini*, the intention to hold as owner, fails to explain the cases of the pledgee, emphyteuta, *sequester* and *precario tenens*, who had possession but did not intend to hold as owners. He first condemned them as 'anomalous', hinted at 'historical reasons', and then suggested that they were cases of 'derivative possession', ie possession 'derived from the owner'. If so, why did not *detentors*, such as the borrower, depositee and the tenant, also get possession derived from the owner? It has been said that the only reason for treating these cases as anomalous was their failure to conform to his theory, and that if this theory failed to take account of them, so much the worse for the theory[8]. Puchta, defending Savigny, took the heroic line that these cases should really have been cases of *detentio*, in effect, that if Roman law failed to conform with Savigny's theory, so much the worse for Roman law[9]. Other disciples of Savigny, perceiving the weakness of the *animus domini* idea, altered it to '*animus possidendi*', the intention to exclude other persons. This got rid of the derivative possession fiction, but remained open to two objections: (a) it still did not explain why the borrower and the tenant had only *detentio*, even though they intended to exclude others just as much as possessors, and (b) it is without support in the texts. Finally, the application of Savigny's rigid theory to the continuation and loss of possession starkly reveals its weakness. Possession did sometimes continue despite the loss of *animus* or *corpus* or even both. The most that his theory could allow was that possession was lost when one or the other was lost. When, therefore, his beloved Paul said in two texts that both *animus* and *corpus* have to be lost before possession was lost, he was forced to say that where Paul said '*utrumque*', each of them, he really meant '*alterutrum*', one or the other[10]. Such an escape from the difficulty is comment enough on his theory. Savigny's qualification that mere temporary loss of one ingredient did not matter, provided there was the ability to reproduce it at will, is also inconsistent with the texts. It does not explain, for instance, the continued possession of a fugitive slave, despite the owner's inability to reproduce the *corpus* element at will, nor the continued possession by a madman.

As said at the beginning, Savigny's theory bears little relation to Roman law.

IHERING'S THEORY

It is agreed that Ihering succeeded in demolishing Savigny's theory. He himself approached possession as a sociological jurist[11]. He posed the question why Roman law protected possession by means of the interdicts. They were devised, he said, to benefit owners by protecting their holding of property and so placing them in the advantageous position of defendants in any action as to title. Persons who hold property would be owners in the majority of cases and possession was attributed to them in order to make the interdicts available. Accordingly, he concluded that whenever a person looked like an owner in relation to a thing, he had possession of it, unless possession was denied him by special rules based on practical convenience. The *animus* element was simply an intelligent awareness of the situation. It will be seen at a glance that this is more consonant with the facts of Roman law than

8 Bond 'Possession in the Roman Law' (1890) 6 LQR 259 at 269.
9 Quoted by *Bond* at 270.
10 *D* 41.2.8 and 50.17.153; *Savigny* pp 247, 253.
11 Ihering *Grund des Besitzesschutzes* (1868) *Der Besitwille* (1889).

Savigny's theory. It is flexible: it explains the case of the fugitive slave, who to outward appearances resembles one going on an errand for his master, and above all Ihering did grasp the great point about policy and convenience.

The comment to be offered on this theory is that it appears to be unduly coloured by the angle of his approach, namely, the interdicts. The special reasons of policy that lay behind the interdicts required that the person in control should be protected. To that extent possession for interdictal purposes had a factual basis, but outside that sphere, the factual basis ceases to help. In the case of the usucaptor who pledged a thing, the pledge-creditor, who looked like an owner since he actually had the thing, was in possession for the purpose of the interdicts; but the usucaptor too had possession, though he no longer resembled an owner. He was a person who, though no longer resembling an owner, was allowed to have possession for one special purpose. If this is regarded as an 'exception', based on policy or convenience, to a general rule that whoever looked like an owner in relation to a thing had possession of it, that overlooks the fact that the main rule itself is just as much a rule of policy and convenience as the departures from it. Ihering's main rule can, therefore, be dispensed with and possession described in terms of policy and convenience alone. His formula is an appropriate explanation of interdictal possession. As a more general description, it seems needlessly narrow, but none the less it is superior to Savigny's view.

POSSESSION IN ENGLISH LAW

Notwithstanding the frailty of Savigny's theory as an explanation of Roman law, a modified version of it has exercised considerable influence on English writers. Ihering's hint has passed unheeded by all save a few. The same shift in the meaning of possession has occurred in English as in Roman law: the term is not confined to physical control. As Roskill LJ has said, 'Having something in one's possession does not mean of necessity that one must actually have it on one's person'[12]. This is to some extent reflected in the phrases sometimes encountered, such as 'possession in fact' and 'possession in law'. The former suggests the presence of some factual basis for 'possession in fact', and it may be some such supposition that has paved the way for the acceptance of the ready-made *corpus* and *animus* formula of Savigny, not only by writers but even in some of the cases[13]. The objection to *corpus* and *animus* as comprising possession is that their content has varied so much that they cannot provide a reliable criterion. *Corpus* and *animus* mean different things for different purposes so much so that even possession in fact has come to be no more than a variable concept of the law.

> 'Possession', said Erle CJ 'is one of the most vague of all vague terms, and shifts its meaning according to the subject-matter to which it is applied — varying very much in its sense, as it is introduced either into civil or into criminal proceedings'[14].

---

12 *R v Purdy* [1975] QB 288 at 298, [1974] 3 All ER 465 at 473; and further references on p 272 n 3 ante.
13 *The Tubantia* [1924] P 78 at 89; *Brown v Brash and Ambrose* [1948] 2 KB 247 at 254, [1948] 1 All ER 922 at 925.
14 *R v Smith* (1855) 6 Cox CC 554 at 556.

Lord Parker CJ has expressed the same view:

> 'For my part I approach this case on the basis that the meaning of 'possession' depends on the context in which it is used'[15].

Both statements are apt summaries of the thesis of this chapter. The evidence in support may now be considered, subject to the caution that some of the examples to be given refer to rules and doctrines no longer in force: they are merely historical illustrations.

The question may first be considered how far the holding of a key gives possession of the thing or the place to which it gives access. In *Ancona v Rogers*[16] X was allowed to put her goods in certain rooms in Y's house. X sent them by an agent, who locked them in the rooms allotted for that purpose in Y's house by Y, and took away the key. It was held that X was in possession of the rooms. The court indicated that the delivery of the key accompanied by other facts, such as the appropriation of the rooms by Y to X's use and the acquiescence by Y in the whole proceeding, were sufficient to vest possession in X. The delivery of a key may also be sufficient by itself to pass possession of the contents of a room or a box, at all events if it provides the effective means of control of the goods[17]. On the other hand, for the purpose of satisfying the doctrine of part performance of an unenforceable contract to transfer or dispose of an interest in land, entry into possession is a sufficient act of part performance; but having the key to the premises will not of itself constitute possession of them. The policy of the law is different in part performance. For these contracts are not actionable unless evidenced by a note or memorandum in writing signed by the party to be charged or his agent. The absence of such evidence can be got round by acts of part performance of the agreement, but since these are a substitute for written proof of the contract, they must be unambiguously referable to the contract[18]. Entry into possession of the premises could amount to part performance, for which purpose possession means actual, physical entry[19]. Having only the key will not suffice, for this is open to many interpretations, eg to view the premises.

The old Rent Acts provided instructive examples. It is necessary to distinguish between possession in a landlord of rent-controlled premises and possession in a tenant. Under the Rent and Mortgage Interest Restrictions Act 1923, if the landlord regained possession of the premises, they became decontrolled. Section 2 (3)[20] specified that 'For the purposes of this section, the expression 'possession' shall be construed as meaning 'actual possession', and a landlord shall not be deemed to have come into possession by reason only of a change of tenancy made with consent'. The policy behind this provision was probably what Scrutton LJ thought it was:

15 *Towers & Co Ltd v Gray* [1961] 2 QB 351 at 361, [1961] 2 All ER 68 at 71, approved by Lord Pearce in *Warner v Metropolitan Police Comr* [1969] 2 AC 256 at 304, [1968] 2 All ER 356 at 387; by Fisher J in *Hambleton v Callinan* [1968] 2 QB 427 at 432, [1968] 2 All ER 943 at 945; by Ashworth J in *Woodage v Moss* [1974] 1 All ER 584 at 588, [1974] 1 WLR 411 at 415; and Lord Widgery CJ in *Sullivan v Earl of Caithness* [1976] QB 966 at 969–970; [1976] 1 All ER 844 at 846–847.
16 (1876) 1 Ex D 285.
17 *Jones v Selby* (1710) Prec Ch 300; *Re Mustapha, Mustapha v Wedlake* (1891) 8 TLR 160; *Wrightson v McArthur and Hutchinsons* [1921] 2 KB 807; *Re Lillingston, Pembery v Pembery* [1952] 2 All ER 184; *Re Wasserberg, Union of London and Smiths Ltd v Wasserberg* [1915] 1 Ch 195.
18 *Wakeham v Mackenzie* [1968] 2 All ER 783, [1968] 1 WLR 1175.
19 *Morphett v Jones* (1818) 1 Swan 172 at 181–182; *Brough v Nettleton* [1921] 2 Ch 25.
20 See now the Rent Act 1977.

'I think Parliament in using the phrase 'actual possession' intended to reject the legal right to possess and to require actual control or apparent dominion in fact'[1].

Nevertheless, the courts took the line that if the landlord merely got the key, even momentarily, he got 'actual possession' within the meaning of this section. It was held in *Jewish Maternity Home Trustees v Garfinkle*[2] that having the key for some time amounted to 'actual possession' of the premises. In *Thomas v Metropolitan Housing Corpn Ltd*[3] it was held that dropping the key into the letter box of the office of the landlord's agent, which was closed for the week, was sufficient to give the landlord 'actual possession'. In *Holt v Dawson*[4] the outgoing tenant gave up the key to the landlord's agent, who handed it to the new tenant, and the landlord was held to have come into 'actual possession'. In *Goodier v Cooke*[5] the outgoing tenant and the new tenant met the landlord's agent by appointment five days before the former left the premises. She handed the key to the agent, who immediately handed it over to the new tenant. It was held that the landlord had come into 'actual possession'. It must not be supposed that control of the key is the sole criterion of a landlord's possession, for as Scott LJ was careful to say in *Holt v Dawson*:

'Each of these cases as to actual possession by the landlord must be decided on its own particular circumstances, and the fact that in one case a court or judge has taken a certain view is of little guidance in other cases'[6].

Thus, it was held in *Boynton-Wood v Trueman*[7] that the handing over of the key to the landlord to carry out repairs was not surrender of possession; and in *Michel v Volpe*[8] the possession of a key to a room in a house was held not to give exclusive occupation amounting to a subtenancy.

Possession of controlled premises by tenants was viewed differently from possession by landlords because the policy of the law differed in the two situations. With regard to landlords, the old Rent Acts used originally to be viewed with disfavour as restricting the freedom of property owners to deal with their property as they wished. Judicial policy, which at the time was more vigilant in safeguarding interests in private property than in furthering social experiments, appeared to have sought to minimise the legislative restriction on the freedom of landlords. In possession was found a handy device for pursuing this policy, and a nominal view was adopted of what amounted to regaining possession so that landlords might be freed from the statute on the easiest conditions. With tenants, on the other hand, the judges pursued another line. They sought to protect tenants and to ease the housing shortage, but also to prevent them from taking unfair advantage from their protection. It was summed up by Sir Raymond Evershed MR (as he then was):

'The reason for such a provision, I think, is not far to seek. No one has better laid down the principles of the Rent Restrictions Act than Scrutton LJ and he

---

1 *Hall v Rogers* (1925) 133 LT 44 at 45.
2 (1926) 42 TLR 589.
3 [1936] 1 All ER 210.
4 [1940] 1 KB 46, [1939] 3 All ER 635.
5 [1940] 2 All ER 533.
6 [1940] 1 KB 46 at 53, [1939] 3 All ER 635 at 639.
7 (1961) 177 Estates Gazette 191. Cf *Stadium Finance Ltd v Robbins* [1962] 2 QB 664, [1962] 3 All ER 633 (possession of a car was retained by retaining the ignition key); and *obiter* in *Walker v Rountree* [1963] NI 23.
8 (1967) 202 Estate Gazette 213.

has pointed out that their object was to protect persons who were tenants from eviction, and not to provide some mean whereby tenants could make financial gain out of dealings with rent-controlled property'[9].

To further this aim the courts construed the tenant's possession more strictly than that of the landlord; they even adopted a *corpus* and *animus* view of it. What constituted *corpus* and *animus* in any given case depended on whether the court thought that the tenant was trying to take an unfair advantage or not. In *Brown v Brash and Ambrose*[10], the tenant went to gaol for two years, leaving his mistress in occupation, and after a time she also left. His claim that he remained in possession during that time was rejected by the court. When the tenant was not being unfair, the courts were prepared to protect him and to say that he continued in possession by viewing his *corpus* and *animus* more liberally. In *Tennant v Whytock*[11], where the tenant went to live in Germany with her husband, who was serving with the British Army of Occupation, it was held that she remained in possession. In *Tickner v Hearn*[12] the tenant left the premises to visit her daughter and was taken from there to a mental home. The daughter maintained the premises so that the tenant could eventually return. It was held that the tenant had not lost her possession in the circumstances.

The possession of tenants is also affected by policy with regard to husbands and wives and morality in general. A husband is bound to provide a home for his wife. If, therefore, a tenant deserts his wife and leaves the premises, but she remains, he is deemed to remain in possession through her so that she can be protected against eviction[13]. If, however, the wife has been divorced, she is not protected and the tenant will have lost possession[14]. Nor is protection given to a mistress, and a tenant who leaves the place, but leaves his mistress behind, will have lost possession[15]. There is also another special rule: if a tenant sublets, he is still in possession of the whole of the premises as long as he occupies at least a part, but not otherwise[16].

Turning to the law of tort, the axiom is that possession is the basis of

9 *Regional Properties Co Ltd v Frankenschwerth and Chapman* [1951] 1 KB 631 at 636, [1951] 1 All ER 178 at 181. For similar statements, see *Brown v Brash and Ambrose* [1948] 2 KB 247 at 254, [1948] 1 All ER 922 at 925; *Dixon v Tommis* [1952] 1 All ER 725 at 727; *Paisner v Goodrich* [1955] 2 QB 353 at 357, [1955] 2 All ER 330 at 332; *Gofor Investments v Roberts* (1975) 119 Sol Jo 320.

10 [1948] 2 KB 247, [1948] 1 All ER 922, approved in *Poland v Earl Cadogan* [1980] 3 All ER 544. See also *Thompson v Ward* [1953] 2 QB 153, [1953] 1 All ER 1169; *Bushford v Falco* [1951] 1 All ER 957; *SL Dando Ltd v Hitchcock* [1954] 2 QB 317 at 322, 325, [1954] 2 All ER 335 at 336, 338: *Cove v Flick* [1954] 2 QB 326n, [1954] 2 All ER 441; *Gofor Investments v Roberts* (1975) 119 Sol Jo 320.

11 1947 SLT (Sh Ct) 83; *Hoggett v Hoggett* (1979) 39 P & CR 121, CA.

12 [1961] 1 All ER 65. See also *Langford Property Co Ltd v Tureman* [1949] 1 KB 29; *Wigley v Leigh* [1950] 2 KB 305, [1950] 1 All ER 73; *Dixon v Tommis* [1952] 1 All ER 725; *Beck v Scholtz* [1953] 1 QB 570, [1953] 1 All ER 814.

13 *Old Gate Estates Ltd v Alexander* [1950] 1 KB 311, [1949] 2 All ER 822; *Middleton v Baldock* [1950] 1 KB 657, [1950] 1 All ER 708; *Wabe v Taylor* [1952] 2 QB 735, [1952] 2 All ER 420; *SL Dando Ltd v Hitchcock* [1954] 2 QB 317 at 322, 325, [1954] 2 All ER 335 at 336-337, 338.

14 *Robson v Headland* [1948] WN 438.

15 *Thompson v Ward* [1953] 2 QB 153, [1953] 1 All ER 1169; *Colin Smith Music Ltd v Ridge* [1975] 1 All ER 290, [1975] 1 WLR 463. But see *Dyson Holdings Ltd v Fox* [1976] QB 503, [1975] 3 All ER 1030, CA.

16 *Baker v Turner* [1950] AC 401, [1950] 1 All ER 834; *Berkeley v Papadoyannis* [1954] 2 QB 149, [1954] 2 All ER 409; *Crowhurst v Maidment* [1953] 1 QB 23, [1952] 2 All ER 808; *Cove v Flick* [1954] 2 QB 326n, [1954] 2 All ER 441; *Michel v Volpe* (1967) 202 Estates Gazette 213.

trespass[17], and the policy of this branch of the law is to compensate the party whose interests have been affected. In order to enable such persons to recover, the courts have contrived to attribute possession to them. Bailment is a good illustration. A bailee is a person who gets possession of a chattel from another with his consent. A bailment may be at will, ie revocable by the bailor at any time, or for a term, ie a fixed period of time. Even where a bailment is at will, the bailee, who by definition has possession, can sue a third party in trespass. Since it is revocable at will, the bailor, too, has an interest worth protecting. In order that he might bring trespass, his 'right' to possess is treated as being possession itself. Nothing could be clearer than the words of Viscount Jowitt in *United States of America v Dollfus Mieg et Cie SA*:

> 'Under English law, where there is a simple contract of bailment at will the possession of the goods bailed passes to the bailee. The bailor has in such a case the right to immediate possession, and by reason of this right can exercise those possessory remedies which are available to the possessor. The person having the right to immediate possesis, however, frequently referred to in English law as being the 'possessor'—in truth English law has never worked out a completely logical and exhaustive definition of 'possession'[18].

Lord Parker CJ reiterated the point when he said:

> 'In other cases it may well be that the nature of the bailment is such that the owner of the goods who has parted with the physical possession of them can truly be said still to be in possession'[19].

Where, on the other hand, the bailment is for a term, only the bailee can bring trespass, not the bailor[20], so a special action had to be devised.

Where a master has temporarily handed a thing to his servant it is well known that possession remains in the master and the servant gets only 'custody'. *Meux v Great Eastern Rly Co*[1], shows that it is the master who can sue in trespass for an injury to the thing committed by a third party; but A L Smith LJ said *obiter* that he had no doubt that the servant could also have sued in trespass, implying thereby that possession is concurrently in the servant, although the question would be, as he admitted, as to the quantum of damages[2]. There is also a *dictum* in the earlier case of *Heydon v Smith*[3] that a servant is capable, on these facts, of bringing trespass or an appeal of larceny. *Moore v Robinson*[4] actually decided that a servant could maintain trespass, but the facts suggest that the servant had been constituted a bailee by his master.

Lost property provides another example. A person who loses a thing retains his ownership of it. For the purpose of suing the person who takes it in

17 *Rooth v Wilson* (1817) 1 B & Ald 59 at 62; *Wilson v Lombank Ltd* [1963] 1 All ER 740, [1963] 1 WLR 1294.

18 [1952] AC 582 at 605, [1952] 1 All ER 572 at 581, approved by Lord Wilberforce in *Warner v Metropolitan Police Comr* [1969] 2 AC 256 at 309, [1968] 2 All ER 356 at 391–392. See also YB 2 Edw IV, 25 (Laicon *arg*); *Lotan v Cross* (1810) 2 Camp 464 at 465; *Ancona v Rogers* (1876) 1 Ex D 285 at 292. Cf D 41.2.17 *pr*, where the 'right' to possess was treated as possession for the purpose of an interdict.

19 *Towers & Co Ltd v Gray* [1961] 2 QB 351 at 361–362, [1961] 2 All ER 68 at 71. The bailor may retain his possession even though the bailment is not gratuitous: *Wilson v Lombank Ltd* [1963] 1 All ER 740, [1963] 1 WLR 1294.

20 *Gordon v Harper* (1796) 7 Term Rep 9.

1 [1895] 2 QB 387.

2 [1895] 2 QB 387 at 394.

3 (1610) 13 Co Rep 67 at 69.

4 (1831) 2 B & Ad 817.

conversion his 'right' to regain possession will suffice, and for the purpose of suing such a person in trespass it seems probable that the 'right' to possess will once more be regarded as possession. On the other hand, for the purpose of claiming from the insurance company for the loss, he will be regarded as having lost possession within the terms of the contract, if the thing is not in fact found[5].

In connection with land, the doctrine of 'trespass by relation' is another example of the artificial manipulation of the concept of possession so as to provide a remedy in trespass to one deserving of compensation. When a person with a 'right' to possess enters in pursuance of it, he is deemed to have been in possession from the time when his title originally accrued so that he can sue for any trespass that has been committed between the accrual of the title and entry. 'Entry' is purely technical, and is satisfied merely by making a formal claim so that, in effect, the 'right' to possess here also is being treated as equivalent to possession itself. Again, if two persons are on a piece of land and both do acts to assert possession, the question to whom it is to be attributed is determined according to which of them is entitled to the land[6]. This shows that there is nothing in the factual situation that determines the incidence of possession. It is determined on the basis of title because, as between the two of them, it is the person entitled to the land who deserves compensation by means of an action in trespass against the other. If it is sought to establish possession without proof of title, the 'exclusiveness' of the plaintiff's possession depends on the facts[7].

Professor Goodhart suggested two further rules[8]. (a) A possessor of land possesses everything attached to or under the land. In *Elwes v Brigg Gas Co*[9], a prehistoric boat embedded in the soil, and in *South Staffordshire Water Co v Sharman*[10], two rings buried in the mud in a pool were held to be in the possession of the respective landowners. In *London Corpn v Appleyard*[11] banknotes contained in a wooden box, which was inside a locked safe in the wall of a building, were held to be in the possession of the party who had possession of the land. On the other hand, in *Hannah v Peel*[12] a brooch, which was found by a soldier on requisitioned premises, was held not to have been in the possession of the landowner, who was not at the time in possession of the premises. (b) Things lying loose on the land are not in the possession of the landowner, but fall into the possession of the first finder, at any rate if he is lawfully on the land. In *Armory v Delamirie*[13] a chimney-sweep, while cleaning a flue, discovered a jewel and was held to have acquired possession. In *Bridges v Hawkesworth*[14] a pocketbook was dropped in a shop and was later

5 See Parker in the 9th edn of Salmond's *Jurisprudence* p 388.
6 *Jones v Chapman* (1849) 2 Exch 803 at 821; *Newcastle City Council v Royal Newcastle Hospital* [1959] AC 248 at 255, [1959] 1 All ER 734 at 736; *Ocean Estates Ltd v Pinder* [1969] 2 AC 19, [1969] 2 WLR 1359; *Portland Managements Ltd v Harte* [1977] QB 306, [1976] 1 All ER 225. Cf *D* 41.2.49 *pr*: '*plurimum ex jure possessio mutuetur*', possession borrows a great deal from the right.
7 *Fowley Marine (Emsworth) Ltd v Gafford* [1968] 2 QB 618, [1968] 1 All ER 979.
8 'Three Cases on Possession' in Goodhart *Essays in Jurisprudence and the Common Law* pp 88- See also the 8th Report of the Law Reform Committee (Conversion and Detinue) Annex 1.
9 (1886) 33 ChD 562.
10 [1896] 2 QB 44. Cf *Re Cohen* [1953] Ch 88, [1953] 1 All ER 378.
11 [1963] 2 All ER 834, [1963] 1 WLR 982. But if the owner was known he would have had a better claim: *Moffatt v Kazana* [1969] 2 QB 152, [1968] 3 All ER 271.
12 [1945] KB 509, [1945] 2 All ER 288.
13 (1722) 1 Stra 505.
14 (1851) 15 Jur 1079.

picked up by a customer. It was held that it had never been in the possession of the shopkeeper, and that it was possessed by the finder. So, too, in *Bird v Fort Frances*[15] a boy found some banknotes lying on a sill in private premises, and it was held that he acquired possession of them. In *Grafstein v Holme and Freeman*[16] X found a box in the basement of a building and informed his employer, who instructed him to put it on a shelf. Two years later X investigated the contents and discovered banknotes. It was held that the employer had come into possession when X had reported the find and had placed the box on the shelf. *Crinton v Minister for Justice*[17] shows that if in fact the finder finds as agent for his principal, possession vests in the latter. In *Byrne v Hoare*[18] a police constable, who found a gold ingot on private land, was held entitled to it as against all save the owner[19]. He was not acting as a Crown officer, so the Crown had no claim. Finally, in *Parker v British Airways Board*[20] a passenger, waiting in the lounge of an airways terminal occupied by the defendants, found a gold bracelet, which he handed to an employee of the defendants and gave his name and address. It was held that he had acquired possession of it and not the defendants.

The old law of larceny, which has now been replaced by the Theft Act 1968, provided abundant examples of the manipulation of possession to suit policy, but these need only be summarised[1]. The savagery of the old punishments for even trifling thefts led judges to mitigate the rigour of the law by making it difficult to hold persons guilty. This understandably humane attitude shaped larceny, which required the coincidence of three conditions at the same point of time: (i) a taking of possession, (ii) without the consent of the owner or possessor, and (iii) with intent to steal at the time of the taking. Later the penalties became milder and there was a reversal of policy. The result of making it difficult to secure convictions meant that many obviously dishonest persons escaped punishment. So judges began to juggle with possession so as to make the three requirements coincide with the consequence that possession became completely nebulous. Thus, in cases where a person took possession of a thing innocently and only later formed his intention to steal, several strange rules were evolved. Where the taking of possession was a civil trespass (ie without consent), it was said that this gave rise to a continuing series of fresh takings thereafter so that the subsequent intention to steal could coincide with a taking that was occurring at the moment. In this way it amounted to larceny[2]. In another famous case it was held that a person who received a sovereign in the dark, when both giver and taker believed it to be a shilling, only took possession of the sovereign when he later realised what it was and at that moment intended to appropriate it[3]. Again, a servant, who was handed a thing by his master, could not be guilty of larceny if he was thought to have received possession with consent and

15 [1949] 2 DLR 791.
16 (1958) 12 DLR 727.
17 [1959] Ir Jur Rep 15.
18 (1965) 58 QLR 135.
19 Cf *Moffatt v Kazana* [1969] 2 QB 152, [1968] 3 All ER 271, where the owner was known and was held entitled.
20 [1982] QB 1004, [1982] 1 All ER 834.
 1 For fuller treatment, see the 2nd edn of this book, pp 320-325.
 2 *R v Riley* (1853) Dears CC 149, especially the judgment of Parke B.
 3 *R v Ashwell* (1885) 16 QBD 190; *R v Hudson* [1943] KB 458, [1943] 1 All ER 642; *Russell v Smith* [1958] 1 QB 27, [1957] 2 All ER 796. Cf *Warner v Metropolitan Police Comr* [1969] 2 AC 256, [1968] 2 All ER 356.

without any intention to steal at that moment. In order to catch the servant, who formed his intention to steal later, it was said that he had received only 'custody', not possession, from the master, but that when he formed his dishonest intention, then and only then did he take possession without consent. If, however, a third party took it from the servant, the latter was deemed to have both possession or 'special property' to justify holding the former guilty of larceny from him[4]. Finally, a bailee by definition has possession with consent. Accordingly, to convict the dishonest bailee the courts invented the doctrine of 'breaking bulk'[5], which was to the effect that if the bailee took the thing bailed apart in any way ('broke bulk'), this determined the bailment, possession revested in the bailor and the bailee then took a new possession without consent and with intent to steal.

Larceny also required that possession be 'laid' in someone from whom the theft took place. This, too, was artificially extended. For instance, a loser of a thing was deemed still to be in possession so that a dishonest finder could be held guilty[6]. Things lying loose on land were likewise deemed to be in the possession of the landowner, unlike the rule in tort[7]. These and the foregoing examples should demonstrate the attitude of the old law of larceny towards possession: it was viewed in whatever way was most apt for punishing wickedness. Happily, the Theft Act 1968, has relegated them all to the historical shelf.

An important contemporary concern of the criminal law with possession is in connection with the statutory offence of being in possession of prohibited drugs. The difficulty arises in cases where the accused is shown to have been in possession of a parcel, but he asserts that he did not know it contained drugs. In *Warner v Metropolitan Police Comr*[8] the House of Lords held that the Drugs (Prevention of Misuse) Act 1964, laid down absolute prohibition of possessing drugs, but they in effect mitigated the severity of this by importing a mental element into possession in the context of this particular branch of the law. Approval was given to dicta of Lord Parker CJ that

> 'a person cannot be said to be in possession of some article which he or she does not realise is, or may be in her handbag, in her room, or in some other place over which she has control. That, I should have thought, is elementary; if something were tipped into one's basket and one had not the vaguest notion it was there at all, one could not possibly be said to be in possession of it'[9].

---

4 *Heydon and Smith's Case* (1610) 13 Co Rep 67 at 69; *R v Deakin and Smith* (1800) 2 East PC 653; *R v Harding* (1929) 21 Cr App Rep 166.
5 Attributed to *The Carrier's Case* (1473) YB 13 Edw 4, fo 9, Pasch pl 5; doctrine abolished by statute in 1857. See also Larceny Act 1916, s 1.
6 *R v Thurborn* (1849) 1 Den 387. If a third party took from a finder, the indictment could properly lay the thing either in the loser or the finder: *R v Swinson* (1900) 64 JP 73.
7 *R v Rowe* (1859) Bell CC 93; *R v Foley* (1889) 26 LR Ir 299; *Hibbert v McKiernan* [1948] 2 KB 142, [1948] 1 All ER 860.
8 [1969] 2 AC 256, [1968] 2 All ER 356. See also *Hambleton v Callinan* [1968] 2 QB 427, [1968] 2 All ER 943; *R v Hussain* [1969] 2 QB 567, [1969] 2 All ER 1117; *R v Marriott* [1971] 1 All ER 595, [1971] 1 WLR 187.
9 *Lockyer v Gibb* [1967] 2 QB 243 at 248, [1966] 2 All ER 653 at 655. Contrast two earlier statements by Lord Goddard CJ in *Hibbert v McKiernan* [1948] 2 KB 142 at 150, [1948] 1 All ER 860 at 862; and in *Russell v Smith* [1958] 1 QB 27 at 34–35, [1957] 2 All ER 796 at 799. See, too, *R v Peaston* (1978) 69 Cr App Rep 203, CA. *Quantity* may be a factor in determining possession: *R v Boyesen* [1982] AC 768, [1982] 2 All ER 161, HL; need for knowledge: *R v Ashton-Rickardt* [1978] 1 All ER 173, [1978] 1 WLR 37, CA. In *R v Buswell* [1972] 1 All ER 75, [1972] 1 WLR 64, a man who had lost some tablets and found them ten months later at the back of a drawer was held to have continued to be in possession. For

Finally, in connection with adverse possession of land for the purpose of the Statute of Limitations, the policy of the law requires that possession should consist of overt acts which are inconsistent with the title of the owner. Far more is needed to constitute adverse possession against an owner than is needed by an owner to continue his own possession. 'The overall impression created by the authorities', said Ormrod LJ 'is that the courts have always been reluctant to allow an incroacher or squatter to acquire a good title to land against the true owner, and have interpreted the word 'possession' in this context very narrowly'[10]. Much will depend on the nature of the case, particularly the enjoyment of the land concerned. Thus, in *Leigh v Jack*[11], the fact that the defendant had placed his own materials on the land, inclosed a portion of it and had even fenced in the ends, did not amount to adverse possession. In *Littledale v Liverpool College*[12], the erection and locking of gates did not amount to adverse possession; nor in *Convey v Regan*[13] did the cutting and removal of turf. On the other hand, in *Williams Bros Direct Supply Ltd v Raftery*[14] minor acts by the plaintiff owners, such as measuring the land on two occasions and once dumping rubbish on it, were held to constitute continued possession in them as against the defendant's acts of cultivation, putting up of a shelter, some sheds and a fence for keeping in greyhounds. Indeed, *Wuta-Ofei v Danquah*[15] shows that as against a trespasser even the slightest evidence is sufficient to continue possession.

In the light of all this the conclusion must be that in English law, as in the Roman, possession is no more than a device of convenience and policy. This has been appreciated by a few writers and most clearly by Shartel, who said,

> 'I want to make the point that there are many meanings of the word 'possession'; that possession can only be usefully defined with reference to the purpose in hand; and that possession may have one meaning in one connection and another meaning in another'[16].

---

possession of premises for the purposes of the Act, see *Sweet v Parsley* [1970] AC 132, [1969] 1 All ER 347, HL; *R v Mogford* [1970] 1 WLR 988 (disapproved in *R v Tao* [1977] QB 141, [1976] 3 All ER 65, CA).

10 *Wallis's Cayton Bay Holiday Camp Ltd v Shell-Mex and BP Ltd* [1975] QB 94 at 114, [1974] 3 All ER 575 at 589.

11 (1879) 5 Ex D 264.

12 [1900] 1 Ch 19.

13 [1952] IR 56. See generally, *George Wimpey & Co Ltd v Sohn* [1967] Ch 487, [1966] 1 All ER 232; *Hayward v Chaloner* [1968] 1 QB 107, [1967] 3 All ER 122; *Paradise Beach & Transportation Co Ltd v Price-Robinson* [1968] AC 1072, [1968] 1 All ER 530; *Hughes v Griffin* [1969] 1 All ER 460, [1969] 1 WLR 23.

14 [1958] 1 QB 159, [1957] 3 All ER 593. See also *West Bank Estates Ltd v Arthur* [1967] 1 AC 665, [1966] 3 WLR 750; *Bligh v Martin* [1968] 1 All ER 1157, [1968] 1 WLR 804; *Techbild v Chamberlain* (1969) 209 Estates Gazette 1069; *Wallis's Cayton Bay Holiday Camp Ltd v Shell-Mex and BP Ltd* [1975] QB 94, [1974] 3 All ER 575 (distinguished in *Treloar v Nute* [1977] 1 All ER 230, [1976] 1 WLR 1295, CA).

15 [1961] 3 All ER 596, [1961] 1 WLR 1238. See also *Murland v Despard* [1956] IR 170; *Western Ground Rents v Richards* (1961) 177 Estates Gazette 519; *Edgington v Clark (Macassey Trustees of Whitley House Trust)* [1963] 3 All ER 468; *Ocean Estates Ltd v Pinder* [1969] 2 AC 19, [1969] 2 WLR 1359; *Portland Managements Ltd v Harte* [1977] QB 306, [1976] 1 All ER 225. Acts done on parts of land may be evidence of possession of the whole land: *Higgs v Nassauvian Ltd* [1975] AC 464, [1975] 1 All ER 95. Cf *British Railways Board v G J Holdings* (1974) 230 Estates Gazette 973.

16 Shartel 'Meanings of Possession' (1932) 16 Minnesota Law Review 611 at 612. See also Bentham *Works* III, p 188; Lightwood *A Treatise on Possession of Land* passim; Gray *The Nature and Sources of the Law* p 4; Bingham 'The Nature and Importance of Legal Possession' (1915) 13 Michigan Law Review at 638; Kocourek *Jural Relations* p 389; Parker in Salmond on *Jurisprudence* (9th edn) at pp 381, 388, 390; G L Williams 'Language and the Law' (1945) 61 LQR at 391; Fifoot *Judge and Jurist in the Reign of Queen Victoria* p 108.

These are, however, isolated voices in the wilderness, for the classic theories in English law have been dominated by the Savigny-ian *corpus* and *animus* doctrine. Implicit in this are two assumptions: firstly, that Savigny's analysis was correct for Roman law, which it was not; and, secondly, that it must necessarily be correct for English law. English authority is conspicuously lacking. Markby avowedly based his treatment of the subject on Savigny, saying:

> 'Notwithstanding criticisms to which Savigny's conception of possession has been subjected, it seems to me to be still the only one which is clear and consistent and to be in the main that which is accepted by English lawyers. Savigny's treatise is founded upon the Roman law'[17].

The 'clear and consistent' (paying no heed to the fact that the Roman law itself was anything but consistent), 'founded upon the Roman law', 'accepted by English lawyers', are all remarkable propositions. The overriding objections to all these theories are that they are based on the fallacy that the word 'possession' must have some direct physical counterpart, and that the attempt to force the inconsistencies of the law within the four corners of a rigid formula distorts the law.

SALMOND'S THEORY

Salmond[18] began by distinguishing between 'possession in fact' and 'possession in law'[19]. He treated possession in fact as a 'conception', which it undoubtedly is, but this, as Professor G L Williams has pointed out, is as much a conception as possession in law[20]. He also denied that there are two different conceptions of possession. There is only one conception and that is possession in fact, which is possession 'in truth and in fact'. This is no more than the 'one proper meaning' fallacy of language. Having assumed that possession in fact is possession 'in truth and in fact', he was driven to say that possession in law is 'fictitious'. As will have become evident, possession is no longer tied to fact; it has become a concept of the utmost technicality.

Salmond then distinguished between possession of physical objects, which he called 'corporeal possession', and possession of 'rights', which he called 'incorporeal possession'. Corporeal possession is 'the continuing exercise of a claim to the exclusive use of it'. The exercise of this claim involves two ingredients, *corpus possessionis* and *animus possidendi*. Hence, corporeal possession 'is' *corpus* and *animus*. The only authority quoted in support is *D* 41.2.3.1 from Paul. The cases which might have been used in support were decided after Salmond wrote and these, in any case, cannot be generalised.

The *animus possidendi* is an intent to exclude other people, which is simply an adoption of the modified *animus domini* of Savigny. Arguing on this assumption, he explained *Bridges v Hawkesworth*[1] on the ground that the shopkeeper had no intention to exclude people from the pocketbook because he was unaware of its existence, a reason which Professor Goodhart has shown to be a misrepresentation of its *ratio decidendi*[2].

---

17 Markby *Elements of Law* s 347. Even the shrewd Austin eulogised Savigny on possession: *Lectures on Jurisprudence* I, p 53. See also Holland *The Elements of Jurisprudence* p 199.
18 Salmond *Jurisprudence* (7th edn) chs 13 and 14; (12th edn) ch 9.
19 Salmond p 318.
20 Williams 'Language and the Law' (1945) 61 LQR 391.
 1 (1851) 15 Jur 1079.
 2 Goodhart 'Three Cases on Possession' in *Essays in Jurisprudence and the Common Law* pp 82–83.

He dealt with the *corpus possessionis* under two headings. (a) The relation of the possessor to the thing, which must admit his making such use of it as accords with its nature. In this connection he said

> 'Whether the possession of one thing will bring with it the possession of another that is thus connected with it depends upon the circumstances of the particular case'[3].

Here there is a glimpse of the truth, but so obsessed was he with his preconception that he failed to develop its significance. (b) The relation of the possessor to other persons. 'I am in possession of a thing', he said, 'when the facts of the case are such as to create a reasonable expectation that I will not be interfered with in the use of it'. This led him to invent reasons to explain *Elwes v Brigg Gas Co*[4] and *South Staffordshire Water Co v Sharman*[5]. Further, an expectation of non-interference is not necessary for the continuation of possession for, as Mr Parker, a former editor of Salmond, pointed out, a man continues to possess his pocketbook although he is being pursued by swifter bandits, who will interfere with his use of it in a few moments[6]. Nor is it necessary even for the commencement of possession for, taking an example from Holmes[7], a child and a ruffian may both make for a purse lying in the road, but if the child is the first to pick it up, can it be doubted that he gets possession even though the ruffian is certain to interfere the very next second?

The trouble arises from the assumption that *corpus* and *animus*, which are only conditions for the acquisition of possession, 'are' possession itself. Salmond denied that possession means one thing at its commencement and something else later on, and he therefore declared that possession is lost when either *corpus* or *animus* is lost[8]. Professor G L Williams, the learned editor of the 11th edition, altered the text on this point, and said that assuming that both *corpus* and *animus* are required to initiate possession, 'the possession once acquired may continue even though *animus* or *corpus*, or even both, disappear'[9]. This, it is submitted, is true, but it destroys the foundation of Salmond's contention that possession 'is' *corpus* and *animus*.

HOLMES'S THEORY

Holmes[10] began promisingly by rejecting *a priori* philosophical criteria. He also perceived that fewer facts are needed to continue possession than to acquire it. He said that the facts which constitute possession are best studied when possession is first gained, and followed this up with the remark:

> 'To gain possession, then, a man must stand in a certain physical relation to the object and to the rest of the world, and must have a certain intent. These relations and this intent are the facts of which we are in search'[11].

The 'then' is probably only a rhetorical flourish, but apart from that, the fallacy recurs that the facts needed to acquire possession 'are' or 'constitute'

3 *Salmond* (7th edn) p 304.
4 (1886) 33 ChD 562.
5 [1896] 2 QB 44; *Goodhart* pp 84–88.
6 *Salmond* (9th edn) p 377.
7 Holmes *The Common Law* p 235.
8 *Salmond* (7th edn) pp 314, 318.
9 *Salmond* (11th edn) p 339.
10 Holmes *The Common Law* ch 6.
11 *Holmes* p 216.

possession. The statement is thus tantamount to an adoption of the Savigny-ian *corpus* and *animus* theory, but whereas Salmond at least cited Paul as authority, Holmes offered no authority at all. Having earlier rejected the *a priori* adoption of doctrines, he proceeded to do that very thing himself.

The physical relation to the object he described as 'a manifested power co-extensive with the intent', and treated it as of less importance than the intent. It should be noted, all the same, that the illustrations given of this power[12] show such variety as to render it useless as a criterion.

The intent was said to be an intent to exclude others. On that basis he, like Salmond, was forced into a false explanation of *Bridges v Hawkesworth*[13]. The American case law fared even worse at his hands, particularly *Durfee v Jones*[14], which he admitted was against him, and then alleged to have been wrongly decided, and finally explained in a manner which pretty nearly makes nonsense of both the case and the explanation. The crowning touch comes when, in the midst of his misinterpretation of these cases on the basis of his theory derived from Savigny, he pointed an accusing finger at Stephen for having misinterpreted two other cases on the basis of 'a reason drawn from Savigny, but not fitted to the English law'[15].

POLLOCK'S THEORY

Pollock[16] laid stress, not on *animus*, but on *de facto* control, which he defined as physical control[17]. A general intent seems to suffice. Even the reduction of possession to a general criterion like *de facto* control involved Pollock in two difficulties. The first was the 'custody' of servants and such like. They have *de facto* control, and Pollock was driven to treat these cases as 'anomalous', and then to argue that it is the master who exercises *de facto* control using his servant as an instrument[18]. This explanation is only a device for fitting these cases into the theory, and there is no warrant for treating servants in this mechanical way. Moreover, it fails to explain how it is that servants have 'custody' for some purposes and 'possession' for others. The second difficulty, which Pollock encountered, was the case law, in particular, *Bridges v Hawkesworth*[19]. He reconciled it with his theory on the ground that the shopkeeper had no *de facto* control of the pocketbook, which again is not a reason to be found in the case itself[20].

A recent writer who makes control the central idea of possession is Professor Tay[1]. For her, possession 'is the present control of a thing, on one's own behalf and to the exclusion of all others'[2]. She concedes that not all uses of the term can be reduced to the fact of control, but her thesis is that these are best understood when matched against the paradigm case, which is control

12 *Holmes* pp 217-218.
13 (1851) 15 Jur 1079; *Goodhart* pp 79-81.
14 11 Rhode Island 588; *Holmes* pp 225-226.
15 *Holmes* p 225 n 3.
16 Pollock & Wright *Possession in the Common Law*.
17 *Pollock & Wright* p 26.
18 *Pollock & Wright* p 18.
19 (1851) 15 Jur 1079.
20 *Pollock & Wright* pp 39-40; *Goodhart* pp 81-82.
 1 Tay 'The Concept of Possession in the Common Law: Foundations for a New Approach' (1964) 4 Melb ULR 476. See also 'Possession and the Modern Law of Finding' (1964) 4 Sydney LR 383.
 2 *Tay* (1964) 4 Melb ULR at 490.

so that departures on policy grounds can be openly acknowledged. The argument against this, however, is that control is an idea so variable in its interpretation that it ceases to serve as a 'paradigm case'. In the light of the vagaries, such as the 'key' cases, how does one construct a 'paradigm'? In any case, even if it were possible to construct one, the departures from it would be so numerous that little, if anything, would be gained by having such a concept. Although it is true that control was the primitive factor to which significance attached in law, it did not continue to serve as the anchor. As Maitland observed, 'it is argued in one case that a man has an action of trespass because he has possession, in the next case that he has possession because he has an action of trespass'[3]. The point which Professor Tay seems to overlook is that the nature of possession came to be shaped by the need to give remedies; and this was so in both Roman and English law. It is because of this that possession is sometimes said to be in X or Y simultaneously in different branches. Further, it is submitted with respect that she under-estimates the influence of policy considerations.

CONCLUSIONS

Enough has been said to show how the Roman and English lawyers have handled the concept of possession, and how widely the theories err. Most striking is the correspondence between the two systems, considering the fact that they are separated by centuries, and English law has not borrowed from the Roman. This shows how the law has developed to meet the needs of society, and not in accordance with theories. Only thus could two such widely different systems have arrived at similar results.

There is now so much flexibility in the use of this concept that certainty over a good part of the law in which it figures has disappeared. Such certainty as there may be is preserved by the fact that particular rules prescribe in the particular contexts where possession shall reside. It is therefore submitted that all that is needed are these rules, which determine what view should be taken of different situations of fact. Reference to possession becomes superfluous. Possession was a mould in which the earliest doctrines were shaped, but these have now so outgrown their beginnings that the mould has become a redundant relic. What matters now are the rules which determine the incidence of possession. Analysis reveals the influence of policy behind these rules.

The melancholy record of theorising on this topic should serve as a warning against an *a priori* approach. The jurists, whose theories have been discussed, proceed on the assumption that words always have to refer to some referent and are concerned to discover what this 'thing' is; the law, on the other hand, has proceeded functionally. The result has been misquotation, misinterpretation and allegations of wrong decision in order to force the law as it is into a preconceived pattern. To conclude that Roman and English lawyers reached similar ideas as to possession is one thing; but quite another to twist the rules of both so as to fit them into a single misconceived theory. No single theory will explain possession. The danger to be avoided at all costs is to argue from one branch of the law to another[4].

---

3 *HEL* ii, 31.
4 Lord Diplock: 'These technical doctrines of the civil law about possession are irrelevant to this field of criminal law': *DPP v Brooks* [1974] AC 862 at 867, [1974] 2 All ER 840 at 843.

Corpus and *animus* are not irrelevant. They have no fixed meaning, but are conditions which the law generally requires for the commencement of possession. Two questions should be distinguished: What is possession? and How is possession acquired? The *corpus* and *animus* theory is only *an* answer, by no means the only one, to the second question.

Possession carries with it the claim to possession and not to be interfered with until someone else establishes a superior title. 'The general principle appears to be that, until the contrary is proved, possession in law follows the right to possess'[5]. It should be noted that the 'right' to be in possession is different from the 'right to possess', ie to be put in possession. It has been seen how, for reasons of policy, the term 'possession' is used to cover both, and this is done when the party concerned is, or has been in possession at one time or another. The earlier possession gives the possessor a 'better right' to possess than any later possessor; even a trespasser has a 'better right' to possess than any subsequent taker. The question to be decided is which of several persons have had possession and when. The answer is determined by considerations of policy and convenience[6]. When the question of the 'right to possess' falls to be decided on grounds other than the mere fact of prior possession, it is said that such right has to derive from ownership[7]. Possession then becomes *prima facie* evidence of title. In this way the role of possession in achieving distributive justice gets subsumed under ownership. For the rest, in relation to justice in deciding disputes and adapting to change, the flexibilities in its use have been amply demonstrated.

In the light of all the foregoing it may be asked whether possession is a matter of law or of fact. The Romans disputed it, and neither in Roman nor in English law is there any simple answer. Possession has three aspects: firstly, the relation between a person and a thing is a fact. Secondly, the advantages attached by law to that relation is a matter of law. Thirdly, these advantages are also attributed to a person when certain other facts exist. What they are in any given type of case is a matter of law.

5 Per Ormrod LJ in *Wallis's Cayton Bay Holiday Camp Ltd v Shell-Mex and BP Ltd* [1975] QB 94 at 114, [1974] 3 All 575 at 589.
6 Harris has given nine points which amplify the kind of factors that courts take into account. (1) The degree of physical control which the person claiming possession actually exercises, or is immediately able to exercise; (2) this has to be weighed against the degree of physical control actually or potentially exercised by any other person; (3) the claimant's knowledge (a) of the existence of the chattel, and (b) its major attributes or qualities, and (c) its location at the relevant time; (4) his intention in regard to it; (5) knowledge of another person of its existence, its attributes and location; (6) that person's intention in regard to it; (7) the legal relationship of the claimant, compared with that of another person, to the premises where the chattel is; (8) other legal relationships between the parties, or special rules applicable to the facts; (9) the policy behind the rule: 'The Concept of Possession in English Law' in *Oxford Essays in Jurisprudence* (ed Guest) pp 72–80.
7 *Portland Managements Ltd v Harte* [1977] QB 306, [1976] 1 All ER 225.

READING LIST

J W Bingham 'The Nature and Importance of Legal Possession' (1915) 13 Michigan Law Review 534, especially 549–565, 623 et seq.

H Bond 'Possession in Roman Law' (1890) 6 LQR 259.

A L Goodhart *Essays in Jurisprudence and the Common Law* ch 4.

D R Harris 'The Concept of Possession in English Law' in *Oxford Essays in Jurisprudence* (ed A G Guest) ch 4.

O W Holmes *The Common Law* ch 6.

R von Ihering *Der Besitwille* (trans O de Meulenaere).

R von Ihering *Grund des Besitzesschutzes* (trans O de Meulenaere).

A Kocourek *Jural Relations* (2nd edn) ch 20.

J M Lightwood 'Possession in Roman Law' (1887) 3 LQR 32.

G W Paton *A Text-Book of Jurisprudence* (4th edn G W Paton and D P Derham) ch 22.

F Pollock and R S Wright *An Essay on Possession in the Common Law* Part I.

J W Salmond on *Jurisprudence* (7th edn) chs 13–14.

F C von Savigny *Possession* (trans E Perry).

B Shartel 'Meanings of Possession' (1932) 16 Minnesota Law Review 611.

A E S Tay 'The Concept of Possession in the Common Law: Foundations for a New Approach' (1964) 4 Melbourne ULR 476.

CHAPTER 14

Ownership

The concept of ownership is of both legal and social interest. Not only have courts utilised the idea in such a way as to give effect to views of changing individual and social interest, but so great are its potentialities that in recent times it has become the focus of governmental policy. It is proposed in this chapter to show how its use as an instrument of judicial policy has come to be eclipsed by its political significance.

Ownership consists of an innumerable number of claims, liberties, powers and immunities with regard to the thing owned. Accordingly, some jurists analyse the concept out of existence. When it is said, for example that a person who owns a house has various claims, etc in respect of it, these jurists argue that his ownership means just those claims etc; that there is no point in talking of ownership apart from them. Such a view, it is submitted, is undesirable and inadequate. For the connotation of 'ownership' does not correspond simply with its component elements any more than the word 'team' connotes just a group of individuals. The term is a convenient method of denoting as an unit a multitude of claims etc in a way similar to the term 'person' examined earlier. Another reason is that the various claims etc constitute rather the content of ownership than ownership itself. A person may part with the claims etc to a greater or lesser extent, while retaining the right of ownership. Thus, a person who has the ownership of land, namely the fee simple, may grant the leasehold of it to another with the result that his ownership is denuded of most of its content. As long as he has the fee simple he is 'owner', which shows that his right of ownership is distinct from its contents[1]. Also, it is misleading to talk as if ownership meant only the claims etc; it would be truer to say that a person is entitled to these claims etc by virtue of the right of ownership. Lastly, ownership as an asset has value apart from its component claims etc. It is no doubt true that the exact value of a person's ownership will be affected by the extent of the advantages that he is able to derive, but that is another matter. It is therefore meaningful and necessary to speak of a 'right of ownership' as distinct from a collection of jural relations. The discussion that follows will concern the analysis of ownership as it has been shaped by the progressive adjustment of competing interests, and then its function and functioning in the social regulation of an owner's use and enjoyment of the thing owned. Reference will be mainly to English law, though some of the points may well apply to other systems as well. Ownership is an institution that is generally recognised, so it is not surprising that certain features are shared.

---

1 It should, perhaps, here be remarked that there are such expressions as 'limited ownership', but these, as will appear, refer to special types of interest.

ANALYSIS OF OWNERSHIP

Ownership in English law has to be approached historically, for its evolution is bound up with the remedies that used to be available. The piece-meal development through actions prevented the formation of a clear-cut conception. The peculiarity of English law is that it did not achieve an absolute ownership, as did Roman law for example. Save in the case of land, the common law knew of no real action corresponding to the Roman *vindicatio*, damages in trespass, or one of its variants, being the usual remedy. The basis of trespass was possession, or entitlement to retain or obtain possession.

Moreover, the idea of ownership did not evolve in the same way in relation to land and chattels. Land used to be held in feudal tenure, which was a system of land holding in return for service. This holding was known as 'seisin', which originally meant no more than possession and denoted the state of affairs that made enjoyment possible. If the person seised was dis-possessed, he had to rely on his seisin to get back on the land, and for this the old remedy was the writ of right in which success depended on the claimant being able to establish a superior title to that of the possessor. In the reign of Henry II the possessory assizes were introduced, 'police measures' as they have been described, which were directed at discouraging the use of self-help. They led to a shadowy distinction between seisin and possession, between the respective bases of the writ of right and of the possessory assizes. This, however, was very obscure, since even possession carried with it the 'right' not only to be in possession but also to regain it if dispossesssed until someone else proved a better 'right'. As suggested in the last chapter, this could be 'better' by virtue of being the prior possession; but if it was 'better' for any other reason it gave rise to ideas of ownership. At this early period there was no talk of ownership as such. The earliest known use of the word 'owner', according to Maitland, quoting Dr Murray, occurred in 1340, and 'ownership' in 1583[2]. A further step in the differentiation of seisin and pos-session came with the tenant for a term of years. Whereas seisin was protected by the writ of right, the termor's interest was protected by a form of trespass, *de ejectione firmae*. His interest was not seisin, it was styled possession, which sharpened the contrast between seisin and possession[3].

In time new remedies replaced the old, trespass came to protect the pos-sessor and ejectment was available to a person out of possession, who could prove a better 'right' to possess than the possessor. These were based on the old principles, so much so that even in modern law there are many cases which show that ownership of land is only a question of the 'better right' to retain or obtain possession relative to the other party to the dispute[4]. Holds-worth, however, argued that the action of ejectment introduced a new idea. He said that in this action a defendant in possession could set up a *jus tertii* in answer to the plaintiff's claim to obtain possession, ie a superior title in a third party. Therefore, according to him, a plaintiff was required to establish a better claim than anyone else and in this way English law may be said to

---

2 Pollock & Maitland *History of English Law* II p 153n.
3 For further modifications of seisin, see Holdsworth *History of English Law* VII, ch 1, §2.
4 *Doe d Burrough v Reade* (1807) 8 East 353; *Doe d Hughes v Dyeball* (1829) Mood & M 346; *Doe d Harding v Cooke* (1831) 7 Bing 346; *Asher v Whitlock* (1865) LR 1 QB 1; *Perry v Clissold* [1907] AC 73; *Tickner v Buzzacott* [1965] Ch 426, [1965] 1 All ER 131 (possibly *Delaney v T P Smith Ltd* [1946] KB 393, [1946] 2 All ER 23: not a dispute as to ownership).

have arrived at the conception of an absolute right, namely ownership[5]. Professor Hargreaves challenged this assertion, firstly, on the ground that, except in cases where title has been registered or is derived from statute, no one is able to prove an absolute title which is good against all the world[6]. Secondly, he alleged that the cases do not bear out Holdsworth's contention about the *jus tertii*[7]. The dispute seems to hinge largely on the interpretation of these cases. Leaving these aside, however, there seems to be one respect in which there may be absolute ownership in land, and that is through registration of title under the property legislation of 1925. Subject to certain exceptions, where title is registered proof of a superior right does not assail the registered title, though it may ground some other form of relief.

Another development was the extension of the idea of seisin to certain interests, or collections of claims, liberties etc. These were conceived of as 'things' distinct from the land itself, and the person in whom they were vested was regarded as holding a 'thing' on its own, namely, the totality of his particular interest. This made possible the doctrine of 'estates' in land. The interest which a person enjoyed over a piece of land was treated as an estate, an incorporeal thing, and he was seised of the land for an estate of a certain duration. The same land could thus be subjected to several concurrent ownerships, each person being seised of it for an estate. In this way the concept of 'estates', and with it 'ownership', was shaped by the need to accommodate overlapping interests in land.

The development of the law relating to chattels took a different line. There was nothing resembling a doctrine of estates. Land-holding, not the possession of chattels, was the index to a person's public and political position. Chattels were of comparatively little significance and there was, originally, no ownership in them. They had a fungible character, that is to say, the transfer or restoration of equivalent chattels sufficed, and later money. This was because, in the nature of things, the interest of a person in a particular chattel was neither so important nor so permanent as his interest in land. Indeed, Maitland doubts 'whether there was any right in movable goods that deserves the name of ownership'[8]. When trespass was introduced, the basis of it was, as always, possession. The idea of title as the 'better right' to obtain or retain possession evolved through trover and detinue: the plaintiff succeeded if he could establish a 'better right' to have the possession than the defendant. Once again, this enabled the defendant to raise the *jus tertii* as a defence and, as in the case of land, there has been dispute as to how far this required a plaintiff to prove an absolute right[9]. The Torts (Interference with Goods) Act 1977, s 8, has abolished the restrictions that used to exist on pleading *jus tertii*. The rules of court may require the plaintiff to give particulars of his title and/or identify anyone whom he knows to have or to claim any interest in the goods. Putting *jus tertii* on one side, it would appear that the law has arrived at a more absolute conception of ownership of

---

5 *Holdsworth* VII, pp 30, 62, 79; *Historical Introduction to the Land Law* p 182; 'Terminology and Title in Ejectment—A Reply' (1940) 56 LQR 480.

6 Hargreaves 'Terminology and Title in Ejectment' (1940) 56 LQR 376.

7 *Hargreaves* pp 379, 397. The Australian case of *Allen v Roughley* (1955) 29 ALJ 603, is in support of Hargreaves: see note by H W R Wade [1956] CLJ 177. For the operation of estoppel, see *Industrial Properties (Barton Hill) Ltd v Associated Electrical Industries Ltd* [1977] QB 580, [1977] 2 All ER 293.

8 *Pollock & Maitland* II, p 153.

9 *Holdsworth* VII, p 425; Atiyah 'A Re-Examination of the Jus Tertii in Conversion' (1955) 18 MLR 97, and reply by Jolly 'The Jus Tertii and the Third Man', at p 371.

chattels, at any rate for some purposes, than of land. The Sale of Goods Act 1979 (replacing the 1893 Act), for instance, refers to 'the property' in goods, which in this context means ownership[10]. Sir Raymond Evershed MR (as he was then) has said:

'Although it is, no doubt, true in a sense, and certainly in its original medieval conception, that when one speaks of property in chattels one has in mind the right to their immediate possession, nevertheless the sense of property in chattels is now well understood. It is, of course, involved in the Sale of Goods Act 1893'[11].

In *Raymond Lyons & Co Ltd v Metropolitan Police Comr*[12] X left a ring with jewellers for valuation and they handed it to the police. X did not return and no one claimed it. Accordingly, the jewellers alleged that they were 'owner' within the Police (Property) Act 1897, s 1(1), since they had a better title against the whole world except the true owner. The court rejected the claim saying that 'owner' in the Act had its popular meaning and that they were not 'owner'.

The position, therefore, seems to be that the idea of ownership of land is essentially one of the 'better right' to be in possession and to obtain it, whereas with chattels the concept has moved towards a more absolute one. Actual possession implies a right to retain it until the contrary is proved, and to that extent a possessor is presumed to be owner[13]. Where the question is one of obtaining possession, the 'better right' may be derived from prior possession, and, if not, it is said to derive from ownership; but where the question is one of retaining a thing, the 'better right' is associated with ownership[14]. The idea of ownership as a right in a comprehensive sense is useful for indicating the whereabouts of certain types of interest. With land, in particular, it has been evolved in such a way as to enable the adjustment of concurrent interests. There are also certain further points to which attention should be drawn.

1. The term 'ownership' is used with reference to 'things'. 'Thing' has two meanings depending upon whether it is used with reference to physical objects, 'corporeal things', or certain rights, 'incorporeal things'[15]. Since

---

10 'Property' has had many meanings at various times. There is no clear-cut conception, for, as Lord Porter said, 'In truth the word 'property' is not a term of art, but takes its meaning from its context and from its collocation in the document or Act of Parliament in which it is found and from the mischief with which that Act or document is intended to deal': *Nokes v Doncaster Amalgamated Collieries Ltd* [1940] AC 1014 at 1051, [1940] 3 All ER 549 at 574. 'Property' has meant variously (1) rights *in rem* and *in personam*, eg Blackstone *Commentaries* III, 143, whose use of the term is wider than even '*res*' in Roman law (usually an element in wealth capable of estimation in money for the purpose of the *condemnatio* clause in the *formula* of an action); Hobbes: life, limb, conjugal affection, riches and means of living: *Leviathan* ch xxx; Locke: life, liberty and estate: *Treatise on Civil Government* II, ch v, s 27; (2) rights *in rem* and *in personam*, excluding those relating to personal condition; (3) rights *in rem* only, excluding personal condition; (4) ownership, eg Sale of Goods Act 1979; (5) alienable rights (though pensions and annuities are 'property', but inalienable); (6) physical objects; (7) 'things', as to which see below.
11 *Jarvis v Williams* [1955] 1 All ER 108 at 111. Note that s 61(2) of the Sale of Goods Act 1979, contrasts 'the property', ie the 'general property', with 'a special property', ie a limited interest of a bailee. The term 'owner' is not used in the Act. Cf eg Bills of Exchange Act 1882, s 80, where the term is undefined.
12 [1975] QB 321, [1975] 1 All ER 335.
13 See *Roadways Transport Development Ltd v A-G* [1942] Ch 208, [1942] 1 All ER 52; revsg [1941] Ch 392, [1941] 2 All ER 313.
14 *Moffatt v Kazana* [1969] 2 QB 152, [1968] 3 All ER 271.
15 Cf *Re Knight's Question* [1959] Ch 381, [1958] 1 All ER 812.

ownership is only of 'things', it, too, is 'corporeal' or 'incorporeal', which is but an elliptical way of saying that the ownership is of corporeal or incorporeal things. The former refers to physical objects, the latter to certain groupings of claims, liberties etc. The use of the phrase 'corporeal ownership' with reference to physical objects is simple, and had the term 'incorporeal ownership' embraced *all* claims etc, that too would have been simple. However, the term 'incorporeal ownership' is only applied to some types of claims etc in so far as these are 'things'; but it does not apply to others, because they are not 'things'. This complicates matters by introducing an element of arbitrariness into the use of 'thing' and 'ownership'. There is said to be ownership of copyrights and patents, because these are treated as 'things'; there is no ownership of bodily security or reputation, because these are not 'things'[16].

The history of the common law relating to land shows that different interests came to be treated as 'things' in themselves, known as 'estates', and so there came to be what is describable as ownership of estates. In addition to this, the idea of 'thing' was also shaped by the interaction between remedy and concept—the grant of a remedy stretched the concept, the concept was the basis for granting a remedy. Thus, a feudal tenant performed services for his lord, who was said to be seised of the land in service. The remedies in respect of the sevices were taken over from those available for the land itself. To make these available, the lord was said to be seised of the services as well as of the land. Since seisin meant possession, the services too came to be thought of as capable of being possessed and hence 'things'. Similarly, a lord was seised of rents, non-payment of which was treated as a disseisin of the lord of his rental. On the other hand, it is equally a matter of historical development that the same did not happen with chattels. The use of the term ownership is thus arbitrary so far as it follows the concept of 'thing', and one has to know the conventions of terminology to know how it is used.

Something should be said at this juncture of Salmond's analysis. Analytically, ownership consists of a bundle of claims, liberties powers and immunities. Salmond said that

> 'Ownership in its most comprehensive signification, denotes the relation between a person and any right that is vested in him. That which a man owns in this sense is in all cases a right'[17].

Ownership is, therefore, 'incorporeal'. He then went on to say that to speak of the ownership of physical objects is a figure of speech. What is meant is that that certain claims etc are vested in a person. 'We identify by way of metonymy the right with the material thing which is its object'[18]. Salmond was of course free to give the word 'ownership' any meaning he liked, and he preferred his first wide meaning. The usual meaning, however, is not as wide as that, as Salmond would probably have agreed. There is more cause to quarrel with his statement that the 'ownership of material objects' is a metonymy. He seems to have assumed that his wide meaning is the 'proper'

16 There is talk now of 'property' in a job, but it is not clear whether it is regarded as a 'thing': *Hill v C A Parsons* [1972] Ch 305 at 321, [1971] 3 All ER 1345 at 1355, per Sachs LJ. The liberties of licensed pilots to provide pilotage services and to employ others as pilots are not 'property' according to the Privy Council in *Government of Malaysia v Selangor Pilot Association* [1978] AC 337, [1977] 2 WLR 901.
17 Salmond *Jurisprudence* (7th edn) p 277.
18 *Salmond* (7th edn) pp 278–279.

meaning of 'ownership', which is why he was led to allege that the other must be a figure of speech. That is misleading, because, as Professor G L Williams points out, a word can have more than one usual meaning[19]. He raises another objection that Salmond's way of stating it suggests that the idea of ownership of rights preceded that of physical objects, whereas historically the reverse would seem to have been the case[20].

Professor Williams objects to the suggestion here advanced that ownership follows the concept of 'thing'. He rejects it as a verbal point and as amounting to a substitution of the word 'things' for 'rights'. It is submitted that this objection overlooks the fact that not *all* 'rights' are treated as 'things'. The meaning of 'ownership' is coterminous with that of 'things', which is narrower than that of 'rights'.

2. Ownership is needed to give effect to the idea of 'mine' and 'not mine' or 'thine'. One aspect of it is that the idea becomes necessary only when there is some relation between persons. A man by himself on a desert island has no need of it. It is when at least one other person joins him that it becomes necessary to distinguish between things that are his and those that are not his, and also to determine what he may do with his things so as not to interfere with his companion. Without society there is no need for law or for ownership[1]. Just as the one is an institution of society, so is the other. The social dimensions of ownership will be discussed later in this chapter. The other aspect is the relativity of 'mine' and 'thine'. If X hires a chattel to Y, even during such time as Y may hold it, X is entitled to say, both in law and in ordinary talk, 'That is mine'; and Y would not counter the assertion by claiming it as his as against X. On the other hand, if Y sees Z picking it up, Y may well say to him 'That is mine', meaning that as between the two of them he is more entitled to it than Z. As between the three of them the law would answer the question, 'Whose thing?', in favour of X as far as ownership goes, but would also give Y such remedies as are based on possession. In the case of hiring land, on the other hand, Y's interest might be so substantial, eg a long lease, that even as against X he would be entitled to say 'That is mine'. No accepted linguistic usages apply to these situations, and both in law and in ordinary talk the idea of 'mine' and 'thine' is relative to the kind of thing and kind of interest.

3. The right of ownership comprises benefits and burdens. The former consist of claims, liberties, powers and immunities, but the advantage these give is curtailed by duties, liabilities and disabilities. It is unnecessary to list these in detail and this aspect will be considered later in connection with the social aspects of ownership.

4. The claims etc which comprise the content of ownership may be vested in persons other than the owner. Whether these others may themselves be treated as 'owners' depends on whether the conventions of the law treat their interests as 'things'.

5. An owner may be divested of his claims etc to such an extent that he

---

19 Williams 'Language and the Law' (1945) 61 LQR 386. See also *Salmond* (11th edn) p 304n.
20 *Williams* (1945) 61 LQR 386.
1 'Property and law are born and must die together. Before the laws, there was no property: take away the law, all property ceases': Bentham *Works* I, p 309. See also M R Cohen 'The Process of Judicial Legislation' (1914) 48 American Law Review 193; Turner 'Some Reflections on Ownership in English Law' (1941) 19 Can BR 342.

may be left with no immediate practical benefit. He remains owner none the less. This is because his interest in the thing, which is ownership, will outlast that of other persons, or, if he is not presently exercising any of his claims etc these will revive as soon as those vested in other persons have come to an end. In the case of land and chattels, if the owner is not in possession, his ownership amounts to a better claim to possession than that of the defendant. It is 'better' in that it lasts longer. This is substantially the conclusion reached by many modern writers, who have variously described ownership as the 'residuary', the 'ultimate', or the 'most enduring' interest[2]. This idea needs elucidation. So far as property escheats to the Crown in default of any other owner, the Crown must be said to have the ultimate interest. So even the fee simple absolute in possession, the widest right possible in land, would not be 'full' ownership. Yet, for all legal purposes the holder of the fee simple is regarded as being the ultimate owner. One consideration would be to see whether what reverts is still the same 'thing' or simply a collection of claims etc. When, for instance, a life interest falls in, the ultimate owner resumes the claims, etc corresponding to those which had been enjoyed by the owner of the life interest, but not the life interest as a 'thing'. Another and better way of regarding the whole matter is to say that the way in which the terms 'ownership' and 'thing' are used is governed by convention and policy.

6.   The ways in which ownership arises differ in different systems. These variations depend upon historical and policy considerations. Thus, it is a peculiarity of English law that a contract for the sale of specific goods can in certain circumstances pass immediate ownership without the need for any further conveyance[3], but the same does not apply in the case of land; again, special ceremonies were required in Classical Roman law for the transfer of civil law ownership in certain kinds of things known as *res mancipi*.

Summing up, it may be said that a person is owner at English law when he becomes entitled in specified ways to some thing designated as such, the scope of which is determined by policy; and his interest, constituted in this way, will outlast the interests of other persons in the same thing.

FUNCTION OF OWNERSHIP IN SOCIAL ORDERING

It has been stated that ownership as a right in itself, distinct from its component jural relations, has always been useful for identifying certain groups of interests and for distinguishing them from others. This is because ownership of these special groups was originally an index, not merely to wealth, but to social position, and it was socially significant in other ways as well. Possession, as has been seen, is a juridical concept and an instrument of judicial policy. Ownership is more than that; it is also a social concept and an instrument of social policy. In the words of Lord Evershed 'Property like other interests has a social obligation to perform'[4]. In English law the various forms of landholding designated a man's social standing, whereas chattels, being fungible, did not have this function. Ownership of land was also a

---

2 *Salmond* (7th edn) pp 280-281; Pollock *A First Book of Jurisprudence* p 180; Kocourek *Jural Relations* p 330; Turner 'Some Reflections on Ownership in English Law' (1941) 19 Canadian Bar Review 352. Cf Buckland's definition of *dominium: A Text-Book of the Roman Law* p 188.
3 Provided the contract is unconditional and the goods are in a deliverable state: Sale of Goods Act 1979, s 18, r 1.
4 Evershed 'The Judicial Process in Twentieth Century England' (1961) 61 Col LR 786.

means of controlling government in so far as the qualification to vote was based upon it. *Dominium* in Roman law connoted sovereignty, which is essentially a social concept and something more than just ownership[5]; and *res mancipi*, 'things of ownership', the earliest forms of Roman property, were precisely the things that were important to a primitive agricultural community.

Ownership and the allocation of benefits and burdens

The social aspects of ownership reveal the manner in which its content came to be regulated over the years so as to determine how and to what extent an owner shall enjoy his interest in a manner compatible with the interests of others. It has been stated that this content consists of innumerable jural relations, which establish relationships between the owner and other persons in society. The extent of these reflects the social policy of the legal system. Broadly speaking, ownership normally carries with it claims to be given possession, against interference, and to the produce, rents and profits. There are

5 It is submitted that the association with sovereignty derived from a primitive identity, or at least a very close connection, between *dominium* and *patria potestas*. The family being the social unit, the social significance of the *potestas* wielded by the *paterfamilias* needs no demonstration. If this and *dominium* were one and the same, the social significance of the latter becomes apparent. There are many indications in support. (i) *Mancipatio* and *cessio in jure* were modes of acquiring both *patria potestas* and *dominium*. In form these were not *transfer*, but creation of a new authority in a new sovereign; which would explain why it was the acquirer who did the talking. (ii) The publicity of these ceremonies indicates that they dealt with matters of social concern, which is obvious if a change of sovereignty was involved. This might explain the presence of five witnesses in *mancipatio*, who probably represented the original five Servian clans that made up the ancient state; and might also account for the presence of the thirty lictors attending on the praetor in the *cessio in jure* ceremony in that they were made to represent the thirty tribes, which later formed the expanded state. (iii) The appointment of an heir looks as if it was treated as the appointment of a successor to sovereignty, which would explain the rule that no one could die partly testate and partly intestate, and also why disherisons had to be justified on grounds of unworthiness (ie unfitness for sovereign power). It may also explain why questions of succession came before the Centumviral Court composed of representatives of the clans (*querela inofficiosi testamenti* and *hereditatis petitio*). (iv) One year's uninterrupted prescription was a means of acquiring *dominium* (*usucapio*) and *patria potestas* over a wife (*manus*). (v) *Patria potestas* originally included the power of life and death, sale and pledge of those *in potestate* as well as the same actions for recovery and theft of them as of property. What is this but ownership? (vi) Acquisitions by slaves (under *dominium*) and by children (under *patria potestas*) both vested in the paterfamilias. (vii) *Capitis deminutio* involved loss of both *dominium* and *patria potestas*. (viii) Etymology: the primitive term for *dominus* was '*erus*' (*D* 9.2.11.6), which means 'head of family'; '*dominus*' and '*dominium*' mean respectively 'lord' and 'lordship', not 'ownership'; the full title of *dominium* was '*dominica potestas*' (G 1.52, 55), which shows that like *patria potestas*, it was a form of *potestas*; '*liber*' is the Latin for both 'child' and 'free', suggesting that originally the whole *familia* was under one jurisdiction, but that the children were distinguished from slaves and animals as being the 'free' members, *liberi*. If, on this thesis, *dominium* and *patria potestas* were one and the same, why did they separate? The answer may lie in the different social policies towards the free and unfree members of the *familia*. Public opinion and laws discouraged harsh treatment of the former long before they did so in the case of the latter. When in time a sufficiently wide gap developed in the treatment of the two categories, the types of authority over them came to be distinguished. This early association with sovereignty accounts for the great respect which Roman lawyers continued to pay to *dominium*. Thus, servitudes were never treated as burdens on *dominium*, but as qualities of the *land*, *jura in re*. There could be servitudes over unowned land: *D* 8.5.6.2. The restrictions on usufruct, especially the vesting of produce only on actual gathering by the fructuary and the denial of *possessio*, were arbitrary limitations on a powerful interest in property with a view to conserving as much benefit as possible for the *dominus*.

liberties to use and misuse and to exercise various powers. There are also powers of alienation and disposal, creation of limited interests, and so forth. There are also immunities, eg against deprivation.

The scope of these benefits is bounded by corresponding burdens, which are an integral part of ownership. There are various duties, liabilities and disabilities, which prescribe and regulate how an owner should utilise his property for the benefit of other individuals or society[6]. An example of a liability in favour of another person is liability to execution, which is leviable only on property owned by a debtor; and examples of liability in the social interest is liability to pay rates, to various forms of wealth and property tax. In modern times landowners are under increasing disabilities as to renting or disposing of their property[7]. In countries where a racial policy obtains there are restrictions on the ownership of certain kinds of property, or the exercise of various liberties and powers pertaining thereto, by members of a particular race.

An important restriction on ownership in the interest of another person is seen in the distinction between 'legal' ownership at common law and 'equitable' ownership at equity. This occurs when there is a trust, which is the result of the peculiar historical development of English law. A trust implies the existence of two kinds of concurrent ownerships, that of the trustee at law and that of the beneficiary at equity, and is perhaps the outstanding product of the policies and values of judges of the old Court of Chancery. The ownership at law of the trustee was admitted in equity, but considerations of justice demanded that the content of his ownership should be exercised for the benefit of another person, who did not enjoy ownership at law. The interest of such a beneficiary was at first merely a personal one availing against the trustee alone, but the increasing need to protect that interest in ever-widening spheres led to it being regarded as a kind of ownership. The question is what it is that the beneficiary owns. The short answer is—the totality of his interest, which consists mainly of the due performance and exercise by the trustee of his duties and powers. The nature of this interest is largely tied up with the other question whether the beneficiary's interest is *in personam* or *in rem*. To those who assert that it is *in personam* there is no difficulty whatever. The beneficiary's interest is simply the totality of claims *in personam* against the trustee. The term 'beneficial ownership' is therefore either a misnomer, or else a novelty bearing no analogy with ownership at law. There is no 'thing' which he owns. To those who accept that equitable interests can be *in rem* the problem remains. One solution might be to treat the totality of the interest as a 'thing' in itself, which is what the beneficiary owns, and there is also the point that, on certain occasions at any rate, he owns concurrently at equity the very things which are owned by the trustee at law[8].

The beneficiary might himself be a trustee of his interest for a third person, in which case his equitable ownership is as devoid of advantage to him as the legal ownership is to the trustee. So, when described in terms of ownership, the distinction between legal and equitable ownership lies in the historical factors that govern their creation and function; in terms of advantage,

---

6 See Aquinas *Summa Theologica* 11a, 2ae, 66.2.
7 Eg Community Land Act 1975.
8 *Miller v Collins* [1896] 1 Ch 573; *Re Fox, Brooks v Marston* [1913] 2 Ch 75; *A-G v Farrell* [1931] 1 KB 81. Cf *Gresham Life Assurance Society v Crowther* [1915] 1 Ch 214.

the distinction is between the bare right, whether legal or equitable, and the beneficial right[9].

Ownership and liberty

At the height of the individualist era the tendency was to give 'fundamental rights' the fullest possible scope. This is reflected, *inter alia*, in the way in which ownership, as a 'fundamental right of property', was regarded. An example is the definition of Austin, who wrote at the beginning of the nineteenth century. Ownership he described as

'a right—indefinite in point of user—unrestricted in point of disposition—and unlimited in point of duration—over a determinate thing'[10].

Such limitations as undoubtedly did exist were treated as exceptions and restrictively. English law, with its continuous history for many centuries, has a large number of principles reflecting the liberties of the individual and the sanctity of property.

From about the middle of the nineteenth century onwards, emphasis began to shift with ever-increasing momentum towards society and away from the individual. The preoccupation was with the wants of people, with one's duties towards others, rather than with one's 'rights'. A person can only do what he likes with his thing within certain limits, which are determined by the interests of others, and which have become increasingly severe. These limitations are integral to the concept of ownership and not exceptions to an otherwise unlimited right. Austin, in fact, was careful to emphasise that the liberties of user are not *unlimited*, but *indefinite*[11]. The limitations may have been fewer in the past than they are now, but they have always represented the need to compromise between individual interests and life in society.

The common law and statutory duties restricting liberty that now exist need not be gone into in detail. An owner may not destroy or damage his own property to injure another[12]. The fact of ownership can give rise to duties. Thus, the tightening of nuisance, for instance, the rule in *Rylands v Fletcher*[13] (both assuming their present form since the latter part of the last century), the rule in *Donoghue v Stevenson*[14], and many other such rules will be familiar to any student of the law of tort. Statutory restrictions are legion, on building, farming etc. Clear illustrations of social policy are to be found in the restrictions imposed in the interests of public health and safety, the drastic restrictions in times of national peril, restrictions on the use, misuse and non-use of patents, and so on. Judicial interpretation of statutory limitations on ownership used to incline in favour of the individual, but there is now a greater awareness of the social purpose behind them.

Ownership and power

Social reformers, notably those who accept the teachings of Karl Marx, have drawn attention to the evil role which ownership has played. The most

9 Campbell 'Some Footnotes to Salmond's *Jurisprudence*' (1940) 7 CLJ at 217.
10 Austin *Jurisprudence* II, p 790.
11 Austin *Jurisprudence* I, p 371.
12 Malicious Damage Act 1861, ss 3, 59; superseded by the Criminal Damage Act 1971, ss 1 (2), 3.
13 (1868) LR 3 HL 330.
14 [1932] AC 562.

reasoned exposition is that of Renner[15]. It is convenient to begin the Marxist analysis with the individual, who at first provided his own tools, raw materials and labour. With these he manufactured a product which he traded at a profit to himself. When he had accumulated sufficient profit in this way, he was in a position to provide the tools and raw material and get other people to provide the labour. The manufactured product, however, was still in his ownership, not in that of the labourers, and he continued to trade with it for his own profit. In this way the worker became alienated from his labour. It is the concept of ownership, coupled with the institution of hire, that enabled this to happen. Ownership of the means of production, ie tools and raw material, thus came to be a source of power over persons for private profit. The power is manifested chiefly in the inequality of the contract of employment, for by utilising the power of dismissal and the threat of unemployment and consequent starvation, the employer was able to dictate unequal terms of service. Also, owners of the means of production tend to grow into industrial commanders, wielding power that strikes at the foundations of society. By obtaining a monopoly in a certain commodity such an owner can corner the market and hold society to ransom as it were. Renner predicted that law would have to take account of the increasingly public character of ownership of property by investing it with the characteristics of public law. Ownership of other forms of capital can also become sources of profit, for instance, by way of interest on loans or rent from letting and hiring. Such a state of affairs, especially the power over persons for private profit, is anathema to socialists. They point to the unified concept of ownership as being the villain of the piece. 'Private property is robbery, and a state based on private property is a state of robbers who fight to share in the spoils': so said Lenin[16]. The remedy, which they advocate, is to apply in varying degrees two concepts of ownership, a public and a private one. Ownership of the means of production should be public, ie nationalised, and only ownership of consumer goods should be open to private individuals. The distinction lies, not in the nature of ownership, but in the things capable of being owned[17].

Some of the tendencies outlined in Renner's analysis can be said to have taken place, especially with regard to the increasingly public character of industrial property and the growth of combines; but Marx's gloomier forebodings have not materialised in Western countries because of developments in curbing profit and power and in certain other directions, which were either unforeseen or not taken into account sufficiently. Professor Friedmann examined the chief of these at some length[18].

With regard to curbs on power, there has been some removal of the old inequalities that used to prevail between employers and employees. Equality of bargaining in industry has been restored by the growth of trade unions and by the recognition of a liberty to strike[19]. Some of the fears of unemployment have been removed, especially since the introduction of unemployment and other welfare benefits. The dictation of terms by employers has become

15 Renner *Institutions of Private Law and their Social Functions* (1949 edited by Kahn-Freund), on which see Friedmann *Law and Social Change* ch 2.
16 Lenin 31 *Collected Works* (3rd edn) p 300.
17 The USSR recognises private ownership: Constitution (Fundamental Law) of the USSR art 12.
18 Friedmann *Law in a Changing Society* ch 3.
19 This kind of control is not possible in Soviet Russia, where union activities are limited to welfare and strikes are forbidden.

a thing of the past owing to the use now of standardised contracts hammered out between unions and employers, and also owing to the power of unions in other ways. Moreover, judges interpret terms of employment more favourably towards employees than was once the case, as pointed out in Chapter 10. Various duties are imposed on employers by statute and common law in the interests of employees, and out of some of these employers cannot contract.

With regard to curbs on profit, it might be noted that legislative controls now exist as to profits, interests and rents. Income tax, and value added tax and rates are arguably a means of forcing people to put their profits to public use, scaled taxation has helped to level the unequal distribution of wealth, while levies of various sorts compel people to discriminate in the national interest between essential and non-essential commodities.

Several other methods have been evolved of controlling power[20]. For instance, the courts now exercise vigilance on the power of owners to forbid competition by means of restrictive covenants in contracts of service; and in the chapter on Persons mention was made of judicial and statutory 'lifting the mask' of corporate unity to check abuses[1].

The most important method of control has been nationalisation of ownership of means of production. As a curb on the misuse of power, its value has proved to be limited owing to the separation of power from ownership, which was mentioned in connection with corporations[2]. Thus, company A can acquire a controlling number of shares in company B with the result that power resides in A and not B, although B remains owner at law. Further, ownership of a share in A carries more power than ownership of one in B, which is deprived of even such power as it had[3]. With complex and highly technical undertakings power now lies, not in the corporation, which owns the property, or in its shareholders, but in managerial experts. The capitalist has become alienated from his capital. One of Marx's more remarkable insights was that he foresaw this very development, only he treated it as an internal development within capitalism and part of the increasing alienation of the worker[4]. Therefore, nationalising ownership has not provided the hoped-for control of power, and the managerial revolution has had a wider and different impact than Marx had envisaged. What is needed is not nationalisation of ownership, but control of power by managers[5]. In multi-party systems of government it is essential that the managerial boards of nationalised concerns should be independent of the government of the day if they are to enjoy continuity and function efficiently. Governmental control of them, therefore, poses problems[6]. In addition to all this, nationalisation has other drawbacks, previously mentioned, in that it adds political power

20 There has been a recent tendency towards profiteering in 'anti-social' ways by means of terms in standard form contracts, eg exclusion clauses, minimum payment clauses in hire-purchase contracts etc. The courts have sought to curb such abuses in various ways— insistence on reasonable notice, strict interpretation, *contra proferentem* rule and, possibly, avoidance for unreasonableness. See also The Unfair Contract Terms Act 1977.

1 See pp 256 et seq ante.

2 See p 256 ante.

3 See p 255 ante.

4 Marx *Capital* III, ch 27, iii. Cf. Burnham *The Managerial Revolution*, on which see Avineri *The Social and Political Thought of Karl Marx* pp 177–179.

5 Eg the Transport Act 1947, Sch 13, attached obligations directly to controlling companies and not to the owner companies; the Health and Safety at Work etc. Act 1974 s 37, makes managers and directors personally responsible for breaches of safety regulations.

6 See H.C. Debates of 3rd March 1948.

to economic power and brings in its train increased bureaucracy and all it entails; and it may also, arguably, hinder rational planning. Besides, nationalisation fails to get rid of one of the very dangers anticipated by Marx. Workers still only receive wages, not ownership in the product, so that they remain alienated from their labour; and they are still open to exploitation, the only difference being that this is not for private profit. Removing the element of profit does not touch the problem of power, which is why workers continue to strike against nationalised concerns as much as they ever did.

The Marxist analysis is thus not wholly applicable to Western societies because it is out of date. It was certainly put into practice with success in Soviet Russia, but easy parallels should not be drawn from this. For one thing, nationalisation was carried out there while the Russian concept of ownership was still in the potentially dangerous state that ownership had been in the West over a hundred years before. Since then in Western countries most of the potential evils have either been removed or curbed. Historically, too, there is an important difference. Owing to the vast area of Russia and the diversity of races and cultures and their traditional resistance to 'Russification', it was the Tsars who inaugurated industrial enterprises and then sold or leased them to individuals. Therefore, nationalisation in 1917 only restored to the state what had historically been its property. The same would not be true of Western countries. The one-party system of government in Russia enables continuous supervision to be exercised over the managerial boards of nationalised concerns, which, as pointed out, cannot obtain in Western type democracies. Nationalisation certainly facilitates a planned economy; but capitalist states have also adopted planning, and a few of them, eg Great Britain, have shown how nationalisation can work within a capitalist framework.

From all that has been said it should be clear that formal analysis of ownership alone fails to convey any idea of the part it has played in society. A functional study is indispensable to a complete understanding, for it reveals that the concept of ownership is full of potentialities as an instrument of policy and social regulation on a large scale. Modern developments, especially the severing of control from ownership, now indicate that it is a man's position and role in society that determines his relation to things, and not *vice versa* as used to be the case.

READING LIST

L C Becker *Property Rights: Philosophical Foundations.*

A A Berle and G C Means *The Modern Corporation and Private Property* Parts I and II.

M R Cohen *Law and Social Order* 41.

W Friedmann *Law in a Changing Society* ch 3.

J N Hazard *Law and Social Change in the USSR* ch 1.

A M Honoré 'Ownership' in *Oxford Essays in Jurisprudence* (ed A G Guest) ch 5.

J M Lightwood *A Treatise on Possession of Land* chs 5–6.

F S Philbrick 'Changing Conceptions of Property in Law' (1938) 86 University of Pennsylvania Law Review 691.

K Renner *The Institutions of Private Law and their Social Functions* (trans A Schwarzschild, ed O Kahn-Freund).

J W Salmond on *Jurisprudence* (7th edn) ch 12.

J W C Turner 'Some Reflections on Ownership in English Law' (1941) 19 Canadian Bar Review 342.

CHAPTER 15

Justice in adapting to change

The fourth task in the achievement of justice, outlined at the start of this book, is adapting to change. Just as consonance with accepted ideas is an inducement to obey, so also when these change, tensions arise between the law on the one hand, and needs and outlook on the other, and there is then an inducement to ignore the law or to disobey. Failure to use power to adapt to change is in its own way an abuse of power. The issue is thus not one of change or no change, but of the direction and speed of change. The Laws of the Medes and Persians were said to be immutable; but unless a system is capable of adapting itself to changing conditions, it can only go the way of the Laws of the Medes and Persians. Adaptability is truly a condition *sine qua non* of the continued existence of a legal system. Lord Justice Scarman epitomised this thesis at the start of his Hamlyn Lectures when he posed the blunt question:

> 'I shall endeavour to show that there are in the contemporary world challenges, social, political, and economic, which, if the system cannot meet them, will destroy it. These challenges are not created by lawyers; they certainly cannot be suppressed by lawyers: they have to be met either by discarding or by adjusting the legal system. Which is it to be?'[1].

Change within a legal system may come in various ways, by day-to-day adjustment of detail and tinkering with the concepts used in legal reasoning, which is appropriate in a slow moving society; or by reform on a larger scale, which becomes inevitable when the whole social structure begins to change. The system itself may be changed, in which case the change may be constitutional or revolutionary. Before considering the ways in which changes may be accommodated within a legal system, it would be as well to pay attention to some of the forces of change.

SOCIAL EVOLUTION

No society is static. Changes develop gradually over the years in practically every sphere brought about by evolution in environmental, economic and political circumstances, national and global, as well as in religious and moral ideas. They may occur slowly or rapidly; they may be ephemeral as with passing fashions, or permanent. What happens is that practices evolve which influence the ways in which laws actually operate, eg trade practices. When the behaviour of people has moved away from the law with a sufficient degree of permanence, tensions arise with varying results. The law itself may be stretched to take account of the development, or it may be ignored until

---

1 Scarman *English Law—the new Dimension* p 1. See also 'Law and Administration: a Change in Relationship' (1972) PA 253. For change in International Law, see E Lauterpacht 'The inevitability of change in International Law and the need for adjustment of interests', 51 ALJ 83.

it becomes a dead letter, or it may be repealed and a new law substituted. In these ways evolution gives direction to future development.

Evolutionary change has long been the subject of attention by Continental jurists, chiefly German. Savigny, who is accredited as the Father of the Historical School, adopted a conservative approach. Law, he said, is a manifestation of the *Volksgeist*, the spirit of the people, so that it alters with the development of this spirit. Of its very nature such a process is bound to be slow. Although he did not oppose conscious efforts at law reform, he preached that this should always follow the *Volksgeist*, or else it was doomed. His doctrine thus had a depressing effect on law reform. The flaw in his thesis lies in the idea of the *Volksgeist* itself, which is so amorphous as to be unascertainable and meant that reform had to await the clarification of something that could never be clarified. A more acceptable version of evolutionary change came from Ehrlich, who distinguished between what he called 'formal law' and 'living law': the former is represented by laws in statutes, precedents and books, the latter by the way these actually work in social life. The views of Savigny and Ehrlich will be dealt with later[2].

Both these approaches are unable to cope with the palpitating state of society today. Even that of Ehrlich, superior though it is to Savigny's, can only apply while society is evolving comfortably within its legal system. Today, galvanic changes are taking place, each of which can radically alter the system itself. It will require a volume to deal with these changes in detail, but for the purpose of illustrating the theme of this chapter it is only necessary to point to a few examples. For many years business and commercial dealings have been referred to arbitration in the event of dispute, rather than to the courts. This is because the rules and procedures of the latter are not the most suitable means of reaching acceptable solutions. The law still has a supervisory jurisdiction, which in the main is not used. In the sphere of labour relations the movement began in the first decade of this century to oust the jurisdiction of the courts. In torts this had to be done by legislation, in contracts the agreements themselves provide for it. This has dangers. For each union to be able to pursue its own course unhampered is not conducive to a planned economy, while protection of individual workers from abuse of power by their unions disappears. The need for controls in these matters is imperative if industrial and economic chaos is to be avoided. The question is how far a legal framework is suitable in the prevailing climate.

The changes that will have to be made in the wake of the welfare activities of the state are still being realised. Planning, compulsory acquisition, benefits and such like are throwing up increasing problems as between the state and individuals. Lord Justice Scarman in his Hamlyn Lectures drew attention to an important point. The courts can only play a modest role, since from time immemorial their work has been geared to disputes between adversaries, one of whom must be in the wrong, ie their function has been to dispense corrective justice. With welfare-type problems all the parties involved are more or less in the right, ie the function is to adjust distributive justice[3]. The courts are accustomed to deal with the individual, socialism deals with the mass. Legal principles, orientated to safeguarding the interests of the former, are likely to fail even in that task in the areas of planning and social welfare unless the collectivist outlook on such problems is appreciated and new

2 See pp 376, 425, post.
3 *Scarman* ch 3. He also deals with some of the matters mentioned above.

principles evolved. It is not enough to keep adapting the law; there has to be an adaptation of lawyers' thinking. In the sphere of marriage, the law did change its attitude to divorce when the concept of matrimonial offence was replaced by that of irretrievable breakdown[4]. The recent development towards sex equality is bound to have repercussions on family life; the positions of husbands and wives in relation to each other and children are bound to alter. In addition, events are taking place nationally and internationally, which are likely to alter the very constitutional structure of the country. Devolution of power to Scotland and Wales will obviously entail a change in governmental institutions as well as in jurisdiction and authority. These will involve, not just new laws effecting the necessary changes, but a new outlook. It has been pointed out earlier that membership of the European Economic Community, is already having an effect, embryonic as yet, on Parliamentary sovereignty, binding authority, and other cherished dogmas[5]. The courts, too, as acknowledged by Lord Denning, will need to adapt themselves to thinking along unfamiliar lines.

It will be evident from these examples how vital is the need for the law to adapt itself to social change if it is to survive. In a different sphere, consideration should also be given to changes occasioned by scientific advances. What needs to be pointed out is their impact on concepts and doctrines, rather than the host of new laws. It is not possible to deal with each and every such development, but brief allusion will be made to two, namely the introduction of computers and certain medical advances, both of which are likely to have far-reaching effects.

Computers

The influence of computers on law has already effected significant changes, and there is likelihood that there will be many more with the increasing sophistication of equipment and techniques. Analysis of their impact should be sought in specialised works[6]. Computers have brought with them a new jargon: 'input', 'print-out', 'processing', 'programming', 'storage', 'retrieval', 'software', 'hardware'. A fear that needs to be dispelled is that computers will replace the warmth of human justice with an alien philosophy. On the contrary, all that is claimed for them is that they can help and improve human justice and relieve people of drudgery by performing routine jobs more efficiently.

One of the most important facilities provided by computers is the storage and retrieval of information at a greater range and depth than hitherto[7]. The drawback is that however a question is programmed and re-programmed too much tends to be retrieved, which still leaves a formidable job of sifting through it. Certain practical advantages are that computers can assist practitioners by timing and costing interviews with clients; they make light work of conveyancing and patent searches and in drafting documents and letters of a routine nature; they assist with the tasks of crowd control and the detection and prevention of crime. More arguably, they can be used

4 Divorce Reform Act 1969.
5 See pp 104 et seq. ooo ante.
6 For early assessments, see Tapper *Computers and the Law*; also Dickerson 'Some Jurisprudential Implications of Electronic Data Processing' (1963) 28 Law and Contemporary Problems 53; Allen *Computers and the Law* (ed Bigelow) p 167.
7 As provided by Lexis.

to give provisional solutions to problems, but this depends on how the problems are programmed.

Several areas of law have changed and are changing. The threat to privacy, in particular, is giving rise to increasing concern[8]. Copyright and patent law need revision on such questions as the moment at which protection should be available, whether at the input or print-out stage, and patent protection for software. Rules of evidence and procedure, too, have needed modification in important respects, eg enlarging the concept of 'document'; discovery of documents, especially when the information is stored in a neutrally owned data bank; the contemporaneous evidence rule; and the rule against hearsay[9].

Finally, it remains to be seen what effect computers will have on law reporting and the concept of law. The decision whether or not to report a case rests at present with the reporter, which means that what becomes 'law' through *stare decisis* depends on the choice of individual reporters. If every decision were stored in a computer, this would broaden the basis of what becomes 'law', besides eliminating the embarrassments caused by overlooked authorities and divergences sometimes found in different reports of the same case[10]. The further possibility is that because of their ability to collate rapidly masses of heterogeneous information the day may come when computers are able to pick up in detail the prevailing social *mores* and values and relate these to judicial decisions. Decisions will then cease to be 'laws' in themselves and will become only evidence of current value-patterns[11], ie a direct link will have been established between values and the concept of law, which may even yield a new 'social' natural law. Such possibilities are as yet afar, but there is no doubt that computers have brought lawyers to the threshold of exciting new developments.

Medical advances

Medical science has provided examples of the way in which modern developments are forcing the law to restructure certain concepts hitherto supposed to be so obvious and straightforward that few lawyers, if any, even dreamed that they would be seriously challenged. What, for instance, is an 'act' and 'omission', what is 'death', or 'man', or 'woman'? These are now in the melting pot and it remains to be seen in what form modified concepts will emerge. Lawyers must understandably hold back with their revision while the problems are still in ferment, for the profoundest moral, social and scientific issues have still to be resolved. Traditional concepts, however, no longer provide the best tools with which to handle the kind of problems that are emerging.

Taking, first, the terms 'act' and 'omission', it is necessary to begin with

8 Miller 'Personal Privacy in the Computer Age: the Challenge of a New Technology in an Information Oriented Society' (1969) 67 Mich LR 1091; Westin *Privacy and Freedom*; Warner and Stone *The Data Bank Society*; *Tapper* ch 3; 'Computers and Privacy'. (Cmnds 6353, 6354).
9 See eg Criminal Evidence Act 1965, s 1 (4) (for a gap: *R v Pettigrew, R v Newark* [1980] Crim LR 239); Civil Evidence Act 1968, s 5; *The Statue of Liberty* [1968] 2 All ER 195, [1968] 1 WLR 739; *Grant v Southwestern and County Properties Ltd* [1975] Ch 185, [1974] 2 All ER 465; *Barker v Wilson* [1980] 2 All ER 81, [1980] 1 WLR 884 ('bankers' books' in the Bankers' Books Evidence Act 1879, s 9, include microfilm); *R v Wood* [1982] Crim LR 667 (a computer print-out is not hearsay).
10 Hudson 'Some Reflections on Information Retrieval' (1968) 6 Osgoode Hall LJ 259.
11 *Hudson* 267.

their accepted usages in order to appreciate the difficulties that have arisen. As with other concepts, 'act' has no one meaning, but a range of applications. (i) The narrowest is 'a bodily movement controllable by will'[12]. (ii) 'A bodily movement controllable by will in relation to circumstances', eg the 'act of shooting' includes the bodily movement of lifting one's hand and flexing one's finger and the attendant circumstances of there being a gun in the hand. (iii) 'A bodily movement controllable by will in relation to circumstances and results, eg the 'act of battery' includes the bodily movement of flexing one's finger in the circumstances of that finger being round the trigger of a gun and the result of the bullet hitting another person. The 'act of killing' requires the further result of death within a year and a day[13].

The element common to these applications is controllability by will. Whenever an action is controllable by will it is classed as 'voluntary', as opposed to 'involuntary', eg sleep-walking. The need for controllability, as distinct from control, is seen with unthinking rather than unconscious actions. An example is tapping a table when one is engrossed in something else; such action is controllable as soon as one thinks of it. So, too, with breathing up to a point; one can consciously hold one's breath, though for a short time only, since unconsciousness will supervene and breathing will then recommence automatically. The point of controllability is that the purpose of the law is to ascribe responsibility justly. It is also to be noticed that voluntariness only comes to the fore when it is sought to excuse an actor from responsibility on the ground that his action was involuntary. In general, legal responsibility attaches only where conduct has been voluntary. Thus, a man is not answerable in trespass to land if he has been carried there by others[14] but he is liable if he has been compelled to enter by threats[15]. In the latter case, the threats only provide the motive for what is regarded in law as his 'voluntary' action in the sense that he was still in control of the movement of his limbs. On the other hand, where an actor is not in control of his movements, eg sleep-walking or in a fit, he is excused as his conduct is involuntary[16]. As a test for ascribing responsibility, controllability is clumsy and gives rise to difficulties. It could lead to absurdity, as where a man who leaps over a fence on to private property to escape from a bull is answerable in trespass, but not if he is tossed over by the bull. To avoid such a conclusion, the concept of necessity will have to be widened. Another difficulty is presented by a case where a man points a loaded gun at another with the sole object of frightening him, but an unexpected noise so startles him that he jerks the trigger. Ascription of responsibility here is better determined with reference to the course of conduct as a whole and not with reference to

---

12 'An act is always a voluntary muscular contraction, and nothing else': Holmes *The Common Law* p 91 and also p 54. See also Austin *Jurisprudence* I, pp 366, 414–415, 419; Warren and Carmichael *The Elements of Human Psychology* p 419.

13 *R v Robert Millar (Contractors) Ltd* [1970] 2 QB 54, [1970] 1 All ER 577.

14 *Smith v Stone* (1647) Sty 65; *Gibbons (Gibbon) v Pepper* (1695) 2 Salk 637.

15 *Gilbert v Stone* (1647) Sty 72. See also Hale *PC* I, 434. As the Digest aptly puts it, *coactus volui: D* 4.2.21.5.

16 *R v Charlson* [1955] 1 All ER 859 especially at 861, 864. See also *R v Harrison-Owen* [1951] 2 All ER 726; *Hill v Baxter* [1958] 1 QB 277 at 282–283, [1958] 1 All ER 193 at 195; *R v Spurge* [1961] 2 QB 205 at 210–211, [1961] 2 All ER 688 at 690; *Watmore v Jenkins* [1962] 2 QB 572, [1962] 2 All ER 868; *Burns v Bidder* [1967] 2 QB 227 at 240–241, [1966] 3 All ER 29 at 36; *R v Quick, R v Paddison* [1973] QB 910, [1973] 3 All ER 347; *R v Isitt* [1978] Crim LR 159.

the controllability of the action of pulling the trigger[17]. Both these examples show that the requirement of 'voluntariness' is in need of revision.

A different kind of problem is raised by automatism. When through disease or other such affliction a person is deprived of consciousness, then, as just explained, he is not 'acting' in the eyes of the law. Should he be prone to such attacks he constitutes a menace to others. There are two ways of dealing with this situation. One is to impress upon persons the need to provide in advance against the recurrence of the affliction while they are still able to take precautions[18]. Thus, automatism will not be a defence unless the defendant as a reasonable man had no grounds for anticipating the onset of an attack[19]. It will apply when uncontrollability results from wholly extraneous causes, such as a blow on the head. The other way is to hold that every case in which there is evidence of disease likely to produce recurrent attacks should be treated as one of insanity rather than automatism[20]. In this way, as pointed out earlier, the defence of insanity has been given a new dimension.

In contrast to an 'act', an 'omission' is a failure to act. In this sense omission would cover everything that is not an act, which is clearly too wide. It has, therefore, to be restricted and at once becomes technical. The limits become apparent when it is realised that, as with act, lawyers are concerned with omissions for the purpose of ascribing responsibility justly. They are relevant only when there has been a failure to comply with duties to act. Such duties are encountered in various situations and their existence is, as always, a matter of policy. 'An omission on the part of one or other of the defendants' said Willmer LJ 'would not furnish the plaintiff with any cause of action in the absence of some duty to act by the defendant to the plaintiff'[1].

The dividing line between acts and omissions is not clear cut. In the first place, omissions should be distinguished from failures which are incidental to larger activities. A motorist who fails to stop at a 'halt' sign and collides with another vehicle will be answerable, not for an omission as such, but for the bad execution of the active operation of driving. The situation is viewed as a whole, the omission, which is incidental to the larger activity, rendering it a misdoing rather than a pure not doing[2]. The position may be viewed differently in other circumstances. In *Fagan v Metropolitan Police Comr*[3] the

---

17 For a case similar to this example, see *Ryan v R* (1967) 40 ALJR 488, and especially the judgment of Windeyer J. See also Elliott 'Responsibility for Involuntary Acts: *Ryan v R* (1967-68) 41 ALJ 497.

18 So, voluntarily doing an act, such as taking a drug capable of inducing harmful involuntary conduct, is punishable: *R v Lipman* [1970] 1 QB 152, [1969] 3 All ER 410.

19 *Jones v Dennison* [1971] RTR 174, where the defendant was held not to be negligent in driving a car when he was totally unaware of a tendency to blackout. See also *R v Sibbles* [1959] Crim LR 660. Cf *Hill v Baxter* [1958] 1 QB 277, [1958] 1 All ER 193; *Green v Hills* (1969) 113 Sol Jo 385; *Moss v Winder* [1981] RTR 37; *Boomer v Penn* (1965) 52 DLR (2d) 673.

20 *R v Kemp* [1957] 1 QB 399, [1956] 3 All ER 249; *Bratty v A-G for Northern Ireland* [1963] AC 386, [1961] 3 All ER 523; and see p 202 ante.

1 *Zoernsch v Waldock* [1964] 2 All ER 256 at 262, [1964] 1 WLR 675 at 685. No one is under a duty to play the good Samaritan and rescue another who is in peril: 'Thou shalt not kill, but needst not strive officiously to keep alive'. It has been held in a Canadian case that once a person embarks upon an active task of rescue, he could be liable if the method of rescue, or its abandonment, leaves the party in danger worse off than he would otherwise have been: *The Ogopogo* [1971] 2 Lloyd's Rep 410 (affg [1970] 1 Lloyd's Rep 257). Cf Roman law where also there was no general answerability for omissions: *D* 7.1.13.2.

2 The same view was taken in Roman law: *Coll* 12.7.7; *D* 9.2.8. *pr*.

3 [1969] 1 QB 439, [1968] 3 All ER 442.

Divisional Court was divided in its opinion as to whether the appellant committed an assault by driving his car accidentally on to a policeman's foot and then spitefully letting it remain there. The majority thought this was an assault because it was a continuing act, which became intentional after he realised what he had done; but Bridge J thought that it was at most an intentional omission to remove the car.

Another difficulty lies in applying the idea of voluntariness to omissions. (i) Just as action is excused as involuntary when something is done to or befalls an actor, so too an omission is involuntary when that which is done to or befalls a person prevents him from doing what he should do. Thus, a professional singer may be prevented from fulfilling an engagement through a sudden illness on the eve of a performance. (ii) When a person is aware of the duty to act and abstains, the omission may be said to be voluntary. (iii) When a person is aware of the circumstances that give rise to the duty and abstains, the omission is likewise voluntary. (iv) When a person is not mindful of the duty to act or of the circumstances giving rise to it, the ascription of responsibility to such an omission depends upon whether he should have been mindful or not. Here the terms 'voluntary' and 'involuntary' cease to be appropriate.

Notwithstanding these difficulties, the law has so far managed to steer a clumsy course. Certain medical developments in recent years have necessitated a radical rethinking of act and omission. Ways have now been devised of keeping death at bay by artificial means with the result that the question whether or not to prolong life in the case of terminal diseases has stirred up issues of the deepest concern. For instance, an intentional act, which terminates a 'living death', is *prima facie* punishable as murder. Liability is not quite so automatic in the case of an omission since there has to be a duty to act, which depends upon the circumstances, including, among other things, the relationship between the parties. In this way flexibility enters into the question of liability for an omission; but not for an act, where such considerations come in, if at all, only by way of excuse for *prima facie* liability, or in mitigation of sentence. There is much force in the contention that the same considerations should apply to acts, which end terminal diseases, as to omissions. To achieve this result, however, any such act will have to be regarded as a form of omission, a failure to prolong life. Act or omission, the moral issues remain the same, so there is no justification for a difference in approach. As an acute observer has asked, if difference there has to be, why should it turn simply on whether a person switched off a life-sustaining machine, or failed to switch it on[4]? Two considerations support the treatment of such actions as omissions. One is that some omissions are treated as being absorbed into acts, eg failure to stop at a 'halt' sign. Why, then, should not some acts be absorbed into omissions? The other is that linguistically there is a distinction between 'causing' harm, eg by shooting a person, and 'permitting' harm to occur, eg by not giving help to a wounded person[5]. Acts are generally associated with 'causing' harm and omissions with 'permitting' harm to occur. Consonant with linguistic usage, some omissions may also be spoken of as 'causing' harm, eg failure to take insulin 'causes' a diabetic coma. Likewise, there would be no violation of linguistic usage in saying that some acts 'permit' harm to occur, eg switching off a mechanical respirator,

4 Fletcher 'Prolonging Life' (1967) 42 Wash LR 999.
5 *Fletcher.*

which permits death to supervene. This way of looking at the matter might pave the way towards their acceptance as a species of omission, in short, for a revision of the concepts of act and omission[6].

Techniques of organ transplantation have created other conceptual difficulties. There must always remain a distinction between removing tissue, which is still living, from a dead body and out of a live body, which dies as a result. Organ transplants have raised in an acute form the question: At what point is a body dead?[7] Is it when the EEG recording of the electrical activity of the brain gives a flat reading? What of a person whose brain still registers the barest activity, but who is in an irreversible coma and has lost all meaningful life?[8] Donations by living persons of their organs for life-saving purposes, eg kidney donations, create a problem as to the defence of consent. The accepted rule is that no person may legally consent to the infliction of grievous bodily harm on himself[9]. *Bona fide* surgical operations are exceptions because they are performed in the interest of the person consenting. In the case of organ donation, however, the question is whether a person can consent to the infliction on himself of what is, after all, grievous bodily harm for the benefit, not of himself, but of another. May a third party, eg the parent of a young child, validly consent to the removal of organs from the child? If these are permissible, then the scope of consent will have been enlarged[10]. Finally, some allusion might be made to the possibility of effecting a 'sex change' by means of surgical and hormone treatment. A British court was confronted for the first time with the question, What is a 'woman'?, when a man had himself converted into a 'woman' and then married. The decision that he remained a 'man' turned, not on the application of rules or precedents, but on complex medical criteria and socio-moral considerations of the purpose and function of marriage[11].

---

6 Switching off a life support machine where the patient was the victim of an assault does not constitute an intervening act. Hence the assailant is regarded as having caused death: *R v Malcherek, R v Steel* [1981] 2 All ER 422, [1981] 1 WLR 690, CA. So, too, *R v Blaue* [1975] 3 All ER 446, [1975] 1 WLR 1411, CA.

7 The South African Anatomical Donations and Post-mortem Examinations Act 1970 (No 24 of 1970) speaks of donations and removal of tissue from dead bodies, but provides no test of death.

8 The quality of life appears to have been the point in the American case of Karen Quinlan, who was in this condition and whose father applied to court for permission to disconnect the life-sustaining machine. The New Jersey Court refused, saying that no one had a constitutional right to die, and that 'there is a presumption that one chooses to go on living'. The court also cast on the doctors the decision whether Karen was to be removed from the machine or not: The Times, 11 November 1975. This was reversed by the Supreme Court, which left the decision to her legal guardian in consultation with doctors: The Times, 1 April 1976. The machine was switched off, but she died only in 1985. See also the case of Judith Ann Debro, whose brain was apparently biologically dead. Both the trial and appellate courts refused to decide whether her husband should be allowed to disconnect the life-sustaining machine by ruling that they had no jurisdiction: The Times 10 November 1975. It would seem that in her case the courts failed to measure up to their responsibility.

9 *R v Donovan* [1934] 2 KB 498.

10 For both points, see the South African Anatomical Donations and Post-mortem Examinations Act 1970. According to the Congenital Disabilities (Civil Liability) Act 1976, s 1, a child is prevented from suing in respect of a preconceptional occurrence, which results in the child's disability, if the parents had accepted the particular risk.

11 *Corbett v Corbett* [1971] P 110, [1970] 2 All ER 33. See also *W v W* 1976 (2) SA 308; *R v Tan* [1983] QB 1053, [1983] 2 All ER 12, CA.

CHANGE THROUGH DISOBEDIENCE

Civil disobedience has become a problem in many societies in recent times, and changes have been brought about in consequence. The question is how far, if at all, disobedience can be accommodated within a theory of law. On the face of it, there is an obvious contradiction here; but if law is thought of in a continuum and ability to change is regarded as a condition of the continuity of law, then disobedience could, within limits, be included among the phenomena inducing legal change.

It is necessary, first, to consider what 'disobedience' means. It is in permissive societies that disobedience begins to assume the proportions of a problem. In them, the emphasis on liberty inevitably inspires resistance to duty, and coupled with this there tends to be in such societies an amelioration of sanctions and consequent weakening of fear of them. The fear motive should not be exaggerated, but equally it should not be ignored. Also, where there are deep-seated religious or social antagonisms, a permissive attitude sharpens the tensions by encouraging minorities. Finally, a permissive society fosters rapid changes in moral ideas, thus producing increasing tensions between laws and behaviour.

There are different ways of disobeying. Disobedience could be directed at a particular law, or at all laws; it could be disobedience of a duty not to do something, or of a duty to do something; it could be in secret, as in ordinary criminality, or open and coupled with a readiness to undergo the penalty, which is defiance of the law. Further, individuals may disobey in any of these ways, or there may be mass disobedience. In the case of the latter, if the challenge is to all laws, the position is one of revolution; but so far as the challenge is of a particular law or group of laws, the aim is change rather than destruction. In the view of those advocating a change of system, it is not enough for individuals to disobey and show themselves willing to accept the penalty, for they are thereby submitting to the system. If the system needs to be changed, then everyone should disobey. It need not amount to revolution; it could be a process for remedying an evil and is, therefore, connected with morality. So far as mass disobedience stops short of permanent anarchy, there is implicit in it a willingness to abide by a better system. Also, if laws cannot bind conscience, it would seem that conscience is guided by some other superior dictate, which is somehow knowable. Such a dictate has to be something other than self-interest, which is incompatible with any kind of order. Finally, it is questionable whether mere non-co-operation should be treated as a form of disobedience.

Non-co-operation is a means of challenging some policy and may even succeed in changing it, eg the refusal by trade unions to co-operate under certain industrial legislation. Perhaps it is better not to treat non-co-operation as disobedience.

Two questions that have been distinguished earlier in this book are: why people *do* obey law, and why they *ought* to do so. The former has been considered[12]. The problem of disobedience concerns the latter.

It is meaningless to ask whether there is a legal duty to obey the law; the question is how far there is a moral duty to obey the legal duty, or preferably, how far disobedience should be allowed[13]. As has been pointed out, even

---

12 See pp 48 et seq. and 248 ante.

13 See *Law and Philosophy, A Symposium* (ed Hook) Part I; Wasserstrom 'The Obligation to Obey the Law' in *Essays in Legal Philosophy* (ed Summers) p 244.

where there is a legal duty, the individual has the inner moral liberty to obey or disobey[14]. The inquiry thus becomes a socio-moral one into the limits of disobedience to which there is no easy answer. Disobedience of an immoral law would not necessarily be thought immoral even by those who would still deem it 'law', though they would treat it as illegal; but neither would it necessarily be immoral to obey such a law, eg because of the need to prevent social disruption[15]. There could be moral justification either way, so other considerations have to come in.

One reason why people ought to obey may be dismissed at the outset. This is the charismatic authority of the law-giver, eg the divine right of kings. Another reason is consent, which looks plausible, but does not bear examination. Why should consent make obedience obligatory? The answer cannot be a legal one, since any rule that makes consent obligatory would itself require some other rule to make it obligatory, and so on. Consent makes contractual agreements obligatory because of a rule of law to that effect; the point is why this other rule is obligatory. To offer instead a moral justification for consent can only work in cases where consent has actually been given, eg contracts. The implication of the consent argument is not so much that consent is the reason why people ought to obey laws, but that once consent is withdrawn laws cease to be binding[16]. This is unreal since in vast areas of law, such as criminal law, torts and so on, no one has ever been asked if he or she consents to laws which are treated as binding, legally and morally, irrespective of consent or its withdrawal. If some people declare that they no longer consent to abide by certain laws, then the organised force of the state can be brought to bear on them thereby making consent or its absence immaterial. The real question is when it is justifiable for people to challenge the organised force of the state and when it is justifiable for the state to use its force, since there may be reasons why it is not always politic to use force. The problem thus moves away from consent and becomes one of striking a balance, ie fixing the limits within which disobedience can be tolerated.

Leaving consent aside, another reason sometimes offered for obedience is that disobedience sets a bad example. In so far as obedience by others exerts a psychological pressure to obey, disobedience relaxes that pressure. While it is true that disobedience of *this* law at *this* moment does not imply that it may be disobeyed all the time, still less that all laws may be disobeyed, nevertheless disobedience of this law now may inspire another to disobey in circumstances in which the first person would still have obeyed. In this way it could be the first step along the slippery slope towards breakdown and anarchy[17]. Again, it is said that disobedience may inflict hardship on others, and may entail undue expense in preventing or minimising its effects. Professor Rawls advances a 'fair-play' argument[18]. A just legal order, he says, is a system of co-operation by which people are bound as long as they accept its benefits. Such an order is founded on two Basic Principles: (1) Each person is to have the most extensive liberty compatible with a similar liberty in others; (2) social and economic inequalities must be for the greatest benefit

14 See pp 118 et seq ante.
15 This point seems to be overlooked by Wasserstrom. Cf Allen *Legal Duties* p 198; St Thomas Aquinas, p 474 post.
16 On the 'binding force' of law, see p 248 ante.
17 Goodhart *English Law and the Moral Law* p 25.
18 Rawls *A Theory of Justice* discussed at pp 480–484 post.

of the least advantaged (subject to the 'just savings principle'[19]) and should attach to positions and offices equally open to all. If an order is just, or nearly just, according to these criteria, fair play requires that those who accept its benefits are bound to obey laws of which they disapprove, provided that the burdens are evenly distributed and not too onerous and do not violate the Basic Principles. Professor Rawls would thus support limited disobedience, ie when these Principles are violated, if other means of obtaining redress fail and injury is not inflicted on the innocent. Similar to this is the argument put forward by Singer that the duty to obey derives from participation in a system which represents a fair compromise[20]. If one accepts decisions of which one approves, one is bound by a kind of quasi-consent or estoppel not to protest at decisions of which one disapproves. Singer would accept disobedience in order to restore the fair compromise basis of the system, because if this fails the reason for participation fails too[1]. Dworkin does not address himself primarily to obedience, but argues a case for disobedience deriving from what he calls 'the right to equal concern and respect', which is promised to minorities by the majority[2]. Based on this, he says, there are certain 'fundamental rights', which are akin to principles and are 'rights' against government. In these cases people have the liberty to follow conscience and to disobey the law, and it is wrong for government to punish them. The limits are, first, infringements of the 'fundamental rights' of others and, secondly, restrictions imposed by government to prevent catastrophe or to obtain a clear and major public benefit. No justification short of these will suffice. Finally, Raz says that 'there is no obligation to obey law', nor do moral or prudential reasons invest it with moral authority. In his view, obedience derives from 'respect for law', which is an aspect of loyalty to society analogous to friendship, which likewise presupposes mutual loyalty[3].

Are there situations of justified disobedience?

Two American authors have argued that some actions are, as they put it, 'legitimated' by law even when they are departures from it[4]. In addition to linguistic usages, which they say support their contention, they cite examples not all of which are convincing. A troublesome case is necessity, where a person does something which, but for necessity, would be illegal. If the limits of necessity are prescribed by law in advance of the action in question, then, assuming that the act falls within those limits, it cannot be described as disobedience since the law permits it. If, however, a court interprets necessity

---

19 This is that each generation must not only preserve the gains of culture and civilisation, but must also set aside 'a suitable amount of real capital accumulation': *Rawls* p 285. For the Basic Principles, see pp 60, 302.
20 Singer *Democracy and Disobedience*.
1 Singer goes on to argue that in large communities direct participation by every member has to yield to representative participation, which weakens the participation basis. Thus, representatives have to act according to conscience rather than the wishes of constituents when these are irreconcilable. Even if they act according to the wishes of the majority, those whose wishes are disappointed cannot be said to participate through their representatives. Singer contends further that in Western countries fair compromise tends to be negatived and participation weakened still further by the political party system and pressure groups.
2 Dworkin *Taking Rights Seriously*; and see p 501-503 post.
3 Raz *The Authority of Law, Essays on Law and Morality* Part IV. On respect for law see *Duport Steels Ltd v Sirs* [1980] 1 All ER 529, [1980] 1 WLR 142, HL.
4 Kadish and Kadish *Discretion to Disobey, A Study of Lawful Departures from Legal Rules*.

retrospectively in such a way as to cover the act, there are two ways of looking at the matter. It could be said that since the act was held to be justified, it was not illegal and hence not disobedience; but this is applying hindsight. At the time of the act itself, it looked like disobedience, may have been thought to be disobedience by the authorities and may well have been intended to be such by the actor. The most that can be said is that where the law is uncertain, an action may be performed to provide a test case with full acceptance of the consequence of it being held to be disobedience. In *R v Bourne*[5] a doctor performed an abortion on a girl, who was pregnant as a result of rape, knowing full well that as the law then stood he was committing a crime. He was in fact held not guilty because the court retrospectively enlarged the scope of necessity. A more difficult case is *Johnson v Phillips*[6] where a policeman was held to be justified on grounds of necessity in requiring a motorist to reverse in the wrong direction down a one-way street; and the motorist was convicted of obstruction when he refused. The value consideration behind the decision was the sanctity of life and limb, which had been endangered by an affray in a public house. It would seem that the policeman had not disobeyed traffic regulations by ordering the motorist to go against them. If the motorist had complied, would he have been convicted of disobeying regulations? One hopes not. A different situation, but similar in principle, is where an act is done in contravention of a statute, but is later held not to have been illegal since the statute is declared unconstitutional. (This cannot happen in Britain.) The same alternative ways of looking at the situation apply here as in necessity.

Non-enforcement or non-prosecution of some offences, eg unauthorised parking or the Attorney General entering a *nolle prosequi*, is also offered by the authors as an example of 'legitimated' disobedience, but this needs careful examination. To some extent it seems that their argument is based on a failure to distinguish between duty and the operation of sanction. Failure of the latter does not 'legitimate' the fact of a breach of duty. The argument tacitly assumes that the actual operation of a sanction is the test of a breach of duty; which it is not[7]. Further, a distinction has to be drawn between officials, who refuse to take action, and offenders. With regard to the former, their refusal cannot be 'legitimated' disobedience of the law by them as long as they have a discretion to take action or not given by law[8]. Similarly, another example given by the authors, that of juries acquitting in defiance of directions to convict, is not 'legitimated' disobedience since juries, too, have discretion. Where there is no discretion, officials who refuse to act are liable[9].

On the other hand, from the point of view of offenders, there does appear to be some substance in the argument, though the position is arguable. If acquittal by a perverse jury 'legitimates' an offender's disobedience, then every failure of the legal process, such as lack of evidence, or acquittal for

5 [1939] 1 KB 687, [1938] 3 All ER 615.
6 [1975] 3 All ER 682, [1976] 1 WLR 65.
7 P 237 ante. This might also be the answer to their example of a judge refusing to follow a precedent.
8 *R v Metropolitan Police Comr, ex p Blackburn* (1980) Times, 7 March, CA. Even when they have a discretion, if they exercise it carelessly they will be liable: *Smith v Jago* (1975) 11 SASR 286 (transport inspectors ordering the driver of a large vehicle to execute a dangerous manoeuvre at night without taking adequate precautions).
9 *R v Metropolitan Police Comr, ex p Blackburn* [1968] 2 QB 118, [1968] 1 All ER 763, CA.

misdirection or on a technicality, 'legitimates' disobedience. However, the point in all such cases is that there is no proof in law that a disobedience had been committed, so on the face of it there is nothing to be 'legitimated'. It has also to be remembered that refusal by officials to take action is generally no bar to a successful civil action by the aggrieved party. In what sense, then, does failure of official action in enforcing or prosecuting 'legitimate' the disobedience? The situations, which do seem to support the authors, are those in which there is undoubted disobedience and officials refuse to act for reasons of policy and no private actions lie. The Attorney General's *nolle prosequi* could be one example, but an outstanding case is *Gouriet v Union of Post Office Workers*[10]. The House of Lords upheld the Attorney General's political discretion in refusing to invoke the law in the face of a threatened criminal offence in deliberate defiance of an Act of Parliament and organised on a national scale by two trade unions. The House also refused to allow the plaintiff to proceed personally on the ground that he had no 'right' recognised at law. In the event the threatened disobedience did not take place, but if it had, presumably it would have been 'legitimated'.

Limits of disobedience

In the light of the foregoing, it is submitted that the following considerations should apply to disobedience. (1) Obedience should always be the norm so that disobedience needs to be justified. If a society is to continue, there must be law and order and conformity with it. As Fox LJ has said: 'The proposition that citizens are free to commit a criminal offence if they have formed the view that it will further what they believe to be the public interest is quite baseless in our law and inimical to parliamentary authority. I do not disregard the existence of what is called the moral imperative. But such cases are rare in the extreme'[11]. (2) Available means of obtaining redress must be tried first, and in this connection the degree of likelihood of their success has to be taken into account. (3) Action by way of disobedience should not impair the equal liberty of others to continue to obey. (4) Disobedience in order to provide a test case is acceptable. (5) When disobedience is resorted to as a plea for the reconsideration of some decision, the disobedience should cease when reconsideration has been given, even if the result is that the decision should stand. (6) Disobedience is persuasive when it is designed to gain publicity and a hearing when other means fail. It has been pointed out[12], however, that there is a danger that the public will in time grow used to this kind of demonstration with the result that disobedience will keep intensifying in order to hold public attention. (7) Disobedience should not involve violence or infliction of hardship on others, because it then becomes coercive and not persuasive. 'Hardship' includes breakdown of social existence, social services or undue expenditure in preventing or repairing the effects of disobedience. (8) Disobedience of a national law in order to protest against some evil in another country, especially if it inflicts hardship or inconvenience on innocent persons, is not permissible[13].

10 [1978] AC 435, [1977] 3 All ER 70, HL. For the implications of this on the freedom of the subject, 'rule of law', judicial independence and the authority of Parliament, see the author's paper, '*Götterdämmerung*: Gods of the Law in Decline' (1981) 1 Legal Studies 3.
11 *Francome v Mirror Group Newspapers Ltd* [1984] 2 All ER 408 at 415, also 412–413, [1984] 1 WLR 892 at 901, also 897.
12 *Singer* p 81.
13 This is what was threatened in the *Gouriet* case: see supra and note 10.

When disobedience reaches the point of successful revolution, there is an overthrow of the régime and an end of its legal system. The situation raises entirely new problems concerning legality, which are discussed elsewhere in this book[14].

MACHINERY OF CHANGE

Change may be effected judicially or through legislation. Judicial methods include conceptual tinkering, use of fictions and equity. The first of these has been demonstrated in the foregoing chapters. With regard to the rest, it was Sir Henry Maine who propounded the classic thesis that what he called 'progressive societies' develop beyond the point at which 'static societies' stop through the use of fiction, equity and finally legislation[15]. Modern authorities question whether these stages ever were as clearly separated as he had imagined[16], but whatever the sequence, as agencies of legal development they merit attention.

Fiction

Maine defined this as 'any assumption which conceals or affects to conceal, the fact that a rule of law has undergone alteration, its letter remaining unchanged, its operation being modified'[17]. Fictions need to be distinguished from shifts in the meanings of words. For example, the word 'possession' was originally applied to physical control; then it came to be applied to situations where there was no physical control[18]. There was no pretence about the facts of either situation; there was simply the application of a word to a new situation. Adoption, on the other hand, is not a shift in meaning, but the name for a pretended fact, namely, that the adopted child was born into the family. A more difficult case is that of the corporate person. One application of the word 'person' is to a human being, and it was submitted in Chapter 12 that its application to a corporation is best treated as a shift in meaning. Supporters of the 'fiction theory', however, seek to explain it on the ground that a corporation is treated 'as if' it is a human being.

Are fictions something to be ashamed of? In the opinion of Bentham the answer was yes, and he repeatedly attacked them in various parts of his many writings. Vaihinger, on the other hand, contended that they are indispensable to the working of the human mind[19]. In the workings of the law there is an additional reason behind the use of fictions, namely, to introduce change behind the façade of adherence to existing law. It is thus a manifestation from early times of how the law can be adaptable and also stable. Both adaptability and stability are responses to different calls of justice. In the words of Coke '*in fictione juris semper aequitas existit*'.

Professor Fuller detected the following motivations behind the use of fictions[20].

14 See chs 5 and 17. For the Marxist 'philosophy of revolution', see ch 18.
15 Maine *Ancient Law* (ed Pollock) p 31.
16 Eg Diamond *Primitive Law* (2nd edn) p 346. Kahn-Freund 'Recent Legislation on Matrimonial Property' (1970) 33 MLR 601, 630, points out that in matrimonial property the courts appear to have moved from equity to fiction.
17 *Maine* pp 32–33.
18 See p 272 ante.
19 Vaihinger *The Philosophy of 'As If'* (trans Ogden); Fuller *Legal Fictions* ch 3.
20 *Fuller* pp 57 et seq.

POLICY. Bentham believed that judges resorted to fictions in order to conceal something from others, and pointed to the fiction that judges do not make law, but only declare what has always been law. Maine himself thought that this fiction may have had some justification in the past, but was now so threadbare that everyone could see through it[1]. The point that most fictions in fact deceive no one weakens the charge of concealment. Besides, there are other reasons of policy behind fictions, eg the rule that husband and wife are one. Even the old rule that a wife was deemed to have committed a crime under her husband's compulsion was not originally introduced in order to deceive anyone, although the absurdity of it did wring from Mr Bumble the comment 'If the law says that, the law is an ass'.

EMOTIONAL CONSERVATISM. Fuller said this is the judge's way of satisfying his own craving for certainty and stability. If there is any deceit, it is not intended to deceive anyone but himself; it is at most a process of self-deception.

CONVENIENCE. This consists of making use of existing legal institutions by pretending that certain facts exists. Ihering gave the example of the Roman *hereditatis petitio*, the action by which an heir claimed the estate. When later it became necessary to enable the purchaser of a bankrupt's estate (*bonorum emptor*) to claim the estate, the same action was made available, but with the pretence that the *bonorum emptor* was heir[2]. Adaptation of existing institutions reflects at bottom the need to preserve respect for the law; open innovations are unsettling, while novel applications of established institutions are not.

INTELLECTUAL CONSERVATISM. 'A judge', said Fuller, 'may adopt a fiction, not simply to avoid discommoding current notions, or for the purpose of concealing from himself or others the fact that he is legislating, but merely because he does not know how else to state and explain the new principle he is applying'[3].

Equity

In one sense equity is synonymous with justice. In so far as the purpose of law is to do justice, Cicero spoke of *aequitas* as the principle which makes possible any systematised administration of law, namely, deciding like cases alike[4]. However, there develops before long a need for justice over and above that available at law, and it was in the sense of this further justice needed to correct legal justice that Aristotle spoke of equity[5]. Maine defined it as 'any body of rules existing by the side of the original civil law, founded on distinct principles and claiming incidentally to supersede the civil law in virtue of a superior sanctity inherent in those principles'[6]. Broadly stated, one function

1 *Maine* p 38.
2 *Geist des römischen Rechts* (6th edn) III, pp 301 et seq. So also in the *actio Publiciana* the lapse of the period of prescription was assumed. Cf. *mancipatio* and *cessio in jure*, which were actual conveyancing forms put to new uses without pretended facts. Early English law was full of procedural fictions, eg the writ *latitat*. The law of quasi-contract is based on pretended contract. 'Deeming' provisions in statutes are fictions. So is 'summer time'.
3 *Fuller* pp 63-64.
4 Cicero *Topica* 4.23.
5 Aristotle *Nicomachean Ethics* V.
6 *Maine* p 34.

of equity is to mitigate in various ways the effects of the strict law in its application to individual cases[7]. Another function is to procure a humane and liberal interpretation of the law itself[8].

It is clear, therefore, that equity arises out of the processes of law-applying, and is fashioned by the hands of those charged with that task. In Roman law the rigidity and shortcomings of the civil law were remedied by the Praetors; in English law similar deficiencies were remedied by the Chancellors. As with the Roman civil law, the common law, too, became technical, so appeals were addressed by aggrieved litigants to the King himself, as the 'fount of justice', to give relief as a matter of conscience. The King handed these petitions to the Chancellor, who as an ecclesiastic in the early days and as 'Keeper of the King's conscience', was best fitted to deal with them. Thus, there grew up a new jurisdiction in Chancery, as the Chancellor's court came to be called, and this is why English equity can be identified historically as the body of rules evolved by the court of Chancery. The Praetors and Chancellors are the parallel sources of equity in the two systems[9].

The description given by the jurist Papinian of the function of praetorian equity is equally apt for the Chancellor's equity. 'Praetorian law', he said 'is what the praetors introduced for the purpose of assisting, supplementing and correcting the civil law': *jus praetorium est quod praetores introduxerunt adjuvandi vel supplendi vel corrigendi juris civilis gratia*[10]. It is not possible here to do more than instance a few, almost random, examples of the ways in which the equitable influence worked in the two systems. The Praetors 'assisted' the civil law in many ways. For example, they aided the owner at law by devising interdictal protection of possession, since by protecting possession they were in most cases protecting title. In English law the equitable remedy of injunction protects various rights at common law; so also specific performance reinforces certain contractual claims at common law. The Praetors 'supplemented' the civil law and filled out its deficiencies by inventing new doctrines. Outstanding among these was the institution of praetorian ownership side by side with civil law ownership. The Praetors also gave protection to minors and other persons not capable of looking after themselves; they recognised doctrines of fraud, coercion and mistake; and they invented as well as extended existing remedies by means of *actiones in factum* and *utiles*. The most important creation of the Chancellors was the trust, but they also recognised fraud, coercion and mistake. More rarely the Praetors 'corrected' the civil law and in effect nullified it. Their most drastic remedy was *restitutio in integrum* by which a completed transaction at law could be erased and the parties allowed to begin afresh. The Praetors could also refuse to allow plaintiffs to proceed with actions at law if it was unconscionable for them to do so: *denegatio actionis*. The entire civil law of intestate succession was nullified in favour of a fairer scheme of distribution which, unlike the civil law, took account of the entitlement of blood relations: *bonorum possessio*. In English law the question of conflict between common law and equity has been the subject of some controversy. The Judicature Act 1873, s 25[11] provided: 'Generally in

7 It was in this sense that Aristotle dealt with equity: V, 10. 3–8.
8 *D* 50.17.90.
9 The parallel should not be pushed too far: Buckland *Equity in Roman Law*; 'Praetor and Chancellor' (1939) 13 Tulane LR 163. See also Stein 'Equitable Principles in Roman Law' in *Equity in the World's Legal Systems* (ed Newman) p 75.
10 *D* 1.1.7.1.
11 See now Supreme Court of Judicature (Consolidation) Act 1925, s 44.

all matters not hereinbefore particularly mentioned, in which there is any conflict or variance between the rules of equity and the rules of the common law with reference to the same matter, the rules of equity shall prevail'. The implication of this provision clearly is that some conflict at any rate did exist. Nevertheless, Maitland contended that this provision was only added *ex abundanti cautela*, since the relationship between law and equity, to use his own words, 'was not one of conflict'.

> 'Equity had come not to destroy the law, but to fulfil it. Every jot and every tittle of the law was to be obeyed, but when all this had been done something might yet be needful, something that equity would require'[12].

This is a debateable statement, and perhaps the argument turns on what exactly is signified by 'conflict'. Hohfeld showed, it is submitted successfully, that there were many instances where the position was indeed what one might fairly describe as conflict[13].

During the formative periods of Roman and English law the creative function of equity was most marked. In the more developed law it tended to be less active, but remained in the form of a cloud of principles to guide and ameliorate the application of the law, eg no one shall profit from his own wrong, nor be unjustly enriched at the expense of another. These and other such principles were crystallised in the concluding Title of the Digest, and it was these that came to be absorbed as the fundamental principles of modern civilian systems[14]. In English law, which did not 'receive' Roman law, equity solidified in time in much the same way as the common law had done, so much so that there has been a call for a revival of the old spirit of equitable justice. Lord Denning, in particular, ever since he became a High Court judge, has been foremost in striving to inject a new equity into the law.

> 'If the rules of equity have become so rigid that they cannot remedy such an injustice, it is time we had a new equity, to make good the omissions of the old'[15].

Some of his experiments have met with success[16], others have not[17]. Perhaps the reluctance of some of his colleagues to go along with him reflects the age-old need to strike a balance between certainty and adaptability.

Legislation

Even while social conditions were relatively stable, the gradual dimming of the fires behind the forces of fiction and equity in keeping law adaptable

---

12 Maitland *Equity* (ed Brunyate) p 17.
13 Hohfeld *Fundamental Legal Conceptions as Applied in Judicial Reasoning* (ed Cook) pp 115 et seq and for a few examples, see p 31 ante.
14 Stein 'The Digest Title, *De diversis regulis juris antiqui* and General Principles of Law' in *Essays in Jurisprudence in Honor of Roscoe Pound* (ed Newman) pp 1 et seq. See also *Regulae Juris: From Juristic Rules to Legal Maxims*.
15 *Solle v Butcher* [1950] 1 KB 671 at 695, [1949] 2 All ER 1107 at 1121. In another place he said, 'It may be that there is no authority to be found in the books, but, if this be so, all I can say is that the sooner we make one the better': *Re AG's Application, A-G v Butterworth* [1963] 1 QB 696 at 719, [1962] 3 All ER 326 at 329. See also his paper 'The Need for a New Equity' (1952) 5 Current LP 1.
16 Eg *Central London Property Trust v High Trees House* [1947] KB 130, [1956] 1 All ER 256; and see now *Crabb v Arun District Council* [1976] Ch 179, [1975] 3 All ER 865.
17 The 'deserted wife's equity', which he introduced in *Bendall v McWhirter* [1952] 2 QB 466, [1952] 1 All ER 1307, was overruled in *National Provincial Bank v Ainsworth* [1965] AC 1175, [1965] 2 All ER 472. For a partial remedy by statute, see the Matrimonial Homes Act 1967.

made that task devolve increasingly on legislation. With the rapid changes now taking place, this is the only efficient way of dealing with the problem. In addition to the aspects of legislation dealt with in Chapters 5 and 8, something should also be said about its application to law reform and codification.

LAW REFORM. There is a great deal of room for improvement short of drastic change of the system itself. It is in the business of law reform that all the insights of legal and sociological analysis, philosophy and morality are called into service.

The task of making proposals for law reform used to be in the hands of *ad hoc* bodies, and this is still possible. Royal Commissions may be cited as an outstanding example[18]. The first permanent arrangement came in 1934 when the Law Revision Committee was set up to report on matters referred to it by the Lord Chancellor. This was superseded in 1952 by the Law Reform Committee, and also in that year the Private International Law Committee was established. These were followed in 1959 by the Criminal Law Revision Committee. Then, in 1965 by the Law Commissions Act two Law Commissions (one of them the Scottish Law Commission) were set up as permanent, independent bodies, charged with keeping 'under review all the law with which they are respectively concerned with a view to its systematic development and reform, including in particluar the codification of such law, the elimination of anomalies, the repeal of obsolete and unnecessary enactments, the reduction of the number of separate enactments and generally the simplification and modernisation of the law': s 3 (1)[19]. These bodies have shown considerable activity.

A prerequisite to deciding what the law ought to be is to discover what it is at present. To this extent positivist philosophers, notably Bentham and Austin, were correct[20]. There is a difficulty raised by the fact that in a large number of matters where the rule is not clear, the rule is stated to be what it ought to be[1]. The distinction between what the law is and what it ought to be is thus by no means sharp, but for practical purposes this difficulty does not and, indeed, should not stand in the way of reform. If the law on a point in unclear, then that is how the position has to be accepted.

Information about existing law includes the collation of all rules likely to be affected by the topic being reformed. Here, computers can be of help, since they are able to gather information at great depth and range in next to no time. However, the difficulties that were mentioned earlier apply here too. Two bases of information retrieval are the 'key-word' basis and the 'full text' basis. The former operates by identifying relevant documentary material through key-words; but this depends on the human element in choosing the appropriate key-words and also requires co-ordination and consistency in choice. To avoid this difficulty, the alternative is the 'full text' basis, which is that entire texts of documents are stored, not by page, but by

18 Eg in 1973 a Royal Commission was set up to consider the law relating to compensation for personal injuries: *On Civil Liability and Compensation for Personal Injury* (Cmnd. 7054).
19 For development, see *The Reform of the Law* (ed G L Williams); *Law Reform and Law Making, A Reprint of a Series of Broadcast Talks; Law Reform* Now (eds Gardiner and Martin). On the Law Commissions, see Chorley and Dworkin, 'The Law Commissions Act 1965' (1965) 28 MLR 675; Scarman 'Law Reform—the Experience of the Law Commission' (1968) 10 JSPTL(NS) 91; Farrar *Law Reform and the Law Commission* chs 1–4.
20 See ch 16 post.
1 See p 333 post.

sentences. All relevant matter can thus be retrieved, but the drawback is that a vast quantity of irrelevant matter is dredged up as well. Experiment so far has shown that human techniques retrieved little that was irrelevant, but could not guarantee to be comprehensive; computers guaranteed comprehensiveness but brought in far too much irrelevant matter; which meant that the task of sifting still remained[2].

After collating the existing law, its adequacy has to be assessed. Of course, it must have been thought unsatisfactory, else it would not have come up for review; but the matter has to be thoroughly explored. The criterion of 'adequacy' is ability to fulfil some purpose. Morals, ethics, social needs and all other relevant considerations have to be pressed into the service of such evaluation. Sociological research is needed to discover how the law has been working and how far behaviour has corresponded with legal norms. Law reform is thus a collective job[3].

In the actual business of reforming the law, the first and most difficult decision concerns the basis on which reform should proceed: should there be a completely new restructuring of the law?, or should reform be carried out within existing categories, such as contract, criminal law etc? The Law Commission has opted for the latter course, and has proposed a beginning with the reform and codification of the general principles of contract[4]. A more radical proposal was put forward by Professor Jolowicz, who argued that reform should be based on the factual problems involved, rather than on the artificial categories of the law[5]. He pointed out that if, for instance, the category of 'nuisance' was being reformed, the case of a person hit by a tile off a roof would come within the ambit of the review if he happened to be standing one foot outside the gate on the pavement, but not if he happened to be one foot inside the gate, for then the case would come under 'occupiers' liability'. A wider example would be 'consumer protection'. This is a social problem, which straddles contract, torts, criminal law etc. Reforming contract alone would leave many aspects of the factual social problem untouched. The existing divisions of the law into contract, torts etc were products of historical problems, chiefly procedural, which have disappeared. If, as the Law Commissions are charged with doing, the whole law is going to be overhauled, then the opportunity should be seized of restructuring it according to contemporary problems. There is much substance in this view, but there are also considerations the other way[6]. One is that the existing divisions are so ingrained in the law and, indeed, have even become parts of social life, eg business and industry, that so radical a restructuring might be impractical. Another is that experiments in teaching law along the sort of lines suggested have not been successful. However, a cogent point has been raised, to which too little attention seems to have been paid as yet.

Another matter, which it may become necessary to consider, is the best machinery for implementing reform. In what way might the purpose be achieved, or better achieved than hitherto? Are the existing courts, for instance, the most suitable institutions, or should there be some new kind of

2 Tapper *Computers and the Law* Ch 4, discussing the pioneering experiments of Professor Horty; see also p 307 ante.
3 Scarman (1968) 10 JSPTL(NS) 91 *passim; Farrar* Ch 6.
4 First Annual Report, para 31.
5 Jolowicz 'Fact Based Classification of Law' in *The Division and Classification of the Law* (ed Jolowicz).
6 See the other contributions to *The Division and Classification of the Law* especially Ch 2.

tribunal? The Restrictive Practices Court and a Registrar of Restrictive Trading Practices were created by the Restrictive Trade Practices Act 1956, which introduced a much needed reform. Should there be special industrial courts[7], family courts, and courts for dealing with sexual deviance? Even if separate bits of machinery were to be created in this way, it is important that there should remain some overall control, otherwise too much fragmentation could destroy the system as a system. In connection with all these matters there is a core of truth in Savigny's doctrine that reforms at least have a better chance of success if they keep within the traditions and stream of continuity of the society. Those which go against deeply-rooted ideas are likely to be sloughed off[8].

Finally, there is a problem of the language in which the reform is to be drafted. Legal language is peculiar in that it seeks to control behaviour, but is non-emotive[9]. Laws are communications designed to have continuing operation; they are addressed to different audiences, those who are expected to act on them, and those who have to apply them. With regard to the former, it has previously been pointed out that the language of drafting should take account of different kinds of measures[10]. Traffic laws are expected to be understood by the motoring public and should, therefore, be drafted in language intelligible to a lay audience. On the other hand, with technical matters of the sort that laymen would be ill-advised to tackle without expert advice, the language could afford to be what experts would readily understand. There is peril in trying to make highly technical matters comprehensible to laymen. With regard to those who are called on to apply laws, eg judges, it has to be remembered that the wording of laws should leave room for doing justice according to values and at the same time provide a measure of precision. The selection of suitable concepts becomes important here. Concepts are retrieval tools in that they are generalised means of referring to groups and types of situations. They should provide the right balance between precision and vagueness, which requires that they be appropriately structured.

A word might also be added about drafting[11]. This is far more than putting something into words. It has a substantive aspect and the draftsman can help the policy-makers. Consistency of terminology, expression and lay out induces consistency in policy and thought. The division of a measure into Parts, Headings, Sub-headings, Sections and Provisos requires decisions as to the relative importance of various points of substantive policy. All these assume special importance in long and complicated statutes.

CODIFICATION. This is a phenomenon, which is found at various stages of development. Undeveloped systems often start with codes. The 'start' of Roman law, for instance, is usually taken to be the Twelve Tables. Maine opened his classic work with the remark, 'The most celebrated system of jurisprudence known to the world begins, as it ends, with a code'[12]. In

---

7　The court set up by the Industrial Relations Act 1971, was abolished with that Act.
8　As to which, see pp 377–378 post.
9　For the semantic problems, see Scarman *Law Reform—the New Pattern* (Lindsay Memorial Lecture, University of Keele) p 56; *Farrar* ch 5.
10　See p 185 ante.
11　Dickerson *The Fundamentals of Legal Drafting*; Smith 'Legislative Drafting: English and Continental' [1980] Stat LR 16.
12　Maine *Ancient Law* p 1.

pre-Norman Britain there were various Anglo-Saxon codes. Codes are also introduced in mature systems to unify diverse jurisdictions, an outstanding example of which is the Uniform Commercial Code of America, unifying the diversities that had grown up in the jurisdictions of the several states. Codes may also be introduced in systems which have exhausted their powers of development.

Codification is said to provide a 'fresh start', but this must not be misunderstood. 'Fresh start' cannot mean an entirely new kind of law, for, in the first place, it is impossible to invent such a thing 'out of the blue'; and, secondly, the new law must keep within the stream of continuity of existing law, especially in commercial and other such long established areas.

Codification, therefore, must be of the existing law, and the question is what shape and form it should assume. This makes the problem inseperable from law reform. Reform must precede codification[13]. Clearly, conflicts, anomalies and complexities will have to be ironed out, but this is only a prelude. More important is the question, previously considered, of the basis of codification: should the law be completely restructured, or should codification proceed within the established divisions of the law? One of the earliest, and still most radical, proposals for restructuring was Bentham's. He began by elucidating the nature of 'a law'. This is not the same as a statutory provision, which is compounded of parts of other laws created at different times. Thus, the provision against being drunk when in charge of a car is made up of laws establishing a police force, breathalyser tests, courts etc. He accordingly sought to isolate 'a law' in a jurisprudential sense, which he did by assigning each law to a separate act-situation[14]. Codification on this basis would restructure the law beyond all recognition, existing categories would disappear, and even the distinction between 'penal' and 'civil' laws would acquire a wholly unfamiliar appearance. A less radical proposal is that of Professor Jolowicz, who proposed restructuring according to factual and social problems[15]. The alternative to wholesale restructuring is to codify within the existing divisions; and this is the course favoured by the Law Commission. The chosen field with which they propose to make a start is the general law of contract. The wisdom of this is not self-evident. The issue is whether codification of general principles of contract law should precede codification of particular types of contracts, eg hire-purchase, marine insurance etc. There may be some case for suggesting that the latter should come first, since attention will thereby be focused on problems in particular contracts, which will provide a better informed and meaningful basis for the codification of general principles[16]. Against this, it has been pointed out by one of the original Law Commissioners that it is unsatisfactory to impose codes, eg Sale of Goods Act, on the *corpus* of an uncodified general law of contract, and that it is absurd that there should be fundamental differences between English and Scots law[17].

Another debate surrounds the degree of generality of a code. Are the detailed rules, already evolved in case law, to be included? If they are, this would make codification incline towards consolidation. Or are there going

---

13 *Reform of the Law* (ed G L Williams) p 19; *Law Reform* Now (eds Gardiner and Martin) p 12.
14 See pp 342, 343 post.
15 See p 323 ante.
16 Wilson 'Evolution or Revolution?—Prospects for Contract Law Reform' (University of Southampton 1969).
17 Gower 'A Comment' (1967) 30 MLR 259.

to be only general principles? On the one hand, if the wisdom contained in the rich storehouse of case law is to be reduced to a few simple formulae, much of it will be lost. Answers to problems of detail will have to be sought outside the generalisations of the code, which, it is said, would be a waste of effort if the answers had already been worked out in the earlier cases. The code will inevitably accumulate an increasing volume of 'secondary' rules, which for practical purposes will represent the 'living law' (to use Ehrlich's phrase). This is bound to keep growing, not only in volume, but also in complexity, which means that the simplicity of the original conception will get progressively swamped by the rising tide. In the French Code, for example, the law of torts is contained in five sections, but for all practical purposes the 'law' is to be found in the case law and doctrine. On the other hand, if the code tries to preserve the accumulated wisdom of the case law, it will simply be a restatement minus anomalies etc. This is hardly preferable, since the complexity of such a restatement will be considerable, and it will not get rid of the pevious law, which will remain to be consulted on doubtful points. A compromise might be to keep the code itself to broad, general principles, but to couple it with a detailed commentary referring to previous case law, or else with selected examples which could serve as analogies. In any case, the previous law will cease to be authoritative, but it might be permissible to refer to it for the purpose of elucidating the wording of the code[18]. A related point concerns the status, not of pre-code cases, but of post-code cases. It was argued in an earlier chapter that *stare decisis* was inappropriate to statute interpretation[19]; this is *a fortiori* the case with a code[20]. It must be remembered, however, that *stare decisis* is so ingrained in the habit of thinking of British lawyers that it may not prove easy to abandon. It will take time; codification is a lengthy process.

What, finally, is the case for and against codification as such? This has been a well-gnawed bone of contention. In Germany in the early 19th century the proposal for codification propounded by Thibaut was powerfully opposed by Savigny, whose doctrine gave rise to the Historical School[1]. Towards the end of that century in America the Thibaut–Savigny controversy was parallelled by the Field–Carter controversy[2]. There is little new that the protagonists are able to advance even today, and little can be offered as factual evidence, which means that empirical support for a good many contentions is hard to find. It is thus very much a matter of preference. The degree of persuasiveness of an argument depends on the reader: if he is pro-code minded, it will be less of an effort for him to see the weaknesses in the case for the other side, and *vice versa*. The problem is the psychological one of how to convert people from positions they already hold. One of the stock arguments in favour of a code is its accessibility, intelligibility and simplicity, as well as its general convenience[3]. Simplicity is undoubtedly a boon when, as in America, there is much diversity[4]. However, there are some

18 *Bank of England v Vagliano Bros* [1891] AC 107 at 145, per Lord Herschell; Scarman *Law Reform—the New Pattern*. Cf the American Restatements.
19 See p 184–185 ante.
20 Scarman *English Law—the New Dimension* p 80. See also his 'Codification and Judge-made Law' (University of Birmingham 1966).
1 See ch 18 post.
2 For references, see the companion *Bibliography* pp 261–262.
3 Diamond 'Codification of the Law of Contract' (1968) 31 MLR 361; *Farrar* ch 5.
4 Eg Uniform Commercial Code.

considerations the other way which weaken the force of the general point. 'Accessible', 'intelligible' and 'simple' to whom? Technical matters, for instance, cannot be made intelligible and simple to laymen[5]. Problems of 'fringe' meanings in unforeseen situations will always be matters for experts. It has also been pointed out that there is bound to be a period of uncertainty after the introduction of a code until case law clarifies one by one the many doubts and obscurities: a point which is not disputed by proponents of codification, but which they think can be exaggerated[6]. A further point is that the inevitable silting-up of case law will gradually reduce accessibility and simplicity. As to general convenience, it has been objected that the cost, time and labour spent in preparing a code will be disproportionate to its value, and that lawyers and others will have to put in an immense effort in re-educating themselves to think along the new line; but these points, too, as proponents of codification point out, are exaggerated and, in any case, very much a matter of opinion[7].

Another claim in favour of codification is that it will unify the law by providing 'a logically articulated skeleton for the law' as well as 'an authoritative point of departure' from which practitioners can find answers to problems[8]. The value here will depend on the basis of the codification. It might be worth considering the relative value to practitioners of a code unified on the basis of factual and social problems and one unified on the basis of existing categories. The answer must remain speculative since there is no evidence which could give a pointer one way or the other.

Finally, there is a claim that a code will have the beneficent effect of facilitating and expediting future reforms[9]. This again may well prove to be so, but such evidence as there is does not bear out the hope. In France, there was no revision of the Code for 140 years; in Germany, the problem of exception clauses had to be dealt with judicially as in Britain. To speak of future reform being facilitated raises the query: what sort of reform—reforms within the structure of the code, or recodification? Society is never still, and as new developments take place, the unifying pattern of the code will tend to become out-moded and new unification needed. Such an argument seems somewhat unrealistic, and should not stand in the way of codification now. In view of the balance between these various considerations, perhaps one ought to ask whether there is a risk that a code would actually do harm and whether such risk, if there is one, is worth taking. All in all, codification of English law will be an act of faith.

5 Hahlo 'Here lies the Common Law. Rest in Peace' (1967) 30 MLR 241.
6 *Hahlo* p 249; contra *Gower* p 261; Topping and Vandenlinden '*Ibi Renascit Jus Commune*' (1970) 33 MLR 175.
7 *Hahlo* p 253; contra *Topping and Vandenlinden* pp 174–175.
8 *Topping and Vandenlinden* pp 173–174.
9 *Diamond*; *Topping and Vandenlinden*.

READING LIST

A L Diamond 'Codification of the Law of Contract' (1968) 31 Modern Law Review 361.

F R Dickerson *The Fundamentals of Legal Drafting*.

J H Farrar *Law Reform and the Law Commission*.

G P Fletcher 'Prolonging Life' (1967) 42 Washington Law Review 999.

L L Fuller *Legal Fictions*.

H R Hahlo 'Here Lies the Common Law. Rest in Peace' (1967) 30 Modern Law Review 241.

J F Handler *Social Movements and the Legal System: A Theory of Law Reform and Social Change*.

H S Maine *Ancient Law* (ed F Pollock).

J Rawls *A Theory of Justice* pp 350-391.

L G Scarman *English Law—the New Dimension*.

L G Scarman *The Law in Transition* (The Child & Co Lecture 1974).

P Singer *Democracy and Disobedience*.

C F H Tapper *Computers and the Law*.

M R Topping and J P M Vandenlinden '*Ibi Renascit Jus Commune*' (1970) 33 Modern Law Review 175.

J F Wilson 'Evolution or Revolution?—Prospects for Contract Law Reform' (University of Southampton publication).

Law Reform Now (eds G Gardiner and A Martin).

More Law Reform Now (eds P Archer and A Martin).

The Division and Classification of the Law (ed J A Jolowicz)

PART III

Legal theory

SUMMARY

CHAPTER 16

Positivism: British theories

The start of the nineteenth century might be taken as marking the beginning of the positivist movement. It represented a reaction against the *a priori* methods of thinking that characterised the preceding age. Prevailing theories of natural law shared the feature of turning away from the realities of actual law in order to discover in nature or reason principles of universal validity. Actual laws were then explained or condemned according to these canons. Unverified hypotheses of this sort failed to satisfy the intelligence of an age nurtured in the critical spirit of new scientific learning. Scrutiny of natural law postulates had damaging results, for they were shown to be without foundation or else the products of extrapolation.

The term 'positivism' has many meanings, which were tabulated by Professor Hart as follows[1]: (1) Laws are commands. This meaning is associated with the two founders of British positivism, Bentham and his disciple Austin, whose views will be considered in this chapter. (2) The analysis of legal concepts is (a) worth pursuing, (b) distinct from sociological and historical inquiries, (c) distinct from critical evaluation. (3) Decisions can be deduced logically from predetermined rules without recourse to social aims, policy or morality. (4) Moral judgments cannot be established or defended by rational argument, evidence or proof. (5) The law as it is actually laid down, *positum*, has to be kept separate from the law that ought to be. Whatever meanings are ascribed to positivism, it is contrasted with natural law, which also has different meanings[2]. In view of these differences one needs to be chary of classifying any particular writer as positivist or naturalist. However, subject to that general caution, it would be safe to assert that the authors discussed in this and the following chapter are commonly regarded as positivists. What matters are their views on particular issues, not how they are labelled[3].

The fifth meaning given above seems to be the one currently associated with positivism. It may spring from a love of order, which aims at the clarification of legal conceptions and their orderly presentation. To insist that 'what the law is' is one question, 'what the law ought to be' is another, looks neat thd tidy. Precision may be elusive but striving towards it whenever possible is commendable and profitable. Positivism flourishes in stable social conditions; the difficulties of maintaining a rigid separation between 'what is' and 'what ought to be' are only projected to the forefront when conditions are in turmoil. It is worth remarking that neither Bentham nor Austin should be thought of as writing in periods of particular stability. What they represent is the intellectual reaction against naturalism and a love of order and precision. Bentham was a tireless campaigner for reform, and both he and

1 'Positivism and the Separation of Law and Morals' (1957-58) 71 Harvard Law Review at p601 n25.
2 See p470 post.
3 J Hall *Foundations of Jurisprudence* ch 2.

Austin insisted that prior to reform there has to be a thorough-going clarification of the law as it is. The significance of stable conditions might conceivably be seen in the fact that the Austinian theory made no headway until after his death, until after the Chartist movement had collapsed, and it then rapidly reached the zenith of its influence in the serene atmosphere of Victorian England.

Whether a separation between the 'is' and the 'ought' is tenable or not is a debateable issue to which allusion will be made on several occasions. It is necessary, therefore, to try and clarify what that issue is. The preceding portions of this book, especially the analysis of 'Duty', will have shown that a large part of law consists of prescriptive patterns of behaviour, ie models of conduct to which people ought to conform and by which their actual behaviour is judged. Therefore the 'is', which positivists are anxious to preserve inviolate, is largely composed of 'oughts'. So far most positivists would agree[4], but they would add that only those 'oughts' acquire the character of 'law' which have filtered through certain accepted criteria of validity. In English law these are precedent, legislation and immemorial customs. The distinction, in other words, between an 'ought' proposition that 'is' law and an 'ought' proposition that 'ought to become' law lies solely in the fact that the former has passed through one or other of the media which regulate the use of the label 'law'. It follows that positivists need not deny that judges make law; indeed, the majority admit it[5]. They also acknowledge the influence of ethical considerations on judges and legislators, and that generally it is because a proposition was thought to be moral and just that a judge or legislator adopted it. What they do say is that it is only incorporation in precedent, statute or customs that imparts the quality of 'law'. This quality follows from such incorporation irrespective of morality, so that even if an unjust proposition were embodied in precedent or statute, it would be 'law' none the less because it would exhibit the formal stamp of validity. Therefore, they maintain, every proposition which passes through one or other of the accepted media is 'law' irrespective of all considerations which go towards saying that it should be, or should not be, law. It is this contention which touches the heart of a modern controversy to which some anticipatory reference is necessary. Natural lawyers would assert that a proposition is 'law' not merely because it satisfies some formal requirement, but by virtue of an additional minimum moral content. According to them an immoral rule would not be 'law' however much it may satisfy formal requirements[6].

It is also thought to follow from the positivist obsession with the 'is' that they distinguish between formal analysis on the one hand, and historical and functional analysis on the other. Those who assert this do not deny the value of the latter, but contend that these should be kept apart from the former. Any such attempt, however, suffers from the inherent difficulty that it is seldom possible to study institutions as they are except in the light of their history and function. Many can only be understood in the light of their origins and past influences, which is especially the case with common law institutions, reaching back as they do unbroken for centuries. The suggested

4 Though not, perhaps, some of the early 'realists', whose views are considered in ch 21 post.
5 Positivism has sometimes been taken to refer to the doctrine that judges do not make law, but this has been discredited.
6 Sajjad Ahmad J in *Jilani v Government of Punjab* PakLD (1972) SC 139 at 261; pp 500—501 post. See also pp 87 et seq ante.

division between 'analytical' and 'functional' study is unhappier still. The preceding chapters should have demonstrated that legal conceptions are shaped by the way in which they are used and the ends which they serve, all of which import social, moral and other value considerations[7]. This leads to a more general objection. If the analysis of legal conceptions as they are inevitably brings in a consideration of their function, which in turn as inevitably brings in considerations of what ought to be law, what then becomes of the alleged distinction between formal and functional analysis?

Some further objections to the 'is'/'ought' distinction may also be mentioned at this juncture. It is said that a law is what its maker thought it ought to be, whether it be moral or immoral, as with Herod's decree for the massacre of the innocents. In so far as this assertion relates to the content of a law, no positivist need disagree. The real thrust of the objection, however, becomes apparent when one considers the structures of concepts, which are shaped by the ends which they serve. This is not a mere matter of content, but of the texture of the law itself. The point is also apparent in the judicial process which, as pointed out, is guided by values. In a situation uncovered by authority, for instance, a judge will enunciate as law an appropriate rule, which will lead to the desired decision; but the point is that he states the rule *to be* what he feels it *ought to be*. As far as he is concerned he accepts it as law already because it appeals to his sense of right and *before* it is made into a precedent. As Sir Garfield Barwick CJ said 'the common law is what the court, so informed, decides that it should be ... For where no authority binds or current of acceptable decision compels, it is not enough, nor indeed apposite, to say that the function of the court in general is to declare what the law is and not to decide what it ought to be'[8]. As has been suggested, the same sentiment may underlie the converse situation: what ought not to be law cannot have been law, which may be the explanation of the retrospective effect of overruling[9]. Even where there is a rule of law, its application blurs the line between the 'is' and the 'ought'. As should have been evident from the discussions of precedent, statutory interpretation and values, rules are occasionally shaped and reshaped so as to yield the desired conclusion, ie the rule is stated as being what it ought to be to lead to the decision. Another point is that principles and doctrines operate differently from rules in that they exert pressure as to the direction in which rules ought to develop[10]. No one disputes that they, too, are part of law, so what 'is' law here are statements as to what it ought to be. If, then, for these reasons a total separation of the 'is' and the 'ought' cannot be maintained, any assertion that they are separate does not represent the position that 'is', but only what positivists think ought to be; which makes positivism itself an ideology[11].

When considering this debate two questions have to be asked: How far is there a separation? and, Is it desirable that there ought to be a separation? With regard to the first, the relationship between the 'is' and the 'ought' is close, as both sides will agree. It is submitted that if the matter is viewed in a temporal perspective a reconciliation may be found. There is no separation in a continuum, since the continuity of laws, their application and even their

7 See pp 16–18, 226 ante.
8 *Mutual Life & Citizens Assurance Co v Evatt* (1968) 42 ALJR 316 at 318.
9 See p 156 ante.
10 See p 46 ante.
11 Silving *Sources of Law* pp 298 et seq.

criteria of validity are in the long run dependent on conformity with moral and other such dictates. In this time-frame the naturalists can make out a case[12]. On the other hand, in the present time-frame positivists can likewise make out a case for at least some degree of separation for the practical purposes of here and now. They themselves must concede that total separation is difficult to maintain in the day to day business of applying rules. So their contention narrows itself to the *means of identifying* 'law' at any given point of time, in short to the criteria of validity. When the matter is reduced in this way, the two questions can be restated as follows: Are the criteria of validity purely formal and separate from moral considerations? and, Should they incorporate a minimum moral criterion? Identification of that which is 'law' is the concern of lawyers in their daily business, and in this context the answer to the first question is on the side of the positivists. Even so, it may be possible to draw a slight distinction between precedent and statute as criteria of identification. A lower court is bound to apply an undistinguishable precedent of a superior court, however wrong it may be, so that, with regard to such court, there is a distinction between what 'is' and what 'ought to be' law[13]. A superior court, however, when overruling the unjust precedent declares that it never was law notwithstanding the formal stamp of validity which it had borne until then. With regard to such a court the 'is'/'ought' separation in precedent as a criterion of identification breaks down at that point. Repeal of a statute, on the other hand, takes effect only from the date of repeal, and even when the effect of repeal is expressly made retroactive, there is no denial that the repealed statute was law until it was repealed. Summing up, therefore, one may say that the answer to the first question is that, within the limits of here and now and for the purpose of identifying laws, there is a separation in the criteria of identification (subject to the suggestion to the contrary with regard to precedent). It is for this reason that ways had to be explored in Chapter 5 for introducing a moral element into the criteria of identification (validity).

The second question is whether such a separation is desirable. The arguments that it is undesirable have been considered and need not be rehearsed[14]. In this chapter it is necessary to consider why positivists contend that separation is desirable. Their arguments are practical. (a) Valid laws are what those charged with administering laws identify as such, and the principal reason for keeping the means of identification as clear cut as possible is convenience. For otherwise no one could know how to regulate his or her daily actions and the task of lawyers when advising clients, law-teachers instructing pupils, businessmen conducting their affairs etc would be impossible. The importance of being able to tell as clearly and simply as possible whether this is, or is not, a 'law' at any given point of time is obvious. The introduction of morality into the criterion of identification presents difficulties. Morality is a diffuse idea and no one, not even a naturalist, maintains that everything which is moral is 'law'. Since the area of 'law' is bound to be narrower than that of morality, its boundary should be made as clear as possible. (b) There is a difference in the application of formal and moral criteria. Establishing the validity of a precept by means of a formal test and a moral test involve different processes. Courts have neither the time nor the

12 See pp 498 et seq.
13 *Miliangos v George Frank (Textiles) Ltd* [1976] AC 443 at 478, [1975] 3 All ER 801 at 822.
14 See p 89 ante.

training to undertake the latter. (c) A separation between the 'is' and the 'ought' is useful in providing a standard by which positive law can be evaluated and criticised. Even naturalists concede that there will always be some discrepancy between law as it is and as it ought to be, and as long as this is so the latter can be used to evaluate the former[15]. This argument is thus not conclusive.

The above is an attempt to clarify what is perhaps the most important contention of contemporary positivism. In considering positivist theories it should not be forgotten that although there is value in identifying laws clearly for practical purposes, there is more to law besides that; but these are matters which will have to be dealt with in due course.

BENTHAM

Analytical positivism in Britain will be associated to posterity with the names of Jeremy Bentham (1748–1832) and John Austin (1790–1859). The latter used to be styled until recently the 'Father of English jurisprudence', but it is clear from a work of Bentham first published in 1945 that it is he, if anyone, who deserves such a title. Bentham was a champion of codified law and of reforming English law, which to him was in chaos. He saw, however, that there could be no reform of substantive law without reform of its structure: so analysis of structure was an essential prelude to reform. Accordingly, he distinguished between what he termed 'expositorial' jurisprudence (what the law is) and 'censorial' jurisprudence, or the art of legislation (what law ought to be)[16]. In the course of writing *An Introduction to the Principles of Morals and Legislation* he was moved to ask:' 'What is a penal code of laws? What is a civil code'[17]? In seeking the answer he had to investigate the nature of 'a law', which led him into a maze through which he mapped out a path in *Of Laws in General*. Thus, what was originally conceived as a substantial appendix developed into a major contribution on its own and which was finished more or less in 1782. It remained unpublished and was disinterred fom the vaults of University College, London, by Professor C W Everett in 1939 and published under the title *The Limits of Jurisprudence Defined* in 1945. A revised edition was published as *Of Laws in General* in 1970 under the editorship of Professor Hart[18].

Bentham's analysis of a law has to be approached through his *Theory of Fictions*, which in modern terminology would be styled semantics. There is a tendency to believe that each word corresponds to some object. Indeed, some words do: 'real entities'. Other words stand for 'fictional entities'. These have to be understood in terms of real entities by a process called 'paraphrasis'[19], a new method of elucidation with a new name made necessary by the inapplicability of the traditional *per genus et differentiam* technique[20].

15 Unless it is said with Hobbes that no positive law can be unjust: *Leviathan* ch 30. Cf Kelsen 'The Pure Theory of Law' (1934) 50 LQR at 482.
16 Bentham *An Introduction to the Principles of Morals and Legislation* (eds Burns and Hart) p 293.
17 *Bentham* p 299.
18 References will be to this edition (*OLG*).
19 Bentham *The Theory of Fictions* (ed Ogden) pp 86 et seq, 138 et seq; *OLG* pp 251–252. Cf 'low-order' and 'high-order' referents of Ogden and Richards. *The Meaning of Meaning.* In a letter to the author shortly before his death in 1956, Ogden expressed the view that Bentham's work would reveal him to have been one of the greatest semanticists. See also the Introduction to his edition of *The Theory of Legislation* pp xi et seq.
20 *OLG* pp 294–295.

Parenthetically it might be remarked here that Bentham anticipated modern linguistic philosophy in a remarkable way by his insight that the meaning of words depends on how they are used in statements in which they occur[1]. 'A law', as distinct from 'law', was to him a real entity, and so was an 'act'; rights and duties, on the other hand, were fictional[2]. 'Law' is a fictional entity made up of an aggregate of individual laws[3]. At this point a comment has to be made. As pointed out earlier, 'law' in the sense of 'legal system' is much more than the sum-total of laws, just as a railway system is more than the sum-total of tracks and rolling stock[4]; it is the pattern of their linkage and a good deal more besides. By assuming that the clue to 'law' lies in the nature of 'a law', it would seem that Bentham overlooked a significant and different set of phenomena.

'A law may be defined' said Bentham 'as an assemblage of signs, declarative of a volition, conceived or adopted by the *sovereign* in a state, concerning the conduct to be observed in a certain *case* by a certain person or class of persons, who in the case in question are or are supposed to be subject to his power'[5]. Bentham's concept of a law is thus an imperative one, for which he himself preferred the term 'mandate'[6]. This definition is flexible enough to cover 'a set of objects so intimately allied and to which there would be such continual occasion to apply the same propositions', eg not only laws made by legislators, but also judicial, administrative, domestic orders as well as declaratory laws[7]. It also isolates a unit in terms of which more complex phenomena may be analysed. An important point is that permissions are included; but this so waters down the idea of mandate that it seems inappropriate to rank Bentham among the imperative jurists. Indeed, the imperative aspect of his theory, such as it is, is its least happy part, as will appear. Finally, every law may be considered in eight different respects: source, subjects, objects, extent, aspects, force, remedial appendages and expression[8].

SOURCE

The source of a law is the will of the sovereign, who may conceive laws which he personally issues, or adopt laws previously issued by former sovereigns or subordinate authorities ('susception'), or he may adopt laws to be issued in future by subordinate authorities ('pre-adoption')[9]. Pre-adoption may take the form of (a) permission given to the subordinate in the negative sense of his 'not being made the subject of a law commanding him not to issue the subordinate mandate which is in question'; or (b) a more positive permission to issue the mandate (which may be reinforced by permission to punish offenders, and by commands to others to assist); or (c) a mandate issued to the subjects of the subordinate to obey[10]. Pre-adoption in senses (b)

1 Bowring edition, vol 8, p 322; Hart *Bentham*.
2 *OLG* pp 293–294.
3 Bentham *Collected Works* p 141. Cf Jolowicz: 'For him, as for his disciple Austin, there is no law but laws': *Jeremy Bentham and the Law* (eds Keeton and Schwarzenberger) p 10.
4 See pp 60–62 ante, and pp 503–505 post.
5 *OLG* p 1.
6 *OLG* pp 10–16.
7 *OLG* pp 4–10.
8 *OLG* p 1.
9 *OLG* pp 21, 22.
10 *OLG* pp 22, 27, 28.

and (c) can be accommodated within Bentham's broad version of an imperative theory. The difficulty is with susception and pre-adoption in sense (a). Where a sovereign consciously allows a prior law to continue, or a subordinate to continue issuing laws, he may be said to exercise his will not to interfere; but where such continuance goes by default, this can hardly be said to be an exercise of will, except by way of an exceedingly tenuous fiction.

Bentham's sovereign is 'any person or assemblage of persons to whose will a whole political community are (no matter on what account) supposed to be in a disposition to pay obedience: and that in preference to the will of any other person'[11]. There is a difficulty about this in that 'political community' is defined elsewhere as follows: 'Where a number of persons (whom we may style *subjects*) are supposed to be in the *habit* of paying *obedience* to a person, or assemblage of persons of a known and certain description (whom we may call *governor* or *governors*), such persons altogether (*subjects* and *governors*) are said to be in a state of political *society*'[12]. The result is partly circular: 'sovereign' is defined partly in terms of 'political society' and the latter is defined partly in terms of the former. Also, it is not clear what exactly is meant by 'supposed'.

The attributes of sovereignty are interesting. Such power is indefinite unless limited by express convention or by religious or political motivations[13]. The sovereign may consist of more than one body, each of which is obeyed in different respects. Habitual obedience may thus be divided and partial, ie owed in certain areas of conduct[14]. When divided in this way the power of each is limited by the other and each has a limited power to prescribe for the other[15]. These laws are of a special kind: 'The business of the ordinary sort of laws is to prescribe to the people what *they* shall do: the business of this transcendental class of laws is to prescribe to the sovereign what *he* shall do'[16]. Thus, there is created a form of self-bindingness which has legal quality. This fascinating piece of analysis seems to have been lost on Bentham's disciple Austin, whose simplification in this and other respects long stultified British jurisprudence by providing nothing better than an arid basis for exploration and criticism.

SUBJECTS

These may be persons or things[17]. Each of these may be 'agible' (active) or 'passible' (passive) subjects, ie the agent with which an act commences or terminates. Thus, a person may be the striker or the party struck, a thing may be the instrument of destruction or the thing destroyed. They may be direct or indirect, the latter constituting the circumstances of an act.

OBJECTS

It is crucial in understanding Bentham's analysis to appreciate that each act-situation (including forbearance) is the object of an individual law[18].

11 *OLG* p 18.
12 *A Fragment on Government* ch 1, para 10.
13 *A Fragment on Government* ch 4, para 23 and n 1; *OLG* pp 68–70.
14 *OLG* pp 18 n *b*, 168 n *n*.
15 *OLG* p 68 n.
16 *OLG* p 64.
17 *OLG* pp 34 et seq.
18 *OLG* pp 41 et seq.

This was because he believed that 'a law' is a 'real entity', and so sought to reduce it to its factual basis. It is perhaps unfortunate that he did not apply here his own insight into the way words are used rather than seek their reference. An act originates in persons, but may end in a person or thing. (He might perhaps have amplified the part played by forbearance in this respect.) All laws regulate conduct positively or negatively, by imposing duties or granting permissions, 'imperatively' or 'de-imperatively'. To classify act-situations would be too cumbrous a task, but it is possible to classify the sovereign's reactions to them so that they become offences or not. These reactions are the 'aspects' of the sovereign's will.

EXTENT[19]

Direct extent means that a law covers a portion of land on which acts have their termination; indirect extent refers to the relation of an actor to a thing, eg being in a certain place at the time of the act, in short the circumstances. Bentham also alluded in passing to extent in point of time, or duration of a law[20]. He was thinking of time only as a way of determining the subjects of a law. It has been pointed out that time is significant in another way. Whatever the intended duration, the very concept of duration is dependent on certain factors, which, following Bentham's own line of thought, could be regarded as a part of every law[1]. At this point Bentham seems casually to have opened a door without pausing to peer at the vistas that it reveals.

ASPECTS

Every law has a 'directive' and a 'sanctional' or 'incitative' part. The former concerns the aspects of the sovereign's will towards an act-situation; the latter concerns the force of a law. Command is only one of four aspects of the sovereign's will, permutations of which comprehend the whole range of laws. These four are related by 'opposition' (incompatibility) and 'concomitancy' (compatibility); and Bentham evolved a 'deontic logic' with which to demonstrate the relationship between command, prohibition and permission[2].

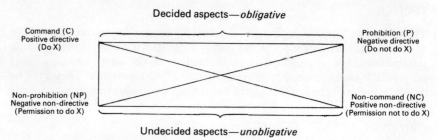

Decided aspects—*obligative*

Command (C)
Positive directive
(Do X)

Prohibition (P)
Negative directive
(Do not do X)

Non-prohibition (NP)
Negative non-directive
(Permission to do X)

Non-command (NC)
Positive non-directive
(Permission not to do X)

Undecided aspects—*unobligative*

The logic of imperation is as follows:
(1) C   ('Do X')
        (a) can co-exist with NP ('Permission to do X')—an obligative duty is not cancelled (de-obligated) by an unobligative liberty to do the same thing;

19 *OLG* pp 72 et seq.
20 *OLG* pp 74, 75.
 1 See p 21 ante.
 2 *OLG* pp 95 et seq.

(b)   cannot co-exist with P ('Do not do X')—an obligative duty is cancelled (de-obligated) by an obligative duty to do the opposite;

(c)   cannot co-exist with NC ('Permission not to do X')—an obligative duty cancels (de-obligates) the unobligative liberty to do the opposite.

(2) P   ('Do not do X')

(a)   can co-exist with NC ('Permission not to do X')—for the same reason as in (1) (a);

(b)   cannot co-exist with C ('Do X')—for the same reason as in (1) (b);

(c)   cannot co-exist with NP ('Permission to do X')—for the same reason as in (1) (c).

(3) NC   ('Permission not to do X')

(a)   cannot co-exist with C ('Do X')—an unobligative liberty is cancelled (de-obligated) by an obligative duty to do the opposite;

(b)   can co-exist with P ('Do not do X')—an unobligative liberty is not cancelled (de-obligated) by an obligative duty to do the same thing; *or*

(c)   with NP ('Permission to do X')—an unobligative liberty is not cancelled (de-obligated) by an unobligative liberty to do the opposite;

but *not* both together, since (b) and (c) cannot co-exist.

(4) NP   ('Permission to do X')

(a)   cannot co-exist with P ('Do not do X')—for the same reason as in (3) (a);

(b)   can co-exist with C ('Do X')—for the same reason as in (3) (b); *or*

(c)   with NC ('Permission not to do X')—for the same reason as in (3) (c);

but *not* both together, since (b) and (c) cannot co-exist.

The difficulty of reconciling permissions with an imperative theory, even in the extended sense of mandate, has been mentioned. This weakness, however, is a minor blemish when set against the depth and incisiveness of this demonstration of jural opposition and contradiction, which is more acute than Hohfeld's depiction of it 131 years later[3].

FORCE OF A LAW, SANCTIONAL OR INCITATIVE PART

A law is dependent upon motivations for obedience[4]. The sovereign's wish in respect of a class of acts is a law as long as it is supported by a sanction, even if this is not explicit, though usually, of course, it would be. It includes physical, political, religious and moral motivations[5], comprising threats of punishment (commination, coercion) and rewards (invitations, allurements)[6]. There is, however, a difference which appears to be glossed over. The failure to do, or not do, what a law supported by punishment requires

3 See p 28 ante.
4 *OLG* pp 133 et seq.
5 *OLG* pp 68–70, 248. Cf *An Introduction to the Principles of Morals and Legislation* ch 3.
6 *OLG* pp 134–136.

is illegal; but it is not illegal to do, or not do, what a law supported by reward requires.

Regulation of conduct and stipulation of sanction govern different act-situations, so they require separate laws: one saying 'You shall not murder', and the other 'If you do, you shall be punished'. Non-prohibitions and non-commands are unobligative aspects of the sovereign's will and are supported by sanctions affecting, not the subjects of the laws, but others who are subjects of 'corroborative' laws not to interfere. From the legislator's point of view, actual punishment is a prediction, since it is outside his province to carry out the threat. Accordingly, he issues subsidiary laws, eg that a judge must verify that the accused did murder. The judge in turn is assisted by various officials all of whom are likewise under subsidiary laws. If no one obeys these subsidiary laws, the principal law becomes a dead letter. Now, even though it is true to say, in Bentham's view, that all these subsidiary laws are expressions of sovereign wishes, the inescapable fact is that they add up to no more than a prediction, dependent on probability, of punishment as prescribed in the sanctional part of the principal law. In other words, the functioning of a law is implicitly a part of Bentham's own concept of a law, and this imports many considerations of a social and psychological character[7]. This further dilutes the imperative character of a law. Nevertheless, he should be given credit for an illuminating hint. For yet again he anticipated the twentieth century to a remarkable degree. His analysis of sanction resembles that of Kelsen and the implication that sanction is a prediction based on probabilities foreshadows the views of the American Realists[8]. On the other hand, he differed from both these in separating the regulation of conduct and the stipulation of sanction into two distinct laws. It is a matter of opinion which view is preferable, but it will be submitted in due course that Bentham's is better.

REMEDIAL APPENDAGES

Sanctions are provided by subsidiary laws. They themselves require a further set of subsidiary laws, 'remedial appendages', addressed to judges with a view to curing the evil (compensation), stopping the evil or preventing future evil[9].

EXPRESSION

The ways in which the sovereign's will may be expressed are various[10]. The connection with will immediately raises the problem of discovering the will from the expression, which is a root difficulty encountered by any imperative theory. Expression may be 'complete', ie the matter to be regulated coincides with one law. In all such cases a judge should adopt a literal interpretation. Only where expression is incomplete may he adopt a liberal interpretation. Bentham, the relentless enemy of judge-made law, sought to minimise judicial discretion by trying to ensure that laws were complete, not only in expression, but also in 'connection' and 'design', and this feature of his analysis needs to be considered separately.

7 See p 21 ante.
8 See pp 449 et seq post.
9 *OLG* pp 149 et seq.
10 *OLG* pp 152 et seq.

Individuality of a law

What, then, is a 'complete law', ie 'complete' in a jurisprudential sense? The individuality of a law he says 'results from the *integrality* and the *unity* of it laid together'[11]; and the purpose of individuation 'is to ascertain what a portion of legislative matter must amount to in order on the one hand not to contain less, on the other hand not to contain more than one whole law'[12].

INTEGRALITY. This means that a law should be complete in expression, connection and design. With regard to the first, the standard of reference is whether the actual will of the legislation has been completely expressed. Every law contains an imperative provision which may be qualified or unqualified, further expounded or unexpounded. If it is unqualified and unexpounded, it is complete in expression in itself; if it requires qualification or exposition, it is incomplete without these. Qualifications and expositions cannot, of course, be complete in themselves without the principal provision.

With regard to completeness in connection, Bentham said that more often than not parts of a law 'lie scattered up and down at random, some under one head, some under another, with little or no notice taken of their mutual relations and dependencies'[13]. Moreover, these parts may have been brought into existence by different bodies at different times. Thus, a statutory prohibition of driving while under the influence of liquor includes, *inter alia*, a police force, courts, judges, breathalysers, procedures etc, each of which has been brought into existence by different laws at different times. They need to be co-ordinated before a law can be said to be complete in point of connection. One implication of this is that the individuation of every law imports a temporal dimension.

If the legislator's general idea of the mischief deviates from that which, in the light of the particular case, he should and might have formed, the law in question is incomplete in design. The deviation may be that it does not go far enough, in which case it is incomplete in point of amplitude; or it may go too far, in which case it is incomplete in point of discrimination. All exceptions must therefore be set down[14].

Judicial interpretation of laws is made to depend on their completeness. Interpretation is strict when the will attributed to the legislator is that which he really entertained. Interpretation is liberal when the will attributed by a court is that which he inadvertently failed to entertain, but which he would have entertained had the particular case been presented to him, ie when the law is incomplete in point of design. When it is incomplete in point of amplitude, liberal interpretation has to be 'extensive'; when it is incomplete in point of discrimination, interpretation has to be 'restrictive'. In all such cases incompleteness results from the legislator's inadvertence. If, however, incompleteness is only supposed, ie when what is thought to be a shortcoming or an overstatement was intended, then liberal interpretation ceases to be interpretation and amounts to overruling the legislator. The weakness of all this lies in the assumption that the wish which the legislator 'really' entertained is somehow knowable independently of its expression. To start on the

---

11 *OLG* p 156; and see pp 59–60 ante.
12 *OLG* 'description of that which is to be looked upon as neither more nor less than one entire law': p 247.
13 *OLG* p 159.
14 *OLG* p 168.

basis that the mode of expression has to be interpreted according to the legislator's will, and then to discover that it is often impossible to discover what this is apart from the mode of expression frustrates the whole exercise. Such is the consequence of any imperative approach, requiring as it does the 'ascertaining of the intention of the legislator'[15].

UNITY. 'The unity of a law' said Bentham 'will depend upon the unity of the species of the act which is the object of it[16]. The way in which different species of acts are designated is largely a matter of wording dictated by convenience. His point was that each act-situation is the object of a separate law. Here lies the difference between the unity of a law and its integrality[17]. Also, nowhere did he assert that one species of act could give rise to only one offence. Two different laws can create two separate offences out of the same act, as where a criminal offence is also a tort.

If an act-situation is the object of every law, what of the 'laws' of contract or property, which deal with the requirements of a contract and title to property? These neither impose duties nor grant permissions. Bentham's answer was that these are not laws in themselves, but parts of laws. Laws forbid breaches of contracts and interferences with property[18]. Statements as to what a contract is and those determining title to property are 'expository' (amplifying and limiting the acts and sanctions) and 'qualificatory' (limiting the scope of the laws forbidding interference). Such 'parts of laws' are often very complex and pertain to different laws, which is why they are set out on their own for convenience. Ingenious as this explanation is, it is unsatisfying. The point that it cuts across traditional usage and habits of thought might be countered to some extent by the reply that he was trying to straighten out the tangle resulting from traditional thought and that divergences from accepted terminology is only to be expected. Nevertheless, the divergence should not be too great[19]; indeed, Bentham himself at various points did make concessions to convenience. The point is whether such wholesale divergence oversteps the limits of convenience. More serious is the objection that this classification only follows from squeezing the concept of a law into the strait-jacket of an imperative theory: all laws have to be either commands or permissions. It takes no account of powers, eg powers to make contracts, create title etc[20].

Customary laws received short shrift at Bentham's hands. In his view they could never be complete[1].

At the end of his analysis he returned to the question with which he began: 'What is a penal code of laws? What is a civil code?' He concluded that the former consists of laws creating 'offences' (those composed of directive and sanctional or incitative parts), while the latter consists of expository and qualificatory matter. 'Offences' in this context are wider than crimes. The characteristic of criminal offences, as distinct from civil offences, lies not in their intrinsic nature, but in the degree of mischief they occasion, the degree of displeasure they evoke and the degree of punishment meted out. To the

15 See pp 166–168 ante.
16 *OLG* pp 166, 170.
17 *OLG* p 171.
18 *OLG* pp 176–182.
19 Raz *The Concept of a Legal System* pp 115, 142.
20 Cf identifying 'legal material' (not 'laws') with reference to function: pp 11, 23 ante.
 1 *OLG* pp 184 et seq.

category of civil offences belong 'such offences as it is not judged necessary to punish with any extraordinary degree or species of punishment: to the criminal, such offences as it is judged necessary to punish with some extraordinary degree or species of punishment'[2]. It may be asked how such a distinction is applicable to the gradations of treatment, penal, reformative and curative, meted out to criminals. It also breaks down in the case of a tort visited by exemplary damages[3], whereas pulling the communication cord in a train needlessly can only be visited by a £50 payment. Why is the former civil and the latter criminal? Or are they both 'civil'? The proposed distinction will lead to a formidable restructuring, which seems scarcely worth the price.

Bentham's ultimate objective was an ideal code. His analysis of a law led him to conclude that such a code should consist of laws analysable jurisprudentially, and its penal and civil branches should be separated[4]. Its advantages would be to minimise the risk of incompleteness of laws and consequently what he termed 'licentiousness' of interpretation; to exhibit a common standard by which different systems might profitably be compared; and to create and improve the method of teaching the art of legislation. Whether, in the light of the difficulties that have been pointed out, this kind of code would indeed be ideal is a matter of opinion. So strong were his feelings as to the merits of a code that he remained a life-long enemy of judge-made law, which he hoped would be largely eliminated, thereby reducing the judicial function. The likelihood of his hopes being realised in present-day Western-type societies may be doubted; but should these be replaced by forms of totalitarianism, in which the judiciary only reflects governmental values, those hopes may well become a reality.

An assessment of his work is not easy. His main interest lay in advocating reforms, but he also examined problems of international law. In fact, it was he who coined that name[5]. The current resurgence of interest in his work is leading to a great deal of re-evaluation, while his remarkable anticipations of modern thought in so many directions make one wonder whether a final judgment is yet possible. Even as it is, the breadth and depth of his analyses and brilliant insights are such that it does not seem too extravagant to say that had all his writings been known, he could well have been the greatest single contributor to European jurisprudence; which makes it all the more regrettable that the world of scholarship lost so much for so long.

AUSTIN

Throughout the nineteenth century Bentham's *Of Laws in General* remained hidden in London University and British positivism came to be dominated by the views of his disciple John Austin (1790–1859) until virtually the outbreak of the 1939–45 war. As will appear, his work is largely derivative and far less satisfying than Bentham's. The first six lectures, the most influential part of his work, were published in 1832 under the title of *The Province of Jurisprudence Determined*, and the rest were published posthumously in 1861[6].

2 *OLG* p 211.
3 Within the limits of *Rookes v Barnard* [1964] AC 1129, [1964] 1 All ER 367.
4 *OLG* pp 183, 232 et seq.
5 Bentham *An Introduction to the Principles of Morals and Legislation* ch 17, para 25.
6 Austin *Lectures in Jurisprudence* (5th edn, ed Campbell).

Austin, in sympathy with Bentham as to law reform, conceived his initial task to be a critical analysis of the law as it is. The time he had spent in Germany preparing for his lectures and his study of Roman law brought home to him the contrast between the orderliness of Roman law and the chaos in England. Commentators on Roman law had Justinian's codification as their starting point, while their British counterparts were groping amidst a thicket of statutes and diverse and often poor law reports. German lawyers had behind them centuries of exegetical work, while Blackstone's *Commentaries* was still the only attempt at a systematic arrangement of English law.

Accordingly Austin set himself the task of making a beginning with the analysis of the principal concepts of English law. Before doing so he felt it necessary to demarcate the province of 'law' and to distinguish it from what it ought to be. In his first six lectures he sought to elucidate 'law' in the light of which its concepts would then be analysed. Although his fame rests on these preliminary lectures, they were only a prologue to the study of jurisprudence which, to him, meant the analysis of concepts. His concept of law is an imperative one influenced by his preparatory studies, which had impressed upon him the powerful position occupied by the sovereign in municipal law. In Roman law the authority of the *Princeps* and later of the Emperor was seen to have been unquestionable. European writers had preached in like vein. Bodin, for instance, said that sovereignty was the absolute and perpetual power within the state and, perhaps most importantly, in the work of Hobbes was to be seen the connection between the law of the state and enforcement by organised power. He had also spoken of law as being grounded in 'natural reason', but that it became 'law' only by virtue of the command of a sovereign. Bentham's approach, too, was an imperative one based on sovereignty. With these influences behind him Austin's adoption of a similar basis is hardly surprising.

Like Bentham, Austin believed that 'law' is only an aggregate of individual laws. In his view, all laws are rules the majority of which regulate behaviour. These are either directives or those imposed by general opinion. Directives have to be laid down 'posited'; and a directive, whether general or particular, is 'the expression or intimation of your wish' that another shall do or forbear, issued in the form of a command. Accordingly, a law in its most comprehensive signification is 'a rule laid down for the guidance of an intelligent being by an intelligent being having power over him'[7]. This can only be accomplished by a determinate person or body, since an indeterminate body cannot express wishes in the form of commands.

Austin proceeded to distinguish between what he called 'laws properly so called' and 'laws improperly so called'[8]. The key to a law 'properly so called' lies in obligation, which was approached as follows. Every wish with regard to conduct is favourable to conduct which is desired, and unfavourable to conduct which is not desired. Such wishes may emanate from directives or from general opinion, but wishes that are directives are distinguishable in that they render conduct obligatory. A person is under an obligation, not simply when consequences harmful to him ensue, for, if so, there would be an obligation not to put one's hand in the fire. An obligation exists when another has the power and purpose of inflicting an evil on any actor, who fails to conform to the desired conduct[9]. This other may be God, or human

7 *Austin* p 86.
8 *Austin* pp 79, 86 et seq. 3 p 89. 4 p 96.
9 *Austin* p 89.

beings acting as political superiors, ie a sovereign person or body of persons in an independent political society, or private persons acting in pursuance of rights conferred upon them by political superiors. General opinion cannot create obligations. Every directive, then, is a command, the threat of evil is a sanction, and the party commanded and threatened is under an obligation or duty. Duty and sanction are correlative and fear of sanction is the motive for obedience.

A command may be particular (addressed to one person or group of persons) or general. General commands are addressed to the community at large and enjoin classes of acts and forbearances[10]; they are also continuing commands. A particular command is effective when the commanded person or group obeys; a general command is effective when the bulk of a political society habitually obeys it. A commander, who receives 'habitual obedience from the bulk of a given society', is sovereign in that society. It is not necessary for general opinion to authorise the issue of commands, since a person can command and threaten without such authority. From all this Austin concluded that a law is a general command of a sovereign backed by a sanction.

He subdivided laws 'properly so called' into laws set by God, Divine laws, and laws set by men to men acting as political superiors or in pursuance of rights conferred by political superiors. To every law set by men to men he applied the term 'positive law' or 'law simply and strictly so called' so as to distinguish them from the laws of God[11]. 'Positive laws' are the subject matter of jurisprudence. Separate from all these are laws set by men to men neither as political superiors, nor in pursuance of rights conferred upon them by such superiors, eg those set by a master to a servant or the rules of a club. They are still laws 'properly so called', because they are commands, but he distinguished them from positive law by giving them the term 'positive morality'.

Under the heading of laws 'improperly so called' he placed, first of all, 'laws by analogy', ie laws set and enforced by mere opinion, such as the laws of fashion, international law and so forth. These also he somewhat confusingly termed 'positive morality'—'positive' so as to distinguish them from the laws of God, 'morality' so as to distinguish them from positive law or law strictly so called. Laws 'improperly so called' also included 'laws by metaphor', which covered expressions of the uniformities of Nature.

Austin's model is open to several comments. The first is that the distinctions which he drew were arbitrary. Not that there is any objection to doing this provided clear indications are given of what they mean; and Austin was scrupulous in this respect. He did, however, commit two errors. Although he did not specifically say so, it is clear that he fashioned his concept out of the material of English law with an occasional sprinkling of Roman law, but he proceeded to use it as a criterion of 'law in general' and so excluded, eg international law. He was also misguided in applying the epithet 'proper' to what was, after all, his own stipulative definition of 'a law'.

Austin was seeking to provide a means of identifying a law for the purposes of the moment, but to link this with the means of securing obedience is to confuse identification with functioning. Obedience is a factor relevant to the latter, and in this context, as has been pointed out, fear of sanction is not the sole, or even principal, motive for obedience[12]. Many objections may also be

10 *Austin* p 96.
11 For this and the subsequent divisions, see *Austin* pp 86 et seq, and Lecture V.
12 See pp 51–52, 248 ante.

levelled at the association of duty and sanction, which have been developed earlier[13]. Another weakness is the fact that he found himself compelled to treat nullity as a sanction in order to accommodate, eg the rule, 'You must make a gratuitous promise under seal', within his command-duty-sanction model[14].

LAWS AS COMMANDS

This idea has encountered the heaviest criticism. Austin's association of duty with command was probably the result of his having been misled by the imperative form in which duties are expressed: 'You must', or 'You shall'. Professor Olivecrona has pointed out that everyone has a store of experiences of actual commands addressed in the imperative form, so that whenever one encounters that form of expression there is a tendency to suppose that it must have emanated from a command. He points out that duties are 'ought' propositions which are phrased imperatively, and it is a *non sequitur* to suppose that such phraseology of itself implies command[15].

With regard to the wider aspects of the command theory, it may well be that the idea at the back of Austin's mind was, in Buckland's words, 'primarily an English criminal statute'[16]. Even so, there is a difference between this sort of law and command. The function of a law is to regulate future conduct indefinitely and to serve as a standard by which to judge deviance; a command is more usually directed to a specified individual or individuals with reference to a particular act or forbearance and does not serve as a general standard of judgment. Apart from this, there are laws which are not commands. Austin himself was somewhat exercised by declaratory statutes, repealing statutes and 'laws of imperfect obligation', which include laws defining, eg what a contract is, or a crime, or a law which says that no action shall succeed after the lapse of a limitation period. He concluded that these were exceptions[17]. In this he was perhaps unduly hesitant, for, as Buckland pointed out, declaratory statutes could have been treated as repeating earlier commands, while repealing statutes may be said to create fresh claims and duties by their cancellation of earlier ones and so be said to command[18]. Nevertheless, Austin's hesitation and the fact that he was driven to admit exceptions betray some uneasiness with the command thesis. The question of custom troubled him not at all. To him customs were laws when commanded either directly by incorporation in statutes, or indirectly in judicial decisions[19].

Command presupposes a commander. Austin perceived clearly that 'no indeterminate party can command expressly or tacitly, or can receive obedience or submission'[20]. The question is whether a determinate person, or body of persons, can be discovered who might be regarded as having commanded the whole *corpus* of the law. Never at any point in history is such a person or

13 See pp 236 et seq.
14 *Austin* p 505, criticised on p 44 ante.
15 See p 231 ante. There is also the duty accompanying all types of legal material that they shall be treated as 'law'.
16 Buckland *Some Reflections on Jurisprudence* p 4.
17 *Austin* pp 98-100.
18 *Austin* pp 49-51.
19 *Austin* pp 101-102, 199.
20 *Austin* Lecture V especially pp 183, 194-195.

group discoverable. Who, for instance, commanded the rule that precedents shall be binding? A sovereign is sovereign within a 'state', and 'state' is a legally defined organisation consisting of territory, population, government and a measure of independence in external relations. Who commanded these requirements? Again, it might be thought that the present monarch and members of both Houses of Parliament can command any law they please. However, as Professor Olivecrona pointed out, the individuals who comprise the sovereign body have attained their positions by virtue of laws. Who, then, commanded these laws? Whoever commanded them in turn owed their authority to command to the observance of other laws. There is no sense in saying that the laws which brought them to their positions were their own commands[1]. Even if the Crown in Parliament as a composite entity is taken to be the uncommanded commander, a study of the events of 1688–1689 shows that this body in no sense commanded the rule that its commands shall be law. It was acceptance of it as the supreme commander, particularly by the judges, that entitled it to command henceforth[2]. Moreover, it is artificial to pretend that any member of Parliament believes that the law of the land has emanated from his commands, for the vast majority of laws existed before he was born. To attribute commands to people, who have neither commanded nor believe that they have done so, is a fantasy.

Although the Crown in Parliament was accepted in 1689 as the Austinian commander, the bulk of the common law and much legislation was already in existence and continued to exist unaffected. Even if it is assumed with Austin that these laws had emanated from earlier commands, the question is why and how commands of a former sovereign continue to be laws under his successor. Austin's reply was that this comes about by virtue of 'tacit command': what the sovereign permits, he commands[3]. This implies that the sovereign knows of the earlier commands and decides not to interfere. When does he so decide? It cannot be when their applicability comes before a judge (who, according to Austin, is the sovereign's delegate), since he has no choice in the matter: a previous enactment, however ancient, is always accepted by a judge as being law already. If so, the decision, assuming that there was one, not to interfere with this prior command, and which thereby invests it with fresh authority, can only be that of the sovereign himself. Professor Hart has demolished the idea of 'tacit command'[4]. (i) A sovereign may consciously permit the continuance of a former law, or (ii) such a law may continue by default simply through not being repealed. Tacit command may superficially fit case (i); though it will be noticed that even an actual decision not to repeal is a decision *not to command*. How, then, can a decision not to repeal impart fresh law-quality to something which never ceased to possess it? Tacit command ceases to be even superficially applicable to case (ii), since non-repeal by default is in no sense 'the expression of a wish', which was Austin's own description of command. The continuance of the majority of the laws of a previous sovereign are instances of (ii). In any case, tacit command fails to explain why the laws and system which continue are the *same* laws and

1 Olivecrona *Law as Fact* (1939) pp 36–37; (1971) pp 67–77. For further objections, see 'The Imperative Element in Law' (1964) 18 Rutgers LR 794.
2 Hart points out that for a successor sovereign's commands to be 'laws' there must have been acceptance of a rule which entitles the successor to succeed: *The Concept of Law* p 54; p 352 post.
3 *Austin* p 102; ch 30.
4 *Hart* ch 2, ss 2–4.

system. If, then, tacit command is rejected, as it must be, what remains is the proposition that laws remain in force until repealed.

Finally, it has been pointed out that even actual commands of a sovereign only acquire the character of laws when certain procedures have been followed[5]. If the Queen, Lords and Commons unanimously assent to a measure at a garden party in Buckingham Palace, it would not become a law, because the appropriate Parliamentary procedures have not been gone through. If these procedures are laws, it is difficult to square them with command (still less with sanction save by way of nullity). If they are not laws, they are indistinguishable from the dictates of etiquette and morals. Yet, distinguished they must be. What all this shows is the inadequacy of the command doctrine.

SOVEREIGNTY

Austin's distinction between positive law and positive morality was that the former was set by a political superior. In elaborating this notion he evolved his theory of sovereignty.

Sovereignty has a 'positive mark' and a 'negative mark'. The former is that a determinate human superior should 'receive habitual obedience from the bulk of a given society', and the latter is that that superior is 'not in the habit of obedience to a like superior'[6]. The reference to 'habitual obedience' touches obliquely on the point that every legal system is ultimately founded on some social fact for which no legal justification can be adduced[7]. The addition of 'the bulk of a given society', however, is arguable, since this is hardly the body that matters. For instance, it was obedience on the part of the judges after 1689 that established the sovereignty of the Crown in Parliament. On the other hand, it has been pointed out that Austin confused the *de facto* sovereign, or the body that receives obedience, with the *de jure* sovereign, or the law-making body[8]. In Britain the Crown receives allegiance from its subjects, while the Crown in Parliament is the supreme law-maker. When Austin talked of the uncommanded commander who makes laws, he was referring to the *de jure* sovereign. Another criticism is that the 'negative mark' is not so much the concern of municipal lawyers as of international lawyers. For the former the question is, Whose enactments constitute 'laws'? It is a matter of indifference to them that the law-maker obeys some other body in the international sphere as long as he can make laws in the municipal sphere. Finally, it has been questioned whether it is necessary to have a sovereign in a state. The answer depends on the meanings of 'necessary' and 'state'. A sovereign may be 'necessary' because definition has made it so. In another sense the question is whether a sovereign is 'necessary' as a practical matter. The word 'state', too, has shades of meaning into which it is not proposed to enter. The short answer to the question is that there is no need for only one law-making body, though in practice this might be convenient.

Austin went on to assert that a sovereign cannot command himself, ie place himself under an obligation. Further, to confer a power on another is to specify the conditions under which other persons may create obligations, subject to sanctions specified by the sovereign. Delegation of authority is thus

5 See pp 52 et seq.
6 *Austin* pp 220–221.
7 Cf acceptance of the Crown in Parliament in 1689: pp 53–54 ante.
8 Bryce *Studies in History and Jurisprudence* II, pp 51–60.

commanding that people shall obey the commands of another. The attributes of sovereignty, which followed from this, are that it is illimitable, indivisible and continuous; and he has encountered criticism in each respect. His denial that the sovereign could be limited[9] relegated substantial areas of constitutional law to positive morality. The sovereign cannot be under a duty, since to be under a duty implies that there is another sovereign above the first who commands the duty and imposes a sanction; in which case the first is not sovereign. Jethro Brown argued that the sovereign could well be bound by a duty; Buckland, supporting Austin, denied it[10]. As to this, it is to be observed, in the first place, that Austin overlooked limitations through disabilities rather than duties[11]. Secondly, the exercise of sovereign powers may be limited by special procedures[12]. Thirdly, Bentham showed how sovereignty may be divided in such a way that each component has a limited power to prescribe for the other, and how this creates legal self-bindingness on a sovereign[13]. Connected with duties is the question whether the sovereign can have claims. Austin again denied it since, in his view, a claim has to be conferred by a sovereign on someone, therefore to say that one sovereign confers a claim on another is to deny the sovereignty of the latter. It may be thought that the sovereign may confer a claim upon itself, to which Austin replied that this would be to confuse 'might with right'. Buckland pointed out that this answer is inconsistent with his concept of claims and duties according to which a person is under a duty if he is subject to an evil, which the party with the claim could cause to be inflicted in the event of disobedience. There is no contradiction in saying that the sovereign could fulfil both roles. Accordingly, Buckland himself suggested that since the situation looks like one in which there is a claim-duty relation, there is no point in denying that the sovereign can have a claim[14]. The question may also be asked whether anything of practical moment turns on the issue. It is also to be noted that in most of these discussions there has been a tendency to refer to the Crown as the Austinian sovereign, which it is not; the Crown in Parliament is the sovereign[15].

The attribute of indivisibility creates other difficulties. The question is whether sovereign authority can be vested in more than one body, not

---

9 *Austin* p 263.
10 Brown *The Austinian Theory of Law* p 194; *Buckland* pp 107–109.
11 See pp 39, 102 ante.
12 See pp 93 et seq ante.
13 See p 337 ante.
14 *Austin* pp 282 et seq; *Buckland* p 110.
15 It has been contended by Professor Paulson that the rejection by the War Crimes Tribunal at Nuremberg of the defences of act of state, superior orders and *ex post facto* law making was tantamount to a rejection of the Austinian doctrines of sovereignty and of law as command backed by sanction. (1) The defence of act of state presupposes the Austinian thesis that a sovereign cannot be subject to a duty since there is no sovereign superior to a sovereign state. The Tribunal's answer was to point to instances where sovereign states are under duties; which leads to a rejection of the Austinian thesis. (2) The defence of superior orders by the accused is based on the thesis that the validity of a sovereign's order cannot be impugned on moral groundss. The Tribunal rejected this defence on the ground that the test was whether a moral choice was open to the accused persons individually. (3) The defence that the trial amounted to *ex post facto* law making is based on the concept of law as command backed by sanction, the answer to which was that there had been laws forbidding the kind of conduct that was on trial although they lacked effective sanctions. The absence of sanction in no way impugns the quality of 'law'; the Nuremberg Charter did not create offences *ex post facto*, but only provided sanctions: 'Classical Legal Positivism at Nuremberg' (1975) 4 Phil & Pub Affairs 132.

whether it can be exercised by more than one, which Austin would have admitted[16]. Bentham showed how sovereignty could be divided; besides, there are obvious examples, eg the old Roman assemblies, the United States of America and the concurrent powers of a colonial legislature and the Westminster Parliament[17].

Finally, the attribute of continuity may be questioned by asking where sovereignty resides during a dissolution of Parliament. Austin fell into contradiction in trying to anticipate the objection by saying that sovereignty lies with the Queen, Lords and Electorate. This is contrary to his assertion that it lies with the Queen, Lords and Commons, and it also renders the whole concept meaningless[18]. Who, on this view, is the commander, and who the commanded?

In assessing Austin's contribution, it is to be noted that he helped to propagate the positivist doctrine that it is necessary, to some extent at least, to separate the law as it is from what it ought to be. His concept of a law, shorn of its sovereignty, command and sanction attributes, is reducible to a prescription of conduct phrased in imperative form; but this is not a sufficient basis for drawing the distinction he desired between the 'is' and the 'ought'. His method of logical analysis, ie of deducing the nature of legal conceptions from his conception of a law, is, as Julius Stone pointed out, no more than the use of a model to reveal the logical consistency of a system[19]. The value of any such model depends on the degree of correspondence between it and the way in which laws and legal conceptions are actually used. Austin presented his scheme in the belief that, notwithstanding some discrepancies, there was a sufficient measure of correspondence with actuality. In this he was mistaken. Also, he did not reveal the reasoning which led him to his concept of a law; he simply made certain assertions and applied them logically. It is always more interesting to probe and test the reasoning behind premises than to follow out their logical implications. The material of his book consists mainly of contemporary English law with occasional bits of Roman law thrown in. The concept of a law which he fashioned out of these data should have been confined within those limits. Unhappily, he extrapolated them into a test of law in general. Even so, what he was doing was, in effect, to give a stipulative definition of how he proposed using the term 'a law'. By proffering it as 'law properly so called' he assumed that 'law' has a 'proper' meaning and he also utilised the emotive connotation of 'proper'. His exclusion of international law and portions of constitutional law from 'law properly so called' was logical according to his premise; and had he said that he was only doing this because they fell outside the subject as he saw it, it would have been a permissible attitude for him to have adopted. To exclude them, as he did, on the ground that they were not 'law properly so called' was needlessly provocative[20].

16 *Austin* p 238.
17 Eg *Madzimbamuto v Lardner-Burke*, [1969] 1 AC 645, [1968] 3 All ER 561; pp 54–55 ante. Since a colonial legislature can delegate its power to legislate, it is not itself a delegate of Westminster, *delegatus delegare non potest: Powell v Apollo Candle Co* (1885) 10 App Cas 282. Indivisibility of sovereignty was rejected by Lord Evershed MR in *Re Mwenya* [1960] 1 QB 241 at 298, [1959] 3 All ER 525 at 533–534. See too *R v Secretary of State for Foreign and Commonwealth Affairs, ex p Indian Association of Alberta* [1982] QB 892, [1982] 2 All ER 118; *Manuel v A-G* [1983] Ch 77, [1982] 3 All ER 786, 822.
18 *Austin* pp 245–246.
19 Stone *Legal System and Lawyers' Reasonings* ch 2.
20 The international lawyers must shoulder some responsibility for the fruitless controversy which developed: see pp 495–498 post.

Austin paid lip-service to 'general jurisprudence', by which he meant 'the exposition of the principles, notions and distinctions which are common to systems of law; understanding by systems of law, the ampler and maturer systems'[1]. This is unhelpful without a criterion for 'amplitude and maturity', and some indication as to whether the 'common' principles are those which are in fact found to be common, or those which for some reason are 'necessarily' common. Nor did he provide evidence that the notions which he did put into his book are in truth shared by 'ampler and maturer systems', whatever these may be. Indeed, Austin to some extent belied his own thesis by confining his demonstration to English and a little Roman law. Perhaps, he thought that in so far as the legal orders of the Old and New Worlds were based, as far as he knew, on these two systems, they would furnish between them a sufficient basis for general jurisprudence. However, as Buckland observed, Austin and others like him, who profess general jurisprudence, seldom adhere to it[2].

A comparison of Bentham and Austin must lead to the conclusion that the former provided a deeper and more adaptable theory. His concept of sovereignty was flexible in that it avoided the shackles of indivisibility and illimitability. He was thus able to accommodate the division of authority between organs, as in a federation, or division in certain areas, as well as restrictions of authority and self-bindingness. His concept of a law was broader than Austin's and he avoided the absurdity of 'law properly so called'. His sanction was both wider and less important than Austin's: laws are still laws even though supported by moral or religious sanctions, they may even be accompanied by rewards. He thus had no need to resort to 'sanction by nullity'. The imperative foundation is a weakness in his theory, as has been pointed out, but it was so much broader and less uncompromising than Austin's that he was able to accommodate permissions up to a point; and he certainly avoided the 'tacit command' fiction.

Austin's successors in the positivist tradition have abandoned his concept in favour of other formulations. Holland concentrated, not on command, but on 'enforcement by sovereign political authority'[3]. This suffers from all the difficulties concerning enforcement that were previously examined[4]. Salmond spoke of law as consisting of 'the rules recognised and acted on by courts of justice'[5]. The reference to justice is not clear. It may be no more than an embellishment of 'courts', for nowhere does Salmond appear to make justice a criterion of identification. A minor difficulty is that courts often apply, for example, rules of arithmetic in the course of giving their decisions, but these do not thereby become 'law'. What is required is the addition of a rider to the effect that the rules are 'recognised and acted on' as *law* by the courts.

HLA HART

Professor Hart (1907–) may be regarded as the leading contemporary representative of British positivism. In his influential book, *The Concept of Law*, published in 1961, he brought to bear the training of a philosopher, barrister

---

1 *Austin* p 1073.
2 *Buckland* pp 71–72.
3 Holland *The Elements of Jurisprudence* p 43.
4 See pp 235 et seq ante.
5 Salmond *Jurisprudence* p 36.

and jurist to the elucidation of jurisprudential problems. As a linguistic philosopher he belongs to the school which sees how words are used rather than what they refer to[6], and he subscribes to the view that a word possesses, not a 'proper meaning', but an inner 'core' of agreed applications surrounded by a 'fringe' of unsettled applications. As an analytical jurist, he is keenly appreciative, *inter alia*, of Hohfeld's distinctions, the influence of which is evident throughout his writings.

He approached his concept of law as follows. 'Where there is law', he says, 'there human conduct is made in some sense non-optional or obligatory'[7]. Thus, the idea of obligation is at the core of a rule. He commences his book by taking Austin's command theory to task. The idea of command will explain a coercive order addressed to another in special circumstances, but not why a statute applies generally and also applies to its framers. Secondly, there are other varieties of laws, notably powers. Thirdly, the continuance of pre-existing laws cannot be explained on the basis of command; as pointed out, he was able to demolish completely the 'tacit command' myth[8]. Fourthly, Austin's 'habit of obedience' fails to explain succession to sovereignty because it fails to take account of important differences between 'habit' and 'rule'. Habits only require common behaviour, which is not enough for a rule. A rule has an 'internal aspect', ie people use it as a standard by which to judge and condemn deviations; habits do not function in this way[9]. Professor Hart maintains that the significance of 'rule' has been neglected. Succession to sovereignty occurs by virtue of the acceptance of a rule entitling the successor to succeed, not because of a habit of obedience. He also uses 'rule' to distinguish between 'being obliged' and 'having an obligation'. Austin's command-duty-sanction thesis fails to explain why, if a gunman threatens X with 'Your money or your life', X may be obliged to hand over his purse, but has no obligation to do so. The reason is that one has an obligation only by virtue of a rule.

Rules of obligation are distinguishable from other rules in that they are supported by great social pressure because they are felt to be necessary to maintain society[10]. How, then, do they acquire the character of 'laws'? Regulation of behaviour is by means of what are called 'primary rules'. Societies which possess only these are in a 'pre-legal' condition and suffer from three drawbacks[11]. One is uncertainty as to what these rules are and their scope; but this can be met by having a 'secondary rule of recognition' by which to identify primary rules. Secondly, primary rules are static; but this can be met by having secondary rules providing powers to change primary rules[12]. Thirdly, the maintenance of primary rules is inefficient because of the absence of authoritative arbiters of disputes; but this can be met by having secondary rules of adjudication. Thus, primary rules acquire the character of a legal system through their union with secondary rules, ie the union of rules creating duties and rules creating powers to create, extinguish, modify and adjudge, as well as a rule of recognition with which to

6 Cf his elucidation of 'right': 'Definition and Theory in Jurisprudence' (1954) 70 LQR 49.
7 Hart *The Concept of Law* p 80.
8 See pp 347–348 ante.
9 *Hart* pp 55–56, 99; see p 48 ante.
10 *Hart* p 84; p 228 ante.
11 *Hart* pp 90 et seq.
12 Cf Maine's distinction between 'static' and 'progressive' societies. The latter develop beyond this stage through fiction, equity and legislation: Maine *Ancient Law* (ed Pollock) p 31. See also pp 318 ante.

identify primary rules. Thus 'law' for Professor Hart is equivalent to 'legal system'. Also, the union between primary and secondary rules is more than a plus sign; primary rules acquire the unity of a system through their union with secondary rules[13]. Moreover, there can be primary rules without a rule of recognition, which 'is not a necessity, but a luxury, found in advanced social systems'. His point is that 'in the simpler form of society we must wait and see whether a rule gets accepted as a rule or not; in a system with a basic rule of recognition we can say before a rule is actually made, that it *will* be valid *if* it conforms to the requirements of the rule of recognition'[14]. He also attaches much importance here to the 'internal aspect' of rules, ie their acceptance as standards, since what is crucial is that *officials* should have the internal point of view[15].

The volume of discussion which Professor Hart's concept has evoked is comment in itself on the stimulating quality of his contribution[16]. It is unnecessary to marshal all that has been said about different aspects of his work, but some remarks are needed on those relevant to the purposes of this book. In the first place, it is to be observed that a private club prescribes patterns of behaviour for its members and also possesses machinery whereby such prescriptions are added to, modified, abolished, applied and identified. It would seem, then, that the systems which prevail in a club and in a state exhibit the same characteristics. What is needed is some means of identifying the one as the 'law of the club' and the other as the 'law of the land'. It is not enough simply to incorporate identification by officials into the rule of recognition. A club has officials. What has to be answered is the question: Why is one set of officials 'officials of the state'? In other words, the system of a club can only exist within, and presupposes, a legal system, and Professor Hart does not appear to give an adequate criterion for distinguishing between them. The difference lies in the nature of the institutions, of which his theory takes no account. A club is an institution, so is law and legal system, and it is at the institutional level that the distinction has to be found[17].

Next, it is submitted that the distinction between a legal and a pre-legal state of affairs is not at all clear. If, as is alleged, a rule of recognition is not essential to the validity of primary rules in social systems that have not advanced, what precisely is the criterion? According to Professor Hart, in these societies 'we must wait and see whether a rule gets accepted as a rule or not'; which then raises the question, When do we know the category of a given society, when do we know that there is a rule of recognition? This rule is *not* a hypothesis, but a rule of positive law and, therefore, its own validity cannot relate to itself. The answer to the latter question is that 'for the most part the rule of recognition is not stated but its existence is *shown* in the way in which particular rules are identified, either by courts or other officials or private persons or their advisers'[18]. It is not clear why private persons are included. Since the rule of recognition identifies the rules by which the conduct of private persons is to be judged, it would seem that only courts and officials need be included. Comparison with umpires in a game

---

13 Summers 'Professor H L A Hart's Concept of Law' (1963) 98 Duke LJ at 638.
14 *Hart* p 229.
15 *Hart* p 113.
16 See Dias *Bibliography*.
17 For a way of distinguishing them, see Raz 'The Institutional Nature of Law' (1975) 38 MLR 489.
18 *Hart* p 98.

(Professor Hart's own analogy) brings out another difficulty. One can indeed discover what rules umpires recognise, but they, and still less the players, are not in a position to choose which rules to recognise. Professor Hart's officials and private persons seem free to do just this. The result, then, is not very different from Austin's 'habitual obedience'. If one knows what the rules are in a given legal system, one can discover what its rule of recognition is; the difficulty is to find the rule of recognition *de novo*.

The rule of recognition is grouped under powers as a secondary rule, but it looks more like the acceptance of a special kind of rule than a power[19]. Besides, there appear to be some rules of recognition which are not powers, such as those which indicate the criteria to be applied, eg constitutive rules of procedure[20]. It has even been suggested that the rule of recognition is not a power, but a duty addressed to officials[1].

Professor Hart's concept is based on the distinction between rules creating duties and rules creating powers, since a legal system is constituted by their union. It is questionable whether so sharp a distinction can be drawn. It has been pointed out, for example, that the same rule may create a power plus a duty to exercise it, or a power plus a duty not to exercise it[2]. Professor Fuller instances a situation where the same rule may confer power and duty, or power or duty according to the circumstances[3]. A trust instrument may give the beneficiary power to transfer the estate to himself on a certain condition. The trustee is of course entitled to reimbursement out of the estate and has the power to reimburse himself, correlative to the liability in the beneficiary to have the estate reduced in this way. If, however, the beneficiary exercises his power on the occurrence of the condition but before the trustee has reimbursed himself, the beneficiary comes under a duty to reimburse him. Which, asks Professor Fuller, is the rule creating the power and which is the rule creating the duty? The distinction lies, not in the rule, but in the circumstances. The rule in *Hedley Byrne*[4] is not one rule imposing a duty not to make careless misstatements and another rule conferring a power to disclaim responsibility; on the contrary, it is one rule which is power and duty-conferring—not to inflict pecuniary loss by careless misstatement, except where there is a disclaimer. Some rules abolish one's duty on an event, eg a contract discharged by frustration[5]. Such a rule is neither power nor duty-conferring. There may even be rules about secondary rules, which may be power or duty-conferring, eg a rule requiring a government to change a law on a referendum, or the duty of a judge to hear a case. If, then, in the light of such examples the distinction between rules creating powers and rules creating duties is as fluid as this, one wonders whether it is a sure enough foundation for Professor Hart's concept. The relation between primary and secondary rules seems to be more complex than would appear from his treatment of it.

Professor Dworkin has pointed out that in unprovided cases what the law

---

19 See Cohen's criticism that Hart lumps together powers in the sense of capacities enjoyed by large numbers, eg to make contracts, wills etc, and power conferred on persons specially qualified or in special situations: Review in (1962) 71 *Mind* 408.
20 For the difficulty of rules of procedure and evidence see Singer 'Hart's Concept of Law' (1963) 60 J Phil 197, 209.
1 Raz *The Concept of a Legal System* p 199.
2 See pp 36–38 ante.
3 Fuller *The Morality of Law* pp 134–136.
4 [1964] AC 465, [1963] 2 All ER 575.
5 MacCormick 'Law as Institutional Fact' (1974) 90 LQR 118–120.

is has to be determined with reference to doctrines, standards and principles, which do not derive their law-quality from a rule of recognition. To relegate them to 'discretion' is inconsistent with judicial acceptance of them as 'legal'[6]. Also, at this point it might be appropriate to mention again that insufficient allowance appears to be made for 'institutions', ie a legal system consists of particular ways in which rules and clusters of rules operate[7]. These evolve in many ways which cannot be attributed to a rule of recognition.

Professor Hart's avowed positivism in relation to his concept of law is also open to criticism. He says that the acceptance of a rule of recognition rests on social facts[8], but he does not concern himself with the reasons why, or the circumstances in which it comes to be accepted. Social and moral considerations may well set limits on a rule of recognition at the time of acceptance so that it may have built-in limitations that provide safeguards against certain abuses of power[9]. A different point arises in the light of the thesis of the present book that when legal phenomena are considered in a continuum, moral and social factors, which are indispensable to continued existence, are an integral part of any concept of them. Professor Hart has spoken elsewhere of 'the acceptable proposition that *some* shared morality is essential to the existence of any society'[10]. 'Existence of any society' must mean 'continued existence', and he does concede that a 'minimum morality' is an essential part of every community. This minimum morality is rooted in five facts: human vulnerability, approximate equality, limited altruism, limited resources and limited understanding and strength of will[11]. As a positivist, he excludes morality from his concept of law, for he says that positivists are concerned to promote

> 'clarity and honesty in the formulation of the theoretical and moral issues raised by the existence of particular laws which were morally iniquitous but were enacted in proper form, clear in meaning, and satisfied all the acknow-ledged criteria of validity of a system. Their view was that, in thinking about such laws, both the theorist and the unfortunate official or private citizen who was called on to apply or obey them, could only be confused by an invitation to refuse the title of 'law' or 'valid' to them. They thought that, to confront these problems, simpler, more candid resources were available, which would bring into focus far better, every relevant intellectual and moral consideration: we should say, "This is law; but it is too iniquitous to be applied or obeyed"'[12].

It was pointed out at the beginning of this chapter that the principal call for a positivist concept of law is to identify laws precisely for the practical purposes of the present and that, for this limited purpose, it is desirable to separate the 'is' from the 'ought'. To accomplish this no more would appear to be needed than simply those uses of the word 'law' by courts; which is akin to Salmond's definition alluded to above. Professor Hart's concept, however, is of 'legal system', which is a continuing phenomenon. Indeed, the

6 Dworkin 'Is Law a System of Rules?' in *Essays in Legal Philosophy* (ed Summers) p 25. See also Fitzgerald in *Salmond on Jurisprudence* p 51.
7 See pp 442-443 post. See also articles by Raz and MacCormick referred to above.
8 *Hart* p 107.
9 See ch 5 ante. For a relation of this point to Hart, see *Fuller* pp 137-139.
10 Hart *Law, Liberty and Morality* p 51; p 112 ante.
11 *Hart* pp 190-195.
12 *Hart* p 203. See also 'Positivism and the Separation of Law and Morals' (1958) 71 Harv LR 595. Hart is *not* implying that 'might' (in the form of an unjust enactment) is 'right', but only that 'might' is law'; and to say that it is 'law' does not imply that it has to be obeyed. For difficulties, see pp 114-116 ante.

very union of duties and powers would imply this for, as pointed out earlier, the exercise of a power and the duty created by it can only be brought into focus in a temporal perspective[13]. He concedes also that some morality is essential to the continued existence of society. Is a distinction being drawn between the continued existence of society, for which some morality at least is essential, and the continued existence of a legal system? This cannot be, for while a community (a moral system) could exist without a legal system, a legal system presupposes a community. The relation between morals and a legal system is that the latter only develops within and around the morality of a community. It is submitted that underlying all this is a confusion of time-frames. There is no contradiction in saying that an immoral precept is 'law' here and now and also that its immoral quality is likely to prove fatal to its continuity. When Professor Hart thinks in a continuum, as he does with society, he has to bring in morality; but in order to defend positivism he shifts ground and takes refuge in the present time-frame, for only in this way can he justify the exclusion of morality for the purpose of identifying laws here and now. There would thus appear to be a greater separation between his concept of law and his positivism than ever he alleges between law and morality. For the limited purpose of identifying 'laws' his concept seeks to accomplish more than is necessary; for the purpose of portraying law in a continuum it does not go far enough.

13 See pp 43–44 ante.

READING LIST

J Austin *Lectures on Jurisprudence* (5th edn ed R Campbell) chs 1-6.

J Bentham *Of Laws in General* (ed H L A Hart).

M S Blackman 'Hart's Idea of Obligation and his Concept of Law' (1977), 94 South African Law Journal 415.

J Bryce *Studies in History and Jurisprudence* II, ch 10.

W W Buckland *Some Reflections on Jurisprudence* chs 1, 5, 9, pp 107-110.

S C Coval and J C Smith 'The Completeness of Rules' (1977) 36 Cambridge Law Journal 364.

J Dewey 'Austin's Theory of Sovereignty' (1894) 9 Political Science Quarterly 31.

R M Dworkin *Taking Rights Seriously* chs 2-3.

R A Eastwood and G W Keeton *The Austinian Theories of Law*.

W Friedmann *Legal Theory* (5th edn) chs 20-21.

H L A Hart *The Concept of Law*.

M H James 'Bentham on the Individuation of Laws' in *Bentham and Legal Theory* (ed M H James) 91.

J W Jones *Historical Introduction to the Theory of Law* ch 3.

D B Lyons *In the Interests of the Governed, A Study in Bentham's Philosophy of Utility and Law* chs 6-7.

L J Lysaght 'Bentham on the Aspects of a Law' in *Bentham and Legal Theory* (ed M H James) 117.

N MacCormick *Legal Reasoning and Legal Theory* chs 9-10.

W L Morison 'Some Myths about Positivism' (1959-60) Yale Law Journal 212.

K Olivecrona *Law as Fact* (1939) chs 1-2; (1971) chs 1-5.

J Raz *The Concept of a Legal System*.

W J Rees 'The Theory of Sovereignty Restated' in *Philosophy. Politics and Society* (ed P Laslett) ch 4.

R Sartorius 'Hart's Concept of Law' in *More Essays in Legal Philosophy, General Assessments of Legal Philosophies* (ed R S Summers) 131.

R S Summers 'Professor Hart's Concept of Law' (1963) Duke Law Journal 629.

Law, Morality, and Society. Essays in Honour of H L A Hart (eds P M S Hacker and J Raz).

CHAPTER 17

The pure theory

The theory of Hans Kelsen (1881–1973) represents a development in two directions. On the one hand, it marks the most refined development to date of analytical positivism; on the other, it marks a reaction against the welter of different approaches that characterised the opening of the twentieth century. This is not to imply that Kelsen reverted to ideology. Far from it; he sought to expel ideologies of every description and to present a picture of law austere in its abstraction and severe in its logic.

It is necessary to begin with the premise from which he argued. A theory of law, he said, must deal with law as actually laid down, not as it ought to be. In this, as in some other respects, he agreed with Austin, although he was unaware of Austin's work when he first propounded his views. Insistence on this point has earned him the title of 'positivist'.

A theory of law must be distinguished from the law itself. There is no logic in natural phenomena, but a theory of nature, which purports to take account of them, must be logically self-consistent. In the same way, the law itself consists of a mass of heterogeneous rules, and the function of a theory of law is to organise them into a single, ordered pattern. Kelsen obviously did not evolve his theory of law *in vacuo*, but out of a study of legal material as it was actually found. What he did was to proffer it as a way of regarding the entire legal order and to demonstrate the pattern and shape into which it falls when looked at in the way he suggests[1], and the brilliance and organising power of his concept is best appreciated after the substance of the law and its problems have been studied.

A theory of law should be uniform, ie it should be applicable at all times and in all places. Kelsen thus advocated general jurisprudence. So did Austin, who, as will be remembered, only paid lip-service to it. Kelsen, however, carried out his analysis on an undoubtedly general basis. Austin's concept of law was derived from limited material, namely, English and Roman law, and ran into trouble outside that sphere. Kelsen, who had the advantage over Austin of profiting from roughly a century of varied developments, was able to arrive at generalisations which hold good over a very wide area.

A theory of law must be free from ethics, politics, sociology, history etc; it must, in other words, be 'pure' (*rein*)[2]. This follows from the last point, for if a theory is to be general, it needs to be shorn of variable factors such as those mentioned. One suspects at this point a measure of reaction against the modern introduction of these other influences which has enormously widened the scope of jurisprudence. Not that Kelsen denied their value: all he said was that a *theory* of law must keep clear of them.

Finally, laws being 'ought' propositions, knowledge of law means a knowledge of 'oughts', ie 'norms', and a norm is a proposition in hypothetical

---

1 Philosophically Kelsen is regarded as a neo-Kantian, but in his distinction between 'is' and 'ought' (see p 359 post) he is a descendant of Hume.
2 Kelsen *Pure Theory of Law* p 1.

form: 'if X happens, then Y ought to happen'. The science of law, or what in Anglo-American parlance is called 'jurisprudence', consists of the examination of the nature and organisation of normative propositions as they are found. It includes all norms created in the process of applying some general norm to a specific action. According to Kelsen, a dynamic system is one in which fresh norms are constantly being created on the authority of an original, or basic, norm, a *Grundnorm*; a static system is one which is at rest in that the basic norm determines the content of those derived from it in addition to imparting validity to them.

Around these points Kelsen unfolded his picture of law. It appears as a hierarchy of norms. One should, in his view, distinguish between propositions of law and propositions of science. In his earlier writings the distinction, adapted from Kant, was drawn in a straightforward manner. Propositions of science relate to events which are observed to occur and which do occur. Thus, whenever an apple is parted from a tree, in the absence of support it falls to the ground. If a new fact or event is observed which fails to conform to a scientific 'law', then that 'law' has to be modified to include it. Propositions of science may thus be described as dealing with what does happen, ie what 'is' (*sein*). Propositions of law only deal with what ought to occur, eg if a person commits theft, he ought to be punished. Even though in a given case events may not work out according to the legal 'ought', that does not invalidate it or call for modification. X may commit theft but go unpunished, for he may escape detection, he may bribe the officials who administer the law, or he may die. Even though any of these things may happen, the proposition that 'if a person commits theft, he ought to be punished' remains good. Legal propositions, therefore, deal with what ought to be (*sollen*). 'The principle according to which natural science describes its object is causality', said Kelsen; 'the principle according to which the science of law describes its object is normativity'[3]. It is true that in quantum physics strict causation has been abandoned in favour of the 'principle of indeterminacy', a modified version of causation in terms of probabilities. Accordingly, the Kantian distinction between the 'is' and the 'ought' requires modification too. However, the laws of science, though based on probabilities, remain descriptive of behaviour; juristic laws are not concerned with description, but with imputation of responsibility and are prescriptive of what ought to ensue. So put, Kelsen's distinction can be preserved, for it is a cardinal feature of his theory that laws consist of 'ought' propositions.

Two observations might be made on all this. In the first place, Kelsen in his early writings expressed this distinction rather misleadingly. He said in one place:

> 'The law of nature (meaning causality) runs: If A is, then B must be. The legal rule says: If A is, then B ought to be ... It is evident that this connection is not that of cause and effect. Punishment does not follow upon a delict as effect upon a cause. The legislator relates the two circumstances in a fashion wholly different from causality. Wholly different, yet a connection as unshakeable as causality. For in the legal system the punishment follows always and invariably on the delict even when in fact, for some reason or other, it fails of execution. Even though it does not so fail, it does not stand to the delict in the relation of effect to cause'[4].

---

3 Kelsen *General Theory of Law and State* p 46.
4 Kelsen 'The Pure Theory of Law' (1934) 50 LQR 485.

This kind of expression is misleading and may induce others to do less than justice to his thesis[5]. In more recent works he distinguished between causality and imputation without the disturbing touches as above. 'Under certain conditions' he said later 'a certain consequence ought to take place. This is the grammatical form of the principle of imputation'[6].

A second source of misunderstanding is more important. Legal norms are expressions of 'oughts'. The sense in which this is so will shortly be explained. Such 'oughts' should be distinguished from the 'oughts' of valuation. The legal 'ought' is in the form, 'If X happens, then Y ought to happen'; value 'oughts' shape the content of legal propositions, whether or not they are desirable, and with these Kelsen was not concerned. He did not deny that there are such 'oughts' apart from the formal 'oughts' of the law. What he said was that the latter should be kept separate from these others. Nor did he deny that the 'oughts' of the law may have their origin in these other 'oughts'. To formulate a theory of law account need only be taken of the formal 'ought' without reference to origin or content.

Kelsen found the distinction between legal and other 'oughts' in that the former are backed by the force of the state, the preoccupation of law being with the prospect of disobedience rather than obedience. Thus, it is the prescription of sanction that imparts significance to a norm, or putting it in another way, 'Law is the primary norm, which stipulates the sanction'[7]. Only in this way does 'law arrive at its essential function'[8]. It is true that in the statement, 'If a person does X, then Y ought to happen', there is implicit the idea that a person ought not to do X if he wants to avoid Y, ie not doing X is the effective means of avoiding Y. Yet the law is only invoked when X has been done. What matters in law is what should happen then. In this way a legal norm prescribes conduct by attaching a sanction to contrary behaviour[9]. This, it is urged with respect, is a weakness of Kelsen's scheme. It was argued in Chapter 10, (a) that the 'essential function' of law is by no means confined to dealing with wrongdoing, (b) that the form, 'If X, then Y ought to happen', does not necessarily imply that Y is a sanction for the breach of some duty, and (c) that, in any case, sanction is not essential to duty. As to (a), as will be seen presently, Kelsen made the efficacy of the total legal order a condition of the validity of every norm[10], which means that the very existence of a legal system implies that its laws are in the main *obeyed* rather than disobeyed. This suggests that the main function of laws is to give guidance by prescribing how people ought to behave. Further, prescribing behaviour, even in Kelsen's indirect sense, suggests that moral and social values are indispensable despite his effort to exclude them. The use of force in the event of disobedience becomes very much a secondary function. As to (b), it was pointed out earlier that the form, 'If X, then Y ought to happen', would fit the rule that if one earns more than a certain amount, then one ought to be taxed; but taxation is in no sense a sanction, nor is there a duty not to earn more than that amount. As to (c), it was also pointed out that it is erroneous to associate sanction with duty in view of the numerous instances of sanctionless duties. In the light of all this it is submitted that any

5 Eg Olivercrona *Law as Fact* (1939) pp 17–21.
6 Kelsen *What is Justice?* p 349.
7 Kelsen *General Theory of Law and State* pp 29, 61.
8 Kelsen (1934) 50 LQR 487; *Pure Theory of Law* p 33.
9 Kelsen *General Theory of Law and State* p 59; *Pure Theory of Law* pp 33, 115.
10 Kelsen *General Theory of Law and State* p 119; p 363 post.

concept of law which revolves around sanctions is not an accurate reflection of law as it actually is.

To the extent that the provision of sanctions is regarded as crucial, the theories of Austin and Kelsen agree, but they differ in elaboration. For Austin, a law is a command backed by sanction. Kelsen disagreed in two respects. First, he rejected the idea of command, because it introduces a psychological element into a theory of law which should, in his view, be 'pure'[11]. The most that he conceded was that a law is a

> 'de-psychologised command, a command which does not imply a 'will' in a psychological sense of the term ... a rule expressing the fact that somebody ought to act in a certain way, without implying that anybody really 'wants' the person to act in that way'[12].

Secondly, to Austin the sanction was something outside a law imparting validity to it. To Kelsen such a statement is inadequate and confused. For the operation of the sanction supporting a rule resolves itself into the operation of other rules; and further, the validity of a rule has nothing to do with its sanctions. Thus, Austin would have said that the sanction behind the proposition, 'you ought not to steal', is that if you do steal, you will be imprisoned. To Kelsen, the operation of the sanction itself depends on the operation of other rules of law. One rule prescribes that if a man has committed theft, he ought to be arrested; another prescribes that he ought to be brought to trial; others prescribe how the trial ought to be conducted; another rule prescribes that if the jury brings in a verdict of 'guilty', the judge ought to pass sentence; and another prescribes that some official should carry that sentence into execution. In this way the contrast between law and sanction in the Austinian sense disappears.

With reference to the validity of a rule, Kelsen asserted that the validity of an 'ought' is not to be derived from any 'is' of fact outside the law[13], but from some other 'ought' standing behind it and imparting validity to it. The validity of a norm is ascertained with reference to its authorising norm, which confers a power to create it and may also specify conditions for its exercise. A particular norm, therefore, is 'authorised' if it can be subsumed under a more general norm[14]. The conjecture which this opens up is the end of the progression. Kelsen's solution was that in every legal order, no matter with what proposition one may begin, a hierarchy of 'oughts' is traceable back to some initial, fundamental 'ought' on which the validity of all the others ultimately rests. This he called the *Grundnorm*, the basic or fundamental norm. For example, the validity of each of the rules comprising a sanction

---

11 'The norm is an *ought*, but the act of will is an *is*': Kelsen *Pure Theory of Law* p 5.
12 Kelsen *General Theory of Law and State* p 35.
13 This proposition is traceable to Hume *A Treatise on Human Behaviour* III, I.1.
14 'Authorisation' and 'subsumption' are difficult notions. For a critique of Kelsen, see Harris 'Kelsen's Concept of Authority' (1977) 36 CLJ 353; and Paulson 'Constraints on Legal Norms: Kelsen's View in the *Essays*' (1975) 42 U ChLR 768. In an answer to Harris, Paulson draws distinctions. 'Validity' is looking at the law-quality of the end product; from the point of view of the dynamism of law-creation and application 'validity' is the authorisation of lower-order activities. 'Authorisation' is of two kinds: 'formal', which is given to an organ or institution, eg legislature or courts, to create, apply or validate a norm; and 'material', where a norm has to fall within the limits of the applicability of some higher norm and is derived directly from it. Formal authorisation cannot be questioned by courts, material authorisation can be questioned on judicial review. See Paulson 'Material and Formal Authorisation in Kelsen's Pure Theory' (1980) 39 CLJ 172.

depends on some other rule, which in turn rests on another and so on. Thus, the imprisonment of a person for theft is valid in so far as the prison authorities acted in accordance with the norm 'If a judge so orders, then prison authorities ought to imprison him'. The judge's order is valid in so far as he acted according to rules regulating the competence of the court, rules as to how the legal process ought to be conducted, a rule of law that 'If a person steals, he ought to be punished by imprisonment (or in some other way)'. These rules in their turn are valid in so far as they emanate from certain statutes and precedents. To the question why statutes and precedents are valid no answer can be given in law; they represent the end of the line. The entire legal order in Britain is traceable back to the propositions that statutes and precedents ought to be treated as 'law', with immemorial customs as a possible third. In this way Kelsen's picture of a legal order emerges, not just as a collection of 'oughts', but a hierarchy depending downwards from a *Grundnorm*, or branching upwards from it, whichever way one chooses to depict it.

Kelsen recognised that the *Grundnorm* need not be the same in every legal order, but a *Grundnorm* of some kind there will always be, whether, eg a written constitution or the will of a dictator. The *Grundnorm* is *not* the constitution, it is simply the *presupposition*, demanded by theory, that this constitution ought to be obeyed[15]. Therefore, the *Grundnorm* is always adapted to the prevailing state of affairs. The *Grundnorm* only imparts validity to the constitution and all other norms derived from it, it does not dictate their content. The difference between his positivism and natural law theory is that the latter determines content as well. There is also no reason why there need only be one *Grundnorm*, nor has it to be a written constitution[16]. The fact that in Great Britain the fount of validity rests with statute, precedent and immemorial customs does not contradict Kelsen's thesis, for what he contended was that a system cannot be founded on *conflicting Grundnormen*[17]. In Britain there is no conflict between the authority of the Crown in Parliament, judicial precedent and customs; they take precedence in that order[18].

There are several features about the *Grundnorm* deserving of attention. In the first place, in what sense is the *Grundnorm* a norm? It does not conform to Kelsen's own formulation of a norm: 'If X, then Y ought to happen'; it only empowers and does not impose sanctions. Next, according to Kelsen every rule of law derives its validity from some other rule standing behind it. The *Grundnorm* has no rule behind it. Its validity has therefore to be assumed for the purpose of theory, which is why it is said to be the 'initial hypothesis', 'the postulated ultimate rule according to which the norms of this order are established and annulled, receive or lose their validity'[19]. Put in another way, one cannot account for the validity of the *Grundnorm* by pointing to another *rule of law*. The *Grundnorm* validates the rest of the legal system; one cannot therefore utilise the system, or any part of it, to validate the *Grundnorm*. As

15 Kelsen *Pure Theory of Law* pp 201 et seq; 'Professor Stone and the Pure Theory of Law' (1965) Stanford LR 1128 at 1140–1142.
16 Kelsen *Pure Theory of Law* p 222.
17 *Kelsen* pp 72, 74, 195, where he spoke of 'unity' and 'unified system'; see also *General Theory of Law and State* pp 400, 407.
18 For the formulation of the *Grundnorm* for Britain see Harris 'When and Why does the Grundnorm Change?' [1971] CLJ 103.
19 Kelsen *General Theory of Law and State* p 113. See also pp 115–116, 134, 401; Kelsen *Pure Theory of Law* pp 194–195. Salmond had anticipated this point as early as 1902: *Jurisprudence* (1st edn) p 110.

one writer put it, such an attempt would be like trying to pick oneself up by one's bootlaces. This point has already been considered from another angle, namely, in connection with statute and judicial precedent, where the impossibility of finding a reason in law why these should be able to impart the quality of 'English law' was demonstrated[20].

Kelsen's distinction between validity and effectiveness has only been touched upon. Every norm other than the *Grundnorm* is valid, not because it is, or is likely to be, obeyed by those to whom it is addressed, but by virtue of another norm imparting validity to it. Thus, a norm is valid before it is effective, as is the case with a new statute before it has been applied. Yet, the validity of each norm does depend on the effectiveness of the legal order as a whole. In Kelsen's own words,

> 'It cannot be maintained that, legally, men have to behave in conformity with a certain norm, if the total legal order, of which that norm is an integral part, has lost its efficacy. The principle of legitimacy is restricted by the principle of effectiveness'[1].

He later modified this somewhat to the extent of saying that the legal order has to be 'by and large' effective[2]. It will therefore be seen that, with reference to a given norm, its validity and its effectiveness have to be kept separate. Effectiveness of the order as a whole is a condition, not a reason, of the validity of the *Grundnorm* and of any individual norm: 'a *conditio sine qua non*, but not a *conditio per quem*'[3]. At the level of the *Grundnorm* the question, Why is it valid? is meaningless; what is important is that the *Grundnorm* should secure for itself a minimum of effectiveness, ie a certain number of persons who are willing to abide by it[4]. It is futile to say that the proposition that the will of the Tsar should be accepted as law is the *Grundnorm* in Russia today. On the other hand, the fact that enactments of the Crown in Parliament are in fact disobeyed quite frequently does not render the proposition that the Crown in Parliament is law-constitutive any the less a *Grundnorm* of English law. There must not be a total disregard of the *Grundnorm*, but there need not be universal adherence to it. All that is necessary is that it should command a minimum of effectiveness.

When a *Grundnorm* ceases to derive a minimum of support, it ceases to be the basis of the legal order, and any other proposition which does obtain support will replace it. Such a change in the state of affairs is said to amount to a revolution in law. This is because, as pointed out, the *Grundnorm* is not itself the constitution, but the assumption that this (effective) state of affairs ought to be obeyed, and because, for that reason, the *Grundnorm* is adapted to that state of affairs and not *vice versa*. It follows, therefore, that a change in the situation involves a revolution in the theory adapted to it[5]. This point was demonstrated in Chapter 5, where it was seen that the events of 1688–1689 must be regarded as a revolution in the basis underlying the legal system. It was also illustrated with reference to both the Rhodesian rebellion and the British Commonwealth. The constitutions of the various Dominions derived their validity from statutes of the Crown in Parliament at

20 See chs 5 and 7 ante.
 1 Kelsen *General Theory of Law and State* p 119.
 2 Kelsen *Pure Theory of Law* especially at pp 212 et seq; Kelsen *What is Justice?* p 262; 'Professor Stone and the Pure Theory of Law' (1965) 17 Stanford LR 1128 at 1142; *Harris* at p 124.
 3 Kelsen *General Theory of Law and State* p 119.
 4 Cf Austin's criterion of sovereignty as habitual obedience of the bulk of a given society: p 348 ante.
 5 Kelsen *General Theory of Law and State* p 117; *Pure Theory of Law* p 200.

Westminster, from which it would seem to follow that the *Grundnorm* of the Commonwealth legal order is that enactments of the Crown in Parliament at Westminster are law *ipso jure* for the Commonwealth. The Dominions, how ever, have discarded that doctrine, and their acquisitiom of independence has amounted to a revolution in the legal order of the Commonwealth[6].

The *Grundnorm* is thus a key concept in Kelsen's theory, but it raises many difficulties. The change effected in the British *Grundnorm* in 1689 amounted, according to his thesis, to a revolution in the system, but why did it remain the 'same system'? Kelsen would probably have denied that it is the same; which is not the way lawyers and jurists actually regard the position. It would only be a suggestion as to how they ought to regard it. The point can be illustrated in another way. British courts might abandon *stare decisis* tomorrow, ie the *Grundnorm* that 'precedents ought to be binding', but it would be odd to say that a new system comes into being thereafter[7]. All this, however, harks back to the earlier question: 'What exactly is the *Grundnorm* in Britain[8]?

Some writers have pointed out, with a hint of criticism, that in whatever way effectiveness of the *Grundnorm* is measured, Kelsen's theory has ceased to be 'pure' at this point. For, effectiveness would seem to depend on those very sociological factors which he so vehemently excluded from his theory of law. If, then, the *Grundnorm* upon which the validity of all other norms depends is tainted with impurity, it is arguable that the others are similarly tainted. Another attack on the claim to purity is that Kelsen's scheme is an *a priori* one dependent on empirical observation for confirmation. He offered it as a 'theory of interpretation'[9], which implies that it is not a description but a model and thus evaluative in function. It is possible to make too much of this, for Kelsen's analysis of the structure of the legal system is in no way impaired by these comments. The criticism touches, not the theory, but his claim to its purity. He admits that the *Grundnorm* is founded on factors outside the law[10]. That being the case, whether his theory is said to be pure only from the *Grundnorm* onwards, or partially pure because of its initial impurity, is not very material. The fact is, as the words of Kelsen indicate, that the effectiveness of the legal order as a whole is prerequisite to the validity of each single rule in it.

The objection, though verbal, carries more serious implications. If, as seems clear, some inquiry into political and sociological factors has to precede, or at least is implicit in, the adoption of a particular *Grundnorm* as the criterion of validity, and if the validity of every part of the system is dependent upon the continued effectiveness of the whole, then on his own showing the study of jurisprudence should include the study of the social environment. It might also be pointed out that Kelsen's picture is that of a legal order viewed at any given moment of time showing how the validity of every norm is derived from a *Grundnorm*. This explains his exclusion of moral, sociological and other considerations from the question of the validity of any rule at this or that moment. Yet, he could not avoid having to make some

---

6 Cross objects to the word 'revolution': *Precedent in English Law* pp 206-207. This is scarcely an objection to Kelsen's point, but rather to his choice of words. The real point is whether the system would still be the 'same'.
7 See n 6 supra.
8 On which, see *Harris*.
9 Kelsen *Pure Theory of Law* p 1.
10 Kelsen *What is Justice?* p 294.

measure of effectiveness a decisive attribute of the *Grundnorm* and of the legal order as a whole. It was pointed out in Chapter 5 that effectiveness is only *one* reason why courts will in time accept a *Grundnorm*, ie it is a factor operative in a continuum[11]. If, then, he was prepared to accept one such factor, why did he exclude others, eg morality? The force of this point may be seen when one asks why a particular *Grundnorm* was accepted, especially if this followed on a revolution? Might it not be that the new criterion of validity was able to command a 'minimum of effectiveness' because it was thought to guarantee that measure of justice and morality, which the previous criterion did not[12]? Why could it not be argued that the supremacy of the Crown in Parliament was accepted in 1689 in order that tyrannous and arbitrary acts should no longer be valid as they had been by virtue of the supremacy of the prerogative? On this line of argument the *Grundnorm* is effective, and *continues* to be effective, in so far as an element of morality is built in as part of the criterion of validity[13]. If so, the continued validity of every proposition of law derived from the validating source has an ultimate ethical basis and a total separation of law from morality is untenable. Moreover, apart from the *Grundnorm*, if, in Kelsen's own thesis, a norm in the form, 'If X, then Y ought to happen', is an indirect way of *prescribing* the behaviour needed to avoid Y (assuming Y to be a sanction), then the values that prompted the prescription in this indirect way must also underlie the form; and the same applies to every other such norm. All this amounts to an argument levelled not merely at Kelsen, but at positivism in general. It is sufficient here to observe that it would strike at the foundation of his separation of 'is' and 'ought'.

Kelsen gave no criterion by which the minimum of effectiveness is to be measured. All he maintained was that the *Grundnorm* imparts validity as long as the 'total legal order' remains effective, or, as he later put it, 'by and large' effective. As to this it may be asked, in the first place, what is the measure of 'total' and 'by and large'? The Rhodesian case *Madzimbamuto v Lardner-Burke*[14], exposes the weakness here, for as one judge pointed out, an effective order cannot be said to be totally, or even by and large, effective as long as its judiciary refuses to accept the legality of its basis[15]; which the Rhodesian judiciary did for over two years after the illegal declaration of independence by the Smith regime. Secondly, for how long must effectiveness be maintained for the requirement to be satisfied? In *The State v Dosso*[16] the Supreme Court of Pakistan had held a usurper to be effectively in power and hence lawful on Kelsenian grounds (even though, incidentally, he himself was deposed the day after the judgment was published). Later in *Jilani v Government of Punjab*[17] the Supreme Court declared both the first and second usurpers illegal, repudiated Kelsen *in toto* and overruled *Dosso*, which relied on him so heavily and because of which, as one judge quoted approvingly, 'a perfectly good country was made into a laughing stock'[18]. The court was not saying that the usurping regimes were lawful while they lasted, but

11 See pp 54–55 ante; *Jilani v Government of Punjab* Pak LD (1972) SC 139 at 159, per Hamoodur Rahman CJ and at 232–233, 242, per Yaqub Ali J.
12 Ibid at p 182.
13 See pp 55 et seq ante.
14 1968 (2) SA 284.
15 Ibid at pp 427–428, per Fieldsend AJA.
16 Pak LD (1958) SC 533.
17 Pak LD (1972) SC 139.
18 Ibid at 219, per Yaqub Ali J, who also regarded *Madzimbamuto's* case, as far as it went, as the maximum success of Kelsen's theory: at p 244.

that they were unlawful *ab initio* notwithstanding effectiveness. It is to be noted that by the time of the later decision the usurpers had been overthrown, and it may well be that such pronouncements will nearly always be retrospective, since judges sitting under the power of a regime may have little alternative but to accept it as legal; those who refuse will be replaced, or their judgments will be nullified[19]. Against this must be set the independent stand of the Rhodesian judiciary after UDI and also of some Pakistani judges who, while under the illegal regime, not only voiced doubts but even held particular measures void[20]. Finally, what does 'effectiveness' itself mean? Kelsen drew no distinction between effectiveness, which makes people obliged to obey, and effectiveness which makes them feel under an obligation to do so. A usurper may by force and fear achieve the former, but not the latter, which, as judicially acknowledged, is the kind of effectiveness required by Kelsen. A judge of the Supreme Court of Pakistan, examining the position of the deposed usurper President, said in words reminiscent of Professor Hart, 'He obligated the people to obey his behests, but in law they incurred no obligation to obey him'[1].

Effectiveness is not necessarily a condition of validity even in the context of the here and now. For instance, in the lacuna that exists during a revolution, when the old basis has been overthrown and something has still to replace it, there is no longer a *Grundnorm*, but tribunals may continue to apply 'laws' identified as such by means of some criterion which *they* still recognise, albeit provisionally. It does not matter that that criterion belongs to the order that has gone; as long as it is accepted by the judges as imparting the quality of 'law' to the proposition before them that is all that is needed. This was indorsed in the test case of *Madzimbamuto v Lardner-Burke*[2], which was brought during the Rhodesian rebellion. Here the revolutionary 1965 Constitution was acknowledged to be effective, yet for over two years the Rhodesian courts refused to accept it as 'legal'. During that period the Rhodesian courts were none the less prepared to uphold at least some measures of the illegal regime as 'laws', and the displaced 1961 Constitution, which had ceased to be effective, was still held to possess controlling force to the extent that the laws of the illegal authority had to conform to it. The case is inexplicable on Kelsenian theory. It shows, firstly, that effectiveness is not the criterion of the *Grundnorm*, but what courts are prepared to accept as the fount of validity; and, secondly, that the validity of a law does not necessarily derive from an effective *Grundnorm*, but that this, too, depends on what courts accept as valid. A third point, which emerged since is that validity itself has a temporal dimension. In *The State v Dosso*[3] the Supreme Court of Pakistan accepted the régime, which had usurped power unconstitutionally, as legal on grounds of effectiveness; but later in *Jilani v Government of Punjab*[4] the same court declared it to have been illegal *ab initio* notwith-

---

19 The decision in *Mir Hassan v The State* Pak LD (1969) Lah 786, invalidating a Martial Law Regulation was promptly nullified by an Order retrospectively depriving the courts of jurisdiction in a number of matters.

20 Eg the bold decision in *Mir Hassan*'s case (see n 19 supra).

1 *Jilani*'s case (see n 17 supra) at p 229, per Yaqub Ali J. Also: 'the temporary silencing of the people and the courts is not enough': at p 243.

2 1968 (2) SA 284 at 351, 421; and see p 54 ante. For comment, see Brookfield 'The Courts, Kelsen and the Rhodesian Revolution' (1969) 19 UTLJ 326, 345-346.

3 Pak LD (1958) SC 533.

4 Pak LD (1972) SC 139.

standing effectiveness, and overruled *Dosso*. All this boils down to the fact that validity is a matter to be determined in the context of a given point of time and depends on what judges are prepared to accept at *that* moment as imparting law-quality; which seems a more useful way of regarding the matter than a *Grundnorm* enjoying a minimum of effectiveness.

In the result it would seem that Kelsen's theory does not apply in revolutionary situations, in which case it ceases to be a 'general theory'; or, if general, it ceases to be true. In settled conditions it teaches nothing new; in revolutionary conditions, where guidance is needed, it is useless, for the choice of a *Grundnorm* is not dictated inflexibly by effectiveness but is a political decision, as Kelsen has admitted[5].

It is not clear what is connoted by the description of the *Grundnorm* as a 'hypothesis' or 'postulate' or 'presupposed'. There is no analogy here, be it noted, with scientific hypotheses, which are assumptions used to account for the totality of known facts. It is sometimes the case that two alternative scientific hypotheses may be equally apt to explain the phenomena in question[6], but there is no room for alternative *Grundnormen* as postulates of a given legal system. There must be only one *Grundnorm*, which is supreme and uncontradicted; otherwise there can be no unified theory. As to this, the requirement of effectiveness suggests, on the one hand, that the *Grundnorm* is a fact and not a pretence or asumption[7]. On the other hand, it is not itself the constitution but the presupposition, required by theory, that this constitution ought to be obeyed. As such it is not a social reality and does not march happily under Kelsen's positivist banner[8]. There is a further difficulty. An effective constitution is a fact upon which the *Grundnorm* posits an 'ought'. It has been axiomatic since Hume that an 'ought' cannot be derived from an 'is' without the interposition of a value-judgment that the 'is' is desirable and for that reason ought to be. It looks, therefore, as if Kelsen's theory conceals an ideology that might is right and hence ought to be; which is no different after all from the adoption of *a priori* assumptions by naturalists, besides being an open invitation to revolt and crude force[9]. Many of these difficulties would be avoided if what was said earlier is borne in mind. The criterion of validity refers to the medium or media which impart to a rule the quality of 'law', 'valid' here meaning 'legal'. The 'minimum of effectiveness' refers to the acceptance of such media by those in charge of administering 'law'. This is all that would have been needed for Kelsen's

5 *What is Justice?* pp 366, 368. The policy reasons behind judicial choice were amply demonstrated in the Rhodesian test case, as to which see Dias 'Legal Politics: Norms Behind the *Grundnorm*' [1968] CLJ especially at 254. The personal choice of the judges was admitted by Beadle CJ in *R v Ndhlovu* 1968 (4) SA 525 at 532. As to the alleged disclosure after retirement by Munir CJ, who presided over *Dosso*'s case, that his acceptance of Kelsen's theory had not been based on judicial considerations, see Yaqub Ali J in *Jilani*'s case (see n 4 supra) at 277. 4 supra) at 277.
6 Eg the 'corpuscular' and 'wave' theories of light. It used to be said that scientists applied the one theory on Mondays, Wednesdays and Fridays, the other on Tuesdays, Thursdays and Saturdays.
7 Hart *The Concept of Law* p 246; Stone 'Mystery and Mystique in the Basic Norm' (1963) 26 MLR 34 at 47-48. For judicial comment on its vagueness see Hamoodur Rahman CJ in *Jilani v Government of Pakistan* Pak LD (1972) SC 139 at 179-180.
8 'It is, therefore, only a 'thought norm' which could hardly be recognised as a legal norm furnishing a criteria (*sic*) of validity in any legal system. To give it the status of a legal norm or legal rule was thus, in my opinion, unjustified': ibid per Hamoodur Rahman CJ at 180.
9 So Fieldsend AJA in *Madzimbamuto v Lardner-Burke* 1968 (2) SA 248 at 430; *Jilani*'s case at 172 per Hamoodur Rahman CJ, at 259 per Sajjad Ahmad J.

demonstration, but by using the notion of *Grundnorm* he seems to have inflated a pedestrian simplicity into something misleadingly large.

From all this it will be evident that the *Grundnorm* is a weak point in the theory. Yet such as it is, it provides the start of Kelsen's demonstration. The rest of the system is pictured as broadening down in gradations from it and becoming progressively more and more detailed and specific. The entire process is one of the gradual concretisation of the basic norm and the focussing of it to specific situations *(Stufentheorie)*[10]. It is a dynamic process, for the application of a higher norm involves the creation of new lower norms[11]. Thus, the practical manifestation of the acceptance of a *Grundnorm* as a basis is that it validates the creation of certain general norms, which may be described as propositions of substantive law, as well as the machinery and procedure for the application of these general norms. The application of general norms by this machinery, as represented by a judge or other official, to a particular situation in turn involves a creative element in so far as the judge by his decision creates a specific norm addressed to one or other of the parties. The final stage is the carrying out of the compulsive act. At the end of the progression, therefore, sanction is a permission to someone to execute the coercive act. This means that 'ought' here covers 'may' and 'can'[12]. It is to be noted that in the application of the general norm the judge may be left with an element of discretion, or he may consciously choose between alternative interpretations which the norm permits. The doctrine leaves room for value-judgments in the course of the decisional process. Their exclusion from the theory is not intended to diminish the actual parts they play. Again, the application of a general norm may depend upon the act of the parties, eg an agreement or some form of wrongdoing.

Several implications follow from such a view of a legal system. In the first place, the traditional distinction between 'public' and 'private' law is seen to be one of degree, while at times it disappears. They are both part of the process of concretisation and both are norm-creating. The distinction between them lies sometimes in the fact that they operate at different levels of the structure, and at others in the organs which apply them. With criminal law, for example, the distinction would seem to disappear altogether. Secondly, in a similar way the distinction between legislative, executive and judicial processes appears in a new light. They are all norm-creating agencies, the executive and judiciary being but steps in the concretisation of norms in particular cases. Thirdly, the distinction between substantive law and procedure is relative, procedure assuming greater importance. It is the organs and process of concretisation that constitute the legal system. Fourthly, the distinction between questions of law and fact also become relative. The 'facts' are part of the condition contained in the 'if X' part of the formula, 'If X, then Y ought to happen'. The application of a norm concretises every part of it, including the 'If X' part. Therefore, the finding of fact by a judge is not necessarily what actually happened but what he regards as having happened for the purpose of applying the particular norm.

Fifthly, the legal order is a normative structure which operates so as to culminate in the application of sanctions for certain forms of human

10 Adapted by Kelsen from Merkl *Die Lehr von der Rechtskraft; Allgemeines Verwaltungsrecht*; Kelsen *General Theory of Law and State* pp 123-153; *Pure Theory of Law* ch 5.
11 'Creation of law is always application of law': Kelsen *General Theory of Law and State* p 133; *What is Justice?* p 280.
12 Kelsen *Pure Theory of Law* pp 5, 16, 134.

behaviour. It follows that the idea of duty is of its essence, which is evident in the 'ought'. Kelsen made no specific allowance for powers, while liberty, in his view, 'is an extra-legal phenomenon'[13]. Liberty is the jural opposite of duty, but Kelsen's stand in the matter reflects a wider issue, namely, between an 'open' and a 'closed' concept of law. The former is one in which law concerns only specific regulation so that anything as yet unregulated falls outside law. The latter is one in which all aspects of behaviour are within law, whether positively through specific regulation or negatively through liberties; in short, liberty and duty are two sides of the same coin. Kelsen's theory is an 'open' one[14].

On the other hand, when he turned to the concept of claim, he stood on firmer ground. This, he maintained, is not essential. It appears when

> 'the putting into effect of the consequence of the disregard of the legal rule is made dependent upon the will of the person who has an interest in the sanction of the law being applied'[15].

Claim is only a by-product, as it were, of the law. Kelsen showed how modern criminal law has for the most part discarded ancient ideas of the law being set in motion by the injured person and is now enforced directly by officials, ie the idea of individual claims is no longer the foundation of the criminal law. It is still the basis of the law of property and contract and so on, but in Kelsen's view there is no reason why it need be, and may well be dispensed with in the future.

Sixthly, to Kelsen the concept of 'person' was simply a step in the process of concretisation. This has been previously discussed[16], and it was seen that by 'person' he meant only a totality of claims etc. 'Person' is a legal conception, and he therefore rejected the traditional distinction between 'natural' and 'juristic' persons. The former are biological entities, which lie outside the province of legal theory. They are only the concern of the law in so far as they focus duties and claims etc.

Lastly, a significant feature of Kelsen's doctrine is that the state is viewed as a system of human behaviour and an order of social compulsion. Law is likewise a normative ordering of human behaviour backed by force, which 'makes the use of force a monopoly of the community'[17]. Moreover, a state is constituted by territory, independent government, population and ability to enter into relations with other states, and each of these requirements is legally determined. The inescapable conclusion is that state and law are identical. This is not to say that every legal order is automatically a state, eg highly decentralised orders like primitive communities; only relatively centralised legal orders are states. Kelsen further rejected any attempt to set the state apart from law or to say that law is the 'will of the state'.

Kelsen also applied his theory to the system known commonly as 'international law'. His earliest work did not touch on this field, and it was only after Verdross, one of his disciples, had started to adapt his approach to international law, that Kelsen himself took an interest in it. When applied in this field his theory does reveal some limitations. However assured his

13 *Das Problem der Souveränität* p 247.
14 As to this, see pp 31–32 ante.
15 Lauterpacht 'Kelsen's Pure Science of Law', in *Modern Theories of Law* at p 112; Kelsen *Pure Theory of Law* pp 126–127.
16 See pp 267–268 ante.
17 Kelsen *General Theory of Law and State* p 21.

thesis appears when demonstrated with reference to long established and settled municipal systems of law[18], in the palpitating condition of international relations it has shortcomings. The Pure Theory demands that a *Grundnorm* be discovered. If there are conflicting possibilities, then, as Kelsen himself admitted, his theory provides no guidance in choosing between them. All he said was that the *Grundnorm* should command a minimum of support. In the international sphere there are two possible *Grundnormen*, the supremacy of each municipal system or the supremacy of international law. The argument based on the former, as pictured by Kelsen, would run as follows. Every national legal order cannot *ex hypothesi* recognise any norm superior to its own *Grundnorm*. The English legal order does not apply in France, nor *vice versa*. Nevertheless, the English legal order recognises the validity of the French legal order in France; and if the only *Grundnorm* known to English law is its own, it follows that the English legal order regards the validity of the French legal order in France as being in some way a delegated normative order from the English *Grundnorm*. Similarly, approaching the matter from the French side, the French legal order can only recognise the validity of the English legal order in England as being derived from the French *Grundnorm*. Such is the outcome of the doctrine of national sovereignty and it tends to a state of anarchy in which each national order recognises only its own *Grundnorm* and endures other legal orders as subsidiary to it.

Kelsen would have none of this[19]. He argued instead for a monist view of the relationship between international and municipal law, and declared that the *Grundnorm* of the international system postulates the primacy of international law[20]. Nations in practice, he argued, recognise the equality of each other's legal orders, and the doctrine of equality must mean that they recognise the existence of a *Grundnorm* superior to the *Grundnormen* of their own particular legal orders. The equal force of national systems is an impossible notion unless there is some higher authority, which bestows equality. The same conclusion is arrived at in a different way. Much of international law rests on custom, which consists in rationalisations of the actual practice of states. When a description of the conduct of states is transmuted into a prescription of how they ought to behave, it becomes international law. Now, Kelsen's insistent contention was that the validity of an 'ought' cannot be derived from an 'is', but only from a superior norm. He also maintained that a legal norm is distinguishable from norms of morality, ethics and the like in that it is backed by force. In the international sphere he found the element of force in war and reprisals[1].

All this is questionable. The first thing which his theory requires, is the *Grundnorm* of the international order. This is by no means clear: it may be the principle *pacta sunt servanda*, or 'coercion of state against state ought to be exercised under the conditions and in the manner, that conforms with the custom constituted by the actual behaviour of the states'[2]; but other suggestions have been offered by other writers. As Stone has commented,

---

18 Kelsen admitted that his theory of municipal law applies only to advanced systems: Kelsen *What is Justice?* p 246.
19 *Kelsen* pp 284-285.
20 *Kelsen* pp 283 et seq; *General Theory of Law and State* pp 328 et seq; *Pure Theory of Law* ch 7; 'Sovereignty and International Law' (1960) 48 Georgetown LJ 627.
1 Kelsen *General Theory of Law and State* pp 328 et seq.
2 Kelsen *Pure Theory of Law* p 216. For comment see Hart *The Concept of Law* p 230.

'It is difficult to see what the pure theory of law can contribute to a system which it assumes to be law, but which it derives from a basic norm which it cannot find'[3].

It looks as if Kelsen shifted the meaning of *Grundnorm*. With reference to municipal law it was pointed out that the *Grundnorm* has to possess some basis in fact, namely, a minimum of effectiveness. It would seem that with reference to international law the *Grundnorm* is a pure supposition lacking even this basis. Assuming that a monist legal theory has to be offered to account for the present state of international society, then one way of explaining the assertion of equality by states would be by hypothesising a norm superior to that of each national order from which equality might be said to derive. It is open to doubt, however, whether even an attempt at a monist explanation is worth while, for one is entitled to question whether there is any *Grundnorm* which commands the necessary minimum of effectiveness demanded by Kelsen's theory. States recognise such doctrines as *pacta sunt servanda* or equality only in the sense of paying lip-service to them; they talk about them, but are only too ready to ignore them when it suits their convenience to do so. Indeed, an alternative, and as plausible, a hypothesis to explain equality is that it springs from a sense of mutual forbearance inspired by fear. Indeed, it has been asserted judicially that 'in International Law there is no "legal order" as such'[4]. So the hypothesis of a superior norm of the international order is no more than one possible assumption, and unreal at that. With reference to municipal law, on the other hand, Kelsen's theory is meaningless unless the *Grundnorm* commands a minimum of effectiveness in action and not just in words. *Post hoc* is not *propter hoc*.

It is not easy to accept a monist theory of the primacy of international over municipal law in the face of the conflicts between the two. Kelsen's general theory does allow, it is true, for limited conflicts within a given order, but those between international and municipal law are too extensive to ignore. The case of *Jilani v Government of Punjab*[5] is an illustration, not just of conflict, but of the categorical rejection by a municipal court of Kelsen's monism. An attempt had been made to buttress the effectiveness of a revolutionary régime, and hence its legality, with the fact that it had received recognition at international law. The Supreme Court said that to do this would be to assume the primacy of international law over municipal law, a doctrine which it emphatically repudiated. With reference to the emergence of a new government as well as a new state, it was pointed out that their recognition at international law is irrelevant to their legality at municipal law. 'The validity of a new government is governed by the law of the state', said the Chief Justice[6]. Even when a new state comes into being through secession, the courts of the parent state are not bound by international recognition accorded to it. The creation of the State of Bangla Desh out of East Pakistan was precisely in point, and as to this a judge of West Pakistan said: 'While under International Law, East Pakistan has become an independent state, the municipal courts of Pakistan will not confer recognition on it or act upon the legal order set up by the rebel Government'; and he

---

3 Stone *Legal System and Lawyers' Reasonings* p 130.
4 *Jilani v Government of Punjab* Pak LD (1972) SC 139 at 181, per Hamoodur Rahman CJ.
5 See ibid.
6 Ibid at 181.

added that Kelsen's monistic theory is 'wholly inapplicable to municipal courts'[7].

In view of the absence of a minimum of effectiveness in support of any *Grundnorm* for the international order, there is no reason to prefer a monist explanation to a dualist one, as indeed Kelsen seemed ready to concede. It appears then, that in postulating the primacy of international law Kelsen was making an assumption as to what ought to be the case rather than what actually is. Little wonder that Sir Hersch Lauterpacht, one of Kelsen's own pupils, was moved to question whether he was not here reverting to natural law ideology[8].

These difficulties will be avoided if the idea of a *Grundnorm* is replaced by that of an identifying criterion, accepted by courts, which would regulate the use of the label 'international law'. Propositions concerning the conduct of states would then be 'international law' because the appropriate tribunals accept them as such whenever they satisfy the criterion. It is true that different types of tribunals might view the criterion differently, or might even accept different criteria. Notwithstanding this, there might be here a sufficient basis for constructing a more realistic theory of international law than a monist one.

Finally, to treat war and reprisals as providing the element of force would be acceptable only if resort to them was permitted by the international legal order and forbidden as instruments of national policy. It is true that international law does not forbid war and reprisals entirely as instruments of national policy, not even after the Briand-Kellogg Pact 1928, or the Charter of the United Nations, but the object of international law is to try to prevent these. War represents the breakdown of international law.

In the light of all this, as Professor Friedmann observed:

'Logically Kelsen should have been led to deny the character of law to international law in present international society'[9].

In any case, in view of the differences between the connotation and function of the word 'law' as applied to international and municipal legal orders, it is questionable whether the attempt to construct a unifying theory is feasible.

The conclusion of many writers is that, notwithstanding the logical coherence of Kelsen's structure, he provided no guidance in the actual application of the law. Thus, he showed how, in the process of concretising the general norms it may be necessary to make a choice either in decision or interpretation. The judge or the official concerned is already aware of that necessity; his need is for some guidance as to how he should make his choice. The answer is not to be found in Kelsen's teachings, but in value considerations of one sort or another, which Kelsen sedulously eschewed[10]. One should not level this point as a criticism against Kelsen, who insisted that he was not concerned with that aspect. To criticise him for not having done something which he expressly disclaimed would be unfair. He set out to achieve a limited objective, namely, to present a formal picture of the legal structure, and what he set out to do, he did do. To say that he should have aspired to do more is not a criticism of what he has done, but a comment on his limited objective.

7 Ibid at 230, per Yaqub Ali J.
8 Lauterpacht 'Kelsen's Pure Science of Law' in *Modern Theories of Law* at pp 129–131.
9 Friedmann *Legal Theory* p 279.
10 Laski commented on his theory as 'an exercise in logic and not in life': *Grammar of Politics* p vi.

Another more serious aspect is that a legal order is not merely the sum total of laws, but includes doctrines, principles and standards, all of which are accepted as 'legal' and which operate by influencing the application of rules[11]. Their validity is not traceable to the *Grundnorm* of the order. Are these, then, to be lumped with values and banished from a theory of law, even though they are admitted to be 'legal'? If so, it is a weakness in any such theory.

Finally, although Kelsen has been hailed as having provided the outstanding theory of the twentieth century from a positivist point of view, it has to be remembered that Bentham's *Of Laws in General* only saw daylight after Kelsen had made his contribution. Some differences between them are significant. Kelsen avoided the weakness of Bentham's imperative basis, but in some other respects Bentham's analysis is preferable to Kelsen's. The most important of these is that Kelsen's method individuating a norm, 'If X, then Y ought to happen', minimises the regulatory function of law. This, as has been pointed out, stems from his obsession with sanctions: conduct is only a condition which brings them into play or avoids them. Bentham took full account of the regulatory function and perceived that one law prescribes behaviour and another prescribes a sanction: they are two different act-situations. Bentham kept them apart, while Kelsen rolled them into one. Kelsen was also driven to the difficult conclusion that laws are ultimately permissions to apply sanctions and that 'ought' thus includes 'may' and 'can'; which Bentham avoided. Bentham gave sanction a much broader meaning than Kelsen. On the other hand, both of them perceived that 'constitutional law' is a part of every law as ordinarily formulated, the linkage for Bentham being that such laws are compounded of other laws enacted at other times and in other contexts, while for Kelsen the linkage being their validity traceable through to the *Grundnorm*.

11 See pp 45-46 ante. Cf *Jilani v Government of Punjab* Pak LD (1972) SC 139 at 232-233.

READING LIST

W Ebenstein *The Pure Theory of Law*.

J W Harris 'Kelsen's Concept of Authority' (1977) 36 Cambridge Law Journal 353.

J W Jones *Historical Introduction to the Theory of Law* ch 9.

J W Jones 'The 'Pure' Theory of International Law' (1935) 16 British Year Book of International Law 5.

H Kelsen *General Theory of Law and State* (trans A Wedberg, 20th-Century Legal Philosophy Series I).

H Kelsen 'Professor Stone and the Pure Theory of Law' (1965) 17 Stanford Law Review 1128.

H Kelsen *Pure Theory of Law* (trans M Knight).

H Kelsen *What is Justice?*

H Kelsen 'What is the Pure Theory of Law?' (1959-60) 34 Tulane Law Review 269.

H Lauterpacht 'Kelsen's Pure Science of Law' in *Modern Theories of Law* (ed W I Jennings) ch 7.

S L Paulson 'Material and Format Authorisation in Kelsen's Pure Theory' (1980) 39 Cambridge Law Journal 172.

J Raz 'Kelsen's Theory of the Basic Norm' (1974) 19 American Journal of Jurisprudence' 94.

J Stone *Legal System and Lawyers' Reasonings* ch 3.

J Stone 'Mystery and Mystique of the Basic Norm' (1963) 26 Modern Law Review 34.

Essays in Honor of Hans Kelsen (contributions to (1971) 59 California Law Review 609-819, published in book form).

CHAPTER 18

Historical and anthropological approaches

The theories hitherto considered have sought to depict the formal structure of law and to elucidate the criterion of validity of the legal 'ought'. The theories about to be dealt with in this and the following two chapters are concerned with content and application. These also come under the umbrella of positivism so far as they accept laws as they are found. The difference between these and theories previously considered is one of emphasis, for they are concerned with the analysis of those factors, historical, economic and social excluded by analysis of only form and structure. As will appear, therefore, a conception of law, viewed in this perspective, assumes a material and functional aspect.

The historical outlook will be dealt with in this chapter. It comprises, on the one hand, inquiries into the past and evolution generally with the object of elucidating the position today. The question to be answered is to what extent the 'oughts' of contemporary laws have been fashioned by the past. This is what some of the jurists, who belong to what is known as the Historical School, have purported to do. On the other hand, there are inquiries into the past, especially into primitive and undeveloped communities, which are conducted for their own sake in order to discover what 'law' might appropriately be taken to mean in them. Such inquiries are distinguishable as the Anthropological approach and will be touched on at the end of the chapter.

HISTORICAL SCHOOL

The Historical School arose more or less contemporaneously with Analytical positivism at the beginning of the nineteenth century, and should be regarded as another manifestation of the reaction against natural law theories. It did not emerge as something novel in European thought, for it had been germinating long before then. The reaction against natural law theories provided a rich bed in which the seeds of historical scholarship took root and spread.

The prelude to the historical approach to law is the story of the study and reception of Roman law in Europe. The gradual disappearance and decay of Roman law in the ages which followed the dissolution of the Roman Empire were arrested by a revival of academic interest in that system in the eleventh century in France and in Italy and principally at the law school in Bologna. This new interest took the form of adding to the texts explanatory glosses and commentaries. The Glossators accepted Justinian's boast that conflicts had been eliminated from his codification, and they devoted their ingenuity to reconciling and explaining away the many conflicts that did undoubtedly exist. There was another more significant side to their work, which was that they endeavoured to fit the problems of their feudal society

into Roman terminology and thus paved the way for the later reception of
Roman law into Europe. The work of the Glossators culminated in the *Glossa
Ordinaria* of Accursius in the early twelfth century, which superseded all
previous glosses and came to be accepted as the final resolution of the conflicting opinions of individual Glossators. The scholars who followed them
were known as the Post-Glossators or Commentators. The most interesting
feature of their work is the way in which they attempted to relate the Roman
law to contemporary problems, but they used for this purpose, not the original texts, but the *Glossa*. So it was that when Roman law was eventually
received into Europe in the fifteenth and sixteenth centuries it was a diluted
version adapted from the *Glossa* that was received.

The Renaissance kindled fresh interest in the teachings of the Romans
themselves. The outstanding name in this connection is that of Cujas, a
Frenchman, who resorted to the Roman originals underneath the accumulated silt of commentary and gloss. He did more: he was the first scholar to
understand Justinian's *Corpus Juris* in historical perspective. It is difficult to
appreciate nowadays how lacking in historical sense people were in those
days. The tendency was to regard the *Corpus Juris* more or less as a simul-
taneous product, rather than as a collection of materials which had been
changing and developing over centuries. More than one hundred years
spanned the jurists of the Classical period, whose writings comprise the Digest, while between them and Justinian another three centuries elapsed. This
lack of historical sense led to elaborate and fanciful explanations of differences
which were easily explicable on historical grounds. The admirable work of
Cujas, however, was confined to the academic sphere and failed to penetrate
through to practice. For this there was good reason. As long as Roman law
remained 'the law' in the countries of Europe, inconsistencies had to be
reconciled and historical explanations of their origin were of no avail. The
living law could not be self-contradictory. Accordingly, there developed a
gulf between the academic jurist and the practitioner, which also explains
why the historical approach remained for so long in the background.

The position of Germany at the start of the nineteenth century deserves
special mention, since this was the cradle of the Historical School. Roman
law functioned as the common law subject to canon law, imperial enactments
and customary law, so far as this was still extant. The Roman law was
assumed to have been accepted as a whole, not in fragments, in the form of
Justinian's codification as found in the works of the Glossators and Commentators[1]. The practical problems which lawyers had to solve had altered
with the ages, but the methods of applying the law differed little from that
of the Italian courts in the time of the Glossators. Moreover, the panorama
of the law as a whole was confusing, for local variations were innumerable.
In these circumstances a proposal was made by Thibaut, of Heidelberg, in
1814 for a code on the lines of the Code Napoléon[2]. This was immediately
answered by von Savigny (1779–1861) in an essay entitled *On the Vocation of
our Age for Legislation and Jurisprudence*[3], with which, in the words of Ihering,
a new jurisprudence was born. So powerful was his influence that the move
towards codification was effectively halted and it was not until 1900, after

---

1 Summarised by Windscheid in *Lehrbuch des Pandektenrechts*.
2 For review of the events of 1814 leading to Savigny's publication, see Stammler 'Fundamental Tendencies in Modern Jurisprudence' (1923) 21 Mich LR 623.
3 Savigny *Vom Beruf unserer Zeit für Gesetzgebung und Rechtswissenschaft*, hereafter referred to as
   '*On the Vocation*'.

many years of sustained agitation, that Germany ultimately acquired her code, the *Bürgerliches Gesetzbuch*.

Although Thibaut's proposals were the immediate stimulus for the rise of the Historical School, other factors had combined to prepare the way. The first of these has already been mentioned, namely, the reaction against the unhistorical assumptions of the natural law theorists. As these were exposed as hollow and false, so the need was felt for a realistic investigation into historical truths. Secondly, the attempt to found legal systems based on reason without reference to past or existing circumstances had proved to be revolutionary, culminating in the French Revolution, with all its brutalities. A reaction set in against the rationalism that promoted such barbarity. This was a factor which weighed heavily with Savigny, a conservative nobleman, who acquired a deep and lasting hatred for the revolution. Thirdly, the French conquests under Napoleon aroused the nationalism of Europe. Fourthly, the French had spread the idea of codified law, and the reaction against anything French carried with it hostility to codification. Finally, the influence of certain early pioneers in the new way of thinking should not be ignored. Montesquieu had maintained that law was shaped by social, geographical and historical considerations; Burke in England had voiced the same sentiment by pointing to the importance of tradition as a guide to social change[4]. These factors, boosted by the genius of Savigny, started European thought along a new road.

Savigny was born in Frankfurt in 1779, and was nurtured in the natural law discipline. His interest in historical studies was kindled at the universities, first of Marburg and then of Göttingen, and was greatly encouraged when he became acquainted with Niebuhr at the University of Berlin. He also acquired a lasting veneration for Roman law. In 1803 appeared his first major work, *Das Recht des Besitzes* (*The Law of Possession*), which was considered in Chapter 13, in the last section of which Savigny's distinctive method became apparent. He traced the process by which the original Roman doctrines of possession had developed into the doctrines and actions prevailing in contemporary Europe. Savigny next set himself the task of laying the foundation for future historical labours by producing a basic history of the development of Roman law in mediaeval Europe. It was his thesis that Roman law had been received into Germany so long ago that her legal soul had become a mixture of Roman and local laws. In this great work, *The History of Roman Law in the Middle Ages*, which appeared in six volumes between 1815 and 1831, he analysed the Roman element to its roots, and in his other great work, *The System of Modern Roman Law*, he analysed Roman and local laws. These two together form an imperishable monument to his learning and industry. He was also supremely conscious of his mission, which was *not* opposed to reform; it was to preach the warning that reforms, which went against the stream of a nation's continuity, were doomed[5]. He emphasised that the muddled and outmoded nature of a legal system was usually due to a failure to comprehend its history and evolution. The essential prerequisite to the reform of German law was, for him, a deep knowledge of its history. Historical research was therefore the indispensable means to the understanding and reform of the present, and he said, somewhat belatedly it is true, but none the less clearly:

---

4 *Reflections on the Revolution in France* 1790.
5 Savigny was Prussian Minister of Legislation.

'The existing matter will be injurious to us so long as we ignorantly submit to it; but beneficial if we oppose to it a vivid creative energy—obtain the mastery over it by a thorough grounding in history and thus appropriate to ourselves the whole intellectual wealth of preceding generations'[6].

His warning, then, was that legislators should look before they leap into reform, but he spoilt this advice by over-generalisation. The core of Savigny's thesis is to be found in his essay *On the Vocation*. The nature of any particular system of law, he said, was a reflection of the spirit of the people who evolved it. This was later characterised as the *Volksgeist* by Puchta, Savigny's most devoted disciple. *All* law, according to him, is the manifestation of this common consciousness. He wrote,

'Law grows with the growth, and strengthens with the strength of the people, and finally dies away as the nation loses its nationality'[7].

A nation, to him, meant only a community of people linked together by historical, geographical and cultural ties. The boundaries of some nations may be clearly defined, but not of other nations, and this is reflected in the unity or variety of their respective laws. Even where the unity of a people is clear, there may lie within it 'inner circles' of variations, such as cities and guilds. He then went on to elaborate the theory of the *Volksgeist* by contending that it is the broad principles of the system that are to be found in the spirit of the people and which become manifest in customary rules. From this premise it followed that law is a matter of unconscious growth. Any law-making should therefore follow the course of historical development. Custom not only precedes legislation, but is superior to it, and legislation should always conform to the popular consciousness. Law is thus not of universal application; it varies with peoples and ages. The *Volksgeist* cannot be criticised for being what it is. It is the standard by which laws, which are the conscious product of the will as distinct from popular conviction, are to be judged. An individual jurist may misapprehend the popular conviction, but that is another matter. In place of the moral authority, which the natural lawyers of the preceding age had sought to posit behind law, the Historical School substituted social pressure, which provided the bridge between the work of the Historical School and that of the Sociological School[8].

This view of the nature of law dovetailed with Savigny's historical method of work, for if law is a reflection of people's spirit, then it can only be understood by tracing their history. It is clear, all the same, that in his revolt against the lack of historical sense, which characterised natural law theory, he swung the pendulum of legal thought too much the other way. To point out Savigny's exaggerations, however, is not to detract from the importance of his contribution.

On the idea of the *Volksgeist* several comments should be made.

(1)   There is an element of truth in it, for there is a stream of continuity and tradition[9]; the difficulty lies in fixing it with precision. Savigny,

---

6 Savigny Introduction to *The System of Modern Roman Law*.

7 Puchta *Outlines of the Science of Jurisprudence* (trans Hastie).

8 For American parallels see Sumner *Folkways*, on which see Sawer *Law in Society;* Carter *Law: Its Origin, Growth and Function;* 'The Ideal and the Actual in Law' (1890) 24 Am LR 752.

9 It is interesting to note that the Soviet Union, which claimed to make as complete a break with the past as it is possible to conceive, has found itself unable to slough off its traditions: see p 415 post.

however, made too much of it. As with most pioneers, he drew too sweeping an inference from modest premises. The idea of the *Volksgeist* certainly suited the mood of the German peoples. It was a time of the growing sense of nationhood, a desire for unification, an interest in the dramatic marking the appearance of the Romantic movement. German thinking, also, seems prone to personify the abstract, and to attribute a mystical coherence to ideals. Gierke's personification of corporate existence, considered in Chapter 12, was an example: Savigny's *Volksgeist* is another. The idea of a *Volksgeist* is acceptable in a limited way. Thus, the psychological associations built up around the law-making institutions in a particular state could be regarded as a manifestation of the *Geist* of that community[10]. Savigny, however, extrapolated his *Volksgeist* into a sweeping universal. He treated it as a discoverable thing; but it is common experience that even in a small group (*a fortiori* in a nation) people hold different views on different issues. 'The' spirit does not exist. So Savigny's thesis is probably best treated as the juristic contribution to Romanticism. In this it would appear that his historical sense deserted him, for it amounts, in effect, to the adoption of an *a priori* preconception. It will be remembered that in dealing with possession he did much the same thing, namely, to draw an inference from limited data, and then to use it as an *a priori* talisman[11].

(2) The transplanting of Roman law in the alien climate of Europe nearly a thousand years later is inconsistent with Savigny's idea of a *Volksgeist*. It postulates, if anything, some quality in law other than popular consciousness. His endeavour to establish that the reception of Roman law had taken place so long ago as to make the Germanic *Volksgeist* an expression of it was unconvincing. Apart from this, a survey of the contemporary scene shows that the German Civil Code has been adopted in Japan, the Swiss Code in Turkey and the French Code in Egypt without any apparent violence to popular susceptibilities. The French Code was also introduced into Holland during the Napoleonic era, displacing the Roman–Dutch common law, and it is significant that after the overthrow of Napoleon the Dutch never went back. They had, however, taken Roman–Dutch law to their colonies in the Cape of Good Hope and Ceylon (now Sri Lanka) with the odd result that it flourishes today in two such dissimilar national climates as southern Africa and Sri Lanka, although it has long since disappeared in its homeland. The reception of English law in so many parts of the world is also evidence of supra-national adaptability and resilience[12]. Indeed, the protest in South Africa today is that far too much English law has been allowed to overlay the 'national' Roman–Dutch law.

(3) The *Volksgeist* theory minimises the influence which individuals, sometimes of alien race, have exercised upon legal development.

10 See pp 52 et seq ante; p 465 post.
11 Some of the criticisms that follow have been adapted from chs 1 and 2 of Allen *Law in the Making*.
12 Walton 'The Historical School of Jurisprudence and Transplantation of Law' (1927) 9 JCL (3rd series) 183. Cf Pound 'Comparative Law and History as Bases for Chinese Law' (1947–48) 61 Harv LR 749.

Every man is a product of his time, but occasionally there are men who by their genius are able to give legal development new directions. The Classical jurists of Rome, Littleton, Coke, may be cited as examples. This is especially the case in modern times when new doctrines are deliberately introduced by a handful of policy-makers. Ehrlich pointed out that customs are norms of conduct, juristic laws are norms for decision. They are always the creation of jurists[13].

(4)   The last two points lead to the further objection that the influence of the *Volksgeist* is at most only a limited one. The national character of law seems to manifest itself more strongly in some branches than in others, for example in family law rather than in commercial or criminal law. Thus, the general reception of Roman law in Europe did not include Roman family law. Even more significant is the fact that the successful introduction of alien systems into India and Turkey affected the indigenous family laws least of all[14]. The inference appears to be that very few branches of law, perhaps only family law and succession to some extent, are really 'personal' to a nation. A further distinction may have to be drawn between the creative influence of the *Volksgeist* and its adaptative and abrogative influence. It is undoubtedly the case that new doctrines have been, and are constantly being, introduced by individuals. The most that indigenous tradition can do is to bring about practical modifications of these gradually and by degrees. Turkey provides an example, where new marriage laws, which were contrary to the existing traditional laws, were introduced as a matter of deliberate policy. The result from a juristic point of view was a fascinating process of action and reaction between the old and new law[15]. It might be thought that this bears out Savigny's contention that legislation should conform to existing traditional law, or it is doomed. In a sense so it does, but an example such as this also reveals something else. It shows that in modern times the function of the *Volksgeist* is that of modifying and adapting rather than creating, and that, in any case, even this function manifests itself only in the very 'personal' branches of the law. There is less evidence today of its creative force and none of its influence over the whole body of the law. If one thinks in the time-frame of the moment, the *Volksgeist* is of little or no relevance, for many existing laws have come from 'outside'. Savigny's theory only makes sense to a limited extent in a continuum. Even so, the *Volksgeist* is discernible only in retrospect, but he sought to make it a test of validity, ie to use it in the present time-frame where it is irrelevant. This confusion in his frames of reference left his theory open to attack.

(5)   Law is sometimes used deliberately to change existing ideas[16]; and it may also be used to further inter-state co-operation in many spheres. Even in Germany one may instance Bismarck's shrewd and

---

13   Ehrlich *Fundamental Principles of the Sociology of Law* (trans Moll) ch 19. Cf Weyrauch *The Personality of Lawyers*; Pound *Interpretations of Legal History* ch 6.
14   See Lipstein 'The Reception of Western Law in Turkey' (1956) 6 Annales de la Faculté de Droit d'Istanbul 10, 225; 'The Reception of Western Law in a Country of a Different Social and Economic Background: India' (1957–58) 8–9 Revista del Instituto de Derecho Comparado 69, 213.
15   *Lipstein.*
16   Eg in India, on which see Stone *Social Dimensions of Law and Justice*, pp 112–114.

successful attempt to cut the ground from under the feet of the socialist movement by introducing the Railway and Factories Accident Law 1871, well before social conditions were ripe[17].

(6) Many institutions have originated, not in a *Volksgeist*, but in the convenience of a ruling oligarchy, eg slavery.

(7) Many customs owe their origin to the force of imitation rather than to any innate conviction of their righteousness.

(8) Some rules of customary law may not reflect the spirit of the whole population, eg local customs. Savigny, it will be remembered, did allow for these by recognising the existence of 'inner circles' within a society. The question remains: if law is the product of a *Volksgeist*, how is it that only some people and not all have evolved a special rule? On the other hand, some customs, eg the Law Merchant, were cosmopolitan in origin: they were not the creatures of any particular *nation* or *race*. In short, it is not at all clear who the *Volk* are whose *Geist* determines the law.

(9) Important rules of law sometimes develop as the result of conscious and violent struggle between conflicting interests within the nation, and not as a result of imperceptible growth, eg the law relating to trade unions and industry. Evolution does not follow an inexorably determined path.

(10) A different objection to the *Volksgeist* came from Savigny's opponents. They pointed out that, taken literally, his thesis would thwart the unification of Germany permanently by emphasising the individuality of each separate state and by fostering a parochial sense of nationalism.

(11) An inconsistency in Savigny's work was that, while he was the protagonist of the *Volksgeist* doctrine, he worked at the same time for the acceptance of a purified Roman law as the law of Germany. There was in Germany in his day a vigorous school of jurists who strongly advocated the resuscitation of ancient Germanic laws and customs as the foundation of a modernised German system. The leader of this school, Eichorn, was a fellow professor with Savigny at the University of Berlin. Savigny never opposed the work of Eichorn, but he opposed the expulsion of Roman law[18]. The obvious objection to Savigny is that his endeavour to preserve Roman law as the law of Germany was inconsistent with his idea of the *Volksgeist* of the German nation. One explanation lies in his personal devotion to Roman law. Another is that in his earliest work on possession he had been able to expose the misinterpretations of Roman law by later commentators, and this possibly implanted in his mind the idea that the Romans were better craftsmen than incompetent moderns. Even so the point apparently overlooked by Savigny was that, whatever may have been the case with possession, in other branches of the law these post-Roman interpretations were 'adaptations', rather than 'perversions', to meet contemporary needs. It might even be argued that the so-called 'misinterpretations' were indeed expressions of the *Volksgeist* of each different country. Another and better reason for the preservation of Roman law might have been

17 *Reichshaftpflichtgesetz* 1871.
18 On this see Walton 'The Historical School of Jurisprudence and the Transplantation of Law' (1927) 9 JCL (3rd series) 183.

that, in view of its long established reception, to dispense with it would have unsettled three centuries of development. In order to account for the original reception of an alien system Savigny argued that at that date the Germanic law was incapable of expressing the *Volksgeist*. This questionable proposition fails to show how an alien system was better able to express it than the indigenous law. Far from the law being a reflection of the *Volksgeist*, it would seem that the *Volksgeist* had been shaped by the law.

Such are the objections to Savigny's idea of the *Volksgeist*. Other aspects of his work also need mention. His veneration for Roman law led him to advance certain dubious propositions. For instance, there was in Roman law a strict adherence to the doctrine of privity of contract with few exceptions, ie no one other than parties to a contract can be entitled or obliged under it. The law of negotiable instruments, of course, is a contradiction of this. Savigny accordingly condemned negotiable instruments as 'logically impossible'[19]. This reveals one of the more unfortunate results of devotion to a postulate as well as the limitations of the *Volksgeist* idea. It could hardly be supposed that the populace had any feeling in the matter one way or the other, while the feelings of the commercially minded were strongly in favour of negotiable instruments. Indeed, the crucial weakness of Savigny's approach was that he venerated past institutions without regard to their suitability to the present.

The *Volksgeist*, according to Savigny, only formulates the rudimentary principles of a legal system. He saw clearly enough that it could not provide all the detail that is necessary. He accordingly maintained that as society, and consequently law, becomes more complex, a special body of persons is called into being whose business it is to give technical, detailed expression to the *Volksgeist* in the various matters with which the law has to deal. These are the lawyers, whose task is to reflect accurately the prevailing *Geist*[20]. This is nothing but a fictitious assumption, in no way related to reality, to cover up an obvious weakness in his principal contention. As Sir Carleton Allen said, it is not possible to pretend that the rule in *Shelley's Case*, for instance, is rooted in the instincts of the British[1]. Savigny's thesis, however, contained another and even more awkward implication. The only persons who talked of the *Volksgeist* were academic jurists, unversed in the practical problems of legal administration. Therefore, the *Volksgeist* resolved itself into what these theorists imagined it to be. On the other hand, it is possible that there is a limited sense in which Savigny's contention is acceptable. It has already been pointed out that the *Volksgeist* manifests itself, if at all, only in a few branches of the law and, even in these, by way of modifying and adapting any innovations that may be introduced. So, Savigny's proposition might be taken to mean simply that in these spheres of the law it would be helpful if legislators took account of tradition when framing new laws.

Consistently with this theory, Savigny further maintained that legislation was subordinate to custom. It should at all times conform to the *Volksgeist*. It has been pointed out that he did not oppose legislation or reform by way of codification at some appropriate time in the future, but his attitude was

---

19 Savigny *Obligationenrecht* II, p 101.
20 Cf Carter *Law: Its Origin, Growth and Function*.
 1 *Allen* pp 114-115.

generally one of pessimism[2]. He certainly opposed the project of immediate codification on several grounds. In the first place, he pointed to the defects of contemporary codes which, to his mind, preserved adventitious, subsidiary and often unsuitable rules of Roman law, even while they rejected its main principles. Secondly, in matters on which there is no *Volksgeist*, a code, in his opinion, might introduce new and unadaptable provisions and so add to the prevailing difficulties. Such an argument would appear to have been disposed of by the subsequent experience of many countries. Thirdly, he argued that codification could never cater exhaustively for all problems that are likely to arise in the future and hence was not a suitable instrument for the development of law. Fourthly, he suggested that an imperfect code would create the worst possible difficulties by perpetuating the follies underlying it. On the other hand, when lawyers were in a position to create a perfect code, no code would then be necessary since the lawyers could adequately cope with the problems that arise. Fifthly, he argued, even more oddly, that codification would highlight the loopholes and weaknesses of the law and so encourage evasion. The short answer to the last two contentions is that they leave out of account the possibility of amendment and alteration. Codification, in Savigny's view, should be preceded by 'an organic, progressive, scientific study of the law', by which he meant of course historical study. Reform should await the results of the historians' work. It is true that reformers should not plunge into legislation without paying some heed to the past as well as to the present. Savigny was over-cautious in this respect, for as Allen observed, his doctrines had the unfortunate tendency 'to hang traditions like fetters upon the hands of reformative enterprise'[3]. So little in fact did the historians contribute in the years that followed that drastic legislative action became imperative; which it did in 1900.

Savigny's work, on the whole, was a salutary corrective to the methods of the natural lawyers. He did grasp a valuable truth about the nature of law, but ruined it by overemphasis.

Another writer of whom some mention should be made is Gierke (1841–1921)[4], who was profoundly interested in the 'association', which has always exercised a peculiar fascination for German thinkers. Associations have significance in law, and are sometimes treated as persons. As seen in Chapter 12, Gierke denied that the recognition of an association as a person depended on the state. The reality of social control lies in the way in which autonomous groups within society organise themselves. He then proceeded to trace the progress of social and legal development in the form of a history of the law and practice of associations and propounded a classification of associations on the following lines: firstly, he contrasted groups organised on a territorial basis, such as the state, with those organised on a family or extraterritorial basis: then he contrasted associations founded on the idea of fraternal collaboration (*Genossenchaften*) with those founded on the idea of domination (*Herrschaften*). In his view legal and social history is most accurately portrayed as a perpetual struggle between the *Genossenschaft* and the *Herrschaft*. Thus, in feudal society men were organised in tight hierarchical groups based

2 For a parallel development in America, see Field 'Codification' (1886) 20 Am LR 1; opposed by Carter 'The Province of the Written and the Unwritten Law' (1890) 24 Am LR 1. See further Field (1800) 24 Am LR 255; Williston 'Written and Unwritten Law' (1931) 17 Am BAJ 39; Gray *The Nature and Sources of the Law* (2nd edn) pp 89-93, 233-239, 291.
3 *Allen* p 17.
4 *Natural Law and the Theory of Society 1500-1800* (trans Barker) and Barker's 'introduction'.

on the holding of property; this system was opposed in the Middle Ages by the emergence of collaborative groups such as the guild and the city. These degenerated in turn, and with the Renaissance and Reformation the state appeared as the significant factor in social organisation. In his own day Gierke felt that the collaborative principle had prevailed and that the state encouraged the growth of independent collaborative organisations within its own framework. The pivot of social control, then, lay not in state organisation but rather in these collective bodies within the state.

Gierke represented a collectivist, rather than an individualist, approach. To this extent his work touched on that of the sociologists, but his interpretation of this development on historical lines entitles him to be ranked among the historians. His doctrines of mass psychology, though largely fanciful, anticipated modern inquiries. He also never quite succeeded in reconciling the independence of autonomous bodies with the supreme power of the state. He devised a pyramidal structure, which made society consist of a hierarchy of corporate bodies culminating in the state. He wished at the same time to defend the independent existence of the lesser corporate bodies and to limit absolute state power by arguing that the state was the expression of reason and the sense of right. This, of course, was easily brushed aside by those who wished to use Gierke's doctrines as a justification for absolute totalitarian power.

THE DIALECTIC INTERPRETATION

Savigny and his followers did not face the question of how the *Volksgeist* is formed. His theory therefore appeared to be somewhat incomplete and this opened the way for the reintroduction of a naturalist explanation; it became possible to posit again an immutable ideal behind evolution. Variations in historical development emerge in the course of progress towards the realisation of an ideal. If there is some unchanging ideal at the root of it all, then all systems, notwithstanding their evolutionary variations, should share certain common features; which, according to this view, they do. This is the explanation of such resemblances, not so much conscious borrowing and analogy. Such an idealised historical interpretation of law is associated with the name of Hegel (1770–1831)[5]. It is so abstract as to bear little relation to fact and is far removed from the work of men like Savigny and Gierke[6].

Hegel distinguished between laws of nature and positive laws. The former are outside human consciousness and can neither be improved nor assisted by men; they have to be accepted because they exist. Positive laws, on the other hand, are man-made and, as such, do not have to be accepted because they exist. This would seem to be approaching the distinction between the 'is' and the 'ought', but with Hegel that distinction tends to be blurred. He also proceeded to distinguish between the philosophy of law, which concerns the rationality of law, and the study of the positive law itself. Thought is the rational process of synthesising contradictions and of reconciling the general with the particular, the abstract with the concrete. Legal philosophy, being rational, should conceive of law in a rational way. Philosophy is only concerned with reality so far as this is rational, ie so far as it is the rational reconciliation of appearance and essence. So, mere factual existence is not

5 Hegel *Philosophy of Right* (trans Knox). See also Stace *The Philosophy of Hegel*.
6 In particular, it is noteworthy that Hegel did not share Savigny's hostility to legislation, and denounced such an attitude: *The Philosophy of Right* §211.

'real' in this sense, since it might be the product of fortuitous (irrational) factors. When therefore Hegel asserted, 'That which is rational is real and that which is real is rational', this remark should be understood in the context of his approach and the fact that he was only concerned with ideas.

Hegel sought to explain history on an abstract, evolutionary plane[7]. The idea of evolution as expounded biologically by Darwin was shortly to influence human thinking profoundly. Hegel, however, a little earlier saw it unfolding as a process of action and reaction between opposites, thesis and anti-thesis, which results in their synthesis, the whole broadening slowly towards the realisation of freedom. The 'idea', says Hegel, has as its antithesis the 'idea outside itself', which is nature. The synthesis is 'spirit' (of which Savigny's *Volksgeist* is possibly an aspect). The subjective spirit (thought and consciousness) and its anti-thesis, the objective spirit (legal and social institutions) are synthesised in the absolute spirit. Law comes into the category of objective spirit. Law and other social institutions are the result of free subjective will endeavouring to realise freedom objectively. In this development the starting-point is the idea of freedom, which implies will. Freedom and will are complementary. Personality arises when the will becomes individualised. The idea of freedom has a three-fold sphere of operation. There is, first, the freedom of the individual in relation to himself, which concerns his proprietary rights. Secondly, there is the perception of freedom in others in conformity with the common will of all, which brings in contract. Thirdly, the freedom of the individual opposes itself to the common will, which is wrongdoing. Taken in turn, and stated baldly, the explanations are as follows. As to property, the free will of a person is imposed on a thing, which is unfree and impersonal. A thing has no end in itself and only acquires one from the will of the individual. The right of property is therefore the first manifestation of freedom. Contract is approached from the angle of property. Not only may property be the subject of one person's will, but it may also come within the purview of another person's will. When a thing is held by virtue of the individual's conformity with their mutual will, the matter falls into the sphere of contract. Wrongdoing occurs when the will of the individual is opposed to the general will. The conflict then brings about morality, which is the anti-thesis of freedom. Social ethics is the synthesis between these two. Social ethics starts at the level of the family. When members of the family become independent, society comes into being with its attendant institutions of law etc. Society is then the anti-thesis of family. The synthesis is the state, which combines freedom and social co-existence. In the state Hegel found the highest achievement of human endeavour, and to be a member of the state was to him the supreme objective. The individual is the product of his culture and age, which are realised only through the state. Law and state are thus concrete manifestations of the national spirit, which together with others are in turn a manifestation of a world spirit.

On all this it might be remarked that one seeks in vain for the facts to which these formidable abstractions relate. For the purpose of his demonstration of conflict Hegel attributed objective existence to values and natural phenomena. It should be pointed out that the conflict between thesis and anti-thesis is a logical contradiction, which is not the case with natural phenomena. If he had confined his attention to the action and reaction of

---

7 For a critique of the inevitability of historical development, see Popper *The Open Society and its Enemies*, especially vol II. See also *The Poverty of Historicism*.

ideas as evidenced by historical fact, he might well have been led to other, though less imposing, conclusions. Besides, to treat values as having objective existence is to make an 'is' out of 'ought'. All in all, his highly abstract scheme is nothing but a verbal juggle into which divergent interpretations can be fitted. It is therefore not surprising to find it being utilised in support of two such dissimilar ideologies as Nazism and Marxism[8].

THE BIOLOGICAL INTERPRETATION

A variant of the historical interpretation and one which also sought to find the clue to the nature of contemporary law in evolutionary processes is the so-called Biological approach. The publication of Darwin's *On the Origin of Species* in 1859 was destined to affect human thought profoundly in many directions. Side by side with this there was the rise of psychology as a new fashion in thinking with a concomitant preoccupation with group psychology. Its effect in legal theory is to be seen in the interpretation of law as the product of evolutionary forces in connection with which the work of Herbert Spencer (1820-1903) is characteristic[9].

Darwin's thesis was that evolution was a struggle for existence in which those creatures that are able to adapt themselves to changing conditions survive. In human beings the survival of the fittest called for the development of the social instinct. Spencer also adopted the idea that a collection of individuals form a community. He promulgated three fundamental laws of society, the principles of persistence of force, the indestructibility of matter, and the continuity of motion. The combination of these principles with other laws[10] results in the process of evolution, which is that process by which an amorphous, homogeneous mass evolves into a series of distinct, orderly bodies. Spencer then proceeded to draw parallels between the social organism and biological organisms.

The adaptation of the individual to social conditions is due to heredity. He inherits a social instinct from his ancestors, including ideas of morality, obligation, right and justice. In this way different sociological groups evolve differently and so, too, do their laws and institutions.

There are two stages in the progress of civilisation. In the first, which is primitive, war and compulsion figure prominently; in the second, which is advanced, peace and freedom are prominent. Spencer, however, was a strong individualist with a *laissez-faire* approach to government. He denied the complete absorption of the individual in the state and maintained that the duty of government was to secure the greatest possible amount of individual freedom. He abhorred any form of welfare activities by the state. Each person may do what he likes, provided he does not infringe the equal freedom of others. His theory of evolution together with his *laissez-faire* idea of government led him to a reactionary position with regard to legislative reform. He held that all conscious legislative attempts to improve social organisations were doomed to failure and that Man must await the working out of evolutionary laws.

Whatever may have been left of Spencer's theory has disappeared with the

8 For this perversion, see Friedrich *The Philosophy of Law in Historical Perspective* ch 15.
9 *Social Statics* (1850); *Justice* (1891). See also Sabine *A History of Political Theory* ch 32.
10 The law of the persistence of the relations among forces, the law that force is never lost but only transformed, the law that everything moves along the line of least resistance or greatest attraction, and the law of rhythm or alternation of motion.

advent of the welfare state; his biology would now be dismissed as crude. The objections to his theory were epitomised by Mr Justice Holmes, who said:

> 'The liberty of the citizen to do as he likes so long as he does not interfere with the liberty of others to do the same, which has been a shibboleth for some well-known writers, is interfered with by school laws, by the Post Office, by every state and municipal institution which takes his money for purposes thought desirable, whether he likes it or not. The Fourteenth Amendment does not enact Mr Herbert Spencer's Social Statics'[11].

Spencer's work does represent, however, the transition from the historical approach to the sociological.

THE RACIAL THEORY OF LAW

This was the theory of law that prevailed in National Socialist Germany under Hitler. It was nothing more than an emotional and militant adaptation of theories and ideas in support of the quest for power. From the biological interpretation was derived the idea that law was inherited by blood. The Historical School was made to lend its support in seeking the roots of the law in the past and for the nationalistic flavour that was imparted to it. The writings of Hegel, who showed how the individual could be integrated into society, were utilised so as to suppress individual rights.

The National Socialist theory of law revolved round two cardinal principles, the 'leadership principle' and the 'racial principle'. The application of the first was as follows. The state is a group and a group has no strength or unity without a leader. The leader, therefore, becomes the mystical personification of national unity. Law and state mean the same thing, and since the leader is the embodiment of the state, law is what the leader commands. This had three implications. (a) Unquestioning obedience was demanded. (b) Law should serve political ends. (c) Nothing, not even reverence for statutes, should stand in the way of implementing the will of the leader. According to the 'racial principle' law was inherited by blood. It should (i) serve the ends of the state and its policies. (ii) It should help to preserve racial purity, for the state cannot be strong unless it is racially pure. This was the justification for the persecution of the Jews. (iii) The Code of 1900 was attacked on the ground that its basis was Justinian's Byzantine version of Roman law. Therefore, besides being an alien system, it was condemned as being 'oriental' and 'Jewish' in origin. (iv) The only international system which could be tolerated was a Nordic one, ie one based on a blood tie. The League of Nations could therefore command no respect. Every state has a natural privilege and power to prevail over other states and to take their land as room for its people. Any treaty which attempted to restrict this privilege could rightly be ignored.

It is no longer necessary to dwell on the details of this perverted conception of law, nor to enter into a refutation of it. The answer of a sort that did come at the end of a world shattering war was effective enough.

11 *Lochner v New York* 178 US 45 at 75 (1904).

ANTHROPOLOGICAL APPROACH

Anthropological investigations into the nature of primitive and undeveloped systems of law are of modern origin and might be regarded as a product of the Historical School. Pride of place will here be accorded to Sir Henry Maine (1822–1888), who was the first and still remains the greatest representative of the historical movement in England[12]. It is not easy to place Maine's contributions to the theory of law. He began his work with a mass of material already published on the history and development of Roman law by the German Historical School, and he was able to build upon that and also to bring to bear a more balanced view of history than is found in Savigny. Maine, however, went further. He was learned in English, Roman and Hindu laws and also had knowledge of Celtic systems. In this respect he parted company with the German historians. Instead of stressing the uniqueness of national institutions, he brought to bear a scientific urge to unify, classify and generalise the evolution of different legal orders. Thus he inaugurated both the comparative and anthropological approaches to the study of law, and history in particular, which was destined to bear abundant fruit in the years to come[13].

Maine set out to discover whether a pattern of legal development could be extracted from a comparative examination of different systems, especially between Roman law and the common law. What he sought were laws of historical development. He was led to distinguish between what he called 'static' and 'progressive' societies. The early development of both types is roughly the same and falls, in his thesis, into four stages. The first stage is that of law-making by personal command, believed to be of divine inspiration, eg Themistes of ancient Greece, and the dooms of the Anglo-Saxon kings. The second stage occurs when those commands crystallise into customs. In the third stage the ruler is superseded by a minority who obtain control over the law, eg the pontiffs in ancient Rome. The fourth stage is the revolt of the majority against this oligarchic monopoly, and the publication of the law in the form of a code, eg the XII Tables in Rome.

'Static' societies, according to Maine, do not progress beyond this point. The characteristic feature of 'progressive' societies is that they proceed to develop the law by three methods—fiction, equity and legislation. Ample examples of the use of fiction are to be found in Roman and early English law. The operation of equity and legislation has been considered in the earlier chapters of this book.

As a general inference Maine believed that no human institution was permanent, and that change was not necessarily for the better. Unlike Savigny, he favoured legislation and codification. He recognised that the advance of civilisation demanded an increasing use of legislation, and he often contended that the confused state of English law was due to its pre-eminently judge-made character. Codification is an advanced form of legislative development, and represents the stage at which all the preceding phases of development are woven into a coherent whole. He also did not share Savigny's mystique of the *Volksgeist*.

---

12 The opinion is ventured that neither Maitland nor Holdsworth has made the contributions to legal theory that were made by Maine.
13 Maine *Ancient Law* (Pollock's edn). At the time of its publication his knowledge of Hindu law was not as profound as it became later, for he only took up his Indian appointment in the following year.

Side by side with these doctrines Maine developed another thesis. In early societies, both 'static' and 'progressive', the legal condition of the individual is determined by status, ie his claims, duties, liberties etc are determined by law[14]. The march of 'progressive' societies witnesses the disintegration of status and the determination of the legal condition of the individual by free negotiation on his part. This was expressed in one of Maine's most famous generalisations:

'The movement of progressive societies has hitherto been a movement from *Status to Contract*'[15].

An evaluation of Maine's work must take into account the pioneer character of his comparative investigations. Since his day the study of anthropology has developed into a separate branch of learning. Modern research over a wider field and with better equipment has corrected Maine's work at many points, and departed from it at others. One should be charitable about his errors and marvel at his genius in accomplishing so much. Some comment should, however, be made about the development from status to contract. There was much to support it. In Roman law there was the gradual amelioration of the condition of children, women and slaves, the freeing of adult women from tutelage, and the acquisition of a limited contractual capacity by children and slaves. In English law the bonds of serfdom were relaxed and eventually abolished. Employment came to be based on a contractual basis between master and servant. Maine's own age was one in which legislation was removing the disabilities of Catholics, Jews, Dissenters and married women. He witnessed the triumph in the American Civil War of the North, a community based on contract, over the feudal and status-regulated South. In the modern age, however, a return to status has been detected. In public affairs, and in industry in particular, the individual is no longer able to negotiate his own terms. This is the age of the standardised contract, and of collective bargaining. Such developments, however, should not be held against Maine. He was not purporting to prophesy and, indeed, he expressly qualified his proposition by saying that the development had 'hitherto' been a movement towards contract[16].

Modern anthropologists have had the advantage of following the trails blazed by Maine and by others after him with the added advantage of being able to profit from the researches of fellow-workers in many directions. It is not surprising, therefore, to find that Maine's conclusions about primitive law have now been discredited or modified. The idea that early development passed through the successive stages of personal judgments, oligarchic monopoly and code has been abandoned as drawing too simple a picture. Primitive societies are seen to have been more complex than had been supposed. There have been several forms of such societies, so there is an initial problem of determining what sorts of societies should be classified as 'primitive'. It is now thought that there were seven grades of them, the First and Second Hunters, the First, Second and Third Agricultural Grades, and the First and Second Pastoral Grades. The agricultural and pastoral grades are to some extent parallel. The degree of development of social institutions does

14 Those societies which remain governed by status are 'static'. Note the etymological connection between 'status and 'static'.
15 Maine (Pollock's edn) p 182; but see Graveson *Status in the Common Law* ch 3.
16 Dicey *Law and Public Opinion in England during the 19th Century* chs 7–8; *Law and Opinion in England in the 20th Century* (ed Ginsberg) ch 1.

bear some correspondence with the degree of economic development[17]. From all this it will be gathered that primitive societies exhibit a wide range of institutions; there is nothing like a single pattern as Maine had supposed.

There has also been modification of the sequence, as stated by Maine, of later development, namely by means of fiction, equity and legislation. Deliberate legislation is now seen to have been an early method of law-making with fiction and equity coming in at a later stage. The codes, which one finds at the culmination of the primitive period, were chiefly collections of earlier legislation.

Primitive law was by no means as rigid as Maine had supposed, nor were people inflexibly bound by it[18]. Field-work among 'contemporary primitives' has revealed that considerable latitude is inherent in the content of their customary practices. For instance, Malinowski's first-hand experience of life among certain Pacific islanders enabled him to demonstrate how, eg their practices make allowance for good and bad harvests, or take due account of an excess of generosity on the part of individuals[19]. Observations by Gluckman of the Barotse in Northern Rhodesia have shown that the very indeterminate character of their standards permits a desirable flexibility in application[1]. Rigidity develops at a much later period. Above all, it is generally agreed that even in primitive societies people do control their destinies, that they are by no means blindly subservient to custom. The conscious purpose of achieving some end precedes the adaptation of human behaviour, and the adaptation of behaviour is followed by adaptation of the structure of social organisation[2].

It used to be accepted that law and religion were indistinguishable in primitive societies. This view has given way to an increased recognition of the secular character of primitive law. The exact extent to which law and religion were associated, seems, however, to be in some doubt. Diamond, for example, criticises Maine most strongly for his assertion that they were indistinguishable; the association of the two, in his view, is a comparatively late development[3]. Hoebel, on the other hand, defends Maine on this point[4]. Hocart believed that the dualism between religion and the secular authority (the state) originated in a division of function between a 'sky-king', who was the supreme regulator and as such responsible for law, and an 'earth-king', who was charged with the task of dealing with evil and wrongdoing; the former was reflective and unimpassioned, the latter quick in decision and violent in action. The role of the 'sky-king' would seem to have combined religion and law[5]. Further, if Hocart is right there seems to be implicit in this the distinction between the primitive, prescriptive patterns of conduct and the secondary machinery of sanction; which leads on to the next point.

It is likewise agreed among anthropologists that there is, at any rate as far

---

17 Hobhouse, Wheeler and Ginsberg *The Material Culture and Social Institutions of the Simpler Peoples.*
18 For criticism of Maine's idea of rigidity, see Hoebel *The Law of Primitive Man.*
19 Malinowski *Crime and Custom in Savage Society* pp 1–68.
 1 Gluckman *The Judicial Process among the Barotse of Northern Rhodesia; Politics, Law and Ritual in Tribal Society.* Cf Gulliver *Social Control in an African Society.* On the importance of maintaining social equilibrium, see Driberg 'The African Conception of Law' (1934) 16 JCL (3rd series) 230.
 2 Malinowski 'A New Instrument for the Interpretation of Law—especially Primitive' (1941–42) 51 Yale LJ 1237.
 3 Diamond *Primitive Law; The Evolution of Law and Order*; Lloyd *The Idea of Law* pp 231–239.
 4 *The Law of Primitive Man.*
 5 Hocart *Kings and Councillors.*

as contemporary primitive societies are concerned, a phenomenon that can be isolated from religious and other social observances and for which the term 'law' would be convenient. Bohannan has suggested that law comes into being when customary reciprocal obligations become further institutionalised in a way that society continues to function on the basis of rules[6]. These concern mainly the relations of individuals *inter se* and of groups, ie primary patterns of conduct importing an 'ought'. Gluckman has shown that among the Barotse the laws consist mainly of positive injunctions, 'you ought', rather than negative, 'you ought not'. These 'oughts' of primitive law are distinguishable from others by the nature of the obligation to obey them[7]. It was a cardinal point of Malinowski's thesis, supported by Hogbin, that obedience to customs rests on the reciprocity of services[8]. People do unto others what the law bids them do because they depend on some service in return as part of their mutual co-existence. It is spontaneous and incessant goodwill that promotes and preserves social existence. It is possible that Malinowski underestimated the part played by sanction[9]. It might also be that the ceremonial with which these services are usually rendered underlines their obligatory character, but this is of minor significance. Moreover, it is obedience, not disobedience, that is contemplated by law, the primary rule, not sanction. Yet some mechanism there has to be for dealing with cases of conflict and breach. As long as obedience prevails there is no call for this machinery. Examples of its working are also of interest. For instance, the records kept by Gluckman of the judicial processes among the Barotse show that the main task is reconciliation rather than the ordering of sanctions, which implies that even at the secondary stage an attempt is made to ensure conformity with the primary pattern of conduct[10]. Sanctions apply only when reconciliation has failed or is not possible. One form which these take is to abandon the wrongdoer to the avenger, who has the moral support of the community behind him. In other cases, compensation may be payable to the victim, and it is a matter of dispute whether vengeance preceded compensation or whether they existed side by side. This is why it is difficult to distinguish between civil and criminal wrongdoing in early societies. The question depended on whether the action was thought to affect the society or only the individual. In the result, the conclusion which most anthropologists have reached is that what is called 'law' should be described in terms of its function and the attitude of the people towards it rather than in terms of form or enforcement. It would appear to be something compulsorily observed and certainly far from what is commanded or backed by sanction.

Lastly, another point, which has emerged from modern investigations, is the disposal of the belief in communism as the primitive form of society[11]. This may be seen in many ways, particularly in the prevalence of jealously protected private ownership of socially productive weapons and institutions, such as spells, incantations and, above all, ritual.

6 Bohannan 'The Differing Realms of the Law' (1965) 67 American Anthropologist 6, Part II, p 35.
7 Gluckman *The Judicial Process among the Barotse of Northern Rhodesia*.
8 Malinowski *Crime and Custom in Savage Society;* Hogbin *Law and Order in Polynesia* and Malinowski's 'Introduction'.
9 For this criticism, and for changes in his thinking, see Schapera 'Malinowski's Theories of Law' in *Man and Culture* (ed Firth) 139.
10 For the handling of 'trouble cases' by the Cheyenne Indians, see Llewellyn and Hoebel *The Cheyenne Way*.
11 Lowie 'Incorporeal Rights in Primitive Society' (1927-28) 37 Yale LJ 551.

So far not much has been said, save indirectly, of the organisation of government. In this connection the oustanding contribution of Hocart deserves mention, especially as his name is insufficiently known among jurists[12]. On the evidence collected from a large number of widely separated tribes in many parts of the world, Hocart came to the conclusion that the functions of modern government were gradually fitted into the framework of a machinery that was previously fulfilling other functions. In other words, the framework of government was there before there was any governing to be done. Man does not consciously seek government; he seeks life, and with that end in view he does one thing after another, evolving and adapting special procedures and techniques, till he finds himself governed. The means by which primitive societies sought life was ritual. The lives and well-being of individuals depended on the life and well-being of society. Ritual was therefore a social affair and society had to organise itself for it. The structure of ritual was such that different roles were assigned to different individuals and groups. In all this one may detect the origin of caste; the various castes that one finds, the fisher, the farmer, the launderer, the potter etc, may not have derived from the trades that the people actually pursued, but from the roles they fulfilled in the ritual. There probably was some connection between trade and a role, for no doubt it was usual to assign to a person the role which he was fitted to fulfil whenever this was possible.

It was the organisation, founded on ritual, that was adapted for purposes of government. Since the king could not play every role simultaneously, he assigned to each chieftain a particular role which had a particular objective. The aim of the ritual was the control of nature so as to render it bounteous and abundant. The particular form which the ritual assumed in any given case depended on the aspect of nature which was to be controlled, whether sunshine or rain or harvest or game etc. To the group that was identified with some aspect of nature was entrusted the ritual concerning it. It follows from this, first, that only the group that exclusively owned a particular ritual was competent to perform it; secondly, every ritual had its leader; thirdly, the performers did not merely imitate nature as it happened to be at the moment, but as they wanted it to behave, eg to shed rain at a time of drought—an 'ought' not an 'is'; fourthly, in order to control nature the performers had to become one with nature and identify themselves with it; and fifthly, such equivalence was accomplished by the 'word', which thus acquired special significance.

There was always a tendency for rituals to coalesce in one person or group of persons. The greatest cumulator was the king, and this process of cumulation is centralisation. Even after the king had begun to fulfil several roles, his chiefs had to stand ready to lend their assistance if called on to do so. In the role of the sun the king became the supreme regulator of the world, and this regulative function assumed greater and greater importance and eventually became the mark of the king. The aim of the ritual, as has been remarked, was to make nature bounteous. It followed that nature should itself be amply provided before a generous return could be expected of it. The king being identified with nature, the prosperity of the people could only be achieved by making the king prosperous. Revenue and tribute were the means of making him so.

In these and various other ways Hocart discerned the outlines of govern-

12 Hocart *Kings and Councillors; Kingship; The Northern States of Fiji; Social Origins.*

ment, the organs of which were fitted into the existing framework of ritual. It is not possible in this short space to pursue his demonstration further, nor to consider his parallel investigations into the meaning of ceremonial statements, doctrines and courtesies relating to monarchy even today. One thing which his analysis has indorsed is the prescriptive nature and function of primitive law.

CONCLUSION

Too much attention on those factors of the past that have shaped the content of the 'oughts' of the law of today should not be allowed to throw other factors out of focus. Historical factors are not nearly so important as those factors of today, for it is not so much what shaped an 'ought' in the past that matters as the factors that combine to keep it alive. It is suggested that historical approaches would find their appropriate setting as part of a general sociological approach. Another weakness is the mystical, nationalistic flavour which it imparted to theories about law, but this has not penetrated through to this country. Again, historical interpretation can so easily be made to lend its support to the particular ideology of the interpreter. Savigny's teaching evolved out of his strongly conservative, anti-revolutionary, Civil law bias. Spencer's biological parallels could just as easily have led him to conceive of the state as an unifying organism in which the individual loses his identity; in fact, it was only his individualist outlook that led him to other conclusions. Of the manner in which historical interpretation was used in support of the Nazi ideology it is not necessary to speak.

Against all this, some of the practical contributions of the Historical School, leaving aside its more extreme manifestations, have had lasting effect. It provided the great stimulus to the historical study of law and legal institutions, which has ingrained a sense of historical perspective in the outlook of lawyers. In England it inspired men like Maine, Maitland and Holdsworth and others scarcely less famous. It has demonstrated the perils of over-hasty legislative experiment and has taught the cautionary lesson that development should flow, in some spheres at any rate, within the channels of tradition. As to the nature of law, it has demonstrated the connection between some parts of law and cultural evolution, and the need to delve into the past sometimes in order to obtain a full understanding of the law as it is at present. Above all, it awakened new confidence in convictions relating to the content of law by insisting that formal criteria of validity are of subordinate importance. In this way it may have had an indirect result in paving the way for the resurgence of natural law in this century, which seeks to base even the validity of law on its moral content.

On the question what kind of a concept of law would be apt for historical investigation, it would seem that so far as the study seeks to uncover the factors that have shaped the institutions of today what is needed is a concept which not only identifies the 'oughts' of the law, but also includes the dynamic forces that have shaped and developed them. So far as the investigation is anthropological, a formal criterion of identification does not appear to be appropriate or applicable. A broader conception is needed and one that will distinguish institutions according to function, the scale of their social operation and the social reaction to them. It is clear from what has been said that anthropological inquiries have given to the 'ought' fascinating new interpretations.

READING LIST

C K Allen *Law in the Making* (7th edn), pp 87-129.
J Bryce 'The Interpretation of National Character and Historical Environment on the Development of the Common Law' (1908) 24 Law Quarterly Review 9.
J C Carter *Law: Its Origin, Growth and Function.*
M Gluckman *Judicial Process among the Barotse* (revised edn).
A M Hocart *Kings and Councillors.*
H I P Hogbin *Law and Order in Polynesia.*
H U Kantorowicz 'Savigny and the Historical School' (1937) 53 Law Quarterly Review 326.
J M Lightwood *The Nature of Positive Law* ch 12.
K Lipstein 'The Reception of Western Law in Turkey' (1956) 6 Annales de la Faculté de Droit d'Istanbul 10, 225.
K Lipstein 'The Reception of Western Law in a Country of a Different Social and Economic Background: India' (1957-58) 8-9 Revista del Instituto de Derecho Comparado 69, 213.
H J S Maine *Ancient Law* (ed F Pollock) chs 1 and 5.
B Malinowski 'A New Instrument for the Interpretation of Law—especially Primitive' (1941-42) 5 Yale Law Journal 1237.
E W Patterson *Jurisprudence* pp 403-435.
K R Popper *The Open Society and its Enemies* (5th edn) I and II.
R Pound *Interpretations of Legal History* chs 1, 4.
G H Sabine *A History of Political Thought* (3rd edn) chs 30, 32, 35.
F C von Savigny *On the Vocation of Our Age for Legislation and Jurisprudence* (2nd edn trans A Hayward).
W T Stace *The Philosophy of Hegel* Part IV, pp 374-438.

CHAPTER 19

Economic approach

The discussion of this approach will proceed mainly with reference to the doctrines of Karl Marx and Friedrich Engels with which it is usually associated. It might be regarded as a variant of the historical approach in so far as it has sought to unfold a pattern of evolution; but it also concerns the part which law has played and is playing in society and as such is sociological. This approach, like these others, concerns the content of law, the nature of which is regarded as being but a reflex of an economic substrate. Another point is that the original Marxist interpretation challenged the indispensability of law and foreshadowed its eventual disappearance. 'Law' in Marxist theory lumps together laws and their administration and it is in this sense that the term will be employed herein.

Many factors contributed to the rise of the movement under review. The critical spirit of positivism had accustomed people to challenge existing standards. Advances in contemporary science shed their influence in the same direction. The failure of religious ideals to stand up to critical inquiry led to the substitution of materialist ideals in their place. The new movement had as its object the improvement of the condition of poor and working people, who found in it new hope and encouragement. Formal positivism was largely indifferent to the justice or injustice of existing conditions of life. Although Bentham was more concerned with reform than with formal analysis, his successors in the analytical tradition, notably the Austinians, concerned themselves increasingly with the law as laid down and not with efforts to improve it. In consequence, positivism fell into disfavour with those who were dissatisfied with existing conditions, and was regarded as casting a cloak of legality around injustices. The new movement was iconoclastic and exposed the injustices concealed behind traditional façades. It appealed to a certain type of mind, which for the first time felt enlightened and emancipated. Unfortunately, the enthusiasm which it aroused prevented its own assumptions from being subjected to similar scrutiny. It called for action and change and was revolutionary in purpose and appealed to all who felt inclined to rebel against complacency and monotony.

The interpretation of law as part of an economic interpretation of social evolution is a by-product of the social and political theories of Marx and Engels, which have since been put into practice by Soviet Russia and certain other countries. Russia was the first to do so, and for over twenty years until after the 1939–45 war remained the only one. Other countries have largely copied her, so the ensuing discussion will proceed with reference to Russia. One difficulty in the way of its presentation is the absence of a theory of law worked out on this basis. Neither Marx nor Engels elaborated one for reasons that will shortly become clear. What they say about law is incidental to their views on society generally. Jurists in Russia today, however, are having to work out a theory of law, but as yet none of them has said a great deal that is new: each plays a variation on the basic theme derived from Marx and

Engels. It is therefore to their works that attention should first be paid. The practical application of their doctrines since their day has necessitated certain changes and adaptations, which leads to the next difficulty, namely, deciding into what periods the narrative should fall. On this there is no unanimity[1]. For present purposes it is sufficient to adhere to the following scheme. (1) The period of 'war communism', including the 'theoretical' period from Marx to 1920, ie the establishment of the proletarian dictatorship in Russia. (2) The period from 1921 to 1937, which could be subdivided into the period of the New Economic Policy, the NEP, from 1921 to 1929; and from 1930 to 1937, the 'construction of socialism', during which the NEP was abandoned. (3) The period from 1938 to the present day, which could be subdivided into the period from 1938 until the death of Stalin in 1953, which may be called 'consolidation of socialism'; and the post-Stalin era, which may be called 'construction of communism', at least since 1961.

THE PERIOD FROM MARX TO 1920

The views about law of Karl Marx (1818–1883) and of his great friend, Friedrich Engels (1820–1895), are to be gleaned from their various works. Marx was influenced, so Lenin insisted, by developments in contemporary science, in particular the prevalent belief that the physical world was governed by a universal principle of causation. He believed that social phenomena were likewise governed by some universal principle, namely, the economic principle. In this respect he was a social scientist in that he sought descriptive propositions about social evolution. He was also influenced by the dialectic philosophy of Hegel, but differed from him over the notion that reality and, indeed, history was the unfolding of an 'idea'. On the contrary, said Marx, the 'idea' is a reflection of reality, otherwise the idea is only a distortion or 'ideology''; and this is what he meant when he said of Hegel's dialectics that 'with him it is standing on its head. It must be turned right side up again'[2]. Marx and Engels insisted on being 'scientific'. Although, like Hegel, they visualised history as unfolding according to the recurrent conflict between a thesis and an anti-thesis[3], in place of his ideals they substituted material and economic forces as the determinant factors of development. 'Scientific socialism', so they preached, must replace 'utopian socialism'.

The primitive tribal society, in their view, contained no anti-thesis within itself as long as there was equal distribution of commodities. It was a communist order, an Eden, before it was perverted through selfishness and greed. When distribution became unequal, the society was destroyed and split into classes patterned by the division of capital and labour[4]. Man became avaricious and self-centred with no thought of the common weal[5]. The value of commodities then came to be governed by the cost of the labour required to produce them. The place of the tribal society was taken by the state, which became the instrument of the stronger class, whether this is described as a slave-owner's state, a feudal state, or bourgeois state. The modern capitalist

---

1 See on this Hazard Introduction to *Soviet Legal Philosophy* (20th Century Legal Philosophy Society v) pp xix–xx.
2 Preface to the second German edition of Marx *Capital* vol I.
3 See p 385 ante.
4 For Renner's analysis as to how this came about, see p 302 ante.
5 Engels *The Origin of the Family, Private Property and the State.*

state necessarily involves the domination of the labouring majority by a minority, which controls the economic resources of the country; law is an instrument by which this minority exploits the workers. The tension between capital and labour will eventually break into conflict, a revolt of the majority against the minority, and the majority will gain control of the economic resources and will seek to eliminate the minority. The state thus established is the proletarian dictatorship.

> 'After the proletariat has grasped power, the class struggle does not cease. It continues in new forms, and with ever greater frenzy and ferocity, for the reason that the resistance of the exploiters to the fact of socialism is more savage than before'[6].

The dictatorship of the proletariat is said to represent 'the highest form of democracy possible in a class society'[7], and is also 'substantially the dictatorship of the Party, as the force which effectively guides the proletariat'[8]. The term 'democracy' is here used in a sense different from that in the West. The proletarian dictatorship is indeed a dictatorship, but in so far as it has been formed by the masses and acts in their interests it is a democracy[9]. The distribution of commodities at this stage of development will follow the maxim, 'From each according to his ability, to each according to his work'[10]. Inequality inevitably persists and state organisation continues to be necessary.

Out of this conflict will eventually emerge communism or the classless society. Domination will cease, inequalities will vanish, and with them the state and law will disappear as well. It is not altogether clear when Marx and Engels expected the advent of utopia. It may be when production has reached such a point that all people can be supplied with their needs without having to compel them to work, in short, when the maxim, 'From each according to his ability, to each according to his needs', can be applied. Or it may be when crime and other forms of wrongdoing have been eliminated, for as long as these continue the machinery for their repression will continue to be needed. Lenin believed that after the removal of the economic causes of crime, a great part of, if not all, wrongdoing will disappear. Recent Soviet jurists have tended to postpone the disappearance of the state until capitalism disappears in all, or most other countries, in other words, when the danger of capitalist encirclement disappears[11].

Marx supposed that the defects and inequalities in human society were due to factors that lay in production and economic conditions and outside the nature of Man. This assumes that Man is by nature equal and free, and that only in the communist society would he be able to realise his true self. For, as both Lenin and Stalin asserted, the individual will only be liberated when the mass is liberated. 'Everything' said Stalin 'for the mass'[12].

From all this the following doctrines are deducible as to the nature of law.

---

6 Vyshinsky *The Law of the Soviet State* p 39; see also p 3.
7 *Vyshinsky* p 41.
8 Stalin *Questions of Leninism* I p 33.
9 Civil rights are restricted on class lines: first Constitution 1918 arts 9, 23, 65.
10 Constitution of 1977, Art 13; on the 1936 Constitution see *Vyshinsky* pp 77, 204 et seq.
11 *Vyshinsky* pp 59–62, 65–70; Golunskii and Strogovitch 'The Theory of the State and Law' in *Soviet Legal Philosophy* pp 353, 400.
12 Stalin 'Anarchism or Socialism' i *Collected Works* (1946) p 295; Lenin 24 *Collected Works* (4th edn 1935) p 241.

DOCTRINE OF THE ECONOMIC DETERMINATION OF LAW. Ideas, according to Marx, are reflections of reality; and in this respect he differed, as pointed out, from Hegel, who maintained that reality was but a reflection of an idea. A false or distorted appreciation of reality was to Marx an 'ideology' in a derogatory sense. The bourgeois picture of society is an ideology distorted to suit the situation of those who present it, namely, the ruling class, in whose interest it is to give a false picture and quieten the masses and further their own ends. Law is a superstructure on an economic system; economic facts are independent of and antecedent to law. The notion that law is a reflex of an economic substrate is not an ideology, for it accords with reality. Bourgeois *theories* of law, however, which present it as something other than this, are distortions. There may be other super-structures and other ideologies, eg religion, but they all have their ultimate reality in the economic background.

DOCTRINE OF THE CLASS CHARACTER OF LAW. Law is an instrument used by the economic rulers to keep the masses in subjection. Even after the estab-lishment of the proletarian dictatorship law will continue to be used as the instrument by which the working-class majority can crush and eliminate the capitalist minority. There will still be the need to force people to work, to punish wrongdoing, to stamp out 'counter-revolutionary' and other subversive activities, and to maintain some inequality of distribution, which is still unavoidable. Law is thus an instrument of domination.

DOCTRINE OF THE IDENTITY OF LAW AND STATE. The state came into existence as soon as there was unequal distribution of commodities and class dis-tinctions developed. Law was one of the means whereby the capitalist minority sought to preserve and increase its power, while those who had property sought to protect it against those who had not. So law and the state in capitalist societies together form an apparatus of compulsion wielded by the minority to oppress and exploit the working majority. Even in the proletarian dictatorship these will remain as instruments of com-pulsion and domination. The state, therefore, reflects an essentially une-qual condition of affairs. The depiction of it as a just and fair institution is again a distorted ideology. It will be noticed that this doctrine of the identity of law and the state corresponds with that of Kelsen, but for different reasons.

DOCTRINE OF THE WITHERING AWAY OF LAW AND STATE. When the communist or classless society arrives, there will no longer be any domination or inequality. Therefore, the instruments of domination, ie law and the state, will, in the words of Engels, 'wither away' and be replaced by 'an admin-istration of things'. If it is asked how criminality and wrongdoing will be dealt with, Lenin replied that, in the first place, no special machinery will be needed:

> 'this will be done by the armed people itself as simply and readily as any crowd of civilised people, even in modern society, parts a pair of combatants or does not allow a woman to be outraged': secondly, 'we know that the fundamental social cause of excesses which consist in violating the rules of social life is the exploitation of the masses, their want and their poverty. With the removal of this chief cause, excesses will inevitably begin to 'wither away'[13].

---

13 Lenin *State and Revolution* p 70.

This doctrine of the withering away of the state is an uncomplimentary comment on the dialectics of Hegel. It was observed in the last chapter that his abstractions were such that they can be used to support even two such irreconcilable doctrines as Nazism and Marxism. It is now worth noticing that, whereas to Hegel the state was the highest achievement of human endeavour, Marx used his method of reasoning to arrive at the extinction of the state. It should also be noted in this connection that what will wither away is the proletarian dictatorship, which is, as it were, a step towards the classless society. The bourgeois state will not wither away; this has to be smashed and destroyed.

The reason why neither Marx nor Engels elaborated a theory of law is obvious. Law, in their view, is an instrument of domination, to be done away with, not developed and elaborated. Although they regarded law as reflecting economic conditions, it would not be fair to suggest that they thereby deprived it of all its creative force. It can play, and has played, a creative part, but always conditioned by its economic substrate. In the proletarian dictatorship law should be a means to an end, namely, to prepare the way for the classless society. It is thus in instrument of governmental policy[14]. There is certainly rule *by* law; there cannot be a rule *of* law, for reverence of the law for its own sake is a 'bourgeois fetish'. Since law is but a means to an end, it should on no account hamper the work of the proletarian state. There should be no division between 'public' and 'private' law, because (a) law being a reflection of an economic substrate, there will be no public and private spheres of interests in the economy, and (b) law being an instrument of domination, only the proletarian government will dominate and there is thus only governmental law. Nor will there be any separation of powers. Judicial independence as traditionally understood must go. Judges, like law itself, are instruments of policy and must give effect to this, to which end they have to be strongly indoctrinated before they can be fit for office. Thus, in the early days of the proletarian dictatorship in Russia judges had to apply their 'socialist consciousness' of justice and such Tsarist laws that were useful guides[15] in the absence of decrees of the Soviet government. Even so, they did not have to apply a provision which they considered unsuited to the new conditions[16]. In criminal cases severer penalties were to be inflicted on enemies of the régime than on those who interfered with their fellow citizens from purely personal motives[17]. It was left originally to the judge to decide whether a given act was prejudicial to the régime or was purely personal in character. This was the notorious 'principle of analogy' according to which all socially harmful conduct could be treated as criminal[18]. This doctrine went into decline[19], but it did carry the interesting corollary that conduct which, although technically criminal, was not socially harmful should not be treated as such. Equally drastic was 'guilt by association' whereby members of the family of a person convicted of certain offences

14 'Law is a political measure, it is politics': Lenin 1916; 23 *Collected Works* (4th edn) p 36.
15 Decree No 1 (Courts) 27 November 1917 [1917] 1 Sob Uzak RSFSR, No 4, item 50; also Statute of the People's Court November 30 1918, art 22.
16 Civil Code RSFSR, Decree of 31 October 1922, art 1.
17 Civil Code 1922, art 5.
18 Art 10, Criminal Code RSFSR, operative 1 June 1922 [1922] 1 Sob Uzak RSFSR, No 15, item 153; Decree of November 22 1926 [1926] 1 Sob Uzak RSFSR No 80, item 600, art 16.
19 Excluded in the Criminal Code RSFSR, 1 January 1961; (1961) Sovestskaia Iustitsiia, No 17, pp 5 et seq, art 3.

against the state, who knew of his activities but did not denounce him, were punishable. This, too, has gone. Finally, although it would not be true to aver that individuals should enjoy no liberties other than those expressly conferred upon them, there has to be nevertheless a strict regulation of these, especially in regard to property, according to governmental policy.

The principal difficulty in the way of assessing the doctrines of Marx and Engels lies in sifting the parts that are valuable from irrelevancies. In the first place, causation is no longer the inexorable principle governing the material world. This is similar to the erroneous assumption made by the Historical School. In social phenomena Marx and Engels sought to discover in the economic principle the counterpart of causation. Towards the end of his life Engels admitted that both he and Marx had exaggerated the economic influence and that it was not the *sole* motivating factor in human society[20]. What they would say, then, is that it is the ultimate or most important factor. That depends on the criterion of 'ultimate' and 'most important'. It ceases to be objective and becomes a matter of personal evaluation. The economic factor is undoubtedly important, but other factors have also to be reckoned with. Traffic law, for example, and large parts of criminal law are not based on economics. Indeed, the law which has to deal with violence to the person has been brought about by weaknesses in human nature. It is a wishful pretence to say that impulses such as anger, lust, revenge and jealousy, to mention but a few, are always rooted in economics. Today, the second and later generations of Soviet youth, which never knew capitalism, exhibit the same tendencies as youth elsewhere, and the Russians have started somewhat belatedly to develop criminology. Cupidity is not rooted exclusively in the economics of capitalism, but in human nature; increased availability of the good things of life whets the appetite for more. It has previously been pointed out that Marx's analysis of ownership is outdated in many respects; and although he foresaw the 'managerial revolution', he treated it as part of the dialectic of capitalist development and did not appear to have grasped its implications[1]. Modern economists have long since abandoned Marx's labour theory of value, which has become inapplicable to conditions of mass production and still more so to 'automation'. There can be no other conclusion than that an explanation of history in terms of some single determinant factor will inevitably fail, for it is bound to be an over-simplification.

This leads to another point. Both Marx and Engels purported to be 'scientific' and to expel ideologies. They found the cause of existing ills in economic conditions and suggested that the cure lies in a rectification of the economic system. So far as the economic factor is not the only one underlying law and society, the picture they drew of these in the light of the economic factor alone is incomplete; it is, in other words, a distortion of 'ideology' in Marx's own sense of that term. The degree of distortion is proportionate to the importance of the factors omitted. Marx seems to have confused legal theory, which may be described as an 'idology' in his sense of the term in that it reflects 'reality', and actual laws, which are an integral part of the economic infrastructure of society, ie part of the 'reality' itself. The classless society which he envisaged is the end which he wanted to bring about, and in this is a distortion of another kind, the introduction of a teleological consideration,

20 Engels, Letter to J Bloch, September 21–22 1890, and to H Starkenburg, January 25 1894: Marx-Engels *Selected Correspondence*.
1 See p 303 ante.

of politics into science, carrying with it a moral obligation to further this end; which is why Marxists try to force the pace of events, said to be evolutionary, by fostering revolutions in other countries. The ideological character of Marxism is likewise evidenced by the fact that the Soviet authorities dare not admit that there are flaws in the basic thesis. Their attitude has been that the 'truth' is there if only the correct interpretation can be found, or else to ignore or minimise awkward facts, thereby making the doctrine a religion.

Marx explained the evolution of society on the basis of the class struggle, the struggle between capitalists and workers. It is undeniable that there has been considerable friction between them, but generalisations should only be made with the utmost circumspection. 'The' class struggle is an abstract and misleading expression. 'The' class struggle, or any class struggle, should always be related to the place where it occurred, the period, the persons involved, and other circumstances[2]. It is a shortcoming in this respect that leaves Marx's handling of historical facts open to doubt. There have been many class struggles in the course of human history, all of which have influenced the development of law and society, eg religious struggles and not least between Trotskyists, Leninists and Chinese communists. It is also not clear why 'the class struggle' has to culminate in violence[3]. It may be that human nature being what it is, capitalists will not relinquish their position without force. Against that, Great Britain and the Scandinavian countries have shown a peaceful road to socialism. Although a recurrent pattern of conflict between workers and capitalists can be detected, the danger of erecting it into a principle and of arguing mechanically from it can be seen in the following fact. According to Marx, the tension between workers and capitalists grows more acute with the development of capital. This will tend to become more and more international, and hence the famous call to the workers of the world to unite. This led to the conclusion that the conflict will be precipitated in those countries where capitalism is most developed. Instead, it occurred in Russia, which was at that date semi-feudal and had only the rudiments of capitalism. This was why some orthodox Marxists at the time wondered whether they would not be better engaged in promoting a capitalist revolution instead. For a quarter of a century Russia remained alone, and the next country in which the conflict occurred was China, another backward state, and Cuba. The countries of Eastern Europe, which turned over to socialism at the end of the 1939-45 war, are scarcely examples, since, with the possible exception of Yugoslavia, the presence in those countries of the Russian armed forces at the critical time was no small factor. The other prediction that capitalism will become more and more international has been fulfilled up to a point. It fails, however, to take account of the strong sentiments of nationalism aroused by two world wars. It will thus be evident that there are dangers in erecting 'the class struggle' into a principle for the purpose of drawing the sweeping deductions that Marx sought to make.

Marx and Engels were strictly materialistic and the 'scientific method' figured prominently in their discussions and in those of their followers. Yet

2 See Corbin's appreciation of this in 'Jural Relations and their Classification (1920-21) 30 Yale Law Journal at 227 n 2, quoted p 6 ante.
3 'Evolutionists' maintain that socialism would evolve without the need for a violent revolution, eg the views of the French and Italian delegations to the XXV Communist Party Congress, February 1976; Solzhenitskyn *August 1914*.

they themselves could not escape from *a priori* assumptions in their nature as unscientific as those of the 'ideologists' whom they condemned. The adoption of Hegelian dialectics is one. Hegel treated values and natural phenomena as enjoying objective existence; but to treat values in this way is to derive 'is' from 'ought'. Further, conflicts in natural phenomena are not logical contradictions as required by the dialectic method. Marx would have been better advised not to have linked his 'class struggle' with this, since it is no more than an abstract juggle of words into which almost anything might be fitted[4]. Implicit in his adoption of it are the following assumptions: (a) that the dialectic interpretation of history is correct; (b) that the conflict between 'thesis' and 'anti-thesis' is identifiable with 'capital' and 'labour'; and (c) that the 'synthesis' will be the classless society. All three are open to question. The first two are insufficiently supported by evidence, the third has no evidence at all. Besides, why stop there? Why should not the classless society in turn become a thesis with its own anti-thesis, evolving into some other synthesis? Equally serious is the assumption that primitive society was happy, containing no anti-thesis within itself, communism without state and law; and that Man is so intrinsically nice that once the corrupting influence of economic maladjustment is done away with he will become a paragon of virtue. This looks like a reversion to a natural law theory, and by saying that primitive society had no anti-thesis within itself and that corruption set in with the unequal distribution of commodities, it would seem that the legend of the Fall of Man has been given a new meaning[5]. Besides, as pointed out at the end of the last chapter, this view of primitive society, especially its communist character and the absence of private property, is wholly suppositious. Again, though there is some truth in the assumption that the wickedness of men is prompted, perhaps in large measure, by economic conditions, it is no justification for Lenin's generalisation that all criminality stems from unequal economic conditions.

Actual legal systems usually precede theory. Russian Marxists, however, claim that their philosophical theory came first and that the legal system was modelled on that. This makes reality a reflection of an idea as Hegel had propounded, but whose thesis needed to be turned upside down according to Marx. Be that as it may, while the claim of Russian Marxists is true up to a point it should be noted that from the start, and increasingly since about 1920, legislators and judges were forced to proceed according to social needs, and jurists had to struggle to provide theoretical support[6]. So theory could not help having to follow actual law after all.

The characteristic feature of law in the Marxist picture of things is that it is an instrument of domination and exploitation wielded by capitalists against workers. In this there is a further erroneous inference. Whatever truth there might be in the statement that law has been used as an instrument for the repression of one class by another, it does not follow that this is, or need necessarily be, its sole function. For (a) regulation, and even coercion, is unavoidable to enable the intricate concatenation of interests and activities that make up any society to function efficiently. Engels said that after the advent of communism there will be an 'administration of things', which

4 In this respect there is force in Duhring's comment on which Engels pours such ridicule: *Anti-Dühring* Part I, ch 13.
5 For Kelsen's comment on the illusion of the basic virtue of Man, see *What is Justice?* pp 231 et seq.
6 Eg Pashukanis: see pp 407–408 post.

implies that regulation and judging of conduct will continue, perhaps more through executive than judicial machinery. What is this but 'law' under another name? (b) Law is a means of preserving security and moral standards. Not only is it necessary to set standards, but also to maintain them. This remains true in the proletarian dictatorship, which has to educate the masses in the values of communism, and also in the communist society where each new generation needs education[7]. In the execution of so huge a task law is indispensable. Therefore, it is implicit even in Marx's own teachings that law possesses an educative function other than exploitation and domination. (c) Law also serves to *restrain* oppression by classes or individuals. Rule by law inevitably leads to abuses, which could hamper the task of educating the masses by weakening people's respect and confidence in law. On the contrary, the educational task will be greatly aided if people see in law a bulwark. So, even for Marxist purposes, ideas of 'rule of law' and 'due process' are not so absurd after all. (d) Law gives practical expression to the balance that has to be struck between competing interests; and this is true even in Russia today where there are no classes. Judges no longer simply reflect governmental values, since all values are governmental. Law, then, ceases to be merely an instrument of domination and becomes a means of adjusting interests, and, more important, a measure of judicial independence becomes necessary. Above all (e) law satisfies the ineradicable human craving for justice, ie like treatment in like cases, and certainty; both of which require rules and precedents. Marx it would seem, failed to distinguish sufficiently between the various uses to which law can be put and has sometimes been put; and, in any case, his observations should be limited to the purpose which law was being made to serve, as he saw it, in some countries in his day.

When the proletarian dictatorship was established in Russia the repressive use of law reached greater heights than before, but this was explained as a temporary phase and a means of achieving utopia to which this period of travail would give birth. For there was still a capitalist minority, which the working-class majority had to dominate and eventually eliminate. By the mid-1930s, however, there was no longer a minority left, but law continued to flourish even more vigorously[8]. Indeed, it was possible to say in 1935 that all minorities had been eliminated[9]. The continued need for law, then, was to provide the economic organisation for the new society, which is of slow development; and to discipline the social conscience of people. It is easy to lead the ignorant. Education inevitably teaches people to think, and the more they are taught to do this, the harder it is to keep the power of thought within channels. Precisely for these reasons legal enforcement had to become increasingly ruthless. The state cannot wither by degrees, but has to remain strong until communism is achieved. It was also emphasised that the state is a defence mechanism, which is necessary as long as the Soviet Union is surrounded by enemies. All this was summed up in the Stalinist dialectic: 'The dying out of the State will come not through weakening State authority, but through intensifying that authority to the utmost'[10]. (Stalin did not

7 1977 Constitution, Preamble.
8 For Stalin's creation of 'Special Boards' within the Commissariat of Internal Affairs, see Decree of 5 November 1934 [1935] 1 Sob Uzak SSSR, No 11, item 84.
9 Sidney and Beatrice Webb *Soviet Communism: A New Civilisation?* I, p 83.
10 'Political Report of the Central Committee to the XVI Congress' 1930. This speech was attacked by Krushchev in his speech to the XX Communist Party Congress, 25 February 1956.

regard himself as bound by any law.) It may be that this aggrandisement of the state also lies behind the oft-stated need for a perpetual state of revolution. However, the point remains that law is not necessarily bound up with exploitation. What is left is a picture of law as an instrument of coercion no different from the concept familiar to the West. Modern Soviet disquisitions on the subject now seek to draw distinctions between 'bourgeois' and 'socialist' law and tend, on the whole, to avoid reference to domination and exploitation[11].

The state, according to Marx, is an engine of compulsion by which the economic rulers keep workers in subjection. So the idea of a 'classless state', which developed under Stalin after about 1938 and has become prominent since, undermines the Marxist foundation of state in class conflict. Krushchev adopted the policy of 'peaceful co-existence', which meant that other states were not to be treated as constant enemies[12]. This weakened further the Stalinist justification of the continued existence of the state as a defence mechanism. Krushchev also took the line that the 'classless state' is an intermediate stage, 'a state of the whole people', interposed between the proletarian dictatorship and communism, which might even be called the 'first stage of communism'[13]. This is another contradiction of Marxist doctrine according to which the state is solely an institution of class inequality and oppression. It also contradicts Stalin's thesis of the state as a defence mechanism. The Communist Party has become the 'party of the whole people', which, on the face of it, is a Marxist absurdity, since the party is that part of a class which is organised to serve as its spearhead and guide in the struggle. What was now meant, as explained by Krushchev, was that the Communist Party is one of two 'friendly classes' in an 'all-people's state'. In these circumstances the continued existence of the Party can only be a return to a new ruling class[14]. The 1977 Constitution openly acknowledges the elitist character of the Party in its Preamble and in Art 6. Art 99 confers the power of nominating candidates for election on the Party and other public organisations; but the Party remains the guiding force as Art 6 lays down. The contradiction of Marxist dogma that state and class-conflict are synonymous remains glaringly obvious.

It was predicted that with the arrival of the classless society law will 'wither away', but that there will remain 'an administration of things'. This follows from the thesis that law is but the reflection of an oppressive economic system: once oppression is removed, there will be an economic system without law. As was admitted, however, there will still have to be some regulation of behaviour, which is what Engels referred to as 'an administration of things', and the point has been increasingly recognised in later Programmes of the Soviet Communist Party. According to Krushchev 'Under communism, too, there will remain certain public functions similar to those now performed by the state, but their nature and the methods by which they will be accomplished will differ from those existing in the present stage'[15]. In other words, there will probably be a tendency to deal with more and more areas by

---

11 Golunskii and Strogovitch 'The Theory of the State and Law' in *Soviet Legal Philosophy* (trans Babb) pp 385-386, 392.
12 Now enshrined in the 1977 Constitution, art 28.
13 'A state of the whole people' is in the Preamble to the 1977 Constitution.
14 Cf Djilas *The New Class*.
15 Report to the XXI Extraordinary Congress of the Communist Party of the Soviet Union, reported in *Pravda* 28 January 1959.

ministerial decree than by courts: transfer, not abolition, from the category of private law to public or administrative law. This would appear to be a verbal point: the regulation of conduct which will remain is not to be *called* 'law'. For, if 'law' is defined with reference to domination and oppression, when these have disappeared what remains will not be 'law'. There may be a deeper reason. To Marxists the word 'law' carries a strong pejorative connotation, and because it is so associated in their minds with everything unjust and oppressive, they cannot bring themselves to continue to apply so odious a word once perfection has been reached. Despite all this, it is obvious that a large sphere of human regulation will have to remain even after the arrival of the classless society. Whether this is to be called 'law' or not is immaterial. A similar obsession with the pejorative connotation of 'state' led Lenin to deny that the proletarian dictatorship was anything more than a 'semi-state' or 'commune' state. It has also subsequently been conceded, that there can indeed be 'law' without a state, and in this way it was sought to uphold international law. On the other hand, there developed the theory, which Stalin found convenient, that the state is superior to law. All these are not just deviations from Marx, but denials of the class character of law, its identity with state and its use solely as an instrument of exploitation. One should be chary of levelling accusations of contradiction in a philosophy which is rooted in the Hegelian logic of contradictions; but even so there are contradictions and contradictions.

Finally, the maxim, which embodies the goal towards which all this endeavour is directed, namely, 'from each according to his capacity, to each according to his needs', suffers from the weakness that it is difficult to see how needs are to be measured and what checks there will be on exorbitant demands. One wonders whether there ever will be abundance, for the more people have the more are their appetites likely to be whetted[16].

The theories of Marx and Engels have been dealt with at length because they have dominated subsequent theorising in Russia. Immediately after the Bolsheviks seized power on 7 November 1917 (October 25 according to the Julian calendar which prevailed in Russia), the tendency was to leap into communism without the transitional period. This was due, not just to enthusiasm, but doubts among the Bolsheviks themselves of their permanence. When, however, their reign was assured, they began to appreciate the immensities of the tasks ahead and a more realistic approach set in.

THE PERIOD FROM 1921-1937

After the revolution in Russia, the proletarian dictatorship was established along Marxist lines between the years 1918 and 1920. The period from 1921 to 1937, as already pointed out, can be divided into two parts. The first, which lasted till about 1929, may conveniently be described as the period of the New Economic Policy, the NEP, while the second from 1930 onwards, marks a departure from the NEP and the construction of socialism.

The establishment of the proletarian dictatorship required a 'revolutionary legality' by means of which the victorious majority could dominate and eventually exterminate the capitalist minority. This period did not prove to be as short-lived as had been hoped. So codes were introduced, and

16 See p 67 ante.

professional judges appointed. Whereas in 1918 and 1920 judges had been enjoined to rely on their 'socialist consciousness of justice'[17], they had now to abide by 'the general principles of the Soviet legislation and the general policy of the government of the Workers and Peasants'[18]. Having won freedom from the power of the Tsars, the revolutionaries set up an even more ruthless power-structure to prevent opposition to themselves. The cohesion of the state would be wrecked if divisive values were allowed to develop and people were allowed freedom to act in pursuance of them. Accordingly, severe repression was introduced, which included one of the most effective ways of nipping in the bud the growth of unwelcome values, namely, a secret police to inhibit people from expressing views other than orthodox among themselves. Without communication ideas cannot spread.

There was also what Berman felicitously styles the 'parental' function of law[19]. The Party had to guide the masses to communism by educating and training them rather like children for the part they would have to play in the future[20]. All this was reflected in the administration of law, for it was recognised early that law enforcement had a decisive role to play in this process. The need to educate and train the populace justified virtually unlimited activities by the secret police, trials in secret and the like, and enabled these to flourish notwithstanding constitutional guarantees of free speech and respect for the individual. Side by side with this was an exclusive and ceaseless propaganda campaign coupled with a jealous exclusion of foreign influence and contact. The latter has only been relaxed slightly in very recent times. The work of educating the people for a communist society would be gravely impaired, if not undone, if they were allowed to see that conditions elsewhere were at least not worse, and in some respects perhaps better, than in Russia.

The wave of nationalisation that followed in the wake of the initial revolutionary ardour proved to have been premature. The Soviet state was faced with crises of the first magnitude in the spheres of production and distribution. The only way out was to re-introduce private enterprise and capital to a certain extent. A drastic revision of ideas was called for, and the New Economic Policy was decided on at the Tenth Communist Party Congress in March 1921.

The feature of the NEP was that it constituted a partial compromise between Marxist ideas and capitalism under the strict supervision of the state. The NEP has been happily described as 'state-controlled private enterprise'. It was necessary in the interests of the nation to give scope to private enterprise and at the same time to prevent an abuse of it. Private enterprise and private rights were subordinate to the national interest, and were deemed to be forbidden unless expressly permitted. Alongside this, in the interests of efficiency, Lenin introduced the concept of 'one man management'[1].

Another characteristic of the period was the feeling of tension that pervaded

---

17 Statute of the People's Court, November 30 1918, art 22.
18 Constitution of 1925, art 2. See also Draft of a New Criminal Code of the RSFSR 1930; and Draft of the Fundamental Bases of the Criminal Code of the RSFSR 1930.
19 *Justice in Russia* Part II.
20 To mould the citizen of communist society is one of the 'principal tasks of the state': 1977 Constitution, Preamble.
 1 First Decree on the Trusts, 10 April 1923 [1923] 1 Sob Uzak RSFSR, No 29, item 336; followed by the Second Decree on the Trusts, 29 June 1927 [1927] 1 Sob Uzak RSFSR, No 39, item 392.

the nation, which had just emerged from the throes of an unprecedented upheaval, and was faced with internal crises and surrounded by enemies. Little wonder that a state of emergency was felt to exist, and an attitude of the utmost severity was adopted towards political deviations.

To meet the new situation a theory of law was evolved. The principal contribution of this period was that of Pashukanis (1891–1937)[2] who was strongly influenced by two German writers, Jellinek and Laband. He developed what is known as the 'commodity-exchange theory'. All law, he maintained, was built up of relations between individuals. He followed Marx in believing that law was a reflection of economic conditions, but departed from Marx in supposing it to consist of the exchange of commodities between individuals[3]. Commodity-exchange calls for individual rights and legal relationships. The various aspects of law reflect these relationships. The thesis that commodity-exchange is the basis of law has been challenged by Dr Schlesinger as being historically untrue. He quotes primitive blood-feuds and the payment of *wergild* and asks in what sense these relationships reflect commodity-exchange[4]. Pashukanis also maintained that law presupposes theoretical equality, not subjection. Law is the peaceful means of settling conflicting interests of persons, who are treated as being on an equal footing however much they may be unequal in fact. In the ultimate perfect society individual interests will not conflict, for there will then be unity of purpose. Therefore, there will be no need for law. As Dr Schlesinger points out, Pashukanis's contention leaves unexplained why there cannot be individual relationships apart from commodity-exchange, and the relationships entered into in the course of *production* of commodities as distinct from their distribution[5]. Following from the last point, Pashukanis maintained that once the perfect society is reached the national economy will pass wholly into the hands of the state. Law, however, which presupposes conflict of individual interests, will come to an end. The implications of this are that law and state are distinct, which is a departure from Marx, and that law will wither away before the state. Finally, Pashukanis asserted that 'bourgeois law' had ceased to exist in Russia as far as production was concerned, but that so far as capitalism, and hence the conflict of private interests, was allowed to survive, Russian law still bore characteristics of it.

It is obvious that this theory was adapted only to the peculiar situation during the NEP. By about 1930 the position had altered. The concession made of necessity to private enterprise was withdrawn. The Second Revolution took place to eliminate the capitalists, a 'revolution from above' this time, ie by those in power to exterminate the minority whom they had hitherto permitted to exist. Private capital and private enterprise now became illegal, and the change was justified on the ground that the ultimate interest of the proletarian dictatorship rose superior to the sanctity of its own prior laws. Moreover, it was clear by 1930 that the long-awaited revolutions in other countries would not materialise and that Russia would have to wait a long time in the midst of her enemies. The state and its apparatus were a guarantee of defence and were necessary until all, or most, other countries had turned socialist. The withering away of the state was postponed until the remote future and less and less was said about it. Finally, in December

2 Pashukanis 'General Theory of Law and Marxism' in *Soviet Legal Philosophy* p 111.
3 Anthropologically the commodity-exchange idea is only partially true of primitive societies.
4 Schlesinger *Soviet Legal Philosophy* p 157.
5 *Schlesinger* p 152.

1936 a new Constitution was promulgated and acclaimed as the triumph of socialism. Strict observance of laws was insisted on. 'We need the stability of laws now more than ever' said Stalin[6].

Once the special conditions which had brought the NEP into being had passed, the theory of Pashukanis was outdated. His views were subjected to attacks, both fair and unfair. There was its obvious weakness that law was based on exchange and not on production. Marx himself had laid emphasis on production. There was, moreover, another deviation from Marx in that law was represented as regulating conflicting interests of equals and not as an instrument of domination. Next, law on his doctrine was destined to wither away before the state. By the 1930s law had become a firmly established institution in Russia, which necessitated three important changes in ideas. (a) The essentially sociological concept of Marx, Engels and Pashukanis, which viewed law as the product of the economic structure of society, was beginning to give way to a normative concept. (b) Since there was no longer a capitalist minority left, the idea of law as an instrument of domination began to be replaced by one that identified it with the wishes of the people themselves. (c) Though law was still viewed as an instrument of policy, it was also the means of providing security for expectations as determined by policy. Although law was still viewed as 'a political category ... Nevertheless law can no more be reduced simply to policy than cause be identified with effect'[7]. So law was seen to have an important task to perform and its withering away was something that should be indefinitely postponed, if not forgotten. Pashukanis's doctrine was attacked on the ground that it encouraged 'a nihilistic attitude' towards Soviet law. Some people went so far as to distort what he had said and alleged that he preached the withering away of the state as well, which it was pointed out was dangerous and inexpedient in the face of a hostile world. In view of the fact that law had become an important institution in Russia, it was necessary now to propagate the idea that Soviet law was somehow better and different from capitalist law. It is not surprising in consequence that Pashukanis's statement that Soviet law partook of the character of 'bourgeois law' grew increasingly unpopular. In the result Pashukanis was impeached and disappeared in 1937[8].

THE PERIOD FROM 1938 TO THE PRESENT

This period falls into two parts, from 1938 until the death of Stalin in 1953, and the post-Stalin era from 1953 onwards.

The first part witnessed the consolidation of socialism in the form of a monolithic state with complete subordination of legal theory to political expediency. This was also the period of the 'personality cult', fostered by Stalin. The doctrine of the 'classless state', previously mentioned, was propounded, and the state, represented by the Supreme Soviet, was held to be

---

6 Stalin 'On the Draft Constitution of the USSR 1936' *Leninism* p 402.
7 Vyshinsky 'The Fundamental Tasks of Soviet Law' 1938; Schlesinger *Soviet Legal Philosophy* 329.
8 It is interesting to note the violence of the language with reference to Pashukanis throughout Vyshinsky *The Law of the Soviet State*, especially at pp 54 et seq. Even making allowances for Vyshinsky's volatile nature one suspects that the succession of panegyric and abuse throughout the book is a smoke-screen for an official change of front.

superior to all its laws. A more interesting development was the Yugoslav attack on the Stalinist régime as a counter-revolutionary dictatorship. While differences in the conditions prevailing in different countries must inevitably yield different *applications* of Marxist doctrines, it was accounted 'deviation' to adopt any *interpretation* of them other than that of the USSR. In 1948 Yugoslavia, under Marshal Tito, insisted that each country should be left to interpret Marxism in its own way, and denounced the Soviet model under Stalin as a betrayal of Marxist-Leninism. It was alleged to be nothing but a form of capitalism exploited by a new ruling class of bureaucrats, who have merely substituted a bureaucratic state in place of a bourgeois state[9]. Whereas Russia postponed the decline of state power and law to some distant epoch, Yugoslavia was prepared to phase it into immediate effect as and when it proved feasible. This is the approach which was termed 'Titoism'. It called for new methods: for instance, in place of state ownership there should be 'social ownership' by free associations of producers; and workers should take as much part as possible in economic management. Such 'industrial self-management' is achieved by allowing each enterprise to be run by a workers' council, a measure of overall control and co-ordination being maintained by the appointment of a director by the People's Committee of the Commune[10]. The state as such is still responsible for order and national defence, but its other aspects could well be allowed to wither away. Law and state are not synonymous; the state may go, but law must remain.

After the death of Stalin there was a relaxation of centralisation; Stalin had been a firm believer in it. Krushchev introduced decentralisation in his administrative reforms of 1957, which were criticised as too localised and unco-ordinated. Accordingly, in 1965 centralisation was reintroduced with minor modifications towards giving state enterprises wider powers.

At the Twentieth Party Congress the image of Stalin was dethroned by Krushchev, who denounced him as a criminal and for fostering a 'personality cult'[11]. This made the Russians rather more inclined to self-criticism than they would otherwise have been and readier to admit, to themselves though not openly, that there might be some truth in the Yugoslav gibes after all. Accordingly, the breach with Yugoslavia was patched up by the admission that there could be 'several roads to socialism', although there has been a renewal of differences from time to time. There was also relaxation of some of the other rigid controls. In Russia this had no marked effect, probably because the controls had never been felt to be unduly oppressive by the mass of people, who had no tradition of freedom. In Hungary, on the other hand, the result of de-control was the uprising in 1956, which had to be crushed by massive Russian intervention, and controls were re-imposed. Later in 1968 the doctrine of 'several roads to socialism' was forgotten when Czechoslovakia attempted to introduce a relaxed form of 'communism with a human face'. This, too, was crushed by massive intervention by Russia with somewhat half-hearted support from her Warsaw Pact partners. A different

9 Cf Djilas *The New Class*.
10 One-man management was introduced in Russia by Lenin: see p 406 ante. Under Stalin the 'triangle' doctrine was introduced in the early 1930s whereby the manager had to be guided by the Party secretary and the shop steward. In 1937 this system was abolished and the manager became all-powerful. It was this managerial class which was the principal target for Djilas's attack. Krushchev restored the 'triangle' principle, but after 1965 there was a return to the all-powerful manager. See the Statute on the Socialist State Production Enterprise *Ekonomicheskaia Gazeta* 20 October 1965, p 24, Part V.
11 Speech to the XX Communist Party Congress 25 February 1956.

breach has occurred between Russia and Albania, supported by China, and between Russia and China. The Chinese, too, insist on their own interpretation of Marxism and accuse the Russians of having betrayed socialism. This clash is more than just ideological; it is a bid for leadership of the communist world, the outcome of which remains to be seen.

It has already been pointed out that Krushchev emphasised the classless character of Soviet society where there is now a 'state of the whole people', that the Communist Party is a 'party of the whole people' and one of two friendly partners in the 'all-people's state'[12]. These are all contrary to strict Marxism and only reconcilable with a revised version of it to the effect that a state, differing from the bourgeois state, can and should survive under socialism as the 'first stage of communism'. This is the period of the 'construction of communism'[13], for although socialism has won in Russia, the goal of communism is still afar. Three conditions remain to be fulfilled before its advent. (a) The menace of 'capitalist encirclement' has to be removed, which calls for strict protective measures, within and without; (b) the masses need to be completely re-educated; and (c) economic abundance has to be secured, which necessitates experiments. 1980 was set as a vague, tentative date for the dawn of the New Age; but nothing has happened. The problem is to know who decides, and on what criteria, that the time has arrived. Unless some clear indication of this is forthcoming, the vision of a state-free and law-free society must remain no more than a vision. After the fall of Krushchev, there was a return to severer treatment, but the doctrine of the state of the whole people remains[14].

Soviet jurists are now increasingly confronted with problems similar to those facing lawyers in other countries. Socialist legality is openly proclaimed and the need for theory is increasingly felt. In so far as laws serve the socialist economy they are just and deserve obedience from all bodies and persons; but they are still only instruments of policy, not objects of veneration in doctrine such as the 'rule of law' is still incomprehensible to Soviet jurists. One danger is that this attitude opens the way for an unscrupulous abuse of power by the rulers, as indeed happened under Stalin; another is that the patent association of law with expediency weakens respect for it and may well hamper the task of re-education. So 'due process' now tends to be insisted on[15]. Moreover, it was felt to be expedient to incorporate in the 1936

---

12 1977 Constitution, Preamble, art 1; and see *Program of the Communist Party of the Soviet Union* October 31 1961, II § 3. For the function of law and administration: 'Theses of the Central Committee of the Communist Party on the 50th Anniversary of the Great October Socialist Revolution', June 21 1967, Spravochnik Partunogo Rabotnika (1967) Vyp vii, Thesis 12; *The Theory of the State and Law* (ed Denisov) 247.

13 1977 Constitution, Preamble.

14 1977 Constitution, Preamble; Kanet 'The Rise and Fall of The "All-People's State": Recent Changes in Soviet Theory of the State' (1968) 20 Soviet Studies 81.

15 There were no procedural rules in the early decrees on courts: 24 November 1917 and 15 February 1918 [1917–18] 1 Sob Uzak RSFSR, No 4, item 50; No 28, item 366. The first procedural instruction was issued on 23 July 1918: No 53, item 597, although immediately prior to it judges were told not to let procedure hamper justice: No 52, item 589. The first statute, People's Court Act, was passed on 30 November 1918: No 85, item 889. Principles of civil procedure were enacted in 1922, and principles of criminal procedure were enacted on 31 October 1924 [1924] 1 Sob 1 Zak SSSR, No 24, item 204. General principles were enacted in the Constitution of 1936, arts 103, 110, 111, 127. Stalin's erosions of these were repealed on 19 April 1956 [1956] Vedomosti Verkhovnogo Soveta SSSR, No 9 (851), item 193. See now the Code of Criminal Procedure RSFSR 1961, and of Civil Procedure of the USSR and Union Republics 1962. For substantive criminal law, see the Code of 1922 [1922] 1 Sob Uzak RSFSR, No 15, item 153; replaced by the Code of 1926 [1926] 1 Sob Uzak

Constitution, which was hailed as the final victory of socialism in Russia, and in the 1977 Constitution a bill of fundamental rights[16]. Whether these are likely to have any practical effect may be doubted, for they are subject to the provision that 'Exercise by citizens of rights and freedoms must not injure the interests of society and the state and the rights of other citizens'[17]. Who decides?

There are important differences between the structure of the Soviet state and capitalist states, and these have wrought some changes in the Soviet concept of law. The guiding principle of Soviet law was floridly described as follows:

'In Soviet law such a single and general principle is that of socialism—the principle of a socialist economic and social system resting on socialist property, annihilation of exploitation and social inequality, distribution in proportion to labour, a guarantee to each member of society of the complete and the manifold development of all his (spiritual and physical) creative forces, and true human freedom and personal independence'[18].

The practical working of this principle has resulted in the following broad characteristics. In the first place, a distinction is drawn between ownership of the means of production and ownership of consumer goods. The former is wholly in the state[19], and only the latter is open to individuals, 'the home, garden and a cow'[20], the land belongs to the state, but the individual has title to his house[1]. The resale of consumer goods is subject to strict scrutiny. Some problem remains with producers who employ no labour and with individual artisans[2]. Apart from consumer goods purchased by means of income from labour, there is inheritance. This was forbidden in the *Communist Manifesto* as a method of perpetuating private ownership in means of production[3]; but inheritance has been increasingly recognised over the years[4]. There is another distinction between state ownership and ownership by co-operatives (*kolkhozes*), and there is also ownership by public and social organisations, eg trade unions[5]. Ownership by co-operatives facilitates the performance of functions and tasks. For instance, land is nationalised and

RSFSR, No 80, item 600; and see now the Fundamental Principles of Criminal Law of the USSR and of the Union Republics, 25 December 1968.

16 1936 Constitution, arts 122-135. The 1977 Constitution has a new 'Section II. The State and the Individual', setting out the 'rights', 'freedoms' and 'duties' of citizens.

17 1977 Constitution, art 39.

18 *Vyshinsky* p 77.

19 1977 Constitution, arts 9-10; Fundamental Principles of Civil Law of the USSR and of the Union Republics, 8 December 1961 ([1962] Vedomosti Verkhovnogo Soveta SSSR, No 50 (1085), item 525), art 21; Stalin *Economic Problems of Socialism in the USSR* (1952).

20 1977 Constitution, art 12; Fundamental Principles of Civil Law of the USSR and of the Union Republics, arts 19, 25.

1 Decrees of 19 February 1918 [1918] 1 Sob Uzak RSFSR, No 20, item 346, and of 20 August 1918, No 62, item 674.

2 1977 Constitution, art 17; Rules for Registration of Artisans and Handicraftsmen who are not members of co-operatives 1949 (Annotation to art 54 of the Civil Code 1961); Criminal Code of the RSFSR 1966, arts 153, 162; Decree of the Council of Ministers of the RSFSR, 4 August 1965.

3 Given effect in the Decree of 27 April 1918 [1918] 1 Sob Uzak RSFSR, No 34, item 456.

4 Civil Code 1922, arts 416-418; 1977 Constitution, art 12; Decree of 14 March 1945, 3 Sbornik Zak SSSR, 1945-1947 (1947) p 163; Fundamental Principles of Civil Law of the USSR and of the Union Republics 8 December 1961 [1962] Vedomosti Verkhovnogo Soveta SSSR, No 50 (1085), item 525, arts 117-119.

5 1977 Constitution, art 113 Basic Principles of Civil Legislation, art 20.

belongs to the state; *kolkhozes* have the use of it in perpetuity for the purpose of management and cultivation in strict conformity with state planning. This is a new form of ownership. The promise of abundance requires a centrally directed national economy, which has entailed not only a vast mass of regulations but also severe regimentation of the populace. Whether this helps or hinders the achievement of the ultimate objective is open to argument[6].

Secondly, in the sphere of production, economic and business relationships, eg between transport, producing and manufacturing concerns, are essentially transactions between state organs *inter se*. State organs are of two kinds, those that are subsidised by the state and those that have been made into autonomous bodies known as State Trusts. The latter are legal persons and correspond with the public corporations in other countries. Their property is, as it were, conceded to them by the state. The regulation of relations between these agencies, eg a manufacturing and a transport concern, is conducted on the basis that they are individual bodies.

Thirdly, there are the relations between the state and the individuals, eg between a State Trust and its employees; but these do not present any novel ideas.

Fourthly, industrial contracts are subject to the national economic plan[7]. Sometimes the plan directs that certain 'contracts of supply' shall be entered into and outlines the pattern of the nature, scope and timing of the obligations, leaving only details to be arranged by the contracting enterprises, who know best their own particular needs[8]. To meet the situation where they are unable to agree, a system of state arbitration *(Gosarbitrazh)* has developed, its function being not merely to deal expeditiously with disputes, but also to assist in negotiating the terms of proposed agreements[9]. At other times the plan only posits the goal to be attained and the enterprises are left to decide what contracts, if any, should be entered into and with whom. This leaves greater freedom of contract, though it is bounded by the task fixed by the plan for each enterprise. The freedom to select one's contracting partner promotes competitive efficiency, since an inefficient enterprise will not secure contracts. The achievement of a plan, and not profit, being the basis of contracts, it follows that specific performance, reinforced by penalties, and not compensation, is the accepted remedy. At the other end of the scale, contracts with the consumer public and between private individuals are no different from contracts in Western countries[10]. As consumer goods become increasingly available, these kinds of contracts increase too.

Fifthly, the admission of individual ownership in consumer goods involves a recognition of private rights, albeit to a restricted extent.

Sixthly, the regulation of all these relations, and particularly disputes between parties, have of necessity to be entrusted to tribunals, the courts, which have to be impartial and independent. The familiar doctrine of judicial independence and impartiality has thus gained ground. 'Judges and people's assessors shall be independent and subject only to the law': so runs

6 Cf *The Soviet Legal System* (eds Hazard, Shapiro and Maggs) p 180, where the editors suggest that it has actually hindered rational planning.
7 The Plan was treated as law after 1927 and the Second Decree on the Trusts 29 June 1927 [1927] 1 Sob Uzak RSFSR, No 39, item 392.
8 Decree of 18 February 1931 [1931] 1 Sob Uzak SSSR, No 10, item 102.
9 Decree of 3 May 1931 [1931] 1 Sob Uzak SSSR, No 26, item 203.
10 *Soviet Civil Law* (1959) I, pp 390 et seq; Fundamental Principles of Civil Law of the USSR and of the Union Republics 8 December 1961 [1962] Vedomosti Verkhovnogo Soveta SSSR, No 50 (1085), item 525, arts 14, 33-34, 36-37.

art 154 of the Constitution[11]. In this connection a tribute should be paid to the Soviet Supreme Court, a conscientious and fair-minded body of men, whose restraint and care have done much to raise the standard of the Soviet administration of justice[12]. If the law is to be administered with firmness, it must be certain and predictable.

Finally, observance of legislation is strictly enforced. Even so, the Constitution is not treated as a fundamental law. Both the Praesidium and the Council of Ministers have legislated contrary to it[13].

All this introduces new ideas in some respects, but only a redistribution of emphasis in others. Not only are Soviet jurists now facing the same sort of problems as those in other countries, but many laws themselves have approximated more and more to those obtaining elsewhere. Such has been the case with criminal law, family law, private rights and many other branches. Perhaps the biggest retreats have been in criminal and family law. The abandonment of the idea that crime is only the reflection of capitalist economy has induced a revised approach to the problem of criminality[14]. The vital influence of a stable family background on children has also been recognised[15]. Apart from these the following points may be noted:

(1) The emphasis has shifted from the protection of the interest of the individual in himself and his property to the state's interest in the individual. This does away with the distinction between 'public' and 'private' law; all law is 'public'[16].

(2) The safeguarding of 'socialist legality' and protection against abuses and oppression is entrusted to a body known as the *Prokuratura*, which may be compared with the Ombudsman[17].

(3) The task of counsel in courts is primarily to further the cause of socialism, and this circumscribes his duty towards his client[18].

(4) Since law is a superstructure on an economic foundation, its material sources lie in collectivisation and the presence of a People's State. Its formal source is legislation[19]. There is no doctrine of the separation of powers. Interpretation of legislation has to be in accordance with the principles of 'socialist legality', ie judges are bound to reflect official policy; which is difficult with the bulk, complexity and

---

11 For disciplining of judges, see Statute on Disciplinary Responsibility of Judges of the Courts of the RSFSR, 12 June 1965.

12 Statute of the Supreme Court of the USSR 1957, amended 30 September 1967.

13 Cf Stalin's declaration of the need to 'put an end to a situation in which not one but a number of bodies legislate', see *Leninism: Selected Writings* p 402. For the function of a constitution in a socialist state, see Farber and Rzhevskii *Questions of the Theory of Soviet Constitutional Law* (1967); Kalinychev 'The Principal Distinctive Characteristics of the Soviet Socialist Constitution', Soveskoe Gosudarstvo i Pravo 1967, No 11, p 48.

14 See p 400 ante. For recognition of inheritance, see p 411 ante.

15 Fundamental Principles of Legislation of the USSR and of the Union Republics on Marriage and the Family, 3 July 1968 [1968] Vedomosti Verkhovnogo Soveta SSSR, No 27, item 241, p 401. For the early liberalisation of divorce, see Decrees of 18 and 19 December 1917 [1917] 1 Sob Uzak RSFSR, No 10, item 152; No 11, item 160; Family Code 1926. For reversal of this policy, see Decree of 8 July 1944 [1944] Vedomosti Verkhovnogo Soveta SSSR, No 37, and now the Fundamental Principles 1968. For parental responsibility for crimes committed by children: Decree of 25 November 1935 [1935] 1 Sob Uzak RSFSR, No 1, item 1, ss 4, 6.

16 Lenin 29 *Collected Works* (3rd edn) 419.

17 Statute on the Procurator's Audit in the USSR 24 May 1955, No 9, item 222.

18 Sukharev 'Defend but do not excuse' (1967) Sovetskaia Iustitsiia, No 18, p 15.

19 Shebanov 'Sources of Law' *Encyclopaedia of Legal Knowledge* (1965) 171.

technicality of modern statutes. In this climate the question whether judges should adopt a creative attitude or merely abide by the letter of the law involves a delicate balance of considerations. Since state policy is paramount, it might be said that they are limited to inter-peting, not to creating rules. As pointed out earlier, however, this is not possible owing to the very nature of the judicial process. So what happens is that the judicial authorities, especially the Supreme Court, help to develop law by publishing instructions as to how laws should be applied for the guidance of other courts; and the *Prokuratura* is at hand to guard against aberrations of the courts. This is a new form of precedent in its broad sense and it has a creative function[20].

(5)   The educational function is an important aspect of law. Not only must the parties be made to feel that socialist laws are best and just, but legal administration as a whole has to assist in a thorough-going re-education of social conscience in preparation for communism[1]. Thus, there tends to be more sermonising in Soviet courts than in Western courts; and criminal courts especially are very much courts of morals[2].

(6)   At present custom plays a very minor role, as an occasional aid in the interpretation or application of legislation. Perhaps, in the future truly communist society, when people will have been socially re-educated, custom will come into its own as the principal source of socialist conscience.

All these developments, whether approximating to Western ideas or evolv-ing new ones, should show how far the Russians have gone in legal theory. The only way to reconcile them with traditional Marxism is to say that law will have to flourish before it will disappear. From at least one source ortho-dox Marxists may derive comfort and hope. This is the intervention on behalf of, or against, an accused or suspect person, and the performance of various legalistic and preventive functions by representatives of the group to which he belongs, be it a factory or garage (*obschestvennost*)[3]. The Comrades' (People's) Courts were revived by Krushchev in 1959 wherever there are at least fifty persons living or employed, eg farms, factories, apartment blocks and even schools[4]. They deal with minor matters, such as foul language, drunkenness, lateness for work and some kinds of civil disputes. Use has also been made of the 'public meeting' to denounce 'parasites', ie those living off unearned income[5]. These institutions might be thought to foreshadow a time when law and courts will have vanished and the people themselves deal with problems as they arise. The rationale behind them is that a state advancing

20 Other forms of interpretation are: *Authentic* interpretation by the Praesidium, which is authoritative (Constitution, art 49 (c)); *Doctrinal interpretation*, which is unofficial.
1 Bratus and Samoshchenko *The General Theory of Soviet Law* (1966) pp 86–90; Elivanov 'Our People's University of Legal Knowledge' Sovetskaia Iustitsiia 1966, No 18, p 1; Ryskalina *Radio Lecture Courses* Sotsialisticheskaia Zakonnost 1966, No 12 p 73; *The Theory of the State and Law* (ed Makichev) 497 et seq; Ioffe and Shargorodsky *Soviet Law and Government* II No 2 p 3 (who stress the importance of law 'in the field of ideological education').
2 Fundamental Principles of Criminal Legislation of the USSR and of the Union Republics 25 December 1958, No 1, item 6; Fundamental Principles of Civil Legislation of the USSR and of the Union Republics 8 December 1961, No 50, item 525.
3 1977 Constitution, art 161; see Feifer *Justice in Moscow* ch 4.
4 Statute on Comrades' Courts of 3 July 1961 and 23 October 1963; first introduced into the Red Army by Decree of 3 December 1917 [1917] 1 Sob Uzak RSFSR, No 5, item 87.
5 Beerman 'The Parasites Law' (1961) 13 Soviet Studies 191.

towards communism has to start creating institutions for keeping order according to healthy public morality, which are not those of the state.

Despite the claim that Russia has made a revolutionary break with her past, many aspects of the system reflect a stream of continuity[6]. It has been pointed out that the Tsars had repeatedly inaugurated industrial enterprises, which were sold or leased to individuals. Nationalisation, therefore, in effect restored to the state what had been its property[7]. The diversity of ethnic and cultural groups in Russia is connected with their age-old resistance to 'Russification'. Lenin had encouraged such resistance in order to weaken the Tsarist régime, but later found himself forced to accept them as separate states. Amidst these divergences the Orthodox Church used formerly to function as a unifying spiritual force, and its mantle has now descended on the Communist Party. The fact that communism has become a substitute faith would explain why political dissenters are visited with the same sort of repression and ridicule as that which used to be meted out to religious dissenters. The Tsars had inherited the Mogul tradition of absolute autocracy. There never had been a 'rule of law'; there always was a tradition of 'rule by law'. The traditional identification of crime with sin made criminal courts into courts of morals; which remains very much the case. Equality before the law was unknown, and the tradition was continued into the proletarian dictatorship while class distinctions remained. Even after the disappearance of such distinctions, equality before law could not sprout like a mushroom overnight. Offences against the state had always been specially dealt with; and that is still so. Even the *Prokuratura* is the descendant of an institution of Peter the Great.

In the light of all this it may be asked: How far has the Soviet system achieved justice? With regard to justice in the allocation of benefits and burdens, there is undoubtedly a more even distribution than before, and this might be regarded as its greatest achievement. The amounts of burdens and benefits that have been distributed has been strictly controlled by government policy[8], but the more detailed problem of evaluating different kinds of work and needs is no easier in Russia than elsewhere. With regard to justice in preventing the abuse of power, this has not been achieved at all. As pointed out, the removal of Tsarist power was only succeeded by an even more ruthless power-structure. Further, a centrally directed economy entails a vast bureaucracy and red-tape. With regard to justice in preventing the abuse of liberty, it is true to say that this has been achieved, but only at the cost of allowing very few liberties. With regard to justice in deciding disputes, it would appear from what has been said that the Soviet Union is moving more and more towards the position in Western countries. Finally, with regard to justice in adapting to change, there is no difference between the Soviet Union and other countries in adapting to technological advances. Indeed, it might even be easier in Russia where there can be no strikes against the introduction of new methods and machinery. On the other hand, any move which even hints of political change will receive short shrift. The rigid orthodoxy, which the Soviet Union seeks to impose even on other

6 See especially Johnson *An Introduction to the Soviet Legal System* ch 2. Cf Savigny's *Volksgeist:* pp 378 et seq ante.
7 See p 304 ante.
8 Eg Stalinist policy laid emphasis on heavy industry at the expense of consumer goods. Krushchev relaxed that somewhat, but there has been a return to heavy industry since.

countries under her wing, makes the possibility of this kind of change within her own territory extremely unlikely.

A word might also be said about the Soviet attitude towards international law. The capitalist threat from abroad is not only an explanation of the severity of the measures adopted internally, but also a clue to Russia's insistence on the sovereignty of states and her policy in international affairs. There was an initial theoretical difficulty as to how the idea of law, which was viewed as the product of an economic structure, could apply as between states with widely differing economic systems. This led at first to confusing attempts to introduce the class concept into international relations, which were replaced by the view that international law is simply an instrument of policy. The result has been a highly eclectic selection of principles and interpretations. Thus, while Russia was still militarily weak she made use of international law for protection. To this end she put forward and persisted in claims that were designed to make denials of them by other states appear as aggression; she rejected the League of Nations as a tool of capitalism, but found no difficulty in joining it in the face of the growing German threat in 1934. After the 1939–45 war, by which time she had achieved a position of power, the continued furtherance of her own interests led to the reversal of attitudes previously adopted. During the Korean War in 1950, for instance, in order to support the North Koreans it was found necessary to reject the very definition of aggression which she herself had insisted on in 1933; nor could she bring herself to support the International Declaration of Human Rights. She is a party to the Helsinki accord, but its internal implementation leaves much to be desired.

Two developments are worth noting. The first is that with the establishment of a number of communist states since the 1939–45 war there is increasing talk of a new 'socialist international law'[9]. The economic structures of these countries being more or less alike, the possibility of an international law, between them at any rate, which is not simply an instrument of policy, is now more real. The invasion of Czechoslovakia in 1968 by the Warsaw Pact countries was prompted by Russian fears of 'deviation'. The Brezhnev doctrine of the 'limited sovereignty' of other communist countries, which was propounded to justify the invasion, raises questions as to what the sovereignty of states now means in the communist world. It is an almost open avowal of the satellite status of these other countries. Moreover, this event, even if it stood alone, makes one wonder what is to be made of the familiar and apparently serious charges continuing to be made of Western 'imperialism' and 'aggression'. Secondly, even in relation to capitalist countries, the policy of 'peaceful co-existence'[10], if seriously pursued, should bring about a different attitude towards international law, accentuated perhaps by the realisation of the economic and political inter-dependence of states. Instead of two systems of international law, one for socialist states and another for non-socialist states, there may be only one system after all; but the ingrained Marxist dialectic sees this as a kind of synthesis produced by the economic and political competition between all states. Whatever the type of international law, the underlying question is: Does the Soviet Union regard it as binding and, if so, on what basis? The answer that seems to be given is:

9 Butler '"Socialist International Law" or "Socialist Principles of International Relations"' (1971) 65 AJIL 796. The 1977 Constitution has for the first time a special chapter on 'Foreign Policy': see ch 4.
10 1977 Constitution, art 28.

agreement. This cannot stand up to analysis, but since it is part of a wider question concerning international law in general, it will be postponed until later[11].

CONCLUSION

When considering the nature of law from an economic point of view two questions have to be distinguished. One is the extent of the economic influence on the content of the law. In so far as it has been demonstrated that a great many rules have been shaped by economic factors, perhaps more than had been suspected, this can be accommodated within traditional concepts of law. The other question is what kind of a concept of law would be appropriate for Marxism as practised in contemporary Russia. This would have to be a functional concept, but one that would need to be sharpened with reference to the re-education of the people and the ushering in of a better society. As such, it would be an instrument of executive, rather than class, policy and would centre on the executive rather than on the courts. A concept focused on the latter will unfold a far from satisfactory picture of law as it operates in Russia. For the decisions of Soviet courts can never be fully understood except in the light of the theoretical and ideological background of the principles that are being applied: all of which are dictated by policy. However, at bottom the idea of law still remains very much the expression of an 'ought'.

Apart from this the contribution of the economic approach is varied. The significant point that has emerged is the indispensability of law. The Marxist approach was a thorough-going attempt to do away with it, but the practical experience of Russia has only demonstrated its importance. It may be that the final stage of development, according to Marxist predictions, has not been reached, but it is clear that even if it is reached the prescription of behaviour and a measure of coercion will continue to exist. There is no reason, apart from an emotional one, for refusing to call all this 'law'. The significant difference from Western societies is that law will not serve as a watch-dog on the government—a rule by law rather than a rule of law. How far an effective safeguard against an abuse of governmental power will be evolved remains to be seen.

Marx and Engels painted a confident picture of evolution, 'the' class struggle reaching a point when conflict arises and results in the establishment of the proletarian dictatorship, which in turn develops into communism. Their followers, both in and out of the Soviet Union, have sometimes tried to force the pace of events. These tactics have been somewhat exaggerated by opponents of Marxism, but they do, even in themselves, reflect unfavourably on the doctrines. While it is true that over-enthusiasm of disciples should not discredit the teachings of the prophets, yet to have to force the occurrence of events, which are supposed to follow an evolutionary plan, can only raise doubts as to its correctness. The policy of 'peaceful co-existence', so prominent in Soviet pronouncements in the last two decades, may well be inspired by an appreciation that the events will nevertheless take time.

The Marxist doctrines in their practical content come to this. For reasons good or bad, the existing structure in capitalist countries needs to be altered.

11 See pp 497–498 post.

In Russia it is a fact that the structure was changed and the Russians are seeking to improve upon it still further. This great and praiseworthy experiment is independent of any question as to the nature of law, as the Russians are beginning to perceive. Unfortunately, questions as to the nature of law were unnecessarily dragged into the social experiment at its theoretical stage and were coloured by a strongly emotional element. This intrusion of emotion is nowhere more evident than in the loading of such words as 'law', 'state', 'bourgeois' and some others. Although they approve of the term 'science', it should be realised that there cannot be a 'scientific' discussion of any topic until the emotional element has been expelled[12].

There is no reason to suppose that communism is the universal social panacea. It might well prove to be the answer for some types of societies, but not others. Two points appear to stand out in this connection. The first was well summed up by Dr Schlesinger, who said:

> 'Socialism of the Russian type may be a historical expedient by which nations held back under a capitalist régime may catch up with those more advanced'[13].

Nor is there any reason to suppose that communism will work in the same way, or at all, in countries which have reached a high state of development under a capitalist system. Secondly, the Russian type of communism requires a degree of regimentation of the masses, the success of which inevitably depends on the nature and temper of the people concerned: the more ignorant and traditionally inclined to subservience the better the chance of success, the more educated and independent the greater the difficulty. The Russian peoples throughout their history never knew emancipation in the sense that inhabitants of Western countries have known it. Indeed, the boast of the Revolution was that it freed them from serfdom, which is true; but it is a relative kind of freedom compared with the traditions of certain other countries, which have long been schooled in the pursuit of independence and resistance to dictatorship. Such countries are less likely to embrace a communist régime than those which have long been oppressed or have remained largely ignorant, and they are likely to fare badly for a long time under one. This is one reason why communism succeeds with oppressed peoples; another is the hope which it holds out to them. Even with these an unremitting process of education is needed; how much re-education would be needed for some races of the West can only be guessed. The Hungarians in 1956 and the Czechs in 1968 demonstrated to their cost the reaction of peoples to an uncongenial régime as soon as control was slightly relaxed, while a similar relaxation in Russia evoked no reaction.

The attack on religion and its ideals has only succeeded in substituting one kind of religion for another. It is doubtful if Marx or Engels foresaw, or would have welcomed, the worship they now receive. The adherence to what one wit has described as the 'gospel according to St Marx' has involved Soviet jurists in some strange mental feats in trying to maintain his doctrines as the official creed and at the same time to take account of developments inconsistent with it. The official attitude seems to be that the 'truth' is in Marx if only the right interpretation can be found; but in the very nature of

12 It is in this respect, if for no other, that so authoritative a treatise as Vyshinsky's *The Law of the Soviet State* comes as a disappointment. Even those who read it with the best will in the world cannot but feel that the case is hardly advanced by the vividly emotional tone which is adopted in it.
13 *Schlesinger* p 260.

things, departures from his teachings have proved to be inevitable. As long as these are officially countenanced, they are 'interpretations'; when they cease to have official support, they are denounced as 'deviations'. Even from a Soviet point of view, why should it not be admitted that the teachings of Marx have obvious limitations and have also in some respects become out of date? In 1956 the 'personality cult' was denounced with regard to Stalin. Whether its rejection will extend to Marx, Engels and Lenin and, if so, to what degree, remains to be seen. Indeed, outside religion, the adherence to the belief in the infallibility of one man would be a mark of an immature mentality. One explanation might be that, having erected the whole of their structure on Marx, the Russians are afraid to risk the consequences of admitting the existence of flaws in the foundations. It is also difficult to escape the suspicion that there is in their attitude elements of immaturity and religious fervour, as borne out, for example, by the genuine desire to convert the whole world, the refusal to see or believe that anyone can be right but themselves, and the faith in the inevitability of a communist triumph. In the face of such sturdy and militant enthusiasm it is not easy to sift what is solid and sound from the emotional admixture of eulogy and abuse. Indeed, in contemporary Marxism is to be seen the twentieth-century version of the Crusades.

READING LIST

H J Berman *Justice in the USSR, An Interpretation of Soviet Law*.

M M Bober *Karl Marx's Interpretation of History* (2nd edn).

E Bodenheimer 'The Impasse of Soviet Legal Philosophy' (1952–53) 38 Cornell Law Quarterly 51.

H Collins *Marxism and Law*.

R David and J E C Brierley *Major Legal Systems in the World Today* (2nd edn) Part II.

A Denisov and M Kirichenko *Soviet State Law*.

M Djilas *The New Class*.

F Engels *The Origin of the Family, Private Property and the State*.

V Gsovski *Soviet Civil Law* especially Part I.

J N Hazard *Law and Social Change in the USSR*.

J N Hazard, I Shapiro and P B Maggs *The Soviet Legal System, Contemporary Documentation and Historical Commentary*.

E L Johnson *An Introduction to The Soviet Legal System*.

H Kelsen *The Communist Theory of Law*.

K Marx *Capital* I and II.

K Marx and F Engels *Manifesto of the Communist Party*.

K R Popper *The Open Society and its Enemies* (5th edn) II.

R A Posner *The Economics of Justice*.

R Pound *Interpretations of Legal History* ch 5.

R Schlesinger *Soviet Legal Theory* (2nd edn).

Soviet Legal Philosophy (trans H W Babb 20th Century Legal Philosophy Series V).

CHAPTER 20

Sociological approaches

A common feature of a number of approaches, which have gained increasing popularity in this century, is that in one way or another they concern law in relation to society. This outlook is the product of many factors. In the nineteenth century the focus of attention began to swing away from individual rights towards social duties, and carried with it an emphasis on the function of law in communal existence. The rapid increase in population, inequalities engendered by the industrial revolution on a scale hitherto unprecedented, were factors which, together with others, created new problems. The Historical School had shown an essential connection between law and the social environment in which it develops. Prior to the nineteenth century such matters as health, welfare, education, economics, were not the concern of the state. Now the state came increasingly to concern itself with them. This implied regulation through law, which compelled legal theory to readjust itself so as to take account of such preoccupations. Towards the latter half of that century the shortcomings of purely formal analysis were being felt. The increasing number of social activities with which the law had to deal produced a host of new problems for the solution of which guidance was needed. Traditional approaches, analytical positivism in particular, were forced into confessions of mental bankruptcy in meeting these demands. Finally, revolutions and social unsettlement not only upset any complacency about social stability, but also provoked anxiety about the shortcomings of law.

The diverse character of the various types of inquiries that are styled 'sociological' invites comment. Sociology means, broadly, the study of society of which law is but a part. The founder of sociology, in a sense, is Comte (1798-1857), because he was the first to employ the term 'sociology' to connote an independent discipline, and he also unified the work of earlier men. Comte insisted that advancement of knowledge comes only through observation and experiment and he proceeded to construct a hierarchical classification of the sciences, from mathematics, through physics, chemistry and biology to what he called sociology. Even though it was more difficult to apply the scientific method to sociology, it was still, in his view, the most fruitful. Sociology he defined as the science of social order and progress. It includes two compartments, social statics and social dynamics, the former being the theory of social order and the latter the theory of social progress. Society is a developing organism, whose progress is marked by the specialisation of functions within it. Its distinctive feature is its capacity for improvement and development if guided by proper scientific principles. The task of sociology is to discover and work out these principles. Earlier Montesquieu (1689-1755) in his *L'Esprit des Lois* had endeavoured to trace the effect of social environment on law. He busied himself with legal institutions with the object of offering explanations for them. He stressed the influence of geographical and climatic conditions on law which, in his view, could operate only through the medium of society[1]. He perceived the importance of history as a means of understanding the structure of society and also drew attention to the part played by economic factors. In all this might be seen anticipations of what later developed into the Historical, Economic and Sociological Schools. In his own work, however, they appear as pointers to such studies rather than as studies in themselves.

As a subject sociology is still young and in search of respectability[2]. One step towards this would be to win for its methods the dignity of being able to invoke the magic word 'scientific'. The following are the main resemblances and differences between sociological and scientific methods[3].

(1) Sociology, like science, proceeds from observation to hypothesis, and deductions therefrom are in turn checked back with 'reality'. In this respect the difference between them is largely one of degree, for sociology is still very much at the stage of observation, which indeed is being conducted on a massive scale with all modern techniques, but with as yet only exploratory hypotheses, classifications, models and tentative laws of probabilities[4].

(2) It is theoretical and aims at synthesising other disciplines, some of which are long established, such as history, economics, law etc.

(3) It progresses cumulatively in that new hypotheses are evolved as much out of the correction, extension and refinement of earlier ones as out of new data.

(4) It is non-ethical, ie impartial in evaluation. Just as a scientist puts aside his own values when observing his data, so too the sociologist excludes his own preferences and prejudices when observing his data, which include current values and opinions. Put in another way, the values of a sociologist *qua* sociologist are the same as those of a scientist, namely neutrality and scrupulousness. There are, however, two qualifications. The social observer cannot avoid being personally involved in the society or group which he is observing, of which he is a part and in which he has a role to play *towards* his data. The scientist is not involved with his data in this way. Secondly, social behaviour has causal as well as purposive explanations, ie the questions to be answered are not only 'How?' but also 'What for?' Sociological explanations are therefore sometimes termed 'structural-functional', the structural side being explanatory and descriptive, the functional side being both heuristic and teleological.

(5) It seeks to describe, explain and predict, in short to derive descriptive laws which will predict, as opposed to prescribe, social behaviour:

---

1 Montesquieu *L'Esprit des Lois* especially Books XIV et seq, and XVIII.

2 Selznick *The Sociology of Law*, distinguished between three stages in the sociology of law: (i) outlining broad strategy and perspectives and programs of attack; (ii) evolving methods and techniques; (iii) in the fullness of 'intellectual autonomy and maturity' a return to the problems posed at the outset. A professor of sociology admitted that 'Sociology is still to a large extent in the classifying, ordering and descriptive stage, because we are still not sure what is relevant and what is not. The result is that a great deal of sociologising is more like a kind of random botanising, a collecting of data, ie statistics, personal case histories and the like, uncontrolled by the purpose of verification. This is inevitable, and certainly provides material on which the theorist can build, but at the same time it must be admitted that, while unbased and unverified hypotheses are empty, a mere collection of data is blind': Sprott *Sociology* p 39.

3 For the first four, see Johnson *Sociology: A Systematic Introduction* p 2.

4 Sprott p 39: see n 2 supra.

that which 'is', not that which 'ought to be'. The material out of
which such descriptive laws are derived includes (a) social morphol-
ogy: which concerns the form of social structure as affected by such
factors as the quantity and distribution of population, geography,
climate etc. (b) Social change: which may in turn inspire conscious
or unconscious efforts to resist, adapt to or alter it. So-called 'short-
term' theories of social change confine themselves to changes that
have occurred and the influences behind them without extrapolating
these into some general law of change, whereas 'long-term' theories
aim to do precisely that[5]. (c) Social pathology: which concerns social
disturbance and maladjustment. Criminology is a well-known aspect
of this. (d) Social controls: which include laws, morals, religion,
public opinion, fashions and so on. (e) Group behaviour: which deals
with the problems of the interaction between individuals *inter se* and
groups. Something more about group behaviour will be said towards
the end of this chapter, but social controls raise points which may be
dealt with immediately.

Laws are not the only instruments of control; others, such as morals,
religion etc are at least as effective, if not more so, with the result that they
all figure prominently in sociological study. No less important is the relation
between public opinion, its unifying and divisive power, and the various sorts
of issues on which opinions are held. The point is that all forms of control
are in their nature 'ought' propositions, prescriptive not descriptive. The
concern of sociology is not with prescriptions as such, but with the phenomenon that when such prescriptions are regularly followed, they produce
uniformities of behaviour which recur with such a degree of probability that
they may then be described in terms of the 'is', ie patterns which do occur
as a matter of observation. It might seem from this that sociologists are here
deriving 'is' from 'ought', but this is not so. The sociologist is primarily
concerned with descriptions of social behaviour and only concerned with
prescriptions in so far as these happen to produce regularities which can be
observed. In no sense is he *logically* deriving the one from the other.

This reveals a crucial difference between the point of view of the sociologist
looking at law as the sum-total of legal administration and as a given phenomenon of society ('legal sociologist'), and that of the lawyer looking at the
operation of laws and the conceptual tools of a lawyer's equipment in their
social and functional setting ('sociological jurist'). The former regards society
as a whole, including the part played by legal administration in bringing
about observable patterns of behaviour. He is interested in the fact of the
regular application of force and the fact of the regular use of guides for
determining disputes (norms of decision), both of which help to shape patterns of social behaviour (norms of conduct). Thus, his concept of law tends
to be that of an ideal type, a model of the totality of legal administration,
which can be fitted into a model of society[6]. On the other hand, the sociological jurist is primarily concerned with laws and the tools of a lawyer's
trade; he accepts the former as being prescriptive in their nature and considers their function and functioning in society. The present chapter will be
concerned mainly with the point of view of the sociological jurist, not of the

5 Eg Hegel and Marx; contra Popper *The Open Society and its Enemies* especially vol II.
6 For an attempt to construct one, see King 'The Concept of a Lawyer's Jurisprudence' (1953)
   11 CLJ at 236, 418; 'The Basic Concept of Professor Hart's Jurisprudence' [1963] CLJ 270.

legal sociologist, though works of the latter type cannot be excluded altogether. Needless to say, the authors, whose works will be dealt with, have not themselves maintained any such rigid distinction and in some cases it is arguable into which category they fall. Whether any further distinction is to be drawn between 'sociology of law' and 'sociological jurisprudence' is doubtful. If 'sociology of law' is thought to be concerned with the manner in which laws work in society, there is, it is submitted, no difference between it and sociological jurisprudence: if it is concerned with society and how legal administration as a whole fits into it, then it is synonymous with legal sociology.

The social study of laws has assumed four forms (1) There are inquiries which seek the social origins of laws and legal institutions. They are concerned with the content of the 'oughts' and the factors that have and are shaping them. (2) There are also examinations of the impact of laws on various aspects of society. (3) There are other inquiries which deal with the task which laws should perform in society. The results of these studies generally take the form of prescriptions addressed to persons who make and administer laws and not to members of society at large. Such 'prescriptions for administration' are in a different category from the 'prescriptive oughts' of laws themselves. Lastly (4) there is the attempt to find some social criterion by which to test the validity of laws. So wide is the field that is covered by these categories that it will not be possible to do more than consider the work of some representative writer or writers.

SOCIAL ORIGINS OF LAWS AND LEGAL INSTITUTIONS

The theories which deal with origins fall into three categories. Two of these, namely, the Historical interpretation and the Economic interpretation, have been considered in the last two chapters, where it was pointed out that they are but versions of the sociological approach. Something has still to be said of the theory of Ihering, which sought to explain the origin of laws without resorting to a metaphysical concept like the *Volksgeist* or a single evolutionary principle as Marx had done.

IHERING

Ihering (1818–1892) passed the early part of his juristic career as an orthodox member of the German Historical School, during which time he intensively studied Roman law and published four volumes of a work, *The Spirit of Roman Law*. This he left unfinished, for its execution had convinced him that the origin of laws lay in sociological factors, a thesis which he proceeded to urge for the rest of his life. In the third volume of *The Spirit of Roman Law* he concluded that the basis of a 'right' was an interest, which led him to consider more closely how laws dealt with conflicting interests. His ideas came to fruition in his major work, *Der Zweck im Recht* ('Purpose in Law'), which has been translated into English as *Law as a Means to an End*[7]. The dominant notion to be found in the exercise of human will is that of purpose. Causality in the natural world is governed by a 'because'. A stone falls because, without support, it must fall.

7 By Husik *Modern Legal Philosophy Series* v.

'The stone does not fall in order to fall, but because it must fall, because its support is taken away; whilst the man who acts does so, not *because* of anything, but *in order* to attain to something. This purpose is as indispensable for the will as cause is for the stone. As there can be no motion of the stone without a cause, so can there be no movement of the will without a purpose'[8].

Law is but a part of human conduct, and in the idea of purpose Ihering found the mainspring of laws, which are only instruments for serving the needs of society. Their purpose is to further and protect the interests of society. Purpose should also guide juridical thinking, of which his analysis of possession was an example[9].

The problem of society is to reconcile selfish with unselfish purposes, and to suppress the former when they clash with the latter. Ihering stressed that law does not exist for the individual as an end in himself, but serves his interest with the good of society in view. Man, as a social animal, whether as a member of the state, Church etc, stands on a superior plane to Man simply as an animal[10]. Property, for example, is both a social and individual institution, which justifies expropriation and limitation of the individual's rights[11]. In order to reconcile the individual with society, it is necessary to balance various interests, which he grouped into three categories: individual, state and social[12]. The social activities of people need to be encouraged, and this is accomplished by means of the 'principle of the levers of social motion'. There are four, the first two being the principles of Reward and Coercion. These seek to identify the selfish interest of the individual with some larger social interest. To give an example, since the economic wants of Man need satisfaction trade is instituted to fulfil this need, thus achieving a social purpose by pandering to the selfish profit motive. This is an example of Reward being employed. Coercion is a feature of that part of the social machinery which is called legal administration, namely, coercion organised in a set form by the state. By its side there is also unorganised coercion in the form of social conventions and etiquette. In addition to these there are two altruistic principles, Duty and Love, which also direct men towards social ends.

The point which emerges from Ihering's analysis is that laws are only one type of means of achieving an end, namely social control. There is a distinction between society and state; laws are a feature of the latter. He insisted that laws should be treated from the angle of purpose and convincingly demonstrated the inadequacy of what he called the 'jurisprudence of concepts', that is, mechanical deduction from given premises[13]. He insisted also on the interdependence of all factors that obtain in society, which include (a) extra-legal conditions, ie those under the control of nature, such as the climate and the fertility of the soil; (b) mixed legal conditions, those in which laws do not play a prominent part, such as self-preservation, reproduction, commerce and labour; and (c) purely legal conditions, those interests which are secured solely by legal regulation, such as the raising of revenue. Finally, he stressed the coercive character of legal regulation[14]. His analysis led him to a definition in the following terms:

8 Ihering Law as a *Means to an End* p 2.
9 See pp 276–277 ante.
10 *Ihering* pp 63, 68, 397. Cf his *Kampf ums Recht*.
11 *Ihering* p 391.
12 Cf *Pound*, pp 431 et seq post.
13 He parodied a heaven in which legal conceptions enjoyed a blissful existence: *Im Juristischen Begriffshimmel* in *Sherz und Ernst in der Jurisprudenz* (11th edn 1912) p 245.
14 Ihering *Law as a Means to an End* p 241.

'Law is the sum of the conditions of social life in the widest sense of the term, as secured by the power of the State through the means of external compulsion'[15].

In his approach Ihering was building upon the work of the English thinkers, Bentham and Mill, whose utilitarianism may be said to have influenced his theory of purpose[16]. Ihering, however, insisted on the need to reconcile competing social and individual interests. In this respect he merits the title of 'father of modern sociological jurisprudence', for, as will presently be seen, the problem of the harmonisation of interests plays a prominent part in the theories of some modern writers. Ihering himself did not indicate how this was to be resolved. His social utilitarianism, as it is usually called, stops short of this question and only draws attention to it. His concern, as stated at the beginning, was to examine the origin of laws, not their application. He was also rightly convinced of the futility of *a priori* theories of justice; a law may be bad today and good tomorrow if the social background has shifted in the meantime.

IMPACT OF LAWS ON SOCIETY

EHRLICH

Ehrlich's (1862–1922) thesis[17] was that laws found in formal legal sources, such as statutes and decided cases, give only an inadequate picture of what really goes on in a community, for the norms which in fact govern life are only imperfectly and partially reflected in them. He drew a distinction between norms of decision, which correspond to that which is traditionally understood to be laws, and norms of conduct, which govern life in society[18]. There is often a considerable divergence between them. Thus, a commercial usage may develop, but it is only after the lapse of some time that courts will acknowledge it and import it into contracts. Eventually it may become embodied in a statute, but by this time modifications of it and fresh usages may have developed. So the process goes on. There will always be an inevitable gap between the norms of formal law and of actual behaviour. The point that Ehrlich was seeking to make was that the 'living law' of society has to be sought outside the confines of formal legal material, in other words, in society itself. One learns little of the living law in factories, for example, by reading only the Factory Acts, the enactments and the common law relating to master and servant, trade unions etc. One needs to go into a factory to observe how far the formal law is followed, modified, ignored and supplemented. Only a minute fraction of social life comes before courts, and even then it usually represents some form of breakdown of social life. The task of formal law-makers is to keep it as nearly abreast of the living law as possible.

The existence of a social order ante-dates formal legal provisions and, moreover, certain facts underlie all laws. These are usage, domination, possession and declaration of will. Propositions of law with reference to them arise in three ways, by endeavouring to give effect to the relations they create, by controlling or invalidating them, or by attaching consequences to

15 *Ihering* p 380.
16 See pp 427–429 post.
17 Ehrlich *Fundamental Principles of the Sociology of Law* (trans Moll).
18 *Ehrlich* p 37.

them. A formal concept of law consists of the synthesis of generalisations constructed from the various propositions of law. If it is asked how the living law, as distinct from the formal law, is to be discovered, Ehrlich's answer was: from (a) judicial decisions, which are only evidentiary; (b) modern business documents against which judicial decisions need to be checked; and above all (c) observation of people, by living among them and noting their behaviour.

It follows from all this that state organisation plays but a subsidiary part. The norms emanating from the state and its organs are only one factor of social control and should be considered in conjunction with others such as customs, morality and the practices of groups and associations. When looked at in the context of living law, there is no difference between formal legal norms and those of customs etc, for it is social pressure that ensures obedience to both types in practice. So, to Ehrlish a statute which is habitually disregarded is no part of the living law. Enforcement by the state is not the distinction between formal and living law; the difference resides in social psychology. Some types of rules evoke different feelings from others. So there are many reasons why a person obeys even a legal rule other than fear of state enforced sanction[19]. The characteristic of formal rules lies in the kind of feelings they arouse by virtue of their generality and social significance. It is a fact that different societies, and even the same society at different times, have had different feelings about what is socially important, so the line between legal, on the one hand, and moral and social rules, on the other, has constantly shifted. There is in all this some parallel with the views of Savigny, but Ehrlich's approach is infinitely more practical than Savigny's mystical *Volksgeist*. Such regard for the living law requires that the scope of jurisprudence should be enlarged. It should concern itself with an observational study of society, since formal laws are only an adjunct of the living law.

Ehrlich's work was a powerful influence in inducing jurists to abandon purely abstract preoccupations and to concern themselves with the problems and facts of social life. While acknowledging his beneficial stimulation in this direction, one should not overlook some drawbacks in his theory. While the distinction between formal and living law is necessary and important, there is some danger of a verbal discussion as to whether both should be called 'law', or only one, and if so which. He deprived formal law of any creative activity and gave it too much the appearance of trailing in the wake of social developments. It is true that reforming legislation is sometimes the formal expression of a tide of public feeling, but it is also true that many norms of behaviour have been given shape and direction by the constant enforcement of laws. Ehrlich's distinction between norms of decision and norms of behaviour is important; but he failed to emphasise sufficiently their mutual interaction. Ehrlich's contentions were also somewhat outmoded even when he propounded them. State organisation is now, and has been for a long time, playing an ever-increasing part in the regulation of social life. It is by no means merely ancillary to the living law; it has come to be of transcendent importance. The picture which Ehrlich drew was truer of the past than of today, but it was ceasing to be true even in his own day. He was ready to admit the increasingly important part that was being played by state organisation, but he failed to absorb its implications into his theory. Finally,

19 *Ehrlich* p 21; pp 49 et seq ante.

Ehrlich's conception of jurisprudence could make it unwieldly and amorphous. To urge that laws should be studied in the context of society is proper and beneficial, but the way in which Ehrlich proposed to conduct the study of society would all but submerge the significance of laws and might very well lead to the death of jurisprudence as a subject.

THE TASK OF LAWS IN SOCIETY

No account of the function which laws should perform in society would be complete without some mention of the pioneer contribution of Bentham.

BENTHAM

Jeremy Bentham's (1748-1832) contribution to analytical jurisprudence has already been dealt with[20]. What will be considered now is his social philosophy. He was without doubt a stout individualist who approached the problems of society on that basis. His moral philosophy, social sense and juristic insight cannot be separated, but if there was one theme which ran through his many writings it was his utilitarian outlook on life. Man, in his view, was governed by pleasure and pain[1]. In this one is tempted to detect the influence of Hobbes, who based his philosophy on the innate selfishness of men. The function of laws, according to Bentham, should be the promotion of the greatest happiness of the greatest number[2]. This was only one application of the Principle of Utility, which approves or disapproves of action according as it increases or diminishes happiness[3]. Bentham, be it noted, did not invent the utility principle; he took it from others, notably Hume, and developed it in the minutest detail[4]. It is also worth remembering that his 'pleasure' has a somewhat large signification, including altruistic and obligatory conduct, the 'principle of benevolence'; while his idea of 'interest' was anything promoting pleasure[5]. The task of laws should be to bring about the maximum happiness of each individual, for the happiness of each will result in happiness for all[6]. There is in this the age-old problem of reconciling interests of the individual with those of the community, but it amounts almost to a contradiction to try to harness a selfish pursuit of pleasure and avoidance of pain to the unselfish service of the common weal. One way of avoiding contradiction would be to suppose that individual pleasure-pain motivations by and large would not run counter to those of the community. Perhaps Bentham did believe this, at least when he wrote his *Introduction to the Principles of Morals and Legislation*. It has also been suggested that he may have embraced dual standards, that of community interest in the public and political sphere, and self-interest in private matters[7]. However this may be, as an unremitting reformer, he favoured legislation on a drastic scale to

20 See pp 335–343 ante.
 1 Bentham *An Introduction to the Principles of Morals and Legislation* (eds Burns and Hart) I, para 1.
 2 Bentham *A Fragment on Government* (ed Harrison).
 3 Bentham *An Introduction to the Principles of Morals and Legislation*, paras 2–3.
 4 In one place he ascribed credit to Priestley: Bentham *Works* (ed Bowring) X, p 142; in another to Beccaria: Bentham *A Fragment on Government*, p xx.
 5 Bentham *An Introduction to the Principles of Morals and Legislation* para 5.
 6 Bentham *An Introduction to the Principles of Morals and Legislation* para 6.
 7 Lyons *In the Interest of the Governed* p 20.

remedy the evils which he saw around him, but once these had been eradicated legislation should aim at providing subsistence, abundance, equality of opportunity and security for all. His individualist leaning manifested itself in his insistence that individual and private property were essential. This was necessary, he argued, to ensure the fulfilment of settled expectations.

The utility principle has been subjected to searching examination. In the first place, it is not easy to see how a subjective criterion such as pleasure and pain can be transmuted into an objective one. Pleasure connotes an emotional attitude of approval, pain of disapproval. To judge an action according to the pleasure-pain criterion is to judge it subjectively. To say of a given course of conduct 'I prefer it because it is conducive to pleasure' is no more informative than just 'I prefer it'. For conduct is not loaded with pleasure- or pain-giving qualities; these are dependent on individual reaction. The problem then is: whose reaction should be the criterion? It is true that some types of conduct are generally thought of as conducive to pleasure and others to pain, but the problems arise with reference to conduct as to which feelings are equivocal or divided. This leads to another objection. The consequences of pleasure or pain of an action may well be indefinite in time or unforeseeable; it may give rise to immediate pain with a promise of pleasure or *vice versa*. These factors of time and uncertainty render assessment virtually impossible. Nor is it easy to see how the happiness of the majority increases the happiness of society as a whole. Much will depend on the issue, for on some issues it might well be the case that the happiness of the majority will embitter the minority to the point of provoking disharmony. The converse proposition has also been advanced that by promoting the happiness of others one promotes one's own happiness as well. As a general proposition this, too, is in need of support. Apart from all this, the root difficulty of the principle of ensuring the happiness of the greatest number is how this can be used to apportion three houses, for instance, among four people. Above all, the pleasure-pain categories are too simple in themselves. It led Bentham into artificialities in forcing some very complex problems into these two strait-jackets. It was also naïve to imagine that Man is motivated simply by reaction to pleasure and pain. Bentham appeared to have assumed that there is such a thing as an 'average man'. In truth many actions are done unthinkingly, or from habit; and pleasure and pain come as often as incidents to other actions. It may be that he confused causes of action and reasons for action[8]. He seems also to have assumed that laws could be made to operate on some single principle, which, as is evident in modern times, is an unfounded belief. Lastly, he ignored history and tradition altogether. They should not be exaggerated, but neither should they be excluded.

It is in the light of the limitations of the utility principle, which pervaded his thought, that Bentham's jurisprudential contributions should be assessed. His work in the analytical (expository) field has been examined[9]. This was preliminary to his main interest, which was reform (censorial jurisprudence), and it is to this aspect that the following remarks refer. The utilitarian justification for having laws at all is that they are an important means of ensuring the happiness of the members of the community generally[10]. Hence, the sovereign power of making laws should be wielded, not to guarantee the

8 Milne 'Bentham's Principle of Utility and Legal Philosophy' in *Bentham and Legal Theory* (ed James) p 19.
9 See pp 335–343 ante.
10 Bentham *Principles of Legislation* ch 12, p 64.

selfish desires of individuals, but consciously to secure the common good. 'The public good' said Bentham 'ought to be the object of the legislator; general utility ought to be the foundation of his reasoning'[11]. In order to do this there has to be a balancing of individual interests with communal welfare; he called this the 'felicific calculus'[12]. This idea of the balancing of interests was destined to play an important part in more modern theories[13]. Bentham himself did not solve satisfactorily the problem of how such balancing can be achieved. The pleasure-pain motivation, as has been pointed out, is too simple to explain conduct; so any attempt to work out a calculus of interests on that basis was doomed. The 'weight' accorded to interests differs according to the values of different individuals, and the policies of different countries will yield different results, eg Soviet Russia. Another contribution was his insistence on law-making to achieve social ends. The conscience of the people has to be trained so that they learn to find pleasure in ways that are not anti-social. To this end laws should be made which would make anti-social behaviour unprofitable, in other words, a source of pain to the doer rather than pleasure. On this basis he proceeded to consider punishment, and his views are still of absorbing interest[14]. It will be noted that Bentham, although he would not have gone as far as the Soviet Communist Party in mass re-education, seems to have leaned in that direction. Lastly, he preached that laws should be judged by their consequences. For all these reasons it is clear that this aspect of his work entitles him to rank as a pioneer of functional jurisprudence in addition to his many other pioneering contributions. A very great deal of what has been done since is only development along his lines.

THE TÜBINGEN SCHOOL

It was mentioned earlier in this chapter that Ihering had detected the origins of laws in purpose, namely, the resolution of conflicting social and individual interests. He stopped short of the point of suggesting how such reconciliation is to be effected. Bentham, as just indicated, had previously advanced a pleasure-pain criterion and his views had been introduced into Germany by Edward Beneke, though they only came to be well known through Ihering[15]. A number of practitioners, known as the Tübingen School, attempted to evolve a 'jurisprudence of interests' on the line suggested by Ihering, but stopped short of Bentham's principle of the greatest happiness of the greatest number[16]. Instead, they were content to say simply that laws protect some, but not all, interests. A legal rule is, therefore, in a sense a decision on a prospective dispute and, as such, contains in itself a balance between competing interests. To understand a rule one has to see which social interests gave rise to it and how they were adjusted by the rule. Its interpretation and

11 Bentham *Principles of Legislation* I, p 1; Bentham *An Introduction to the Principles of Morals and Legislation* 1, para 7.
12 Bentham *An Introduction to the Principles of Morals and Legislation* 1, paras 4, 5.
13 Eg his influence on Ihering: see 425 ante.
14 Eg his 'Panopticon' scheme for prison reform; and the recent publication of his views on torture: W L and P E Twining 'Bentham on Torture' in *Bentham and Legal Theory* (ed James) p 39.
15 For the influence of Bentham on Beneke, see Coing 'Bentham's Influence on the Development of *Interessenjurisprudenz* and General Jurisprudence' (1967) 2 Ir Jur (NS) 336.
16 A convenient selection of writings is *The Jurisprudence of Interests* (trans Schoch; *20th Century Legal Philosophy Series* vol II).

application should seek to ensure that those interests, which the law-maker preferred, shall prevail. A number of rules may be unified into a concept and concepts and rules into a system of law. Concepts so unified are useful for the purpose of systematic exposition, but for the purpose of applying and interpreting laws other and different concepts are required. These are 'concepts of guidance' for those who have to administer laws. Unhappily, these functional concepts were never evolved. The reason for this lay in the lack of interest on the part of the Tübingen School in the goal which laws should seek to achieve; for the way in which interests are viewed and assessed is dependent on the end to be achieved. Here Bentham might have given them a lead. Despite the disappointing nature of their work, the problem which they failed to resolve is worthy of mention if only as a prelude to the contribution of Roscoe Pound, the American.

ROSCOE POUND

Nowhere has the study of laws in society been taken up with such industry and enthusiasm as in America. Here, the law school and the jurist enjoy a status akin to that of jurists on the Continent and superior to that of their counterparts in Great Britain. These factors have combined to produce an American movement in sociological jurisprudence of great importance which draws its exponents both from the faculty and the bench. Outstanding among these was Pound (1870–1964), of the Harvard Law School. As with Bentham, his theme was a constant one, maintained in his extensive writings throughout a long period[17].

Sociological jurisprudence, according to Pound, should ensure that the making, interpretation and application of laws take account of social facts. Towards achieving this end there should be (a) a factual study of the social effects of legal administration, (b) social investigations as preliminaries to legislation, (c) a constant study of the means for making laws more effective, which involves, (d) the study, both psychological and philosophical, of the judicial method, (e) a sociological study of legal history, (f) allowance for the possibility of a just and reasonable solution of individual cases, (g) a ministry of justice in English-speaking countries, and (h) the achievement of the purposes of the various laws. This comprehensive programme covers, as is evident, every aspect of the social study of laws. It is not possible to follow Pound's elaboration of each of these aspects, and all that can be done here is to outline his thought.

The common law, he said, still bears the impress of individual rights. So, in order to achieve the purposes of the legal order there has to be (a) a recognition of certain interests, individual, public and social[18], (b) a definition of the limits within which such interests will be legally recognised and given effect to, and (c) the securing of those interests within the limits as defined. When determining the scope and subject-matter of the system the following five things require to be done: (i) preparation of an inventory of interests, classifying them; (ii) selection of the interests which should be legally recognised; (iii) demarcation of the limits of securing the interests so selected; (iv) consideration of the means whereby laws might secure the

17 Perhaps the most convenient references are Pound 'A Survey of Social Interests' (1943–44) 57 Harvard LR 1, and *Jurisprudence* III.
18 Cf Ihering, p 424 ante.

interests when these have been acknowledged and delimited; and (v) evolution of the principles of valuation of the interests.

Pound likened the task of the lawyer to engineering, an analogy which he used repeatedly. The aim of social engineering is to build as efficient a structure of society as possible, which requires the satisfaction of the maximum of wants with the minimum of friction and waste[19]. It involves the balancing of competing interests. For this purpose interests were defined as 'claims or wants or desires (or, I would like to say, expectations) which men assert *de facto*, about which the law must do something if organised societies are to endure'[20]. It is the task of the jurist to assist the courts by classifying and expatiating on the interests protected by law. Pound's arrangement of these, elaborated in detail, was as follows:

A. INDIVIDUAL INTERESTS. These are claims or demands or desires involved in and looked at from the standpoint of the individual life. They concern

(1) **Personality.** This includes interests in (a) the physical person, (b) freedom of will, (c) honour and reputation, (d) privacy, and (e) belief and opinion.

(2) **Domestic relations.** It is important to distinguish between the interest of individuals in domestic relationships and that of society in such institutions as family and marriage. Individual interests include those of (a) parents, (b) children, (c) husbands, and (d) wives.

(3) **Interest of substance.** This includes interests of (a) property, (b) freedom of industry and contract, (c) promised advantages, (d) advantageous relations with others, (e) freedom of association, and (f) continuity of employment.

B. PUBLIC INTERESTS. These are claims or demands or desires asserted by individuals involved in or looked at from the standpoint of political life.

'The claims asserted in title of a politically organised society; as one might say for convenience, the claims of the state, the political organization of society'[1].

There are two of them:

(1) **Interests of the state as a juristic person.** These, as pointed out earlier, are not applicable in this country where the position of the Crown has obviated the need for the personification of the state. They include (a) the integrity, freedom of action and honour of the state's personality, and (b) claims of the politically organised society as a corporation to property acquired and held for corporate purposes.

(2) **Interests of the state as guardian of social interests.** This seems to overlap with the next major category.

C. SOCIAL INTERESTS. These are claims or demands or desires, even some of the foregoing in other aspects, thought of in terms of social life and

19 Pound *Interpretations of Legal History* p 156; Pound *Social Control Through Law* p 65.
20 Pound *Jurisprudence* III, p 15. Cf the earlier definition: 'claims or demands or desires which human beings, either individually or in groups or associations or relations, seek to satisfy, of which, therefore, the adjustment of relations and ordering of human behaviour through the force of a politically organised society must take account': 'A Survey of Social Interests' (1943-44) 57 Harvard LR 1.
1 Pound *Jurisprudence* III, pp 235-236.

generalised as claims of the social group. This is much the most important category, since most, if not all, the interests in category A would be statable here from a social, rather than an individual, point of view. Social interests are said to include

(1) **Social interest in the general security.**

> 'The claim or want or demand, asserted in title of social life in civilised society and through the social group, to be secure against those forms of action and courses of conduct which threaten its existence'[2].

This embraces those branches of the law which relate to (a) general safety, (b) general health, (c) peace and order, (d) security of acquisitions, and (e) security of transactions.

(2) **Social interest in the security of social institutions.**

> 'The claim or want or demand involved in life in civilised society that its fundamental institutions be secure from those forms of action and courses of conduct which threaten their existence or impair their efficient functioning'[3].

This comprises (a) domestic institutions, (b) religious institutions, (c) political institutions, and (d) economic institutions. Divorce legislation might be adduced as an example of the conflict between the social interest in the security of the institution of marriage and the individual interests of the unhappy spouses. Pound pointed out that the law has at times attached disabilities to the children of illegitimate and adulterous unions with the object of preserving the sanctity of marriage. The example is not altogether fortunate, since the extent to which such vicarious suffering has deterred would-be offenders is minimal. Then again, there is tension between the individual interest in religious freedom and the social interest, at any rate in some countries, in preserving the dominance of an established church.

(3) **Social interest in general morals.**

> 'The claim or want or demand involved in social life in civilised society to be secured against acts or courses of conduct offensive to the moral sentiments of the general body of individuals therein for the time being'[4].

This covers a variety of laws, for example, those dealing with prostitution, drunkenness and gambling.

(4) **Social interest in the conservation of social resources.**

> 'The claim or want or demand involved in social life in civilised society that the goods of existence shall not be wasted; that where all human wants may not be satisfied, in view of infinite individual desires and limited natural means of satisfying them, the latter be made to go as far as possible; and, to that end, the acts or courses of conduct which tend needlessly to impair these goods shall be restrained'[5].

Thus this social interest clashes to some extent with the individual interest in dealing with one's own property as one pleases. It covers

2 *Pound* III p 291.
3 *Pound* III p 296.
4 *Pound* III p 303.
5 *Pound* III p 305.

(a) conservation of natural resources, and (b) protection and training of dependants and defectives, ie conservation of human resources.

(5) **Social interest in general progress.**

> 'The claim or want or demand involved in social life in civilised society, that the development of human powers and of human control over nature for the satisfaction of human wants go forward; the demand that social engineering be increasingly and continually improved; as it were, the self-assertion of the social group towards higher and more complete development of human powers'[6].

This has three aspects. (a) Economic progress, which covers (i) freedom of use and sale of property, (ii) free trade, (iii) free industry, and (iv) encouragement of invention by the grant of patents. Now, (i) and (iii) are less marked today than they used to be. Indeed, it might even be said that progress has been achieved by a reversal of them. The policy of free trade, which has as its corollary the disapproval of monopolies, might appear to have been indorsed by legislation against restrictive practices. While this is true of private monopolies, it should be noted that there is an ever-growing demand for monopolies in the state or state-controlled institutions. The encouragement of invention by the grant of patents, too, is somewhat suspect, for it opens the possibility of acquiring patents in order to suppress inventions. On the whole, therefore, item (a) is the least happy.

The interest in general progress also includes (b) political progress, which covers (i) free speech, and (ii) free association; and (c) cultural progress, which covers (i) free science, (ii) free letters, (iii) free arts, (iv) promotion of education and learning, and (v) aesthetics.

(6) **Social interest in individual life.**

> 'The claim or want or demand involved in social life in civilised society that each individual be able to live a human life therein according to the standards of the society'[7].

It involves (a) self-assertion, (b) opportunity, and (c) conditions of life.

Having listed the interests recognised by law, Pound considered the means by which they are secured. These consist of the device of legal person and the attribution of claims, duties, liberties, powers and immunities. There is also the remedial machinery behind them, which aims sometimes at punishment, sometimes at redress and sometimes at prevention. He also addressed himself to the question of how in any given case the interests involved are to be balanced or weighed. Interests, he insisted, should be weighed 'on the same plane', as it were. One cannot balance an individual interest against a social interest, since that very way of stating them may reflect a decision already made. One should transfer the interests involved on to the same 'plane', preferably in most cases to that of the social plane, which is the most general. Thus, freedom of the person might be regarded as an individual interest, but it is translatable as an interest of the society that its members

6 *Pound* III p 311.
7 *Pound* III p 316.

should be free. But, assuming that a choice has been made, the extent to which it can be given effect in any given case depends on the texture of the legal institutions that are involved. Some are more flexible than others and permit a freer play for the balancing process. Elsewhere Pound classified the institutions of the law as follows. There are, first, rules, which are precepts attaching definite consequences to definite factual situations. Secondly, there are principles, which are authoritative points of departure for legal reasoning in cases not covered by rules. Thirdly, there are conceptions, which are categories to which types or classes of transactions and situations can be referred and on the basis of which a set of rules, principles or standards becomes applicable. Fourthly, there are doctrines, which are the union of rules, principles and conceptions with regard to particular situations or types of cases in logically interdependent schemes so that reasoning may proceed on the basis of the scheme and its logical implications. Finally, there are standards prescribing the limits of permissible conduct, which are to be applied according to the circumstances of each case.

Such, then, is the substance of Pound's theory. That his contribution is considerable goes without saying. He more than anyone helped to bring home the vital connection between laws, their administration and the life of society. His work also set the seal on prior demonstrations of the responsible and creative task of lawyers, especially the judges. In so far as his theory laid such heavy emphasis on the existence of varied and competing interests and the need for adjustment between them, it will have enduring value. There are, however, some other respects in which his views are less happy.

In the first place, Pound's engineering analogy is apt to mislead. What, for instance, is the 'waste and friction' in relation to the conflict of interests? Further, the construction, for example of a bridge, is guided by a plan of the finished product, and the stresses and strains to be allowed to each part are worked out with a view to producing the best bridge of that kind in that place. With laws there can be no plan, worked out in detail, of any finished product, for society is constantly developing and changing, and the pressures behind interests are changing too. Therefore, the value or importance to be allotted to each interest cannot be predetermined.

Pound assumed that *de facto* claims pre-exist laws, which are required to 'do something' about them. Some claims, however, are consequent on law, eg those that have resulted from welfare legislation[8]. Besides, what does 'do something' about them mean? It is not enough to say that law has to select those that are to be recognised. 'Recognition' has many gradations, which makes it necessary to specify in what sense an interest is recognised as such. Thus, the cult of Scientology is not outlawed, but it has been officially condemned, which makes it difficult to say in what sense the law recognises or does not recognise it[9].

It is not interests as such, but the yardsticks with reference to which they are measured that matter. It may happen that some interest is treated as an ideal in itself, in which case it is not the interest as an interest, but as an ideal that will determine the relative importance between it and other interests. Thus, whether the proprietary right of a slave-owner is to be upheld or not depends upon whether sanctity of property or sanctity of the person is

---

8 See p 67 ante.

9 For the attitude of a British and the European Court, see *Schmidt v Secretary of State for Home Affairs* [1969] 2 Ch 149, [1969] 1 All ER 904; *Van Duyn v Home Office (No 2)* 41/74 [1975] Ch 358, [1975] 3 All ER 190, [1974] ECR 1337 (European Court).

adopted as the ideal. The choice of an ideal, or even a choice between competing ideals, is a matter of decision, not of balancing; and it is with the choice made by judges and the ideals which they adopt that lawyers are concerned.

The balancing metaphor is also misleading. If two interests are to be balanced, that presupposes some 'scale' or 'yardstick' with reference to which they are measured. One does not weigh interests against one another, even 'on the same plane'. Only with reference to some ideal is it possible to say that the upholding of one interest is more consonant with, or more likely to achieve it than another; which means that with reference to that given ideal the one interest is entitled to preference over the other. This leads to another consideration. The 'weight' to be attached to an interest will vary according to the ideal that is used. For example, with reference to the ideal of freedom of the individual all interests pertaining to individual self-assertion will carry more weight than social interest; but with reference to the ideal of the welfare of society the reverse might be true. The point is that the whole idea of balancing is subordinate to the ideal that is in view. The march of society is gauged by changes in its ideals and standards for measuring interests.

In any case, all questions of interests and ideals should be considered in the context of particular issues as and when these come up for decision. An interest is not presented to a judge preclassified as part of an overall scheme, but in relation to one or more other interests in a given situation. Each situation has a pattern of its own, and the different types of interests and activities that might be involved are infinitely various. It is for the judge to translate the activity involved in the case before him in terms of an interest and to select the ideal with reference to which the competing interests are to be measured. Therefore, the listing of interests is not as important as the views which particular judges take of given activities and the criteria by which they evaluate them.

How does one know when interests exist, how are they made articulate? The answer is: when presented in litigation. Lists of interests can be drawn up, not in advance of, but after the various interests have been contended for in successive cases.

The recognition of a new interest is a matter of policy. The mere presence of a list of interests is, therefore, of limited assistance in helping to decide a given dispute. What this and the last paragraph suggest is that interests need only be considered as and when they arise in disputes; the matter that is of importance is the way in which they are viewed and evaluated by the particular judge.

In any case, lists of interests are only the products of personal opinion. Different writers have presented them differently. With reference to Pound's own elaborate scheme, it is to be observed that his distinction between categories B and C, Public and Social interests, is doubtful[10]. Even the distinction between A and C, Individual and Social interests, is of minor significance. As Pound himself says, in most cases it is preferable to transfer individual interests on to the plane of social interests when considering them. On the suggestion previously made, it is the ideal with reference to which any interest is considered that matters, not so much the interest itself, still less the category in which it is placed. None of these remarks is intended to

10 Pound's disciple, Julius Stone, has abandoned it: Stone *Social Dimensions of Law and Justice* pp 171-175.

detract from the value of Pound's analysis of the interests themselves. All that is urged is that as a guide to the administration of laws the listing of interests is unhelpful.

It is difficult to see how the balancing of interests will produce a cohesive society where there are minorities whose interests are irreconcilable with those of the majority. How does one 'balance' such interests? Whichever interest is favoured, the decision will be resented by those espousing the other; a compromise will most likely be resented by both. There is a different problem where a substantial proportion of the populace is parochially minded and have little or no sense of nationhood. The prime task in such countries is the creation of interests and the emphasis is, once more, on the need for ideals[11]. Pound's theory cannot be accepted too generally.

It is worth while repeating that the criticism here is not that Pound ignored ideals of guidance, but that he seems to have devoted too little attention to them. His awareness of them is evident, for example, in his own distinction between 'natural natural law' and 'positive natural law'. The former, according to him, is 'a rationally conceived picture of justice as an ideal relation among men, of the legal order as a rationally conceived means of promoting and maintaining that relation, and of legal precepts as rationally conceived ideal instruments of making the legal order effective for its ideal end'. The latter is 'a system of logically derived universal legal precepts shaped to the experience of the past, postulated as capable of formulation to the exigencies of universal problems and so taken to give legal precepts of universal validity'[12]. As early as 1919 Pound did offer a set of postulates as underlying contemporary society, but these are far from sufficient today and they have, both in Great Britain and America, been outmoded by the march of events[13]. It is submitted with respect that it would have been preferable had he enlarged on the criteria of evaluating interests instead of developing particular interests. It is possible that his work has not had the practical impact that it ought to have had because of this somewhat sterile preoccupation with interests and too little attention to the criteria of evaluation.

SOCIAL CRITERION OF THE VALIDITY OF LAW

DUGUIT

Duguit (1859-1928) was a professor of Constitutional Law in the University of Bordeaux. He attacked traditional conceptions of state, sovereignty and

11 Stone 'The Golden Age of Pound' (1962) 4 Sydney Law Review 1. Harvey 'A Value Analysis of Ghanaian Legal Development since Independence' (1964) 1 UGLJ 4, points out that in Ghana the need to promote a sense of nationhood has played a paramount role.
12 Pound 'Natural Natural Law and Positive Law' (1952) 68 LQR 330, (1960) Nat LF 70.
13 Men should be able to assume (1) that others will not commit intentional aggressions upon them; (2) that they may control for beneficial purposes what they have discovered, appropriated to their own use, created and acquired; (3) that those with whom they deal will act in good faith, ie carry out promises, carry out undertakings according to the expectations which the moral sentiment of the community attaches thereto, and restore unjust enrichment; (4) that others will act with due care and not create unreasonable risk of injury; and (5) that others will keep under proper control property that is likely to inflict damage if it escapes: Pound *Introduction to American Law* (1919) reproduced in *Outlines of Jurisprudence* (1943). Pound subsequently foreshadowed the emergence of three other principles: (a) assurance of security of employment to employees, (b) responsibility of industrial concerns to make compensation for human wear and tear, and (c) the shouldering of responsibility to compensate misfortune to individuals by society as a whole: *Social Control Through Law*. But the admission of these three will involve important modifications of the previous five.

law and sought to fashion a new approach to these matters from the angle of society.

Social life should be viewed, he insisted, as it is lived, so as to be able to extract the most accurate generalisations. The outstanding fact of society is the interdependence of men. This has always existed and becomes more and more widespread as life grows more complex and as Man's mastery of the world increases. People have common needs, which require concerted effort; they have also dissimilar needs, which require mutual adjustment and accommodation. No one can live at the present time without depending on a far-reaching web of services provided by his fellow-men. Water, food, housing, clothing, recreation, entertainment and so on are dependent on other people. This social interdependence is not a conjecture, but an inescapable fact of human existence. All organisation, therefore, should be directed towards smoother and fuller co-operation between people. This Duguit called the principle of social solidarity[14].

From this platform he launched his assault on traditional conceptions of the state, sovereignty and law. All institutions are to be judged according to how they contribute towards social solidarity. The state can therefore claim no special position or privilege. It is not some mystical entity, but an organisation of men, which can only be justified so far as it furthers social solidarity. When it ceases to do this there is a duty to revolt against it. It is worth pointing out that at no stage did Duguit deny the existence of an organised unity known as the state. This is very much a fact and to deny it would be unreal. What he said was that it is not essential nor entitled to special reverence.

The doctrine of sovereignty has likewise become meaningless. It used to be the personal attribute of a monarch, so such ideas as 'sovereignty of the people' and the like are inappropriate and empty. The idea is, moreover, inadequate for composite and heterogeneous unities such as federal states or the British Commonwealth. Decentralisation makes it difficult to locate sovereignty. The use of the notion of delegation does not alter the fact that parts of sovereignty have been ceded. Nor can sovereignty be reconciled with the increasing responsibilities attaching to the state. For these reasons sovereignty fails to explain the kind of authority that governors now wield over the governed. A better way of looking at it is that all power and organisation are subject to the test of social solidarity. Their existence is functional and does not extend beyond the functions they perform in society. At this point, however, it might be noted that sovereignty is a term with many meanings, and cannot be wholly expelled in this way . There has to be some ultimate source of authority, especially law-making authority, in every society.

In Duguit's view, with the disappearance of sovereignty there disappears also the authority traditionally ascribed to laws, for the basis on which these were thought to rest is then sapped of vitality. If sovereignty is mythical, so too are the notions that a law is (a) the command of a sovereign, single and indivisible, (b) unchallengeable, and (c) the product of a single creative act.

Such is the core of Duguit's thesis. It contains some interesting implications. The first and most obvious is that the state is not indispensable. He drew particular attention to the move towards decentralisation and away from a central machinery of authority in view of the increasingly complex

---

14 Cf Malinowski's doctrine of reciprocity among primitive peoples: p 391 ante.

structure of modern society. A vague parallel might here be detected with the Marxist conception of the 'withering away of the state', though Duguit's approach was different. Against this, it can be argued that totalitarian states of recent times have shown how power can be vested in decentralised groups in such a way as to enhance the power of the central authority.

The state is a useful, though not an essential, organisation, but its power is restricted by social solidarity. Whether such a state of affairs is achieved through a constitution or a judiciary, it is akin to the advocacy of a rule of law. The objection is simply that this is far from being the state of affairs in all countries. It will be remembered that Duguit's own initial contention was that life in society should be viewed as it actually is, so it would seem that his argument is only a plea for what it ought to be. Duguit proceeded to assert that when the state ceased to promote social solidarity there is a duty to revolt against it. Apart from the unreality of basing so drastic an action on a matter of personal evaluation, the point at which disobedience becomes justified is by no means as simple as this[15].

The interdependence of men is a fact, but 'social solidarity' is an ideal. For, in the first place, in practice it becomes a matter of personal evaluation when the question to be decided is whether a given course of conduct is conducive to social solidarity or not. Does a law imposing or forbidding racial segregation promote social solidarity? It is difficult to see how this can be answered objectively and otherwise than in the light of political, religious and moral evaluations. Secondly, whose evaluation of social solidarity is to prevail? There is evidence that the forces of social disruption are as potent as those of solidarity. It would appear that Duguit has unfortunately fallen into the error of enlarging a limited truth into an absolute.

The most significant feature is the way in which Duguit used social solidarity as a criterion of the validity of laws. He asserted that a precept which does not further social solidarity is not law, and denied that statutes and decisions make law in themselves. There are three formative laws, namely, respect for property, freedom of contract, and liability only for fault. The precepts of positive law should conform to these formative laws and they only achieve validity when received and approved by the mass of public opinion. 'A rule of law exists whenever the mass of individuals composing the group understands and admits that a reaction against the violation of the rule can be socially organised'[16]. Public opinion is thus the expression of the social solidarity principle, by which the validity of laws should be judged. This is open to objection. What is this mass opinion? Its vagueness and unsatisfactory nature are obvious. By what means is it discoverable? Situations frequently arise with regard to which no particular feeling exists and others with regard to which opinion is divided. It is unrealistic to suggest that a court will, or will be allowed to, decline to receive an enactment as 'law' because it can be shown that public opinion does not subscribe to it. Once more, it is clear that this is no more than what, in Duguit's opinion, should be the position.

Duguit avoided all imagery of the state as a person with organs and will of its own. The state is nothing more than an organisation of individuals and it is they who issue commands and carry out decisions. He likewise denied the personality of corporations and similar groups. The coherence of all such associations lies, not in some mystic personality, but in social solidarity. It is

15 See pp 313 et seq ante.
16 Duguit 'Objective Law' (1921) 21 Columbia Law Review 22.

ironic that Duguit, who foresaw how personification of the state could lead to totalitarianism, which he abhorred, should have had his own theory used for that very end. Thus, national socialist jurists seized on his minimisation of conflict within society as a justification for the suppression of trade unions and strikes. Employers and workers were pictured as comrades united in their own particular factory or local organisation, which in turn was absorbed in the unity of the state. This created a romantic bond of loyalty to the state and any act against it was treachery. Such a perversion of his doctrines to support the aggrandisement of the state would have horrified Duguit.

His view of the function of government led Duguit to deny the distinction between public and private law. All laws are only means of serving the end of social solidarity and should be judged by that criterion. In the distinction between public and private law Duguit suspected a method of elevating the state above the rest of society and he would have none of it.

Duguit also denied the existence of rights. 'Natural rights' he treated as myths, since modern research has shown that Man has always lived in society and was never entirely independent. The core of the law lies in duty, which is the means of securing that each one fulfils his part in the furtherance of social solidarity. 'The only right which any man can possess, he said, 'is the right always to do his duty'. What are commonly called 'rights' are only incidental to the relations with other people which arise in the course of performing one's social duty. The reality is thus not the right, but the duty. This aspect of Duguit's theory is not only unnecessary, but also verbalistic. He admits, as indeed he could hardly avoid doing, that relationships do arise between individuals. These are commonly described in the language of duties as well as of rights. His objection is merely to the use of the word 'right'.

Finally, Duguit would banish the ethical element from law. All he did, however, was to substitute one ideal in place of others.

Duguit's views have had considerable influence. Their adaptation by Nazi and Fascist jurists has been alluded to. Soviet jurists, too, found parts of his work congenial. His functional approach to laws, his denial of the distinction between public and private law and his advocacy of a form of the 'withering away' of centralised authority and its replacement by a decentralised 'administration of things' had some attraction to Marxist interpreters. His work had influence in another direction as well. The emphasis that he placed on the importance of the group, coupled with advances in later sociological thought, shifted the focus of attention to group behaviour, about which something must now be said.

GROUPS AND INSTITUTIONS

Modern society presents a confusing pattern of different values, which exert different pressures of greater or lesser intensity and of varying application and concern. It is relevant in this connection to have some idea of the influence of groups, roles and institutions.

All groups have some unity. For a start, attention should be paid to the phenomenon known as stratification, which refers to the divisions and cross-divisions of people into degrees of compactness, fluidity, distinctness and separability. They may be temporary or permanent, closed or open (depending upon the ease with which people can pass in and out), occupational (eg teachers, miners), functional (eg income groups), feature (eg racial, religious, caste), and so forth. Stratification influences the social set-up, as where status differences structured feudal society, and racial, religious, or functional differences shape modern societies. It also facilitates social control, as when classifications according to income, race, religion or caste become decisive in the moulding and application of certain types of laws. Other kinds of groups result from co-operative effort on the part of a number of persons to achieve a common purpose, coupled with a sense of belonging to that group. These range from giant, permanent organisations to *ad hoc* and localised bodies, such as a union of residents in a town to oppose a threatened curtailment of some amenity.

Groups and values

A point of jurisprudential interest lies in the intimate connection between group phenomena and values and moral pressures. The values of society are closely connected with power-groups. The aims and ideals of such a group are in the first instance matters of evaluation by its members, but the degree of pressure brought to bear behind the aims and ideals depends on the strength of the group. The stronger the group, the more likely is it that what it stands for will in time begin to prevail outside itself. Powerful economic groups, for instance, have had decisive influence throughout the whole of society, as Marx demonstrated. Once the aims and ideals of a group have become socially accepted in due course of time they cease to be dependent on power, and acquire a life of their own. They in their turn become supports for power and factors *sine quibus non* in the continuance of power or the establishment of new power. Governments, for instance, are generally anxious to associate themselves with accepted values of certain groups, especially those of religion, because they transcend the present power-wielders; which is why the régime in South Africa is anxious to justify *apartheid* by pointing to the support of the influential Dutch Reformed Church. The close association between power-structures and values is also seen in the fact that rebellion against one is often rebellion against the other. Another point is that values evolve slowly and are changed as slowly. In this way they serve as a brake on the exercise of power. This may be illustrated once more with reference to South Africa where the government has found that convictions about *apartheid* now run so deep that they hamper the introduction of any policy which smacks of liberalism.

The pressure on an individual to submit to a group derives, among other things, from his knowledge that others also submit. This generates the feeling of being bound, which the individual either accepts or rejects. Among those who accept, there is the further feeling that there has to be some measure of discipline to preserve the group; while even among those who glory in rejecting it, there is the feeling that non-conformity is rebellion.

Roles

Whenever a person's conduct towards others has some measure of permanence his behaviour becomes, as it were, institutionalised, ie a 'role'. Roles evolve as solutions to problems of interaction between individuals and groups and have been described as 'recognised and established usages governing the relations between individuals and groups'[17]. What becomes institutionalised is a way of going about things and it is, thus, an idea. Not only human beings, but ideas also count, said Renard[18]. The institution may take the form of a role, such as that of chairman, which results from the fact that every group has to have someone to control proceedings; or even a place occupied by a person, such as 'father's place' at table, which may simply be the most convenient place to seat him so that he will not be in the way of those serving the meal. These are very simple examples, but what is common to all forms of institutionalised behaviour is that there has to be general and continuous acceptance of a way of doing things, which comes to serve as a standard of behaviour. This is because roles exert pressure to act in certain ways and carry directions for behaviour. A role may involve a number of relationships ('role-set'), and different roles may overlap. Both social roles and strata tend to have built-in values, so that they are more than just factual situations. Hume illustrated this with an example of the difference between a sapling, which destroys the parent tree, and parricide. In both situations, he said, the factual position is the same, namely, destruction of the parent by its offspring. The difference lies in the disapproval attaching to the one and not to the other, and this comes through regarding the human relationship as a role[19]. Roles exert pressure on performers in various ways. One is the pressure to conform to the traditions and standards of the given role, eg of judge or legal adviser. Likewise certain types of strata influence people to live up to the values, which are part of them, in order to win acceptance or retain acceptability and prestige in them.

While it is true that an 'ought' cannot be derived from an 'is', behaviour-patterns do become so interlocked and inter-dependent that if one person fails to conform, he disrupts the whole to a greater or lesser extent. The structure of society consists of interrelationships between numberless roles and groupings, which are often more durable than human beings. The 'ought' behind 'you ought to conform' to these roles does not express an emotional attitude towards the conduct in question, so much as a condition *sine qua non* of social existence; things being as they are, conformity is the effective way of carrying on together[20]. At this point language takes a hand. Conformity tends to be labelled 'right', 'proper', or 'correct' because it fulfils expectations and is convenient; non-conformity tends to be labelled 'wrong', 'improper', or 'incorrect' because it frustrates other people's expectations and is inconvenient. These words already have powerful moral connotations, and so it comes about that through language there occurs a shift in the meaning from 'right' or 'wrong' behaviour in the sense of being effective or ineffective in achieving an end to such behaviour being thought to be 'morally right' or 'morally wrong'. It should not be forgotten that it is through language that people learn huge numbers of values, which are inherited and propagated by means of verbal symbols. To take an example, in the present social structure in southern Africa *apartheid*, in the opinion of the white races, is the 'right' (ie the only effective) way to preserve stability, since integration with Africans is likely to prove very unsettling; but this has generated the conviction that it must also mean that *apartheid* is 'morally right'. In primitive

17 Ginsberg *Sociology* p 42.
18 Renard *Théorie de l'Institution* p 92.
19 Hume *Treatise on Human Nature* III, 1.1. See also Melden *Rights and Right Conduct*; Emmet *Rules, Roles and Relations* pp 14–15.
20 Cf pp 50–51 ante, and Duguit's 'Social Solidarity' (see p 437 ante).

societies the roles performed in religious ritual patterned social structure. The effective way of achieving certain ends (inducing intervention or non-intervention of the gods) was by performing certain ritual actions. So, as Hocart taught, society was organised on the basis of ritual[1], and the various roles were assigned to different individuals, usually heads of important families. Here, too, the 'ought' behind conformity was that this was a condition *sine qua non* of achieving the desired ends rather than that of obligation. The latter evolved out of the former.

Groups as institutions

Society abounds in institutions of many kinds. An important distinction is that between organised institutions, groupings of people, eg Church, family etc, and conceptual institutions, eg property, ownership etc. Institutions, such as courts, police and the like, perform legal functions, but they consist of persons. Group institutions evolve slowly, for however they come into being, perhaps even by force initially, it takes time for them to become accepted. Such evolution is a social, not a juridical, phenomenon. A sociological theory of institutions is one which explains such data as found in society and is, in effect, an analysis of society; a sociological theory of the law of institutions is concerned with the manner in which laws take account of them.

The pioneer institutionalist was Hauriou (1856–1929), who spoke of an institution as 'an idea of an undertaking which is realised and which persists in a social environment'[2]. To achieve this an authority with organs is called into being; and manifestations of a communion among the members of the social group, who are interested in realising the idea, are directed by the organs and regulated by procedures. Hauriou distinguished between *institutions-personnes*, groups of human beings, and *institutions-choses*, 'institution-things' (eg rules of law, marriage); but the latter he largely ignored. One feature about his theory is that he only took account of those ideas which are innate in men as social animals and in the very nature of social life, ie principles of constitution and regulation without which no kind of group activity would be possible. He further limited his treatment to groups which have achieved a certain degree of development. These features, coupled with an avowed Catholic orientation, gave his theory a natural law tinge, which has been noted by several writers[3]. An Italian, Romano, adopted a more positivist approach and paid attention to 'institution-things'[4]. There are, he said, many more *de facto* institutions in society than enter into Hauriou's analysis. In so far as he tried in this way to take account of all institutions as facts found in any given society, his theory may be said to be empirical and more truly sociological than Hauriou's.

Hauriou's theory is not a theory of group personality, but rather a theory of groups, ie of their social reality; and it is also to be noticed that institutionalism does require the subordination of the individual, to some extent at least, to the institution. There is in this a danger that such a theory may

1 See pp 392–393 ante.
2 Hauriou 'La théorie de l'institution et de la fondation' in *La cité moderne et les tranformations du droit* p 10.
3 Renard *La Théorie de l'Institution*; Jennings 'The Institutional Theory' in *Modern Theories of Law* (ed Jennings) p 68; Stone *Social Dimensions of Law and Justice* p 519.
4 Romano *Ordinamento*.

easily be utilised so as to demand unquestioning obedience to a totalitarian régime in the same way as Duguit's theory was used.

Conceptual institutions

Interest has recently grown in legal concepts and even law itself as institutions. Professor MacCormick[5] has drawn attention to the distinction between an 'institution of law', eg contract, and a particular contract, which is an instance of it. An 'institution of law', according to him, depends on whether there is (a) a set of institutive rules, namely, those specifying what constitutes, eg a contract. Such rules include, but are not co-extensive with, power-conferring rules, since an event may bring a conceptual institution into play. (b) Consequential rules, which specify that when a particular institution exists, then certain jural relations follow in consequence. (c) Terminative rules, which specify how institutions shall end. These, too, include, but are not co-extensive with, power-conferring rules. The important point about institutive rules is that they only indicate the conditions which are 'ordinarily necessary and presumptively sufficient' for the existence or creation of a particular instance of the institution. The qualification leaves flexibility and room for value considerations to play their part. In this way it would seem that there is a return to a study of legal concepts via the treatment of them as institutions.

The institutional nature of laws has been approached by Professor Honoré through the group[6]. To say that something is law is to strike an attitude towards disobedience, and a theory of law is, among other things, a theory about such attitudes. To understand laws one has to begin with a group, since every law is a law of some group, and 'law' is a group structure designed to secure obedience to certain group prescriptions. A 'group' is 'a collection of individuals who share a definite understanding of what is to be done by one or more of themselves in given circumstances, or how the question what is to be done in those circumstances is to be decided'[7]. The 'shared understanding' requires communication of prescriptions, no professed rejection of them, and the prescriptions have to curtail liberty. Further, the prescriptions need to be effective, which requires the interlocking of different types: (i) initial and remedial prescriptions ('Everyone is to do X'—initial; 'If not, Y is to happen'—remedial); (ii) genetic and derivative prescriptions ('Do what X says'—genetic; X says 'All sharpen their knives'—derivative). Such prescriptions need to be institutionalised in the sense that they apply to all members of the group, or in specified circumstances, and there must be group understanding about a rule determining how the group officers are to be appointed and how they function. Nothing is to count as a law which is not an interlocking prescription, or derived from interlocking prescriptions. When, therefore, 'we find prescriptions which are reinforced by genetic or remedial rules of an institutional character (ie supported by group understandings as to the jurisdiction and appointment of the relevant officials) we can speak of the prescriptions and rules that support them as laws'[8].

The above description would fit the arrangements of different kinds of

---

5 MacCormick 'Law as Institutional Fact' (1974) 90 LQR 102.
6 Honoré 'Groups, Laws and Obedience' in *Oxford Essays in Jurisprudence (second series)* (ed Simpson) ch 1.
7 *Honoré* pp 3, 4.
8 *Honoré* p 18.

groups, eg Church, clubs etc. Professor Honoré finds the special status enjoyed by the laws of territorial groups, such as the state, to derive from the fact that such groups are able to institutionalise to a greater extent than other groups the use of force in remedial situations[9].

A different analysis of a legal system as an institution comes from Dr Raz[10]. According to him, the distinctive feature lies in the working of courts. Their decisions are binding even when wrong; but they themselves are bound to apply certain norms prescribing the behaviour of individuals when giving decisions as to whether actual behaviour complies with those norms. So far, the description would fit the institution of a private club as well as the legal system of a state. The distinctive features of the latter are that it is comprehensive, in that it claims authority to regulate every type of behaviour; it is supreme, in that it claims authority over all other institutions and organisations; and it is 'open' in that it provides binding force to certain norms which are not part of it, eg private agreements or foreign laws.

CONCLUSION

Summing up, one might say that the greatest practical contribution of various sociological approaches has been field-work in examining the interaction between law and its social *milieu*. In this respect the position in Great Britain still lags behind that in other countries, but a good deal is now being done[11]. Another outcome is likely to be a pointer to the evolution of ideals on an empirical basis. It has been abundantly demonstrated that laws play a significant and creative role in society, and such a dynamic function presupposes the existence of ideals, even unavowed, to provide directing force. The transcendental idealism of the past suffered a blow at the hands of positivism from which it could never hope to recover; positivism in turn faltered in the face of the problems that confronted it. The rise of sociological study has made possible a synthesis between the two by restoring ideals in a way that could satisfy and give life to the exacting positivist discipline. It is no coincidence that the functional approach has heralded the revival of natural law in this century; it was, indeed, a necessary precursor.

What is it that lawyers, who engage in a social study of their subject, seek to accomplish? To answer this the previous distinction between sociological jurists and legal sociologists is relevant. The former term is convenient to describe those concerned with laws in their social context. They inquire (a) into the circumstances in which laws arise and become differentiated from morality and the like; (b) how the administration of laws is related to justice; (c) what influences are mutually exerted by laws and other types of social phenomena and changes in them. The first of these is essentially a historical type of inquiry and nothing need be added to what has previously been said. The emphasis is very much on the prescriptive content of law. The second question, (b), has two aspects. There is, on the one hand, the question of the criteria which should govern the application of laws. What is needed is a theory for the guidance of administrators. Laws are means for achieving

9 *Honoré* p 20.
10 Raz 'The Institutional Nature of Law' (1975) 38 MLR 489; on which see comment by Reid and Schiff (1976) 39 MLR 118.
11 Eg in the Department of Criminal Science at Cambridge since 1941, which was absorbed into the Institute of Criminology in 1961.

certain ends, and there are thus two sets of 'oughts': those of laws themselves which prescribe the conduct of people in society and by which their actions are judged, and a functional set which prescribes how judges and other administrators should apply the general prescriptive norms so as to achieve certain ends, whatever these might be. In addition to this, there is the question of the social criteria which are thought to govern the very validity of the general prescriptive norms. In connection with the third question, (c), Ehrlich's distinction between norms of decision, which correspond to pre-scriptive rules by which conduct is judged, and norms of conduct according to which people actually behave, is of signal importance. The latter are shaped by the gradual acceptance of the former, but there is also the reverse process whereby the behaviour of people brings about changes in prescriptive rules.

In contrast to all this, the term 'legal sociologist' has been used to refer to those whose main interest is the analysis of society and who seek to fit legal administration as a whole into a concept of society. In this enterprise the differentiation of legal administration from the operation of other forms of social control becomes necessary. It brings in at once the distinctive character of legal enforcement, namely the machinery of sanction, as an important social fact. A caution which must be uttered is that no inferences should be drawn from any such concept of law outside its frame of reference. In brief, one should be wary of deducing from it the nature of laws and legal concepts. It has been pointed out, for example, that the provision of sanctions is part of a concept of 'law in society', but that a misleading picture is presented when inferences are drawn from this as to the nature of the concept of legal duty[12]. The sociologist is concerned with what 'is', ie the totality of legal administration as an observable social phenomenon; but from such an 'is' cannot be derived assertions about the prescriptive 'oughts' behind laws, for the two spheres of discourse are distinct. It would be as erroneous as trying to deduce propositions about actual social behaviour from the prescriptive content of laws. These points may seem obvious enough, but there is a tendency to overlook them.

12 See pp 245–246 ante.

READING LIST

J Bentham *An Introduction to the Principles of Morals and Legislation* (eds J H
Burns and H L A Hart).

J Bentham *The Theory of Legislation* (ed C K Ogden).

L Duguit *Law in the Modern State* (trans F and H J Laski). See also H J Laski's
'Introduction'; pp xvi–xxxiv.

E Ehrlich *Fundamental Principles of the Sociology of Law* (trans W L Moll) especially
pp 489–506.

G Gurvitch *Sociology of Law*.

A M Honoré 'Groups, Laws and Obedience' in *Oxford Essays in Jurisprudence*
(*second series*) (ed A W B Simpson) ch 1.

R von Ihering *Law as a Means to an End* (trans I Husik *The Modern Legal
Philosophy* series V).

H J Laski 'M Duguit's Conception of the State' in *Modern Theories of Law*
(ed W I Jennings) 52.

D N MacCormick 'Law as Institutional Fact' (1974) 90 Law Quarterly Review 102.

E W Patterson 'Pound's Theory of Social Interests' in *Interpretations of Modern
Legal Philosophies* (ed P Sayre) ch 26.

R Pound 'The Scope and Purpose of Sociological Jurisprudence' (1910–11)
24 Harvard Law Review 591; (1911–12) 25 Harvard Law Review 140,
489.

R Pound 'A Survey of Social Interests' (1943–44) 57 Harvard Law Review
1.

R Pound 'Sociology of Law and Sociological Jurisprudence' (1943–44) 5
University of Toronto Law Journal 1.

R Pound *Jurisprudence* I, ch 6; III, pp 79 et seq; 186 et seq; 272 et seq.

J Raz 'The Institutional Nature of Law' (1975) 38 Modern Law Review
489.

A Ross *On Law and Justice* chs 12, 17.

D Schiff 'N S Timasheff's Sociology of Law' (1981) 44 Modern Law Review
422.

J Stone 'The Golden Age of Pound' (1962) 4 Sydney Law Review 1.

J Stone *Social Dimensions of Law and Justice*.

N S Timasheff *An Introduction to the Sociology of Law*.

CHAPTER 21

Modern realism

The two movements in thought dealt with in this chapter are of American and Scandinavian origin respectively. They share the desire to introduce a commonsense approach to problems of and about law, and with that end in view concentrate on 'facts'. Unlike Kelsen, they do not eschew sociology and psychology. On the contrary, these play a prominent part in their interpretations. Not only are they positivist, but also some, at any rate, appear to carry their devotion to facts, and nothing but facts, to extremes. Nevertheless, realism cannot be left out of account; it is a Procrustean term covering various kinds of inquiry which have provided interesting, novel and vigorous stimuli in contemporary legal thought.

AMERICAN REALISTS

A warning is needed against imagining that there is anything like a 'school' of American Realists. The difficulty in the way of a coherent presentation of their views is that there are varying versions of realism as well as changes of front; positions formerly defended have since been forgotten or abandoned. Although the descriptions 'realism' and 'legal realists' are commonly used, this terminology is abandoned in more recent writings. Judge Jerome Frank (1889–1957), a leading exponent, preferred the phrases 'experimentalists' or 'constructive skeptics', and has described his own attitude as one of 'constructive skepticism'. He repudiated the charge that 'the 'realist school' embraced fantastically inconsistent ideas' by pointing out that 'actually no such 'school' existed'. The common bond is, in his words,

> 'skepticism as to some of the conventional legal theories, a skepticism stimulated by a zeal to reform, in the interests of justice, some courthouse ways'[1].

It is this lack of homogeneity that makes presentation difficult. All that will be attempted in these pages is to outline some of the assertions made at various times under the realist label with reference to a few outstanding jurists.

American Realism is a combination of the analytical positivist and sociological approaches. It is positivist in that it first considers the law as it is. Reform is the ultimate aim, but a prerequisite to reform is, in positivist thinking, an understanding of law as it is. On the other hand, the law as it stands is the product of many factors. Inasmuch as the realists are interested in sociological and other factors that influence the law, their approach may also be described as being in part sociological. Their concern, however, is with law rather than with society. They share with sociologists an interest in

---

1 Frank *Law and the Modern Mind* (first English edn 1949) Preface pp vii–viii. It has been pointed out that since the so-called 'realist split' in 1928 'the realist movement lost such coherence as it ever had': Twining *Karl Llewellyn and the Realist Movement* p 67, chs 3–4.

the effects of social conditions on law as well as the effect of law on society, but they emphasise the need for a prior revelation of the actual behaviour of lawyers. Julius Stone calls the realist movement a 'gloss' on the sociological approach[2]. It is part of that aspect of sociology, dealt with in the last chapter, which treats law as a given social phenomenon. Its distinctive feature is the stress that it lays on studies of the behaviour of judges[3].

'Theory' is a means towards understanding, and the test of scientific theory lies in predictability. To understand what 'law' is, one should be able to predict how judges decide cases. Many factors contributed to this spot-lighting of the American judiciary. One is the check imposed upon legislative power by the American Constitution. The judges interpret the Constitution and have power to quash legislation in conflict with it. It is also true that American judges have not enjoyed quite that degree of trust and confidence as their British counterparts. A possible reason is that judges in the lower courts are elected, which opens the door to political influence[4]. Again, American legal institutions are young compared with those in Great Britain. The days when judges were consciously building up the law are still fresh in the minds of American jurists. It is therefore less easy for them than for British jurists to think of the judicial function as being a mechanical application of rules. Also, the divergent and separate common law systems in the different states are evidence of the creative function of the judges. How could these systems have developed along different lines from a common starting point were it not for the creative faculties of judges[5]?

At one time there was a tendency to regard the movement as a thorough-going attempt to dispense with the 'oughts' of the law. Only the 'reality' of law matters in fact, and 'reality' is what actually happens and no more. Ideas of 'ought' and such like were not allowed to distort the perception of clear, simple fact.

The realist approach is highly empirical. Law, ie the decisions of judges, is the product of ascertainable factors. Included among these are their personalities, their social environment, the economic conditions in which they have been brought up, business interests, trends and movements of thought, emotions, psychology and so forth. The importance of the personal element was not new[6], and attention has previously been drawn to the part played by value factors underlying the application of law. Ihering's conversion from his unfinished *Geist* to interests was the truly radical reaction in this direction; and the same might even be said of Pound. The realists gave these, especially the personal element, decisive significance.

Among the techniques, which opened up a new vista in the study of law, the following are the most important. (a) The realists introduced studies of case law from a point of view which distinguished between rationalisation by a judge in conventional legal terminology of a decision already reached, and the motivations behind the decision itself. Unfortunately, the way in which in their early writings they expressed their interest in what judges

2 Stone *Social Dimension of Law and Justice* p 62.
3 For the difference in emphasis, see Radbruch 'Anglo-American Jurisprudence Through Continental Eyes (1936) 52 LQR 530 at 541–542.
4 See Dienstein *Are You Guilty?*, and Vanderbilt CJ 'Court System Reform: a Pressing Problem' *Time* February 21 1955.
5 For an account of these factors, see Goodhart 'Some American Interpretations of Law' in *Modern Theories of Law* 1.
6 See eg Gray *The Nature and Sources of the Law* p 226, and p 221 et seq ante.

actually do (decisions), rather than in what they say they do (reasoning), did create the impression that they were stressing the latter to the exclusion of the former. (b) The inquiry into the motivation behind decisions opened up further lines of investigation. So, the study of the personalities, upbringing and psychology of judges and jurymen assumed significance. (c) The realists also study the different results reached by courts within the framework of the same rule or concept in relation to variations in the facts of the cases, and the extent to which courts are influenced in their application of rules by the procedural machinery which exists for the administration of the law.

'Paper rules' do not produce certainty

This assertion was hardly new, but the way in which it was presented in the early days created an impression that realists were seeking to expel rules altogether.

The seeds were sown in a paper by Mr Justice Holmes (1841-1935) in 1897, in which he put forward a novel way of looking at law. If one wishes to know what law is, he said, one should view it through the eyes of a bad man, who is only concerned with what will happen to him if he does certain things. The traditional description of law is that it consists of rules from which deductions are made.

> 'But if we take the view of our friend, the bad man, we shall find that he does not care two straws for the action or deduction, but that he does want to know what Massachusetts or English courts are likely to do in fact. I am much of his mind. The prophecies of what the courts will do in fact and nothing more pretentious are what I mean by the law'[7].

Mr Justice Holmes was in no sense purporting to give a final definition of law, or do more than give a description suitable for the context in which he was writing. The statement that law is only what courts do is iconoclastic, and suggests that ethics, ideals and even rules should be put on one side. Holmes himself had no such intention, for in the same paper he proceeded to insist on the need to restrict the area of uncertainty and on the need for more theory. 'We have too little theory in the law' he said 'rather than too much'[8]. Nor did he, at the time when he wrote, have any suspicion that he would be hailed as the prophet of a new faith. Yet such was his fate. Another pioneer of the new fashion in thinking was Gray (1839-1915), who drew a distinction between law and source of law. The former is what the judges decide. Everything else, including statute, are only sources of law until interpreted by a court[9]. Pushed to its logical conclusion, the obvious implication of this is that even a judicial decision is 'law' only for the parties in the instant dispute and thereafter becomes a 'source of law', since everything will depend on the interpretation that is put upon it in a later decision.

Frank's *Law and the Modern Mind* (1930)[10] is perhaps as typical of early

---

7 Holmes 'The Path of the Law' in *Collected Legal Papers* at p 173.
8 *Holmes* at p 198.
9 He defined 'the law' as follows: 'The law of the state or of any organised body of men is composed of the rules which the courts, that is, the judicial organs of that body lay down for the determination of legal rights and duties': Gray *The Nature and Sources of the Law* p 84. He said of statute that 'the courts put life into the dead words of the statute': p 125. Other 'sources' include expert opinion, customs and public policy.
10 By the time of the British edition in 1949 his views had undergone some modification. Accordingly, while leaving the original text intact, he included a lengthy Preface indicating his revised opinions.

realism as any other work of that period. His main attack was originally directed at the myth of achieving certainty through legal rules. The traditional picture of a legal order is that rules impart to it at least some measure of certainty and uniformity. There is a difference, pointed out by Beale, a great American jurist, between rules and judicial decisions. The 'law' consists of rules; a judicial decision is in no sense the only law, because it is given by virtue of a rule. Frank was vehement in attacking this notion. In the first place, if judgments were so easy to forecast, no one but litigious maniacs would ever go to court. It is quite untrue to suggest that uncertainty stems from uncertainty in rules. In the majority of cases, even where there is some rule which can be applied, two opposite conclusions are perfectly possible. He gave two examples to contradict Beale's thesis that law is distinct from judicial decisions[11]. The Supreme Court in 1917 was equally divided on the question of the validity of a certain statute. In 1923 the Court by a majority declared it to be invalid. In the meantime the personnel of the Court had varied several times, and had the matter come up between November 1921 and June 1922 the decision would have gone the other way. What, then, was the law during the period from 1917 to 1923? The answer would surely have varied according to the date when the question was asked, and according to guesses as to the personnel of the Supreme Court. His other example was where the Kentucky State Court took one view of the law of Kentucky on a particular point, while the Supreme Court took a different view of the law of Kentucky on the same point. The question What was the law? depended on whether it was asked of the Supreme Court or the Court of Kentucky. Law, therefore, cannot be divorced from judicial decisions; it is not, in the words of Holmes, 'a brooding omnipresence in the sky'. Frank rejected such objectifications of the law, which he despised as 'Bealism'[12].

Frank suggested that this craving for certainty and guidance, which men seek in rules, may stem, in part at any rate, from the yearning for security and safety which is an inescapable legacy of childhood. The child puts his trust in the power and wisdom of his father to provide an atmosphere of security. In the adult the counterpart of this feeling is the trust reposed in the stability and immutability of human institutions. Frank suggested that the quest for certainty in law is in effect a search for a 'Father-symbol' to provide an aura of security, and although he attributed great prominence to this factor, he offered it only as a 'partial explanation' of what he called the 'basic myth', and listed fourteen other explanations as well[13]. He called on lawyers to outgrow these childish longings for a 'father controlled world', and to follow the example of Mr Justice Holmes, the 'completely adult jurist'.

Rules, then, are merely word-formulae. If they are to have any meaning at all, such meaning has to be sought in the facts of real life to which they correspond. Frank adopted a quotation from Holmes:

> 'We must think things not words, or at least, we must constantly translate our words into the facts for which they stand if we are to keep to the real and the true'.

---

11 Frank *Law and the Modern Mind* pp 50, 51.

12 Frank p 55.

13 *Frank* Preface pp xxi–xxii, Part I, ch 2, and Appendix I, p 263. The other explanations are: the religious impulse, the aesthetic impulse, professional habits, protection of vested interests, instinct to seek security and certainty, interest in peace and quiet, imitation, devotion to custom, inertia, laziness, stupidity, mental structure, language and word-magic, the Barry-Watson theory.

If the 'facts' in the world which correspond to talk about law are actual decisions this yields a simple picture of law. Frank's original view was that 'law on any point is either (a) actual law, ie a specific past decision as to that situation, or (b) probable law, ie a guess as to a specific future decision'[14]. Later he showed a reluctance to use the word 'law'.

> 'Instead', he said, 'I would state directly—without an intervening definition of that term—what I was writing about, namely (1) specific court decisions, (2) how little they are predictable and uniform, (3) the process by which they are made, and (4) how far, in the interest of justice to citizens that process can and should be improved'[15].

The above passage, taken from the Preface added nineteen years after the original version, represents a modification of Frank's position, or, alternatively, an attempt to dispel misconceptions about it. Shortly after the first publication, however, statements such as the distinction between 'actual' and 'probable' law not unnaturally created a certain impression, which touched off controversy. In reply to Roscoe Pound's attack Llewellyn protested that his criticism was beside the point as it was not founded on what the realists had actually said, but on what they were supposed to have said[16]. The realists were at least guilty of over-statement; and whether misconceived or not, the polemic is a fact of history, which had the merit of inducing some healthy re-thinking and clarification by both sides. Much of the heaviest fire was brought to bear in defence of rules against a real or imagined onslaught on their existence.

Did the early realists reject rules? It is not clear how many did, if any[17]. The importance of rules may be questioned, but that is a matter of degree. To assert that a judge's 'hunch' determines the way in which he manipulates 'paper rules' and guides the logic of justifying it is unexceptionable; but to assert or imply that 'paper rules' are illusory and that the 'hunch' reigns supreme, is too strong a statement. Judges are largely bound by rules and have little choice, whatever their sympathies; and even when they circumvent rules, they do so in a manner which conceals the fact that they are doing so. In other words, the 'hunch' only operates within the framework of the rules. In another sense, the assertion that the 'hunch' is supreme goes scarcely far enough, for the 'hunch' is itself the product of standards, patterns of behaviour, concepts and rules. Suppose that X rides off on the first bicycle which he finds parked in the street, and which Y had placed there a short while before. There can be no doubt that in an action by Y against X the 'hunch' would come down in favour of Y, because it is born of ideas about ownership, rights of possession and so on. The importance of rules can be demonstrated in another way by asking, How does one know who is a 'judge'? The point is that the position of a judge and, indeed, of every other official is defined by rules. The realists properly drew attention to many factors that influence the judges apart from rules. They rightly indicated that it is fallacious to regard what the judges *say* as an infallible guide to what

14 *Frank* p 46.
15 *Frank* Preface p vi.
16 Pound 'The Call for a Realist Jurisprudence' (1931) 44 Harv LR 697, answered by Llewellyn 'Some Realism about Realism: Responding to Dean Pound' (1931) 44 Harv LR 1222 (reprinted in *Jurisprudence: Realism in Theory and Practice* ch 2). Llewellyn charged Pound with failing to identify the individuals who held the views that he attacked.
17 Llewellyn did not, even in the early days. This is now clear from his later *The Common Law Tradition*, and an unfinished book, *The Theory of Rules*. See *Twining* App B p 488.

they *do*. Yet, it is equally fallacious to assert that what judges say can *never* be a guide to what they do; they sometimes say that they are bound by rules because their decisions have in fact been so governed. The point is that the reasons which particular judges give for doing certain things are very much a part of what they do. To be realist in the full sense of the word would require that allowance be made for the way in which non-realist judges behave, which includes their adherence to rules. So, if anyone were to reject rules, he would be more unrealistic than 'traditionalists'. Much of the trouble seems to stem from misleading impressions created by the way in which some realists expressed themselves, especially in their earlier works. Perhaps, what they were doing was to illustrate the tension between what judges do (pronounce decisions) and who they are (people with human responses).

Preoccupation with the hunches of individual judges tended to obscure the fact that judges do agree by and large on certain yardsticks of evaluation, and also the fact that they consciously strive to put aside personal considerations. Shared values produce an extensive and impersonal background against which instances of personal prediliction are few. Again, a quirk may manifest itself on some occasions and not others and it would be misleading to exaggerate its significance. The point is that rules do act as a brake on caprice. The realists succeeded in filling a minute fraction of the picture of judicial action by looking only at personal and environmental factors; the pressure of rules and other impersonal factors also play a decisive part[18].

A rule is more abstract than a judicial decision and to that extent may be thought to be farther from 'reality'; but both are the concern of lawyers. In cases which never come before the courts they have to advise their clients as to the law. It is true that here, too, much of what is stated to be law has been the subject of previous judicial decisions; but immediately after a new statute comes into force, and before it comes before the courts, it would be possible for a lawyer to advise his client that a new rule of law has superseded the old rule. To argue that it is only a statement as to 'probable law' is unrealistic. A great many daily transactions go forward and are governed by what everyone takes to be 'law' even though few of them ever reach the tribunals.

The contention that 'laws' are only what judges and officials do is a somewhat unusual meaning of the word. Statutes and precedents are followed *because* they are 'laws' already. When it is stated that statutes are accepted by the courts as capable of imparting to propositions the quality of 'law', this implies that a statutory rule *will* be accepted by them as 'law'. Gray and Frank appeared to say that the stamp of 'law' is only applicable after the judge has actually decided; which is not the accepted usage. The fact that judges interpret statutes and precedents and keep shaping and reshaping their contents does not mean that they are not 'laws' until interpreted. Clay is clay before, during and after it has been moulded. Moreover, why is it 'realistic' to apply the word 'law' at the point of interpretation and no other? A decision is no more 'real' in providing the damages, property, or whatever else is sought, than a rule. For the decision has still to be carried out and the officials charged with that task may be bribed, the defendant may be bankrupt etc. Another difficulty is that it may be abundantly clear in advance that because of the insufficiency of evidence the court is certain to acquit, for example, a thief, and in fact does acquit him. If law is what a

18 See pp 213–215, 221–222 ante.

court does, or prediction of what it will do in fact, would it be said in a case such as this that there is no law forbidding theft? If it is said that a court *might have* convicted had there been sufficient evidence, that immediately implies the presence of some rule, independent of the decision, on the basis of which a conviction could have been obtained. To say that the actual decision alone becomes 'law' necessarily means that it forthwith ceases to be 'law' for the future, since it will in its turn be subjected to interpretation and be embodied in another decision. 'Law' then, in the words of one critic, 'never *is*, but is always about to be. It is realised only when embodied in a judgment, and in being realised expires'[19].

Any interpretation based only on things which have come before tribunals overlooks the point that law is very much concerned with regulating future behaviour. Such regulation is guided by policies formulated in prescriptive propositions, accepted as 'laws' by courts. This being the case, the expulsion of the 'ought' from a concept of law is impossible. As pointed out, even the idea of law as what judges do should include the reasons for their actions, which would bring in their acceptance of prescriptive rules. It may be that some realists, at any rate, were seeking to derive *descriptive* rules of judicial behaviour, in which case they and the 'traditionalists' were talking about different things.

Whatever merit there was in Frank's assertion that devotion to rules is a manifestation of a childish craving for certainty and fixity, it would seem that it was only he who craved for a 'Father-symbol' in wanting to pin the word 'law' to something definite and fixed, namely, actual decisions. Few, if any, 'traditionalists' asserted that rules can guarantee certainty; on the contrary, they avow the unavoidability and indeed necessity for some measure of flexibility and discretion. To say that law should aspire towards economy of thought and precision is one thing; to say that nothing is law which is not fixed and precise has no basis whatever. A denial that certainty in law can be achieved through rules is no reason why these may not be *called* 'law'. The point would not be worth mentioning were it not for another misleading impression. Frank's statement, quoted earlier and echoing Gray, that until a court has pronounced on a matter there is only 'probable law', suggested that even a statutory rule is not 'actual law' until it has been the subject of a judicial decision. To change the accepted meaning of the word 'law' in this way would involve rewriting textbooks and reports to no purpose. For rules would still remain, though not called 'law'. In one place Frank was driven to admit the existence of rules, though he deemed it a mistake to call them 'law'[20], thereby reducing the matter to a verbal level. In fairness to Frank, it must be pointed out that this was, at worst, a misleading way of expressing himself. In his later thoughts he forcibly reaffirmed the importance of rules, and in his own words, 'backed out of that silly word battle'[1] which is an admission that he had created a misleading impression.

To look at law solely from the point of view of one who is concerned with predicting judicial reactions is too narrow. If, eg one were to regard law as a judge, it would be futile to say that it consists of predictions as to how he himself will decide and, moreover, his own past decisions and those of other judges would only comprise a fraction of the law in his view. From the point of view of a legislator law will appear, not so much as what judges do, but

19 Cardozo *The Nature of the Judicial Process* p 126.
20 *Frank* pp 130–131.
 1 *Frank* Preface pp vi and xxiv.

what they are made to do. Further, the realist viewpoint is helpful in a system which leaves considerable independence to the judiciary. In a system in which judges are strictly controlled and in which their discretion is greatly reduced, the focus of attention will inevitably shift away from the judges to those who do wield power and discretion.

From all this it should be clear that up to this point the realists said nothing about law which would be denied by 'traditionalists'. That might have been the case had they been able to expel the 'ought' or rules from the law, but they did not succeed in doing either. They denied that certainty can ever be completely achieved through rules, which no 'traditionalist' will controvert.

Once the rule controversy is put on one side, there is a better chance of assessing the solid contribution of the realists, which was to furnish a valuable extension to the work of sociologists. They were seeking the factual bases of decisions with a view to sociological description, which investigates the values and forces that provide the motive power for the working of rules as instruments of social regulation. A study of values alone will not explain the view which particular judges are likely to take of them, nor the degree of importance they may individually attach to one value or another. It is here that the realists were able to uncover innumerable personal and other factors that on occasions determine judicial choice and gave them prominence. In the end, however, the 'is' and the 'ought', the open texture of rules, values, morality, sociology and psychology have all become part of the realist cosmos. As someone remarked, 'We're all realists now'. It is not that all these other aspects have quietly been crowding in under the realist umbrella, but that the realists have been enlarging their umbrella to cover them.

No account of realism can be complete without some mention of Karl N Llewellyn (1893-1962), whose work spanned the movement from its beginnings in the 1930s until his death in 1962. Some of his early writings, too, lent themselves to misinterpretation, but these should be viewed as part of the whole development of his thought[2]. He outlined the principal features of the realist approach as follows[3].

(1)   There has to be a conception of law in flux and of the judicial creation of law.

(2)   Law is a means to social ends; and every part of it has constantly to be examined for its purpose and effect, and to be judged in the light of both and their relation to each other.

(3)   Society changes faster than law, and so there is a constant need to examine how law meets contemporary social problems.

(4)   There has to be a temporary divorce of 'is' and 'ought' for purposes of study. This is necessary in order to clarify the level of discourse and to show how each figures in the judicial process and, indeed, to show ultimately how pervasive is the role of the 'ought'. Perhaps, Llewellyn was also reacting against the belief in a transcendent morality inherent in law. Ideas of justice and teleology are not expelled altogether, but should be put on one side while investigating what the law is and how it works. By this divorce both processes will be

2 On this see Twining 'Two Works of Karl Llewellyn' (1967) 30 MLR 514; (1968) 31 MLR 165, and in more detail in *Karl Llewellyn and the Realist Movement*.
3 Llewellyn 'Some Realism About Realism—Responding to Dean Pound' (1930-31) 44 Harvard LR 1222, reprinted in *Jurisprudence* ch 2.

improved. The realists are interested in the aims and ends of the law, and it was precisely a desire to improve the law that brought the movement into being. Adequate reform, however, has to be preceded by an examination of how the law in fact operates. Such an investigation will be imperfect and clouded if done with 'an intrusion of Ought-spectacles during the investigation of the facts'.

(5)   The realists distrust the sufficiency of legal rules and concepts as descriptive of what courts do. This was always a cardinal point in their approach to law.

(6)   Coupled with this is a distrust of the traditional theory that rules of law are the principal factors in deciding cases. The realists have drawn attention to many other influences which, in their view, play a decisive part. To define law solely in terms of legal rules is therefore absurd.

(7)   The realists believe in studying the law in narrower categories than has been the practice in the past. Different results can be reached within the framework of the same rule or concept in different branches. They feel that part of the distortion produced by viewing the law in terms of legal rules is that rules cover hosts of dissimilar situations, where in practice utterly different considerations apply. So, in the law of contract, topics such as mistake and frustration must be studied in small fields according to their application in different types of transactions. Possession would be another good example[4].

(8)   They also insist on the 'evaluation of any part of the law in terms of its effects' and on 'the worthwhileness of trying to find these effects'.

(9)   Finally, there must be a sustained and programmatic attack on the problems of the law along the lines indicated above.

As Llewellyn admitted, these points were not new. The first three furnished an obvious foundation for any sociological approach to jurisprudence. Perhaps, the main characteristics of realism lay first, in the prominence ascribed to the fourth, fifth, sixth, seventh and eighth points; and, secondly, in the amalgamation of all nine points into a working programme and the actual carrying out of research along these lines.

Improving fact-finding processes in trial courts

Frank urged that too much attention has traditionally been devoted to the processes in appellate courts to the neglect of lower courts. Accordingly, some realists have urged that research be broadened so as to include the activities of lower courts and the relation between their work and those of upper courts. Knowledge of what goes on in the lower courts is needed in order to know what law 'means to persons in the lower income brackets'. Frank thought that there is as much of a contrast between the picture of the law that one gets by studying the work of appellate courts to the exclusion of a study of trial courts as there is between an account of manners in Buckingham Palace and in a New York subway. His comment on Cardozo's account of the nature of the judicial process is:

4 See ch 13 ante.

'Cardozo, most of his days an appellate court lawyer or appellate court judge, suffered from a sort of occupational disease, appellate-court-itis'[5].

Frank accordingly divided realists into two camps, described as 'rule skeptics' and 'fact skeptics'. The 'rule skeptics' rejected legal rules as providing uniformity in law, and tried instead to find uniformity in rules evolved out of psychology, anthropology, sociology, economics, politics etc[6]. Kelsen, it will be remembered, maintained that it is not possible to derive an 'ought' from an 'is'. The 'rule skeptics' avoided that criticism by saying that they were not deriving purposive 'oughts', but only predictions of judicial behaviour analogous to the laws of science. Frank called this brand of realism the left-wing adherents of a right-wing tradition, namely, the tradition of trying to find uniformity in rules. They, too, had to account for uncertainty in the law on the basis of rule-uncertainty. The 'fact skeptics', among them Frank, rejected even this aspiration towards uniformity. It savoured of 'Bealism'. So he abandoned all attempts to seek rule-certainty and pointed to the uncertainty of establishing even the facts in trial courts. These have to be established largely by witnesses, who are fallible and who may be lying. It is impossible to predict with any degree of certainty how fallible a particular witness is likely to be, or how persuasively he will lie. All persons, judges and jurymen alike, form different impressions of the dramas unfolded before them; an inflexion or a cough may awaken subconscious predilictions, varied idiosyncrasies and prejudices. Eternal verities are not to be erected on such a basis. Frank alleged that all those who write on legal certainty, not excepting the 'rule skeptics', overlook these difficulties.

'They often call their writings 'jurisprudence'; but, as they almost never consider juries and jury trials, one might chide them for forgetting 'juriesprudence''[7].

Frank, in his later writings, notably *Courts on Trial*, summed up his objective as being the demonstration, not of the nature of law, but of the difficulties and problems that beset trial rather than appellate judges, and of the inadequacy of existing methods of trial[8]. Not only have the realists given an insight into the judicial process, but they have encouraged and enlisted the aid of statistical inquiries. By all means let the illusion, if indeed it persists, that rules can secure certainty be dispelled, and let daylight be shed on those factors that make for flexibility and variation with a view to the removal of caprice and prejudice; but nothing in all this impairs the prestige of rules or the prescriptive function of law.

Realism as a technology

A decisive stage in the development of Llewellyn's thought came with his notable anthropological investigation in collaboration with Hoebel into the 'law-ways' of the Cheyenne Indians[9], which broke fresh ground in

5 Frank *Law and the Modern Mind* Preface p xxvi. He would have levelled a similar charge against Llewellyn, another realist, who in *The Common Law Tradition. Deciding Appeals*, concentrated exclusively on appellate courts.

6 Twining speaks of a distinction between 'textbook formulations of legal rules and scepticism about the very existence of any rules or principles', and that Frank's phrase 'rule-skepticism' obscures this: pp 32, 408.

7 *Frank* Preface p xi.

8 *Frank* Preface p xxv, and *Courts on Trial*. The *Sacco-Vanzetti* affair 1921–1927, provided an early and powerful stimulus to inquiries into the fairness of trial processes.

9 Llewellyn, Hoebel *The Cheyenne Way* (1941).

anthropology by introducing the case-method of approach. The direction of field-work for this undertaking grew out of his early realism, while his later realism was much influenced by the conclusions that were reached. In particular, the 'law-jobs' theory was evolved side by side with this project[10]. It can be explained as follows. Certain needs have to be met if a group is to survive and achieve its purpose, namely (a) adjustment of trouble-cases, which gives off new material for doing other law jobs. This job is comparable to running 'garage-repair' work. (b) Preventive channelling of conduct and expectations so as to avoid trouble. (c) Preventive rechannelling of conduct and expectations so as to adjust to change. The importance of both these is to be seen in the resistance to certain types of new legislation, eg racial integration. Such legislation introduces 'law' by which trouble-cases are to be decided, but it may fail to channel conduct in advance in accordance with it and so prevent future trouble-cases. (d) Allocation of authority and arranging procedures, ie arranging the 'say' and the manner of its saying (authorities and procedures for decision-making). (e) Providing incentive and direction within the group, ie the 'whither' of the group as a whole. (f) Ways of handling legal tools in these various law-jobs and their upkeep and improvement—the job of juristic method[11]. There can never be one hundred per cent fulfilment of each job, so one difficulty is in knowing at what point shortcoming amounts to failure. Does 'groupness' cease if there is failure in any one or more of the jobs, and, if not, at what point does it cease? Llewellyn became increasingly preoccupied with the problem of method and never ceased to reiterate that realism was not a 'philosophy' but a 'technology'; 'see it fresh. See it as it works'.

He stressed the concept of 'institution', which is 'in the first instance an organised activity built around the doing of a job, or cluster of jobs'[12]. Law-jobs are done by institutions. This makes behaviour the focal point of his jurisprudence, and he probably meant no more than this when he said early on:

> 'This doing of something about disputes, this doing of it reasonably, is the business of law. And the people who have the doing in charge, whether they be judges or sheriffs or clerks or jailers or lawyers, are officials of the law. *What these officials do about disputes is, to my mind, the law itself*'[13].

This was not offered as a credo and was no more than a reaction against what went before. An institution always has a job to do and to do it well. There is, he says, a leeway to *be* wrong or right, but a leeway to *do right* is never a leeway to *do wrong*. Performance of law-jobs is one aspect of the task of law-government in society. There must then be some distinction between law and other social institutions. This lies in the fact that law requires specialists and procedure, supremacy within the group, effectiveness and regularity[14].

10 Llewellyn 'The Normative, the Legal and the Law-jobs: the Problem of Juristic Method (1939–40) 49 Yale LJ 1355; *Law in our Society.*
11 Llewellyn set this to verse: *Jurisprudence* p 214.
12 Llewellyn *Law in our Society* p 21.
13 Llewellyn *The Bramble Bush* (1930) p 3. He later modified this saying that this was 'a very partial statement of the whole truth': 2nd edn p 9. For the continuity of his thought from *The Bramble Bush* to his final position, see Llewellyn *The Common Law Tradition. Deciding Appeals* Appendix B.
14 Llewellyn 'The Normative, the Legal and the Law-jobs' (1939–40) 49 Yale LJ 1355 at 1364; *Law in our Society* p 21.

Predicting judicial decisions

Towards the end Llewellyn was concerned with what he saw as a growing loss of confidence in appellate courts because of the unpredictability of their decisions. This, he thought, was unjustified, so in *The Common Law Tradition. Deciding Appeals*, he sought to restore confidence by showing that there is a 'reckonable' quality about appellate court work. He agreed with Frank to the extent of distinguishing between work in trial courts and appellate courts, but whereas Frank scorned the latter, he concentrated on them. Craftsmanship, he maintained, is possible in litigation. 'A craft is a minor institution. A *major* institution differs in that its job-cluster is fundamental to the continuance of the society (or group) with typical resulting complexities'[15]. Crafts evolve around such major institutions. Craftsmanship in law includes not only the various skills of lawyers, but also tradition, ethos, training etc; and the way in which legal craftsmen use their skills determines their 'style'. There are various ways of dealing with precedents, such as following, distinguishing, expanding and re-directing[16]. A judge's handling of them is not capricious or arbitrary, but is guided by his 'situation-sense', which is a key-concept as well as being the most obscure. It is more than just 'the view taken of the facts'. It seems to include stating the facts in categories which are as close to the actual facts giving rise to the dispute, together with an understanding of the whole background, ie the trade, standard practices etc, and the prevailing opinions and values[17]. The doubt about this is that, whatever it means, a situation-sense may be forthcoming in some types of disputes, but not in others. Apart from situation-sense, a check on arbitrariness and caprice is also maintained by fourteen steadying factors, relating to the whole ethos of the procession, tradition, training and techniques[18]. 'Reckonability' is said to depend on three laws, of which the first is the 'Law of Compatibility', where the application of an appropriate rule is compatible with sense. This increases 'reckonability' of the decision and the direction of its *ratio*. Secondly, there is the 'Law of Incompatibility', where the above does not obtain and where the ground of decision lies outside the rule. Thirdly, there is the 'Law of Singing Reason', where there is a rule with a right 'situation-sense' and clear scope and thus gives maximum 'reckonability'. The judicial craft which results from a right situation-sense, reason and justice is called the 'Grand Style', which is overtly functional and purpose orientated, as opposed to 'Formal Style', which is overtly concerned only with the logical application of 'paper' rules. The 'Grand Style' is one of the fourteen major steadying factors alluded to above, and Llewellyn relied heavily on it to produce 'reckonability'.

From all this it will be evident that Llewellyn's position was far removed from that of Frank. It has been doubted whether there was in fact a crisis of confidence and, if so, whether he succeeded in restoring confidence by

15 Llewellyn *Law in our Society* p 21.
16 Llewellyn gave sixteen distinguishing techniques and sixteen for providing 'a fresh start'; and thirty-two techniques of following and applying: *The Common Law Tradition* pp 77-91.
17 *Twining* pp 226-227.
18 (1) Law-conditioned officials, (2) legal doctrine, (3) known doctrinal techniques, (4) responsibility for justice, (5) one single right answer, (6) an opinion of the court, (7) a frozen record from below, (8) issues limited, sharpened and phrased in advance, (9) adversary argument by counsel, (10) group decision, (11) judicial security and honesty, (12) a known Bench, (13) the general period-style and its promise, (14) professional judicial office: *The Common Law Tradition* pp 19 et seq.

re-establishing the 'reckonability' of appellate decisions. The case law material used in the book consists of a small percentage of appeals. It has been estimated that 70–90 per cent of appeals are 'foredoomed' and 'not worth appealing'. This fact alone, it has been pointed out, 'would have disposed more satisfactorily of the alleged crisis of confidence than his attempts to show that the Grand Style promotes reckonability'[19]. Further, the 'situation-sense', which appears to be basic to this thesis, is too vague, being in every case the product of a shifting balance. Be that as it may, long before the publication of this work, Llewellyn had given practical demonstration of his jurisprudence in the great and successful Uniform Commercial Code of which he was one of the chief architects from 1937 to 1952. His biographer points out that in it may be seen how 'Grand Style' thinking can be utilised, not only in judicial opinions, but also in legislation[20]. Perhaps, one may best sum up by saying that *The Common Law Tradition* is Llewellyn's *magnum opus*, but that the Uniform Commercial Code is his monument.

Mechanical prediction: jurimetrics

In recent years attempts to predict judicial behaviour have taken a mechanical turn for which the term 'jurimetrics' has been invented[1]. It takes the form of different kinds of investigations into legal phenomena by using symbolic logic, behavioural models and mechanical aids[2]. Boolean algebra is used to analyse complex sets of facts, prediction of behaviour has moved away from that of the individual to that of groups, and the use of computers is being explored increasingly. These new directions are not necessarily dependent on realism, but may be regarded as developments along its line.

THE GROUP APPROACH[3]. A group, eg the American Supreme Court, has group reactions. It is difficult to predict the behaviour of an individual, but that of a mass of people is easier. Student groups have been used as models of actual social groups. It is not enough merely to take account of the way in which the members of a group vote; it is necessary to consider the influence of personalities and of reasoned argument. In this connection two types of leadership are thought to be significant: task-leadership, which is directed towards solving a given problem efficiently, and social-leadership, which provides a friendly atmosphere conducive to solving it.

This kind of inquiry can only work so long as there is a constant membership within the group. If this varies, as with the Court of Appeal or House of Lords, and there is no knowledge in advance of the precise composition of the group in a given case, there is no basis for prediction. There is also the difficulty of obtaining adequate information about the inner workings of a group. What is available tends to be fragmentary at most, eg memoirs and biographies, and these, in any case, are not available until after death. Even if it can be discovered who is the task- or social-leader, it is not clear how

19 *Twining* p 250.
20 *Twining* ch 12 and p 340.
 1 By Loevinger 'Jurimetrics—the Next Step Forward' (1949) 33 Minn LR 455.
 2 Kayton 'Can Jurimetrics be of Value to Jurisprudence?' (1964–65) 33 Geo Wash LR 287; Meyer 'Jurimetrics: the Scientific Method in Legal Research' (1966) 44 Can BR 1; Beutel *Experimental Jurisprudence: Jurimetrics* (ed Baade).
 3 Murphy 'Courts as Small Groups' (1965–66) 79 Harv LR 1565; Synder 'The Supreme Court as a Small Group' (1958) 36 Social Forces 232; Schubert *Judicial Behaviour* (1966) Geo Wash LR 593.

one could tell whether these tasks have in fact been performed as well as they should, or performed at all. The use of models could be misleading. When using scientific models, which are simplified abstractions of fixed phenomena, the corrections that have to be made are fixed too. Where, however, the phenomena fluctuate, as with human beings and social phenomena generally, it is impossible to know what corrections need to be made. For this purpose models are useless.

COMPUTER PREDICTION. It has also been suggested that in so far as there is consistency in decision and attitude, the prediction of judicial opinions by computers becomes possible. Computer techniques in this connection have been of fact studies (correlation between the circumstances in particular cases and decisions given in them) and attitude studies (correlation between personal attitudes to policies and decisions given). With regard to the former, it is said that the acceptance of a fact by an appellate court rests on identifiable conditions surrounding the way in which it was presented to the trial court[4]. Further, if the accepted facts are combined in certain ways, the decisions will go one way. Personal attitudes are also said to be capable of being scaled by means of scalogram analysis[5]. The basis of this is that a person who reacts positively to a weak stimulus will react similarly to any stronger stimulus, while a person who reacts negatively to a strong stimulus will react similarly to any weaker stimulus. If a line of cases can be made to scale in this way, this would show that a set of values is shared by members of that court. The future behaviour of that court then becomes predictable, as well as the probable effects of a change in composition.

It is submitted that such attempts at prediction seem destined to fail. The personal element just cannot be eliminated from judicial decisions. (a) Everything depends on how facts are viewed and stated. The same set of facts can be stated in different combinations and at different levels of generality. No mechanical aid can predict which combination or level is likely to be chosen. (b) Different *rationes* can be extracted from a decision depending on whether the later court wishes to see resemblances or differences. If it is known which way a judge is going to regard a rule, a computer is not needed; if it is not known, a computer is useless[6]. Another consideration is that the predictability of judicial decisions depends upon consistency in judges' attitudes to values; but people's attitudes change with age and experience[7]. Moreover, computer prediction can only work on the basis of reported decisions, the majority of which, especially those of lower courts, are unreported. This means that the bulk of a judge's early decisions are unlikely to be available, so the basis for predicting his reactions is woefully inadequate. Prediction also requires constant working material; it cannot operate when new matter

4 Kort 'Quantitative Analysis of Fact-patterns in Cases and their Impact on Judicial Decision' (1965–66) 79 Harv LR 1595; Nagel 'Predicting Court Cases Quantitatively' (1965) 63 Mich LR 1411; Schubert *Quantitative Analysis of Judicial Behaviour; Judicial Decision-making* (ed Schubert): Becker *Political Behaviouralism and Modern Jurisprudence.*
5 Tannenhaus 'The Cumulative Scaling of Judicial Decisions' (1965–66) 79 Harv LR 1583.
6 'It is the judge's view of the past and the needs of the present which determine his decision, and neither a study of broad attitudes derived from his decision pattern by external observers, nor a characterisation of 'facts' projected into the decision by observers can hope to correspond closely enough either with his view of the past, or still less with his view of the needs of the future': Tapper *Computers and the Law* p 251.
7 Schmidhauser 'The Justices of the Supreme Court: a Collective Portrait' (1959) 3 Midwest J of Pol Sc 1.

is being introduced, whether by legislation or creative decisions. Computers are of no help here. Finally, even if computer prediction were possible, a by-product may well be what is known as the 'Heisenburg feed-back effect'[8]. Where computer analysis has indicated that a judge's decision will be such and such in a particular case, or type of case, that very fact could induce him either to decide accordingly as if in submission to fate, or else to decide the opposite deliberately so as not to be dictated to by a machine. To produce either reaction detracts from the judicial function.

Even the possibility of trial by computer has been canvassed, the choice being given to the defendant[9]. All that needs to be said on this is that the data programmed into a computer will reflect the personal quirks of the programmer, which will be substituted for the quirks of the judge. At least, the judge works in the open, whereas the programmer works behind the scenes.

SCANDINAVIAN REALISTS

The American Realists were practising lawyers or law teachers, who sought to approximate legal theory to legal practice. In Scandinavia the group of jurists known as realists approached their tasks on a more abstract plane and with the training of philosophers.

HÄGERSTRÖM

Hägerström (1868–1939), who may be regarded as the founder of the movement in Sweden[10], has written at length, especially on Roman law, but much of his work is not available in English[11]. His basic position was as follows. He denied the existence of objective values. There are no such things as 'goodness' and 'badness' in the world. The words represent simply emotional attitudes of approval and disapproval respectively towards certain facts and situations. It is only language form that has erected them into absolutes and has created an illusion of objectivity. So, too, the word 'duty' only expresses an idea, the association of a feeling of compulsion with regard to a desired course of conduct. Language form again gives objectivity, eg 'it

---

8 Heisenberg *Physics and Philosophy* pp 47 et seq, and on the same line Ross *On Law and Justice* p 47.
9 Lawlor (1967) 13, Practical Lawyer 3, 10.
10 For possible earlier origin, see Illum 'Some Reflections on the Method of Legal Science and on Legal Reasoning' (1968) 12 Scand Studies in Law 51, 57 (referring to the influence of Ørsted (1778–1860)). The work of Petrazhitsky anticipated to a remarkable degree the approach of the Scandinavians, but there is no evidence that the latter were influenced by, or were originally aware of his work. This makes the correspondence of their views all the more striking. For his work, see Petrazhitsky *Law and Morality* (trans Babb in 20th Century Legal Philosophy Series vii); Meyendorff 'Leo Petrazhitsky' in *Modern Theories of Law* p 21; Timasheff 'Petrazhitsky's Philosophy of Law' in *Interpretations of Modern Legal Philosophies* p 736, Sorokin 'The Organised Group (Institution) and Law Norms', at p 668, and Laserson "Positive' and 'Natural' Law and their Correlation' at p 434; Northrop 'Petrazhitsky's Psychological Jurisprudence: its Originality and Importance' (1955–56) 104 University of Pennsylvania Law Review 651. For a short critique from a Marxist point of view, see Golunskii and Strogovitch 'The Theory of the State and Law' in *Soviet Legal Philosophy* (trans Babb in 20th Century Legal Philosophy Series v) pp 415–419.
11 A selection of his writings has now been translated into English by Professor Broad and edited by Professor Olivecrona: Hägerström *Inquiries into the Nature of Law and Morals*.

is my duty to do so and so'. Similarly, the idea of 'right' has no factual basis, but derives from a feeling of power associated with it, which has a psychological explanation[12]. This led Hägerström to deny the possibility of any science of the 'ought'. All questions of justice, aims and purposes of law are matters of personal evaluation and not susceptible to any scientific process of examination. In this way many of the traditional problems of legal philosophy become illusory, and must be replaced by an examination of the actual use of legal terms and a psychological analysis of the mental attitudes involved.

Hägerström applied this technique to the study of Roman law[13]. He examined the concepts of Classical Roman law and set forth the thesis that they were rooted in magical beliefs, ie that they were developments of the primitive belief in the power of words to affect happenings in the world of fact. The conception of *obligatio* was, he said, a magical bond, the *'vinculum juris'*, giving power to the creditor over the debtor. This power could only be created in special ways, by the use of magic recitations, such as *stipulatio*, and the debtor could free himself from it by performance or by uttering with the creditor's consent another magic formula. Power over property, *dominium* or ownership, was also a magic power. The archaic mode of conveyance, *mancipatio*, with its formal acts and formula asserting title before its acquisition was a ceremony based on magic. Law starts in religion, eg Mosaic Law, and the monopoly enjoyed by the priestly class, the pontiffs, in early law is also evidence of this idea that law is based on magic.

It is possible that Hägerström was making too much of a point which has some substance. It is probably true that adherence to form and ritual is rooted in word-magic, but how far Roman law in the Classical period should be interpreted along such lines is a matter on which opinion should be reserved. Adherence to ritual was not peculiar to Roman law; it is true that in Classical Roman law some of the early forms of law survived, but whatever their origin, the interpretation of Classical law on the basis purely of word-magic is questionable[14]. Professor Olivecrona, a follower of Hägerström, accepts his leader's explanations of Roman law, but he does say *a propos* of modern law generally that people still retain the outer form of word-magic although the inner belief in it disappeared long ago[15]. That remark might well be applied to Classical Roman law.

As with the American Realists, there is hardly a 'school' of Scandinavian realism. Individuals, who are thought to belong to the group, exhibit important differences among themselves. Notwithstanding these, however, they would in the main agree in denying the possibility of a science of justice or values. To them, these are purely subjective reactions, or else reflective of class or political ideology, and it is not possible to construct a science on such a basis.

LUNDSTEDT

Vilhelm Lundstedt (1882–1955) might be regarded as the most extreme of the Scandinavians. Law is simply the fact of social existence in organised groups and the conditions which make possible the co-existence of masses of

12 *Hägerström* p 5.
13 Hägerström *Der römische Obligationsbegriff im Lichte der allgemeinen römischen Rechtsanschauung.*
14 MacCormack 'Haegerstroem's Magical Interpretation of Roman Law' (1969) 4 Ir Jur (NS) 153.
15 See p 50 ante.

people. He attacked metaphysical ideas in every form. Nothing exists which
cannot be proved as fact, and he was particularly ruthless in dismissing
traditional concepts as being emotive responses or mirages of language. To
say that a person is under a duty 'is only a *feeling* or *sentiment* that he *ought* to
conduct himself in a certain manner, consequently something quite *subjective*.
This subjective element legal writers have been forced to turn into the exact
opposite, into the monstrous contradiction: an *objective duty!*'[16]. To say that a
person has broken a duty is a farrago of words for the plain fact that he is
likely to be punished, or made to pay a sum of money[17]. Similarly, a 'right'
is a term for the favourable position enjoyed by a person in consequence of
the functioning of legal machinery. Law simply consists of rules about the
application of organised force.

The idea of law as a means of achieving justice is chimerical. It is not
founded on justice, but on social needs and pressures. Indeed, 'the feelings of
justice are guided and directed by the laws as enforced, ie as maintained'[18].
In place of justice Lundstedt substituted the method of 'social welfare', which
is 'a guiding motive for legal activities', namely, 'the encouragement in the
best possible way of that ... which people in general actually strive to
attain'[19]. Judges should think in terms of social aims, not 'rights'[20]. He insisted that these are not aims for which people ought to strive, but those
which they are observed to be seeking. They include decent food, clothing,
shelter, security of life, limb and property, freedom of action and protection
of spiritual interests. The method of social welfare strives to attain the best
balance between these and other competing interests without the intrusion
of values.

Lundstedt's iconoclasm is extreme. However true it may be that concepts
such as duty and right have no verifiable content, they are convenient tools
of thought and are used in deciding cases. The wholesale rejection of them,
as he advocated, would only distort what actually goes on. Thus, an answer
to his view that a right is only a word for the favourable position enjoyed by
a person in consequence of the functioning of legal machinery is that everything depends on why a court viewed his position favourably. This is because
success in the action depended on the idea of a right[1]. It happens, too, that
a person may enjoy a favourable position by virtue of a right even though it
is socially undesirable that he should do so[2].

If, as he so vehemently insisted, all conceptual thought is nonsensical, the
same must apply to his own concept of 'social welfare'. However, leaving
that aside, it is not clear how far the method of social welfare represents the
observable pattern of administration and how far it is what Lundstedt himself
would have liked to see. Nor does this method seem very different from what
other writers have said. In any case, as has been pointed out, balancing
interests is just not possible except with reference to yardsticks of evaluation[3].

16 Lundstedt *Legal Thinking Revised* p 62.
17 *Lundstedt* pp 34, 38.
18 *Lundstedt* p 144.
19 *Lundstedt* pp 140 et seq.
20 Lundstedt *Superstition of Rationality in Action for Peace?* p 118.
 1 Olivecrona *Law as Fact* (1939) pp 85-86. For a different objection, see pp 91-93; and 'Law
   as Fact' in *Interpretations of Modern Legal Philosophies* (ed Sayre) ch 25.
 2 Eg *Bradford Corpn v Pickles* [1895] AC 587. For a criticism of Lundstedt which seems to miss
   the point, see G L Williams 'Language and the Law' (1946) 62 LQR 398.
 3 See p 435 ante. Cf Lundstedt's own allusion to useful arrangements 'actually evaluated as a
   social interest' within a given society at a given time: *Legal Thinking Revised* p 137.

The very concept of social welfare is a product of political or socio-moral evaluation. If the actual interests of people are allowed to proliferate to the point of complete social fragmentation and anarchy, that would spell the end of legal activity and, indeed, of social welfare. If this is not to be allowed, then the point at which legal activity has to step in is a matter for decision as to where the line should be drawn, not of observation. Moreover, is a small, but enlightened minority, agitating for reform, to remain outside the endeavour of the social welfare method until, presumably, it attains large enough proportions?

Other Scandinavians have not gone as far as Lundstedt. Even Professor Olivecrona, who perhaps came nearest to his views, does not do so[4]. Indeed, some have reacted sharply against his uncompromising condemnation of any appeal to justice and morality[5].

OLIVECRONA

A less extreme and more acceptable form of scepticism comes from Professor Olivecrona (b. 1897). He expressly refrains from defining law. 'I do not regard it as necessary to formulate a definition of law', he says[6]. 'A description and an analysis of the facts is all that will be attempted'. If one seeks to investigate the nature of law, it begs the question to begin by assuming what it is, and he insists that the facts must be examined first. The method of identifying these 'will be simply to take up such facts as are covered by the expression rules of law'[7].

The question of the validity of law is a matter of much concern to the Scandinavians. Olivecrona approaches it from the angle of bindingness[8]. Law has 'binding force' in so far as it is valid; an invalid law is not binding. This question of the binding force behind law has been a perennial puzzle and is, expressly or impliedly, the foundation of many theories. There is no such thing, says he, as 'the' binding force behind law. Many attempts have been made to find where it resides. Natural lawyers have asserted that it lies in natural law; but if asked why natural law is binding, the answer is a confession of faith. Natural law, whether conceived as an expression of the will of God or as a set of principles based on reason, is said to be binding *per se*. Morality cannot be substituted in place of natural law, for law is treated as binding whether or not it is consistent with morality.

Others have tried to discover the binding force of law in the consent of the governed. This is not wholly true because at no time are the subjects of a system of law asked whether they consent to be bound. Also, it would follow that once consent is withdrawn law ceases to bind, which is not the case.

Another attempt to unravel the binding force is to attribute it to the 'will of the state'. This, too, is imaginary since the 'will of the state' as distinct from the wills of individuals is a myth. The question is whether any individual, or group of individuals, is discoverable in whose will the binding force of law may be said to reside. The answer must be in the negative because,

4 He and Hägerström are the only two jurists who escaped Lundstedt's censure.
5 Vinding Kruse *The Foundations of Human Thought*; Castberg *Problems of Legal Philosophy* pp 110 et seq.
6 Olivecrona *Law as Fact* (1939) p 26.
7 *Olivecrona* p 25, and (2nd edn 1971) pp 3–5; and pp 11–12 ante.
8 *Olivecrona* (1939) Introduction.

in the first place, there never has been and never will be any person or group of persons who can be regarded as having 'willed' the whole law, let alone its binding force. Secondly, it is equally fictitious to imagine that the binding force rests in the wills of legislators or citizens collectively. Such persons have other matters to think of than willing laws or their binding force[9].

It is not meaningful to say that the binding force of law is derived from unpleasant consequences that ensue if law is broken. For unpleasant consequences ensue in a host of situations which have nothing to do with law. A person gets burnt if he puts his hands in the fire, but this does not lead to a binding rule that he should not put his hands in the fire. Conversely, there are occasions when law is treated as binding although unpleasant consequences do not ensue. A person may commit a breach of the law and go undetected, but no one would say that the law is therefore not binding on him. Nor is it satisfactory to say that the binding force is derived from the unpleasant consequences that ought to ensue, for, as Kelsen has shown, the reality of 'ought to ensue' consists of the operation of other rules of law and the binding force of these will in turn have to be sought.

Professor Olivecrona accordingly rejects the idea of 'the' binding force of law as illusory and meaningless. It is not an observable fact in the *milieu* of society. 'The' binding force of law is a mirage of language; it 'exists' only as an idea in individual minds[10]. Laws, too, 'exist' in the form of printed or written words or else in memory. Their importance lies, not in where or how they are stored, but in the fact that they produce behaviour. This results from the fact that most people have a feeling of being bound by law, which is quite different from saying that there is some impalpable binding force existing somewhere outside the mind. It is this feeling of being bound that has to be explained.

Olivecrona accordingly approaches his inquiry by examining the idea of duty, which has been dealt with and need not be repeated[11]. His conclusion, in substance, is that duty involves the idea of action and an imperative mode of expression, and that the feeling of being bound stems from the psychological associations connected with this mode of expression by certain agencies. The picture of law which emerges is of patterns of conduct in imperative form, which are distinguishable from other imperatives by virtue of the nature of the feeling of being bound that is associated with them. This feeling is not the same with regard to any other kind of imperative, eg that one must wear black at funerals. The feeling of being bound by 'law' is psychologically associated with certain agencies when they follow certain procedures, together with the publication of law-texts through certain media, which are assumed to give a true account of them[12]. Law, therefore, is a set of 'independent imperatives' prescribed by these agencies. It is thought, however, that Olivecrona would admit that law prescribes models of conduct. He would, therefore, not deny that it consists of 'ought' propositions.

Nor does he dismiss the idea of rights altogether. He emphasises that it does not correspond with an ascertainable 'thing', that it is, in short, a 'hollow' word[13]. A court could pronounce on a factual situation without

9 *Olivecrona* (1939) pp 22 et seq; (1971) pp 73 et seq. The most powerful attack on 'will theories' was by *Hägerström* pp 1–55, 74–126.
10 *Olivecrona* (1939) p 17.
11 See p 248 ante.
12 See pp 52 et seq ante.
13 Olivecrona 'Legal Language and Reality' in *Essays in Jurisprudence in Honor of Roscoe Pound* (ed Newman) p 157.

calling 'right' in aid. Thus, proof of a right is accomplished by proving certain facts or events whose effects are determined by law. These facts are called 'title'. In a court nothing stands between proof of the facts and judgment; the one is the direct cause of the other. Even in matters which never come before courts, as soon as the facts constituting the title are in existence, the person concerned may do certain things and other persons must not and cannot do certain other things with regard to him. Yet, between the facts and the judgment and between the facts and the behaviour the idea of a 'right' is invariably interposed, and it is said that the favourable decision or the behaviour proceeds *from* the right, which has been *created by* the title. In truth, the idea of a 'right' connotes a multitude of other ideas relating to behaviour patterns, not only for the 'possessor of the right', but also of other persons. It implies directives as to how the right-bearer and others can and should act, it informs people about legal situations, it is purposive in achieving or maintaining a state of affairs, and it is a means of harnessing the force of the state. This analysis, together with that of duty and the feeling of being bound, leads him to conclude that 'law is nothing but a set of social facts'[14] based on the application of organised force.

By way of a general observation, it might be remarked that some people are left with a feeling of dissatisfaction after reading Olivecrona's exposition. Its very simplicity raises a doubt as to whether he may have overlooked some deeper truth. It is submitted, however, that the common sense which he brings to bear in his discussions is the best feature of his work. Obscurity has passed for profundity too often. It is a useful working rule that clarity of expression is an index to clarity of thought. Obscurantist jargon earns much unmerited respect from those who hesitate to condemn as nonsense that which they cannot understand. The clear pages of Olivecrona's presentation are preferable to the turgid complexities of many another. Apart from that, however, one who searches his book for guidance in the solution of legal problems will search in vain. Nowhere is there a hint of values or other such considerations from which the law draws its vitality. It would be unfair to level this as a criticism, for a person should not be criticised for not having said something which he never set out to say and which, in any case, he would not have denied. Olivecrona's object, like Kelsen's, was limited to a formal analysis of law as it is. The picture of law which emerges is that it consists largely of propositions phrased in an imperative form and emanating from certain agencies. It might be said that there is nothing very new in that. Finally, although he repeatedly insists that law is nothing but a set of social facts, nowhere in his book does he explain what he means by 'fact'. Law also provides a model of behaviour which, too, presumably is a social fact. Perhaps, an explanation of the crucial term 'fact' would have been instructive.

The chief merit of his work may perhaps be summed up as follows. He destroyed many traditional myths concerning law, eg 'binding force' and command. He has given a moderate, sane and commonsense approach to some highly abstract problems of legal philosophy. His approach should not be regarded as self-sufficient, but it is an invaluable corrective to some others.

ROSS

The Danish jurist, Alf Ross (b. 1899), also admits the normative character of law (as did Kelsen by whom he was influenced). He distinguished between

14 Olivecrona *Law as Fact* (1939) p 127.

laws, which are normative, and statements about laws in books, which are descriptive. Unlike Kelsen, he confines his attention to particular legal orders. Like Olivecrona, he maintains that laws need to be interpreted in the light of social facts and he, too, is concerned with the problem of validity. Like the American Realists he tends to highlight the position of courts.

'*A norm*' says Ross '*is a directive which stands in a relation of correspondence to social facts*'[15]. To say that a norm exists means that a certain social fact exists; and this in turn means that the directive is followed in the majority of cases by people who feel bound to do so[16]. The principal feature of legal norms is that they are directives addressed to courts. A norm may derive from a past decision, but it follows from this view that all norms, including those of legislation, should be viewed as directives to courts[17]. The judgment or order of the court then forms the basis for action by the state, which is a 'monopoly of the exercise of force'[18]. It follows from this point of view that norms directed at individuals with regard to behaviour are only 'derived and figurative'[19]. In his later work, however, he concedes that 'from a psychological point of view' there is another set of norms directed to individuals, which are followed by them and felt to be binding[20]. Strictly speaking, he adds, there is no need for the latter: to know the former 'is to know everything about the existence and content of the law'[1]. Norms of the law may be further divided into 'norms of conduct', which deal with behaviour, and 'norms of competence or procedure', which direct that norms brought into existence according to a declared mode of procedure shall be regarded as norms of conduct. Thus, norms of competence are indirectly expressed norms of conduct[2].

The crucial concept is 'valid law'[3]. Ross approaches this from the point of view of an observer, ie validity as a describable phenomenon. It can be established in terms of social facts by employing empirical methods of observation and verification. Observation has to show that a rule is effectively followed, and that rule has also to be felt to be binding by those who follow it, just as the validity of the rules of chess is established by showing that they are adhered to by players, who feel bound to do so[4]. Legal norms consist of past decisions and other normative propositions followed by courts and by which they feel bound. The test of their validity is the predictability of decisions.

> 'Valid law', he says 'means the abstract set of normative ideas which serve as a scheme of interpretation for the phenomena of law in action, which again means that these norms are effectively followed, and followed because they are experienced and felt to be socially binding by the judge and other legal authorities applying the law ... The test of validity is that on this hypothesis—that

---

15 Ross *Directives and Norms* p 82.
16 *Ross* p 83.
17 Ross prefers 'directive' to Olivecrona's 'independent imperative', since it is difficult to see how an imperative, which is independent of command, can command a judge; also there are many legal directives which are not imperative: *Ross* p 37.
18 Ross *On Law and Justice* p 34.
19 *Ross* p 33.
20 Ross *Directives and Norms* p 92.
 1 *Ross* p 91. This is reminiscent of Kelsen's view: see p 360 ante.
 2 Ross *On Law and Justice* p 32.
 3 Ross protested against the translation into 'valid law' of what is in Danish 'existing law', or 'law in force': Review in (1961) Yale LJ 1962.
 4 Ross *On Law and Justice* pp 14-15.

is, accepting the system of norms as a scheme of interpretation—we can comprehend the actions of the judge (the decisions of the courts) as meaningful responses to given conditions and within certain limits predict them'[5].

Norms are thus operative 'because they are felt by (the judge) to be socially binding and therefore obeyed[6]. A norm, then, is 'valid' if a prediction can be made that a court will apply it[7]. At this point Ross puts forward an interesting contention. Validity is not an 'all or nothing' concept as it is with other writers; the degree of predictability that a norm will be applied determines the degree of its validity. 'This degree of probability depends on the material of experience on which the prediction is built (sources of law)'[8]. Where the probability is high because the basis is a statute or an established precedent, the degree of validity of a rule is high; where the probability is low because there is no decisive authority, the degree of validity is low.

The criticism originally levelled at Ross that he ignored the regulative function of norms by saying that they are only addressed to courts was partially met by his later modification that, from a psychological point of view, norms are also addressed to individuals. However, his continued insistence that only the former matter still underplays the regulative function. On the other hand, to admit, as he now does, that norms directed at individuals also exist, thereby implying that they, too, are social facts, loosens the foundation of his structure. The thesis that there can be degrees of validity follows from an identification of validity with eventuality, what actually happens. Is this legitimate? The closely related point is his adoption of an exclusively descriptive point of view. As pointed out in connection with American Realism, however, the resulting picture is unsuited to the point of view of a legislator or judge. What does validity signify to them? A judge, for instance, can hardly be predicting his own feelings or behaviour, but it would be quite unrealistic to suggest that validity has no significance for him.

5 *Ross* pp 18, 35. Cf the American Realist position.
6 *Ross* p 35. Cf Hart's 'internal aspect' of rules. Hart points out that his 'internal aspect' is not a matter of 'feelings', but the acceptance of the norm as a standard: 'Scandinavian Realism' [1959] CLJ at 237–238; and pp 48 et seq ante.
7 *Ross* p 49.
8 *Ross* p 45.

READING LIST

A d'Ameto 'The Limits of Legal Realism' (1975) 87 Yale Law Journal 468.

J N Frank *Courts on Trial.*

J N Frank *Law and the Modern Mind.*

L L Fuller *Law in Quest of Itself.*

E N Garlan *Legal Realism and Justice.*

A Hägerström *Inquiries into the Nature of Law and Morals* (trans C D Broad, ed K Olivecrona).

C G Haines 'General Observations on the Effects of Personal, Political, and Economic Influences on the Decisions of the Judges' (1922) 17 Illinois Law Review 96.

O W Holmes *Collected Legal Papers* p 167.

J C Hutcheson 'The Judgment Intuitive: the Function of the 'Hunch' in Judicial Decisions' (1929) 14 Cornell Law Quarterly 274.

J C Hutcheson 'Lawyers' Law, and the Little Small Dice' (1932–33) 7 Tulane Law Review 1.

H U Kantorowicz 'Some Rationalism about Realism' (1934) 43 Yale Law Journal, 1240.

K N Llewellyn *The Common Law Tradition. Deciding Appeals.*

K N Llewellyn *Jurisprudence* chs 1–3, 5, 7–8.

A V Lundstedt *Legal Thinking Revised.*

P Mechem 'The Jurisprudence of Despair' (1935–36) 21 Iowa Law Review 669.

M S McDougal 'Fuller vs the American Realists: an Intervention' (1940–41) 50 Yale Law Journal 827.

K Olivecrona *Law as Fact* (1939); 2nd edn (1971).

R Pound 'Law in Books and Law in Action' (1910) 44 American Law Review 12.

R Pound 'The Call for a Realist Jurisprudence' (1930–31) 44 Harvard Law Review 697.

A Ross *Directives and Norms.*

A Ross *On Law and Justice.*

W E Rumble *American Legal Realism. Skepticism, Reform and the Judicial Process.*

T Schroeder 'The Psychologic Study of Judicial Opinions' (1918) 6 California Law Review 89.

W Twining *Karl Llewellyn and the Realist Movement.*

J N Ulman *A Judge Takes the Stand.*

CHAPTER 22

Natural law

Natural law theory has a history reaching back centuries BC, and the vigour with which it flourishes notwithstanding periodic eclipse, especially in the 19th century, is indicative of its vitality. There is no one theory; many versions have evolved throughout this enormous span of time. Kelsen exposed some of them as masks for political ideologies. Natural law theory, however, should not be dismissed simply on account of its variety. On the contrary, this very fact is a clue to its understanding. No other firmament of legal or political theory is so bejewelled with stars as that of natural law, which scintillates with contributions from all ages. A single chapter cannot possibly do justice to this rich and varied material, so all that will be attempted here is to deploy those portions of it that will help to embroider the topics which seem to be central in contemporary thought. Old ideas have been abandoned or refurbished and new ones put forward, while forgotten lessons have blossomed with new significance.

The term 'natural law', like positivism'[1], has been variously applied by different people at different times. (1) Ideals which guide legal development and administration. (2) A basic moral quality in law which prevents a total separation of the 'is' from the 'ought'. (3) The method of discovering perfect law. (4) The content of perfect law deducible by reason. (5) The conditions *sine quibus non* for the existence of law. It is not always possible to classify a given writer as naturalist or positivist. For instance, it has been pointed out that Scotus, Ockham and Kant have been treated as positivists by some natural lawyers and as naturalists by some positivists; besides which there are differences among those who are normally classed as naturalists or positivists[2]. Also, natural law thinking in one form or another is pervasive and is encountered in various contexts. Values, for instance, as pointed out, play an indispensable part in the development and day-to-day administration of law[3]. In a different sphere natural law theory has tried to meet the paramount needs of successive ages throughout history, and an account has been given of the ways in which it supported power or freedom from power according to the social need of the time[4]. All this is part and parcel of its very nature. Further, natural law thinking could offer indirect help with two contemporary problems, namely, the abuse of power and the abuse of liberty[5]. Positivism, on the other hand, by seeking to insulate legal theory from such considerations refuses to give battle where battle is needed, perhaps wisely, perhaps to its own discredit, depending on the point of view. Nevertheless, the readiness of natural lawyers to meet challenge is a tribute

1 See p 331 ante.
2 J Hall *Foundations of Jurisprudence* ch 2.
3 See ch 10 ante.
4 See pp 71–85 ante.
5 See chs 5, 6 ante.

to the springs of their inspiration, which has a vitality like that of the phoenix[6].

A distinction should be drawn between two kinds of natural law thought, 'natural law of method' and 'natural law of content'. The former was the older, dating from ancient times and was also prevalent in the early middle ages. It concerned itself with trying to discover the method by which just rules may be devised to meet ever-varying circumstances. It is a prescription for rule-making, not a catalogue of rules'[7]. The 'natural law of content' was a feature of the 17th and 18th centuries and was characterised by attempts to deduce entire bodies of rules from absolute first principles. These were manifestations of the then fashionable assertion of 'natural rights' and were accompanied internationally by schemes for ensuring perpetual peace. It was this 'natural law of content' which was the target for damaging criticism, resulting in the eclipse of natural law thinking throughout most of the 19th century, when it reached its nadir and was superseded by positivism. As long as social conditions remained stable, positivism could flourish. This in turn faltered when those conditions were upset by the convulsions that beset nations since the second half of the last century, and a reaction set in against the excesses resulting from a rigid adherence to formalism. It failed through sterility in that it could give no guidance midst the challenge to accepted moral and social beliefs; it failed because it could give no help in avoiding or remedying monstrous abuses of power and liberty that have been, and are still, prevalent. With its decline there has arisen a new preoccupation with social justice, which includes, among other manifestations, a revival of natural law doctrine more in line with the older 'natural law of method' and endeavours to avoid the criticism of the past and to meet the problems of today.

It is against this background that theories of natural law should be approached. Since their concern has always been with the needs of particular ages, only theories with contemporary relevance will be discussed here. Those that were tailored to suit bygone times, eg those of Aristotle and Grotius, will not be dealt with. A start might be made with the doctrine of St Thomas Aquinas (1224/5-1274), which is not only outstanding in itself, but whose enduring value was indorsed in 1879 by Pope Leo XIII, who enabled it to become part of the teaching of the Catholic Church[8].

ST THOMAS AQUINAS

The Thomist scheme has to be set in the context of its time[9]. There was, first, a need for stability in a world emerging from the Dark Ages. Secondly, the struggle between Church and State was beginning and there was need for the Church to establish its superiority by rational argument rather than by force, since secular authority had the monopoly of force. Thirdly, it was necessary for Christendom to unite in the face of the spreading heathen menace and a need was felt for a unifying Christian philosophy. The available philosophic material consisted largely of the natural law philosophies of Greece and Rome. The *Decretum Gratianum* (c 1140) had already identified

6 To say with Ross, 'Like a harlot natural law is at the disposal of everyone' (*On Law and Justice* p 261) is to miss the point.
7 Montrose *Precedent in English Law* (ed Hanbury) p 40, and generally ch 3.
8 Encyclical *Aeterni Patris*.
9 See pp 77-78 ante.

the law of nature with the law of God, which paved the way for resort to classical literature as authority. Aquinas endeavoured to meet all three needs and his doctrine may be presented as follows.

There is a connection between means and ends. There is an unshakeable relation in the nature of things between a given operation and its result. Natural phenomena have certain inevitable consequences: fire burns, it does not freeze. So, one adopts a particular method because of its 'natural' properties. There is also a tendency to develop in certain ways, which is naturally inherent in things: an acorn can only evolve into an oak; it will not evolve into a larch. Appreciation of both these, namely, the relation between means and ends and the process of growth towards fulfilment, is open only to intelligence and the faculty of reason. An acorn does not think, but Man does. He appreciates the relation between means and ends and the destined development of phenomena around him. He can also, within limits, choose for himself the ends which he wants and devise means of achieving them. For example, a person in authority may decide that the health of society is an end worth achieving. He will then consider how best to accomplish this and prescribe appropriate regulations of social behaviour. Laws thus consist of means of achieving ends. The relation between an end and the method by which its fulfilment is sought is initially conceived in the mind of the legislator, but those who are required to conform to his directions can also appreciate the connection by the exercise of their own reasoning faculties. Where the achievement of the end sought by the legislator depends on adherence by others to the prescribed patterns of conduct, it is essential that these should be made known to them. Therefore, law in an all-embracing signification is 'nothing else than an ordinance of reason for the common good, made by him who has the care of the community, and promulgated'[10].

Though Man can to a large extent control his own destiny, he too is subject to certain basic impulses, which can be perceived by observing human nature. At the lowest level there is the impulse towards self-preservation; at the next level there are the impulses, shared with other creatures, to reproduce the species and rear children; at the highest level there is the impulse to improve, to take such decisions as are necessary for the attainment of higher and better things[11]. This last is peculiar to Man by virtue of his reason. These basic impulses point in a definite direction; they are seen to be the means of achieving, not only survival and continuity, but also perfection. They are an inescapable part of human nature and show that Man also, to a lesser extent than an acorn, is limited by nature. If then, the framework of human nature is itself a means to certain ends, the establishment of the ends and these means of achievement could only have originated in the reason of some superhuman legislator. This is the eternal law: 'the eternal law is nothing else than the plan of the divine wisdom considered as directing all the acts and motions'[12] to the attainment of the ends. Man, however, unlike the rest of creation, is free and rational and capable of acting contrary to eternal law. Therefore, this law has to be promulgated to him through reason. This is natural law. There is no need of promulgation to other created things, for they lack the intelligence of Man. 'The natural law is

10 Aquinas *Summa Theologica* I, 2, Q 90, art 4.
11 *Aquinas* I 2, Q 94, art 2.
12 *Aquinas* I, 2, Q 93, art 1.
13 *Aquinas* I, 2, Q 91, art 2.

nothing else but a participation of the eternal law in a rational creature'[13], ie the dictates revealed by reason reflecting on natural tendencies and needs. 'The primary precept of the law is that good should be done and pursued and evil avoided; and on this are founded all the other precepts of the law of nature'[14]. By reflecting on his own impulses and nature Man can decide what is good. In this way he perceives the three basic drives mentioned above. In addition, reason reflecting on experience yields further, more detailed precepts. The moral law thus contains a variety of them of greater or less generality.

Certain doubts might be mentioned at this point. The fact that reason is needed to appreciate the orderings in nature does not necessarily imply that reason established them; nor does the fact that Man by his reason can set himself a goal of his own and utilise the existing ordering of nature as means for its achievement necessarily suggest that the order in nature was appointed by reason. It might conceivably be argued that it is only the faculty of *appreciating* order, implanted in the mind, that should be ascribed to the Deity. On that supposition eternal law would be what Man creates in his own mind, not something external to it and comprehensible by reason. This question, of course, strikes at the root of religious belief and, as such, is too large a matter to be debated here. Another point concerns the nature of the 'ought' behind Aquinas's view of natural law. It amounts to saying: Man's nature is such that he is necessarily impelled to seek good in survival, continuity and perfection; therefore, he ought to do things to achieve these and not do things to frustrate them. Superficially it might seem that this is no more than the functional 'ought' behind the adoption of a certain course of action as the effective means to a certain end[15]. This is not the case here. With the functional 'ought', the failure or refusal to pursue the end is morally neutral. Thus, while it is true that if a person wishes to make a gratuitous promise, he ought to make it under seal, there is no moral failure on his part for not wishing to make such a promise. Aquinas's moral imperative is something different; to go against the ends is morally wrong[16]. It is not wrong because God has forbidden contravention of natural law; God has forbidden it because it is wrong, ie contrary to reason by which He Himself is bound. This being so, Aquinas's argument looks as if he is deriving the 'ought' logically (by reason) from an 'is' (Man's observable nature). Finally, there is the difficulty in that procreation was treated by him as a basic drive of human nature and hence good, but he himself subscribed to clerical celibacy. His answer was that Mankind 'ought not only to be multiplied corporeally, but also to make spiritual progress. Sufficient provision is made if some only attend to generation, while others give themselves to the contemplation of divine things for the enrichment and salvation of the whole human race'[17]. This is tantamount to saying that this natural law is addressed to people generally but nobody in particular. If so, the imperative behind its stands in need of elucidation as well as the connection between sin and contravention of natural law.

In addition to eternal and natural law there is divine law, which is eternal law revealed through the Scriptures; and lastly there is human or man-made law. The latter should conform to reason and thus to the law of God. These

14 *Aquinas* I, 2, Q 94, art 2.
15 See p 44–45 ante.
16 It is also different from Kant's 'categorical imperative': see p 475 post.
17 *Aquinas* I, 2, Q 152, art 2.

four, then, eternal law, natural law, divine law and human law, comprise the Thomist system.

This scheme may justly be regarded as the first of its kind in the history of jurisprudence. Its outstanding features were (1) that it combined ancient philosophy, the law of the Romans, the teachings of the Christian Fathers and contemporary pragmatism with consummate power and skill. Unlike the teaching of St Augustine, law was no longer the product of original sin, but part of the Divine scheme[18]. Nor is there any suggestion that body and natural things are synonymous with corruption and a clog on the spirit. What is striking is its uncompromising appeal to reason. Man was created so that he might strive towards perfection within the limits of mortality. Reason dictates that he has, therefore, to be free. God cannot alter this state of affairs. To do so would contradict His own nature, since God Himself is bound by reason. To match this stupendous assertion one has to go back to the Jewish hypothesis of the Covenant. It is not surprising that, consistently with this, the law of God itself was declared to be 'nothing else than the reason of divine wisdom'; and Christianity was said to be supreme reason: *credo quia rationabilis est*. (2) Natural law furnishes principles rather than rules for detailed application. (3) Another feature is the empirical approach to eternal and natural law. Inferences are drawn from human nature as observable by everybody. (4) Reason becomes the foundation for all human institutions. Social life, whether in the form of families or the state, are founded on human nature. Reason reflecting on this shows that these are necessary for the realisation of Man's full potential and are thus natural institutions[19]. An extension of this is the ideal of a single organisation of all Mankind in a world-state. (5) Aquinas sought to strengthen the authority of the Church by asserting that human dignitaries were responsible to the Church in matters relating to eternal law, and buttressed that contention with the proposition that the Church is the authoritative interpreter of divine law in the Scriptures. Nevertheless, the state, which existed before the Church, is itself a natural institution. It serves the common good, and by means of its laws should bring about the conditions conducive to Man's proper development. (6) The test, then, by which laws are to be judged is the following dictate: 'every human law has just so much of the nature of law, as it is derived from the law of nature. But if at any point it departs from natural law, it is no longer a law but a perversion of law'[20]. (7) The need is stressed for the union of prescriptive patterns of behaviour, ideals and inward obedience if law is to achieve its objectives. In so far as human laws are founded on reason there is a duty to obey them; from which it would follow that if a law is unreasonable and unjust no such duty arises. Interestingly enough, however, Aquinas qualified this inference by saying that there may be subtle dictates of morality which enjoin obedience even to an unreasonable positive law, for instance to avoid social disruption. Unjust laws, he said, 'do not bind conscience unless observance of them is required in order to avoid scandal or disturbance'[1]. The qualification might well have been a concession to the need of the time to preserve social stability. Even more significant, was the implicit recognition of the growing importance of man-made law. (8) The corollary of this was that an unjust ruler may be

18 Gilby '*Principality and Polity*' pp 146 et seq.
19 *Aquinas De regimine principum* 1.1.
20 *Aquinas* I, 2, Q 95, art 2.
 1 *Aquinas* I, 2, Q 96, art 4.

overthrown, unless revolution would create as bad, or worse, state of affairs than before. Sedition is a social evil; and he warned against rebellion in circumstances which do not justify it. As before, the qualification reflects the need of the time. (9) The identification of natural law with reason was destined in later times to bring about a separation of natural law from theology. For with the advent of the Reformation, the Protestants denied the authority of the Church to be the unchallengeable exponent of the law of God; Man was said to have direct access to God through his own reason.

In the era which followed that of Aquinas, the dream of an united Christendom was finally abandoned, Europe emerged from feudalism and there arose the modern municipal state. These developments had to be justified by theories, which were more power-orientated than in the preceding age. Then, abuse of power by sovereigns over their subjects led to revolutionary stirrings and assertion of fundamental rights of the individual, which called for immunity-orientated theories. Both these movements manifested themselves in successive variations of the social contract theory[2]. Side by side with this, there was international chaos produced by the exercise of unlimited freedom of action by states in their mutual relations, which led to the birth of international law and schemes for perpetual peace evolved out of reason. These factors fostered the rise of 'natural law of content' theories, which supposed that by appealing to reason perfect systems could be deduced in detail. Throughout this period the emphasis was very much on the individual and his rights.

TRANSCENDENTAL IDEALISM

The close of this epoch was marked by another line of thought, which was equally uncompromising in its insistence on individual freedom, but wholly idealistic in character. Kant (1724–1804), whose doctrines were developed by Fichte, taught that sensory perception is the avenue to knowledge of the objective world, but that all such perception is shaped by *a priori* preconceptions. Thus, preconceptions of space, time and causation filter one's experience of nature. In so far as Man is part of the world of reality, he is subject to its laws and is to that extent unfree, but his reason and inner consciousness make him a free moral agent. Man thus participates in two worlds, the 'sensible' and the 'intelligible'. Law and morality belong to the latter. The actions of Man as a free agent are governed by aims, and the ethical basis of action has also to be accepted *a priori*. Justice, according to Kant, originates in pure practical reason. People know *a priori* how to act justly. The ultimate aim of the individual should be a life of free will; but it is when free will is exercised according to reason and uncontaminated by emotion that free-willing individuals can live together. People are morally free when they are able to obey or disobey a moral law. Kant propounded two principles of practical reason. (a) 'Act in such a way that the maxim of your action can be made the maxim of an universal law (general action)'[3]. This is his famous 'categorical imperative'. (b) 'An action is right only if it can co-exist with each and every man's free will according to universal law'. This is his 'principle of right'[4].

2 See pp 79–84 ante.
3 Kant *Philosophy of Law* (trans Hastie) p 34.
4 *Kant* p 45.

The first point to note is the emphasis on the individual. A feature of Kant's doctrine is his proclamation of the autonomy of reason and will. Human reason is law-creating and constitutes moral law. Freedom in law means freedom from arbitrary subjection to another, and law is the complex totality of conditions under which maximum freedom is possible for all. To this end a separation of powers is necessary to prevent the emergence of a despotic régime, and the sole function of the state is to ensure the observance of law. Kant proceeded to urge that the individual should not allow himself to be made the means to an end, since he is an end in himself[5]; and that he should, if need be, retire from society if his free will would involve him in wrongdoing[6]; for Kant did perceive the necessity for rules in social existence, guided by a just general policy. Society unregulated by right results in violence. Social existence and violence are incompatible; so reason demands that Man has an obligation to enter into society and to avoid wronging others. Such a society has to be regulated by compulsory laws, and if these laws are derived by pure reason from the whole idea of social union under law, Man will be able to live in peace[7]. What is needed is a rule of law, not of men[8]. The second point is that the Kantian ideal of laws bears no relation to any actual system of law. It is purely an ideal to serve as a standard of comparison, not as a criterion of the validity of law.

NATURAL LAW OF IDEAL CONTENT

Until the beginning of the 19th century natural law theory was a philosophy of content, ie it sought to deduce the contents of just laws from fixed premises. That century witnessed a decline in its popularity. The existence of absolute principles was attacked, notably by Hume (1711-1776), who pointed out that there is no causal connection between facts and ideas. One cannot logically derive an 'ought' from an 'is'. Cause and effect is an empirical correlation to be found in the physical sciences. Conceptions such as good and evil, for example, are subjective emotional reactions. Values are not inherent in nature, nor is justice. Reason can only work out the means that will lead to specified results; it cannot evaluate the latter. It is of some relevance, perhaps, that Hume was writing at a time of comparative tranquillity. Whereas the timorous Hobbes, amidst the alarms of the Civil War, reached for the shelter of an omnipotent sovereign's wing, Hume was concerned, if anything, with preserving stability. He argued against discretion that would allow for justice in individual cases, suspecting a threat to stability in relying on a fluid conception such as justice. He favoured instead the firm and inflexible application of rules, although he conceded that these should be wisely designed in the first place and should be changed when conditions demand. On these lines he attacked the prevailing conceptions of natural law. The conception of a perfect, complete, discoverable system was challenged. If there was such a thing, why are there so many divergent interpretations, and why is positive law needed at all? At the dawn of the 19th century a reaction also set in against excessive individualism, fostered by later natural law theories, which had resulted in the French Revolution. Then, there grew up in the course of that century a new preoccupation with

5 *Kant* p 54.
6 *Kant* p 54.
7 *Kant* p 163.
8 *Kant* pp 230-231.

society, a collectivist outlook on life, which has gathered momentum ever since. Natural law theories of the age immediately preceding, adapted as they were to an individualist outlook, fell into disrepute.

Objections also came from another quarter. The teachings of historians and sociologists laid stress on environment. Historical investigation helped to explode many assumptions; the social contract, in particular, came in for damaging criticism. Research into the early history of society exposed the mythical nature of the contract. The unit in early society was the family, or clan, not individuals. There was, moreover, the technical difficulty that the social contract theory endeavoured to ascribe the validity of law to contract whereas normally the reverse is the case. Some rule has to be presupposed which prescribes that agreements ought to be kept. These objections aside, even as a hypothesis to account for the present state of affairs the theory fell short, since it only heaped fiction upon fiction. Alternative explanations of the origin of society not only fitted the facts but were truer in themselves.

The *a priori* methods of the natural law philosophers were likewise unacceptable to those nurtured in the pragmatic spirit of science. Natural law postulates were subjected to critical examination with disastrous results. Their bases were revealed as unsubstantiated hypotheses or else the results of false inferences. Where, for instance, is the foundation for the assertion that Man must always seek society, or that Man is necessarily selfish? Again, it is a wild inference to assume that because certain institutions in different countries are alike, that must be because they are reflecting some universal law. It has even been suggested more recently that the idea of natural law is no more than a psychological reflex. The very diversity that is observable in systems of positive law raises in the mind, it is said, an anti-thesis of a fixed and changeless law. This coupled with an innate tendency to attribute reality to ideas prepares the way for belief in the existence of natural law. For these reasons it became evident that the increasingly complex problems of the 19th century required a realistic and practical approach, not the easy application of abstract preconceptions.

In the new climate of opinion the prevailing natural law theories could not survive, and in their place arose analytical and historical positivism with increasing stress on a sociological approach to problems. These have been dealt with earlier, but something should now be said of the revival of naturalist doctrines towards the end of the 19th and in the 20th centuries.

One reason for this was the admission of scientists of the extent to which their own subjects were in fact founded on assumptions. Another was the failure of positivists to find answers to the problems that were coming to the forefront. The indispensability of values was increasingly felt as guides for legal development. This need was associated with the increasing use of broad, flexible concepts which admit latitude in application, and also with the realisation that judicial reasoning is creative and not purely syllogistic. The shattering effects of world wars, the decline in standards, a growing insecurity and uncertainty have stimulated anew the quest for a moral order, which was a boon afforded by natural law in the past. The growth of totalitarian régimes, both right wing and left wing, has called for the development of some ideological control which could prevent a cloak of legality being cast around every abuse.

In these circumstances it is hardly surprising that there has been a return to natural law in a new form, which strives to take account, not only of knowledge contributed by the analytical, historical and sociological approaches, but also of the increasingly collectivist outlook on life. A feature is the returning emphasis on a philosophy of method rather than of content, which leaves the details of actual laws to vary with time and place and also opens up a possibility of establishing evaluative criteria empirically.

NATURAL LAW OF METHOD

One form which the revival of natural law has taken is the adaptation of the doctrines of St Thomas Aquinas. In the face of present-day divergences and conflicting tendencies there was some attraction in the method offered by Aquinas whereby philosophical reflection might find a way of synthesising prevailing needs and circumstances from a Christian point of view. Pope Leo XIII's Encyclical *Aeterni Patris* 1879, which drew attention to the value of his synthesis and encouraged the adaptation of his method, gave a stimulus to an intellectual flowering already in bud. Although the philosophy of Thomism has come to be very much associated with Catholicism, it is not in fact officially part of it.

Neo-Thomism

Neo-Thomists, as Aquinas's modern followers are known, are prepared to accept the descriptions of reality provided by scientists, but they maintain that it is for philosophy, starting, like scientists, from certain hypotheses and utilising scientific insights, to give the full explanation of reality through reason and reflection. They also adopt the humanism of Aquinas to steer a course between, on the one hand, an exclusively individualist view of Man and, on the other, a totalitarian view of society in which the individual counts for nothing. Natural law is both anterior and superior to positive law. Aquinas believed that natural law was the attainment of the eternal law of God through the exercise of reason. Following from that the neo-Thomists formulate certain broad generalisations, so abstract that they can be universal. In the evolution from these principles of rules of positive law variations will be found from place to place and from age to age. It is not clear to what extent a dictate of positive law which flouts natural law is void, but the mere fact that a law is unjust does not render it invalid.

One of the principal representatives of this school is Jean Dabin[9], who maintained that the law of nature was 'deduced from the nature of man as it reveals itself in the basic inclinations of that nature under the control of reason'. Since human nature is identical in people everywhere, the precepts of natural law are universal despite historical, geographical, cultural and other such variations[10]. These prescriptions are, however, only generalisations, and their detailed working out is left to the Catholic Church. One of the precepts of natural law is concerned with the good of society[11], which is the purpose of state and law. The state provides order and laws are means to that end: *'ubi jus ibi societas'*[12]. By virtue of this paramount function the

9 Dabin *General Theory of Law* (trans Wilk, *20th Century Legal Philosophy Series: IV*) pp 227–470.
10 *Dabin* para 203.
11 Following Aquinas's definition: see p 472 ante; *Dabin* paras 135 et seq.
12 *Dabin* para 9.

state is superior to all other groups, while state law 'is the sole true law'[13]. The *jus politicum* he defined as

> 'The sum total of the rules of conduct laid down, or at least consecrated, by civil society, under the sanction of public compulsion, with a view to realising in the relations between men a certain order—the order postulated by the end of the civil society and by the maintenance of the civil society as an instrument devoted to that end.[14].

Laws may be expressed variously, eg in statutes, precedents, customs; but they are general regulations of conduct, not of conscience. They are in the main obeyed, but when they are not obeyed, compulsion under the authority of the state has to be employed[15]. By saying that laws are directed to conduct and not to conscience, Dabin was able to argue that there is a moral duty to obey those positive laws which conform to the natural law principle of promoting the common weal. If a law fails to conform to this principle it is not morally binding, because 'everybody admits that civil laws contrary to natural law are bad laws and even that they do not answer to the concept of a law'[16]. This is ambiguous. If they are not 'laws', there is no question of moral bindingness. What is not clear is whether they remain legally valid, though not morally binding[17]. The question whether it would be immoral to disobey even such a law, because disobedience might be injurious to social stability, is not faced.

In order to fulfil the common good laws have to be adapted to the needs and ethos of the particular community. This is a matter of legal technique. So the actual making and applying of positive law with a view to giving effect to the dictates of natural law is an art which only jurists are competent to exercise[18]. For rules of law do not simply put natural law into effect; in most cases practical factors need to be taken into account.

All this reflects the attempt to harmonise the restoration of natural law with the variability of human societies and at the same time to follow the new emphasis on society.

Stammler

Another development was 'natural law with a variable content', of which Stammler (1856–1938) was an exponent[19]. He distinguished between technical legal science, which concerns a given legal system, and theoretical legal science, which concerns rules giving effect to fundamental principles. The former deals with the content of the law, the latter relates them to ultimate principles. He thus proceeded to distinguish between the 'concept of law' and the 'idea of law', or justice, and he approached the concept of law as follows. Order is appreciable through perception or will. Community, or society, is 'the formal unity of all conceivable individual purposes'[20], and by this means the individual may realise his ultimate best interests. 'Law,' says Stammler, 'is necessary *a priori*, because it is inevitably implied in the idea of

13 *Dabin* para 12.
14 *Dabin* para 6.
15 *Dabin* paras 26 et seq.
16 *Dabin* para 210.
17 On this, see Patterson *Jurisprudence* pp 356–358.
18 Cf Savigny's view of the function of lawyers: p 382 ante.
19 Stammler *The Theory of Justice* (trans Husik).
20 *Stammler* p 152.

co-operation'[1]. A just law aims at harmonising individual purposes with that of society. Accordingly, he sought to provide a formal, universally valid definition of law without reference to its content. He defined it as 'a species of will, other-regarding, self-authoritative, and inviolable'. Law is a species of will because it is concerned with orderings of conduct, other-regarding because it concerns a man's relations with other men, self-authoritative because it claims general obedience, and inviolable because of its claim to permanence. The idea of law is the application of the concept of law in the realisation of justice. Every rule is a means to an end, so one must seek a universal method of making just laws. A just law is the highest expression of Man's social activity. Its aim is the preservation of the freedom of the individual with the equal freedom of other individuals. In the realisation of justice the specific content of a rule of positive law will vary from place to place and from age to age and it is this relativity which has earned for the theory the name of 'natural law with a variable content'. In order to achieve justice, a legislator has to bear in mind four principles. These are, firstly, two Principles of Respect:

(1) 'The content of a person's volition must not depend upon the arbitrary will of another.'
(2) 'Every legal demand can only be maintained in such a way that the person obligated may remain a fellow creature.'[2]

Secondly, there are two Principles of Participation:

(1) 'A person lawfully obligated must not be arbitrarily excluded from the community.'
(2) 'Every lawful power of decision may exclude the person affected by it from the community only to the extent that the person may remain a fellow creature.'[3]

With the aid of these four principles Stammler set out to solve actual problems which may confront the law courts. His solutions may sometimes be questioned on the ground that they do not necessarily follow from his principles, or that they are not the only possible just solutions. He did not deny validity to laws which fail to conform to the requirements of justice. His scheme is a framework for determining the relative justness of a rule or a law and for providing a means for bringing it nearer to justice. The approach is Kantian in so far as it is maintained that human beings possess certain *a priori* forms of apprehending the idea of law. The difference lies in the variability that is allowed in its content and in the collectivist, rather than individualist, slant of the whole theory. Despite its ingenuity it has not found wide acceptance.

It is in America that contemporary natural law theory might be said to have found something like a congenial home.

John Rawls

A thorough-going attempt to formulate a general theory of justice is that of Professor John Rawls (b. 1921) of Harvard University, who writes mainly from the angle of philosophy and political science rather than of law[4]. Natural law

1   *Stammler* p 55.
2   *Stammler* p 161.
3   *Stammler* p 163.
4   Rawls *A Theory of Justice.*

is not dealt with as such; but in so far as his scheme is based on reason, concerns social justice and purports to be comprehensive, it is naturalistic in conception. Since its publication in 1971 it has received wide attention.

Professor Rawls assumes that society is a more or less self-sufficient association of persons, who in their mutual relations recognise as binding certain rules of conduct specifying a system of co-operation. Principles of social justice are necessary for making a rational choice between various available systems[5]. The way in which a concept of justice specifies basic rights and duties will affect problems of efficiency, co-ordination and stability. This is why it is necessary to have a rational conception of justice for the basic structure of society. Practical rationality has three aspects, namely, value, right and moral worth. The 'concept of right' relates to social systems and institutions, individuals, international relations and also the question of priority between principles. With regard to social systems and institutions, the concept of right yields 'Principles of Justice' and 'Efficiency'.

The approach to principles of social justice through utilitarianism and intuitionism respectively is considered critically and rejected. The latter in particular is faced with the difficulty of answering, first, Why should intuitive principles be followed? and, secondly, What guidance is there for choosing between conflicting principles in a given case? Professor Rawls endeavours to meet the first question by grounding his own principles in the exercise of reason in an imaginary 'original position'; and the second by calling in aid certain 'principles of priority'. He arrives at his theory as follows.

Fairness results from reasoned prudence; and principles of justice, dictated by prudence, are those which hypothetical rational persons would choose in a hypothetical 'original position' of equality. The insistence on prudence excludes gamblers from participating in the 'original position', but will bring in, on the whole, those who are conservatively inclined. The concept of the 'original position' is not quite a modernised version of the 'social contract', nor is it offered as being anything other than a pure supposition. On the one hand, people in this 'original position' are assumed to know certain things, eg general psychology and the social sciences, but, on the other hand, a 'veil of ignorance' drapes them with regard to certain other things, eg the stage of development of their society and especially their own personal conditions, places in that society, material fortunes etc. In short, all this is designed to exclude personal self-interest when choosing the 'Basic Principles of Justice' so as to ensure their generality and validity. What is needed is a form of justice which will benefit everyone, ie the disinterested individual's conception of the common good. Leaving aside the wholly fictitious nature of this 'original position', it is necessary to question the underlying assumption that what would be judged prudent in these hypothetical circumstances will eventually coincide with what people in actual societies will regard as just[6]. Moreover, the 'veil of ignorance' introduces needless complexities into what is no more than the simple requirement of impartial judgment[7].

The Basic Principles of Justice are generalised means of securing certain generalised wants, 'primary social goods', comprising what is styled the 'thin theory of the good', ie maximisation of the minimum (as opposed to a 'full theory')[8]. These primary social goods include basic liberties, opportunity,

5 *Rawls* p 4.
6 For criticism, see Barry *The Liberal Theory of Justice* pp 15–18.
7 *Barry* p 12.
8 *Rawls* pp 396 et seq. For critical examination, see *Barry* ch 3.

power and a minimum of wealth. The *First Principle* of Justice is: 'Each person is to have an equal right to the most extensive total system of equal basic liberties compatible with a similar system of liberty for all'[9]. The basic liberties include equal liberty of thought and conscience, equal participation in political decision-making and the rule of law which safeguards the person and his self-respect[10]. The *Second Principle* is: 'Social and economic inequalities are to be arranged so that they are both: (a) to the greatest benefit of the least advantaged, consistent with the just savings principle, and (b) attached to offices and positions open to all under conditions of fair equality of opportunity'[11]. The 'just savings principle' is designed to secure justice between generations and is described as follows. 'Each generation must not only preserve the gains of culture and civilisation, and maintain intact those just institutions that have been established, but it must also put aside in each period of time a suitable amount of real capital accumulation'[12]. With the aid of these Principles Professor Rawls seeks to establish a just basic structure. There has to be a constitutional convention to settle a constitution and procedures that are most likely to lead to a just and effective order; next comes legislation; and lastly the application of rules to particular cases[13]. In this way it is claimed that the Basic Principles will yield a just arrangement of social and economic institutions.

Many criticisms have been levelled at various aspects of Professor Rawls's philosophic methods and economics into which it is unnecessary to enter. One attack, launched by more than one critic, has been to question whether his conclusions follow from his 'original position'. For instance, distribution of goods is said to follow need, not merit[14]. How does the 'original position' yield this? Again, would people in this position necessarily choose liberty? Professor Rawls does not specify any particular period in history, so that people may find themselves in a time when there is need for power rather than liberty, or, as one critic suggests, the need may be for food in a time of famine rather than liberty[15]. The answer to the last point might be that, as Professor Rawl says elsewhere, liberty is to have priority only *after* a certain point[16]; but this raises another difficulty with regard to his priority principle, as will appear. Even so, when looked at from an economic or philosophical point of view, it is not easy to see how the balance between liberty and needs follows from the 'original position'[17]. Indeed, the 'veil of ignorance' is so restrictive that one wonders how people in that carefully defined state of nescience could arrive at any of the Rawlsian conclusions. Although they are supposed to know general psychology and social science, they are ignorant of the stage of development of their society: what is not clear is whether people in a primitive state of development are supposed to possess the sophisticated psychological and social scientific knowledge of modern people[18]. The insistence on excluding motivations of self-interest as well as knowledge of the state of society is designed to make the choice disinterested, but

9 *Rawls* p 302.
10 *Rawls* p 205 et seq, 221 et seq, 235 et seq.
11 *Rawls* p 302.
12 *Rawls* p 285.
13 *Rawls* pp 196 et seq; criticised by *Barry* chs 13–14.
14 *Rawls* pp 310 et seq.
15 Raphael Review in (1974) 83 Mind 121.
16 *Rawls* pp 45, 542–543; p 483 post.
17 *Barry* pp 7–10.
18 *Raphael* p 122.

nonetheless it remains personal. It has been pointed out that the fact that something is good for the individual does not imply that it will, therefore, be good for society. Thus, the benefit to an individual of being able to exercise a liberty may be lost to him if it were enjoyed by all[19]. If, then, the Basic Principles do not necessarily follow from the 'original position', their ultimate acceptance (if, indeed, they do come to be accepted) must derive from their intrinsic moral appeal rather than reason. Thus, the fact that particular principles may have been thought suitable in an 'original position' of limited knowledge and uncertainty is no basis for continuing to impose them later in the face of changed conditions and fuller knowledge. If it is contended that people would have chosen the principles anyway even in the light of later knowledge, this can only happen because they are thought to be just *per se*. The 'original position' then becomes irrelevant[20]. All this shows that the concept of the 'original position' and the 'veil of ignorance' and what it covers and does not cover only provide a semblance of justification for reaching certain desired conclusions[1].

An objection to intuitionism is, as Professor Rawls points out, that it gives no guidance in choosing between conflicting principles. To meet this difficulty he offers certain 'Principles of Priority'. Such priority is 'lexical', ie the first has to be fully satisfied before the second falls to be considered[2]. The *First Priority Rule* is the priority of liberty: 'liberty can be restricted only for the sake of liberty'[3]. He continues: '(a) a less extensive liberty must strengthen the total system of liberty shared by all; (b) a less than equal liberty must be acceptable to those with the lesser liberty'[4]. The *Second priority Rule* is the lexical priority of justice over efficiency and welfare: '(a) an inequality of opportunity must enhance the opportunity of those with the lesser opportunity; (b) an excessive rate of saving must on balance mitigate the burden of those bearing this hardship'[5]. These principles, in effect, ensure that as between liberty and need, liberty prevails; as between need and utility, need prevails; and as between liberty and utility, liberty prevails.

An objection to the lexical priority of liberty is that if equal liberty is accorded such priority, then anything involving unequal liberty can never fall to be considered, since the former has to be fully satisfied before one passes to something else[6]. More seriously, Professor Rawls concedes that liberty is to be given this kind of priority only *after* certain basic wants are satisfied[7]; but if liberty is not prior to needs all the time, lexical priority becomes meaningless.

With reference to the individual, Professor Rawls contends that reason yields principles of natural duties and fairness. The former include the duty to uphold just institutions, to help in establishing just arrangements, to render mutual aid and respect, not to injure or harm the innocent. The fairness principle gives rise to obligations, including promises; and in connection with fairness he strikes a topical note when discussing civil disobedience[8]. The

19 Hart 'Rawls on Liberty and its Priority' (1972–73) 40 U Ch LR 534; *Barry* ch 11.
20 Dworkin 'The Original Position' (1972–73) 40 U Ch LR 500.
 1 *Dworkin*; *Barry* p 22; *Raphael* p 123.
 2 *Rawls* pp 42–43, 244.
 3 *Rawls* p 302. On the importance of assessing basic liberties as a whole, see p 203.
 4 *Rawls* p 302.
 5 *Rawls* pp 302–303.
 6 *Raphael* p 126.
 7 *Rawls* pp 45, 542–543.
 8 *Rawls* pp 350–391.

principle is that one should play one's part as specified by the rules of the institution as long as one accepts its benefits ('fair-play'), and provided the institution itself is just, or at least nearly just, as judged by the two Basic Principles of Justice[9]. Civil disobedience is said to be justified when 'substantial injustice' occurs, all other methods of obtaining redress fail and disobedience inflicts no injury on the innocent. In these circumstances disobedience is an appeal to the society's sense of justice, which, it is said, is evidenced by the reluctance of the community to deal with it. This is hardly in accord with observed facts; it is more realistic to say that such reluctance is rooted more often than not in apathy and even fear, no matter how strongly people may condemn the disobedience.

In the result it would seem that Professor Rawls has not succeeded in showing how his principles, desirable as they may be, derive from reason. Leaving that aside, however, it should be noted that the thrust of his theory is for stability, especially in Part Three of his book where he deals with objectives, and in his emphasis on obedience grounded in fair-play.

Law is only one institution of social justice in Professor Rawls's scheme. Professors Clarence Morris and Jerome Hall make it their exclusive concern, which makes their theories less extensive in scope.

Clarence Morris

Professor Morris (b. 1893) begins with the proposition that 'justice is realised only through good law'[10]. Laws without just quality are doomed in the long run; but the implication of his statement that justice cannot exist without good law does not follow. Justice may be realised through many other institutions; indeed, according to Marx and Engels, in a communist society laws will wither away and justice for all will remain. Apart from the likelihood or otherwise of this prediction being fulfilled, it needs to be borne in mind that they were using 'law' in a narrow sense, since, as Engels went on to say, though 'law' will disappear, there will remain 'an administration of things'[11]. Professor Morris, however, uses 'law' in a broader sense. 'I use the word 'law' he says 'to mean more than statutes and ordinances; it includes both adjudicated decisions of cases and social recognition of those legal obligations that exist without governmental prompting' (customs and practices)[12].

Justice is one of three principal justifications of law, the other two being rationality and 'acculturation'. His theory concerns the method of realising justice and is not a theory of just content. 'Doing justice' through law means that law-makers serve the public by advancing its 'genuine aspirations', which are 'deep-seated, reasonable, and non-exploitative'[13]. Law-making contrary to them is doomed to failure, for without public support legislators toil in vain. One difficulty lies in knowing who constitutes the 'public'. Would Jews in Nazi Germany or Africans in South Africa count as the 'public'? 'Genuine aspirations' is a vague phrase, as Professor Morris admits[14]. To speak of them as 'deep-seated, reasonable, and non-exploitative' does not carry the matter much further. Who, for instance, decides what is

9 *Rawls* ch 6; pp 314–315 ante.
10 Morris *The Justification of Law* p 21.
11 See pp 398, 402–403 ante.
12 *Morris* p 23.
13 *Morris* p 23.
14 *Morris* p 58, and ch 3 generally.

'reasonable'? In South Africa today it is not unfair to say that a majority of the European minority regard many African aspirations as unreasonable, and may even feel that some exploitation of Africans is reasonable. Such sentiments are deep-seated. Yet, the tenor of Professor Morris's book seems to be against regarding that régime as just. Another question is why it should be supposed that justice is achieved only so long as legislators follow public aspirations. May they not, with justice, sometimes seek to lead[15]? The point is not faced.

The second justification of law, rationality, concerns the reasoning processes of the law, both judicial and legislative[16]. Reason is a major ingredient of justice, but is of a special kind. By accepting judicial appointment, a judge is said to incur a duty to implement public aspirations within the leeways of the judicial process. Although legislation, too, must reflect them, this does not imply that an unjust law is not a 'law'; a court remains bound to apply it. At this point Professor Morris enters the familiar ground of judicial reasoning and legislative techniques, which need not be rehearsed.

The third justification is 'acculturation', which is conformity with culture. The purport of a statute, for example, can be more easily gathered when one is in tune with the legislator's cultural environment[17], and the point is developed with reference to ancient Chinese legislation. Under the heading of 'acculturation' is included a plea for an awareness in law-making of man's responsibility towards his environment, since destruction and pollution of this will redound on himself[18]. What is not clear is whether the idea of justice is here being stretched to cover conservation.

Professor Morris's general thesis is that law has to be justified morally, socially and technically. He does not specifically assert that just quality is a necessary condition of the continuity of laws, but this seems to be implicit. He certainly stops short of saying that just quality is a requirement of the validity of a 'law', for he does speak of 'unjust laws'. So, mindful of the point made at the start of this chapter, perhaps Professor Morris is not to be classed as either naturalist or positivist, for his thesis would not be rejected by either side.

Jerome Hall

Not only does Professor Hall (b. 1901) insist on unifying moral, social and formal considerations, but he also takes the further step of saying that moral value needs to be included in a definition of positive law[19]. It is certainly appropriate to treat him as a naturalist.

Until the time of Hegel, jurisprudence was treated as part of philosophy. Since then it has become fashionable to diversify different aspects of philosophy, including jurisprudence. The positivist belief in the 'neutrality' of jurisprudence as an autonomous discipline is said to be associated with belief in logical analysis as a 'neutral' method of reasoning. It is obvious, however, that logical analysis will yield neutral results only if the premises are neutral; if values are part of the premises, then the results of logical analysis are likewise value-laden. The real issue is how one should view the premise, ie

15 Cf Plato, Aristotle, Marx: pp 74–75, 403 ante.
16 *Morris* chs 4–6.
17 *Morris* p 151.
18 *Morris* ch 8.
19 Hall *Foundations of Jurisprudence.*

the subject matter of jurisprudence, namely, 'positive law'[20]. The time has come, says Professor Hall, to re-unite disciplines, and to this end he argues that jurisprudence should be 'adequate' in the sense that it will combine positivist, naturalist and sociological study, namely, rules, values and social conduct[1]. The result will be what he calls 'integrative jurisprudence'[2]. The focal point of this is the action of officials, and he calls the concept 'law-as-action'[3]. The word 'action' is preferable to 'behaviour'; 'behaviour' occurs, whereas 'action' brings in the idea of purpose guided by the value of achieving goals[4]. Law-as-action from the point of view of officials relates rules, values and social behaviour in the following way. Rules come in to explain official actions in prescribing, judging and ordering and applying sanctions[5]. Values come into the idea of validity. The way in which validity is understood depends upon whether law is viewed as law-as-rules or law-as-action. The former leads to a Kelsenian-type concept whereas the latter will include moral attitudes, principles and ideals[6]. Thus, it is not sufficient to say of the actions of officials in deciding disputes that their decisions are in conformity with law, one has also to say whether they are correct, fitting or useful. 'Correctness' reflects sound values in the rules, which means that from this perspective rules, too, acquire moral validity. In so far as law-as-action concerns the achievement of goals, 'correctness' also partakes of the morality of the goals[7]. Social behaviour comes in through the idea of the effectiveness of law, which covers a whole range of phenomena, including sanctions, mere conformity, conscious obedience and compliance (obedience plus approval). Obedience has to be gauged in relation to results, which are aimed at, as distinct from consequences, which simply occur. So, probable consequences have to be considered, which necessitates continuous re-assessment. Even the very enforcement of a law alters the facts in the sense that the situation is different after enforcement from what it was at the time the law was made. Laws, therefore, are effective when actual behaviour in accordance with them maximises the values of their goals[8].

The conclusion thus becomes irresistible that, when looked at from the point of view of law-as-action, moral value must be included in any definition of positive law[9]. In addition, Professor Hall points to customary law which, he says, represents experience in settling problems in just and rational ways. 'It is the deliberate blocking out of the history of juridical experience that supports restrictive positivist analysis'[10]. He also points to the avowal of a 'minimal natural law' by at least one modern positivist as 'tantamount to surrender'[11].

The need still remains to distinguish positive law from morality and other

20 *Hall* pp 64 et seq, especially p 67.
1 *Hall* pp 17–20.
2 *Hall* ch 6; and see previously, 'Integrative jurisprudence' in *Interpretations of Modern Legal Philosophies* (ed Sayre) p 313; 'From Legal Theory to Integrative Jurisprudence' (1964) 33 U Cin LR 153.
3 *Hall* pp 20.
4 *Hall* pp 156–157.
5 *Hall* pp 127, 157 et seq.
6 *Hall* pp 173 et seq.
7 *Hall* pp 174–175.
8 *Hall* pp 170–172.
9 *Hall* pp 49, 120.
10 *Hall* pp 50–51.
11 *Hall* p 51. The 'minimal natural law' referred to is that of Hart, as to which see pp 493–494 post.

norms, and to this end he offers six criteria for law: (i) ethical validity reflected in certain attitudes; (ii) functions; (iii) regular (rather than system atic) character; (iv) range and character of public interest expressed in a state's laws; (v) effectiveness, which, if tied to the moral validity of law, has both a descriptive and prescriptive meaning; (vi) supremacy and inexorability in its sphere of relevance[12]. Only law possesses all six features[13].

The main difficulty about Professor Hall's thesis is a practical one. For all the persuasiveness of his theoretical demonstration that a moral value has to be included in a definition of positive law, the question remains: how does this help in the day-to-day business of law-as-action? What is the correct, fitting or useful action to be taken by a judge if he is confronted, eg with a duly enacted decree requiring the killing of all new-born babies in order to save the state from the effects of the population explosion? Nowhere does he say that an immoral law is not 'a law'. Validity in the sense of law-quality for the purpose of deciding this or that case is different from validity in the sense of law-as-action. The practical implications of the latter are unclear. An explanation may lie in the fact that his theory presupposes a continuum of time[14]. His thesis that morality must be included in a definition of law has to be understood in that context. Moreover, his stress on the need to integrate rules, morality and sociology, and the need to study law-as-action (functioning) give striking support to many of the contentions previously advanced in the present book.

Side by side with attempts, such as those considered, to work out a natural law of method, there have also been endeavours to base natural law on fact. Of especial interest in this connection is the theory of *John Wild* (b. 1902)[15]. He proceeds on the idea that 'there are norms grounded on the inescapable pattern of existence itself'[16] and his method of arriving at these is not that of logical deduction, but a different though equally logical process, namely 'justification'. 'How', he asks, 'is moral justification to be explained? We cannot explain it without recognising that certain moral premises must somehow be based upon facts'[17]. The core of his thesis is that 'value' and 'existence' are closely intertwined. Existence has a tendency towards fulfilment or completion[18], and if the completion of existence is considered good, then existence itself must be valuable. The same act is good so far as it is realised, but evil so far as it is frustrated or deprived; an influence that enables something to act is good for it, and one that frustrates it is bad. Goodness, then, is some kind or mode of existence, evil is some mode of non-existence or privation[19].

Tendencies are the facts on which value-statements are founded[20]. All individuals share in a common human nature, which has existential tendencies and which move them to their natural end[1]. Such tendencies are at the root of the feeling of obligation which men possess. From it one can pass back to the values which require the act obliged, from the values to the needs

12 *Hall* pp 137–138.
13 *Hall* p 140.
14 See eg *Hall* p 168.
15 Wild *Plato's Modern Enemies and the Theory of Natural Law.*
16 *Wild* p 107.
17 *Wild* pp 226, 228.
18 *Wild* p 65.
19 *Wild* pp 64–65, 105, 107.
20 *Wild* p 227.
 1 *Wild* p 68.

which they satisfy, and factual evidence can be produced to demonstrate that these needs are essential rights. Accordingly, Wild reaches the following conclusions. (1) The world is an order of divergent tendencies which, on the whole, support one another. (2) Each individual entity is marked by an essential structure which it shares in common with other members of the species. (3) This structure determines certain basic existential tendencies that are also common to the species. (4) If these tendencies are to be realised without distortion or frustration they must follow a general dynamic pattern. This pattern is what is meant by natural law. It is grounded on real structure and is enforced by inexorable natural sanctions. (5) Good and evil are existential categories. It is good for an entity to exist in a condition of active realisation; if its basic tendencies are hampered and frustrated, it exists in an evil condition. When all these principles are applied to human nature, three ethical theses may be derived: (a) the universality of moral or natural law; (b) the existence of norms founded on nature; and (c) the good for Man as the realisation of human nature[2]. Natural law may therefore be defined as 'a universal pattern of action applied to all men everywhere, required by human nature itself for its completion'[3].

Wild's opponents, notably Kelsen and Julius Stone[4], have fastened on the hiatus between fact and norm in his theory. There may be factual grounds for the content of the rules of natural law, but these do not show that natural law *ought* to be binding[5]. Again, it may be a fact that human beings have certain tendencies and have a sense of obligation; but they do not explain why people *ought* to obey this sense[6]. Mere existence is not enough, since, in Wild's view, the fact is the tendency of existence towards fulfilment or completion. How are these to be determined? Opinions will vary so enormously that this tendency ceases to be objective fact and becomes purely subjective. Besides, the fulfilment of existence of one entity may thwart or destroy the existence of another[7], and in such a case one wonders which is the natural law.

John Finnis

A sophisticated version of natural law has been put forward by John Finnis, who admits to having been schooled in the analytical tradition[8]. His theory is in the tradition of Aristotle and Aquinas. Every theorist has to evaluate in order to select or form concepts with which to describe aspects of human affairs, such as law. Without some idea of the practical reasonableness of a concept no theorist can know its central use, in Aristotelian terms, its 'focal meaning'. By 'practical' is meant 'with a view to decision and action'[9].

'In relation to law, the most important things for the theorist to know and describe are the things which, in the judgment of the theorist, make it important from a *practical* viewpoint to have law—the things which it is,

2   *Wild* p 134.
3   *Wild* p 64.
4   Kelsen 'A Dynamic Theory of Natural Law' in *What is Justice?* p 174; Stone *Human Law and Human Justice* pp 196-201.
5   *Kelsen* generally.
6   *Stone* p 199.
7   Kelsen asked how the continued existence of a poisonous snake could be a natural law on Wild's theory when it is so inimical to the continued existence of human beings.
8   *Finnis Natural Law and Natural Rights.*
9   *Finnis* p 12.

therefore, important in practice to 'see to' when ordering human affairs'[10]. He goes on to say that 'a theory of natural law claims to be able to identify conditions and principles of practical right-mindedness, of good and proper order among men and in individual conduct'[11]. It has been argued from the beginning of the present book that lawyers are, and if not they should be, concerned with justice and the moral authority of law. Both these considerations are said by Finnis to import natural law.

According to him, natural law consists of two sets of principles: the first consisting of certain basic values that are good for human beings, the second consisting of the requirements of practical reasonableness. These values are known because they are self-evident. One basic form of good is knowledge itself[12], which is reached, not by intuition, but through experience and reflection. The human mind has the ability to appreciate without demonstration or intuition the fundamental features of a good life and the methods of achieving it. In addition to knowledge, the values in the first set are[13]: life, play, aesthetic experience, sociability (friendship), practical reasonableness and religion, meaning thereby, not any particular faith, but 'recognition of, and concern about, an order of things "beyond" each and every man'[14]. This list is exhaustive. The second set of principles consists of the basic requirements of practical reasonableness[15]. Out of a variety of possible ways to live, it is necessary to choose a rational plan of life to enable people to participate in these goods. Practical reasonableness and its principles are the means of achieving these goods; together they produce morality. The requirements are: a coherent plan of life, no arbitrary preferences among basic values, nor among persons, detachment (avoiding fanaticism), commitment (avoiding apathy and abandoning commitments lightly), limited relevance of consequences (efficiency of means within reason), respect for every basic value in every act, the requirements of the common good, and following one's conscience.

How far would denial of any basic value or requirement of practical reasonableness amount to a denial of natural law? Perhaps, merely restructuring the list, or redistribution of emphasis, would not constitute rejection as long as some (or a majority?) of basic values and requirements of practical reasonableness are accepted as self-evident. Reason may devise different plans for co-ordinating and resolving problems of communal existence, so no particular plan can claim preference. The theory thus allows for varying manifestations of the principles.

Save where unanimity can be achieved, problems of co-ordination have to be resolved by authority[16], which is where law comes in. Authoritative rules can emerge out of customs, which Finnis discusses with reference, *inter alia*, to international law[17]. There has to be convergence of practices and opinions, not only on the need for *a* solution, but also on a particular solution. With custom the process is beset with doubt, so it is simpler to have someone or body to settle co-ordination problems authoritatively and effectively[18]. Since

10 *Finnis* p 16.
11 *Finnis* p 18.
12 *Finnis* ch III.
13 *Finnis* ch IV.
14 *Finnis* p 90.
15 *Finnis* ch V.
16 *Finnis* p 232.
17 *Finnis* pp 238 et seq.
18 *Finnis* p 246.

the central use of a concept is its 'focal meaning', the 'focal meaning' of law is to 'see to' co-ordination for the common good, which reason requires as being necessary, although the different forms which such co-ordination may assume can be left to be worked out.

Justice is 'other-directed', ie it concerns relations with others; it is owed as a duty to another; and it involves equality in the sense of proportionality[19]. All these aspects are directed towards the common good, which reflects basic values and the requirements of practical reasonableness; and 'distributive' and 'commutative' justice are examined in this light. The author's interpretation of these shows that the distinction between them is not as sharp as in Aristotle's presentation and is 'no more than an analytical convenience, an aid to orderly consideration of problems'[20]. For example, compensation in tort on the basis of the allocation of risks involved in communal activities could be classified as distributive or, as is more usual, commutative: just distribution requires compensation for all who suffer injury in the course of such activities, not just making a wrongdoer restore the equilibrium which has been upset by his fault. 'Right' and 'obligation' are also components of the common good, for they are limited by each other and other aspects of common good.

It follows that 'the moral authority of the law depends ... on its justice or at least its ability to secure justice'[1], and derives from the dictate of reason which shows this to be necessary. Law is an aspect of practical reasonableness and there are some goods that can be secured only through law. It also creates conditions for the good society and to that extent is a precondition of it, but part of it at the same time. Coercion and punishment are unavoidably necessary. More important, however, is that law introduces predictability through a framework of rules; it provides for their creation; it also allows individuals to create or modify rules for themselves; and it provides special techniques for regulating the future in an all-sufficient way, without 'gaps', on the basis of past acts of rule-creation. The definition of law derived from all this is that it refers

> 'primarily to rules made, in accordance with regulative legal rules, by a determinate and effective authority (itself identified and, standardly constituted as an institution by legal rules), for a complete community, and buttressed by sanctions in accordance with the rule-guided stipulations of adjudicative institutions, this ensemble of rules and institutions being directed to reasonably resolving any of the community's co-ordination problems (and to ratifying, tolerating, regulating, or overriding co-ordination solutions from any other institutions or sources of norms) for the common good of that community, according to a manner and form itself adapted to that common good by features of specificity, minimisation or arbitrariness, and maintenance of a quality of reciprocity between the subjects of the law both amongst themselves and in their relations with the lawful authorities'[2].

By 'rule of law' is meant a system in which (i) its rules are prospective, (ii) possible to comply with, (iii) promulgated, (iv) clear, (v) coherent with each other, (vi) sufficiently stable, (vii) the making of decrees and orders is guided by rules that are themselves promulgated, clear, stable and relatively general, (viii) those who administer rules are accountable for their own

19 *Finnis* pp 161–162, and generally ch VII.
20 *Finnis* p 179.
 1 *Finnis* p 260.
 2 *Finnis* pp 276–277.

compliance with rules relating to their activities and who perform these consistently and in accordance with law[3].

Social schemes that contravene basic values and practical reasonableness are unjust; so, too, is any infringement of the individual's liberty to assign his own priorities among the basic values. Prima facie there is a moral obligation to obey laws directed to achieving the common good, but as long as common good is not impaired, disobedience on grounds, eg of conscience, would be permissible. The question whether an unjust law is 'law' is said not to be central to natural law thinking. As to this, the author's distinction is best stated in his own words:

> 'The ruler has, very strictly speaking, no right to be obeyed; but he has the authority to give directions and make laws that are morally obligatory and that he has the responsibility of enforcing. He has this authority for the sake of the common good (the needs of which can also, however, make authoritative the opinions—as is custom—or stipulations of men who have no authority). Therefore, if he uses his authority to make stipulations against the common good, or against any of the basic principles of practical reasonableness, those stipulations altogether lack the authority they would otherwise have *by virtue of being his*'[4].

The book concludes by reaching into an explanation of existence and natural law as participation of Eternal Law. What is crucial to its thesis is 'self-evidence' based on experience and reflection. It is not clear how far, if at all, there is room for disagreement about self-evidence itself. On a different point, is it possible to detect in the self-evident basic values and requirements of practical reasonableness the conditions essential to the continuity of a good society? Perhaps, one ought not to read into the theory something not alluded to by the author; but the question serves as a lead into that aspect of natural law.

NATURAL LAW OF CONTINUITY: TEMPORAL APPROACH

The 'natural law of method' is a way of working out just laws, and the 20th century has seen versions of 'natural law with variable content'. The temporal approach is in line with this thinking. Factors but for which a thing would not be and continue to be and function are part of the conception of it as a continuing phenomenon. The nature of things being what it is, such factors dictate a 'natural law of existence'. The 'ought' behind it is that behind the conditions *sine quibus non* of achieving any end—in this case, continuity. It is not the 'ought' of duty, so there is no question of deriving an obligatory 'ought' from an 'is'. Such an approach is politically neutral in that it does not support any particular kind of order. Even if the present one were shattered to pieces and a different one established, the continuance of that, too, will require the same conditions.

A similar line of argument is adopted by Professor Lon L Fuller who might perhaps be regarded as a leading natural lawyer. The core of his thesis concerns the conditions *sine quibus non* for the functioning of laws[5]. For him, law 'is the enterprise of subjecting human conduct to the governance of rules'[6]. Its morality has two aspects, external and internal. 'External morality'

3 *Finnis* pp 270–271. Cf Fuller's 'inner morality' of law, p 230 ante.
4 *Finnis* pp 359–360.
5 Fuller *The Morality of Law* (revised edition).
6 *Fuller* pp 74, 96, 106, 122.

is the 'morality of aspiration', ideals; and towards the end of his book he submits that it is possible to derive a 'substantive natural law' from it. This is more than a recipe for mere survival; it is a recipe for 'meaningful contact with other human beings'[7] whereby men can improve and enrich themselves. This substantive natural law concerns itself with those fundamental rules without which such meaningful co-existence could not obtain. There is also the 'internal morality' of law, which makes no appeal to external standards, but is, in Professor Fuller's own words, 'a procedural version of natural law'[8]. It is the morality that makes the governance of human conduct by rules possible. A judge may well stay neutral with regard to external morality, but it would be 'an abdication of the responsibilities of his office' for him to stay neutral with regard to the internal morality[9]. The content of it, which has been considered in connection with the functioning of duty[10], consists of eight desiderata: (i) generality, (ii) promulgation, (iii) prospectivity, (iv) intelligibility, (v) unself-contradictoriness, (vi) possibility of obedience, (vii) constancy through time, and (viii) congruence between official action and declared rules[11]. This 'inner morality' is not something superimposed on the power of law, 'but is an essential condition of that power itself'; it is, in other words, 'a precondition of good law'[12]. Immoral policies are bound in the end to impair the 'inner morality' and so the very quality of law.

It was argued earlier that these are conditions *sine quibus non* for the functioning of duties. If they are called 'natural law', they are 'natural' in that they are founded on the nature of things—human beings and human society are made in such a way that their natural limitations constitute the conditions for the successful functioning of duty-creating laws. It will be noticed that these conditions apply to the governance of any society of human beings so that they do not of themselves help to distinguish the functioning of the rules of a legal system from those of a club; nor does Professor Fuller claim that they do. The question may be raised, however, as to what a judge should do when faced with a decree violating the 'internal morality', eg that of Caligula, which was promulgated in such a way that no one could read it. Should he refuse to acknowledge it as 'a law'? Professor Fuller does not give an answer. In the sort of régime in which the 'internal morality' is likely to be violated, a judge who refuses to accept a decree on this ground will receive short shrift indeed. So Professor Fuller's thesis seems likely to avail least where it would be most needed.

Professor Hart and others have drawn attention to a different point. The former has pointed out that the eight desiderata are 'unfortunately compatible with very great iniquity'[13], eg Herod's order for the massacre of the innocents satisfied all the conditions. Professor Fuller's reply is to doubt whether an evil ruler could pursue iniquitous ends and also continue to respect the 'inner morality'. He calls for 'examples about which some meaningful discussion might turn' and which would show that 'history does in fact afford significant examples of régimes that have combined a faithful adherence to the internal morality of law with a brutal indifference to justice and

7 *Fuller* p 186.
8 *Fuller* p 96.
9 *Fuller* p 132.
10 See p 230 ante.
11 *Fuller* ch 2.
12 *Fuller* p 155.
13 Hart *The Concept of Law* p 202; Friedmann *Legal Theory* p 19.

human welfare'[14]. This is hardly an answer, but it does reveal an interesting point about the difference of opinion here. His contention is that iniquitous régimes have not *continued* to exist, nor could they *continue* to combine evil policies with fidelity to the 'internal morality'. In other words, he is thinking in a continuum, which is consistent with his idea of conditions needed for the continued functioning of laws. Professor Hart's objection concerns the position here and now of an inquitious decree rather than the question of its continuance. In other words, the two parties are not at issue since they are thinking in two different time-frames.

Professor Hart (b. 1907), who is a leading contemporary positivist, has himself essayed an incursion into natural law[15]. He admits that there is 'a core of indisputable truth in the doctrines of Natural Law'[16], if survival is taken as the minimum aim of human existence[17]. The conditions *sine quibus non* for achieving this end require that account be taken of five 'facts': (i) human vulnerability, (ii) approximate equality of people, (iii) limited altruism, (iv) limited resources, and (v) limited understanding and strength of will[18]. Because of these there is a *'natural necessity'* to protect persons, property and promises in varying degrees. This necessity imposes some limit on the content of laws and this, he says, is the answer to a positivist who thinks that laws may have *any* content[19]. It is by no means clear what this last statement implies. Professor Hart would hardly maintain that a law contrary to any of his five requirements is void, for he has strenuously upheld the positivist separation of law and morality and has urged that it is both intellectually honest and conducive to clarity to say 'This is law; but it is too iniquitous to be applied or obeyed'[20]. Such being his position, it would seem that the five requirements only furnish a standard of evaluating actual laws and guidelines for what they ought to be. Yet, his assertion that they are the answer to a positivist who thinks that laws may have any content suggests something more than this, something quite un-positivist[1]. Another point is that, even as guidelines, the requirements are too vague to offer meaningful guidance. Thus, human vulnerability has not prevented life in most modern societies being made increasingly hazardous through various technological advances. Does vulnerability require that law should be used to discontinue such activities, or only to provide suitable compensation when injuries are sustained? If it is the latter, it seems odd that the minimal natural law should manifest itself, not in seeking to avoid threats to one of its basic 'facts', but only in seeking a remedy in ways which can hardly 'remedy'; for no amount of money can mend broken bones. Again, the 'approximate equality' of people suffers from the weakness, previously noted, that everything depends on the criterion of equality and who applies it[2]. Finally, it is to be observed that survival even as the minimum aim of human existence, as well as the five 'facts' of the human condition, are not supported by any evidence, ie they are intuitive, self-evident. Professor Fuller has doubts about survival,

14 *Fuller* p 154.
15 *Hart* pp 189–195.
16 *Hart* p 176. See also p 196.
17 *Hart* p 188.
18 *Hart* pp 190–193.
19 *Hart* p 195.
20 *Hart* p 203.
 1 See D'Entrèves *Natural Law* App C.
 2 See p 65 ante. For Hart's appreciation of the difficulty, see *Hart* p 202.

even as an assumption: survival may be a means to other ends, but as the core of human striving, he says, it is open to question[3].

It may seem ironic that this account of natural law should end with a leading positivist expounding on the 'core of indisputable truth in the doctrines of Natural Law', but this may at least indicate that the gulf between the two groups is not as wide as it used to be. Positions are less clear-cut now. It further underlines the point that classification into 'naturalist' and 'positivist' applies to views, not individuals. Certain doctrines may be labelled 'naturalist' and others 'positivist', but people may subscribe more or less strongly to one type or the other depending on the issue.

IMPLICATIONS OF A TEMPORAL APPROACH

The temporal approach, as outlined in the first chapter, only offers a way of looking at phenomena and not some new revelation. Jurisprudential study has broadened immeasurably in modern times, and the theme of this book has been to emphasise the essential inter-relation between law and other disciplines, principally philosophy, sociology, politics and ethics. No one can be a good lawyer who only knows the law. It does not require a temporal approach to appreciate the connection between law and these other subjects, but such an approach can provide a framework which will unite their study. Whenever phenomena are viewed in a continuum, factors but for which they would not come into being, continue to be, and function become integral to one's concept of them. Origins include moral and social factors, reaching back perhaps to the very springs of governmental and other established social institutions. Function, or purpose, brings in the study of policies and values and the multifarious parts these play. They help to relate contemporary problems to the whole sweep of human thought from ancient philosophies down to the most modern. Functioning brings in the actual operation of laws in society, including the important parts played by the institutional structure of society, the interplay of social and moral factors, and so on. In this connection the study of legal concepts also comes in, for they are necessary instruments in the task of doing justice in deciding disputes. The idea of an instrument includes its use, and the way it is used shapes the instrument.

Next, a temporal approach might help by assigning inquiries to their appropriate context. It has been suggested, for instance, that statutes should be thought of in a continuum, since they are designed to operate over indefinite periods of time[4]. This will make it easier to see that statutory interpretation is an open-ended process of applying a given set of words to ever-changing situations rather than a linguistic exercise in trying to elucidate the referents of words. There is an *ad hoc* character about the latter, which is quite out of keeping with the nature of the enterprise, which should be one of statute 'application' or even 'construction', not 'interpretation'. It is submitted that the present unsatisfactory position is the result of approaching this task in the wrong temporal context. So, too, the *ratio* of a judicial precedent is not some 'thing', which can be isolated here and now, but an open-ended process of continuous adjustment[5]. Again, the dispute as to whether or not sanction is an essential part of the concept of duty is the

3 *Fuller* p 185.
4 See p 170 ante.
5 See pp 140, 144 et seq ante.

product of a failure to see that each view is appropriate in its own context[6]. Sanction is indeed part of the duty concept when duty is viewed in a continuum, where its functioning falls to be considered and with it the machinery of enforcement. Viewed as a tool of legal reasoning for the purpose of doing justice in this or that case, the concept of duty divorced from sanction is frequently used[7]. The controversy arises when an inference from one time-frame is illegitimately transferred to the other. 'Validity' (law-quality) is a concept which is appropriate in the present time-frame, where the question, Is this proposition 'law'?, is asked with a view to identifying it as 'law' for the purpose in hand, usually the deciding of a dispute. It is necessary to keep the means of identification as clear-cut as possible. One does not have to consider the need to decide of this or that case when thinking in a continuum, so different questions are asked: Why was this criterion of validity adopted? Why does it continue to be adopted[8]? The operation of Savigny's mystical *Volksgeist* is discernible, if at all, only over a continuum, but his mistake, it is submitted with respect, was to utilise a factor operative in a continuum as a criterion of validity here and now[9]. Professor Hart, whose concept of law and society imports continuity, changes his ground in order to defend positivism and he shifts his argument to the need for clear-cut criteria of validity in the day-to-day business of identifying 'laws'[10].

The temporal approach cannot resolve every puzzle, but it might at least shed new light on some. In connection with customs, there is the age-old antinomy between the apparent bindingness of customs and the unlimited discretion which courts appear to have in accepting or rejecting them. At least an explanation of why this problem has arisen, if not a solution, is suggested by a consideration of the requirements of customs in a temporal perspective[11]. Two other famous controversies need separate treatment. They are the question whether international law is 'law', and the positivist-naturalist debate.

THE PROBLEM OF INTERNATIONAL LAW

International law did not fit Austin's definition of 'law properly so called', so he excluded it from further consideration; which was unobjectionable in itself. Unfortunately what he said, in effect, was, 'This is the definition of 'law' which I propose to adopt. It is the proper meaning, and I exclude international law because it is not properly called 'law' '. As might have been expected, international lawyers, incensed at this denigration of their subject, took issue with him. Had they, for their part, simply replied: 'Use the word 'law' how you like, but we shall use it for our subject', no controversy need have arisen. Instead, they took issue with him on the 'proper meaning' of the word 'law'. To this extent the controversy was verbal and sterile.

It is a fact that the respect which states pay to international law is less than that which individuals pay to municipal law. There has always been a need to enhance the prestige of international law by calling in aid the magic of the word 'law', especially in creating a sense of obligation. This is one

6 See pp 245–246 ante.
7 For examples, see pp 240–245 ante.
8 See pp 53–59 ante.
9 See p 382 ante.
10 See pp 355–356 ante.
11 See p 191 ante.

reason why international lawyers are sensitive about Austin's exclusion of their subject from his imaginary paradise and why they are so anxious to avail themselves of the emotive connotation of the word 'law'. Professor G L Williams pointed it out very clearly.

> 'The word 'law' stimulates in us the attitude of obedience to authoritative rules that we have come through our upbringing to associate with the idea of municipal law. Change the word for some other and the magic evaporated. Accordingly these writers felt obliged to embark upon the unprofitable discussion as to the 'proper' meaning of the term 'law'[12].

Hence the attempts to prove that the subject is 'really' law[13].

Professor Hart thinks that the controversy is more than just a disagreement about words, because the application of the general term 'law' to a whole discipline like international law is different from the application of a name to an object. The question, he says, is one of analogies. (a) There are rules prescribing how states ought to behave, which are accepted as guiding standards just as in municipal law. (b) Appeals are made to precedent, writings and treatises as in municipal law; not to rightness or morality. (c) Rules of international law, like those of municipal law, can be morally neutral. (d) Again, like rules of municipal law, they can be changed by conscious act, eg by treaty[14]. Accordingly, Professor Hart submits that there are sufficient analogies of content, as opposed to form, to bring rules of international law nearer to municipal law than to any other set of social rules[15].

Despite these resemblances, two important differences should not be overlooked. One is that the subjects of international law are primarily states, and the disparity in strength between them far exceeds that between individuals in society[16]. Besides, there are other institutions which have claims, duties etc, but which are not states. Examples would be the United Nations Organisation, the Holy See between 1871 and 1929, various other specialised agencies and so on. Individuals as such are increasingly becoming subjects of international law, which enhances the disparity between the various subjects.

The other difference is that whereas the courts of a municipal order appeal to the same criterion, or criteria, by which to identify 'laws', there is no coordination in the ways in which rules of international law are identified. There is no single criterion of identification, because there are unrelated sets of tribunals, each of which identifies international law differently. There is, first, the International Court of Justice, which identifies its rules with reference to art 38 of the Statute of the International Court. Paragraph (1) specifies treaties, custom, general principles of law, and, subject to art 59, judicial decisions and writings of jurists. Paragraph (2) empowers the Court to decide *ex aequo et bono* if the parties agree. There are other international tribunals, such as arbitration tribunals, which are not bound by the Statute of the International Court. They may, and usually do, resort to much the same sources, namely, treaties (especially the treaty setting up the tribunal) custom, general principles of law, judicial decisions and writings of jurists.

---

12 Williams 'International Law and the Controversy Concerning the Word 'Law'' in *Philosophy, Politics and Society* (ed Laslett) at pp 143-144.
13 This idea seems also to underlie the attempt to prove that international law is *'per se'* part of the common law: pp 217-218 ante.
14 Hart *The Concept of Law* ch 10.
15 *Hart* p 231.
16 There is not that 'approximate equality' between subjects which Hart mentions elsewhere: pp 190-191, mentioned p 493 ante.

Municipal courts also are often called upon to apply principles of international law. Their criteria of identification are regulated by their own municipal systems. A British court, for instance, finds rules of international law primarily in statute and precedent. Only in the absence of a rule of statute law or common law applicable to the case in hand will it go outside and, even then, only as a matter of discretion.

When one considers international law in a continuum the differences become more pronounced. In the first place, it follows from what has just been said that no consistent answer can be given to the question why the criteria of identification were adopted. In most cases the adoption is *ad hoc*, for the purpose of the instant dispute, not once and for all. The predictability of decisions in any international tribunal is less than in municipal tribunals because there are fewer agreed rules and because of the greater intrusion of political considerations and national self-interest. Indeed, 'vital interests' and 'national honour' prevent every important issue ever going before courts.

More interesting is the manner in which rules of international law work, with which is associated the question of obedience to it. The basis of the 'binding force' of international law is commonly ascribed to consent, which is not a satisfactory explanation. A basis in consent presupposes some rule which makes consent obligatory; and the basis of that rule then requires elucidation. Again, if consent is the basis, it would follow that once consent is withdrawn, the obligation to obey ceases. It has been pointed out with regard to municipal law that consent is unrealistic[17]. Individuals are never asked if they consent to be bound by municipal laws, which are treated as binding regardless of consent. The point only arises when some dissident declares that he no longer accepts a law, in which event the question is not whether consent makes a law binding, but whether withdrawal of compliance can deprive it of its obligatory force; which is a different matter. Here, the coercive power of the state, manifested in its sanction machinery, comes into play, and this is so overwhelming as to make it quite immaterial what the individual thinks. Accordingly, as has been suggested, there is no point investigating 'the binding force' behind laws as if this is some 'thing' which can be isolated, but it would be more meaningful to ask: Why do people obey? and, What machinery is there for dealing with disobedience[18]? The so-called 'binding force' rests in the psychological reactions inducing people to obey, among which fear of organised force is one factor. In the international sphere, there is no effective machinery for applying overwhelming, organised force. The principal reasons why states choose to obey international law are fear, if at all, of their neighbours and self-interest. Fear operates through war, reprisals, retaliation, pacific blockade and naval and military demonstrations. These have comparatively little effect and, in any case, are calculated to deter weak rather than strong states. Fear of action taken by the United Nations Organisation is very slight, for such action is inhibited by the use of the veto in the Security Council. The greatest shortcoming of international law is the absence of effective machinery to carry out sanctions. In any case, such action as might be taken is more likely to influence weak rather than strong states. The result, therefore, is that whether or not a given state at any time abides by a given rule of international law depends upon a balance between various considerations, eg a

17 See p 314 ante.
18 See p 248 ante.

desire to secure fair treatment for its own nationals at the hands of other states, nationalism, tradition, morality, diplomacy, economic interests and, possibly, fear. All this makes the working of international law very different from that of municipal law. In brief, international law continues in being mainly because states and international lawyers find it useful and profitable.

The result is that when one considers the matter in the present time-frame the resemblances between international and municipal law are such as to tilt the balance in favour of hallowing the former with the sanctity of 'law'; when one considers it in a continuum the functioning of international law is so different from municipal law that the balance gets tilted the other way. The temporal approach does not answer the question whether international law is 'law' or not, but it could account for the persistence of the question and why it resists all efforts to lay it to rest.

THE POSITIVIST-NATURALIST DEBATE

The chapter on Positivism drew attention to the points of conflict[19], some restatement of which is necessary in order to highlight, not just the area of disagreement, but also of agreement. The submission is that the temporal approach will resolve some parts at least of the conflict. It will have become obvious that naturalists think mainly in a continuum and positivists in the time-frame of the present. The former include a moral element in their conception of law since they think of it as an indispensable factor in the continued existence and functioning of law; the latter exclude a moral element since they are mindful of the necessity of having clear-cut means of identifying laws for the practical purposes of the present, unclouded by impalpable moral considerations. So for a good deal of the time the two sides appear to be shadow-boxing on different planes.

In the course of the discussion of the is/ought dichotomy it was pointed out that a *total* separation of the 'is' and the 'ought' is not possible[20]. Law is what its makers think it ought to be. For instance, in rule-making and rule-applying including the constant restructuring of concepts, it is undeniable that moral, social, political and other such factors make them what they are; and where there is no authority on a point, the judge will declare the rule to be what he feels it ought to be[1]. Again, principles and doctrines, as Professor Dworkin has argued, 'are' law now, but they are themselves pointers to what laws ought to be[2].

When naturalists talk of the moral quality of law they are thinking of law in a continuum, ie as a purposive social activity extending over an indefinite period of time. They are certainly able to make out a powerful case[3]. A separation of law from morals is not possible when the moral quality of law is one of the factors that brings it into being and determines its continued existence; all such factors are a part of the concept of law as a continuing, functioning phenomenon. A person may be very ill, and for the purposes of the moment the concept is that of a sick human body. It will not remain so, for forces are at work to get rid of the disease, and should they fail that body

---

19 See pp 332-335 ante.
20 See p 333 ante.
 1 Sir Garfield Barwick CJ in *Mutual Life & Citizens' Assurance Co* (1968) 42 ALJR 316 at 318, quoted p 333 ante.
 2 See pp 45-46, 333 ante.
 3 See ch 5 ante.

will perish. The forces which make for health and continued life are part of the concept of an enduring human body. Similarly, morality is a factor that governs the health and continued life of laws. Is there, or is there not, in every community a morality which will assert itself in the long run however impalpable it may be, just as there is a normal state of healthiness of a human body which tends to re-assert itself in the long run however much the details of that condition may vary? The answer must surely be in the affirmative, if only because experience has shown that immoral régimes just do not last indefinitely[4].

Positivists, on the other hand, think mainly in the present time-frame where the need is to determine whether a given precept is or is not a 'law' for the purpose in hand. Their case for resting identification on a purely formal criterion is overwhelming[5].

So far naturalists and positivists are not at issue, and the fact that they have been operating in two different frames of thought can be revealed by a few sample writings. When Austin declared that 'a law' is the command of a sovereign supported by a sanction, he was only providing a method, inaccurate at that, of identifying what he called a 'positive law'. Nowhere did he concern himself with the conditions of continuance. Kelsen's hierarchical scheme is a demonstration of how the law-quality of every norm at any given moment is derived from the *Grundnorm*; and by insisting on 'purity' for his theory he excluded all dynamic forces that make for continuity. Professor Hart begins by equating 'law' with 'legal system', which is an on-going phenomenon; but in arguing the case for positivism he bases it on the need for a clear-cut method of identifying laws at any given moment of time[6]. Elsewhere he has alluded to 'the acceptable proposition that *some* shared morality is essential to the existence of any society'[7]. Thus, when he thinks of continuity, morality is said to be essential; when defending the need here and now for clear-cut, formal means of identifying laws, he takes refuge in the present time-frame.

On the other hand, when Professor Fuller, a naturalist, proffers his eight conditions, which comprise the 'inner morality' of law, he is stating, as has been pointed out, indispensable requirements for the continued functioning of laws[8]. His positivist critics have not been slow to point out (a) that all these conditions are compatible with very great iniquity, and (b) that there is no reason why an immoral precept may not be likened to a 'sick law', but a 'law' nonetheless. Both objections betray the critics' obsession with the present time-frame of thought in which alone they are meaningful. For they overlook the crucial point that the conditions required to keep a thing going, to cure or kill it are included in any conception involving its endurance. An unjust law may indeed satisfy the eight conditions and even function, but Professor Fuller's point is that it will not continue to function. However, he does not answer the question whether or not an immoral precept is to be

---

4 Fuller *The Morality of Law* p 154. Positivists admit this, eg Savigny's *Volksgeist* moulds or abrogates the law (see ch 18 ante); Hart admits that '*some* shared morality is essential to the existence of any society': *Law, Liberty and Morality* p 51. The Watergate scandal of 1974 in America might be regarded as an instance of the moral sense of the nation asserting itself.
5 See pp 334–335 ante.
6 Hart *The Concept of Law* p 203, (quoted p 355 ante). See also Hart 'Positivism and the Separation of Law and Morals' (1958) 71 Harv LR 595.
7 Hart *Law, Liberty and Morality* p 51.
8 Fuller *The Morality of Law* ch 2. For discussion, see pp 230 et seq ante.

treated as 'law' at this moment. He side-steps that point by asking instead whether 'history does in fact afford significant examples of régimes that have combined a faithful adherence to the internal morality of law with brutal indifference to justice and human welfare'[9]. This is a matter of *continuance* and shows that he, for his part, is thinking in a continuum. The time-frame approach thus shows that the two sides are not on the same plane.

It follows that the relation of morality to a concept of law cannot be stated simply in the form of a stark alternative that the former is *either* externally *or* internally related to the latter. It is both, depending upon the time-frame of reference. Morality tends to be externally related to law in all such identificatory concepts operating in the present time-frame. Thus it is that an immoral precept can be regarded as 'law' in that context. On the other hand, when the question is one of the durability of a law, consonance with morality is one of the conditions which makes for endurance, and here the naturalists have an equally strong case. Morality is then internally related to law in any concept which takes account of the implications of continuity. For, notwithstanding that an immoral precept is 'law' at this moment, it will not continue to be 'law' indefinitely[10]. The inter-relation between law and morality is perceptible by looking backwards over a long period, by retrospective rationalisation. If so, why not also look forwards and prospectively?

The real confrontation comes when naturalists step into the present time-frame and seek to incorporate a minimum moral content in the criterion of validity by which to identify propositions as 'laws' here and now. They do not reject the Positivist attitude, which leads to certainty and hence is an aspect of justice. Nor do they contend that everything which is moral is 'law'; what they say is that validity has to depend on a formal plus a minimum moral criterion[11]. The inclusion of both a formal and moral element will ensure that there will continue to be some separation between what is law and what ought to be law so that the latter can serve as a standard by which to evaluate the former. What naturalists are anxious to secure is that precepts, which violate minimum morality, will not become 'laws'.

It is necessary to separate two questions: Is there presently a minimum moral criterion of validity? and Ought there to be such a criterion? With regard to the first, the answer must be in the negative, save where a moral element has been written into a constitution in some form or other. There have been occasional judicial utterances of wider import, but these are not decisive and should not be generalised.

The second question is whether a minimum moral element ought to be incorporated into the criterion of validity. This has been discussed at length in Chapter 5 in relation to the abuse of power. Naturalists, arguing on the basis of the conditions essential to continuity, advance good reasons why it should be[12]. Positivists, while not questioning the desirability, advance equally cogent reasons why a moral test as such would be impracticable in the daily workings of the law[13]. This casts the onus squarely on naturalists to

9 *Fuller* p 154.
10 Professor Taylor 'Law and Morality' (1968) 43 NYULR 611, approaches this idea when he says that in explaining what is *a law* there should be a separation of law and morals, but that they are re-united when considering *law* as an activity. It is submitted, however, they are united even when *a law* is considered as an enduring phenomenon. The distinction lies in a time-frame.
11 See p 87 ante.
12 See p 89 ante.
13 See pp 334–335 ante.

find a practicable way of incorporating a moral test into a formal criterion of validity. It is proper that they should accommodate themselves to a formal test, since the method of identifying laws for the purpose of daily business has to be clear-cut and impersonal for the compelling reasons given by positivists. Indeed, if naturalists choose to enter the lists in the present time-frame, as they are doing here, they must submit to the requirements dictated by its circumstances. If such a method could be found, then both positivitsts and naturalists should be satisfied, the former because their insistence on a formal test will have prevailed, the latter because their demand for a minimum moral criterion will also have been met. The possibilities of achieving this were considered in Chapter 5 though it is doubtful if any of them can be regarded as providing a wholly satisfactory answer. So, finding such an answer remains an unattained goal in the general pursuit of social justice, but there is no reason why positivists and naturalists should not co-operate in making the quest a joint enterprise.

NATURAL 'RIGHTS'

These came into prominence with the rise of individualism. Each person was thought of as enjoying an area of sanctity. 'Natural rights' are abstract versions of claims, liberties and immunities and at this level of generalisation are akin to principles, standards and doctrines. It is in this sense that they have been embodied in sundry Bills of Rights, Charters of Fundamental Freedoms and Constitutions; they are called 'natural' perhaps because they are thought to be essential to social existence. Rules of law crystallise out of them and it is a mistake to equate them with specific claims, liberties and immunities expressed in rules of positive law. As previously pointed out[14], principles etc exert pressure on the law to develop according to them, but such pressure may be overriden by other pressures in particular instances.

A modern case for 'fundamental rights' has been argued by Professor Dworkin[15]. Although he dislikes the description of his 'rights' as 'natural', his thesis is not dissimilar to 'natural rights' as traditionally conceived. He distinguishes between 'background rights, which are rights that hold in an abstract way against decisions taken by the community or the society as a whole, and more specific institutional rights that hold against a decision made by a specific institution'. Legal rights are institutional rights to decisions in courts. Intuitions about justice presuppose a fundamental right, namely, 'the right to equality, which I call the right to equal concern and respect'[16]. The utilitarian approach to justice is rejected on the ground that the individual has 'rights' against the government, from which it follows that justice cannot lie in the subordination of the individual simply because doing so would, on balance, benefit the common weal. Now, the 'right of free speech' of one individual can indeed be limited by the 'right' of another individual to the integrity of his reputation; and another major qualification is that the 'right' of the individual may be overridden even by government 'to prevent a catastrophe, or even to obtain a clear and major public benefit'. What is not permissible is for government 'to act on no more than a judgment that its act is likely to produce, overall, a benefit to the community'[17].

14 See p 46 ante.
15 Dworkin *Taking Rights Seriously*. See also Finnis *Natural Law and Natural Rights* ch VIII.
16 *Dworkin* p xii.
17 *Dworkin* pp 191–192.

Dworkin also rejects the positivist conception of law as consisting solely of rules. These are not enough in themselves since justice and obligation have a moral dimension. Individual 'rights' are principles, which are required by 'justice or fairness or some other dimension of morality'[18]; and law as a whole incorporates rules and principles. Positivists maintain that in 'hard cases' judges have a discretion to decide on 'policy' grounds. Dworkin disputes this on the ground that there is always a right answer, which entitles one party to the decision on principle. Decisions that look like policy decisions are decisions about existing 'rights' of individuals.

The law has of necessity to reflect the majority view of the common good. 'Fundamental rights' represent the promise by the majority to minorities that their views on this will be respected. Such 'rights' are against government and enjoy authority superior to and independent of government (unlike, eg the 'right' to drive both ways down a street, which is created only by government and can be restricted by it); and they are usually found in guarantees of due process and equal protection, which call for respect for fairness and equality. Where there is a 'fundamental right' a person has the 'right' to do something even though it is forbidden by law. Therefore, with regard to civil disobedience it follows that, subject to the qualification referred to above, the individual has a 'right to follow conscience'. There is, however, a distinction between a person having a 'right to do something' when it would be wrong for government to punish him, and something being 'the right thing for him to do'. If one believes a law to be morally bad, breaking it is 'the right thing for him to do'; and if the majority break it on this ground, respect for law requires its repeal. On the other hand, when the 'right to do something' interferes with another's 'fundamental right', it is no longer 'the right thing to do'.

Dworkin's demonstration of the law-quality of principles and the short-coming of positivism in failing to accommodate them is acceptable; so too is his contention that, unlike rules, they have a dimension of weight, which exerts pressure on the development of rules. The point, however, is that pressures of any kind may be outweighed by others, which does give judges discretion to decide on policy or other grounds[19]. All this falls short of the contention that the choice is only between competing 'rights' so that there is always a correct answer in principle, that policy considerations do not come in, and that such 'rights' have superior weight, which makes it wrong to condemn people for exercising them against government. The issue boils down to whether these 'rights' carry with them, in addition to the duty to accept them as 'law (which is acceptable), a further duty to apply them, or at least to choose only between them, as opposed to a liberty to apply them or not. A mental leap is required from the acceptable part of his argument to these further contentions, which he does not appear to have bridged.

Reservations that might be felt about the practicalities of his 'fundamental rights' have been expressed earlier in connection with disobedience[20]. While the sincerity of some dissidents cannot be doubted, it would be unwise to trust the sincerity of others who often join in 'fundamental rights' actions for motives such as the overthrow of the system, or to gain positions of power which will enable them eventually to deny equal 'rights' to those disagreeing

18 *Dworkin* p 22.
19 See p 46 ante.
20 See p 315 ante.

with them. The presence, or even the (justified) suspicion of the presence, of the latter under the banner of 'fundamental rights' weakens the appeal of the 'right to follow conscience'. The thrust of the Dworkinian thesis is anti-government, which in itself is no bad thing; but in the real world of today the naivety of this kind of attack on authority is like sawing away at the branch on which one is safely ensconced, so far.

Why, it may be asked in the end, is there talk only of 'natural rights'; what of 'natural duties'? Nothing in justice or principle suggests that the slant should only be towards 'rights'. Indeed, social cohesion and better social justice might be achieved by at least equal emphasis on 'natural duties'.

TEMPORAL APPROACH TO LEGAL SYSTEM

The word 'system' implies continuity, since any concept of inter-relationships and organisation is pointless except in the way in which they continue to hold together while functioning. The inclusion of powers in a concept of law makes a temporal perspective unavoidable, since, as pointed out, the power, eg to make an offer and the power to accept and the claim-duty relationship which they create cannot co-exist[1]. If, then, a time dimension has to be introduced, the implications of this have to be faced. The endurance of a legal system is of course on a much larger scale than this limited example suggests. Factors but for which continuity would not be possible are part of the concept of a continuing phenomenon. Positivist and naturalist concepts of law reflect respectively views of law as a piece of machinery and as an activity. A parallel might be drawn between the concepts of a 'motor car' and 'motoring'. The latter implies more than just a 'car'; it imports use, technique, road-sense, destination and the like. Even the concept of a 'car' is incomplete without its motive power. So, too, a legal system is incomplete without its motivating force and all factors that keep it in being. Of these doing justice is not only an important purpose, but also a condition of continuance. It is not possible to maintain a system indefinitely through fear; people must have faith in it as being substantially a just order and as dispensing substantial justice. Doing justice in deciding disputes is the principal concern of lawyers. This is a task which brings into consideration the equipment used in legal reasoning and above all values, which play so decisive a part in the decisional process. Doing justice further involves consideration of what is actually accomplished in social life through the operation of laws and decisions. So the attribute of justice has to be incorporated into any concept of legal system.

The establishment and maintenance of a just order requires for a start a just allocation of benefits and burdens[2]. Two essential prerequisites for this are moral restraint in the exercise of power by those who have to decide these matters, and moral restraint in the exercise of liberties of action by all those who are in a position to wreck any scheme of allocation[3]. Positivists on their own confession are unable to help with these problems. Their purely formal concepts of law and of legal system are like charts depicting the structure of a machine without its motive power. The structure of every machine has to be devised so as to make *controlled* use of motive power, and

1 See pp 43-44 ante.
2 See ch 4 ante.
3 See chs 5, 6 ante.

all formal depictions of structure are based on the *assumption* that there is, or will be, such control. Legal machinery is only partly the product of human calculation; it is also the product of ideological and social forces over which human control is limited, since human beings as members of society are themselves in the grip of these forces. There is thus all the more reason to incorporate control of these forces into a concept of legal system, for otherwise uncontrolled forces can shatter the system and society. The recurrent trage-dies of history have resulted, not from the support given to power or liberty according to the paramount need of the age, but from failure to control whichever movement was in the ascendent. A contented society is the anti-thesis of tyranny and anarchy. It has been observed that natural law theory is in a sense always a reaction against abuse: abuse of power, which is tyranny, or abuse of liberty, which is anarchy.

Two conditions *sine quibus non* for the continuity of any legal system are thus control of power and of liberty. Power is manifested through laws, and in Chapter 5 ways and means were explored as to how disabilities might be built into, or imposed upon, the criterion of validity. If this were to come about, it could be accommodated within a formal concept. This, however, is not enough. A formal structure stands until changed and, as pointed out, failure to adapt to change is as much an abuse of power as direct exercises of it[4]. What is needed is a concept of legal system which transcends formality and embodies the *need* for control of power as an indispensable part of the very idea of law.

The same applies with even greater force to the restraint of liberty, since the problem of its abuse cuts deeper than that of power[5]. One must begin by asking whether one wants society at all; and if one does, the next question is how it would be possible to have a stable society without providing safe-guards against the two most potent forces of destruction, namely, abuse of power and abuse of liberty. Some exercise of power there will have to be in order to suppress certain forms of liberty. Outside the area of prohibition, restraint on liberty can only come from self-restraint and self-discipline, for which there is no alternative but the acceptance of a set of shared values, which results from faith in a just way of life, namely religion. The sooner the implications of this are realised the better.

The question what sort of concept would be appropriate for this purpose will depend, in the first place, on whether liberty is treated as falling within or outside a concept of law. Clearly, it can form no part of a concept which confines 'law' to positive regulation of conduct. It was pointed out in an earlier discussion that there is justification for including all aspects of conduct within 'law', whether positively or negatively regulated[6]. Besides, apart from specific regulation, the law can indirectly influence the exercise of liberties in many ways, and moreover the continued existence of law itself depends on a sense of freedom with responsibility. On this view it is necessary to bring liberty within a concept of law. The choice between the two kinds of con-cepts, that which includes and that which excludes liberty, is not dependent on logic, but is simply a question of which is more suited to the task of law as one sees it. To rule is to educate; that is a lesson which has been preached from ancient times down to the present. Education includes education in

4 See chs 5, 15
5 See ch 6 ante.
6 See pp 31–32, 369 ante.

values and in moderation, which is inspired by breadth of view and dispassionate, reasoned judgment. Abuse of power and of liberty are productive of fear and both hinder the development of ideas. No matter how difficult the task of curbing these may be at present, the failures of today can be made into stepping-stones towards the success of tomorrow. For neither dictatorship nor anarchy can last indefinitely; they carry in themselves the seeds of their own eventual doom.

READING LIST

St T Aquinas *Summa Theologica* (trans Fathers of the English Dominican Province) 1.2.Qq 90–97.

J Dabin *General Theory of Law* (trans K Wilk 20th Century Legal Philosophy Series IV) pp 227–470.

T E Davitt 'Law as a Means to an End—Thomas Aquinas' (1960–61) 14 Vanderbilt Law Review 65.

R M Dworkin *Taking Rights Seriously* chs 4–13.

A P d'Entréves *Natural Law*.

J Finnis *Natural Law and Natural Rights*.

L L Fuller 'Positivism and Fidelity to Law—a Reply to Professor Hart' (1957–58) 71 Harvard Law Review 630.

L L Fuller *The Morality of Law* (revised edition).

A L Goodhart *English Law and the Moral Law*.

C G Haines *The Revival of Natural Law Concepts*.

J Hall *Foundations of Jurisprudence*.

H L A Hart 'Positivism and the Separation of Law and Morals' (1957–58) 71 Harvard Law Review 593.

H L A Hart *The Concept of Law* chs 9–10.

D Hume *A Treatise of Human Nature*.

I Kant *The Philosophy of Law* (trans W Hastie).

C Morris *The Justification of Law*.

R Pound *The Ideal Element in Law* chs 2–6.

R Pound 'Natural Natural Law and Positive Natural Law' (1952) 68 Law Quarterly Review 330; (1960) 5 Natural Law Forum 70.

J Rawls *A Theory of Justice*.

R Stammler *Theory of Justice* (trans I Husik The Modern Legal Philosophy Series VIII).

J D Wild *Plato's Modern Enemies and the Theory of Natural Law*.

Index